About the editor

Andrea Cornwall is professor of anthropology and development in the School of Global Studies at the University of Sussex. She has worked on participation as a researcher and practitioner for many years, and is author of *Beneficiary, Consumer, Citizen: Perspectives on Participation for Poverty Reduction* (2000) and *Democratising Engagement* (2009), and co-editor of *Pathways to Participation: Reflections on PRA* (with Garrett Pratt, 2003), *Spaces for Change: The Politics of Participation in New Democratic Arenas* (with Vera Schattan Coelho, 2007) and *The Politics of Rights: Dilemmas for Feminist Praxis* (with Maxine Molyneux, 2009).

The Participation Reader

edited by Andrea Cornwall

Zed Books
LONDON | NEW YORK

The Participation Reader was first published in 2011 by Zed Books Ltd,
7 Cynthia Street, London N1 9JF, UK and Room 400, 175 Fifth Avenue,
New York, NY 10010, USA

www.zedbooks.co.uk

All reasonable efforts have been made by the publisher to contact the
copyright holders of the work reproduced in this volume.

Set in OurType Arnhem, Monotype Gill Sans Heavy by Ewan Smith,
London
Index: ed.emery@thefreeuniversity.net
Cover designed by Rogue Four Design
Cover image © Fernando Moleres/Panos Pictures
Printed and bound in Great Britain by the MPG Books Group, King's Lynn
and Bodmin

Distributed in the USA exclusively by Palgrave Macmillan, a division of
St Martin's Press, LLC, 175 Fifth Avenue, New York, NY 10010, USA

A catalogue record for this book is available from the British Library
Library of Congress Cataloging in Publication Data available

ISBN 978 1 84277 402 1 hb
ISBN 978 1 84277 403 8 pb

Contents

Table, figures and boxes

Acknowledgements

This book has taken a very long time to finish. For their patience, their belief that it was worth persisting and ultimately for holding me to my many broken promises to deliver, I'd like to thank Tamsine O'Riordan and Jakob Horstmann at Zed Books. For encouraging me to start putting it together in the first place, I'm grateful to their predecessor, Robert Molteno. I enlisted John Gaventa in working on this reader in its early days, and I was sad to lose him when we were both diverted into other projects; I would like to thank him not only for the hours of discussion, which have contributed to the eventual shape of this book, but also for all I have learnt from him over the years about participation. To all of those who so graciously allowed me to reproduce their work, and who helped secure permissions from their publishers, I am very thankful. To the publishers who were so kind as to grant gratis the right to reproduce pieces originally published in their books and journals, a big thanks, and another one to Jakob Horstmann, whose comradeship and humour in the process of gathering permissions was very much appreciated. An earlier version of this reader was double the length: I'm grateful to all of those who allowed me to include their work, and whose pieces have not made it into the shortened version. Laura Cornish gave invaluable assistance in assembling the manuscript. I'd like to say thanks to students and colleagues in the Participation, Power and Social Change Team at the Institute of Development Studies at the University of Sussex for being willing to look at earlier drafts of this reader. Lastly, I am grateful to the Swedish International Development Agency (Sida) and the Swiss Agency for Development and Co-operation (SDC) for their financial support for this publication, which has permitted us to disseminate free copies to libraries and organizations in Africa.

Acronyms

ADC	Area Development Centre
AEC	Anti-Eviction Campaign (Western Cape, South Africa)
APF	Anti-Privatization Forum (South Africa)
AWC	Area Wide Council (Philadelphia)
CAA	Community Action Agency
CBO	community-based organization
CDA	City Demonstration Agency
CSO	civil-society organization
DfID	Department for International Development (UK)
EZLN	Zapatista Army of National Liberation
GAD	Gender and Development
GM	genetically modified
HIPC	Heavily Indebted Poorer Country
HUD	Department of Housing and Urban Development
IBRFP	Indo-British Rainfed Farming Project
ICDS	Integrated Child Development Scheme
IFE	Federal Electoral Institute (Mexico)
IMF	International Monetary Fund
IPPR	Institute for Public Policy and Research
JFM	Joint Forest Management
KRIBP	Kribhco Indo-British Rainfed Farming Project
LDC	less developed country
MDG	Millennium Development Goals
MKSS	Mazdoor Kisan Shakti Sangathan (Rajasthan)
NAFTA	North American Free Trade Agreement
NGO	non-governmental organization
NPM	New Public Management
OEO	Office of Economic Opportunity
PAR	Participatory Action Research
PARC	Palestinian Agricultural Relief Committees
PB	participatory budgeting
PBA	programme-based approach
PLA	Participatory Learning and Action
PM&E	participatory monitoring and evaluation
PPA	Participatory Poverty Assessment
PPME	participatory planning, monitoring and evaluation
PR	Participatory Research

PRA	Participatory Rural Appraisal
PRI	Partido Revolucionario Institucional (Institutional Revolutionary Party, Mexico)
PRSP	Poverty Reduction Strategy Paper
PT	Partido dos Trabalhadores (Workers' Party, Brazil)
RBU	Redd Barna Uganda
RDP	Reconstruction and Development Programme (South Africa)
RKS	Rationing Kruti Samiti (Action Committee for Rationing, Mumbai)
RRA	Rapid Rural Appraisal
SAP	Structural Adjustment Programme
SC	scheduled caste
SRDP	Special Rural Development Programme (Kenya)
ST	scheduled tribe
SWAP	Sector-wide Approach
TFDC	Theatre for Development Centre
UNICEF	United Nations Children's Fund
UNRISD	United Nations Research Institute for Social Development
UPPAP	Ugandan Participatory Poverty Process
USAID	United States Agency for International Development
WMS	Wood Management Structure

Preface by Andrea Cornwall

While writing a short book that traced the history of participation in development, *Beneficiary, Citizen, Consumer: Perspectives on Participation for Poverty Reduction* (Sida, 2000), at the peak of the participation wave of the 1990s, I stumbled across writings on participation from the 1970s and 1980s. I reflected on how much of what I read from this period echoed the debates that were happening all around me at the end of a decade when participation had been 'mainstreamed' by the major donors and lenders. I was also struck by how much there was in these writings that could lend itself to the project of re-politicizing participation with which I and other colleagues were preoccupied at the time. The idea of this Reader was born.

My aim was to gather together classic and contemporary writing into a book that could be used by practitioners, students and scholars – to recover gems from the past, to reprint significant pieces from the 1990s and 2000s, and to bring into this mix some of the methodological writings by activists and practitioners that are so vital to understanding the promise of participation in practice. But in seeking to include as much as possible, I faced a major challenge. So much has been written, from so many different perspectives, it was very difficult to make choices. Such was the diversity of the material that it seemed impossible to do justice to the topic in a single volume. Every time I settled on a short-list, I would end up ruminating on what was missing. And this would prompt another flurry of hunting and gathering, sifting and resifting. This final selection remains provisional. It is informed by the trajectories of my own engagement with participation – from a frustration with the elitism of academic research and a fascination with visual and performative research methods, to a passion for the democratization of knowledge and of governance. It combines old favourites that have stood the test of time with more recent pieces that give some sense of the field as it has evolved. Eclectic as it may seem, my hope is that it will be nevertheless stimulating and interesting.

The Reader is organized in five sections. There is inevitably some overlap between them. The first looks at frameworks, typologies and definitions, and includes pieces that contextualize the adoption of 'participation' as a development buzzword (Cornwall and Eade 2007). The second introduces a range of participatory methodologies and applications. The third section offers a selection of readings on participatory development and community participation. The fourth addresses participation in governance, and includes a focus on institutionalized participation and accountability. The last section enlarges the scope of participatory engagement beyond 'invited participation' (Cornwall 2000) to self-organization, resistance and mobilization in pursuit of rights and citizenship. In what follows, I give a brief account of each of the sections, to contextualize the choices of readings.

'What is participation?' is the question that dominates the opening section of the Reader. Ladders and typologies of participation are tools that can be useful to distinguish deeper and more meaningful forms of involvement from tokenism and manipulation. Sherry Arnstein's (1969) article gives us one of the best-loved and most used ladders of participation, along with a salutary tale that dispenses with the myth that the kind of issues with which international development engages are only experienced in the global South. The next piece, by Matthias Stiefel and Marshall Wolfe, is excerpted from one of the most important books on participation published in the last thirty years, *A Voice for the Excluded: Popular Participation in Development – Utopia or Necessity?* (1994). This book was the culmination of an UNRISD research programme on popular participation that began in the late 1970s, in which 'participation' was defined as:

> the organized efforts to increase control over resources and regulative institutions in given social situations, on the part of groups and movements hitherto excluded from such control. (cited in Stiefel and Wolfe, 1994: 5)

The excerpt from *A Voice for the Excluded* that I chose for this Reader offers another tool that can be used to make sense of what 'participation' amounts to in practice, distinguishing between a range of different kinds of interests and actors. The third chapter, by N. C. Saxena, is useful in unpacking *what* participation is all about. Saxena, like Arnstein, offers an entry point for distinguishing forms of participation that offer little scope for transformation.

I remember coming across John Cohen and Norman Uphoff's (1980) piece almost two decades after it was written and experiencing a significant 'aha' moment as I read their plea for 'clarity through specificity'. I had become frustrated with all the lipservice about participation that was prevalent at the time, and had come to recognize that the devil is in the detail: amid all the vague generalizations, there was very little to hold on to. Spelling it out – participation by whom, for what, in what and so on – offers a way to pin down some of those promises, and a means to hold those who make them to account. Cohen and Uphoff's chapter complements the others in this section by providing such a framework. Further conceptual distinctions are made in the fifth piece in this section, an article that is one of the most widely read articles ever published by the practitioner-focused journal *Development in Practice*: Sarah White's (1996) critical reflection on the politics of participation. White offers us a typology that urges us to look beyond the visions of those who implement participation to what might motivate those on the receiving end to take part, and what they might get out of participating. It also presents some important cautions, which remain as relevant now as when the piece was written.

The last piece in this section, by Pablo Leal (2007), sets participation on a bigger political canvas, exploring the ways in which elements of participatory development taken up in the pursuit of neoliberalism have come to distort the promise of participation as a transformative project. What makes it such a valuable piece is that it combines pungent critique with a sense of what might be needed to reclaim participation from neoliberal mainstream development and instil again in participatory development practice some of the more radical traditions that have been part of its history. Together, these chapters offer us tools for thought, but they also give us more: each provides a sense of some of the issues with which those engaged in debates about participation were grappling at the time of their writing.

Participatory methodologies and applications are the focus of the second section. Methodologies and methods constitute an aspect of participatory practice that has been a particularly significant site for contesting power. This section is intended as a smörgåsbord of examples and consists of a series of short extracts from longer pieces, introductory pieces and articles published in the informal collection of notes from the field established as a way of sharing knowledge and excitement about PRA, which has now become the journal *PLA Notes*. The section opens with a chapter by one of the best-known advocates for Participatory Action Research (PAR), the late Orlando Fals Borda. In this piece, he sets out a critique of orthodox approaches to research and argues for ways of generating knowledge that challenge the entrenched relations of power that are part of the mainstream research establishment. Inspired by the work of Brazilian popular educator Paulo Freire, PAR grew into an international movement in the 1980s. Another of the key figures in the adult education movement, Rajesh Tandon from the Society for Participatory Research in Asia (PRIA), reflects on the precepts that informed the approach taken by this movement, as well as on the trajectories that PAR came to follow. This history has been well documented by others involved in the East African experiments that proved so significant for the development of PAR, such as Marja Liisa Swantz (2003) and Budd Hall (2005).

Tandon's piece is important for its sharp critique of the monopolization of knowledge creation by the research establishment. The next two chapters demonstrate other dimensions of the critique of conventional research. In the next chapter, the manifesto of the New Paradigm Research Group sets out the principles of another strand of participatory research, which emerged in the 1970s as researchers in psychology and sociology in the UK came to articulate disaffection with the neglect of issues of power and inter-subjectivity in conventional research approaches. It is included here both for its historical value and for the acuity with which it points to the limits of the positivism that remains dominant in some parts of the social sciences even today. Patricia Maguire's chapter situates a feminist approach to participatory research at the centre of efforts to address entrenched power relations in the research process. Her chapter also gives a sense of the history of the evolution of participatory action research, reflecting on the 'androcentric filter' that characterized the way the approach was applied when she first encountered it, sidelining questions of gendered power. The challenges she poses remain as salient now as they did when the piece was originally written.

In the next two chapters, and in the series of short chapters that follow them, principles sit alongside accounts of practice. Peter Reason's chapter on cooperative inquiry describes a methodology that has gained applications in a diversity of organizational settings. The intensive group-based inquiry process, involving a small number of people working together over a number of weeks or months, stands in contrast to the approach described in the next chapter, Participatory Rural Appraisal (PRA) which is often used to elicit the participation of large numbers of people, over as little as a couple of days. PRA developed out of Rapid Rural Appraisal (RRA), an approach that was all about finding out fast, guided by two maxims: 'optimal ignorance' (we don't need to know everything) and 'appropriate imprecision' (we don't need to know everything exactly). The shift from RRA to PRA emphasized the importance of participation in the process of knowledge production; as PRA developed, there was an increasing emphasis on power relations in the research encounter, and on what came to be known as 'ABC' (Attitude and Behaviour Change) on the part of researchers – what Robert Chambers (2006) was to go on to call 'a pedagogy for the powerful'.

Of all that has been written on PRA – and there is a lot of very accessible and interesting material, much of which is featured in the journal *PLA Notes* (back issues of which are available at www.iied.org) – the piece I have chosen for this Reader is in my view one of the best. Its authors are Robert Chambers, whose tireless championing of PRA as an alternative to 'survey slavery' was a major force in the rise and rise of this approach, and Irene Guijt, member of a dynamic team at the International Institute of Environment and Development that played a critical role in innovating and spreading the approach in the 1990s. Their chapter brings together an account of what PRA is all about – and what it is not – with a critical appraisal of what was beginning to happen as the PRA boom took off. The following chapter, Ian Scoones's 'Ten Myths about PRA', is a useful piece to read alongside the critiques of PRA that were to gain such currency among academics, most famously Bill Cooke and Uma Kothari's (2001) *Participation: The New Tyranny?*.

One of the commonly voiced criticisms of participatory methodologies is that over-enthusiasm about methods can result in a lack of attention to local political and cultural dynamics. Janet Symes and Sa'ed Jasser's article not only addresses an area of application of participatory methods that became very significant in the late 1990s and early 2000s, as development agencies sought to engage beneficiaries more closely in monitoring and evaluating projects and programmes (see Estrella et al. 2000). It also sets the application of participatory methods in a context in which everyday oppression and dispossession characterizes people's experiences of state intervention: occupied Palestine. This chapter is as useful for its critique of the strictures of the Logframe – what Symes and Jasser dub the 'illogical framework' – which spread through the development agency world like wildfire in this period, as it is for its grounded account of the process of participatory M&E in this context.

The next chapter takes us to an entirely different kind of application of participatory methodologies and principles: community exchanges, a method used by the international network of slum dwellers, SPARC. In it, Sheela Patel, founder-director of SPARC, explains how the kinds of participatory methods developed by the slum dwellers themselves differ from those employed by external agencies. This article is a powerful reminder of the significance of people coming together to share experiences as a fundamental starting point for analysis and action, something that underpins all participatory methodologies. Tom Wakeford introduces us in the next chapter to another entirely different context, the UK, and to the use of a methodology known as 'citizens juries' to foster public deliberation on complex policy issues.

The last two chapters in this section provide a snapshot of participatory methodologies that bring another ingredient to the mix: creative practice. Oga Steve Abah draws on the traditions of participatory theatre, which weave together principles common to all participatory research with use of the medium of theatre to amplify voice. Abah and his colleagues at Ahmadu Bello University in Nigeria played an important role in putting Theatre for Development on the development map, and this piece is especially resonant in its portrayal of the possibilities for using theatre for social change. Renuka Bery and Sara Stuart's account of participatory video demonstrates the power of people taking charge of the means of representation – all the more feasible as technology becomes cheaper and more accessible. The communications revolution offers enormous opportunities for people to find, amplify and broadcast their voices, versions and demands, and this chapter evokes some of the possibilities.

'Participatory development' is the theme of the third section. It focuses on community and local-level participation in activities that are generally initiated by development agencies or the state. This is in itself interesting: there was barely any consideration in the literature on participatory development of 'participation' happening at any other level than at the 'local' (Mohan and Stokke 2000). And while ideals of self-organization and self-reliance were part of the discourse, the reality was more often of external facilitation and, often, direction. It was only with aspirations to influence national and international policy processes in the late 1990s and early 2000s that participatory development practitioners began conceiving of participation as something that could happen at other levels. Accordingly, the contributions to this section are largely about local-level community participation and participatory development through community-based projects.

Looking back at the literature on community participation – which dates back some fifty years to the late colonial era – it is striking how contemporary some of it feels. When I came across Robert Chambers's (1974) classic book *Managing Rural Development* and read the section on participation, it chimed so much with what I had come to see as the gap between rhetoric about participatory local governance and reality on the ground in many countries, that it was an obvious first choice for this section. James Midgley's writings on community development first came to my attention as I looked for materials exploring the ways in which participation had been used historically as a technique of rule. Midgley's (1986) book *Community Participation, Social Development and the State* provides a valuable account of the evolution of ideas about community participation, and an excerpt from it is included here for this reason.

In the next three chapters in this section, case studies offer critical insights into the dynamics of participatory development in practice. David Mosse gives readers a glimpse into the world of development bureaucracy as he delves into the relationship between funding agency expectations and project delivery in a rural south Indian setting. Andrea Cornwall's 'Whose voices? Whose choices?' addresses some of the paradoxes of gender and participatory development, while Tlamelo Mompati and Gerard Prinsen highlight some of the exclusions that mark notionally 'inclusionary' participatory development initiatives. The last chapter in this section, by Glyn Williams, revisits the *Participation: The New Tyranny?* critique and explores avenues for repoliticizing participatory development.

Participatory governance is the focus of the fourth section. For many years, participation was the provenance of *social* development. It was understood to be about communities, and about issues that were often regarded by those working on issues of governance as 'soft' and even a bit 'fluffy'. By the end of the 1990s, and especially in the wake of the landmark 1998 World Development Report on the state, things began to change. An interesting convergency began to emerge between work on deliberative and inclusionary governance in response to evident democratic deficits in the global North, and development interests in democracy, accountability and 'good governance' in the global South. Out of this came agendas for participatory governance that brought together exciting new thinking and a desire to learn about and spread innovations that were taking place in countries such as India and Brazil. John Gaventa's 'Towards participatory local governance' captures some of the key ideas that came to animate the field, and provides a point of reference for the pieces that follow.

Through a series of case studies, this section addresses some of the main 'story-lines' of participation in governance. Jesse Ribot's chapter reveals the extent to which some of what goes on in the name of participation displays strong resemblances with colonial indirect rule. It also provides insights into the institutionalization of participation in natural resource policy in Francophone West Africa, providing a counterpoint to the examples from Anglophone countries that dominate much of the literature in English. The politics of inclusion, and of whose 'voices' are elicited and listened to in participatory processes, is as much a strand in the literature on citizen engagement in governance as it is in participatory development. Ranjita Mohanty's account of the politics of domesticating participation also traces the trajectory of institutionalization back to colonial institutions, and offers an insightful account of the dynamics of exclusion in 'participatory' governance.

Nowhere are the claims that are made to inclusion more evident than in rhetoric about 'civil society' participation – all the more so because 'civil society' is such a residual category, so filled with normative promise and yet so often ill-defined (Chandhoke 2003). Elaina Mack's account of civil society participation in the Poverty Reduction Strategy Paper (PRSP) process in Tanzania addresses the aims, claims and uses that are made of 'civil society participation' by development agencies. Mack's account can be read alongside Bruce Lubinda Imboela (2005) on the Zambian PRSP process, which shows quite how shallow and manipulative the use and abuse of 'participation' can be, and Nadia Molenaers and Robrecht Renard (2006) on the governance preconditions for meaningful engagement. By showing that Tanzanian civil society was able to make some use of the policy space opened up by the process, for all its limitations, Mack's piece illustrates a point that tends to be forgotten: the outcomes of participation are always contingent, and there can be times when the least promising participatory process can yield positive outcomes.

Participatory governance is, in theory, the area over which one might imagine the greatest ideological contestation, as it ought to bring into clear view the political differences that pervade the field of participation. And yet, there has been remarkable consensus on the merits of citizen engagement, as common concerns with mobilizing and articulating citizen voice and enhancing the responsiveness and accountability of the state have evolved into a productive engagement with institutional innovation. At the heart of this convergence is the idea of accountability, rather than participation per se – or rather, of participation for accountability.

Gianpaolo Baocchi's ethnography takes us to a very different context, and into the heart of the action in a context that has become synonymous with the ideals of participatory governance: participatory budgeting in Porto Alegre, Brazil. It explores some of the gains and challenges involved in one of the most ambitious and successful experiments in engaging citizens in participation in governance.

John Ackerman closes this section with a range of examples from around the world of where initiatives to enhance accountability have strengthened both the capacity of citizens to make demands on their government and that of governments to respond, which include cases from the United States. Ackerman's analysis underscores the importance of institutional frameworks – policies, laws and institutionalized mechanisms – for effective participation in governance, while none the less making it quite clear that institutional designs are only as good as the people who convene and populate participatory institutions.

Participation as collective action is the focus of the final section, expanding the frame for how we view participation beyond 'invited participation' to mobilization, insurgency and struggles for rights and citizenship. Marion Barnes looks at self-organizing among service users, drawing on social movement and citizenship theories to address some of the dynamics of power and exclusion that emerge in their interactions with the state. The activist dimensions of participatory engagement are again a theme in Faranak Miraftab and Shana Wills's account of the Western Cape anti-eviction campaign in South Africa. Their analysis is a reminder that the forms that participatory action can take – and indeed that it sometimes needs to take in order to be effective – may be spontaneous, chaotic and unruly, a far cry from the image of organized, orchestrated involvement that is often associated with participation in development. It also highlights the disciplining effects that authorities seek to have in determining who can participate, and in trying to exclude or marginalize would-be participants who are more likely to challenge than comply.

By bringing contentious politics back into the heart of debates about participation, the contributions to this section – and the bigger literature on social movements and activism from which they are drawn – make an important conceptual contribution to development, challenging the limited instrumentalism of much of mainstream development's applications of participation and foregrounding issues of power. In her piece on the Mexican Zapatista movement as 'pedagogical guerrillas and revolutionary counter-publics', Josee Johnston takes us further still into thinking about the potentialities of participation in relation to the public sphere. Introducing us to Nancy Fraser's (1997) notion of 'subaltern counter-publics' and to radical democratic understandings of participation and deliberative democratic practice, this article offers valuable food for thought about mobilization, resistance and democracy. Shireen Huq's moving account of the Bangladeshi women's rights movement, told through the story of the engagement of one of the country's leading women's organizations, Naripokkho, reveals some of the tensions, contradictions and challenges faced by those who organize to make demands. In doing so, Huq addresses questions of gender, identity and power, issues of difference and the negotiation of engagement from a perspective informed by decades of activism in the women's movement in Bangladesh.

The last piece, by Evelina Dagnino, explores participation as the expression of citizenship and picks up on themes that run throughout this Reader. Highlighting the 'perverse confluence' between radical democratic notions of citizenship and neoliberal appropriations of communitarian ideals when it comes to participation of civil society, Dagnino's account reveals paradoxes of participation that run throughout many of the contributions to this book. Her analysis invites us to reflect carefully on the meanings of citizen and civil society engagement, and to look beyond acts of participation to the bigger political picture. It is an appropriate place to end this Reader, addressing questions and issues that will remain an intense source of debate no doubt for decades to come.

References.

Chambers, R. (1974) *Managing Rural Development: Ideas and Experience from East Africa*, Uppsala: Scandinavian Institute of African Studies.
— (2006) 'Transforming Power: From Zero-Sum to Win-Win', *IDS Bulletin* Volume 37(6): 99–110.
Chandhoke, N. (2003), *The Conceits of Civil Society*, New Delhi: Oxford University Press.
Cooke, B. and U. Kothari (eds) (2001) *Participation: The New Tyranny?*, London: Zed Books.
Cornwall, A. (2000) *Beneficiary, Citizen, Consumer: Perspectives on Participation for Poverty Reduction*, Stockholm: Sida.
Cornwall, A. and D. Eade (eds) (2007) *Deconstructing Development Discourse: Buzzwords and Fuzzwords*, special issue of *Development in Practice*, Vols 3–4.
Estrella, M., J. Blauert, D. Campilan, J. Gaventa, J. Gonsalves, I. Guijt, D. Johnson, and R. Ricafort (eds) (2000) *Learning from Change: Issues and Experiences in Participatory Monitoring and Evaluation*, London: Intermediate Technology Publications.
Fraser, N. (1997) *Justice Interruptus*, London: Routledge.
Guijt, I. and M. K. Shah (eds) (1998) *The Myth of Community: Gender Issues in Participatory Development*, London: IT Publications.
Hall, B. (2005) 'In from the Cold? Reflections on Participatory Research from 1970-2005', *Convergence*, 38(1): 5–4.
Imboela, B. L. (2005) 'Poverty Reduction in Zambia: A Conceptual Analysis of the Zambian Poverty Reduction Strategy Paper', *Bulletin of Science, Technology and Society*, 25(5): 435–45.
Mohan, G. and K. Stokke (2000) 'Participatory Development and Empowerment: The Dangers of Localism', *Third World Quarterly* 21(2): 247–68.
Molenaers, N. and R. Renard (2006) *Civil Society and the PRSP: A Readiness Assessment Framework*, Discussion Paper, Institute of Development Policy and Management, University of Antwerp.
Stiefel, M. and M. Wolfe (1994) *A Voice for the Excluded: Popular Participation in Development – Utopia or Necessity?* London: Zed Books.
Swantz, M. L. (2003) 'My Road to Participatory Action Research, in A. Cornwall and G. Pratt (eds), *Pathways to Participation: Reflections on Participatory Rural Appraisal*, London: Intermediate Technology Publications.

PART ONE

What is participation?

1 | A ladder of citizen participation

Sherry R. Arnstein

Citizen participation is citizen power

Because the question has been a bone of political contention, most of the answers have been purposely buried in innocuous euphemisms like 'self-help' or 'citizen involvement'. Still others have been embellished with misleading rhetoric like 'absolute control' which is something no one – including the President of the United States – has or can have. Between understated euphemisms and exacerbated rhetoric, even scholars have found it difficult to follow the controversy. To the headline reading public, it is simply bewildering.

My answer to the critical 'what' question is simply that citizen participation is a categorical term for citizen power. It is the redistribution of power that enables the have-not citizens, presently excluded from the political and economic processes, to be deliberately included in the future. It is the strategy by which the have-nots join in determining how information is shared, goals and policies are set, tax resources are allocated, programs are operated, and benefits like contracts and patronage are parceled out. In short, it is the means by which they can induce significant social reform which enables them to share in the benefits of the affluent society.

FIGURE 1.1 French student poster. In English, 'I participate, you participate, he participates, we participate, you participate ... they profit'

3

Empty refusal versus benefit There is a critical difference between going through the empty ritual of participation and having the real power needed to affect the outcome of the process. This difference is brilliantly capsulized in a poster painted last spring [1968] by the French students to explain the student–worker rebellion (see Figure 1.1). The poster highlights the fundamental point that participation without redistribution of power is an empty and frustrating process for the powerless. It allows the powerholders to claim that all sides were considered, but makes it possible for only some of those sides to benefit. It maintains the status quo. Essentially, it is what has been happening in most of the 1,000 Community Action Programs, and what promises to be repeated in the vast majority of the 150 Model Cities programs.

Types of participation and 'non-participation'

A typology of eight levels of participation may help in analysis of this confused issue. For illustrative purposes the eight types are arranged in a ladder pattern with each rung corresponding to the extent of citizens' power in determining the end product (see Figure 1.2).

The bottom rungs of the ladder are 1) Manipulation and 2) Therapy. These two rungs describe levels of 'non-participation' that have been contrived by some to substitute for genuine participation. Their real objective is not to enable people to participate in planning or conducting programs, but to enable powerholders to 'educate' or 'cure' the participants. Rungs 3 and 4 progress to levels of 'tokenism' that allow the have-nots to hear and to have a voice: 3) Informing and 4) Consultation. When they are proffered by powerholders as the total extent of participation, citizens may indeed hear and be heard. But under these conditions they lack the power to insure that their views will be heeded by the powerful. When participation is restricted to these levels, there is no follow-through, no 'muscle', hence no assurance of changing the status quo. Rung 5) Placation is simply a higher level tokenism because the ground rules allow have-nots to advise, but retain for the powerholders the continued right to decide.

Further up the ladder are levels of citizen power with increasing degrees of decision-making clout. Citizens can enter into a 6) Partnership that enables them to negotiate and engage in trade-offs with traditional powerholders. At the topmost rungs, 7) Delegated Power and 8) Citizen Control, have-not citizens obtain the majority of decision-making seats, or full managerial power.

Obviously, the eight-rung ladder is a simplification, but it helps to illustrate the point that so many have missed – that there are significant gradations of citizen participation. Knowing these gradations makes it possible to cut through the hyperbole to understand the increasingly strident demands for participation from the have-nots as well as the gamut of confusing responses from the powerholders.

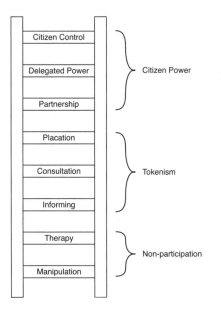

FIGURE 1.2 Eight rungs on the ladder of citizen participation

Though the typology uses examples from federal programs such as urban renewal, anti-poverty, and Model Cities, it could just as easily be illustrated in the church, currently facing demands for power from priests and laymen who seek to change its mission; colleges and universities which in some cases have become literal battlegrounds over the issue of student power; or public schools, city halls, and police departments (or big business which is likely to be next on the expanding list of targets). The underlying issues are essentially the same – 'nobodies' in several arenas are trying to become 'somebodies' with enough power to make the target institutions responsive to their views, aspirations, and needs.

Limitations of the typology The ladder juxtaposes powerless citizens with the powerful in order to highlight the fundamental divisions between them. In actuality, neither the have-nots nor the powerholders are homogeneous blocs. Each group encompasses a host of divergent points of view, significant cleavages, competing vested interests, and splintered subgroups. The justification for using such simplistic abstractions is that in most cases the have-nots really do perceive the powerful as a monolithic 'system', and powerholders actually do view the have-nots as a sea of 'those people', with little comprehension of the class and caste differences among them.

It should be noted that the typology does not include an analysis of the most significant roadblocks to achieving genuine levels of participation. These roadblocks lie on both sides of the simplistic fence. On the powerholders' side, they include racism, paternalism, and resistance to power redistribution. On the have-nots' side, they include inadequacies of the poor community's political socioeconomic infrastructure and knowledge-base, plus difficulties of organizing a representative and accountable citizens' group in the face of futility, alienation, and distrust.

Another caution about the eight separate rungs on the ladder: In the real world of people and programs, there might be 150 rungs with less sharp and 'pure' distinctions among them. Furthermore, some of the characteristics used to illustrate each of the eight types might be applicable to other rungs. For example, employment of the have-nots in a program or on a planning staff could occur at any of the eight rungs and could represent either a legitimate or illegitimate characteristic of citizen participation. Depending on their motives, powerholders can hire poor people to co-opt them, to placate them, or to utilize the have-nots' special skills and insights. Some mayors, in private, actually boast of their strategy in hiring militant black leaders to muzzle them while destroying their credibility in the black community.

Characteristics and illustrations

It is in this context of power and powerlessness that the characteristics of the eight rungs are illustrated by examples from current federal social programs.

Manipulation In the name of citizen participation, people are placed on rubberstamp advisory committees or advisory boards for the express purpose of 'educating' them or engineering their support. Instead of genuine citizen participation, the bottom rung of the ladder signifies the distortion of participation into a public relations vehicle by powerholders.

This illusory form of 'participation' initially came into vogue with urban renewal when the socially elite were invited by city housing officials to serve on Citizen Advisory Committees (CACs). Another target of manipulation were the CAC subcommittees on minority groups, which in theory were to protect the rights of Negroes in the renewal program. In practice, these subcommittees, like their parent CACs, functioned mostly as letterheads, trotted forward at appropriate times to promote urban renewal plans (in recent years known as Negro removal plans).

At meetings of the Citizen Advisory Committees, it was the officials who educated, persuaded, and advised the citizens, not the reverse. Federal guidelines for the renewal programs legitimized the manipulative agenda by emphasizing the terms 'information-gathering', 'public relations', and 'support' as the explicit functions of the committees.

This style of non-participation has since been applied to other programs encompassing the poor. Examples of this are seen in Community Action Agencies (CAAs) which have created structures called 'neighborhood councils' or 'neighborhood advisory groups'. These bodies frequently have no legitimate function or power. The CAAs use them to 'prove' that 'grassroots people' are involved in the program. But the program may not have been discussed with 'the people'. Or it may have been described at a meeting in the most general terms; 'We need your signatures on this proposal for a multi-service center which will house, under one roof, doctors from the health department, workers from the welfare department, and specialists from the employment service.'

The signatories are not informed that the $2 million-per-year center will only refer residents to the same old waiting lines at the same old agencies across town. No one is asked if such a referral center is really needed in his neighborhood. No one realizes that the contractor for the building is the mayor's brother-in-law, or that the new director of the center will be the same old community organization specialist from the urban renewal agency.

After signing their names, the proud grassrooters dutifully spread the word that they have 'participated' in bringing a new and wonderful center to the neighborhood to provide people with drastically needed jobs and health and welfare services. Only after the ribbon-cutting ceremony do the members of the neighborhood council realize that they didn't ask the important questions, and that they had no technical advisors of their own to help them grasp the fine legal print. The new center, which is open 9 to 5 on weekdays only, actually adds to their problems. Now the old agencies across town won't talk with them unless they have a pink paper slip to prove that they have been referred by 'their' shiny new neighborhood center.

Unfortunately, this chicanery is not a unique example. Instead it is almost typical of what has been perpetrated in the name of high-sounding rhetoric like 'grassroots participation'. This sham lies at the heart of the deep-seated exasperation and hostility of the have-nots toward the powerholders.

One hopeful note is that, having been so grossly affronted, some citizens have learned the Mickey Mouse game, and now they too know how to play. As a result of this knowledge, they are demanding genuine levels of partici-pation to assure them that public programs are relevant to their needs and responsive to their priorities.

Therapy In some respects group therapy, masked as citizen participation, should be on the lowest rung of the ladder because it is both dishonest and arrogant. Its administrators – mental health experts from social workers to psychiatrists – assume that powerlessness is synonymous with mental illness. On this assumption, under a masquerade of involving citizens in planning, the experts subject the citizens to clinical group therapy. What makes this form of 'participation' so invidious is that citizens are engaged in extensive activity, but the focus of it is on curing them of their 'pathology' rather than changing the racism and victimization that create their 'pathologies'.

Consider an incident that occurred in Pennsylvania less than one year ago. When a father took his seriously ill baby to the emergency clinic of a local hospital, a young resident physician on duty instructed him to take the baby home and feed it sugar water. The baby died that afternoon of pneumonia and dehydration. The overwrought father complained to the board of the local Community Action Agency. Instead of launching an investigation of the hospital to determine what changes would prevent similar deaths or other forms of malpractice, the board invited the father to attend the CAA's (therapy) child-care sessions for parents, and promised him that someone would 'telephone the hospital director to see that it never happens again'.

Less dramatic, but more common examples of therapy, masquerading as citizen participation, may be seen in public housing programs where tenant groups are used as vehicles for promoting control-your-child or cleanup campaigns. The tenants are brought together to help them 'adjust their values and attitudes to those of the larger society'. Under these ground rules, they are diverted from dealing with such important matters as: arbitrary evictions; segregation of the housing project; or why is there a three-month time lapse to get a broken window replaced in winter.

The complexity of the concept of mental illness in our time can be seen in the experiences of student/civil rights workers facing guns, whips, and other forms of terror in the South. They needed the help of socially attuned psychiatrists to deal with their fears and to avoid paranoia.

Informing Informing citizens of their rights, responsibilities, and options can be the most important first step toward legitimate citizen participation. However, too frequently the emphasis is placed on a one-way flow of information – from officials to citizens – with no channel provided for feedback and no power for negotiation. Under these conditions, particularly when information is provided at a late stage in planning, people have little opportunity to influence the program designed 'for their benefit'. The most frequent tools used for such one-way communication are the news media, pamphlets, posters, and responses to inquiries.

Meetings can also be turned into vehicles for one-way communication by the simple device of providing superficial information, discouraging questions, or giving irrelevant answers. At a recent Model Cities citizen planning meeting in Providence, Rhode Island, the topic was 'tot-lots'. A group of elected citizen representatives, almost all of whom were attending three to five meetings a week, devoted an hour to a discussion of the placement of six tot-lots. The neighborhood is half black, half white. Several of the black representatives noted that four tot-lots were proposed for the white district and only two for the black. The city official responded with a lengthy, highly technical explanation about costs per square foot and available property. It was clear that most of the residents did not understand his explanation. And it was clear to observers from the Office of Economic Opportunity that other options did exist which, considering available funds, would have brought about a more equitable distribution of facilities. Intimidated by futility, legalistic jargon, and the prestige of the official, the citizens accepted the 'information' and endorsed the agency's proposal to place four lots in the white neighborhood.

Consultation Inviting citizens' opinions, like informing them, can be a legitimate step toward their full participation. But if consulting them is not combined with other modes of participation, this rung of the ladder is still a sham since it offers no assurance that citizen concerns and ideas will be taken into account. The most frequent methods used for consulting people are attitude surveys, neighborhood meetings, and public hearings.

When powerholders restrict the input of citizens' ideas solely to this level, participation remains just a window-dressing ritual. People are primarily perceived as statistical abstractions, and participation is measured by how many come to meetings, take brochures home, or answer a questionnaire. What citizens achieve in all this activity is that they have 'participated in participation'. And what powerholders achieve is the evidence that they have gone through the required motions of involving 'those people'.

Attitude surveys have become a particular bone of contention in ghetto neighborhoods. Residents are increasingly unhappy about the number of times per week they are surveyed about their problems and hopes. As one woman put it: 'Nothing ever happens with those damned questions, except the surveyor gets $3 an hour, and my washing doesn't get done that day.' In some communities, residents are so annoyed that they are demanding a fee for research interviews.

Attitude surveys are not very valid indicators of community opinion when used without other input from citizens. Survey after survey (paid for out of anti-poverty funds) has 'documented' that poor housewives most want tot-lots in their neighborhood where young children can play safely. But most of the women answered these questionnaires without knowing what their options were. They assumed that if they asked for something small, they might just get something useful in the neighborhood. Had the mothers known that a free prepaid health insurance plan was a possible option, they might not have put tot-lots so high on their wish lists.

A classic misuse of the consultation rung occurred at a New Haven, Connecticut, community meeting held to consult citizens on a proposed Model Cities grant. James V. Cunningham, in an unpublished report to the Ford Foundation, described the crowd as large and mostly hostile:

> Members of The Hill Parents Association demanded to know why residents had not participated in drawing up the proposal. CAA director Spitz explained that

it was merely a proposal for seeking Federal planning funds – that once funds were obtained, residents would be deeply involved in the planning. An outside observer who sat in the audience described the meeting this way: 'Spitz and Mel Adams ran the meeting on their own. No representatives of a Hill group moderated or even sat on the stage. Spitz told the 300 residents that this huge meeting was an example of "participation in planning." To prove this, since there was a lot of dissatisfaction in the audience, he called for a "vote" on each component of the proposal. The vote took this form: "Can I see the hands of all those in favor of a health clinic? All those opposed?" It was a little like asking who favors motherhood.

It was a combination of the deep suspicion aroused at this meeting and a long history of similar forms of 'window-dressing participation' that led New Haven residents to demand control of the program.

By way of contrast, it is useful to look at Denver where technicians learned that even the best intentioned among them are often unfamiliar with, and even insensitive to, the problems and aspirations of the poor. The technical director of the Model Cities program has described the way professional planners assumed that the residents, victimized by high-priced local storekeepers, 'badly needed consumer education'. The residents, on the other hand, pointed out that the local storekeepers performed a valuable function. Although they overcharged, they also gave credit, offered advice, and frequently were the only neighborhood place to cash welfare or salary checks. As a result of this consultation, technicians and residents agreed to substitute the creation of needed credit institutions in the neighborhood for a consumer education program.

Placation It is at this level that citizens begin to have some degree of influence though tokenism is still apparent. An example of placation strategy is to place a few hand-picked 'worthy' poor on boards of Community Action Agencies or on public bodies like the board of education, police commission, or housing authority. If they are not accountable to a constituency in the community and if the traditional power elite hold the majority of seats, the have-nots can be easily outvoted and outfoxed. Another example is the Model Cities advisory and planning committees. They allow citizens to advise or plan ad infinitum but retain for powerholders the right to judge the legitimacy or feasibility of the advice. The degree to which citizens are actually placated, of course, depends largely on two factors: the quality of technical assistance they have in articulating their priorities; and the extent to which the community has been organized to press for those priorities.

It is not surprising that the level of citizen participation in the vast majority of Model Cities programs is at the placation rung of the ladder or below.

Policy-makers at the Department of Housing and Urban Development (HUD) were determined to return the genie of citizen power to the bottle from which it had escaped (in a few cities) as a result of the provision stipulating 'maximum feasible participation' in poverty programs. Therefore, HUD channeled its physical-social-economic rejuvenation approach for blighted neighborhoods through city hall. It drafted legislation requiring that all Model Cities' money flow to a local City Demonstration Agency (CDA) through the elected city council. As enacted by Congress, this gave local city councils final veto power over planning and programming and ruled out any direct funding relationship between community groups and HUD.

HUD required the CDAs to create coalition, policy-making boards that would include necessary local powerholders to create a comprehensive physical-social plan during the first year. The plan was to be carried out in a subsequent five-year action phase. HUD, unlike OEO [Office of Economic Opportunity], did not require that have-not citizens be included on the CDA decision-making boards. HUD's Performance Standards for Citizen Participation only demanded that 'citizens have clear and direct access to the decision-making process'.

Accordingly, the CDAs structured their policy-making boards to include some combination of elected officials; school representatives; housing, health, and welfare officials; employment and police department representatives; and various civic, labor, and business leaders. Some CDAs included citizens from the neighborhood. Many mayors correctly interpreted the HUD provision for 'access to the decision-making process' as the escape hatch they sought to relegate citizens to the traditional advisory role.

Most CDAs created residents' advisory committees. An alarmingly significant number created citizens' policy boards and citizens' policy committees which are totally misnamed as they have either no policy-making function or only a very limited authority. Almost every CDA created about a dozen planning committees or task forces on functional lines: health, welfare, education, housing, and unemployment. In most cases, have-not citizens were invited to serve on these committees along with technicians from relevant public agencies. Some CDAs, on the other hand, structured planning committees of technicians and parallel committees of citizens.

In most Model Cities programs, endless time has been spent fashioning complicated board, committee, and task force structures for the planning year. But the rights and responsibilities of the various elements of those structures are not defined and are ambiguous. Such ambiguity is likely to cause considerable conflict at the end of the one-year planning process. For at this point, citizens may realize that they have once again extensively 'participated' but have not profited beyond the extent the powerholders decide to placate them.

Results of a staff study (conducted in the summer of 1968 before the second round of seventy-five planning grants were awarded) were released in a

December 1968 HUD bulletin. Though this public document uses much more delicate and diplomatic language, it attests to the already cited criticisms of non-policy-making policy boards and ambiguous complicated structures, in addition to the following findings:

1 Most CDAs did not negotiate citizen participation requirements with residents.
2 Citizens, drawing on past negative experiences with local powerholders, were extremely suspicious of this new panacea program. They were legitimately distrustful of city hall's motives.
3 Most CDAs were not working with citizens' groups that were genuinely representative of model neighborhoods and accountable to neighborhood constituencies. As in so many of the poverty programs, those who were involved were more representative of the upwardly mobile working-class. Thus their acquiescence to plans prepared by city agencies was not likely to reflect the views of the unemployed, the young, the more militant residents, and the hard-core poor.
4 Residents who were participating in as many as three to five meetings per week were unaware of their minimum rights, responsibilities, and the options available to them under the program. For example, they did not realize that they were not required to accept technical help from city technicians they distrusted.
5 Most of the technical assistance provided by CDAs and city agencies was of third-rate quality, paternalistic, and condescending. Agency technicians did not suggest innovative options. They reacted bureaucratically when the residents pressed for innovative approaches. The vested interests of the old-line city agencies were a major – albeit hidden – agenda.
6 Most CDAs were not engaged in planning that was comprehensive enough to expose and deal with the roots of urban decay. They engaged in 'meetingitis' and were supporting strategies that resulted in 'projectitis', the outcome of which was a 'laundry list' of traditional programs to be conducted by traditional agencies in the traditional manner under which slums emerged in the first place.
7 Residents were not getting enough information from CDAs to enable them to review CDA developed plans or to initiate plans of their own as required by HUD. At best, they were getting superficial information. At worst, they were not even getting copies of official HUD materials.
8 Most residents were unaware of their rights to be reimbursed for expenses incurred because of participation – babysitting, transportation costs, and so on. The training of residents, which would enable them to understand the labyrinth of the federal-state-city systems and networks of subsystems, was an item that most CDAs did not even consider.

These findings led to a new public interpretation of HUD's approach to citizen participation. Though the requirements for the seventy-five 'second-round' Model City grantees were not changed, HUD's twenty-seven-page technical bulletin on citizen participation repeatedly advocated that cities share power with residents. It also urged CDAs to experiment with subcontracts under which the residents' groups could hire their own trusted technicians.

A more recent evaluation was circulated in February 1969 by OSTI, a private firm that entered into a contract with OEO to provide technical assistance and training to citizens involved in Model Cities programs in the north-east region of the country. OSTI's report to OEO corroborates the earlier study. In addition it states:

> In practically no Model Cities structure does citizen participation mean truly shared decision-making, such that citizens might view themselves as 'the partners in this program.'
>
> In general, citizens are finding it impossible to have a significant impact on the comprehensive planning which is going on. In most cases the staff planners of the CDA and the planners of existing agencies are carrying out the actual planning with citizens having a peripheral role of watchdog and, ultimately, the 'rubber stamp' of the plan generated. In cases where citizens have the direct responsibility for generating program plans, the time period allowed and the independent technical resources being made available to them are not adequate to allow them to do anything more than generate very traditional approaches to the problems they are attempting to solve.
>
> In general, little or no thought has been given to the means of insuring continued citizen participation during the stage of implementation. In most cases, traditional agencies are envisaged as the implementers of Model Cities programs and few mechanisms have been developed for encouraging organizational change or change in the method of program delivery within these agencies or for insuring that citizens will have some influence over these agencies as they implement Model Cities programs ... By and large, people are once again being planned for. In most situations the major planning decisions are being made by CDA staff and approved in a formalistic way by policy boards.

Partnership At this rung of the ladder, power is in fact redistributed through negotiation between citizens and powerholders. They agree to share planning and decision-making responsibilities through such structures as joint policy boards, planning committees and mechanisms for resolving impasses. After the groundrules have been established through some form of give-and-take, they are not subject to unilateral change.

Partnership can work most effectively when there is an organized power-base in the community to which the citizen leaders are accountable; when the citizens group has the financial resources to pay its leaders reasonable honoraria for their time-consuming efforts; and when the group has the resources to hire (and fire) its own technicians, lawyers, and community organizers. With these ingredients, citizens have some genuine bargaining influence over the outcome of the plan (as long as both parties find it useful to maintain the partnership). One community leader described it 'like coming to city hall with hat on head instead of in hand'.

In the Model Cities program only about fifteen of the so-called first generation of seventy-five cities have reached some significant degree of power-sharing with residents. In all but one of those cities, it was angry citizen demands, rather than city initiative, that led to the negotiated sharing of power. The negotiations were triggered by citizens who had been enraged by previous forms of alleged participation. They were both angry and sophisticated enough to refuse to be 'conned' again. They threatened to oppose the awarding of a planning grant to the city. They sent delegations to HUD in Washington. They used abrasive language. Negotiation took place under a cloud of suspicion and rancor.

In most cases where power has come to be shared it was taken by the citizens, not given by the city. There is nothing new about that process. Since those who have power normally want to hang onto it, historically it has had to be wrested by the powerless rather than proffered by the powerful.

Such a working partnership was negotiated by the residents in the Philadelphia model neighborhood. Like most applicants for a Model Cities grant, Philadelphia wrote its more than 400-page application and waved it at a hastily called meeting of community leaders. When those present were asked for an endorsement, they angrily protested the city's failure to consult them on preparation of the extensive application. A community spokesman threatened to mobilize a neighborhood protest against the application unless the city agreed to give the citizens a couple of weeks to review the application and recommend changes. The officials agreed.

At their next meeting, citizens handed the city officials a substitute citizen participation section that changed the ground rules from a weak citizens' advisory role to a strong shared power agreement. Philadelphia's application to HUD included the citizens' substitution word for word. (It also included a new citizen-prepared introductory chapter that changed the city's description of the model neighborhood from a paternalistic description of problems to a realistic analysis of its strengths, weaknesses, and potentials.) Consequently, the proposed policy-making committee of the Philadelphia CDA was revamped to give five out of eleven seats to the residents' organization, which is called the Area Wide Council (AWC). The AWC obtained a subcontract from the CDA for more than $20,000 per month, which it used to maintain the neighborhood organization, to pay citizen leaders $7 per meeting for their planning services, and to pay the salaries of a staff of community organizers, planners, and other technicians. AWC has the power to initiate plans of its own, to engage in joint planning with CDA committees, and to review plans initiated by city agencies. It has a veto power in that no plans may be submitted by the CDA to the city council until they have been reviewed, and any differences of opinion have been successfully negotiated with the AWC. Representatives of the AWC (which is a federation of neighborhood organizations grouped into sixteen neighborhood 'hubs') may attend all meetings of CDA task forces, planning committees, or subcommittees.

Though the city council has final veto power over the plan (by federal law), the AWC believes it has a neighborhood constituency that is strong enough to negotiate any eleventh-hour objections the city council might raise when it considers such AWC proposed innovations as an AWC Land Bank, an AWC Economic Development Corporation, and an experimental income maintenance program for 900 poor families.

Delegated power Negotiations between citizens and public officials can also result in citizens achieving dominant decision-making authority over a particular plan or program. Model City policy boards or CAA delegate agencies on which citizens have a clear majority of seats and genuine specified powers are typical examples. At this level, the ladder has been scaled to the point where citizens hold the significant cards to assure accountability of the program to them. To resolve differences, powerholders need to start the bargaining process rather than respond to pressure from the other end.

Such a dominant decision-making role has been attained by residents in a handful of Model Cities including Cambridge, Massachusetts; Dayton, and Columbus, Ohio; Minneapolis, Minnesota; St Louis, Missouri; Hartford and New Haven, Connecticut; and Oakland, California.

In New Haven, residents of the Hill neighborhood have created a corporation that has been delegated the power to prepare the entire Model Cities plan. The city, which received a $117,000 planning grant from HUD, has subcontracted $110,000 of it to the neighborhood corporation to hire its own planning staff and consultants. The Hill Neighborhood Corporation has eleven representatives on the twenty-one-member CDA board which assures it a majority voice when its proposed plan is reviewed by the CDA.

Another model of delegated power is separate and parallel groups of citizens and powerholders, with provision for citizen veto if differences of opinion cannot be resolved through negotiation. This is a particularly interesting coexistence model for hostile citizen groups too embittered toward city hall – as a result of past 'collaborative efforts' – to engage in joint planning.

Since all Model Cities programs require approval by the city council before HUD will fund them, city councils have final veto powers even when citizens have the majority of seats on the CDA Board. In Richmond, California, the city

15

council agreed to a citizens' counter-veto, but the details of that agreement are ambiguous and have not been tested.

Various delegated power arrangements are also emerging in the Community Action Program as a result of demands from the neighborhoods and OEO's most recent instruction guidelines which urged CAAs 'to exceed [the] basic requirements' for resident participation. In some cities, CAAs have issued subcontracts to resident-dominated groups to plan and/or operate one or more decentralized neighborhood program components like a multipurpose service center or a Headstart program. These contracts usually include an agreed-upon line-by-line budget and program specifications. They also usually include a specific statement of the significant powers that have been delegated; for example: policy-making; hiring and firing; issuing subcontracts for building, buying, or leasing (some of the subcontracts are so broad that they verge on models for citizen control).

Citizen control Demands for community-controlled schools, black control, and neighborhood control are on the increase. Though no one in the nation has absolute control, it is very important that the rhetoric not be confused with intent. People are simply demanding that degree of power (or control) which guarantees that participants or residents can govern a program or an institution, be in full charge of policy and managerial aspects, and be able to negotiate the conditions under which 'outsiders' may change them.

A neighborhood corporation with no intermediaries between it and the source of funds is the model most frequently advocated. A small number of such experimental corporations are already producing goods and/or social services. Several others are reportedly in the development stage, and new models for control will undoubtedly emerge as the have-nots continue to press for greater degrees of power over their lives.

Though the bitter struggle for community control of the Ocean Hill-Brownsville schools in New York City has aroused great fears in the headline-reading public, less publicized experiments are demonstrating that the have-nots can indeed improve their lot by handling the entire job of planning, policy-making, and managing a program. Some are even demonstrating that they can do all this with just one arm because they are forced to use their other one to deal with a continuing barrage of local opposition triggered by the announcement that a federal grant has been given to a community group or an all-black group.

Most of these experimental programs have been capitalized with research and demonstration funds from the Office of Economic Opportunity in cooperation with other federal agencies. Examples include:

1 A $1.8 million grant was awarded to the Hough Area Development Corporation in Cleveland to plan economic development programs in the ghetto and

to develop a series of economic enterprises ranging from a novel combination shopping-center-public-housing project to a loan guarantee program for local building contractors. The membership and board of the nonprofit corporation is composed of leaders of major community organizations in the black neighborhood.

2 Approximately $1 million ($595,751 for the second year) was awarded to the Southwest Alabama Farmers' Cooperative Association (SWAFCA) in Selma, Alabama, for a ten-county marketing cooperative for food and livestock. Despite local attempts to intimidate the coop (which included the use of force to stop trucks on the way to market) first-year membership grew to 1,150 farmers who earned $52,000 on the sale of their new crops. The elected coop board is composed of two poor black farmers from each of the ten economically depressed counties.

3 Approximately $600,000 ($300,000 in a supplemental grant) was granted to the Albina Corporation and the Albina Investment Trust to create a black-operated, black-owned manufacturing concern using inexperienced management and unskilled minority group personnel from the Albina district. The profit-making wool and metal fabrication plant will be owned by its employees through a deferred compensation trust plan.

4 Approximately $800,000 ($400,000 for the second year) was awarded to the Harlem Commonwealth Council to demonstrate that a community-based development corporation can catalyze and implement an economic development program with broad community support and participation. After only eighteen months of program development and negotiation, the council will soon launch several large-scale ventures including operation of two supermarkets, an auto service and repair center (with built-in manpower training program), a finance company for families earning less than $4,000 per year, and a data processing company. The all-black Harlem-based board is already managing a metal castings foundry.

Though several citizen groups (and their mayors) use the rhetoric of citizen control, no Model City can meet the criteria of citizen control since final approval power and accountability rest with the city council.

Daniel P. Moynihan argues that city councils are representative of the community, but Adam Walinsky illustrates the non-representativeness of this kind of representation:

Who ... exercises 'control' through the representative process? In the Bedford-Stuyvesant ghetto of New York there are 450,000 people – as many as in the entire city of Cincinnati, more than in the entire state of Vermont. Yet the area has only one high school, and 50 per cent of its teenagers are dropouts; the infant mortality rate is twice the national average; there are over 8000 buildings abandoned by everyone but the rats, yet the area received not one dollar of urban renewal funds during the entire first 15 years of that program's operation; the unemployment rate is known only to God.

Clearly, Bedford-Stuyvesant has some special needs; yet it has always been lost in the midst of the city's eight million. In fact, it took a lawsuit to win for this vast area, in the year 1968, its first Congressman. In what sense can the representative system be said to have 'spoken for' this community, during the long years of neglect and decay?

Walinsky's point on Bedford-Stuyvesant has general applicability to the ghettos from coast to coast. It is therefore likely that in those ghettos where residents have achieved a significant degree of power in the Model Cities planning process, the first-year action plans will call for the creation of some new community institutions entirely governed by residents with a specified sum of money contracted to them. If the groundrules for these programs are clear and if citizens understand that achieving a genuine place in the pluralistic scene subjects them to its legitimate forms of give-and-take, then these kinds of programs might begin to demonstrate how to counteract the various corrosive political and socioeconomic forces that plague the poor.

In cities likely to become predominantly black through population growth, it is unlikely that strident citizens' groups like AWC of Philadelphia will eventually demand legal power for neighborhood self-government. Their grand design is more likely to call for a black city achieved by the elective process. In cities destined to remain predominantly white for the foreseeable future, it is quite likely that counterpart groups to AWC will press for separatist forms of neighborhood government that can create and control decentralized public services such as police protection, education systems, and health facilities. Much may depend on the willingness of city governments to entertain demands for resource allocation weighted in favor of the poor, reversing gross imbalances of the past.

Among the arguments against community control are: it supports separatism; it creates balkanization of public services; it is more costly and less efficient; it enables minority group 'hustlers' to be just as opportunistic and disdainful of the have-nots as their white predecessors; it is incompatible with merit systems and professionalism; and ironically enough, it can turn out to be a new Mickey Mouse game for the have-nots by allowing them to gain control but not allowing them sufficient dollar resources to succeed. These arguments are not to be taken lightly. But neither can we take lightly the arguments of embittered advocates of community control – that every other means of trying to end their victimization has failed!

[Originally published as Sherry R. Arnstein, 'A ladder of citizen participation', *Journal of the American Institute of Planners*, 35(4), July 1969, pp. 216–24]

2 | The many faces of participation

Matthias Stiefel and Marshall Wolfe

The term 'popular participation' entered into international discourse on development during the 1960s and achieved wider currency during the 1970s, at a time when the myth of development itself was experiencing contradictory impacts of utopian redefinition ('another development') and disillusionment with state capacity to control or plan. The term itself and the actions it suggested were adaptable to quite different ideological frames of reference and immediately came under suspicion for the same reason. Different actors in the development drama conceived of participation in very different ways and promoted or opposed participatory initiatives with different time perspectives and expectations. The hopes for participation derived from and renewed a long historical evolution of theories and practice of democracy, co-operation and communitarian and socialist utopias, but the 1970s discourse paid only sporadic attention to this history.

During the 1980s participation lost ground in international discourse, sharing in the eclipse of development conceptions oriented to social justice and human welfare. A United Nations International Seminar on Popular Participation, held in Ljubljana in 1982, focused on government policies and expectations from participation, rather than on the 'popular' dimension. At the beginning of the 1990s hopes for participation as a way out of otherwise insoluble crises of human relationships and livelihood are reviving. In February 1990, the African governments, together with various United Nations agencies, non-governmental organizations and African people's organizations, held an International Conference on Popular Participation in the Recovery and Development Process in Africa, at Arusha, Tanzania. In May 1990, the United Nations Children's Fund (UNICEF), which has been particularly concerned at the paucity of beneficiary initiative in its own local projects, organized a Global Seminar on Participatory Finance in Florence, Italy. The documents of these meetings show that long-standing ambiguities remain concerning tutelage by the state or by NGOs and other external allies vs. popular spontaneity and autonomy; and in regard to the requirements of a market-ruled kingdom of necessity vs. popular aspirations to social justice and security. The following sections will discuss the main conceptions of our approaches to popular participation as they emerged in the 1970s and earlier, and as they manifested themselves in the UNRISD (United Nations Research Institute for Social Development) debates and research.

Pluralist democracy

The conception with the longest history and widest acceptance has focused on participation as the ideal functioning of pluralist representative democracy. Political parties competing within codified rules of the game then become the main channels through which the whole adult population can have a voice in the selection of leaders and policies. This conception has supposed free competition in ideas and criticisms; protection of the rights of minorities; two-way communication between the citizens and their elected leadership through a wide range of organizations representing different constituencies, in addition to the competing parties; and many kinds of formal and informal consultations among citizens. It has also supposed a broad underlying consensus that allows all major social groups to feel themselves represented within the system in spite of obvious differences in ability to make themselves heard. It has been compatible with widely differing degrees and kinds of government intervention in society, but thus far has been associated with capitalist or 'mixed' welfare state systems. It has implied a distrust of concrete utopias and blueprints for their achievements, including centralized planning, that might endanger the majority's right to change course.

Pluralist democracy has been formally endorsed and at least intermittently practised by the majority of states since World War II. Governments and social scientists in the First World prescribed it almost as a matter of course for new countries emerging through decolonization. Its application has met with well-known reverses and criticisms, of which the following are particularly relevant for present purposes. First, it has been argued, particularly in regard to countries with rural majorities and high illiteracy, that only educated and well-off minorities are able to enter the political competition. If the rural majority and the urban poor vote at all they do so at the dictate of landowners, caciques or government officials. The 'participating' minorities are then able to serve their own interests at the expense of the voiceless majority. (With economic and demographic changes generating large underclasses practically excluded from employment and even from shelter, similar arguments are now being applied to significant minorities in certain 'rich' countries.) It has been argued that the excluded are more likely to gain from mobilizing regimes, motivated to seek their support to counter-balance the power of the previous élites. This argument has applied particularly to agrarian reforms, since one can find at least a few instances of decisive action by dictatorships and many instances of delay and emasculation of programmes by parliamentary allies of landowning élites. In general, however, the weight of evidence does not suggest that the dispossessed have fared better under mobilizing dictatorships than under élite-controlled democracies, in which clientelistic networks may offer them appreciable rewards and some sense of participating.

A related argument against pluralist representative democracy, linked to the reasoning discussed under 'legitimization of power' below, is that the divisiveness of competition by rival parties clashes with the cultural background of 'non-Western' peoples accustomed to decisions by consensus or by reliance on traditional authorities. It has also been argued, from the experience of multiethnic African and Asian countries, that the formation of competing political parties almost unavoidably becomes linked with ethnic divisions rather than policy choices or class interests, so that pluralist democracy cannot function as it does in more homogeneous societies.

As electoral participation widens with the advance of urbanization, literacy and exposure to mass media, without significant narrowing of the gap between the élites and the majority or the incorporation of the latter into autonomous class-based organizations, different arguments against pluralist democracy come to the fore. Charismatic populist leaders gain the confidence of the majority through extravagant promises and some real benefits, once they come to power. Mobilized voting then displaces more structured efforts to gain control over resources and institutions. The populist leadership tolerates minority opinion only grudgingly, identifying it with 'enemies of the people'. The antipopulists interpret their own exclusion as an evil consequence of excessive participation. In practice, the populist regimes have commonly brought about some changes in the composition of élites but no sustainable redistribution of power to the majority. Their propensity to incoherent economic policies, arbitrariness and corruption has generally brought about their breakdown and replacement by overtly anti-participatory regimes, although mass loyalty to populist leadership has persisted or recurred. A few regimes, such as that of Mexico, have managed to institutionalize original combinations of populist appears, co-option or repression of opposition, and technobureaucratic management to achieve over relatively long periods political stability and economic growth, but at a price of growing popular alienation and apathy.

In the 1970s the advocates of 'another development' looked to China and Tanzania as models and the Velasco military government in Peru had embarked on participatory schemes with apparent innovativeness and conviction. In a good many other countries authoritarian regimes were so well entrenched and so adverse to pluralism that only participatory initiatives too localized and unobtrusive to attract their suspicion seemed practicable, and this limitation influenced many organizations that aspired to bring practical help to the dispossessed. Since then the resurgence of pluralist democracy has been extraordinary, in national societies with quite different past trajectories. It has become more widely agreed that other forms of participation, however legitimate and promising, cannot do without political means of making themselves heard at national level, if only to fend off bureaucratic arrogance and corruption. Ability to give or withhold votes, for all its shortcomings, is indispensable to the efforts of the hitherto 'excluded'.

Modernization

A conception widely influential among policy-making élites and social scientists has viewed participation as a dimension of modernization. If capital formation and transfer of technology were to generate self-sustaining 'development', they would have to go hand in hand with cultural, political and social modernization: including the transfer of democratic political institutions from the West, and the transfer of values emphasizing efficiency and consumerism. Popular participation then became a therapy, to transform 'backward', 'traditional', 'unresponsive' populations into citizens ready to assume their duties and seize their opportunities in a predetermined development process. In this process, the majority would receive diverse incentives as well as compulsions to participate in activities outside the family and the neighbourhood, gradually gaining in ability to organize and defend perceived interests.

This conception has implied that some groups, at least for a few generations, would remain unable or unwilling to be incorporated into a 'modern' and 'efficient' social order; that is, they would be excluded or bypassed by history. Advocates of this conception have generally devalued or distrusted traditional community and extended family ties as forms of participation. Such ties would or should disintegrate in the course of modernization. They have also shared a preoccupation that participation in politics and in consumption might run ahead of participation in production and in technological innovation. Participation might then stifle development by stimulating premature struggles over distribution and preventing accumulation of a surplus for investment.

By the 1970s this conception had lost a good deal of credit through the rise of dependency theory and related attacks on the 'Western' bias of modernization. The long-term viability of continually expanding and modernizing production and consumption was coming into question. The proportion of the world's population able to participate to some degree was obviously growing, but ecological and demographic trends made it seem unlikely that the laggards would ever be able to catch up by following available route-maps of modernization. The dilemmas presented by modernized consumption patterns accessible to minorities prepared to guard their privileges by force versus expanding political participation and demands for redistribution seemed likely to be permanent rather than transitory, both within countries and between countries in the world system. Democratically legitimized regimes that see increasing inequality through the unleashing of market forces as the only way forward are now confronting new versions of these dilemmas.

'The missing ingredient'

Policy-making élites have also viewed participation as a means or set of techniques available to government agencies for the purpose of making development programmes function better and the development process itself more efficient and more equitable. That is, popular participation has been seen as a 'missing ingredient' to be achieved through foolproof or bureaucrat-proof ways of adding 'participation components' to projects and activities. In fact, this approach is associated with a conception of development itself as an aggregation of 'development projects' rather than as a complex process of societal change. It introduces participation only at the stage of implementation of projects handed down from above, and defines the people affected as 'target groups' or 'beneficiary groups'.

Advocates of this approach have generally looked to traditional communities and systems of reciprocity as more adaptable to their purpose than modern party and interest-group organizations. Applications go back to the community development and *animation rurale* programmes embarked on in many countries in the 1950s, some of them backed by considerable public resources and high-level government support. Their generally disappointing results generated diagnoses pointing to their subjection to centrally imposed targets and techniques, their failure to allow for cultural traits and conflicts of interest within the communities they served, and their propensity to manipulate rather than liberate. Since then, programmes using different labels and purporting to meet the criticisms of their predecessors have waxed and waned. Repeated experience of the inefficiency and costliness of the bureaucratic apparatuses available for implementing 'planned' development programmes, particularly in rural settings, and of the lack of communication between these apparatuses and the intended beneficiaries, have kept alive the hope of accomplishing objectives more cheaply, defusing popular discontent and tapping the potential of human imitative.

In spite of its negative evaluation of bureaucratic agents, this conception could not dispense with a supposition of basic state rationality, benevolence and representativeness in society, and of societal consensus on development goals. Programmes whose experience cast doubt on these suppositions risked disavowal by their government sponsors. Practically none of the initiatives could solve the problem of duplicability of localized successes, or shield them against political and economic instability in the wider society. The supposition of a 'missing ingredient' became less plausible with rising scepticism concerning the capacity of the state to manage development.

More recently the forced abandonment of state responsibilities for social services and subsidies to the levels of living of the poor has thrown attention back to the potential of localized self-help with modest support from the state or non-government organizations. This trend, accompanying a shrinkage in the planning capacity and aspirations of the state, becomes rather a substitute for a development policy than a missing ingredient. It has at least meant greater appreciation of the survival strategies of the poor, and has involved a wide range of small-scale initiatives close to the approaches discussed under 'conscientization' below.

The self-reliant poor

Even before the crises of the 1980s, a good many governments looked to a more restricted version of the conception summarized above, viewing participation as a means of relieving pressures for social services and subsidies under conditions in which the style of development could not offer satisfactory livelihood or 'modern' employment to a large part of the population. Self-help, self-reliance and reciprocity were then encouraged for the production and exchange of goods among the poor and for the provision of housing and community services: areas in which participation did not perturb the existing distribution of power and wealth. The poor were to maintain themselves in a kind of parallel economy, functioning under laws quite different from the modern economy, until the latter might become ready to absorb them. Policies of this kind encountered a persistent misunderstanding between the parties: governments supported them to some extent so as to relieve themselves of responsibilities; the poor participated to some extent in the hope of being rewarded by resources from the government. Under present conditions, however, governmental hopes of this kind can reach an uneasy coexistence with strivings from below, when groups of the dispossessed and their allies find no alternative to organized survival strategies and can expect from the authorities not much more than toleration of these strategies.

Legitimization of power

Authoritarian governments have viewed popular participation (although not overtly) as a set of techniques (plebiscites, mass demonstrations of support for the regime, mobilizations of 'voluntary' labour for public purposes, revival or invention of 'traditional' consensual community institutions, etc.) legitimizing their rule and allowing for controlled expression of popular sentiments while eliminating autonomous channels for organization and representation. The rhetoric of participation and also of national cultural uniqueness is thus used to promote manipulated alternatives to 'divisive' pluralist democracy. A good deal of self-deception may enter in, and the degree of authenticity in the participation and the cultural traditions may be unclear even to the sponsoring authorities as well as the groups called on to participate. This approach has been used to some degree by all populist regimes and one-party states and quite systematically in regimes such as the 'New Society' of the Marcos period in the Philippines. It was present in 'African Socialism' and similar ideologies adopted by the ruling élites of various newly independent African countries (Bangura 1991). Authoritarian participatory rhetoric has motivated rejection of the term by some adherents to other conceptions, as indicated below under 'mystification'. This approach differs from the conception next to be discussed in its lack of a coherent rationale for societal transformation in the interest of the majority.

Revolutionary and post-revolutionary mobilization

A conception widely influential in the Third World during the 1960s and 1970s held that 'participation', if it were to bring about real gains for the dispossessed majority, would have to consist of revolutionary mobilization under the guidance of a vanguard party or enlightened élite. The currents of opinion adhering to this proposition generally relied on variants of Marxist-Leninist theory, but it was also advocated independently of such theory. It was argued that the intolerable poverty of the Third World majority, the urgency of transformation, the complexity of the policy choices involved, the threat of imperialist aggression and counter-revolutionary subversion from defeated classes, and the necessity of comprehensive planning did not leave room for more pluralistic, localized autonomous or open-ended approaches. This argument entered into the UNRISD programme through a sub-debate on the 'urgency factor', but none of the field researches confronted its applications to reality, with the partial exception of an exploratory mission to China.

While the conception called for empowerment of the hitherto excluded majority, it left this majority no scope for choice of what to do with its empowerment. It offered no safeguards against arbitrary and unrealistic decisions by an infallible leadership and conformist ritualism substituted for autonomous and critical participation. Its pretensions have collapsed with astonishing rapidity, through the self-admitted impasses of the regimes supposed to exemplify it. An examination of the erratic trajectories of policy in such regimes and their human costs indicate that the alleged advantages of planning and ability to act decisively were illusory, and even the real achievements in social equality and security have come under attack as causes of productive stagnation and psychological antipathy to innovation. Moreover, in a good many Third World countries, 'urgency' has justified military and bureaucratic élites with little or no revolutionary authenticity or claim to majority support. Authentic participation for the defence of perceived popular interests could survive only in the interstices left by the inability of the formal mobilizing and planning mechanisms to regulate all aspects of social intercourse.

Conscientization and self-liberation

A family of conceptions very different from those summarized above has viewed participation mainly in terms of local groups defending and/or transforming their own lifestyles and sources of livelihood, evolving their own ideas and tactics in the course of struggle against exploitative power structures, ideologies and economic systems. These conceptions have supposed a very high potential for popular creativity and also for traditional knowledge and indigenous technology. They have denied the capacity of bureaucratized state power, whether under capitalist or socialist forms of economic and political organization, to achieve just social orders. In general, they have limited the legitimate role of external allies to that of catalysts helping in the early stages of organization. They have generally been reluctant to speculate on the future management of complex societies. They have either disregarded the constraints imposed by national states within the world system, or hoped that these would wither away as local groups become more autonomous and form 'networks' among them. Differences have emerged mainly concerning the degree of spontaneity to be expected and the legitimacy of guidance from outside the group, i.e. 'conscientization'. One activist and participant in the UNRISD programme has affirmed: '... it is concluded, without further ado, that communities must be guided towards social responsibility, or "conscientized". I utterly disagree with this conclusion and with the neologism coined by Paulo Freire [conscientization], because I consider that the appearance of a conscience, whether individual or collective, is not an induced event, but a spontaneous occurrence' (Angulo 1990).

The real initiatives corresponding to these conceptions have proved vulnerable but also resilient and remarkably varied during the past two decades. They have been easy to repress, and have touched upon the lives only of shifting minorities within most national societies. The contradictions between the ideal of autonomy and the real dependence of local groups on external allies have been recurrent, as have the contradictions between the concrete aspirations of the local groups and the egalitarian anti-consumerist ideologies of their allies. The conceptions themselves have come under criticism for their anti-political bias, isolating the local groups from national class-based organizations and making them paradoxically dependent on the state as the only institution capable of responding to their needs for services and subsidies.

At the same time, the ties between local self-defensive movements of the dispossessed and national or international movements with religious, gender, ethnic and environmental agendas have become remarkably complex. The potential of conscientization or self-liberation to transform for the better the lives of the majority remains an open question, but the efforts are bound to persist, both as one dimension in popular survival strategies and as one dimension in the international effort to rethink or replace the myth of development.

Social movements

Conceptions having considerable affinity to the above go back to social upheavals in the First World during the 1960s when a wide range of new movements focusing on 'quality of life' issues or anti-militarism seemed to displace traditional class antagonisms and struggles over distribution as the main focus of challenge to the existing systems of domination. Some of the studies sponsored in Latin America by the UNRISD programme viewed participation mainly as an evolving process of the emergence of 'social movements' and their coming together into broader 'popular movements' capable of challenging the national power structures and eventually controlling the state in the interest of the majority. Their authors argued for the necessity of combining many different bases and motivations for 'organized efforts' (class, local, regional, ethnic, gender, student status, etc.). Their hopes emerged from a period of disillusioning experiences with political parties, electoral mechanisms, revolutionary strategies and development planning.

In a good many countries in Latin America military governments had eliminated previous channels for political and interest-group participation and forced a search for viable alternatives. The resulting distrust of centralized 'vanguard parties', state planning and theoretical blueprints for the future led to a high valuation on spontaneous popular action and on civil society as opposed to the state, but gave more importance to power and transformation at the national level than did the advocates of conscientization and self-liberation. Political parties were looked to as components but not manipulators of the eventual 'popular movements'. Class struggle was viewed as an important but not unique dimension of social transformation. These conceptions were inherently pluralist but viewed pluralism rather differently from the advocates of representative democracy, since popular choice between competing political parties would be less important than interactions between social and popular movements seeking common ground.

Trade unions and other collective action for limited ends

Collective action focused on the advancement of class or group rights and interests through collective bargaining, organized pressures on the authorities, and co-operatively managed production, buying and selling, has a long history and corresponds closely to the UNRISD definition of participation. Participation here takes the form of a continuing struggle over the distribution of incomes and access to livelihood and services, in which solidarity gives strength to a numerous social group engaged in production whose members individually have neither assets nor power. The participants may also act in accordance with one or more of the other conceptions of participation, but their immediate struggle leaves open the question of their acceptance or rejection of the existing economic and political order, and also the question of a liberating transformation of their values. Collective action for limited ends also leaves open the question whether the organized participants should go out of their way to incorporate weaker and less easily organized categories of the disadvantaged, or take a stand on questions outside the area of production, such as ecological menaces or the rights of women and minorities. The contradiction between motivations to broaden solidarity and motivations to maintain group advantages seems inherent in this form of participation. More recently, of course, economic crises have eroded union capacity to defend employment security and income levels.

Worker management

A relatively well-defined movement with its own body of experiences and techniques, more influential in Europe than elsewhere and central to national policy in Yugoslavia until recently, has concentrated on participation in the sense of worker management in industry and other economic enterprises, in the expectation that this could eventually become the main form of organization of production and distribution, and the basis of a new society. Various successful enterprises have been presented as models, but their number and influence do not seem to have increased significantly since the 1970s. Roles for trade unions as administrators of social services for their members, financed by dues and sometimes state contributions, and participation by union representatives in the directorates of industries have been more widespread but do not seem to have brought about significant empowerment of members. Hopes that worker management would replace bureaucratized 'real socialism' during the recent disintegration of the latter seem to have been ephemeral. The approach has been briefly incorporated in national policies in a few Third World countries, as in Peru during the 1970s. In these countries, however, worker management has more often appeared as a dimension of survival strategies: workers, particularly in public transport, have taken over bankrupt enterprises abandoned by their owners or by the state and kept them going as best they could. Small enterprises in the informal sector are also sometimes managed co-operatively by their workers, although even in this part of the economy capitalist entrepreneurial management seems to be more common.

Defence of the natural order

According to one line of argument among social scientists, authentic participatory movements usually derive from a shared set of beliefs justifying group defence or recovery of an imagined traditional social order, based on natural rights and forms of hierarchy and reciprocity, that is threatened by outsiders or by unintelligible forces disrupting lifestyles and sources of livelihood. The resulting 'organized efforts' do not necessarily aim at control of the state or transformation of the economic system, but the consequences can be either revolutionary or reactionary according to interactions with other forces and ideologies and with the state's efforts to maintain order.

Periods of questioning of the legitimacy and viability of the existing political and economic order naturally bring forth a resurgence of national myths and quests for bases of collective identity, which may be partly spontaneous, partly manipulated by the state itself or by movements seeking power. Movements of this kind can take on extremely 'excluding' and xenophobic forms, clashing violently with participatory currents that hold to more universalistic and forward-looking conceptions of human rights and social justice, in particular those calling for gender equality and religious freedom. The revolutionary-religious transformation of Iran is the most obvious case in point. At the same time, advocates of conscientization and of the spontaneous development of social movements have insisted on the need to draw on the historical memories and cultural resources of the oppressed. The movements combining demands for cultural autonomy and defence of traditional means of livelihood have found allies particularly among environmentalist movements. A struggle for popular consciousness may then ensue between rival articulators of historical myths and ethical-religious doctrines. The various outcomes are likely to be as inspiring, baffling and horrifying to proponents of other conceptions of participation in the future as in the past.

Mystification

Ever since the cry of the French students in 1968 – *'Je participe ... ils profitent'* – 'participation' has undergone criticism as a deliberately misleading slogan masking an evasion of the realities of power or the laws of economics. Criticisms have come from economic and political orthodoxy, insisting on the incompatibility of premature or spontaneous participation with governability and development, and from the Marxist left, insisting on the futility of participation divorced from a strategy for the taking of power and transformation of relations of production. At the same time, advocates of self-liberation, direct democracy and autonomous social movements have objected mainly to the contamination of the term itself in international and national political usage. They have argued that the purposes of the organizations and governments endorsing it deprive it of legitimacy as a focus for research and action. More narrowly, 'participation' might amount to a source of livelihood and status for activists and researchers whose previous schemes for development were reaching an impasse.

The various conceptions of or approaches to popular participation summarized above reflect the views of intellectual-ideological activists, social scientists, politicians and administrators who have codified them and tried to act on them. They have manifested themselves in projects and expressions of solidarity with minorities among the dispossessed classes and groups whose 'participation' is hoped for. Here they interact with organizational initiatives from below whose extent and continuity can only be guessed at. The results of this interaction for the dispossessed, depending on real experiences and the capacity of the wider environment to reward participation, are unavoidably contradictory. They include a generalized distrust of outsiders based on past manipulation and unfulfilled promises; a more sophisticated evaluation of outsiders as needed but undependable allies; and an internalization of the vocabularies and views of these allies, whether from conviction or as a means of manipulating them and forging links with more influential components of the societies. The clash of conceptions of participation and the competition of governmental, non-governmental, and anti-governmental allies/manipulators have become part of the environment within which the 'excluded' struggle to survive and adapt to or escape from their exclusion.

[Extract from Matthias Stiefel and Marshall Wolfe, *A Voice for the Excluded: Popular Participation in Development*, Zed Books, 1994]

References

Angulo, Alejandro (1990) *An Experience in Participatory Development*, UNICEF Innocenti Global Seminar on Participatory Development, Florence: UNICEF.

Bangura, Yusuf (1991) *Authoritarian Rule and Democracy in Africa: A Theoretical Discourse*, UNRISD Discussion Paper No. 18, Geneva: UNRISD.

3 | What is meant by people's participation?

N. C. Saxena

'People's participation' has become a standard rhetoric in India today. Different actors interpret it differently. One view is that participation means getting people to agree to and go along with a project that has already been designed for them, or to get support of a few leaders. This has been the approach in many development schemes that did not work. People did not identify themselves with the assets created such as the hand pump or trees planted, nor did they undertake the responsibility of maintenance of assets. 'I manage, you participate' was the dominant underlying principle behind such projects. These tended to try to make people aware of their responsibility without giving them any authority to spend funds or to manage assets. People's participation was then expressed not in a manner that would establish their rights over assets, land or its produce. The important question is, participation for whose benefit, and on what terms?

Participation should include the notions of contribution, influencing, sharing, or redistributing power and of control, resources, benefits, knowledge, and skills to be gained through beneficiary involvement in decision-making. Participation is a voluntary process by which people, including the disadvantaged (in income, gender, caste, or education), influence or control the decisions that affect them. The essence of participation is exercising voice and choice and developing the human, organizational and management capacity to solve problems as they arise in order to sustain the improvements.

Half-hearted measures towards people's participation have only resulted in wastage of funds with no gains. It must be therefore understood as a process by which the people are able to organize themselves, and through their own organization are able to identify their own needs, and share in the design implementation and evaluation of the participatory action. Thus, various elements of participation and decision-making at various stages, control and management of funds and resources, share in usufruct and final produce and certainty of benefits. In other words, participation should not stop at information sharing or consultation; decision-making and initiating action are important and essential components of participation.

Initiating action Initiating action by the people represents the highest level of participation that surpasses involvement in the decision-making process. Self-initiated actions are a clear sign of empowerment. Once people are empowered, they are more likely to be proactive, to take initiative, and to display confidence for undertaking other actions to solve problems beyond those defined by the project. This level of participation is qualitatively different from that achieved when people merely carry out assigned tasks.

Why participate Participation engenders financial, social, and psychological costs, as well as benefits. People or beneficiaries are likely to participate when the benefits outweigh their costs, just as a government department is likely to foster beneficiary participation when the benefits of doing so (for the Forest Department, for instance, higher rate of survival, greater sustainability, and improved public image) outstrip the costs to the agency. However, knowledge about the costs and benefits of participation remains limited; little guidanceabout budget allocations appropriate to induce participation is available to the people or even field staff of government departments. Nevertheless, from the perspective of both, government department and NGO, people's participation (as an input or an independent variable) can contribute to the achievement of four main objectives: effectiveness; efficiency; empowerment; and equity.

Who participates The most important characteristic that brings people together to take action is commonality of interest. This is the glue that binds people who may otherwise not have much in common in terms of geography, wealth, power, readership, degrees of organization, social cohesion, caste, income, gender or education. Commonality of interest may supersede other distinction, including the entity of 'community' (or village or other administrative label of convenience).

Outcomes and indicators of participation Participation in decision-making is an important capacity-building process. As people participate in making new decisions and solving problems, learning takes place. This learning is internalized, because it is accomplished experientially. It therefore leads to changes in attitude, behaviour, confidence, and leadership. Newly acquired knowledge is therefore the first outcome of participation.

Empowerment is a result of participation in decision-making. An empowered person is one who can take initiative, exert leadership, display confidence, solve new problems, mobilize resources, and undertake new actions. Empowerment, it is hypothesized, is an important outcome of high levels of participation involving control over decision-making for a range of activities. Hence, empowerment is a leading outcome of successful capacity-building at the individual and institutional levels.

The third outcome is organization-building. Decentralized programmes require strong local organizations. When local organizations get the opportunity to manage resources and support development, they can become stronger. Participation in decision-making is hypothesized to strengthen the capacity of local organization to call out activities. Local organizations can have a few people working on joint management committees, or a village council, or organizations of several villages.

These three outcomes of participation – learning, empowerment, and a vibrant organization – need to be measured through observable indicators, which will vary from project to project. Each project must develop a clearly observable indicator on people's participation, so as to judge whether they are on track or not. Such indicators should then be given to monitors and evaluators, who have to do mid-course and impact assessment.

When to participate One of the characteristics of participation is that it cannot be turned on and off like a tap, that is, 'now you participate, now you don't'. Participation is an evolutionary process that gathers momentum and defies breakdown into neat, self-contained categories, except for analytical purposes. Establishing participation is particularly important in the early stage, because expecting responsible behaviour in the later stages is not only misguided but may result in ineffective projects. Participation should be viewed as a process that starts with planning of mangrove projects and ends with maintenance and usufruct sharing, rather than as an element that can be injected in the later stages of a project whenever outsiders determine.

[Originally published as N. C. Saxena, 'What is meant by people's participation?', *Journal of Rural Development*, 17(1), 1998, pp. 111–13]

4 | Participation's place in rural development: seeking clarity through specificity

John Cohen and Norman Uphoff

Popularity without clarity

Concern with problems of 'participation' in rural development has been growing in recent years. Ever more documents and pronouncements proclaim the virtues of participation. The UN's Economic and Social Council has recommended that governments should 'adopt popular participation as a basic policy measure in national development strategy' and should 'encourage the widest possible active participation of all individuals and national non-government organizations, such as trade unions, youth and women's organizations, in the development process in setting goals, formulating policies and implementing plans'.[1]

In what came to be called 'the Congressional mandate', the US Congress in its 1973 Foreign Assistance Act made clear that American development assistance is to be extended in ways that involve the intended beneficiaries in the planning and implementation of project efforts, as well as in the gains of development. Other donors take the same position.[2] As the strategy of development moves to what is called a 'basic-needs' approach, we find participation identified as an essential element of this strategy.

Concern with participation is certainly popular, and one can hardly be against the concept, broadly conceived. However, there is a real danger that with growing faddishness and a lot of lip service, participation could become drained of substance and its relevance to development programmes disputable.

Anybody dealing with problems of participation in development quickly finds that the term itself is very ambiguous. Those who study participation are increasingly under pressure to define it, often so that indicators can be generated to measure. We have been more concerned with developing insightful ways of thinking about participation and have not become absorbed in definitional efforts. For us, asking 'what *is* participation?' may be the wrong question, since it *implies that participation is a single phenomenon.* We prefer to focus on what specific but multiple activities and outcomes can be meaningfully understood, and supported, under this rubric.

It seems instructive to think in terms of *three dimensions of participation*: (1) *What kind* of participation is under consideration; (2) *who* is participating in it;

and (3) *how* is this participation occurring? Further, it is necessary to consider closely the *context* in which participation is occurring, or intended to occur. This calls for careful attention to the *characteristics* of the rural development project and the ways in which the *environment* will condition the kinds of participation that are more or less likely, and more or less appropriate.

This view recognizes that participatory situations and actions may vary widely. The term refers to involvement by individuals, but it presumes that more than just a few persons are involved; otherwise the situation or action is one entailing relatively little participation.

In the sections which follow, we first review issues and approaches to participation that have shaped current concerns. Then we shall summarize a way to map out and clarify this complex but critical development notion and to make it applicable to rural development projects.

Origins of concern

Questions about the relationship between participation and social and human development have been around since the ancient Greeks. One of the most extended considerations of the effects of participation remains that of Aristotle. He analysed the Greek city-states to assess what arrangements most likely contributed to human happiness and 'the good life'. In his view, participation in the affairs of state as a citizen was essential to the development and fulfilment of the human personality. To be excluded from politics, as slaves were, meant that one would not develop fully the faculty of reason, a sense of responsibility for others' welfare, a disposition toward prudent and balanced judgements. While participation did not unfailingly produce such virtues in all persons, its denial contributed to ignorance and selfishness.

At the societal level, however, Aristotle found no clear relationship between the extent of participation and the creation of 'the good life'. He did not consider rule by the many to be better than rule by the few if the majority were oppressive and disrespectful of individual rights. Conversely, an enlightened monarchy or aristocracy was preferable to rule by the mob; yet rule by only one or a few persons contained its own dangers of tyranny or oligarchy, denying to the majority the opportunity for economic and personal improvement. So in Aristotle's view, the best state in the final analysis was one where there was broad participation, with no class dominating others. The conditions for this appeared to be a reasonably equitable distribution of wealth and widespread education, conditions commonly associated with development.

Aristotle's analysis showed some relationship between participation and development but did not answer any questions of causation. It appeared that some conditions of development at the societal level were necessary for there to be productive participation, yet such participation was needed for development at the individual level. Could a society be 'developed' if its members

35

were not? We should not blame Aristotle for leaving us with this riddle: which comes first – development or participation?

The relationship is complex for many reasons. Participation, like development, has economic, social and political dimensions, and what contributes to participation at one level may not do so at another. Macro- and micro-dynamics are not necessarily the same. Moreover, most considerations and conclusions are shot through with value judgements. We can try to be as empirical and value-free as possible, and yet no assessments can escape normative implications. It is no wonder that conclusions about participation and development are still arguable.

Participation in Aristotle's time was a matter of voting, holding office, attending public meetings, paying taxes, and defending the state. Those who were to get the benefits of citizenship were expected to bear the costs of maintaining the public realm, and vice versa. In those days, there was little consideration of 'development'. Rather, one hoped and worked for prosperity through agriculture, trade and artisan manufacturing. Ideas of development have obviously changed a great deal, particularly in recent decades, owing to improvements in technological possibilities and infrastructure as well as in social organization and human aspirations. Development theory has undergone considerable change even in recent years, and its implications for the role of participation in development have also been changing.

Although the following characterization is simple, we think it represents the recent evolution of thinking about development. When the US and other more industrialized countries became concerned about problems of 'under-development' following World War II, they focused on differences in the level of *technology*. A 'technology gap' between the more and less developed countries was perceived. Foreign assistance was conceived as filling this gap through *transfer of technology*.

The requisite participation by people was primarily the *adoption* of new technologies. This assumed that these technologies would invariably be more productive or more beneficial, an often incorrect assumption. Rather than examine whether the new technology was indeed appropriate and productive, social scientists and practitioners all too often tried to explain why people in less developed countries (LDCs) did not adopt it. Issues of people's participation in development were commonly framed in terms of people's 'traditionalism' contrasted with the 'modernity' of their rulers. Non-participation was attributed to people's 'traditionalism' and 'resistance to modernity', concepts by now thoroughly disputed.

By the 1960s, development efforts and foreign assistances began to focus on *resources*, and theories dealt with various 'resource gaps' – between government revenue and expenditure, between exports and imports, between savings and investment. Increased investment in modern capital formation was regarded as the crucial ingredient for development, and the corresponding participation required from the people was accordingly measured in terms of resource contributions.

The public in this perspective was expected to pay taxes, consume domestic products, produce more for export, save and invest, and hold down personal consumption. This approach to participation, which was thought to justify exclusion of the public from decision-making participation, was hardly one to be enthusiastically approved by the public, whose members might prefer to consume rather than abstain from consumption.

Both of these technology- and resource-based theories of development which are essentially capital-centred imply a passive role for the majority of people who are not highly trained technologically and not skilled in managing national resource flows. There were, during the 1950s and 1960s, two important approaches to rural development introduced in a number of countries – community development and *animation rurale* – which aimed at mobilizing local people's participation. But neither had any strong influence on national or donor policies and resource allocations. Here we note in passing that they both held fairly narrow views of participatory activities and have been judged largely ineffective in transforming rural sectors.

As nearly two decades of experience with development effort could be examined by the late 1960s, a considerable revision of thinking occurred. Among the conclusions reached was that there appeared to be a critical 'organization gap' in LDCs (Cohen and Uphoff 1974). Relations in most countries between national centres and dispersed rural communities were weak or truncated, thus stunting development potential and response. All too often, what linkages there were were only one-way, top-down and extractive, in keeping with prevailing development theory, rather than being co-operative and mutually supportive.

The emerging new approach to development put participation into a more active and complete role, which we will be considering here. The greater concern with the use of labour as an abundant resource, with greater employment generation and with the distribution of benefits, was markedly different from the development theory that emphasized technology and physical capital formation, and which relegated popular participation to a derivative role.

Political participation

Aside from experiments like community development and *animation rurale*, when participation was discussed in the social sciences during the 1950s and 1960s, what was usually referred to was political participation, activities centred around electoral and other decision-making processes. There was also some concern with what was called 'social participation'. But neither focus encompassed what might be called *development* participation. Social-science theory regarded different levels of political participation – represented by voting, organizational memberships, etc. – as a *consequence* of development or as a characteristic of different *kinds* of political systems. As long as participation was defined operationally in terms of voting, memberships, office holding, financial contributions and other activities relating to the workings of a (presumably liberal democratic) political system, and as long as it was treated essentially as a dependent variable, it was not really very relevant to development.

The prevailing view was that political participation would increase as development proceeded, accepting Aristotle's theory at the societal level. Probably the most important work along these lines was by Almond and Verba (1963), *The Civic Culture.* In this, they found that citizen participation was greater in the US and Great Britain than in Germany, Italy and Mexico. These two countries happened also to be the most advanced economically and educationally. A 'participant' political culture was seen as growing out of economic and social development, as roles became specialized and persons became oriented to the inputs and outputs of government.

That a more active citizenry would result was also argued on the basis of cross-national analysis by Deutsch (1961). He had found that political activity and demands increased as a concomitant of such factors as economic growth, spread of mass communications, and occupational mobility. There was thought to be a bundle of orientations and actions associated with 'traditional' society, which would be replaced by a new, more participatory set with the advent of 'modernization'.

This theory fitted conveniently with the prevailing economic development theory, stressing technology transfer and capital formation. These instruments for development could be wielded only by a highly educated ruling elite, able to understand advanced technology, to formulate national development plans, and to manage the fiscal manipulations which would accelerate capital formation. The 'big push' for development was to be made possible by the 'big squeeze' put on the majority.

What were seen as the requirements of economic development justified a 'strong' state in which popular participation, unless controlled by the government elite, was an unnecessary luxury and quite possibly an impediment to increasing the GNP. Lacking technological sophistication and having a strong desire for improved living standards like those of the elite, the majority was either to be mesmerized by charismatic leadership into accepting the dictates of 'modernization' or to be kept in check by institutional channels controlled from above. This would amount to 'guided' participation or even de-participation.

It is instructive that an extensive analysis of political participation done under the auspices of the US Agency for International Development (USAID), in furtherance of its mandate under Title IX, concluded that having *either more or less* participation was likely to contribute to political instability, with attendant adverse implications for economic development. This ambivalent conclusion may have derived from misspecifications of both 'participation' and 'development'. Certainly, economic-development theory has undergone considerable change since the late 1960s. But participation theory has unfortunately lagged behind, being largely fixed on a fairly narrow view of political participation.

Development participation

Around the turn of the decade [the 1960s], more and more economists came to challenge the prevailing view that capital was the prime mover in development. They stressed rather than savings and investment the productive utilization of labour, LDCs' most abundant resource, as a way to achieve economic growth which was more socially efficient but also more equitably distributed. The dominant role of advanced technology was modified to emphasize 'appropriate' technology, which if not always smallest in scale was more manageable by the majority. Instead of relying on top-down planning, there was more attention given to decentralized, local approaches to development. In this theoretical and practical context, popular participation became important, having been peripheral when capital formation occupied centre stage.

Still, the impetus for concern with participation came not from economists or political scientists so much as from development practitioners and members of Congress. Title IX of the Foreign Assistance Act of 1966 clearly recognized and supported the contribution of popular participation in development:

> Over the years, in exercising legislative oversight with respect to the administration of the Foreign Assistance Program, the House Committee on Foreign Affairs has observed that there is a close relationship between popular participation in the process of development, and the effectiveness of that process.
>
> ... it has become increasingly clear that failure to engage all of the available human resources in the task of development not only acts as a brake on economic growth but also does little to cure the basic causes of social and political instability which pose a constant threat to the gains being achieved on economic fronts.
>
> ... Unless the people benefit from development efforts, no meaningful progress can result from foreign aid. It is equally true that unless the people contribute to development efforts, no meaningful progress can result from foreign aid ...
>
> The great potential for planning and implementation of development activities, contained in the mass of the people of the developing countries, is still largely untapped [and] slows down the achievement of the objectives of the foreign assistance programme.[3]

The amendment called for USAID to assist in furthering popular participation in connection with development efforts overseas. But there was little clarity to the concept, and it gained little operational effectiveness within the agency. To the extent that it was equated with political participation and with political development, it was liable to some criticism as unacceptably interventionist or ideologically ethnocentric, pushing American 'liberal' ideals on the Third World.

To some, it seemed part of a larger effort to persuade late developing nations to base their revolutions on Locke rather than Marx. And, to be sure, it was influenced by the Jeffersonian myth of small-town democracy and the view of participatory America preserved in the writings of de Tocqueville. Still, in so far as it challenged purely economic or technocratic ways of approaching development projects, it was resisted by many practitioners.

One of the few tangible results of Title IX was the report of a conference on its implementation, held at MIT in the summer of 1967 (Hapgood 1969). This report offered some useful definitions of 'development participation', but there was no evident impact on USAID programming. Experience of practitioners and observers of development continued to mount, however. In a trenchant analysis focused on African development experience, David Hapgood addressed some cogent questions about development participation:

> Advocates of peasant participation in decision-making run into the inevitable objection that there are many decisions peasants are not competent to make. This is true: if one asks how peasants can run an agricultural research station, the answer obviously is that they cannot. But participation (or decentralization, or 'peasant power') is not anarchy. In any decentralized system of agricultural development, the state would continue to make a great many decisions. Participation simply means that peasants would take part in the design of agri-cultural projects at the local level, where their knowledge in some respects is greater than that of the technicians. In addition to producing better plans, this might also release the latent creative and managerial energy of the farmers. (Hapgood 1968: 10)

It was becoming apparent that trying to proceed with development in most LDCs by use of coercive efforts was bearing little fruit. Perhaps some pro-gress could be made in the industrial sector by emulating Soviet or Japanese methods. But most developing countries, for better or worse, depended on the growth and efficiency of their agriculture for overall economic develop-ment, and this sector was not amenable to centrist or command approaches. In the absence of popular support and co-operation, the result could indeed be stagnation.

In the field, at the project level, it was also becoming clearer that success was critically affected by the extent of participation (or lack of it) in various aspects of development efforts. In her review of rural development projects in Africa for the World Bank, Uma Lele found the element of popular participation to be consistently important, noting for example the experience of the Special

Rural Development Projects in Kenya: 'the neglect of local input has had an unfavourable effect on the performance of the rural development effort' (1975: 150). In general she found:

> Local participation may mean involvement in planning, including assessment of local needs. Even if local people do not participate in planning, at the very minimum, they should be informed of the plans designed for their areas if they are expected to consent and to co-operate in program implementation. Participation in planning and implementation of programs can develop the self-reliance necessary among rural people for accelerated development. (Lele 1975: 162)

An analysis of 50 programmes for introducing technological change found that the only effective strategy for doing this was with popular participation (Lance and McKenna 1975).

Certainly, there were cases where attempts at fostering such participation were unsuccessful in terms of development outcomes and, perhaps more often, the institutions and roles set up for participation did not really provide this. Much of what was called participation, through village development committees or consultations in village assemblies or local planning exercises, was superficial or cosmetic. Still, the climate of opinion was becoming ever more favourable toward participatory approaches. The alternative, non-participatory approaches had been unsuccessful so often that practitioners were becoming ready to try something else.

The content of development efforts was also changing, to be more suitable for local initiative and management. Technology is usually simpler when more appropriate. There is support now for more reliance on labour for production and infrastructure creation, and this must *ipso facto* be more participatory. It has been seen that, given conditions of security and profitability, poor people can save and invest. The benefits of development are to be more broadly distributed now that economists no longer agree that this would hold back development. Such a spread of benefits appears likely to result with wider participation and to require it as well.

There are still grounds for specific criticism and objections to participatory approaches. The evidence is not one-sided or overwhelming. But the tide of thinking has been turning. Whether it will remain 'in' or will go 'out' again remains to be seen. In part, this will depend on how clearly and how effectively participation is conceived and applied.

Getting specific about participation

Because participation is essentially a descriptive term, including numerous different activities and situations, there is much room for confusion about its causes and effects, and its amounts and distribution. It is necessary to be quite specific about what is meant or referred to in any particular situation if we are to speak usefully about it in regard to any particular kind of rural development effort.

Our framework is based on the key assumption that 'participation' is not a *thing* that either exists or does not exist and which can be measured in the same way as a dam's capacity or an amount of agricultural production. While some studies treat participation as a clearly defined concept capable of measurement, we have chosen to treat it as a *rubric* under which a number of clearly definable elements can be assembled.

While these elements can be related together under a framework called 'rural development participation', it would be quite misleading to try to define the framework in such a way that a single summary measure would result. Rather, empirical indicators of different dimensions are sought. In this sense, participation is an overarching concept best approached by looking at specific, more concrete components.

At the heart of our elaboration of rural development participation is the distinction between dimensions and contexts of participation. Briefly, *dimensions* of participation concern the *kinds* of participation which are taking place, the *sets of individuals* who are involved in the participatory process, and then the various *features* of how that process is occurring.

The *context* of participation focuses on the relationship between a rural development project's characteristics and the patterns of actual participation which emerge. The context of participation also includes the *task environment* in which the project operates. This directs concern to historical, environmental and social characteristics which frequently have a strong effect on emerging patterns of participation in a given rural development effort.

Dimensions of rural development participation

The framework that we have devised delineates three dimensions of participation (see Figure 4.1). Basically these frame the questions: *what kinds* of participation are occurring or desired?; *who* participates in them?; and *how* is the process of participation taking place? The latter set of questions introduces important qualitative considerations.

What kinds of participation? The main kinds of participation that warrant major concern are: (1) participation in *decision-making*; (2) participation in *implementation*; (3) participation in *benefits*; and (4) participation in *evaluation*. We find that the first three kinds of participation are reasonably well defined in the approaches of development assistance agencies up to now, and there appear to be no grounds for objecting to the fourth. While evaluative participation occurs less frequently than the others, it deserves increased attention if development efforts are to be progressively improved. Its underscoring here is

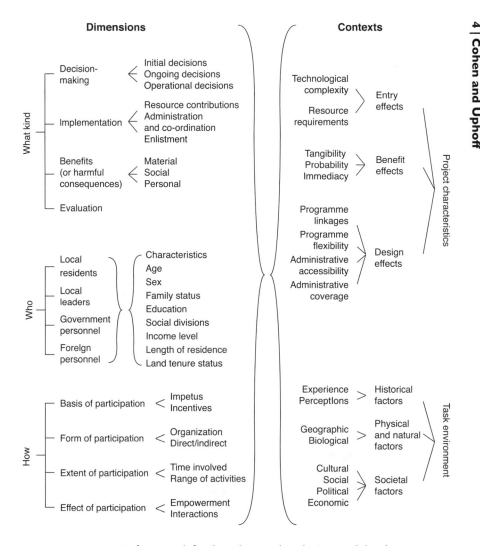

FIGURE 4.1 Basic framework for describing and analysing rural development participation

consistent with efforts being made in the development community to introduce systematic evaluation into most or all of its activities (see Figure 4.2).

Together, these four kinds of participation constitute something of a cycle for rural development activity. In practice, there is seldom a consistent or complete cycle of interactions. Participation in these different activities is often quite limited or unequal. Yet they constitute a tangible set of things to focus attention on and represent the major ways in which participation in rural development can be assisted and assessed.

Participation in decision-making is what political scientists most often refer to when they think of 'participation', whereas administrators are likely to focus

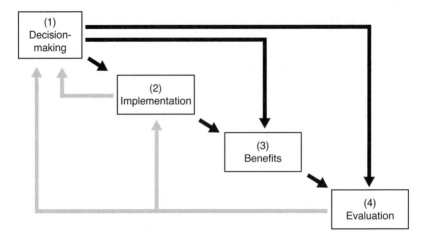

FIGURE 4.2 What kinds of participation?

on implementation participation. On the other hand, economists have in the past stressed participation in benefits as the most important thing. Nobody has been much concerned about participation in evaluation, just as evaluation itself has been neglected.

Participation in *decision-making* and *implementation* pertains to the 'inputs' of rural development, to plans, labour and other resources, while people's involvement in *benefits and evaluation* of development activity concerns the 'outputs' of this. (When considering 'benefits', we note the importance of recognizing that harmful consequences, and not just benefits, can flow from development programmes.)

Decision-making: Specifically, this kind of participation centres on the generation of ideas, the formulation and assessment of options, and making choices about them, including the formulation of plans for putting selected options into effect. For this reason, we distinguish three types of decisions: (1) initial decisions; (2) ongoing decisions; and (3) operational decisions.

Initial decisions begin with the identification of local needs and how they will be approached through a particular project. For most projects, this is the most crucial stage. Very early decisions or implicit assumptions, when a project is only a 'gleam in the eye' of those persons conceiving it, cast much of the project in concrete and remove a large number of options from the decision-making processes which are to follow.

For this reason, initial decisions generally described as 'project identification' need to be carefully distinguished and focused upon. Such involvement at an early stage can provide vital information on the local area and prevent misunderstandings as to the nature of the problem and the strategies proposed for its resolution. Among the initial decisions in which local people can be involved are whether the project should start, where it should be located, the ways it should be financed and staffed, the paths by which individuals and groups will participate in the project, and the contributions that they are expected to make.

It is possible that local people who did not participate in the initial decision may be asked to participate in the *ongoing decisions* once the project has arrived in the locality. There is some evidence that participation in ongoing decisions which occur after initial decisions have been made may be more critical to project success than such participation in initial design decisions. Various opportunities exist for searching out new needs and priorities that the project might respond to, as well as in operating the project in ways that best meet people's needs.

We conceive of *operational decisions* as relating to specific local organizations which have been established by the project or linked to the project in an effort to involve people in the delivery aspects of the enterprise. Here, the focus is on voluntary associations, co-operatives, traditional associations, women's clubs and other organizations involved in the substantive activities of the project. The framework we have elaborated points to participation with regard to such matters as membership composition, meeting procedures, leadership selection, and influences of such organizations.

Implementation: Rural people can participate in the implementation aspects of a project in three principal ways: (1) resource contributions; (2) administration and co-ordination efforts; and (3) programme enlistment activities.

Resource contributions can take a variety of forms, such as the provision of labour, cash, material goods, and information. All such inputs are vital to projects seeking to incorporate local resources in the development enterprise. Through such participation, local people lend their labour to the digging of wells, give land for a school, contribute timber for the construction of the health station, donate tools for working on a local road or money for financing community grain storage bins, or provide crucial information on such topics as crop yields, tenure arrangements, pest problems, sources of nutrition, and so on.

The relationship among the three dimensions of participation is illustrated clearly with regard to resource contributions. It is particularly important to know *who* is contributing and *how* their contributions are made, whether they are voluntary, remunerated or coerced, the degree to which they are provided on an individual or collective basis, and whether they occur on an intermittent or continual basis. These are particularly important questions since resource contributions can often be both unequal and exploitative.

Participation in *project administration and co-ordination* is a second way in which rural people can be involved in implementation. Here they can participate as either locally hired employees or as members of various project advisory or decision-making boards. They can also be members of voluntary associations which are playing a role in co-ordinating their activities with those of the project. By having local people involved in administration and co-ordination, a project may not only increase the self-reliance of the local people, by training them in techniques of project implementation, but valuable inside information and advice may also be gained concerning local problems and constraints affecting the given project.

Finally, perhaps the most common form of implementation participation is through *enlistment* in programmes. It seems essential to distinguish between such enlistment and participation in benefits because enlistment does not necessarily ensure benefits. Indeed, harmful consequences may result for persons who have enlisted in project programmes.

Benefits: Enlistment in a project can lead to at least three kinds of possible benefits: (1) material; (2) social; and (3) personal. While we would agree that participation in benefits is one of the more passive kinds of participation, it has such a long tradition in the economic literature that it should not be overlooked. Perhaps the only danger in focusing on this kind of participation is that it can sometimes be quite high and lead observers to overlook the fact that participation in other important aspects of the project, such as decision-making, has either not occurred or has been quite limited.

Material benefits are basically private goods. They can, perhaps, be summarized as an increase in consumption, income or assets. Consumption increases can result from higher yields of food grain, and income benefits can result from the sale of surplus production. Increased assets can be seen in the acquisition of land, livestock, implements, improved farm dwellings, savings, and so on. As with all other aspects of participation discussed in this paper, it is essential to break down aggregate data on material benefits by analysing *who* is participating and the process by which it is occurring.

Social benefits are basically public goods. They are usually characterized as services or amenities such as schools, health clinics, water systems, improved housing, and better roads. Increasingly, as rural development projects are designed to be more 'integrated', and as efforts are increased to improve the 'quality of life' for poorer sections of the population, there will be more need to assess participation in such benefits. Particular attention should be given to the amount, distribution and quality of these services and amenities.

Personal benefits are usually greatly desired though often not attained on an individual basis, coming rather to members of groups or sectors as these acquire more social and political power through the operation of a project. We term them 'personal' benefits to distinguish them from 'material' and 'social' benefits, but this does not imply that they are necessarily 'individual' in their causes or effects. Among several possible project-generated benefits of this sort, three kinds appear particularly important: self-esteem, political power, and sense of efficacy.

It is essential that a focus on benefits does not lead to a frame of reference that overlooks the large number of possible harmful consequences that can follow from participation in a project. These range from seeds that do not germinate or cross-bred dairy cattle that do not survive, to the erosion of the local culture or the eviction of tenant farmers. While harmful consequences tend to be obvious to many careful observers, they are often not studied in the same way that benefits are.

As suggested earlier, we concluded that in attempting to assess participation in benefits, harmful consequences should also be studied. If they are, any differential rates of participation in them will be significant data to determine. The main concern will be *who* is participating in these adverse outcomes of the project. Once this is known, one will want to try to establish *why*, so that remedies can be found if possible and can be built into a redesigned project.

Evaluation: Because there is little written on participation in evaluation, it is difficult to conceptualize how this kind of participation might be analysed and measured. It appears that there are three major activities through which rural people can participate in project evaluation.

Direct or indirect participation can occur in relation to actual *project-centred evaluation*. If there is any formal review process, one would want to know who participates in it, how continuously, with what power to achieve action on suggestions and so on. There may be informal consultation only, in which case we would want to know the same kinds of things. Most probably, unless specifically provided for in the project design, there will be no direct or indirect evaluation in which local people or local leaders can participate. Government personnel may themselves participate in annual budget reviews that fulfil a certain kind of evaluative function, but local-level officials are generally not involved.

It is more likely that whatever local efforts and involvement in project evaluation there are will occur through *political activities* of one sort or another. Where there are elected officials such as members of parliament, local people and/or local leaders can voice complaints and suggestions through this channel. Possible participation in elections at local, regional or national (constituency) level can provide some opportunity for favourable or unfavourable local evaluations to be fed into policy processes. Such inputs, however, are likely to be rather gross, reflecting simply dissatisfaction or satisfaction with what the project has accomplished.

Where there are no participatory political processes available, local people and/or local leaders can engage in lobbying activities – possibly through some organization like a co-operative or peasant league – to communicate their views to the project or the government. Alternatively, although not necessarily more effectively, there can be demonstrations or protests if dissatisfaction is high enough to try to force officials to give attention to local grievances. Indeed, sustained conflict and violence have been stimulated by some projects. When any of these activities occur, they should be studied to determine if they provide important *indirect* evaluation of the project or reflect other issues in the task environment. If the former, the content of the protest, as well as the characteristics of those making it, should be the subject of inquiry.

Less direct would be participation in evaluative activities that aim at *influencing public opinion* with the hope this will have the desired ramifications for continuation or possible modification of a project. Usually such efforts seek to use the media, for example, through a 'letter to the editor', to promote a favourable or unfavourable opinion of the project or to suggest some improvement. This is a very diffuse approach, but it might be regarded as one possible form of participation in evaluation and as better than no such participation at all.

Who participates? The participation about which most development agencies and governments are concerned these days is that of the 'rural poor' or the 'poor majority'. If they are considered in such an aggregated mass, it is very difficult to assess their participation in any respect, since they are a large and heterogeneous group. Their being considered as a group is not, indeed, something they would themselves be likely to suggest. There are significant differences in occupation, location, land tenure status, sex, caste, religion or tribe which are related in different ways to their poverty. To talk about 'the participation of the rural poor' is to compound one complex and ambiguous term with another, even more complicated and amorphous. If we want to deal usefully with the problems of the rural poor, we need to begin making some analytical distinctions among them.

Our framework begins with a differentiated and flexible scheme intended to analyse the entire rural community in general, as well as important groups such as the rural poor. We would start by distinguishing four general *types* of participants whose *characteristics* warranted specific attention. Depending on the setting and the goals of the project, certain characteristics of participants would be more significant than others.

We would distinguish the categories of: (1) local residents; (2) local leaders; (3) government personnel; and (4) foreign personnel. Each of these sets of persons can be, in turn, subdivided into a number of groups. Moreover, they can be further classified with regard to a number of important background characteristics that are known to be essential to the analysis of individual participation.

The first two sets of people are those who have local roots, whereas the latter two are, to varying degrees, outsiders. *Local residents* form a residual category that includes a large and heterogeneous group made up of self-sufficient farmers, tenants of landowners, farm labourers, herdsmen, craftsmen, and so on. It is this group of people who are usually the target of a rural development project. *Local leaders* have a long-run involvement in the area in which they work. Usually they are people who are considered local elites, such as landowners, merchants and professionals.

The definition of what a local leader is will vary from area to area. Basically there are three types of such leaders: (1) *informal leaders*, such as clan chiefs, religious figures, influential professionals and local notables; (2) *associational heads* elected or appointed for a formal organization, such as a co-operative league president, the chairman of a voluntary association, or the leader of a local trade union; or (3) *local office holders*, such as headmen, elders, mayors or tax-collectors. Sometimes the nature of officeholding, given requirements to uphold government interests, makes it difficult to distinguish such local leaders from government personnel.

Government personnel are assigned to an area for a certain period of time. Even if they are from the local area, their career rests with the bureaucracy at the centre, and their future is not usually determined by what happens in the area. This being the case, they are subject to transfer. They usually have higher education and social status than do locals. It is important to look at the participation levels of these people to evaluate what role they may be playing in promoting, controlling, or blocking project activity.

Some consideration should be given to *foreign personnel*. While often not important, they can at times play a crucial participatory role. Among them would be included foreign donor employees, heads of private voluntary associations, missionary personnel, expatriates, or immigrants who live and work at the local level.

What personal background characteristics are important in a given situation depends on the circumstances and the kinds of participation possible. A wide range of such characteristics exists, and the analyst must make judgements about *which* are the most significant in the given case.

Among the most important of the background characteristics that we would suggest are: (1) age and sex, with special attention to male–female differences; (2) family status (household head vs. other members); (3) educational level (functional literacy, formal schooling); (4) social divisions, if relevant, according to ethnicity, religion, caste, language or region of origin; (5) occupation; (6) level of income and sources; (7) length of residence, and distance of resident from the project, service or activity; and (8) land tenure or employment status (tenant with or without security, casual vs. permanent labourers, etc.).

Each of these background characteristics can be subdivided and amplified in a number of ways. Perhaps the best illustration of this would be the division of the *occupational* characteristic into agriculturists and non-agriculturists. Here important distinguishing features may be: (1) size of holding; (2) ownership status; or (3) percentage of income from agricultural production only. Likewise, one could distinguish among: (1) large-scale landowners; (2) small-scale owner cultivators; (3) tenants, either renters or sharecroppers; and (4) agricultural labourers. Even tenants might be subdivided into those without permanent leases and those who have considerable security on the land.

Non-agriculturalists might be subdivided in a similar way into: (1) business-men; (2) artisans or craftsmen; (3) professionals; (4) day labourers or domestic servants; (5) students; and so on, into a number of relevant classifications. This kind of breakdown could be applied to any of the suggested background characteristics. The degree to which one engages in such a breakdown depends on the type of project one is evaluating and the important characteristics relevant to that project.

Several principles are involved in deciding which information to gather for assessing who participates in what activities. First, *not all of these characteristics are relevant for all projects*. Obviously, age and sex would be crucial for a family-planning programme, while one might want to know whether certain ethnic minorities or immigrant groups or casual labourers and their families were utilizing health facilities. Second, often the data are not readily available for making some of these distinctions, although some fairly simple, even observational, data can be used to make meaningful categories. Finally, where persons are using services such as schooling, credit or clinics, the data on participant characteristics can be gathered. Rather than make complete enumerations, simple sampling (like three random days a month) can be done. Where surveys are conducted, most of the information on characteristics can be obtained.

How is participation occurring? The how dimension adds something qualitative to the analysis of participation. Attention to it generates insights into such questions as why participation takes place, continues or declines, and why it has the particular patterns which it does. The amount, distribution and trends of participation can be assessed basically by looking at the *who* and *what* dimensions. But one would not want to be oblivious to the ways in which participation is occurring, such as: (1) whether the *initiative* for participation comes mostly from above or from below; (2) whether the *inducements* for participation are more *voluntary* or *coercive.* It may be relevant to analyse and compare over time: (3) the *structure* and (4) the *channels* of participation – whether it occurs on an individual or collective basis, with formal or informal organization, and whether it is direct participation or indirect representation. Further consideration should often be given to: 5) the *duration* and (6) the *scope* of participation – whether it is once-and-for-all, intermittent or continuous, and whether it extends over a broad or narrow range of activities. Finally, it will usually be useful to consider (7) *empowerment*: how much capacity people have to obtain the results which they intend to obtain from their involvement in decision-making and implementation.

It is important to focus on who instigates participation. Does the initiative come from the *grass roots* or from the *national centre*? More specifically, does it flow from the people themselves, from local leaders, from project staff, from local or national officials, or from foreign personnel? Basically, this particular characteristic focuses on the distinction between *top-down* and *bottom-up* initiatives for a project or programme. As a project progresses, one frequently finds an increasingly number of initiatives coming from the grass roots level, although the opposite trend may emerge.

Incentives to participation are particularly important to consider. Usually one is interested to know whether, or to what extent, the participation is *voluntary* or *coerced.* However, often this is not easy to distinguish as there can be a continuum between voluntarism and coercion, since participation usually flows from a combination of positive and negative inducements. Indeed, there can be *remunerated* participation which is somewhere in between (pure) voluntarism and coercion.

Coerced participation is generally regarded as inconsistent with democratic values, yet there might be cases where it is productive and justifiable, such as ensuring compliance with a range management scheme that pools cattle, adhering to herd size limits and following rotational grazing requirements. Participation in the regeneration of forest areas or watersheds could be voluntary, remunerated or coerced. Actually, *impetus* to participate and people's motivation for participation can be combined to reveal several different types ranging from volunteered participation initiated from below to enforced participation initiated from above.

The *organizational pattern* greatly affects the process of participation, contributing to effectiveness as well as sustainability. One of the first questions here is whether a person enters into participation as a member of the group. For example, can any farmer get credit from the project directly, or must he belong to a co-operative in order to be eligible? Another question concerns the complexity of the organization. Are there well-defined leadership roles and rules governing activities, and are there fairly clear standards for evaluating the performance of leaders? If organizations are too complex, it may be difficult for local people to engage in any meaningful participation in them. Local elites can often 'capture' more complex organizations and use them to promote their own ends. Indeed, complexity might be designed into a project to keep participation under close control.

The process of participation is also affected by whether one participates *directly* or is *represented* by someone selected by oneself and others. Direct participation probably has greater impact on building individual capacity. Unfortunately, it is often very difficult to achieve because of the numbers of participants who might be involved. It is also often difficult to get this kind of participation in rural areas without adequate infrastructure, because people may have a great deal of trouble finding time and means to journey to far-away meetings. In general, indirect participation is more likely to occur with decision-making activities, and direct participation is more typical of participation in either benefits or implementation.

The *time* required of the participant affects the amount of participation which occurs. The longer the participatory experience continues, and the more regular it is, the greater the likelihood that there will be some formal organizational basis for this. Projects should carefully monitor changes in the frequency of participation, giving particular attention to the emergence of more regular and continuous patterns of involvement as well as to any trends in the opposite direction.

The *intensity* of participation that one finds in a given project is frequently related to the range of project activities involving participation. Here, one should consider the number of possible situations in which various members of the groups being analysed could participate. It is also important to determine whether project procedures make participation in one activity a precondition for participation in other activities. For example, farmers may have to belong to the project co-operative society before they or other members of their families can attend adult education classes.

Careful attention should be given to the number of activities that people are participating in as well as to the effects of that range on their overall participation activities. It may be that multiple participatory activities will lead to inadequate participation in all of them. On the other hand, the multiple activities may reinforce each other in a way that not only returns more concrete benefits to the participant, but also raises his or her awareness about the importance of actively seeking to engage in and affect the broader society.

Careful evaluation should also be given to the degree of *power* which participants have. Empowerment of participation ranges from no power or influence to extensive power, and it is important to know whether or not participation is simply a formal action with little meaning, or an activity which allows the individual to gain greater control over situations that would alter his or her life.

From our reading of experience we would give particular attention to the structure and channels for participation. That participation can be individual and unorganized is quite clear; but it is not so evident that it will be effective or sustained in the absence of some organized expression and support. One of the hypotheses that is most worth examining is the extent to which *organization* is a crucial factor conditioning the amount, kind and success of participation, recognizing that these may vary for different tasks or for different groups.

It is submitted that considering these several *how* characteristics will illuminate the possibilities, dynamics and consequences of participation if applied appropriately to the assessment of *who* participates in *what* rural development activities. They may be combined in interesting and different ways, or compared to each other in various matrices.

The dimensional nature of the *how* dimension means that making just a single qualitative assessment is seldom worthwhile. According to most views of participation, that which is initiated from below, voluntary, organized, direct, continuous, broad in scope, and empowered would be the 'most' participatory. But judgements about anything diverging from this ideal can differ widely, and it may not be ideal for all situations.

This is not only because people have different values and expectations about participation, but because the relevance of different aspects will vary. Indirect participation through representatives may be quite appropriate and satisfactory in some situations, and not in others. For maintaining irrigation canals, periodic participation may suffice, whereas continuous participation may be needed for handling the distribution of water.

By analysing the *how* dimensions, we want to alert persons to the ways in which participation by certain groups (who) in given activities (what) can differ. Even if no quantitative value is attached to these aspects, one should be sensitive to what they are, and particularly to such shifts as may occur from a bottom-up to a top-down initiative, or from a voluntary to a more coerced performance.

Participation for what? It is essential to consider also the *purposes* of participation. Indeed, *for what* may prove to be a critical fourth dimension of participation. Because purposes are essentially normative, disagreement when assessing them is even more likely than with the more descriptive dimensions discussed above. Quite a range of different purposes for participation can be listed, such as Chambers (1974) offers in his book on rural development.

The difficulty with constructing a standard analytical framework for *purposes* is that their assessment and even their factual basis shift, depending on whose perspective one takes. Farmers taking credit for use of new maize varieties may be seen as reducing national food deficits or even as helping to stabilize the regime from a governmental point of view, while the farmers can see it as possibly augmenting family income and consumption.

As with all objectives, they may be intended or unintended, stated or unstated and achieved or unachieved. It is certainly useful to consider the purposes for which participation is undertaken or advocated, but as yet their analysis cannot be as rigorous as for the three dimensions outlined already. One of the key questions to ask is whether the purpose which the authorities have in mind for getting people to participate is the same as, or compatible with, the purpose the people themselves would accept as their own.

Where governments want things from or for the people that the people do not want for themselves, we know right away that certain ambiguities and even obstacles affecting the intended participation are likely. We can imagine sinister purposes such as encouraging critical participation from the public in order to identify malcontents (some thought this was done during the campaign in China to 'let a thousand flowers bloom'). On the other hand, the opportunities for participation provided by a government to bolster its support could be used to try to bring its downfall.

Questions can be raised about participation's purposes in terms of *who* is supposed to benefit from it – participation for *whom*? According to Holm (1972), the Village Development Councils in Botswana were allowed to operate only under tight political and administrative control and the government gave no funds for local projects. So popular participation appeared to be mostly an instrument for bureaucratic domination of the village modernization process according to Holm. This may or may not be true, and it may or may not be common elsewhere, but it is certainly a valid question to consider in evaluating participation.

Some would dismiss activity such as Holm describes as not constituting 'participation'. But we think it more appropriate to make assessments of the kind of activity involved and with what effect, regarding participation as *a matter of degree* rather than being simply present or absent, or assessed according to a single metric, given that there are various *kinds* of participation possible (and not all are equally desirable). An analysis which identifies *who* is participating *how* in decision-making and implementation, and *who* is participating in benefits and evaluation, should concretely illuminate 'participation for whom and for what?'

In the original article, we included in our analysis a consideration of how the environment of participation – i.e., its *context* – also has a bearing on the planning and assessment of participation. Here we simply note that one should also take account of the setting(s) of participation as well as its purpose. This extends the three-dimensional framework for understanding participation into a fourth and even fifth dimension.

Emerging generalizations

Based on what we know so far, we would set forth the following major points:

1. *Participation is not a single thing.* It is, rather, a rubric or heading under which a number of distinct, though related, activities can be analysed and promoted.
2. *Participation for development is not the same thing as participation in politics.* The voting, campaigning, lobbying and so on associated with institutionalized politics may be part of developmental participation, but more and different things should be considered with regard to participation in development.
3. *Participation is not just an end in itself, but it is more than a means.* The debate as to whether participation is to be regarded as an end or only as a means is fruitless, since people can consider it as either or both. Pronouncing it one or the other will not end what is essentially an ideological dispute.

4 *Participation is not a panacea.* While its neglect has often been devastating to project results, simply introducing it will not necessarily make projects successful. In many instances, participation appears to be necessary but not sufficient for good results. There are many reasons why getting productive participation started is difficult, and why the results are not always those intended. Having 'more' participation is not always 'better' as its value depends on what kind of participation, under what circumstances and by and for whom?

5 *There is a connection among different kinds of participation.* This has not been well demonstrated, in part because participation has not been analysed and studied in a disaggregated way. But there is a good deal of fragmentary evidence that in projects, *ex ante* participation such as in decision-making is related to *ex post* participation in benefits. This seems especially true when one is concerned with the poor majority, as paternalistic approaches neglecting the organization and mobilization of the poor to work and act on their own behalf seem to produce limited results. We would be the first to say, however, that more work needs to be done on understanding these relationships. We need to know more to be able to specify what kinds of participation, and under what conditions, produce the desired results.

6 *Participation even in 'development' terms is inescapably 'political'.* Broader participation is likely to change the use and allocation of resources in society. Indeed, this is why it is often advocated, since such change is associated with the development process. Such change is subject to wide-ranging differences in the value judgements that people make about it, and these should be openly acknowledged. If persons refuse to recognize and accept this aspect of participation, their co-operation in participatory development approaches is doubtful. We are not saying that participation is always political in the sense that it will adversely affect the government. Indeed, support of participation can have the opposite effect of building a stronger political base. However, participation is likely to have some effect on political relationships one way or the other, or in many ways.

Our overall conclusion is that participation is possible and under many conditions desirable to achieve the development goals set by development agencies and LDC governments. It can be difficult to promote and the results are not always predictable. The knowledge base to work from is not yet consolidated. But there is enough experience and theory so that incorporating more elements of participation into development strategies is feasible and appropriate.

[Abridged from J. Cohen and N. Uphoff, 'Participation's place in rural development: seeking clarity through specificity', *World Development*, 8, 1980, pp. 213–35]

Notes

1 Commission for Social Development, Report of the 24th Session, January 1975, Official Records of the Economic and Social Council 58th Session, Suppl. No. 3, UN Document No. E/CN.5/525, para. 4. This resolution was in response to a report by the UN Secretary General on 'Popular participation and its practical implications for development', UN Document No. E/CN. 5/496 (August 1974).

2 See, for example, World Bank (1975) and HMSO (1975).

3 These statements are from reports on Title IX, cited in Hapgood (1969).

References

Almond, G. A. and S. Verba (1963) *The Civic Culture*, Princeton, NJ: Princeton University Press.

Chambers, R. (1974) *Managing Rural Development: Ideas and Experience from East Africa*, Uppsala: Scandinavian Institute of African Studies.

Cohen, J. M and N. T. Uphoff (1974) *Rural Development Participation: Concepts and Measures for Project Design, Implementation and Evaluation*, Ithaca, NY: Rural Development Committee, Cornell University.

Deutsch, K. W. (1961) 'Social mobilization and political development', *American Political Science Review*, 55(3): 493–514.

Hapgood, D. (1968) 'The politics of agriculture', *Africa Report*, 13.

— (ed.) (1969) *The Role of Popular Participation in Development, Report of a Conference on the Implementation of Title IX of the Foreign Assistance Act*, Cambridge: Massachusetts Institute of Technology Press.

HMSO (Her Majesty's Stationery Office) (1975) *Overseas Development: The Changing Emphasis in British Aid Policies*, London: HMSO.

Holm, J. (1972) 'Rural development in Botswana: three basic political trends', *Rural Africana*, 18: 80–92.

Lance, L. M. and E. E. McKenna (1975) 'Analysis of cases pertaining to the impact of western technology on the non-western world', *Human Organization*, 34(1): 87–94.

Lele, U. J. (1975) *The Design of Rural Development: Lessons from Africa*, Baltimore, MD: Johns Hopkins University Press.

World Bank (1975) *Rural Development: Sector Policy Paper*, Washington, DC: International Bank for Reconstruction and Development.

5 | Depoliticizing development: the uses and abuses of participation

Sarah White

Introduction

The Bangladeshi NGO leaders are in a dilemma. They are unhappy with the official agencies' new plan. Neither social nor environmental questions have been given the consideration they deserve. As happens more and more often, they have been invited to attend a meeting to discuss the plan. Flattered at first by official recognition, they are now uneasy. If they do not go, they have no grounds to complain that the interests of the poor have been ignored. But if they go, what guarantee do they have that their concerns will really be heard? Too many times they have seen their discussions drain away into the sand. The plans are left untouched; but their names remain, like a residue, in the list of 'experts' whose opinions the scheme reflects.

'We are all democrats today' was John Dunn's (1979) ironic opening to an essay on political theory. With its universal acceptance, he argued, what democracy meant *in practice* was increasingly elastic. Rather than describing any particular type of political order, democracy had become 'the name for the good intentions of states or perhaps for the good intentions which the rulers would like us to believe that they possess' (Dunn 1979: 12).

These days, the language of democracy dominates development circles. At national level it is seen in the rhetoric of 'civil society' and 'good governance'. At the programme and project level, it appears as a commitment to 'participation'. This is trumpeted by agencies right across the spectrum, from the huge multi-laterals to the smallest people's organizations. Hardly a project, it seems, is now without some 'participatory' element.

On the face of it, this appears like success for those committed to 'people-centred' development policies. But stories like the one above should make us cautious. *Sharing through participation does not necessarily mean sharing in power.* As with gender and with the 'green' movement, the 'mainstreaming' of participation has imposed its price. In all three cases, the original movement was one of protest against the existing orthodoxy. Some are still fighting for this. But in the mainstream, 'women in development' or 'win-win' environmental policies appear with the sting taken out of their tail. What began as a political issue is translated into a technical problem which the development enterprise can accommodate with barely a falter in its stride. Incorporation, rather than exclusion, is often the best means of control.

The status of participation as a 'Hurrah' word, bringing a warm glow to its users and hearers (Turbyne 1992), blocks its detailed examination. Its seeming transparency – appealing to 'the people' – masks the fact that participation can take on multiple forms and serve many different interests. In fact, it is precisely this ability to accommodate such a broad range of interests that explains why participation can command such widespread acclaim. If participation is to mean more than a facade of good intentions, it is vital to distinguish more clearly what these interests are. This will help to show what many have long suspected: that though we use the same words, the meaning that we give them can be very different.

Interests in participation

There are two main ways in which the politics of participation are admitted in development planning. The first is the question of *who* participates. This recognizes that 'the people' are not homogeneous, and that special mechanisms are needed to bring in relatively disadvantaged groups. The second regards the *level* of participation. This points out that the involvement of the local people in implementation is not enough. For a fully participatory project, they should also take part in management and decision-making.

Both of these dimensions are important. The problem is that they do not go far enough. In lending themselves to technical solutions (which is, of course, their attraction), they can again obscure the politics of participation. A quota for the inclusion of poor women on the executive board, for example, seems to provide the answer. But of course, simply *being there* does not ensure that those women have a real say; and, even if they do, there is no guarantee that they will speak for others in a similar situation. At their best, such measures can only facilitate fuller participation, they cannot deliver it. More critically, framing the problem in these terms ties us to observing the mechanisms for participation: it gives us no means of assessing its content.

Table 5.1 aims to move beyond this in drawing out the diversity of form, function, and interests within the catch-all term 'participation'. It distinguishes four major types of participation, and the characteristics of each. The first column shows the form of participation. The second shows the interests in participation from the 'top down' : that is, the interests that those who design and implement development programmes have in the participation of others. The third column shows the perspective from the 'bottom up': how the participants themselves see their participation, and what they expect to get out of it. The final column characterizes the overall function of each type of participation. In the following sections I describe practical examples in which the different types of participation can be observed.

TABLE 5.1 Interests in participation

5 | White

Form	Top-down	Bottom-up	Function
Nominal	Legitimation	Inclusion	Display
Instrumental	Efficiency	Cost	Means
Representative	Sustainability	Leverage	Voice
Transformative	Empowerment	Empowerment	Means/end

This framework is, of course, simply an analytical device. In practice, the uses (and abuses) of participation may be very varied. Any project will typically involve a mix of interests which change over time. Rarely will any of these types appear in 'pure' form. I hope, none the less, that setting them out in this way will highlight some important distinctions. It is in the ambiguity of participation, as both concept and practice, that the scope for its colonization lies.

Nominal participation

An example of this type of participation is found in Zambia. Large numbers of women's groups have been formed by various government departments over the past thirty years. The existence of these groups demonstrates that the departments are 'doing something' and have a 'popular base', which may be significant in their claims for personnel or financial support. Their interest in women's participation, therefore, is largely for *legitimation*.

Many of the women go along with this. They say they are members of groups, but rarely attend any meetings. It serves their interests of *inclusion*, however, to keep their names on the books. From time to time they may 'check in' to see if any new loans or other inputs are on offer. How many of these groups actually exist in a functional sense is far from clear. In most cases, it seems, the women's participation is nominal, and the groups mainly serve the function of *display*.

Instrumental participation

Under the terms of Structural Adjustment Programmes (SAPs), government funding for essential infrastructure and services in many African countries has been sharply reduced. People's participation may therefore be necessary, to provide the labour for local schools. This serves the *efficiency* interests of outside funders. The people's labour is taken as 'local counterpart funds', which guarantee the people's commitment to the project. The funders' input can be limited to financing raw materials, and the programme can therefore be far more 'cost effective'.

For the local people, participation is seen as a *cost*. The time which they spend building the school has to be taken away from paid employment, household work, or leisure. But if they want the school, they see that they have little option. Participation in this case is instrumental, rather than valued in itself. Its function is as a *means* to achieve cost effectiveness, on the one hand, and a local facility, on the other.

Representative participation

A Bangladeshi NGO wished to launch a cooperatives programme. It invited the local people to form their own groups, develop bylaws, and draw up plans for what they would do. The function of participation was to allow the local people a *voice* in the character of the project. From the NGO's side, this would avoid the danger of creating an inappropriate and dependent project and so ensure *sustainability*.

A group of fishing families decided to apply. They wanted to form a co-operative for loans and fish marketing. For them, taking an active part both in their own meetings and in discussions with the NGO was important to ensure *leverage*, to influence the shape which the project should take and its subsequent management. Participation thus took on a representative form, being an effective means through which the people could express their own interests.

Transformative participation

The idea of participation as *empowerment* is that the practical experience of being involved in considering options, making decisions, and taking collective action to fight injustice is itself transformative. It leads on to greater consciousness of what makes and keeps people poor, and greater confidence in their ability to make a difference. An example from the Philippines indicates how this can happen.

Encouraged by a community organizer, 25 hillside families decided to form a consumers' cooperative. Prices at the local store were 50 per cent higher than those in the town, but the town was four hours' walk away. They took some training in cooperative management from the local NGO, and gradually devised their own constitution, bylaws, roles, and responsibilities. As their confidence grew, they decided to take on other projects. Then a presidential election was called. The local mayor and some other officials visited the area. They had only one message: 'Vote for Marcos'. They had no time to listen to the villagers' questions or enter into discussion with them. After they left, the villagers decided to boycott the election.

When the election came, all 398 villagers spoiled their ballot papers. The community organizer visited them two days later. The election was widely viewed as a public relations exercise, but she had never discussed it with them, so was surprised and impressed by what they had done. She asked them for their reasons. One of the farmers explained:

In the co-operative, we discuss problems. We look at them from different angles. When we think that we have understood the situation, we try to come to a consensus. We avoid voting as much as possible. When the government officials came, we asked for an explanation of why we were given other than what we asked for. We asked for a school, teachers, and a road. The Mayor sent us the army, guns, and bullets. He refused to answer our questions. He just told us to vote for Marcos. We want the government to be run the way we manage our co-operative store. (Tiongo and White 1997)

Empowerment is usually seen as an agenda controlled 'from below'. This is because empowerment must involve action from below. However supportive, outsiders can only facilitate it, they cannot bring it about. None the less, as shown in Table 5.1, empowerment may also be identified as the interest in participation 'from above', when outsiders are working in solidarity with the poor. From Marx's analysis of alienation, to Freire's work on conscientization, to the 'alternative visions' of organizations like DAWN (Sen and Grown 1987), it is in fact not usually those who are poor or disadvantaged themselves who identify empowerment as the key issue. The latter generally have far more immediate and tangible interests and goals. This case is therefore typical, in that empowerment of the poor was initially the concern of the local NGO. It was only through their experience in the cooperative that the hillside families came to see empowerment as being in their interests. In this form, participation is therefore at one and the same time a means to empowerment and an end in itself, so breaking down the division between means and ends which characterizes the other types. In another sense, of course, this process never comes to an end, but is a continuing dynamic which transforms people's reality and their sense of it.

Dynamics in participation

All of the above examples are positive. There is a degree of match between the interests from 'top down' and 'bottom up'. This is because the stories are told as a way of clarifying the framework in Table 5.1. They are snapshots, abstracted from their wider social context, and even their own history as development programmes. Only one set of interests is focused on, and presented as though this were all there is to say. The stories, as much as Table 5.1, are a device, highlighting some points, but throwing others into shadow. Stated in this way, the framework itself runs the risk of depoliticizing participation, which it was designed to overcome.

What needs to be injected into Table 5.1 is a sense of dynamic, along (at least!) four dimensions. These are presented in Figure 5.1. Here, clusters of circles show the interests from top-down and bottom-up, and the forms and functions of participation. The small arrows between the circles indicate the first dynamic, that each of the clusters is internally diverse, and there is tension over which element – or combination of elements – will predominate at any one time. In particular, as seen already in the case of the election boycott, the character of participation typically changes over time. The second dynamic is shown by the arrows coming into the 'form and function' cluster from either side. These indicate that the form or function of participation is itself a site of conflict. The third pair of arrows comes out of the 'form and function' cluster, and into the 'interests' clusters, showing that the outcomes of participation feed back into the constitution of interests. The final dynamic is indicated by the arrows feeding into the diagram from the outside. These show that interests reflect power relations external to the project itself. The rest of this section discusses each of these dynamics in turn.

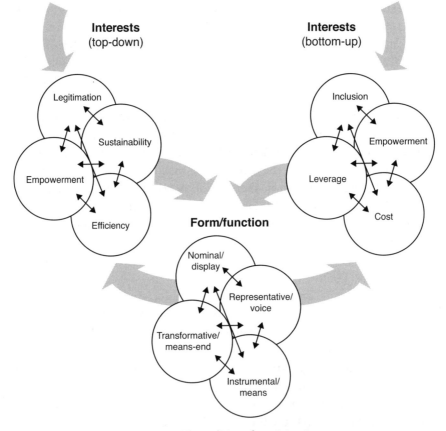

FIGURE 5.1 The politics of participation

The diversity of interests

In all the cases cited above, the Zambian women, the African villagers, and the fishing and hillside families are presented as though they were homogeneous groups. In reality, they are diverse, with differing interests and expectations of participation. This is clearest to see in the Zambian case: it is in the hopes of individual gain that the women occasionally 'check in' to the groups. Also, those women who do remain more active – the chair, secretary, and treasurers of the groups – are likely to identify their participation as instrumental, and may even have some expectations of its being representative.

For outsiders similarly, there is a mix of interests. The NGO in the Philippines case certainly gains legitimacy by having large numbers of group members. Its interests in efficiency and sustainability, as well as empowerment, are met by the hillside families developing and managing their own projects. In addition, there will be different interests among the local organizers and the NGO management. National leaders, for example, may talk more readily of empowerment than field workers who are aware of the dangers of reprisals from the local elite. The NGO may also 'package' the form and functions of participation differently for different 'markets'. In dealing with their radical Northern funders, they stress the transformative aspect. When engaging with the local elite and the national government, they may place more emphasis on the efficiency and sustainability dimensions. There is politics, therefore, not simply in the form and function of participation, but also in how it is represented in different quarters.

Changes in participation over time

As participation is a process, its dynamic over time must be taken into account. Seen at its simplest, there is a strong tendency for levels of participation to decline over time. This is clearest in the Zambian case: thirty years ago, or even twenty, those same groups were highly active, with the enthusiasm of project workers matched by that of the women themselves. This change may be due to disillusionment with the project, but it can also mean that people choose positively to use their time in other ways. There is a tendency in the rhetoric of participation to assume that it is always good for people to take an active part in everything. People do, however, have other interests, such as in leisure. People often participate for negative reasons: they do not have confidence that their interests will be represented unless they are physically there. One can grow tired of being an 'active citizen'!

Withdrawal from participation is not, however, always a positive choice. Women with heavy domestic responsibilities, for example, may find that they cannot sustain the expenditure of large amounts of time away from home. Also, even if power relations have been challenged by a successful exercise of participation, there is a danger that new patterns of domination will emerge over time. This is particularly so where the project itself creates new positions, with some people being far more involved than others. The Bangladeshi fishing cooperative has a relatively good chance of sustaining representative participation, because all of the members are actively involved. In other projects which rely on the management of a few leaders, wider participation over time is much more likely to dwindle to a point where it becomes nominal.

It may also be that the level of participation increases over time. All their lives the fishing families had taken loans from a middle trader, and had to sell their catch back to him. He then kept a proportion of the sale price as profit, before selling on to a larger trader. Through their cooperative, the fishing families could apply for loans to the local NGO. Bypassing the middle trader, they then took loans from their own group, and sold the fish back to it. The cooperative itself then accumulated the profit, and they were able to use the money for other collective projects. Their successful exercise of representative participation led on to transformation.

In a similar way, the Philippine families first encountered the NGO in a health education programme. After a year, an evaluation was held and they approved the programme. They saw that poverty was the underlying cause of their poor health. Having gone through the initial programme largely out of the interests of inclusion, they developed the confidence to move to representative participation, in stating that their more immediate need was a cooperative store. The action and reflection process of organizing and managing the store involved them in transformative participation. This affected not only their economic position, but also their political consciousness.

In practice, the interests from 'top down' and 'bottom up' do not match neatly. Probably more often, the interests that one group identifies are not served by the participation that occurs. The first example, of the Bangladeshi NGO leaders and the official agencies' plan, gives an instance of this. The NGO leaders desire representative participation, to gain leverage. The official agencies, however, require their presence simply for legitimation. This is probably the dominant pattern, but it is not always the 'top-down' interests that prevail. While participation may be encouraged for the purposes of legitimation or efficiency, there is always the potential for it to be 'co-opted from below', and for a disadvantaged group to use it for leverage or empowerment.

The Philippines election boycott gives an instance of this, though with a twist. Here, the interests of President Marcos and his cronies in the nominal participation of the villagers is frustrated. The hillside families see the mayor's visit as an opportunity for representative participation. When they see there is no opportunity for dialogue, they simply refuse to play the game. This draws attention to another important point. It shows that participation is not always in the interests of the poor. Everything depends on the type of participation, and the terms on which it is offered. In cases like this one, exit may be the most empowering option.

Power and the construction of interests

The final dynamic in participation is more complex and more abstract. It is clear that power is involved in the negotiation to determine which interests are favoured over others. What is less clear is that *power is involved in the construction of interests themselves*. This has two dimensions, which will be discussed in turn. The first is external to the model, represented in the figure by the arrows coming from the far left and the far right. These show that interests are not just 'there', but reflect the power relations in wider society. The second dimension is shown by the arrows coming from the form and function cluster back into the 'top-down' and 'bottom-up' interests. These indicate that the participation process itself shapes the constitution of interests.

When asked why they joined the women's groups, many of the Zambian women say that they hoped to get fertilizer or credit from them. Their interests in inclusion therefore reflect their practical interests as village women with a major role in food production (see Molyneux 1985). These interests are determined by the local gender-based division of labour, as well as by their class positions. Limiting their involvement to nominal levels also reflects their wider social context. With their domestic and productive responsibilities, many have little time to spend 'sitting around'. The timing of the groups' meetings recognizes this: most are (even nominally) inactive from November to March, the main agricultural season. It is no coincidence that it is mainly groups whose members are older, and thus freer of responsibilities in the home, that continue to meet throughout the year.

In practice, access to credit or fertilizer rarely comes through the groups. Instead, most of them spend their time working on handcrafts, which they sell locally at marginal profit. The women's acceptance of this work again reflects the wider gender-linked division of labour, in which control over significant resources is reserved for men. It is also shaped by the limited marketing opportunities in the rural areas. The women have other potential interests, for example in using the groups to put pressure on government departments to provide real services to the rural areas. The fact that women do not express these interests – and may not even recognize them – is not random, but reflects their low expectation of any change, born out of a general sense of powerlessness or earlier disappointments. While the women may identify their interests as semi-detached inclusion in the existing project, therefore, this is not a free choice. To understand it, we have to see it in the wider social context in which the women live their lives. From the other side, the government departments' interest in legitimation comes from their competition with each other for resources. Also, however, it expresses their complacency that no real demands will be made on them, either from the poor or from the powers-that-be.

The other cases tell a similar story. In the shadow of the SAP, the local people's participation in building the school clearly shows the absence of other options. It is probable that those who do have alternatives (such as a relatively well-paid job) are able to evade participating, perhaps by paying someone else to do their share. Whatever the collective rhetoric, it is well recognized that it is rare for the whole community to take part equally. Some will be excused for being too young or too old. But others will be able to call on their status: it is no coincidence that such 'community' labour projects in practice often fall to the women and poorer men. Wider power relations condition the interests of the outside agency, too. Its concern for efficiency might indicate its limited budget. But it also clearly draws on the international supremacy of free-market ideology, and the awareness that it could easily take the funds elsewhere, if the local people do not cooperate.

That the experience of participation acts back on the construction of interests is clearest to see in the cases of the fishing and hillside families' cooperatives. In both instances, undertaking successful projects enabled them to see new opportunities that they had not at first imagined. There are also less positive examples. It is quite common, for example, that agencies, when they 'ask the people' what kind of project they would like, get very conventional answers. Women do ask for sewing machines, however much feminists wish that they wouldn't! This may in part reflect the wider gender-determined division of labour, but it also draws on what the people have seen of development projects, and so what they expect them to look like. The NGOs' negative experience of co-option through the official agencies' 'consultation' processes, in the first example, similarly shapes their choice as to whether to participate in discussions of the latest plan.

It may be that the most profound renegotiation of interests occurs where transformative participation achieves empowerment. While external agencies may genuinely desire the people's empowerment, they may find it rather uncomfortable when empowerment actually occurs. In the Philippines, for example, there is now considerable tension between some People's Organizations and the national NGOs that fostered them. The former now wish to communicate directly with the funders. The NGOs do not wish to lose control. Similarly, some Northern NGOs have found the language of partnership to be double-edged. It can, for example, lead to their Southern counterparts rejecting as 'imperialist' any demand for funding accountability. In some cases this may be legitimate; in others it is not. But if one takes seriously the fact that both parties have been shaped by unjust power relations, there is no particular reason to expect that the form which empowerment takes will be benign. Former friends, rather than common enemies, may be the first and easiest point of attack. Top-down commitment to others' empowerment is therefore highly contradictory. It is likely to lay bare the power dimensions of the relationship which the dominant partner would prefer to leave hidden.

If it is genuine, the process must be transformative, not only for the 'weaker' partner but also for the outside agency and for the relationship between them.

The underlying message of this section is simple: however participatory a development project is designed to be, it cannot escape the limitations on this process that derive from the power relations in wider society. That people do not express other interests does not mean that they do not have them. It simply means that they have no confidence that they can be achieved (as discussed in more depth by Gaventa 1980).

Participation: what counts and what doesn't

Before concluding this discussion, I want to point out a final anomaly in the new pursuit of participation. Like the Women in Development (WID) agenda, it is founded on the assumption that those who have been excluded should be 'brought in' to the development process. It represents the people in the bad, non-participatory past as passive objects of programmes and projects that were designed and implemented from outside. As the literature on women in development now recognizes, however, the people have never been excluded from development. They have been fundamentally affected by it. But more than this, people have also always participated in it, on the most favourable terms they can obtain. They await with a mixture of expectation and scepticism what the new agency in their area is offering, and what it will want in return. They have opted in or out of projects as they judged that it suited their interests. At least some of what agencies may see as project 'misbehaviour' (Buvinic 1986) can from another standpoint be viewed as their co-option from below.

In Bangladesh, for example, an NGO introduced a hand-tube-well programme for irrigation. The pumps were located in the fields to be used for vegetable production. The villagers, however, considered water for domestic use a higher priority. They therefore moved the pumps from the fields to their homes. Rather than recognizing this as the expression of people's genuine interests, the NGO began to issue plastic pipes, which could not be relocated. Applications for the tube wells rapidly declined, and the programme was deemed a failure. This is not an isolated example. In the same area, shallow tube well engines destined for irrigation were adapted by the local people to power rice mills and small boats. People have never simply been a blank sheet for development agencies to write on what they will.

There is, of course, a need for more space for poorer people to participate in development programmes in representative and transformative ways. They should not need to resort to manipulation and covert resistance, the 'weapons of the weak', to express their interests (see Scott 1985). Recognizing that people have always used such tactics, however, suggests that the problem is not simply 'enabling the people to participate', but ensuring that they participate *in the right ways*. This underlies, for example, some official agencies' current enthusiasm for programmes in 'community-based resource management'. These explicitly recognize that unless people are 'brought in' to the programme, they may actively sabotage it, by cutting trees or embankments, killing animals in nature reserves, and so on. The fact that the way in which people have participated is so often classified as illegitimate should lead us to question quite carefully: on whose terms is the current agenda, and whose interests are really at stake?

Conclusion

This article suggests three steps in addressing the 'non-politics' of participation. The first is to recognize that participation is a political issue. There are always questions to be asked about who is involved, how, and on whose terms. People's enthusiasm for a project depends much more on whether they have a genuine interest in it than in whether they participated in its construction: participation may take place for a whole range of unfree reasons. The second step is to analyse the interests represented in the catch-all term 'participation'. Table 5.1 sets out a framework for this. It shows that participation, while it has the potential to challenge patterns of dominance, may also be the means through which existing power relations are entrenched and reproduced.

The third step is to recognize that participation and non-participation, while they always reflect interests, do not do so in an open arena. Both people's perception of their interests, and their judgement as to whether or not they can express them, reflect power relations. People's non-participation, or participation on other people's terms, can ultimately reproduce their subordination. The form and function of participation can themselves become a focus for struggle.

If participation means that the voiceless gain a voice, we should expect this to bring some conflict. It will challenge power relations, both within any individual project and in wider society. The absence of conflict in many supposedly 'participatory' programmes is something that should raise our suspicions. Change hurts. Beyond this, the bland front presented by many discussions of participation in development should itself suggest questions. What interests does this 'non-politics' serve, and what interests may it be suppressing?

[Originally published as Sarah C. White, 'Depoliticizing development: the uses and abuses of participation', *Development in Practice*, 6(1), 1996, pp. 6–15]

Acknowledgements

My thanks to Ken Cole, Marion Glaser, Charlotte Heath, Tone Lauvdal, Arthur Neame, Jane Oliver, and Romy Tiongo for comments on earlier drafts of this paper.

References

Buvinic, M. (1986) 'Projects for women in the third world: explaining their misbehaviour', *World Development*, 14(5): 653–64.

Dunn, J. (1979) *Western Political Theory in the Face of the Future*, Cambridge: Cambridge University Press.

Gaventa, J. (1980) *Power and Powerlessness: Quiescence and Rebellion in an Appalachian Valley*, Oxford: Oxford University Press.

Molyneux, M. (1985) 'Mobilisation without emancipation? Women's interests, the state and revolution in Nicaragua', *Feminist Studies*, 11(2): 227–54.

Scott, J. (1985) *Weapons of the Weak: Everyday Forms of Peasant Resistance*, London: Yale University Press.

Sen, G. and C. Grown (1987) *Development, Crises and Alternative Visions: Third World Women's Perspectives*, London: Earthscan.

Tiongo, R. and S. White (1997) *Doing Theology and Development: Meeting the Challenge of Poverty*, Edinburgh: St Andrew's Press.

Turbyne, J. (1992) 'Participation and development', University of Bath (unpublished mimeo).

6 | Participation: the ascendancy of a buzzword in the neo-liberal era

Pablo Alejandro Leal

Somewhere in the mid-1980s, participation ascended to the pantheon of development buzzwords, catchphrases, and euphemisms. From that moment on, and throughout the greater part of the 1990s, the new buzzword would stand side by side with such giants as 'sustainable development', 'basic needs', 'capacity building', and 'results based'. Participation entered the exclusive world of dominant development discourse; it had gained currency and trade value in the competitive market struggle for development project contracts, an indispensable ingredient of the replies to requests for proposals that issued from multilateral aid agencies everywhere. Development professionals and consultants rushed to attend workshops on how to employ a multiplicity of methodological packages such as Participatory Rural Appraisal (PRA), Participatory Learning and Action, Appreciative Inquiry, Community Based Needs Assessment, and Stakeholder Analysis. Other professionals rushed to lead these workshops, given the growing market for them. There was no doubt: participation was hot, it was in, and it was here to stay – or at least, until it was displaced by another, newer buzzword.

That this happened should be of no surprise to anyone, since the development industry has made an art of reinventing itself in the face of its failure to reduce or alleviate poverty, social and economic inequity, and environmental degradation after more than five glorious development decades. What is striking is the time and manner in which it came upon the institutional development scene, and this article seeks to explore this particular issue.

The historic and systemic failure of the development industry to 'fix' chronic underdevelopment puts it in the challenging position of having both to renew and reinvent its discourse and practice enough to make people believe that a change has, in fact, taken place and to make these adjustments while maintaining intact the basic structure of the status quo on which the development industry depends. This explains why we have seen, over the past 50 years, a rich parade of successive development trends: 'community development' in the post-colonial period, 'modernization' in the Cold War period, and 'basic human needs' and 'integrated rural development' throughout the 1970s. The neo-liberal period (1980s to the present day) witnessed a pageant of such trends as 'sustainable development' and 'participatory development' from the late 1980s and all through the 1990s; 'capacity building', 'human rights', and 'good governance' throughout most of the 1990s; and, we must not forget, 'poverty reduction/alleviation' in the dawn of the twenty-first century.

Michel Chossudovsky (2002: 37) explains the phenomenon in simple and lucid terms:

> The 'official' neoliberal dogma also creates its own 'counter-paradigm' embodying a highly moral and ethical discourse. The latter focuses on 'sustainable development' while distorting and stylizing the policy issues pertaining to poverty, the protection of the environment and the social rights of women. This 'counter-ideology' rarely challenges neoliberal policy prescriptions. It develops alongside and in harmony rather than in opposition to the official neoliberal dogma.

It is clearly more than coincidence that participation appeared as a new battle horse for official development precisely at the time of the shock treatment of Structural Adjustment Programmes (SAPs) inflicted on the underdeveloped world by the World Bank and the IMF. SAPs were the operational methodology that, in practice, implemented neo-liberalism in poor nations. By using the re-negotiation of Third World debt as leverage, the international financial institutions were able to force poor countries to do things that were clearly against their best interest. Thus the wave of privatization, denationalization, elimination of subsidies of all sorts, budgetary austerity, devaluation, and trade liberalization initiated a deep social desperation throughout the Third World. The anti-SAP riots in Caracas in 1989, which left more than 200 people dead; the bread riots of Tunis in January 1984; the anti-SAP riots led by students in Nigeria in 1989; the general strike and popular uprising against the IMF reforms in Morocco in 1990; and the Zapatista uprising of 1994 against the signing of the North American Free Trade Agreement (NAFTA) are but some of the most emblematic examples of the social and political backlash that the SAPs produced.

In participation, official development found what Majid Rahnema has called 'a redeeming saint' (Rahnema 1990: 20). Development's failures were now to be explained by its top-down, blueprint mechanics, which were to be replaced by more people-friendly, bottom-up approaches that would 'put the last first', as Robert Chambers (1983) coined in his well-known book *Rural Development: Putting the Last First*.

What perhaps sets the ascendancy of participation apart from other co-opted development concepts are its radical roots. Arising from the emancipatory pedagogy of Paulo Freire, the Marxist-oriented school of Participatory Action Research (PAR), the principal objective of the participatory paradigm was not development – or 'poverty alleviation' – but the transformation of the cultural, political, and economic structures which reproduce poverty and marginalization.

'The basic ideology of PAR', according to Muhammad Anisur Rahman (1993: 13), 'is that a self conscious people, those who are currently poor and oppressed, will progressively transform their environment by their own praxis'. Or, in more Freirean terms, development can only be achieved when humans are 'beings for themselves', when they possess their own decision-making powers, free of oppressive and dehumanizing circumstances; it is the 'struggle to be more fully human' (Freire 1970: 29).

Development per se is not excluded from the equation but is seen as something that stems from and is functional to the advancement of social transformation. According to Fals-Borda et al. (1991), in the context of the global state of victimization and oppression of the poor by power-wielding elites, development comes only as a result of individual self-awareness and subsequent collective action. In other words, social transformation can and should produce development, while institutional development historically has not led to social transformation. The reason for this is very clear: institutional development was simply never intended to do so.

Radical neo-liberalism

> The World Bank praises the privatization of Zambia's public health system: 'It is a model for Africa. Now there are no more long line-ups in the hospitals.'
> The *Zambian Post* completes the idea: 'There are no more long line-ups at the hospitals because people now die at home.' (Galeano 2002)

When taking into consideration the radical nature of the participatory proposal for social transformation and the neo-liberal structural-adjustment context in which it has been co-opted, the incompatibility between the two might seem far too deep-seated to permit such a co-optation to take place. But if we factor in the growing social discontent, popular mobilizations, and anti-SAP riots that were taking place across the Third World, we begin to understand how the development industry could not simply ignore the increasing critiques and challenges to its reigning paradigm. In Rahnema's words (1990: 200), the challenge that participation posed to development orthodoxy was 'too serious to be brushed away or frontally imposed'.

Yet, what exactly does Rahnema mean when he identifies participation as 'a threat too serious to be brushed away'? In what way did participation represent a challenge to the reigning orthodoxy? To understand this issue, we must locate ourselves in the context of the Cold War, whose most significant disputes (which were anything but 'cold') took place not in the First but in the Third World. National liberation struggles were on course in Africa in countries like Namibia, Angola, and Guinea Bissau. Tanzania had undertaken its historic project of Ujaama socialism under the leadership of Julius Nyerere. In Central America, the Sandinista rebels had triumphed in Nicaragua, and revolutionary insurgencies in El Salvador and Guatemala were underway. In South America, the brutal dictatorships of the Southern Cone were confronting an increasingly belligerent popular opposition. In all of these cases, popular education and participatory grassroots action were playing an active role.

In 1971, Freire would travel to Tanzania and, along with Budd Hall, a renowned PAR activist and thinker, would assist the socialist government in the design of its educational programme. In the mid-1970s, Freire would serve as an adviser to the revolutionary government of Guinea Bissau. He would later provide similar services for the Sandinista government of Nicaragua. Popular education would play a significant role in the construction of grassroots guerrilla support in El Salvador and Guatemala throughout the 1980s, while it would help to consolidate popular resistance to the fascist dictatorships in South America throughout the 1970s and 1980s (see Freire 1978; Hall 1997; Hammond 1998). In 1977, radical Colombian sociologist and participatory research pioneer, Orlando Fals-Borda, would be instrumental in organizing a world conference on PAR which, according to Budd Hall, reflected the decision of researchers and activists to 'use their intellectual skills and connections to strengthen the political movements associated with revolution and democracy of the time' (Hall 1997). From this conference, the participatory action-research movement received a global push and expansion.

It was clear that in the Cold War dispute, participation and popular education had taken sides with the Left and not the Right, and, in the world run by the ultra-reactionary Reagan–Thatcher politics of the 1980s, the very decade in which participation began its ascendancy, this would not go unnoticed. The threat was real and palpable and needed to be reckoned with.

If we add to the above the fact that the SAP politics of the 1980s and 1990s would only serve to heighten popular resistance throughout the Third World, it would become imperative for the global power elites to seek some kind of palliative solution, to put a 'human face' on inhumane policies; at the very least, to create the illusion that they were not indifferent to the suffering inflicted upon the poorest of the poor by the new neo-liberal shock treatment (Leal and Opp 1999). Consequently, a 1989 World Bank Report entitled *Sub-Saharan Africa: From Crisis to Sustainable Growth* advocated creating new institutions and strengthening civil-society organizations (CSOs), inclusive of groups such as NGOs and voluntary organizations such that these might create channels of participation, by establishing 'links both upward and downward in society and [voicing] local concerns more effectively than grassroots institutions' (World Bank 1989: 61, cited in Leal and Opp 1999). According to the Bank, with the creation of a proper 'enabling environment', poor nations can 'channel the energies of the population at large', and 'ordinary people should participate more in designing and implementing development programs' (ibid.).

But the mutations of the official discourse did not stop there, and the irony that they produced was indeed something to behold. By employing the language of 'empowerment', 'self reliance', and 'participation', the Bank assumed a populist appearance reminiscent of PAR. The new rhetoric assumed a pseudo-political stance in its suggestion that the 'crisis of governance' in many countries is due to the 'appropriation of the machinery of government by the elite to serve their own interests', and went so far as to state that a 'deep political malaise stymies action in most countries' (ibid.). At a first glance, one might naively infer that the logical implication is to call for people to be empowered to overturn the current and oppressive state of affairs through increased political participation. However, the actual intent is somewhat different. By having identified the nasty state as the culprit, the World Bank was not advocating a popular government, but rather creating a populist justification for the removal of the state from the economy and its substitution by the market. As Moore (1995: 17) asserts:

> the World Bank is not about to give the state to these people even though it contends that the state has taken the resources from them. Rather than have the state controlled by the common people, the World Bank would control the local state's withdrawal from the economy. Resources must be taken away from the state and placed in the 'market,' where all citizens will supposedly have equal access to them.

Thus liberation or empowerment of poor people in this rationale is not linked with political or state power. Rather, the implication is that empowerment is derived from liberation from an interventionist state, and that participation in free-market economics and their further enlistment into development projects will enable them to 'take fuller charge of their lives', and it is this which is cast as inherently empowering (Leal and Opp 1999).

The World Bank would go on to manufacture products such as the *Participation Source Book* in 1996, a methodological guide to 'doing' participatory development. And later it would produce the stirring report *Voices of the Poor* (Narayan et al. 2000), making heart-felt calls for all development institutions to pay closer attention to the needs, aspirations, and subjectivities of the planet's marginalized classes and to consider how these might influence development policy. Linked to *Voices of the Poor* were the Poverty Reduction Strategy Papers (PRSPs), an initiative also led by the World Bank, that sought to articulate poverty reduction with participation, 'with empowerment as an implicit adjunct' (Cornwall and Brock 2005: 1045). And finally, the cherry on the cake, were the Millennium Development Goals (MDGs), ratified by the United Nations General Assembly in 2000, in which the world's governments committed themselves to the goal of halving global poverty by 2015. The declaration is peppered with buzzwords such as 'sustainability', 'participation', 'empowerment', 'equality', and 'democracy', but it makes no reference to what might be the forces that produce and perpetuate poverty. Maintaining a politically and conceptually ambiguous stance, the MDG declaration affirms that 'the central challenge' faced by the planet's governments and respective institutions is 'to ensure that [neo-liberal] globalization becomes a positive force for all the world's poor' (United Nations General Assembly 2000: 2).

People's participation and empowerment filter into all of the above equations, sometimes implicitly, but more often than not explicitly identified as foundational pillars of the global poverty reduction crusade. According to Cornwall and Brock (2005: 1046), by remaining 'politically ambiguous and definitionally vague, participation has historically been used both to enable ordinary people to gain agency and as a means of maintaining relations of rule'. However, in the hands of the development industry, the political ambiguity has been functional to the preservation of the status quo.

Preserving the hegemony of the status quo, in the Gramscian sense, entails the reproduction of discourse through various channels in order to create and maintain a social consensus around the interests of the dominant power structures, which in the twenty-first century are encased in and are functional to the neo-liberal world order. Thus, the manipulations required to neutralize challenges and threats to its dominant rationale and practice cannot afford to lack sophistication. Whatever the method used to co-opt, the dominant order has assimilated an historic lesson, as White (1996) affirms with simple clarity: 'incorporation, rather than exclusion is the best form of control'. Since frontal negation or attacks to those challenges to the dominant order often serve only to strengthen and legitimate the dissent in the eyes of society, co-option becomes the more attractive option for asserting control. Counter-ideology is thus incorporated as part of the dominant ideology, as Chossudovsky (2002: 37) argues:

> Within this counter-ideology (which is generously funded by the research establishment) development scholars find a comfortable niche. Their role is to generate within this counter-discourse a semblance of critical debate without addressing the social foundations of the global market system. The World Bank plays in this regard a key role by promoting research on poverty and the so-called 'social dimensions of adjustment'. This ethical focus on the underlying categories (e.g. poverty alleviation, gender issues, equity, etc.) provides a 'human face' to the World Bank and a semblance of commitment to social change. However, inasmuch as this analysis is functionally divorced from an understanding of the main macro-economic reforms, it rarely constitutes a threat to the dominant neoliberal economic paradigm.

For participation to become part of dominant development practice, it first had to be modified, sanitized, and depoliticized. Once purged of all the threatening elements, participation could be re-engineered as an instrument that could play a role within the status quo, rather than one that defied it. Co-optation of the concept depended, in large measure, on the omission of class and larger social contradictions. As such, participation became another ingredient in the prevailing modernization paradigm. This conceptualization holds that poverty, inequity, and marginalization are results of a lack of application of technology, capital, and knowledge combined successfully through appropriate policy and planning mechanisms, leading to pertinent reforms of institutional structures (i.e. SAPs) (Escobar 1995; Tandon 1996). The dominant discourses of mainstream development hold as fundamental the assertion that the pattern for these types of intervention are found in the Western rationalist tradition which focuses on behavioural models of rational choice rather than structural inequity or the human response to oppression (Cowen and Shenton 1995; Porter 1995; Pieterse 1991).

As such, institutional development opts for the route of technocracy or the technification of social and political problems. By placing emphasis on the techniques of participation, rather than on its meaning, empowerment is thus presented as a de facto conclusion to the initiation of a participatory process – part and parcel of technical packages like PRA, PLA, and stakeholder analysis. Power – or political – issues are thus translated into technical problems which the dominant development paradigm can easily accommodate (White 1996).

Freed from its originally intended politics and ideology, participation was also liberated from any meaningful form of social confrontation, aside from the very superficial dichotomy between 'outsiders' and 'insiders', or 'uppers' and 'lowers'. Power, in the current global context, and especially so in the context of Third World societies, implies significant degrees of social confrontation and contradiction which are inherent and imminent in processes of social change and transformation. However, for reasons that should by now be self-evident, social confrontation is an issue that the development industry has never been able or willing to address.

This process of depoliticization has been well documented in a series of critiques, culminating with Cooke and Kothari's (2001) *Participation: The New Tyranny?* Nevertheless, to say that institutional development effectively 'depoliticized' participation is not entirely true. Either tacitly or overtly, participation is either functional to the dominant social order or it defies it. The 'depoliticized' versions of participatory action (participatory development, PRA, etc.), 'liberated' from their transformative elements, are still, in fact, political, since they inevitably serve to justify, legitimize, and perpetuate current neo-liberal hegemony. As such, by having been detached from its radical nature, participatory action was consequently re-politicized in the service of the conservative neo-liberal agenda. As Williams (2004: 1) states: 'If development is indeed an "anti-politics machine", ... participation provides a remarkably efficient means of greasing its wheels.'

Returning to politics and power

It should come as no surprise then, that a very relevant and legitimate call has been made to politically relocate participation and rescue its transformative potential. One good example is the edited volume *From Tyranny to Transformation? Exploring New Approaches to Participation* (Hickey and Mohan 2004). This book is based on the idea that while the critical backlash has been legitimate and necessary, one must be careful not to throw the baby out with the bathwater and discard participation in its entirety. The merits of participation as a political and methodological approach that makes social transformation possible remain, but participation must be re-articulated to serve broader struggles, as Hickey and Mohan (2004: 1) point out:

> participatory approaches are most likely to succeed where they are pursued as part of a wider (radical) political project and where they are aimed specifically at securing citizenship rights and participation for marginal and subordinate groups.

Since it is abundantly clear that 'wider radical political projects' are unlikely ever to be on the agenda of development industry, the re-politicization of participation must take place outside the institutional development agenda and within the social, political, and cultural context of grassroots struggle.

Power is, as it has always been, at the centre of the participation paradigm. But, as we have discussed, the institutionalized understandings of empowerment seek to contain the concept within the bounds of the existing order, and empowerment becomes the management of power when in the hands of the powerful. Institutionalized development, unable to accept or assume the original connotations of power and empowerment that participation carried with it, manoeuvred to create new interpretations of the concept. Principal among them is the idea of power as something which could be 'given' by the powerful to the powerless. Of course, as Tandon (1996: 33) points out, this is highly problematic:

> Those who 'give' power condition it; it has to be taken. It is through the active struggle for rights that you secure those rights. It is through the active struggle for resources that you secure those resources. That is the lesson of history.

Empowerment, disassociated from the broader societal issues that generate poverty and disenfranchisement, is reduced to sharing in the cycle of development projects; but, as White (1996) notes, 'sharing through participation does not necessarily mean sharing in power'. If empowerment, as Guijt and Shah (1998) state, is about the transformative capacity of people or groups, and there is no collective analysis of the causes of oppression or marginalization and what actions can be taken to confront and affect those causes, then any efforts are unlikely to be empowering. Genuine empowerment is about poor people seizing and constructing popular power through their own praxis. It is not handed down from the powerful to the powerless, as institutional development has conveniently chosen to interpret the concept. Those who give power condition it, for, as Paulo Freire (1970) best put it himself: 'Freedom is acquired by conquest, not by gift.'

Towards other, better possible worlds

> I am not a subject but rather I create myself as one, as a subject. I continually become; I continually place myself as a subject. There is no subject without becoming one as such. To become is a verb and not a noun. If others place me as a subject, I am not a subject but an object, because I have been placed as one. All domination is based on positioning the other as an object. (Drí 1998: 1)

Today's globalized world is characterized by a vast concentration of wealth that implies a parallel concentration of political power. This has led to the exclusion of the global majorities, denying them any meaningful economic or political participation. The inability of these expanding majorities to attain a dignified life, not in consumer-led opulence espoused by the modernization paradigm, but at least free from misery, renders political democracy meaningless. Rather than being subjects of their own political power, the global poor are objects of neo-liberal capital, overwhelmed by global forces that they do not see or comprehend. After all, political power is nothing if it does not serve as a vehicle to assert control over – or govern – one's present and future life. One cannot speak of participation when a few global power brokers decide the fates of more than two-thirds of the world's population.

Most Third World societies are experiencing crisis in governance, brought on by militarization, transnational corporate control, and corrupt governments created in the service of neo-liberal globalization. These phenomena have undermined all democratic capacity at the formal institutional level and created a sort of political vacuum. This political vacuum could be interpreted as a strategically favourable situation for building upon local people's decision-making capacity and grassroots action, for building popular power and self-governance. However, this first political vacuum is related to a second, which can be called the absence of spaces and a culture for meaningful participation. In societies with historically paternalistic or authoritarian structures or current de-democratized neo-liberal regimes, the spaces for meaningful social and popular participation are constantly reduced. As a consequence, the necessary culture of participation is displaced by the Freirean 'culture of silence'.

The above raises the question: What exactly do we wish to participate in? Can we continue to accept a form of participation that is simply added on to any social project, i.e. neo-liberal modernization and development, creating an alibi for development by transferring ownership to the poor in the name of empowerment? Or should participation be re-located in the radical politics of social transformation by reaffirming its counter-hegemonic roots?

We must not lose sight of the fact that the underlying principle of those approaches to participation was the struggle for deep social transformation. This is something quite different from institutional reform, or development. The context of the global political economy of power and powerlessness places new responsibility on participatory activists and practitioners to reconstitute participation as an instrument for promoting social transformation. The recovery of the emancipatory meaning of participation implies re-grounding in the radical roots of liberatory/popular education and participatory action research, to re-situate the transformative proposal in the twenty-first century neo-liberal world order and reconstruct the spaces and culture for participation and the exercise of popular power. In this logic, Orlando Fals-Borda (2000), the renowned PAR pioneer, creates the concept of people's SpaceTimes as the 'place' where we, as grassroots practitioners and activists, can initiate our political-pedagogic work:

> people's SpaceTimes are concrete social configurations where diversity is part of normality, and 'where people weave the present into their particular thread of history' (Sachs, 1992: 112). Local affirmation, collective memory, and traditional practices are fundamental in such SpaceTimes. Here life and cultural identities, mutual aid and cooperative institutions are formed, personality is shaped, and collective rights have priority over individual rights. Hence it is not surprising that many of the mechanisms used in SpaceTimes by the common people to defend themselves are those to which they have had recourse throughout the centuries, mechanisms and practices which they know best for survival in basic struggles such as those for land, power, and culture. (Fals-Borda 2000: 628)

The struggle to fill people's SpaceTimes is the struggle to counteract the hegemony of global capitalist power. It is thus the struggle for political power; it is the struggle for cultural recognition or affirmation of alternative constructs of 'the good life'; it is the struggle for control over territories, communities, and their resources or the defence of the space of material and cultural reproduction (Fals-Borda 2000). For local people to construct this type of popular power, they must engage in their own political and economic analysis of the local, national, and global realities, which will in turn determine their capacity to influence and affect power relations at higher social levels.

As such, there lies before us the historic task, as participatory practitioners and activists, to be active protagonists in the reconstruction and re-dimensioning of the social subject which will frontally engage the world of twenty-first-century capitalist society by creating new political and cultural imaginaries and make the push towards transformation. This juncture drives us all to make value-based, philosophical, and ideological stands with respect to our own praxis, beginning with the recognition that our primary task is, as it should always have been, not to reform institutional development practice but to transform society.

[Originally published as P. A. Leal, 'Participation: the ascendancy of a buzz-word in the neo-liberal era', *Development in Practice*, 17(4), 2007, pp. 539–48]

References

Chambers, Robert (1983) *Rural Development: Putting the Last First*, London: IT Publications.

Chossudovsky, Michel (2002) *The Globalization of Poverty: The Impacts of IMF and World Bank*, London: Serpent a Plume.

Cooke, Bill and Uma Kothari (eds) (2001) *Participation: The New Tyranny?*, London/New York: Zed Books.

Cornwall, A. and K. Brock (2005) 'What do buzzwords do for development policy? A critical look at "participation", "empowerment" and "poverty reduction"', *Third World Quarterly*, 26(7): 1043–60.

Cowen, Michael and Robert Shenton (1995) 'The invention of development', in Jonathan Crush (ed.), *Power of Development*, London: Routledge.

Drí, Ruben (1998) 'Crisis y reconstrucción del sujeto político popular', Paper presented at Primeras Jornadas de Teoría y Filosofía Política, Buenos Aires, 21–22 August, Facultad de Ciencias Sociales, Universidad de Buenos Aires. Available at: www.clacso.org/wwwclacso/espanol/html/biblioteca/sala/sala2.html.

Escobar, Arturo (1995) 'Imagining a post-development era', in J. Crush (ed.), *Power of Development*, London: Routledge.

Fals-Borda, Orlando (2000) 'People's SpaceTimes in global processes: the response of the local', *Journal of World-Systems Research*, 3 (Fall/Winter), pp. 624–34.

Fals-Borda, Orlando and Muhammad Anisur Rahman (eds) (1991) *Action and Knowledge: Breaking the Monopoly with Participatory Action-Research*, New York: Apex Press.

Freire, Paulo (1970) *The Pedagogy of the Oppressed*, New York: Continuum.

— (1978) *Pedagogy in Process: Letters to Guinea Bissau*, New York: Continuum.

Galeano, Eduardo (2002) 'Paradojas', *La Jornada*, Mexico City, 19 October.

Guijt, Irene and Meera K. Shah (1998) 'Waking up to power, conflict and process', in I. Guijt and M. K. Shah (eds), *The Myth of Community*, London: IT Publications.

Hall, Budd L. (1997) 'Reflections on the origins of the International Participatory Research Network and the Participatory Research Group in Toronto, Canada', Paper presented to the Midwest Research to Practice Conference in Adult, Continuing and Community Education, Michigan State University, East Lansing, Michigan, 15–17 October.

Hammond, John (1998) *Fighting to Learn: Popular Education and Guerrilla War in El Salvador*, Piscataway, NJ: Rutgers University Press.

Hickey, S. and G. Mohan (eds) (2004) *From Tyranny to Transformation? Exploring New Approaches to Participation*, London: Zed Books.

Leal, Pablo and Robert Opp (1999) 'Participation and development in the age of globalization: institutional contradictions and grassroots solutions', available at www.

pdforum.org. Abridged version published in *Development Dialogue*, published by CIDA.

Moore, David (1995) 'Development discourse as hegemony: towards an ideological history – 1945–1995', in David Moore and Gerald Schmitz (eds), *Debating Development Discourse: Institutional and Popular Perspectives*, London: Macmillan.

Narayan, Deepa, Raj Patel, Kai Schafft, Anne Rademacher and Sarah Koch-Schulte (2000) *Voices of the Poor: Can Anyone Hear Us?*, New York: Oxford University Press/ World Bank.

Pieterse, Jan Nederveen (1991) 'Dilemmas of development discourse: the crisis of developmentalism and the comparative method', *Development and Change*, 22(1): 5–29.

Porter, Doug J. (1995) 'Scenes from childhood: the homesickness of development discourses', in Jonathan Crush (ed.), *Power of Development*, London and New York: Routledge.

Rahman, Muhammad Anisur (1993) *People's Self-Development: Perspectives on Participatory Action Research*, London/Dhaka: Zed Books and Dhaka University Press.

Rahnema, Majid (1990) 'Participatory action research: the "Last Temptation of Saint Development"', *Alternatives*, 15: 199–226.

Sachs, Wolfgang (1992) *The Development Dictionary: A Guide to Knowledge as Power*, London: Zed Books.

Tandon, Yash (1996) 'Poverty, process of impoverishment and empowerment', in Vangile Titi and Narech Singh (eds), *Empowerment for Sustainable Development: Toward Operational Strategies*, London: Zed Books.

United Nations General Assembly (2000) United Nations Millennium Declaration: Resolution adopted by the General Assembly, www.un.org/millennium/declaration/ares552e.pdf.

White, Sarah C. (1996) 'Depoliticising development: the uses and abuses of participation', *Development in Practice*, 6(1): 6–15.

Williams, Glyn (2004) 'Towards a re-politicization of participatory development: political capabilities and spaces of empowerment', in S. Hickey and G. Mohan (eds), *From Tyranny to Transformation? Exploring New Approaches to Participation*, London: Zed Books.

World Bank (1989) *Sub-Saharan Africa: From Crisis to Sustainable Growth*, Washington, DC: World Bank.

PART TWO

Participatory methodologies: principles and applications

7 | Production and diffusion of new knowledge

Orlando Fals Borda

External animators, government officials and ordinary experts, such as academic intellectuals, are faced with no major problems concerning the production and diffusion of the knowledge and techniques which they acquire. They simply write a report or a book under their own responsibility, see that it reaches their colleagues or higher authorities, publish it themselves or through a third party and then wait until the critics take note of their contribution to 'knowledge', with their subsequent inclusion in the respective technical bibliographies. Politicians likewise have no difficulties in this respect. They simply decide what to offer to the masses according to their own superficial impressions and proceed accordingly to dispense the crumbs of power through offers, gifts and miscellaneous promises which encourage traditional subservience.

[... I]n participatory action research these academic and political rituals are incongruent with the search for people's power. PAR activists claim that all the knowledge obtained in the communities and subsequently sifted, systematized and fully elucidated does not belong to the researchers or to the activists themselves, but continues to be the property of the investigated community, which has the first right to know the results, discuss and direct them for its own purposes, and authorize their publication.

There is an obligation to 'return' the processed information to its rightful owners, that is, to disseminate in the communities concerned, through a respectful, responsible popularization of good quality, the acquired knowledge and resulting techniques. This 'devolution' is an intrinsic part of participatory research *praxis* because it is another aspect of the emphasis on collective experience which leads to the goal of social change. The classic separation between survey activities and the publication of results has thus no part to play here. In PAR all elements converge, and publication is also evaluated within the context of action and its continuation.

In the same way, the process by which obtained knowledge is systematized, that is, made formally scientific, is not the monopoly of the external agents because the grassroots can and must in one way or another play a critical role in this process. Of course, they do not follow the principles of 'universal scientific' rationality (whether Cartesian or Kantian) but rather their own empirical methods. But these procedures may be more effective and exact than the former in the context of grassroots action. However, it is clear that the patient and imaginative counselling by external animators is more significant during this process than at other stages of the fieldwork, provided that they do not saturate and overwhelm the analytical processes with their own techniques and specialized concepts and that they bear in mind the objectives of increased conscientization, integration and politicization which are being sought by people's power. In other words, both rationalities – the academic and the empirical – appear indispensable if we are to proceed from common sense to the 'good sense' and informed action postulated by Gramsci for transforming societies.

[...]

In this context, the devolution and popularization of knowledge and techniques are a practical, communal and collective exercise resulting from the combined and convergent knowledge of different groups and classes. These groups and classes produce, apply and diffuse the systematic knowledge thus obtained in various ways at the grassroots level.

For this reason, the devolution of knowledge and techniques should not be limited to books or pamphlets. It takes many other different forms, from graphic maps ('taking maps') to films produced by the communities themselves and various other projects and activities for economic advancement. They are *informal adult education* techniques in which the work of participatory investigators complements the efforts of the teachers and the promoters of popular commitment and liberation.

[...]

The political effects of communication are not obtained by separating discourse from the people's concrete necessities or from their own forms and symbols of expression. Shouting slogans and hurling accusations, let us say, against imperialism in the way that activists of the left often do may, in such circumstances, become incongruous. The desired effect is better obtained through a well-composed song, for instance, or an inspired poem denouncing exploitation by foreign business interests which pollute or destroy the environment of a region.

The *attitude* of the speaker often conveys more than vociferous slogans. This is another form of recognizing the role of symbols in folk culture and in horizontal communication. Thus gestures count as much as words. There is even a tactile code: ways of embracing and shaking hands (learned instinctively by clever politicians), and of expressing physical affection or rejection, are patterns of regional behaviour which every animator, educator and participatory researcher should know because they are part of the communication code with base groups which they seek to activate.

[...]

Folk tales and stories are an inevitable and infinite part of all men [sic.].

Thus at the popular level there are never two identical versions of the same story; they never become fossilized or acquire a final shape but remain ever alive and changing.

All these techniques of international oral communication, through appropriate gestures and symbols, are handed down in folk culture from one generation to the next. Since they run in the blood, it is difficult but not impossible for outsiders to assimilate them. It is therefore advantageous to join forces with local narrators for the purpose of increasing political conscientization and commitment, if one wishes to communicate new ideas at the base level.

[Extract from Orlando Fals Borda, *Knowledge and People's Power: Lessons with Peasants in Nicaragua, Mexico and Colombia*, Indian Social Institute, New Delhi, 1985, ch. 4]

8 | The historical roots and contemporary urges in Participatory Research

Rajesh Tandon

History

Participatory Research began to gain visibility in the early–mid 1970s. It challenged the very premises on which social science research methodology was created: of neutrality and objectivity, and of the possibility of value-free inquiry. The distance between the researcher and the researched, the dichotomy of the subject and object, the reliance on statistical and quantifiable techniques – all were subjected to comprehensive critique. Six significant trends converge to contribute to the evolution of the concept and the practice of Participatory Research.

The *first* was a debate about the sociology of knowledge and its implications in terms of epistemology. The debate suggested that knowledge is conditioned by historical context. Therefore, the ways of knowing about a given human phenomenon also change with human history. It is within this framework that alternative views of the history of struggle for social transformation were posited. The most famous came to be known as Subaltern Studies, which presented the view of society, human order and human history from the point of view of the marginalized, the weak, the poor and the deprived as opposed to the dominant form of knowledge produced and articulated throughout history from the point of view of the ruler, the kings, the Brahmins.

The *second* historical trend, which stimulated the very first articulation of the phrase 'Participatory Research', came from the practice of adult education in the countries of the South. As genuine believers in adult learning and in facilitating a horizontal dialogue between the teacher and the learner, adult educators evolved a methodology of learning and education that helped to establish the control of the learner over his or her own learning process. Those adult educators who trained as professionals and engaged in systematic research, particularly around the outcome of their own interventions, began to face a contradiction that was rooted in their training as researchers. They observed how professional training encourages researchers to distance themselves from the learner, establish one-way control over the research process and carry out their research in a manner that has little or no impact on the learner. This contradiction began to result in the reformulation, both in theory and in practice, of a view of research that was sympathetic to, integrated and congruent with the premises on which the practice of adult education was based. It was thus in this field that, in 1974/75, the phrase Participatory Research was first projected and disseminated through this group of adult educators and subsequently promoted through the International Council for Adult Education and its national and regional member organizations through the world.

The *third* support to the ideas and practice of Participatory Research came from the work of Paulo Freire and Ivan Illich. Illich's critique of schooling in modern societies and Freire's contribution to an alternative pedagogy became the basis for linking Participatory Research as an educational process with the framework of popular education. A number of contributions related to this theme emerged in the late 1960s and early 1970s and paved the way for strengthening the arguments in favour of Participatory Research. In particular, the process of knowing and the process of education were shown to be interlinked. This gave further reinforcement of the argument promoted by adult educators in support of Participatory Research.

Another contribution was that of Action Research. Proponents of Action Research had challenged the myth of a static notion of research and inquiry, arguing for 'acting' as a basis of learning and knowing. This formulation of Action Research, going back to the work of Kurt Lewin, was recaptured in Latin America and subsequently became the basis for the formulation of Participatory Action Research. It emphasized the notion of action as a legitimate mode of knowing, taking the realm of knowledge into the field of practice.

Another significant epistemological contribution came from the work of phenomenologists, from the legitimacy they lent to experience as the basis of knowing. This gave impetus to the recognition of human emotions and feelings as legitimate modes of knowing. Subsequently this stream of work developed in a significant way as a body of knowledge and practice within the frame of Experiential Learning.

Finally debates within the development paradigm began to place the question of participation as a critical variable in human development in the mid and late 1970s – people's participation, women's participation and community participation, repositioning the participation of those whose development is being attempted as central actors in their own development. This received significant support from those who had observed the emerging failures of top-down, expert-designed development projects and programmes. A fundamental tenet in the promotion of participation as a central concept in development was that it required the use of knowledge and skills of those who are critical participants and central actors in the development process.

[These] historical trends in the evolution of Participatory Research are worth recalling because they represent the complexity in the evolution of the theory and practice of Participatory Research over the last two decades. Each trend had made its own unique and important contribution, both in the practice of Participatory Research throughout the world as well as in elaborating its theoretical principles, methodology and epistemology.

Contemporary urges

Participatory Research in the contemporary context has been further reinforced with other influences. Many of these derive their roots from the historical trends noted earlier.

The *first* important trend, one that has been rearticulated in the last few years, is the 'new politics of science'. This shows that science based on instrumental rationality, on the logic of manipulation and control of nature (both material and human nature), has been the basic instrument of ensuring the continued hegemony of the ruling classes. It is this science that has also been the basis of an expert-led, top-down, centralized model of development.

The *second* contemporary urge is part of the long-standing historical trend of linkages between ideology and education. It has been revised in the contemporary context where a large number of people in the South are beginning to be integrated into a global education order. Two contrasting streams of education have become visible once again: a system of education that perpetuates the status quo and socializes people into acceptance of the dominant order, based on the positivistic notions of modern science and knowledge enterprise; and an alternative system of education, which links education to social transformation and is based on the traditions of popular knowledge and popular education. In a world divided between conflicting frameworks of desirable futures for humanity, the role of education and its links to ideology have become once again crucial instruments of regulation and control.

The *third* contemporary urge that has enriched the theory and practice of participatory research has its roots in feminist perspectives, struggles and contributions. On the one hand, feminist researchers have significantly critiqued the male bias and patriarchal roots of dominant science. They have challenged formulations about human endeavour and modes and forms of knowing. Contributions from feminist ways of knowing and changing reality have strengthened the work of Participatory Research in the contemporary context.

The *fourth* contemporary urge, one that has reinforced many premises of Participatory Research, has arisen from the ecological movement and the frameworks that it has developed. Research into sustainable human life, ecological balance and harmony has demonstrated the relevance of indigenous knowledge systems. The frameworks of knowledge acquired over centuries of struggle and survival by tribals and other indigenous communities throughout the world have found new support in the light of the growing critique of ecological degradation and destruction in modern societies.

The *fifth* contemporary urge, one that has expanded the scope of original formulations of Participatory Research, is demonstrated in many new methodological labels that have emerged in recent times. There is now a growing body of literature available on Participatory Rural Appraisal. This approach to analysing rural reality has evolved innovative techniques and tools that make the process of village-based investigation of local reality far more accessible and practical. Similarly, new strength has been given to formulations of Action Research and its practice in diverse settings. Some of the most interesting formulations of this have emerged in the work that has come from aboriginal education systems, institutional development and community organizations.

Another stream of work has been labelled 'New Paradigm Research' and has brought together a number of trends of Participatory Research in its practice of human social service, including counselling, therapy, learning for those with learning difficulties and so on.

Finally a number of practical applications of Participatory Research have grown in the last decade. These have focused on evolving examples of people-centred development in organizing and mobilizing women, youth, workers and the marginalized. Applications of Participatory Research in training programmes and in systems of monitoring and evaluation have also grown immensely and further enriched the original formulations.

[This is an edited version of a chapter published in Korrie de Koning and Marion Martin (eds), *Participatory Research in Health*, Zed Books, London, 1996. It is based on a keynote address delivered at the International Symposium on Participatory Research in Health Promotion held at the Liverpool School of Tropical Medicine, UK, September 1993.]

9 | New Paradigm Research Manifesto

New Paradigm Research Group London

1. Research can never be neutral. It is always supporting or questioning social forces, both in its content and by its method. It has effects and side-effects, and these benefit or harm people.

2. Even the most static and conventional research discovers and exposes rigidities and fixed patterns, which are thus enabled to change. This is so whether change is intended or not.

Knowing and participation

3. New paradigm research involves a much closer relationship than that which is usual between the researcher and the researched: significant knowledge of persons is generated primarily through reciprocal encounter between subject and researcher, for whom research is a mutual activity involving co-ownership and shared power with respect both to the process and to the product of the research.

4. The shared language and praxis of subject and researcher created 'the world' to be studied.

Knowing and action

5. We know that people have the capacity for self-awareness and for autonomous, self-directed action within their world, that they may develop the power to change their world. The whole thrust of new paradigm research is to produce the kind of active knowing which will preserve and enhance this capacity and this power. Thus the knowing acquired in new paradigm research is helpful to the flourishing of people and to the politics of self-determination.

6. We see human inquiry not only as a systematic come-to-know process but also as learning through risk-taking in living. Since theoretical and practical knowing are dialectically related, we seek knowledge which can be used in living, and regard knowledge separated from action as in need of special justification. That is why we more often speak of 'knowing' than 'knowledge'.

Knowing and softness

7. The old paradigm research regarded certain kinds of research as 'soft' (loose-construing, qualitative, hypothesis-generating, informal, discovery-oriented aspects of research) and as fit only for preliminary pilot work. The new paradigm approach says that beyond this one-sided objectivity there is a new kind of tight and rigorous synthesis of subjectivity and objectivity. It seeks to develop a new rigour of softness.

Knowing and the holistic

8. The intense particularity of individual situations is respected and celebrated. In studying persons and groups in situation we emphasize tacit understanding, phenomenological exactitude, including acceptance of ambiguities, contradictions and imprecision, which are uniquely valuable sources of insight and change. They need to be used to the full, even though they may be painful. This points to the need for emotional support to be built into the research process.

9. We are interested in generalization, not in order to make deterministic predictions, but as general statements about power, possibilities and limits of persons acting as agents. We are interested in describing the general patterns within which the particular may exist, and accept that often the most personal and particular is also the most general.

10. We make every effort to do justice to the person-in-context as a whole, and find in practice this entails the use of multi-level, multi-disciplinary models of understanding.

Knowledge and values

11. What we contend for most of all is awareness of what is being done to self and others, and what follows from that – both meant and unmeant. We do not want to give up important ideas like truth and checkability, but we want people to recognize that these things can have human costs when they are narrowly applied. For too long social science has treated people like things, and persists in not treating them like people.

12. The outcome of research is knowledge. Knowledge is power. The wrong kind of research gives the wrong kind of power. The right kind of research gives the right kind of power. Research can never be neutral.
This is the ninth draft of the Manifesto. We expect further drafts to emerge as ideas crystallize.

[The New Paradigm Research Group met for several years in the UK in the late

1970s. It was in many ways the initiative of John Rowan, and included among its members at various times John Heron, Peter Reason, Jo May, James Kilty and Michaela von Britzke. The main purpose of the group was to develop and articulate an alternative humanistic approach to inquiry methods in the social sciences. After several years of meeting and discussing different approaches to inquiry, the group articulated its emerging beliefs in the New Paradigm Manifesto.]

10 | Doing feminist participatory research

Patricia Maguire

For years I have been nibbling around the edges of the question of what more could the many feminisms contribute to participatory research (PR) practices, theories and debates. Put another way, how might PR and its advocates be any different if feminism was incorporated more intentionally? Feminisms are about attempting to bring together, out of the margins, many voices and visions of a more just, loving, non-violent world. In that sense, feminism/s and PR share emancipatory, transformative intentions. Yet in practice and theory, PR has often ignored the gender factor in oppressions. This chapter asks: can there truly be emancipatory PR or PR advocates without incorporation of feminisms' perspectives and issues?

The androcentric filter

When I first became curious about PR in the early 1980s, I had been active in the US women's movement and in development work in Jamaica, the USA, and West Africa (Maguire 1984). Eventually I got deeply involved in working against violence against women through direct involvement with Native American, Hispanic and Anglo battered women in rural northwest New Mexico. Although a feminist, I was not much of a feminist theorist; my struggles with and sense of inadequacies in grasping the theoretical debates and underpinnings of development assistance and adult education led me to the Center for International Education, University of Massachusetts, Amherst, an amazing place which openly struggles with the internal practice of the participatory and emancipatory approaches it promotes externally. In the early 1980s the centre saw a regular flow of male guest speakers such as Rajesh Tandon, Paulo Freire, Miles Horton and Ira Shor. In that context, many of us grappled with the contradictions of doing traditional, non-participatory doctoral research or actual project evaluation when the centre's approach to education and development was premised on participatory philosophies and practices. This struggle to find congruency among our education, development and research practices brought many of us to the door of PR.

When I moved to Gallup, New Mexico in 1984 to live and work, I was determined to attempt PR. Working in the community with the local battered women's shelter, I eventually attempted a PR project with a small, multicultural group of former battered women. As we worked together, I began noticing and questioning seriously what seemed to be male or androcentric bias in the PR literature, perhaps in the work itself. At first I felt just a vague annoyance as I devoured accounts of the early PR work. I kept wondering, where are the women? In many case studies, the voices of women were silent or invisible. Gender was hidden in seemingly inclusive terms: 'the people', 'the oppressed', 'the campesinos', or simply 'the community'. It was only when comparing separate descriptions of some projects that it became clear that 'the community' was all too often the male community. In instances where projects dealt only with women, they were usually more clearly identified; 'women villagers', for example. The written PR accounts clearly had a male bias as did, in some cases, the work itself. My understanding of feminism, which grew first out of my daily life and activism, was like a dry cloth on a foggy window. Feminism helped me to *see* things differently.

I believe that in many instances the exclusion of women and gender from much of the early PR literature and work was more than a semantic or logistical oversight (Hall 1993). If women, in all our diversity, were being excluded or marginalized from question-posing, problem-posing community forums of some PR projects, then women's diverse voices, visions and hopes were also excluded. Exactly whose problems and questions was PR addressing? If women had unequal access to project participation, then women no doubt had unequal access to any project benefits. How can you share in the supposed empowerment from a project which continues your silence and marginalization? I found myself wondering, was this potentially emancipatory research approach intended only for the male oppressed? Exactly which systems and structures of oppression would PR attempt to dismantle or replicate? Would men engaged in PR ever seek to dismantle patriarchy? At issue was and still is more than the exclusion of women as women. It is the exclusion of, or minimal attention to and understanding of, gender relations, as context-bound as they are, and subsequent efforts intentionally to shape more just gender relations.

I also delved into PR's theoretical debates and critiques of positivist social science. Feminist theories, critiques, and the growing body of feminist research were largely absent. Would they have us think that only men create emancipatory approaches to knowledge creation? Was PR to become yet another male monopoly? PR acknowledges the centrality of power in the social construction of knowledge. But it is feminist research which alerts us to the centrality of male power in that construction, a power which PR too often ignores. Likewise there is a peculiar silence on exploring how male power still manifests itself behind the scenes in the world of PR advocates.

Feminism has taught me to pay attention to my vague annoyances. Without an intentional space for a multiplicity of voices and visions explicitly including feminism/s, just what kind of worlds would PR have us create? Put another way, can any PR effort and its advocates, real human beings, be considered emancipatory if leaving unchallenged and intact oppressive gender relations and the host of systems and structures which sustain them? There is no way to challenge power relationships within the research process, for example power between the researcher and the researched, without also being intentionally self-conscious of our own behaviour in all our social relationships, each of which have power dimensions. Self-reflection is not only for 'those people, out there', it is for all of us, in here, in the world of advocating for, conferencing about, practising, training others, writing and reading about PR. And it is for us, in here, when out there in our institutions, agencies, networks, friendships, families and love relationships.

Feminisms' challenge to me continues to be to hold myself accountable for congruency between my avowed philosophies and my actual daily behaviours, to recognize the interconnections between the private and public, the personal and the professional. In essence, feminism challenges me to fight fragmentation not only in the knowledge creation process but within myself. Of course I often fall short. I am not suggesting in any way that feminists and feminisms have no flaws or inconsistencies. PR may recognize that seeing and knowing grow out of our specific experiences, situationally complex and shaped by our many multifaceted identities. Yet the profound challenge of knowing differently is then to act and be differently in the world, in our many contexts and relationships. What might it mean for PR advocates and practices if we link being with knowing more explicitly, if we demand greater congruency of ourselves in all our relationships, not merely relationships within our research efforts?

I understand now that one of feminisms' gifts is more than a way of seeing, a way of knowing. It is more than interactive knowledge. It is attention to concrete ways of being in the world of relationships. It is not merely that knowing differently requires acting differently on and with that knowledge (praxis). Seeing and knowing differently pushes us to be differently at our very core, who and how we choose to be daily in all our circles of relationships. And therein lies the ontological challenge. Can we embrace that challenge?

[This is an abridged version of a chapter published in Korrie de Koning and Marion Martin (eds), *Participatory Research in Health*, Zed Books, 1996. For an inspiring account of what a feminist approach to participatory research involves, see P. Maguire, *Doing Participatory Research: A Feminist Approach*, Center for International Education, University of Massachusetts, Amherst, 1987.]

References

Hall, B. (1993) 'Introduction', in P. Park et al. (eds), *Voices of Change: Participatory Research in the United States and Canada*, Westport, CT, and London: Bergin & Garvey.

Maguire, P. (1984) *Women in Development: An Alternative Analysis*, Amherst: Center for International Education, University of Massachusetts.

11 | Cooperative inquiry

Peter Reason

Epistemological groundings

The primary tradition of [social] research [...] has emphasized the separation of subject and object, observer from what is observed, in a search for objective truth. In this tradition, it is the researcher who makes all the decisions about what to study, how to study it, and what conclusions may be drawn; and the 'subjects' contribute only their responses to the situation in which they are observed, without knowing anything about the ideas that inform the inquiry. However, another inquiry tradition, which we can broadly call participatory research, has placed a contrasting emphasis on collaboration between 'researcher' and 'subject', so that this distinction is done away with, and all those involved in the inquiry endeavour to act as co-researchers, contributing both to the decisions which inform the research and the action which is to be studied. Thus, the experiential basis on which participative forms of inquiry are based is 'extended'; extended beyond the positivist concern for the rational and the empirical to include diverse ways of knowing as persons encounter and act in their world, particularly forms of knowing which are experiential and practical.

Many writers have articulated different ways of framing an extended epistemology from pragmatic, constructionist, critical, feminist and developmental perspectives. While these descriptions differ in detail, they all go beyond orthodox empirical and rational Western views of knowing, and embrace a multiplicity of ways of knowing that start from a relationship between self and other, through participation and intuition. They assert the importance of sensitivity and attunement in the moment of relationship, and of knowing not just as an academic pursuit, but as the everyday practices of acting in relationship and creating meaning in our lives (Reason and Bradbury 2001).

The methodology of cooperative inquiry draws on a fourfold extended epistemology: experiential knowing is through direct face-to-face encounter with a person, place or thing; it is knowing through empathy and resonance, that kind of in-depth knowing which is almost impossible to put into words; presentational knowing grows out of experiential knowing, and provides the first form of expression through story, drawing, sculpture, movement and dance, drawing on aesthetic imagery; propositional knowing draws on concepts

99

and ideas; and practical knowing consummates the other forms of knowing in action in the world (Heron 1996). However, as well as being an expression of an extended epistemology within a participative world-view, it has a political dimension. The relationship between power and knowledge has been well argued by Habermas, Foucault, Lukes and others (Gaventa and Cornwall 2001). Participative forms of inquiry start with concerns for power and powerlessness, and aim to confront the way in which the established and power-holding elements of societies worldwide are favoured because they hold a monopoly on the definition and employment of knowledge:

> This political form of participation affirms people's right and ability to have a say in decisions which affect them and which claim to generate knowledge about them. It asserts the importance of liberating the muted voices of those held down by class structures and neo-colonialism, by poverty, sexism, racism, and homophobia. (Reason and Bradbury 2001: 9)

So participatory research has a double objective. One aim is to produce knowledge and action directly useful to a group of people, through research, adult education and socio-political action. The second aim is to empower people at a second and deeper level through the process of constructing and using their own knowledge: they 'see through' the ways in which the establishment monopolizes the production and use of knowledge for the benefit of its members.

This is the meaning of consciousness raising, or *conscientização*, a term popularized by Paulo Freire (1970) for a 'process of self-awareness through collective self-inquiry and reflection' (Fals Borda and Rahman 1991: 16). As Daniel Selener emphasizes, while a major goal of participatory research is to solve practical problems in a community, 'another goal is the creation of shifts in the balance of power in favour of poor and marginalized groups in society' (Selener 1997: 12). Greenwood and Levin also emphasize how action research contributes actively to processes of democratic social change (Greenwood and Levin 1998: 3). Participative research is at its best a process that explicitly aims to educate those involved to develop their capacity for inquiry both individually and collectively.

These four dimensions of a science of persons – treating persons as persons, a participative world-view, an extended epistemology and a liberationist spirit – can be seen as the basis of contemporary action research. Action research itself is currently undergoing an exciting resurgence of interest and creativity, and there are many forms of inquiry practice within this tradition. In one attempt to provide some order to this diversity, we have elsewhere described three broad pathways to this practice. First-person action research/ practice skills and methods address the ability of researchers to foster an inquiring approach to their own lives, to act awarely and choicefully, and to assess effects in the outside world while acting. Second-person action research/ practice addresses our ability to inquire face-to-face with others into issues of mutual concern. Third-person research/practice aims to extend these relatively small-scale projects to create a wider community of inquiry involving a whole organization or community (Reason and Bradbury 2001: xxv–xxvi).

Cooperative inquiry is one articulation of action research. The original initiatives into experiential inquiry were taken around 1970 by John Heron (Heron 1971). This developed into a practice of cooperative inquiry as a methodology for a science of persons (Heron 1996), which places an emphasis on first-person research/practice in the context of supportive and critical second-person relationships, while having the potential to reach out toward third-person practice. In this chapter, I will first set out the logics of the cooperative inquiry method, and then endeavour to show how this takes place within the learning community which is a cooperative inquiry group.

The logics of cooperative inquiry

Cooperative inquiry can be seen as cycling through four phases of reflection and action. In phase 1 a group of co-researchers come together to explore an agreed area of human activity. They may be professionals who wish to develop their understanding and skill in a particular area of practice or members of a minority group who wish to articulate an aspect of their experience which has been muted by the dominant culture. They may wish to explore in depth their experience of certain states of consciousness, to assess the impact on their well-being of particular healing practices, and so on. In this first phase, they agree on the focus of their inquiry, and develop together tentative questions or propositions they wish to explore. They agree to undertake some action, some practice, which will contribute to this exploration, and agree to a set of procedures by which they will observe and record their own and each other's experience.

Phase 1 is primarily in the mode of propositional knowing, although it will also contain important elements of presentational knowing, as group members use their imagination in story, fantasy and graphics to help them articulate their interests and to focus on their purpose in the inquiry. Once they have clarified sufficiently what they want to inquire about, group members conclude phase 1 with planning a method for exploring this in action, and with devising ways of gathering and recording 'data' from this experience.

In phase 2, the co-researchers engage in the actions agreed. They observe and record the process and outcomes of their own and each other's experience. In particular, they are careful to hold lightly the propositional frame from which they started, to notice both how practice does and does not conform to their original ideas and also to the subtleties of experience. This phase involves primarily practical knowledge: knowing how (and how not) to engage in appropriate action, to bracket off the starting idea, and to exercise relevant discrimination.

Phase 3 is in some ways the touchstone of the inquiry method as the co-researchers become fully immersed in and engaged with their experience. They may develop a degree of openness to what is going on so free of preconceptions that they see it in a new way. They may deepen into the experience so that superficial understandings are elaborated and developed. Or they may be led away from the original ideas and proposals into new fields, unpredicted action and creative insights. It is also possible that they may get so involved in what they are doing that they lose the awareness that they are part of an inquiry group: there may be a practical crisis, they may become enthralled or they may simply forget. Phase 3 involves mainly experiential knowing, although it will be richer if new experience is expressed, when recorded, in creative presentational form through graphics, colour, sound, movement, drama, story or poetry.

In phase 4, after an agreed period engaged in phases 2 and 3, the co-researchers reassemble to consider their original propositions and questions in the light of their experience. As a result, they may modify, develop or reframe them; or reject them and pose new questions. They may choose, for the next cycle of action, to focus on the same or on different aspects of the overall inquiry. The group may also choose to amend or develop its inquiry procedures – forms of action, ways of gathering data – in the light of experience. Phase 4 again emphasizes propositional knowing, although presentational forms of knowing will form an important bridge with the experiential and practical phases.

In a full inquiry, the cycle will be repeated several times. Ideas and dis-coveries tentatively reached in early phases can be checked and developed, investigation of one aspect of the inquiry can be related to exploration of other parts, new skills can be acquired and monitored, and experiential competencies can be realized. The group itself may become more cohesive and self-critical, more skilled in its work and in the practices of inquiry. Ideally, the inquiry is finished when the initial questions are fully answered in practice, and when there is a new congruence between the four kinds of knowing. It is, of course, rare for a group to complete an inquiry so fully. It should be noted that actual inquiry practice is not as straightforward as the model suggests: there are usu-ally mini-cycles within major cycles, some cycles emphasize one phase more than others and some practitioners have advocated a more emergent process of inquiry which is less structured into phases. Nevertheless, the discipline of the research cycle is fundamental.

The cycling can really start at any point. It is usual for groups to get together formally at the propositional stage, often as the result of an invitation from an initiating facilitator. However, such a proposal is usually birthed in experiential knowing, at the moment that curiosity is aroused or incongruity in practice noticed. And the proposal to form an inquiry group needs to be presented in such a way as to appeal to the experience of potential co-researchers.

The human process of cooperative inquiry

In a science of persons, the quality of inquiry practice lies far less in impersonal methodology, and far more in the emergence of a self-aware, critical community of inquiry nested within a community of practice. So while cooperative inquiry as method is based on cycles of action and reflection engaging four dimensions of an extended epistemology as described above, cooperative inquiry as human process depends on the development of healthy human interaction in a face-to-face group. The would-be initiator of a cooperative inquiry must be willing to engage with the complexities of these human processes as well as with the logic of inquiry. This requires us to recollect our understanding of group processes.

Many theories of group development trace a series of phases of development in the life of a group. Early concerns are for inclusion and membership. When and if these needs are adequately satisfied, the group focuses on concerns for power and influence. And if these are successfully negotiated, they give way to concerns for intimacy and diversity in which flexible and tolerant relationships enable individuals to realize their own identity and the group to be effective in relation to its task (see, for example, Srivastva et al. 1977). This phase progression model of group behaviour – in which the group's primary concern moves from issues of inclusion to control to intimacy; or from forming to norming to storming to performing (Tuckman 1965); or from nurturing to energizing to relaxing (Randall and Southgate 1980) – is a valuable way of understanding group development (although all groups manifest these principles in their own unique way, and the complexity of an unfolding group process will always exceed what can be said about it).

The creative group can be described as a cycle of nurturing, energizing, a peak of accomplishment, followed by relaxing: the nurturing phase draws people together and helps them feel emotionally safe and bonded. At the same time, early, preparatory aspects of the group task and the organizational issues which allow the group to continue its life and work are attended to. The nurturing phase is about creating a safe and effective container for the work of the group, and leadership is primarily focused on those concerns. In the energizing phase, interaction intensifies as the group engages in its primary task. A degree of healthy conflict may arise as different views, experiences and skills are expressed.

Leadership concerns are with the requirements of the task at hand, with containing and guiding the increasing levels of emotional, physical and intellectual energy which are being expressed. The peak in the creative group occurs at points of accomplishment, those moments when the emotional, task and organizational energy of the group comes together and the main purpose to hand is achieved. These are moments of utter mutual spontaneity. In the relaxing phase, members attend to those issues which will complete the emotional, task and organizational work of the group. Emotionally, the group needs to wind down, to celebrate achievements, to reflect and learn. The task needs to be completed – there are always final touches that distinguish excellence from the merely adequate. And the organizational issues need completion – putting away tools and paying bills. Leadership makes space for these issues to be properly attended to, and usually those naturally gifted as 'finishers' come forward to lead celebrations and complete the task.

A group which lasts over a period of time will experience cycles at different levels: mini-cycles associated with particular tasks and major cycles of action and reflection. These will be set in the context of a long-term developmental cycle of birth, maturation and death, with early concern from inclusion, through conflicts and cliques of the influence stage to (possibly) the maturity of full intimacy and on to dissolution. This creative group nurturing/energizing/relaxing cycle interacts with inquiry phases of action and reflection to produce a complex rhythm of cooperative inquiry.

A creative group is also characterized by an appropriate balance of the principles of hierarchy, collaboration, and autonomy: deciding for others, with others and for oneself (Heron 1996). Authentic hierarchy provides appropriate direction by those with greater vision, skill and experience. Collaboration roots the individual within a community of peers, offering basic support and the creative and corrective feedback of other views and possibilities. Autonomy expresses the self-directing and self-creating potential of the person. The shadow face of authority is authoritarianism; that of collaboration, peer pressure and conformity; that of autonomy, narcissism, wilfulness and isolation. The challenge is to design institutions which manifest valid forms of these principles; and to find ways in which they can be maintained in self-correcting and creative tension.

Research cycling

Heron (1996) suggests that inquiry groups need to draw on both Apollonian and Dionysian qualities in their research cycling. Apollonian inquiry is planned, ordered and rational, seeking quality through systematic search: models are developed and put into practice; experiences are systematically recorded; different forms of presentation are regularly used. Dionysian inquiry is passionate and spontaneous, seeking quality through imagination and synchronicity: the group engages in the activity that emerges in the moment rather than planning action; space is cleared for the unexpected to emerge; more attention is paid to dreams and imagery than to careful theory building; and so on. Apollonian inquiry carries the benefits of systematic order, while Dionysian inquiry offers the possibility of stretching the limits through play. To the extent that co-inquirers can embrace both Apollo and Dionysus in their inquiry cycling, they are able to develop diverse and rich connections with each other and with their experience.

Research cycling builds the energetic engagement of the group with its inquiry task and with each other, and thus meets the emotional needs of the group as it moves into energizing. As the group adventures into deeper exploration of the inquiry topic, to the extent that nurturing has built a safe container, members will become both more deeply bonded and more open to conflict and difference. Deep and lasting friendships have started in inquiry groups, but relationships which are already stressed may fracture. When conflict arises between members, the group needs to find a way of working through, rather than ignoring or burying differences, and different members will be able to offer skills of mediation, bridge-building, confrontation and soothing hurt feelings. The deepening engagement with the inquiry task may itself raise anxieties, for, as people start to question their taken-for-granted assumptions and to try out new forms of behaviour, they can disturb old patterns of defence, and unacknowledged distress may seriously distort inquiry. Inquiry groups will need to find some way to draw the anxieties which arise from both these sources into awareness and resolve them – one of the best ways of doing this is to allow group process time in every meeting for such issues to be raised and explored.

Cooperative inquiry is based on people examining their own experience and action carefully in collaboration with people who share similar concerns and interests. But, you might say, can people not fool themselves about their experience? Isn't this why we have professional researchers who can be detached and objective? The answer to this is that, certainly, people can and do fool themselves, but we find that they can also develop their attention so they can look at themselves – their way of being, their intuitions and imaginings, and their beliefs and actions – critically and in this way improve the quality of their claims to fourfold knowing. We call this 'critical subjectivity'; it means that we do not have to throw away our personal, living knowledge in the search for objectivity, but are able to build on it and develop it. We can cultivate a high-quality and valid individual perspective on what there is, in collaboration with others who are doing the same.

Inquiry skills and validity procedures

We have developed a number of inquiry skills and validity procedures that can be part of a cooperative inquiry and which can help improve the quality of knowing. The skills include:

- Being present and open. This skill is about empathy, resonance and attunement, being open to the meaning we give to and find in our world.

- Bracketing and reframing. The skill here is holding in abeyance the classifications and constructs we impose on our perceiving, and about trying out alternative constructs for their creative capacity; we are open to reframing the defining assumptions of any context.
- Radical practice and congruence. This skill means being aware, during action, of the relationship between our purposes, the frames, norms and theories we bring, our bodily practice, and the outside world. It also means being aware of any lack of congruence between these different facets of the action and adjusting them accordingly.
- Non-attachment and meta-intentionality. This is the knack of not investing one's identity and emotional security in an action, while remaining fully purposive and committed to it.
- Emotional competence. This is the ability to identify and manage emotional states in various ways. It includes keeping action free from distortion driven by the unprocessed distress and conditioning of earlier years.
- The cooperative inquiry group is itself a container and a discipline within which these skills can be developed. These skills can be honed and refined if the inquiry group adopts a range of validity procedures intended to free the various forms of knowing involved in the inquiry process from the distortion of uncritical subjectivity.
- Research cycling. Cooperative inquiry involves going through the four phases of inquiry several times, cycling between action and reflection, looking at experience and practice from different angles, developing different ideas and trying different ways of behaving.
- Divergence and convergence. Research cycling can be convergent, in which case the co-researchers look several times at the same issue, maybe looking each time in more detail; or it can be divergent, as co-researchers decide to look at different issues on successive cycles. Many variations of convergence and divergence are possible in the course of an inquiry. It is up to each group to determine the appropriate balance for their work.
- Authentic collaboration. Since intersubjective dialogue is a key component in refining the forms of knowing, it is important that the inquiry group develops an authentic form of collaboration. The inquiry will not be truly cooperative if one or two people dominate the group, or if some voices are left out altogether.
- Challenging consensus collusion. This can be done with a simple procedure which authorizes any inquirer at any time to adopt formally the role of devil's advocate in order to question the group as to whether any form of collusion is afoot.
- Managing distress. The group adopts some regular method for surfacing and processing repressed distress, which may get unawarely projected out, distorting thought, perception and action within the inquiry.

- Reflection and action. Since the inquiry process depends on alternating phases of action and reflection, it is important to find an appropriate balance, so that there is neither too much reflection on too little experience, which is armchair theorizing, nor too little reflection on too much experience, which is mere activism. Each inquiry group needs to find its own balance between action and reflection.

- Chaos and order. If a group is open, adventurous and innovative, putting all at risk to reach out for the truth beyond fear and collusion, then, once the inquiry is well under way, divergence of thought and expression may descend into confusion, uncertainty, ambiguity, disorder, and tension. A group needs to be prepared for chaos, tolerate it, and wait until there is a real sense of creative resolution.

As the group matures, it will be able to engage in inquiry more energetically and robustly, adapting it to the members' own needs and circumstances. There is always a complex interplay between the logic of inquiry and the process of the human group, as is described in many of the accounts of cooperative inquiry (for a collection of these, see Reason 2001).

Outcomes

The practical knowing which is the outcome of a cooperative inquiry is part of the life experience and practice of those who participated: individual experience will be unique and reflect shared experience. The inquiry will continue to live (if it is successful), and the knowledge be passed along, in the continuing practice of participants as informed by the inquiry experience: doctors practise differently and this affects their patients, colleagues and students; black women discover more about how to thrive and this changes how they are as professionals and as mothers; police professionals see how leadership is a practice of continued learning with others; young women are empowered to speak from their experience; and so on.

So the first thing to remember about all forms of representation is not to confuse the map with the territory. The knowing (the territory) is in the experience and in the practice, and what we write or say about it is a representation. Sometimes action research is seen – wrongly, in my view – as primarily a means to develop rich qualitative data that can be put through the processes of grounded theory or some other form of sense-making; but in action research the sense-making is in the process of the inquiry, in the cycles of action and reflection, in the dialogue of the inquiry group.

[This is an abridged version of a chapter that originally appeared in Jonathan A. Smith (ed.), *Qualitative Psychology: A Practical Guide to Methods*, SAGE Publications, 2008]

References

Fals Borda, O. and A. Rahman (eds) (1991) *Action and Knowledge: Breaking the Monopoly with Participatory Action Research*, Rugby: ITDG Books.

Freire, P. (1970) *Pedagogy of the Oppressed*, New York: Herder and Herder.

Gaventa, J. and A. Cornwall (2001) 'Power and knowledge', in P. Reason and H. Bradbury (eds), *Handbook of Action Research: Participative Inquiry and Practice*, London: Sage.

Greenwood, D. and M. Levin (1998) *Introduction to Action Research: Social Research for Social Change*, Thousand Oaks, CA: Sage.

Heron, J. (1971) *Experience and Method*, Guildford: University of Surrey.

— (1996) *Co-operative Inquiry: Research into the Human Condition*, London: Sage.

Randall, R. and J. Southgate (1980) *Co-operative and Community Group Dynamics ... or your meetings needn't be so appalling*, London: Barefoot Books.

Reason, P. (ed.) (2001) 'Special issue: the practice of co-operative inquiry', *Systemic Practice and Action Research*, 14(6).

Reason, P. and H. Bradbury (2001) 'Inquiry and participation in search of a world worthy of human aspiration', in P. Reason and H. Bradbury (eds), *Handbook of Action Research: Participative Inquiry and Practice*, London: Sage.

Selener, D. (1997) 'Farmer Participatory Research', in *Participatory Action Research and Social Change*, Ithaca, NY: Cornell Participatory Action Research Network, Cornell University.

Srivastva, S., S. L. Obert and E. Neilson (1977) 'Organizational analysis through group processes: a theoretical perspective', in C. L. Cooper (ed.), *Organizational Development in the UK and USA*, London: Macmillan.

Tuckman, B. (1965) 'Developmental sequence in small groups', *Psychological Bulletin*, 63: 384–99.

12 | PRA five years later

Robert Chambers and Irene Guijt

The use of participatory approaches has exploded in recent years. Exciting, innovative and important new approaches to development research, planning and action are evolving rapidly all over the world but this is not happening without difficulties and concerns. This article highlights some important emerging issues, and is based on the thoughts and experiences of many trainers and practitioners of Participatory Rural Appraisal (PRA) around the world. It is not, in any way, a 'final statement' on PRA. The practice of PRA is evolving too rapidly to be captured in anything but a momentary update. We are continually learning through action and critical debates, improving our skills and sharpening our thoughts. As experiences spread and deepen so does our understanding of the issues involved. Your critical reflections are most welcome in this process.

Why RRA and PRA developed

Rapid Rural Appraisal (RRA) evolved in the late 1970s and 1980s, and is one of the precursors of PRA. With accelerating global change and greater awareness of the value of local knowledge, the need for good and timely information and insights became more clearly evident. Four decades of 'development' work, despite its isolated successes, was obviously not solving the problems. Large-scale questionnaire surveys were costly, and generated information that was usually late, inaccurate and little used. Rural development tourism, quick countryside visits, with its anti-poverty biases, was recognized as part of the problem. Outsiders collected information about rural people's realities by visiting places close to urban centres and on main roads, often at successful project sites, during the more prosperous time of the year and by talking to better-off farmers, almost always men.

The failings of these approaches insulated and isolated senior and powerful people, most of whom are men, from rural realities. The failings of this approach above all helped many development professionals to recognize that 'we', as people external to the community where development was intended, and our confidence in our own knowledge, are much of the problem, and that local people, and their knowledge, are the basis of the solution. RRA developed as a research approach to help minimize such biases, an alternative that was cost effective and provided sufficiently accurate information quickly.

At the end of the 1980s, PRA began to evolve in the search for practical research and planning approaches that could support more decentralized planning and more democratic decision-making, value social diversity, work towards sustainability, and enhance community participation and empowerment. PRA can be described as a growing family of approaches and methods to enable local people to share, enhance and analyse their knowledge of life and conditions, to plan and to act. In most cases, the use of PRA is initiated by outside development workers. But when used well, PRA can enable local people (rural or urban) to undertake their own appraisal, analysis, action, monitoring and evaluation. It can draw marginalized people better into planning processes, giving them more control over their own lives.

Both RRA and PRA have built on a wide range of disciplines. In the early 1980s approaches used by agro-ecologists, development planners and geographers provided many of the methodological insights. Since then social science influences (anthropology, sociology, psychology, public administration, etc.) and community development practice (from diverse fields, notably health care and agriculture) have made contributions. The real basis of evolution has proven to be staff of NGOs and some innovative government agencies, whose interaction with villagers has encouraged improvisations, adaptations and new inventions.

Many methods have developed, such as participatory mapping, matrices, wellbeing ranking, causal and linking diagramming, and have been combined in many sequences and an amazing range of applications. These experiences have shown clearly that there are advantages to methods that are flexible rather than rigid, visual rather than verbal, based on group rather than individual analysis, and that compare rather than measure. A major learning for outsiders has been that local people have a far greater capacity to use these methods and to conduct their own analysis than had been supposed.

Beside the basic principles that RRA and PRA share (see Box 12.1), the more recent experiences with PRA suggest additional key principles:

Facilitation. The importance of good facilitation skills, which aims to enable local people to do more or all of the investigation, mapping, modelling, diagramming, ranking, scoring, quantification, analysis, presentation, planning and to own the outcome. Analysis by them is shared with outsiders and the information stays with the people who generated it, being taken away only with their permission.

Sharing. A culture of sharing of information, of methods, of food, of field experiences between and among NGOs, government and villagers, without clinging to the ownership of ideas and information which is common to much development work.

> ### Box 12.1 Basic principles of RRA and PRA
>
> - Off-setting biases – spatial, project, person (gender, elite), seasonal, professional, courtesy.
> - Rapid progressive learning – flexible, exploratory, interactive, inventive.
> - Reversal of roles – learning from, with and by local people; eliciting and using their criteria and categories; and finding, understanding and appreciating local people's knowledge.
> - Optimal ignorance and appropriate imprecision – not finding out more than is needed and not measuring when comparing is enough. We are trained to make absolute measurements but often trends, scores or ranking are all that are required.
> - Triangulation – using different methods, sources and disciplines, and a range of informants in a range of places, and cross-checking to get closer to the truth through successive approximations.
> - Principal investigators' direct learning from and with local people.
> - Seeking diversity and differences.

Behaviour and attitudes. The behaviour and attitudes of external facilitators are of primary importance, more important than methods. And indeed, PRA practitioners and trainers are increasingly stressing personal behaviour and attitudes. These all-important attitudes include: critical self-awareness and embracing error; sitting down, listening and learning; not lecturing but 'handing over the stick' to villagers, who become the main teachers and analysts; having confidence that 'they can do it'; and a relaxed and open-ended inventiveness. It means asking local people to help outsiders learn, respecting them. Self-criticism means learning to accept doubt, acknowledging and learning from errors, continuously trying to do better, and building active learning and improvement into every experience.

All this implies considerable professional and often personal change, and requires good training skills of the PRA trainers. It means that outsiders must take time to reflect on how their role in community interactions changes and what they must learn to do and to stop doing, if local people are to benefit from this. It also often means that community members must adapt to their new, more powerful roles, shedding images of handouts and dependency on outside-led activities.

RRA and PRA

RRA and PRA are very different, despite the similarity in the methods that are being used. The difference lies in their purpose and process. RRA began and continues to be a better way for outsiders to learn. It enables outsiders to gain information and insights from local people and about local conditions. This information is an important input into their own planning so that they will be able to respond more effectively to the needs and priorities of the people they are meant to serve. The greater the understanding that decision or policy-makers have of local reality, the more responsive they may be. Participatory methods, like participatory mapping, can be used in an RRA study. But the emphasis of an RRA exercise lies with the collection of local information. Analysis is carried out by the outsider, later, outside the area of study.

The way PRA has evolved means that it generally refers to a process that empowers local people to change their own condition and situation. It is intended to enable local people to conduct their own analysis and often to plan and take action. It has, therefore, come to encompass more than a single, short, field-based exercise. It means transforming the old dependency roles and recognizing local people, both men and women, as active analysts, planners and organizers. A PRA field exercise is not only for information and idea generation, but it is about analysis and learning by local people. It is about building the process of participation, of discussion and communication, and conflict resolution. This means that the process grows and evolves out of the specifics of the local context.

This does not mean that the external agents are neutral or do not engage in discussions during a PRA process. They are also active, like any of the other interest groups, and have their opinions and ideas. But outsiders have a role to play in, above all, facilitating this analysis by community members. For this they have to learn to keep quiet, to encourage and foster confidence and, especially at first, to restrain their desire to put forward their own ideas. The issue is a subtle one of relative power and devolving analysis and decision-making consciously, at every possible opportunity.

This means that the focus of analysis in PRA-based work is not just the data that are collected but also reflecting on the process. Processes are just as important in the development of a community action plan as the 'data'. Processes do not start and end during a short field exercise and they are not always easy to understand. This understanding is built up over a longer term. PRA itself becomes part of a process, of development, and of empowerment. Learning to see 'process' as one of the 'products' of PRA means a reorientation for fieldworkers. They need to develop skills to see processes and to facilitate them, where appropriate. It also means seeing the use of PRA methods as taking place within a longer time span.

So participatory approaches are not substitutes for but are rather an integral part of long-term dialogue and sustained interaction. Yet many agencies naively assume that a single, brief participatory exercise with a group of local people will lead to positive and lasting change. No participatory approach offers a

Box 12.2 PRA is a learning process

Redd Barna's work with PRA in Kyakatebe and Akoboi in Uganda is based on trying to understand and include intra-communal difference in the development of Community Action Plans. The work is undertaken with 5 community groups: younger women (often unmarried mothers), older women, younger men, older men, and, importantly, children. What seems essential to date is to create an appreciation amongst these groups of the uniqueness and importance of each group's priorities, so that older men will not, for example, oppose the needs that younger women might feel for community family planning activities. Redd Barna's approach is evolving towards a multi-stage process of dialogue with and between these social groups, with about 2–3 weeks between each stage.

Step 1: initial field-based use of PRA methods to start situation analysis with 5 groups, with government extension staff who work in and with those communities and Redd Barna staff (who are all seconded to the National Council for Children).

Step 2: deepen discussions, identify those that have not yet been involved, and seek to draw them into the existing groups, where appropriate. Separate discussion groups might be needed where this is not considered possible by local people.

Step 3: draw up initial Group Action Priorities and Plan (GAPPs) in the groups.

Step 4: share these initial GAPPs amongst the groups, so that all the groups will have a chance to see, discuss, criticize, and, if necessary, laugh about the priorities of others, in order to come to a greater appreciation of the diversity of local concerns and, above all, the validity of all of them. This means that there are 5 sets of GAPPs being shared and discussed within the 5 groups, privately.

Step 5: revise, if necessary, GAPPs as a result of understanding the needs and priorities of other social groups.

Step 6: meeting of (representatives of) the 5 social groups to merge the GAPPs into a Community Action Plan which will be submitted to the Sub-district for funding. At this meeting, the following are identified: areas of totally shared interest (where all 5 groups express a need), areas of partially shared interest (where 2, 3 or 4 groups have overlapping needs), and areas of unique interest (with needs specific to a particular group). This allows for collective action on areas of common interest, while valuing unique needs and acting on them, if necessary, only by the group who expressed them.

quick solution to complex problems. There is no shortcut to success. The first participatory encounter between an external enabling agency and a local community should be seen as the start, not the end, of a long complicated but mutually beneficial journey of joint analysis, self-critical awareness, capacity strengthening, and resource mobilization. This is a learning process that develops and promotes new methods and changes the prevailing attitudes, behaviour, norms, skills and procedures, both within the agency as well as within the local community.

Why is PRA spreading so quickly?

PRA appears to answer a widely felt need that seems to know no boundaries of discipline or of geography. Although it has mainly developed in Asia, Africa and Latin America, the approaches are now spreading and being used in Europe and Australia. Some even talk of a 'revolution' in local (rural and urban) research methods and action.

When done well, with good rapport, these approaches and methods work, involving local people in their own analysis and planning, leading to action, and giving outsiders good insights. The experience is often enjoyable for all concerned. But many of those who have had the opportunity to take part in a PRA (often a training exercise) have found it to be not only fun; it was also an eye-opener. Many missed opportunities become apparent as the knowledge and capacity of local communities to contribute to their own development are revealed. (That we ever thought otherwise!)

Not only donors but also government organizations, training institutes and universities see the important opportunities inherent in PRA and have requested training and are using and evolving variants of PRA. PRA-based work has been carried out in almost every domain of local action and development including community planning, watershed development and management, social forestry, tank rehabilitation, women's programmes, credit, client (stake-holder) selection and deselection, health programmes, water and sanitation, animal husbandry, agricultural research and extension, emergency programmes, food security, institutional development and development staff training. Training institutes are interested in adopting and adapting the approach and methods for fieldwork and field experience of their students. Universities were at first slow to show interest but this is now changing fast.

PRA practitioners and trainers have, in general, strongly emphasized sharing of experiences, so much informal networking has helped the approach to spread quickly. Learning experience workshops have been convened in many places and countries. For example, five international South–South field workshops have been hosted, four in India and one in Sri Lanka. These were organized by Action Aid, AKRSP, MYRADA, OUTREACH and Self-Help Support Programme (Inter-cooperation). Participants came from over 20 countries from

Box 12.3 A menu of methods

- Find and critically review secondary data. They can mislead. They can also help a lot especially in the earlier stages, e.g. deciding where to go, and where gaps or contradictions in understanding exist.
- Observe directly (see for yourself). This can be most effective if combined with self-critical awareness of personal biases that are a result of our own specialized education and background, and consciously trying to compensate for these.
- Seek those who are experts about specific issues. This is so obvious and yet often overlooked, perhaps because outsiders assume that they do not exist. For example: What mechanisms for conflict management/ resolution exist and who in the community is involved?
- Key probes: questions that can lead directly to key issues again based on the assumption that local people are doing something, e.g. 'What new practices have you or others in this village experimented with in recent years?', 'What happens when someone's house burns down?'
- Case studies and stories: a household history and profile, a farm, coping with a crisis, how a conflict was resolved.
- Groups (casual or random encounter; focus; representative or structured for diversity; community, neighbourhood or a specific social group; or formal). Group interviews are often powerful and efficient, but relatively neglected, perhaps due to continued focus on counting through individual questionnaire-based interviews.
- Do-it-yourself: roles of expertise are reversed, with local people as experts, and outsiders as clumsy novices. Local people supervise and teach skills (to fetch firewood, cut and carry fodder grass, level a field, transplant, weed, mud a hut ...), allowing others to learn about their realities, needs and priorities.
- Mapping and modelling: people's mapping, drawing and colouring on the ground, with sticks, seeds, powders, etc. to make social, health or demographic maps (of a residential village), resource maps of village lands or forests, maps of fields, farms, home gardens, topic maps (for water, soils, trees, etc.), service or opportunity maps, making three-dimensional models of watersheds, etc. These methods have been one of the most widely used and can be combined with or lead into household listing and wellbeing ranking, transects, and linkage diagrams.
- Local analysis of secondary sources: participatory analysis of aerial photographs (often best at 1:5000) to identify soil types, land conditions, land tenure, etc.; also satellite imagery.

- Transect walks: systematically walking with key informants through an area, observing, asking, listening, discussing, learning about different zones, local technologies, introduced technologies, seeking problems, solutions, opportunities, and mapping and/or diagramming resources and findings. Transects take many forms: vertical, loop, along a watercourse, sometimes even the sea bottom!
- Timelines and trend and change analysis: chronologies of events, listing major local events with approximate dates; people's accounts of the past, of how customs, practices and things close to them have changed; ethno-biographies – local history of a crop, an animal, a tree, a pest, a weed ..., diagrams and maps showing ecological histories, changes in land use and cropping patterns, population, migration, fuel uses, education, health, credit ..., and the causes of changes and trends, often with estimation of relative magnitude.
- Seasonal calendars – distribution of days of rain, amount of rain or soil moisture, crops, women's, children's and men's work including agricultural and non-agricultural labour, diet, food consumption, sickness, prices, migration, income, expenditure, etc.
- Daily time use analysis: indicating relative amounts of time, degrees of drudgery, etc., activities sometimes indicating seasonal variations.
- Institutional or Venn diagramming. Identifying individuals and institutions important in and for a community or group, or within an organization and their relationships.
- Linkage diagrams: of flows, connections, and causality. This has been used for marketing, nutrient flows on farms, migration, social contacts, impacts of interventions and trends, etc.
- Wellbeing grouping (or wealth ranking): grouping or ranking households according to local criteria, including those considered poorest and worst off. A good lead into discussions of the livelihoods of the poor and how they cope.
- Matrix scoring and ranking: especially using matrices and seeds to compare through scoring, for example different trees, or soils, or methods of soil and water conservation, varieties of a crop or animal, fields on a farm, fish, weeds, conditions at different times, and to express preferences.
- Team contracts and interactions: contracts drawn up by teams with agreed norms of behaviour; modes of interaction within teams, including changing pairs, evening discussions, mutual criticism and help; how to behave in the field, etc. (The team may consist of outsiders only, local people only, or local people and outsiders together.)

- Shared presentations and analysis: where maps, models, diagrams, and findings are presented by local people and/or outsiders, especially at community meetings, and checked, corrected and discussed. Brainstorming, especially joint sessions with local people. But who talks? And how much? Who dominates? Who interrupts whom? Whose ideas dominate? Who lectures?
- Contrast comparisons: asking group A to analyse group B and vice versa. This has been used for gender awareness, asking men to analyse how women spend their time.
- Drama and participatory video-making on key issues: to draw together the problems analysis and explore solutions.

(*Participatory Learning and Action: A Trainer's Guide*)

Asia, Africa and Latin America. They stayed in villages, facilitated the use of PRA methods, and shared their experiences. There are now plans for more workshops on a regional basis, including in Mexico and the Philippines.

As more and more people try out these approaches the need for exchanging experiences and ideas is growing. Networks, both formal and informal, are evolving at national and regional levels, and efforts are made by many to document and share their personal experiences.

Accepting that there is no one right answer to be applied PRA stimulates inventiveness. People, both local and outsiders, have been developing their own varieties of methods, sequences, and processes. The list of approaches and methods is long and continues to grow. It provides practitioners with a varied menu from which they can choose, try out and explore. Some of the methods are common sense. Others are ingenious and not obvious. Some are quite simple, others less so. The rate of innovation makes it impossible to keep up to date.

But if attitudes are rigid and focus on mechanical use of the methods, many of these methods will not work. Where attitudes are open and focus on getting the process and rapport right, then new opportunities appear. With appropriate attitudes and behaviour, each specific situation provides much scope for adapting and inventing new variations.

The opportunities

One of the strengths of PRA is that many of the methods are visual and, therefore, accessible to a larger group of people. The group debates that ensue further stimulate improvisation, resulting in new combinations and applications. The visual methods can be summarized as six main activities:

mapping and modelling; sequencing (chronologically); listing; sorting and ranking; using objects (seeds, stones, sticks, etc.) to count, estimate and score; and linking or relating. These activities have been combined in many different sequences, often using two or three together. In a matrix of famines and their relative characteristics villagers in Senegal combined sequencing of the famines, listing of their characteristics, and scoring these for their intensity. On farm maps that they had drawn, farmers in Kenya drew linkage lines for nutrient flows to and from their compost pits, and then placed seeds on these lines to indicate the volume and importance of each flow. A farmer in Vietnam listed causes and effects of deforestation on cards, drew these on the ground, scored each card for significance with seeds, and also placed the cards around the deforestation circle to signify relative contribution. A group of herders in Somaliland listed 25 water supplies which had been improved, then 45 criteria for assessing their quality and utility. They then scored each criterion out of 10 in the resulting matrix, with two scores in each box, one for before the improvement and one for after improvement. As these examples suggest, the more the visual activities are used in combinations, the more local people can share and analyse their views on the diversity and complexity of their reality.

The stories about the effective use of combinations and sequences of methods in drawing out people's views are many. Community members' own words capture the power of these approaches:

'At the beginning I thought it was just fun but now I have seen the map helped us to generate a discussion on our problems.'

'I never knew that even you [referring to another man in the group who looked very poor] could talk in public.'

'I don't agree with what is depicted in the diagram. I did not go to school but I am not necessarily poor.'

'This is just astonishing. We know each of these pieces because they are part of our existence. But we have never thought of it all put together like this. This is our life and our history.'

Benefits ... and challenges

Some of the benefits of the use of PRA have included the following:

Empowering the poor and weak. Enabling a group (e.g. labourers, women, poor women, small farmers, etc.) or a community themselves to analyse conditions, giving them confidence to state and assert their priorities, to present proposals, to make demands and to take action, leading to sustainable and effective participatory programmes.

Diversification. Encouraging and enabling the expression and exploitation of local diversity in otherwise standard programmes, although this is not automatic. One big limitation of much PRA work to date is the tendency to seek different views but then to compress them all into 'the community perspective'. There is rarely, if ever, a single community perspective on any issue. This obscures key differences and can make subsequent action beneficial for only a few.

The community process. This includes, in theory, identification, appraisal, planning, implementation, monitoring and evaluation, all in a participatory mode. Again, this does not magically and automatically occur. Efforts must be made to carry through beyond the appraisal stage, and such efforts have been made by only a very limited number of organizations.

Research priorities. Identification of research priorities and initiating participatory research has been an important area of positive change, with especially natural scientists more receptive to local knowledge and farmers' ability to design, carry out, and evaluate their own experiments.

Organizational changes. These are occurring, with a reorientation of students, NGO workers, government staff and university and training institute staff towards a culture of open learning with each other and with community members. Direct learning and updating for senior professionals and officials, especially those trapped in headquarters, is taking place, enabling them to change their understanding of, and attitudes towards, community realities.

Policy review. This is happening, in some cases, with the changing and adapting of policies through new, timely and accurate insights from field-based discussions and planning processes. Policy changes are taking place within organizations, and at different levels within government: locally, regionally, and nationally. An example is the Participatory Poverty Assessment (PPA) in Zambia which used PRA methods in representative communities and generated insights which have led to changes in national policy.

The challenges

There seems to be no doubt about the effectiveness of these participatory approaches. This has resulted in increased interest from donors, government organizations, and NGOs who are now requesting, and even requiring, that PRA be used in their programmes and projects. This brings both opportunities and dangers. The opportunities are to initiate and sustain processes of change: empowering disadvantaged people and communities, transforming organizations, and reorienting individuals.

But the dangers and pitfalls are where the real challenges lie. Too much is being demanded, too fast, and with little understanding of participatory development and its implications. Concerns have been voiced about:

- the need to recognize and work at personal responsibilities and professional ethics, such as developing self-critical attitudes and seeking peer review;
- the interaction with community members, which requires dealing with ethics and equity, and careful consideration of the preconditions for engagement, practice, and local human resource support and development;
- the need for the organizations involved to ensure long-term commitment to process, to adapt their organizational culture, management styles, incentives, and procedures, and to seek outward links actively;
- the quality of some training, which forgets the analysis of social differences and the importance of behaviour, and often happens as a one-off event;
- the contradictory demands of donors for both quick visible results and slow participatory development, with donors' and governments' pressures to disburse funds and achieve targets again and again weakening and destroying participation;
- the need for more sharing of good and poor experiences, and networking.

Despite its power when well done PRA is not a quick fix to complex problems, although there are many who wish this were the case. The implications of this new way of working, which emphasizes processes rather than outputs, diversity rather than conformity, attitudes rather than quantifiable targets, have not always been taken equally seriously by the various actors involved. Unfortunately the continuing search for quick fixes has allowed many myths to take hold, myths which are undermining the very spirit of PRA and the potentials which it holds.

Conclusions

Clearly, PRA, or any participatory development approach for that matter, is not a bandage to stick together old failing concepts and approaches. Saying 'first we'll do a PRA and then we can transfer the technology' is simply not an option. Nor is it possible for community members to say, 'First we'll participate in their PRA and then we will take the free seed and fertilizer they are bound to offer.' Both groups need to adapt to different roles, different processes, and different relationships.

Where does all this lead? How crucial is it that outsiders should be aware that rural people should and do conduct their own investigations and analysis and that this needs to be taken into consideration by decision- and policy-makers? Does PRA provide a strategy for local empowerment and sustainable development? Is it feasible on a large scale? Many of these questions are being answered by experience.

We have reached a critical point in the history of humankind. We, as development professionals, face enormous challenges in this period of unprecedented change. Increasing numbers of people are living in abject poverty with little influence over their lives and seemingly few possibilities to improve their situation. Environmental problems are undermining the very life systems on which everyone depends. With government development efforts stagnating the world over, local communities are where many of the changes will have to start. RRA can help to generate relevant information more quickly to help make wiser decisions about what each can do to contribute to solutions. PRA can help to enable local analysis and planning, within and by communities, where much is possible, even without seeking outside resources. Neither approach can nor should do everything, but both can make a meaningful contribution.

[This is an abridged version of an article originally published in *Forests, Trees and People Newsletter*, 26/27, April 2005, pp. 4–15]

Acknowledgements

The authors wish to thank Daphne Thuvesson for her considerable contributions to the content, organization and detail of this article, and for her sustained help with its completion.

13 | Ten myths about PRA

Ian Scoones

1. *That it's quick* While many of the methods associated with PRA may be relatively cost-effective in encouraging dialogue, joint analysis and learning, the processes of participatory development are slow and difficult.

2. *That it's easy* PRA methods are appealingly simple, explaining in part their popularity. They are useful for many people, from villagers to field practitioners to academics. But even experienced PRA practitioners know that the successful use of the approach requires many other skills, especially in communication, facilitation and conflict negotiation.

3. *That anyone can do it* Anyone can help make a map or do a matrix scoring with some success. But this does not mean that learning takes place or changes occur. Using the language of participation, as many consultancy groups and large aid bureaucracies do, does not mean that fieldwork will be successful. Wider issues of organizational change, management and reward systems, staff behaviour, ethics and responsibilities also have to be addressed.

4. *That it's 'just' fancy methods* The popular and visible image of PRA is the range of methods that have emerged over the past decade. These have proved effective and widely applicable. However, methods are only part of a wider shift being seen within both government and non-government agencies. This has deeper implications. In addition to the use of participatory methods, conditions for success seem to include an open learning environment within organizations, and institutional policies, procedures and cultures that encourage innovation.

5. *That it's based on the perspectives of particular disciplines* PRA has grown not out of university departments but from practical field experiences. The main innovators have been field workers and local people in the South (but also increasingly in the North). PRA has drawn on and combined elements from a variety of disciplinary perspectives. The lack of a conventional disciplinary focus has been considered unrigorous and unpublishable, and the experimental and interactive nature of PRA has been sensed as threatening by some academics.

While students increasingly seek to use PRA methods, teaching professionals sometimes resist. Universities have been among the last to take up participatory approaches in their courses.

6. *That it has no theoretical basis* PRA is usually associated with practical situations and with people engaged in practical development activities. But this does not mean that it is without a rich theoretical basis. PRA is based on an action-research approach, in which theory and practice are constantly challenged through experience, reflection and learning. The valuing of theory over practice in most academic disciplines (you've heard the joke about the economist who lies awake at night mulling over whether that which works in practice will also work in theory) means that practice-oriented PRA approaches are often not taken seriously. Yet recent theoretical work shows that participatory approaches raise deep philosophical issues important in social science debates.

7. *That it's just old wine in new bottles* Although PRA, in its ongoing evolution, has been inspired by many sources, it is not simply old hat. As with all major shifts in thinking and practice, PRA is uniting wide-ranging debates and practices in a novel manner. Its emphasis on free visualization and continual improvisation contrasts with other approaches using predetermined diagrams mechanically. Its focus on attitudes and behaviour of external agents contrasts with approaches that disregard this key aspect of local interaction. The extensive range of applications in research and planning on, for example, land tenure, HIV, urban planning, natural resource management, and domestic violence, and subsequent sharing of experiences enriches methodological development. It has proven adaptable to diverse contexts, and accessible and acceptable to a wide range of development professionals.

8. *That training is the answer* One common response to 'new' ideas is to train everyone in their use. The demand for training in PRA is phenomenal. This carries several risks. First, inexperienced trainers are threatening the quality of training and subsequent practice. Second, a training course alone will not ensure appropriate follow-up. Too often, organizations have not explored the implications for themselves in terms of support after the training. Successful training requires encouraging new ways of learning within organizations. Training courses are always only part of the answer.

9. *That people involved are neutral* The myth of the neutral, detached, observing researcher or practitioner is incorrect. People are never neutral, whether they are village participants or external agents. Everyone is unavoidably a participant in some way or other, and these roles and implications need to be understood. This will affect the information gathered and the analyses carried out. In participatory

development, everyone is responsible for her/his actions. The political and ethical implications of participatory action-research must therefore be discussed openly and responded to.

10. *That it is not political* The actions of people engaged in participatory research or development have consequences which are in a broad sense political. Power, control and authority are all part of participatory processes. Conflicts, disputes and tensions may be raised when becoming involved in such a process. Ignoring this is dangerous. Everyone should be aware of the issues of power and control, conflict and dispute that are part of an action-research approach to development. All participants must learn and be ready to deal with these issues. This may mean taking sides or taking a mediating or negotiating role, which are all political acts.

[Excerpt from an article originally published as 'PRA and anthropology: challenges and dilemmas', *PLA Notes*, 24, 1995, pp. 17–20]

14 | Growing from the grassroots: building participatory planning, monitoring and evaluation methods in PARC

Janet Symes and Sa'ed Jasser

Introduction

The Palestinian Agricultural Relief Committee, PARC, is a Palestinian NGO with almost two decades of experience working in agriculture in rural areas of the West Bank and Gaza. PARC targets poor and marginalized farmers – both men and women – and works with them to improve their ability to make a living from farming and to develop a strong Palestinian agricultural sector.

The Palestinian context – the people's struggle

Since 1967, the West Bank and Gaza have remained under Israeli military occupation. As a result, the economy has become almost totally dependent on Israel. It has suffered from a lack of development with poor infrastructure, a negative investment climate and the restrictions imposed by the military administration. During the *intifada* (the popular uprising against the occupation) in the late 1980s and early 1990s curfews were imposed and movement within or between towns, villages or refugee camps was prevented for extended periods of time.

Contrary to expectations there has been little 'peace dividend'. Since the 1993 signing of the Oslo Accords, a closure has been in force which restricts movement. Total closure was in place for most of 1996. The West Bank and Gaza are now a complex patchwork of zones with different degrees of autonomy. The closures, curfews and blockades have had a huge impact on marketing of agricultural produce. These circumstances have many implications for agricultural development and the use of participatory methods. This article discusses how, within PARC, we are slowly developing a more participatory approach to monitor our rural work.

Participation under occupation

The occupation severely limits the control people have over their lives leading to a 'culture of occupation' in which people feel powerless to promote change. On the other hand, the *intifada* saw a huge mobilization of popular power. Men, women and children alike struggled together to promote their

Palestinian identity and tried to build a Palestinian nation that would give them back control over their own future. It is within this context that PARC built its close ties with the rural people, through day-to-day support during the *intifada* and efforts to counter Israeli policies that were destroying Palestinian agriculture. Voluntary committees were set up in villages which were responsible for local decision-making. As a result the work was in direct response to the identified needs and priorities of the rural communities and was carried out by them.

PM&E in PARC

The need for PM&E The concentration on emergency work during the *intifada* led to a limited focus on the development process and the project cycle. The extremely unpredictable and volatile situation meant that planning was very difficult. The combination of these factors did little to encourage the development of participatory monitoring and evaluation (PM&E). The more stable situation of the peace process encouraged a longer-term outlook. PARC began to focus on programmes and project with longer-term goals, re-emphasized its agricultural extension work and concentrated on building a sustainable and viable agricultural sector. PARC also shifted from voluntary work, and expanded its employment of professional field workers.

The voluntary committees were separated from PARC's organizational structure and became the basis for establishing an independent farmers' union. Although this was seen as an essential move, both for PARC to move forward and for the farmers to have an independent voice, this meant that PARC's decision-making process was now one step removed from the rural communities. PARC had to develop new ways of working and, as a result, began to develop participatory techniques. It also became increasingly interested in measuring and understanding the impact of its work, both from a desire to learn from its experiences and ensure that it maintained its relevance to the community, but also because of an increasing interest by PARC's donors in the impact of its work.

Building an organizational commitment to PM&E Although people were very much involved in PARC, many of its methods, and particularly those of planning, monitoring and evaluation, saw participation in terms of 'consultation'. In general, the community was seen as an information source, but not as key actors playing a central role in the decision-making processes of the organization. Much of the early monitoring and evaluation work centred on the collection of data through questionnaires. However, PARC quickly realized the limitations of these methods, and began to introduce more participatory techniques.

The Consultancy Unit was set up with the specific task to develop PM&E.

The Unit has been working to support the use of participatory techniques and to build an understanding of the concepts involved. This process involved several aspects, which are described below.

Interactive methods We needed to make the communication process between our staff and the communities more effective. We found that community or interest group workshops were a particularly useful way of working because they gave people the opportunity to discuss and formulate ideas about the projects and work. In particular they enabled women to gain an equal voice. Due to the conservative nature of rural Palestine, women and men meet separately. In the evaluation of an integrated programme in one village, men had decided what the women could do, but the women redefined their activities for themselves. The men then realized how women had asserted their views, and concluded that it had been the women who had accomplished the most: they had been innovative and successful in getting their ideas off the ground. They appreciated the women's involvement in the evaluation, and even started discussing how women could become involved in the all-male village co-ordinating committee.

The techniques used in workshops were designed to encourage in-depth analysis and to develop future directions for the work. We often use variants on SWOT analysis (Strengths, Weaknesses, Objectives, Threats), but mostly designed group activities specifically for each workshop using a range of tools, such as key points on cards and ranking for prioritization. We are aware that consensus can actually cover up dispute, so try to build in opportunities for individual expression of ideas through various media, as well as group discussion.

Team work: sharing experiences is sharing lessons When we carry out evaluations of specific programmes and projects, a team is set up to lead the process. The team usually comprises at least one person each from the Consultancy Unit, programme, field staff and the community. Outside evaluators are only used if there is a specific reason (e.g. at the request of a donor or if a specific issue would benefit from an alternative or mediating perspective).

The importance of community involvement is illustrated in an evaluation undertaken with the Farmers' Union. The initial idea for an evaluation came from PARC, but once the Farmers' Union joined the team, it became clear that what they wanted was very different to PARC's aims. So we redefined the aims to cover both requirements. New working relations between PARC and the Union developed and the farmers who had participated in the evaluation team went on to lead a planning process for the Union.

From number crunchers to listeners: developing the skills of our staff Successful PM&E requires much more than using different methods; it can only work with an understanding of what participation means, and this often means developing the skills of those involved. In PARC, monitoring was initially understood as a process of collecting quantitative data on projects, such as how many trees were planted. The methods used tended to encourage this approach and reinforced the idea that 'scientifically' calculated data were the only valid information. Furthermore, monitoring and evaluation was seen as simply bureaucratic procedures required by management. In Arabic, the word most commonly used for monitoring conveys a meaning related to 'controlling'. This, among other factors, has contributed to a general feeling that monitoring is a negative process, designed to 'check whether we are working to the rules'. This is aggravated by perception that monitoring and evaluation is the work of a separate unit within PARC. By introducing participatory methods, the staff started to see the benefits of alternative monitoring approaches for both themselves and their projects. We also ensured that programme and field staff are fully involved in all stages in monitoring and evaluation.

This involvement enables them to take on responsibility for the PM&E work and to see it as an essential part of the project process. The Women's Unit of PARC in Gaza decided to use some of the participatory techniques to evaluate their unit's work in more detail after participating in an organizational self-evaluation. Currently, the role of the Consultancy Unit is often just to provide support and advice to the staff's own initiatives and not be the sole driver of the process. By using participatory techniques with senior management, we were able to encourage greater involvement of all staff. For example, during an organizational evaluation, there was an initial reluctance for all the staff to be involved, despite a willingness to encourage the participation of the target group. Now many of the ideas developed in the staff workshops are forming a key part of PARC's on-going strategic planning.

Moving forward: linking planning to PM&E

M&E in the project cycle The project cycle is usually presented as a circle linking planning, monitoring and evaluation. This depiction often leads to the unfortunate image of projects going round in circles! Unfortunately the crucial link between planning and monitoring and evaluation is often not that easy to achieve. In our experience, monitoring and evaluation are seen as ways of measuring how a plan (and by implication a project) is implemented. If they are perceived to come after implementation, then the vital step of moving to the next phase of development is overlooked.

The 'learning loop' We find that simply providing recommendations for future actions in an evaluation is simply not sufficient. The learning loop must extend to include clear plans about what to do next. It is important to include discussions and decisions about how to move forward after a PM&E activity, and to clearly identify the roles of each of the groups involved. We found that the strongest push for clarity of plans often comes from the community themselves. They are rarely content to allow the process to only look at 'impact' without including the question of 'what next?'.

A process approach, rather than a project by project approach, is essential. In this way planning, monitoring and evaluation become part of a continual learning process. The trajectory may shift, but the momentum should be forward. By using a participatory approach, the engine for this momentum becomes the community, and they can control its direction.

Linking levels We are setting up a participatory planning, monitoring and evaluation (PPME) system within PARC that will help us to ensure that planning, monitoring and evaluation are seen as intrinsically linked as one process. An essential part of this system is the linking of different levels of planning, monitoring and evaluation. This helps us to ensure that participation is not limited to the project level, but features in all levels in PARC's work.

Breaking free of the illogical framework One of the difficulties we face in developing a PPME system for PARC is building a suitable framework. Much of the work on PPME systems has been developed by donor agencies and designed with their own reporting and monitoring in mind. However, this concentration on organizational needs is not just confined to the donors; in PARC, the main incentive for developing a PPME system stems from the need to administer money well and to meet our donors' reporting and monitoring requirements. Consequently, although participation is recognized as important, and the donors we work with encourage this in our work, the frameworks used are based more on organizational aspects, and, in reality, tend not to promote participatory techniques.

This is partly due to the predominance of logical framework analysis (LFA) as a tool that links planning, monitoring and evaluation. The logical framework may be useful in some situations, and certainly emphasizes the need to have clear objectives and indicators. However, we have found that it is not a useful tool when working from a participatory premise. In most practical applications we came across, people find it far from logical. Consequently, the framework is developed by programme managers; the field staff and programme participants are alienated from the planning process and control is concentrated in the hands of the 'LFA Expert'. This discourages participation in – and community ownership over – the development process.

LFA also implicitly encourages those who use it to fall into the trap of seeing M&E as a mechanism for checking planning, rather than a process of learning from experience. People tend to focus on whether they have fully implemented each step of the plan. The aim becomes fulfilling the plan, not promoting participatory development. Flexibility is discouraged and the need for introducing change into a programme is considered negatively rather than being viewed as a positive outcome of a progressive monitoring process. In the real world, it is very rare that a plan is implemented with no changes, however carefully conceived. Indeed we often found that projects implemented exactly as planned had more to do with a lack of M&E than with them being exceptionally well planned. This lack of flexibility is a particular problem in the present Palestinian context, where circumstances can change very rapidly. There are so many aspects that can affect a plan over which people have no control. In such circumstances, planning needs to have a degree of fluidity and responsiveness. If PM&E techniques are adopted within such a rigid framework, the alienation of the participants can become a real problem.

By offering people the tools, and encouraging their understanding of the concepts involved, they can build their own framework. Part of this involves finding out what other people's (including the donors) PM&E needs are, ensuring that these are met and that the system is both relevant and practical. This can be achieved by encouraging a participatory approach and cultivating the communities' ability to control the development process.

Conclusions

The transition from working in emergency relief during a conflict situation to an increased focus on building civil society and the development process provided a stimulus for PARC to develop its PM&E. But we still have a long way to go before we can be confident that the community is really playing the central role in PPME and that they are defining the work of PARC. We need to strengthen and widen the scope of participatory methods used, continue to develop organizational commitment to 'participation'; and create a framework that encourages participation. There are several points that emerged from our experience in developing and using PM&E:

- Despite a background as a grassroots organization and working with rural people as part of a popular struggle it is still vital to work with participatory techniques. The process of organizational 'scaling up' does not invalidate the use of participatory techniques, but reinforces the need for them.
- Monitoring and evaluation cannot be separated from planning since all are an intrinsic part of the development process. The linkages are crucial in establishing a learning process that can enable the development process to move forward.
- The nature of the PPME is key. The framework and methods used must have the ability to encourage real participation and give control to the community.

[This is an abridged version of an article that was originally published in *PLA Notes*, 31, 1998, pp. 57–61]

15 | Tools for empowerment: community exchanges

Sheela Patel

Introduction

This paper describes tools and methods developed and used by organizations and federations of slum, squatter and pavement dwellers over the last 20 years. It focuses mainly on the use of these tools by an alliance of three organizations in India – the National Slum Dwellers' Federation (NSDF) (and its many member federations), Mahila Milan (savings cooperatives formed by women slum and pavement dwellers) and the Indian NGO, SPARC (see www. sparcindia.org). This alliance is active in over 50 cities in India and engaged in a variety of initiatives to reduce urban poverty involving millions of urban dwellers. These tools and methods were developed by the 'slum' and pavement dwellers and their own organizations to ensure that they remained at the centre of planning and managing initiatives (including conceiving how participation should be done) and of the negotiations with all external agencies (including local governments).

These tools and methods developed by the urban poor or homeless federations are participatory in two senses. First, in the sense of encouraging and supporting widespread involvement of urban poor groups and the community organizations and the federations which they form in designing and implementing initiatives. Second, in ensuring that the organizations of the urban poor and homeless retain the central role in what is designed and implemented, and how it is managed and evaluated, when working with local governments, national agencies or international donors. The tools described below are to contribute to more equal relations between urban poor groups and the other (usually more powerful) groups with whom they have to work and negotiate.

Background

In India, the development of these tools and methods drew on the same questioning of conventional 'development' and of the role of external professionals that fuelled Participatory Learning and Action and its predecessors. From the mid- and late 1980s as the alliance of SPARC, Mahila Milan and the National Slum Dwellers' Federation in India developed, the tools and methods they used had certain characteristics that made them different from most of the early experiences with participatory tools:

- The main focuses from the outset were strengthening community organizations formed by the (urban) poor (also ensuring that these were democratic and accountable to their members) and supporting these groups, changing their relationship with local governments (and where relevant with other official bodies, including international agencies).
- The tools and methods were designed, implemented and refined by the homeless and the 'slum-dwellers'. They were done for particular purposes or projects but always within a broader concern to create a more equal and productive relationship with local government agencies. So they were very political from the outset and concerned with 'governance' but as this paper describes, generally not a politics of confrontation but of negotiation and of showing alternatives.
- The tools and methods were rooted in addressing problems that low-income groups face in urban (mostly large city) contexts.
- The change in tactics, adopted by community leaders. In the mid-1980s, many leaders within the slum dwellers' federations in India recognized that they had to move from making demands of government (with changes in government policy towards 'slum' dwellers seen as the solution) to demonstrating their own solutions, working with governments.
- The innovators and teachers of these new tools and methods were the urban poor, both within and between nations (with teaching and training done mainly through community-to-community exchanges).
- The role of (local) NGOs was to avoid doing anything that the representative organizations of the urban poor could do themselves ...

Community exchanges

Exchange visits between community organizations have been continually developed because they serve many ends. They:

- are a means of drawing large numbers of people into a process of change, supporting local reflection and analysis, enabling the urban poor themselves to own the process of knowledge creation and change;
- enable the poor to reach out and federate, thereby developing a collective vision and collective strength; and
- help create strong, personal bonds between communities who share common problems, both presenting them with a range of options to choose from and negotiate for, and assuring them that they are not alone in their struggles.

Since 1988, there has been a constant process of exchanges between slum and pavement communities in India (the federations and women's cooperatives have members in over 50 cities). Representatives from savings groups formed by women pavement dwellers in Mumbai were the first to travel to other settlements in their own city and later to other cities in India to visit other communities. They shared their knowledge about the savings and credit groups they had developed and managed themselves and found many people who were interested in acquiring their skills. Although most exchanges are within cities or between cities, there have also been many international exchanges, with community organizers from India visiting many other countries (including South Africa, Thailand, Cambodia, Laos, Uganda, Zimbabwe and Kenya), and community organizers from these and from many other countries visiting slum and pavement communities in India.

These exchanges build upon the logic of 'doing is knowing'. Exchanges lead to a good sharing of experience. One particularly significant international exchange was the visit of senior officials from Kenyan Railways and senior planners from Nairobi to Mumbai in April 2004, to see how the resettlement of the people from beside the railway tracks was organized there. Thousands of low-income households living in informal settlements close to the railway tracks in Nairobi have been threatened with eviction – and this visit showed the Kenyans the possibilities of community-managed resettlement which benefits those who are resettled, as well as clearing the tracks to allow faster and more frequent train services.

In the exchange process, communities and their leadership have the potential to learn new skills and share teaching. The exchanges maintain a rapid learning and teaching curve, within which the Alliance's core team supports new learning and helps more people to teach and to learn from each other. From the first community exchanges between the pavement dwellers on the streets of Mumbai, there has now developed Shack/Slum Dwellers International, an umbrella organization to support all the federations. This links the urban poor organizations in different countries through community exchanges (including many visits to nations where federations have not yet developed or are only in early stages of development) and supports them in their negotiations with international agencies.

[Excerpt from an article originally published as 'Tools and methods for empowerment developed by slum and pavement dwellers' federations in India', *PLA Notes*, 50, pp. 117–30. The original article describes a number of tools, including 'slum' enumerations/surveys, mapping, pilot projects, house modelling, community exchanges and precedent setting; this excerpt focuses on community exchanges as a participatory method for which SPARC has gained particular recognition.]

16 | Citizens juries: a radical alternative for social research

Tom Wakeford

Over the past few years, citizens juries have become a widespread yet controversial method of action research in the UK.[1] While some juries have been one-off attempts to exploit the symbolic legitimacy of a jury as part of a public relations exercise, others have contributed to wider programmes to validate citizen analysis and hold the powerful to account. Key to their future is the development of citizens juries that are not only fair, representative and transparent, but are able to form part of longer-term initiatives particularly aimed at those currently excluded from political processes.

Since its origins in the positivism of the nineteenth century, social scientific research has usually treated its objects of research as subjects of study, rather than as citizens (Barnes 1979). Though they may produce rich qualitative insights, focus group and participatory appraisal techniques do not in themselves change the passive status of the people being studied. Drawing on the symbolism of the system of trial by jury, citizens juries have been seen as potentially challenging this separation between analyst and subject. Having the potential to be a tool of social justice and the legitimization of non-specialist knowledge as much as a method of participatory research, citizens juries are a radical alternative that could contribute to the reining-in of the unaccountable exercise of power.

Like a legal jury, the cornerstone of a citizens jury is the belief that once a small sample of a population have heard the evidence, their subsequent deliberations can fairly represent the conscience and intelligence of the community. This age-old reasoning contrasts with today's most common quantitative and qualitative methods for representing the public's views: the opinion poll and the focus group.

Citizens juries draw on the tradition of representation most famously described in the Magna Carta in 1215, which enshrined every person's right to trial by a jury made up of his or her peers. Today, jury trials are practised in the UK, US, and many other democracies around the world including Russia, Spain, Brazil and Australia. No other institution of government rivals the jury in placing power so directly in the hands of citizens, or wagers more on the truth of democracy's core claim that the people make their own best governors.

The jury process

In most citizens juries a panel of non-specialists meets for a total of thirty to fifty hours to examine carefully an issue of public significance. The jury, made up of between twelve and twenty people, serves as a microcosm of the public. Under the model of the citizens jury most commonly used in the UK and US, jurors are often recruited via a more or less randomized selection of people taken from the electoral roll (Kuper 1996). To encourage recruitment from as broad a range of backgrounds as possible, various provisions are available including an honorarium payment, crèche facilities, and easy-access jury locations.

Jurors hear from a variety of specialist witnesses and are usually able to discuss as broad or narrow a range of issues as they see fit. The distinguishing characteristics of participants in a citizens jury compared with other methods of qualitative research or deliberative democracy are that jury members are:

- given time to reflect and deliberate freely with each other on the questions at hand, occasionally assisted by a neutral advisor;
- given the opportunity to scrutinize the information they receive from witnesses, whom they interrogate themselves;
- expected to develop a set of conclusions or 'vision' for the future – which need not be unanimous.

The statistical representativeness of most quantitative research arises from the large numbers of people that are surveyed. The concept of a citizens jury relies instead on the participatory representativeness of twelve citizens. Because the decision is reached after extensive opportunity for deliberation, the conclusion is arguably of greater validity than when an instantaneous response is obtained from a thousand uninformed citizens. Unlike opinion polls or focus groups, citizens juries are designed to allow participants to represent their own views directly to policy-makers.

The method by which members of the jury are recruited is a vital component of their ability to be representative. Selecting members at random from the electoral register is the standard means of ensuring this, but it suffers from two disadvantages. Around a tenth of the voting population in the UK is not registered and so citizens who are already voiceless risk being excluded from potential membership of the jury. Supplementary methods may be used to ensure that marginalized groups are properly represented (Pimbert and Wakeford 2002). Secondly, even if people are registered to vote, they may be excluded or put off for other reasons, including sensory impairment or physical disability, illiteracy, or lack of confidence. Sensitivity to the situation of potential jurors is therefore crucial for everyone involved in the jury selection process.

In a legal trial the decision that frames the jury's deliberations is simple – the defendant is either guilty or not guilty. However, in a citizens jury, the presentation of the question can, as in an opinion poll, risk influencing the response. For example, in a jury largely funded by a pharmaceutical company, run by the Welsh Institute for Health and Social Care (WIHSC 1997), and evaluated by Dunkerley and Glasner (1998), the jury was asked 'What conditions should be fulfilled before genetic testing for people susceptible to common diseases becomes available on the National Health Service?' This phrasing may have discouraged jurors from discussing arguments opposing all human genetic tests (cf. Irwin 2001; MORI 1999). Another jury attempted to overcome this pre-framing of deliberations by asking jurors merely to discuss the future of the food system, although the majority of the evidence subsequently presented related to GM crops (Genetics Forum 1999). The way in which discussions are framed by witnesses and the information provided can also have an influence on the extent to which citizens have opportunities to develop their own visions for the future (Wakeford, in Pimbert and Wakeford 2001: 79).

The extent to which jurors are allowed to interrogate the sources of information available to them, rather than being merely the passive recipients of written briefings and specialist testimonies, is another important element of citizens juries. One measure of the extent to which this is allowed to take place is the proportion of a jury deliberation that is devoted to the presentation of witness evidence compared with the time that is allocated for the interrogation of witnesses by the jurors. In ActionAid's citizens jury in rural India, for example, the ratio was roughly one-to-one, which appeared to jurors and observers to be enough for the jurors to become informed about the issues (Satya-Murty, in Pimbert and Wakeford 2001: 46). This interactivity, along with the jury's opportunity to demand additional witnesses on topics they themselves have specified, contrasts with the role of a legal jury who may only listen passively to the prosecution and defence cases.

As in criminal trials, citizens juries work best when evidence is communicated in a clear and accessible manner. This confirms legal research findings, which suggest that, even in cases where it is claimed that trial by jury is inappropriate because of the scientific nature of evidence, problems can usually be overcome if the manner of presenting the evidence is given careful consideration (Edmond and Mercer 1997).

Following the jury's verdict in a legal trial, the side that loses the case may suggest that the trial has somehow been unfair. Citizens juries and other similar processes are frequently undertaken on contentious issues, and similar accusations have been made not only by stakeholders (Wallace, in Pimbert and Wakeford 2001: 61), but also by external evaluators (Barns 1995). Three additional elements of jury design are important in ensuring such conflicts are minimized.

In most cases in which a conflict over the conclusions arises, the organizers have not followed a key guideline developed by the Institute for Public Policy Research (IPPR), which suggests that the process should be overseen by an advisory group composed of all relevant stakeholders (Coote and Lenaghan 1997: 79). This oversight panel plays a crucial role in ensuring that the trial is fair and is seen to be fair. In the Genetics Forum (1999) jury, the oversight panel included representatives from a major UK supermarket, the largest farmers' and farm-labourers' unions, an organic farming association, a national consumer rights group, a wholefood manufacturer and a GM laboratory that received both private and public sector funding. When the jury's conclusions were critical of two of the stakeholders, it was difficult for them to dismiss the fairness of the 'trial', since they had overseen, and been given a right of veto on key elements of, the jury process.

Deliberative processes have a natural tendency towards consensus. In legal juries this may be seen as desirable, but when discussing a policy issue it is important to allow the full diversity of opinions on a topic to emerge. Given the time and resource constraints of any deliberative process, this is a major challenge.

The public availability of complete audio or video recordings of all jury hearings (though not of 'jury room' deliberations if participants would prefer privacy) is an important aid to transparency. Multiple sources of funding help to ensure that the jury's organizers are not seen as having a financial interest in producing a verdict that supports the interests of a single funding body. To maximize the scrutiny they provide, the two or more funders should have somewhat opposing interests regarding the subject likely to be under discussion.

The moment in a citizens jury that is most important for its participants is the point at which they deliver their recommendations to those in power. A jury in which jurors are not only allowed to present their conclusions themselves at a press conference, but also undertake work towards ensuring that some of their conclusions are implemented, is a far more empowering process than one in which their verdict is merely extracted by researchers and written up without further input from the jurors. The extent to which juries have been used by participants as part of an ongoing process of holding decision-makers to account varies considerably (Armour 1995; Pimbert, in Pimbert and Wakeford 2001: 81).

Impacts

Although first conceived in the US in the 1970s and developed during the 1980s in Germany, it was not until they began to be piloted by the IPPR in 1994 that citizens juries began to be used in the UK. Yet the appeal of juries was such that within four years of the election of New Labour in 1997 over one hundred juries had taken place in the UK on issues as diverse as Northern Ireland educational reforms, health rationing, waste disposal and genetic testing. Many of the academics, local authorities and non-governmental agencies who led this first wave of experiments based their enthusiasm on the supposed potential of citizen juries to combine citizen deliberation, the interrogation of specialist evidence, and participatory approaches to problem-solving (Smith and Wales 2000).

However, having seen that juries' conclusions can often contain criticisms of Government, and are often announced very publicly, Whitehall's funding for such experiments has now largely been transferred back to safer, more controllable methods such as focus groups. A partial exception to this general trend has been the 'Consumers in the NHS' initiative (Baxter et al. 2001).

At a local level, by contrast, some UK councils and health authorities undertook 'quick and dirty' citizens juries that generated sympathetic publicity and the appearance of public consultation. However, evaluations have questioned the extent to which many of them achieved representativeness in their selection of participants, transparency in their provision of information, or independence, given the limited extent to which jurors could express their opinions without them being channelled through the commissioning body (Barnes 1999). Some suspect that citizens juries have sometimes been used as show-trials that allow those in power to avoid engaging in processes that might hold them accountable to communities (Delap, in Pimbert and Wakeford 2001: 39).

Future challenges

As with many social research tools, the widespread uptake and diversity of methods that use the label 'citizens jury' has raised concerns about whether the approach has become devalued. In contrast to opinion polls and focus groups carried out for commercial clients, citizens juries carried out with emancipatory aims often fail to provide opportunities for communities to evaluate the process.

Yet, despite suspicion about the motives and conduct of some of those involved in their early years of development, the core elements of citizens juries have the potential to provide a powerful participatory tool. Perhaps the greatest danger for its enthusiasts is that they see it as a magic bullet, rather than a contribution to a wider process of community self-analysis and democratic renewal.

Experiments are now being undertaken on the extent to which citizens juries can be made into more bottom-up 'do-it-yourself' processes that are designed by marginalized communities themselves. The basic principles of a fair trial are of common sense to most citizens. If grassroots forums are given the opportunity to determine what question the jury will be asked to address, and help choose the witnesses that provide evidence, they are also more likely to feel empowered to use the results of the jury for advocacy work. Unlike methods such as focus groups and most participatory appraisals, citizens juries appear to offer a method of action-research that has a high potential for methodological transparency, participatory deliberation and subsequent citizen advocacy. Ironically, given that a citizen's legal right to trial by jury is currently being threatened, apparently because the UK Government believes it is often too expensive, citizens juries are increasingly being seen as offering a cost-effective and legitimate means of enhancing both democratic account-ability and social justice.

[This article originally appeared in *Social Research Update*, the quarterly news-letter of the Sociology Department at the University of Surrey, Issue 37, 2002]

Note

1 Details of a range of issues, local contexts and political controversies that have been addressed using jury-type methods can be found at www.jury.org.uk.

References

Armour, A. (1995) 'The Citizens' Jury model of public participation: a critical evalu-ation', in O. Renn, T. Webler and P. Widemann (eds), *Fairness and Competence in Citizen Participation*, Dordrecht: Kluwer Academic Publishers.

Barnes, J. A. (1979) *Who Should Know What? Social Science, Privacy and Ethics*, London: Penguin.

— (1999) *Building a Deliberative Democracy: An Evaluation of Two Citizens Juries*, London: Institute for Public Policy Research.

Barns, I. (1995) 'Manufacturing consensus: reflections on the UK National Consensus Conference on Plant Biotechnology', *Science as Culture*, 12: 199–216.

Baxter, L., L. Thorne and A. Mitchell (2001) *Small Voices Big Noises: Lay Involvement in Health Research: Lessons from Other Fields*, Winchester: Help for Health Trust, www.conres.co.uk/pub.htm.

Coote, A. and J. Lenaghan (1997) *Citizens' Juries: From Theory to Practice*, London: IPPR.

Dunkerley, D. and P. Glasner (1998) 'Empowering the public? Citizens juries and the new genetic technologies', *Critical Public Health*, 8: 181–92.

Edmond, G. and D. Mercer (1997) 'Scientific literacy and the jury: reconsidering jury "competence"', *Public Understanding of Science*, 6: 327–59.

Genetics Forum (1999) *Citizen Foresight: A Tool to Enhance Democratic Policy Making*, Genetics Forum and University of East London.

Irwin, A. (2001) 'Constructing the scientific citizen: science and democracy in the biosciences', *Public Understanding of Science*, 10: 1–18, www.iop.org/EJ/S/UNREG/1uxNT1mXdjkt6y7owAri.g/toc/0963-6625/10/1.

Kuper, R. (1996) *Citizens Juries: The Hertfordshire Experience*, Working Paper, University of Hertfordshire Business School.

MORI (1999) *Public Consultation on Developments in the Biosciences*, London: Office of Science and Technology & MORI, www.dti.gov.uk/ost/ostbusiness/puset/public.htm.

Pimbert, M. P. and T. Wakeford (eds) (2001) 'Deliberative democracy and citizen em-powerment', Special issue of *PLA Notes 40*, Commonwealth Foundation/ActionAid/DfID/Sida/IIED, www.iied.org/NR/agbioliv/pla_notes/pla_backissues/40.html.

— (2002) *Prajateerpu: A Citizens Jury/Scenario Workshop on Food and Farming Futures for Andhra Pradesh, India*, London: IIED, www.prajateerpu.org.

Smith, G. and C. Wales (2000) 'Citizen juries and deliberative democracy', *Political Studies*, 48: 51–65.

WIHSC (1997) *Report of the Citizens Jury on Genetic Testing for Common Disorders*, WIHSC, University of Glamorgan.

17 | Voices aloud: making communication and change together

Oga Steve Abah

Introduction

People are always talking; talking about many different things (work, joy, pain, freedom, etc.). But it is also a common observation that people's voices are always ignored and not heard when they are crying against injustice, against oppression and suppression of freedom. Authorities would normally prefer to ignore voices when they are calling for change. And, based on our experience of working on issues of development failures and on issues of disenchantment with political practice, we have come to understand the difficulty of communication, especially when the aim is change. The manner and structure of popular communication for change must therefore respond to the context in which the work is taking place; for it is determined by the nature of the society, community and target groups in which one is working.

The context of communication and change in Nigeria

One of the reasons why making communication in Nigeria is a difficult enterprise is that we probably live where the tower of Babel broke! There are about 474 officially categorized languages in a country of approximately 140 million people. It is believed that unofficially there may be over 500 languages. In official circles we speak English, which was bequeathed to us by the British people who colonized us. But once outside of such official environments, and especially in the villages, it is a different story. Secondly, the very multiplicity of languages tells of different nationalities and cultures that have been aggregated to form the country Nigeria. In this common plate where beans, maize and rice, etc. are mixed, each one still remains its own self. The colonial legacy of amalgamating different parts and peoples of the region into one country called Nigeria has also created a legacy of difference that nationhood has not yet been able to obliterate. There is one more factor that makes communication in Nigeria difficult. This is the fact that the majority of Nigerians, about 60 per cent, are still non-literate. So, citizenship, language and education remain points to negotiate in the choice of tools and methods to employ in discussing development, participation and rights.

Very often we go for a methodology that has roots and resonance among the group we are working with. This means that the communication forms, which may include different performative modes, are employed. We also deal with issues that are of concern to them. Although very often these issues may be of national importance, they must have relevance and significance at the local level. Democracy, governance and citizenship have been some of the areas of concern. These have relevance to every Nigerian in broad terms. But when we pull them down to what they mean in the lives of the ordinary men and women in rural communities and urban slums, we are talking about the lack of basic amenities and infrastructures such as drinking water, roads, electricity and blown roofs in village primary schools. In talking about all these, moving from the abstract to the concrete, we have employed a combination of participatory approaches such as Theatre for Development (TFD), Participatory Learning and Action (PLA) and the traditional survey method of questionnaires (or checklists, as we prefer to call them) to make communication with people on issues of development and change in their lives. So how does one really do communication for change?

Making communication and change together

The work that we have done with communities, both from within the academic environment and as members of nongovernmental organizations in the Nigerian Popular Theatre Alliance/Theatre for Development Centre, has been characterized by collaboration, negotiation and talking aloud through the performance arts. Increasingly also we have been asking the different methodologies to converse with each other. One critical feature is collaborative development and use of accessible communication strategies. However, as outsiders we are not offering a ready-made package for 'low intelligence people' to use. We take from what already exists, adopt and adapt it collectively. Perhaps the first level of communication in this exercise is between community members and facilitators who have come from the outside. The first step is learning from each other to set the agenda. The first line of educators that this learning consists of are the community members, and the learners are the animators from outside. One of the thrills of this learning for me has always been the collapse of intellectual and knowledge arrogance when we go into the communities as 'experts' with all our baggage of preconceived notions of the nature of rural people and their problems. This arrogance is best exemplified by the objective and indeed a declaration of superiority when the students say '*We are going to conscientize the villagers. We will educate them on their problems and teach them how to solve them!*' And of course, many of us who teach the theory of engagement and change have conditioned as well as premised the students' understanding in prejudice and lack of experiential knowledge by some of these same scholars! So, Freire's concept of dialogics, out of which emerges conscientization (knowledge/consciousness and action), is taken only to mean information and alas we fall victim to what Freire called the 'banking system' of education!

The joy of this conscientization crusade is that it works in reverse in the field! The students are the ones who end up being educated. For one, they do not understand the community issues and must learn from the people what these are. Secondly, they are hardly able to answer the questions which the community members raise concerning their neglect by government. So, they have to learn more about the relationship between government, the people and development. However, what the students know and are able to do is to improvise drama on the basis of existing information about the community joys and problems. Even with this skill the students and TFD animateurs have to acknowledge that the dynamics of theatre in rural and urban squatter communities is a different one from that in academic campuses.

Such learnings have shaped our practice of TFD; so the practice now follows a process of research, of negotiation and of performing in communities in which power play that shapes community life is understood. Over the many years that we have done this, we know that in broad terms there may be a common agenda between animateurs and communities. However, there may be differences in the way the issues are perceived and understood. There may be variations in opinions on how best to talk about the issues, and there may also be differences in how to reach the people in power who should hear the voices. To make communication for purposes of change it is therefore imperative to arrive at a common understanding. This demands negotiation. The strategic direction is how the common agenda developed by facilitators and communities would lead to communication with people in power (PIP). So, we need to first agree with each other.

Stage one: what are the issues?

The first step in understanding the community concerns is to generate information from community members. Our approach is to first identify community-based organizations (CBOs) that have respect within the community. Such CBOs would then be our guides as well as the core group of people who will constitute the resource team to undertake follow-through actions. The approach that we have evolved, and which has worked quite well, is the combination of approaches which I have called methodological conversations. All of these approaches engaging in the conversations may be put under the homestead label. The array of instruments/approaches has included focused group discussion, participant observation and interviews, transect walks, mapping and storytelling. I have always enjoyed this combination because of the many layers of conversation that go on and the amount of information it is capable of generating. The next step is for the community, with the input of the animateurs, to prioritize the issues that have emerged.

The issues that they consider to be the most critical are the ones that the drama will focus on.

We have passed one level of conversations. The conversations here have been between community and animateurs. They have also been between and amongst animateurs debating some matters that are not quite right, and arguing over what to do next. One such debate that I have always witnessed and contributed to is the confrontation between textbook prescription of the number of people with whom to conduct focused group discussions and the reality of the village, in which passers by would stop and join in the discussion through the duration of the exercise or move on after one or two interjections. The textbook says not to allow such interjections or uninvited members. But the community experience tells you that exclusion may alienate and jeopardize your project. I never cease to marvel as well as enjoy myself at the many contradictions that normally emerge and the discomfort of the 'experts' that they got it wrong!

Stage two: TFD, PLA, et al.

The drama creation is the next stage in the process. However, we see it as a continuation of the first section. It is also another level of the conversation in which drama and performance will serve several purposes (research, analysis, community engagement and entertainment). After my parents had taught me how to talk, to communicate, respond to instructions and run errands, I think the other milestone in my knowledge of communication was as a young boy sitting at sessions of folk tale performances in the village. The story sessions allowed communication between the story performer and the 'audience' on the one hand and between the characters in the fictional world of the story and every one at the event on the other. Both the performer and the audience knew the characters, corroborated their knowledge and existence by declaring at different points in the performance that they were present at the events the storyteller was describing! But they also challenged the performer when his performance of the story they all knew threatened to abort the harmony of the cosmos that the story had been devised to uphold. This threat was very often perceived by the 'audience' when the narrative plot and the content that support the message began to deviate from the norm. The difference between this age old moral position and TFD is that the one affirms while the other problematizes. Nonetheless, what interests me, and what I believe TFD has learnt from storytelling performances, is the provision of a site for tapping community wisdom and information. The other lesson is the democratization of participation by allowing others to enter into the performance to engage in a critical change of course and the collective ownership of the story and the performance. I believe that TFD and PLA have used these lessons well.

Take an example: it is 2000 in Birnin Kebbi and the Nigerian Popular

Theatre Alliance is conducting a capacity-building workshop for about six community-based organizations on their capacity needs to engage in governance, as promised by the new democratic dispensation after the withdrawal of the military from politics in 1999. It was a desire to enter the political as well as the development spaces that had opened up. We began by asking what sort of capacity the groups needed and for what purpose. The list ranged over 'We want to talk to government, we want to claim our rights, we are not getting the promises and development that the politicians promised us at elections'. The catalogue that came out was a combination of problems and intentions. So we needed to unpack these to actually know what capacity the CBOs were looking for. We broke into small groups to discuss some of the issues generated above. When we discussed and clustered the many issues that emerged, we arrived at five key concerns as follows:

- forced marriage and gender discrimination;
- the culture of silence and the attendant lack of self-esteem among ordinary members of various communities and CBOs;
- lack of freedom of choice, and of association and action;
- poor education; and
- absence of accountability and transparency in governance.

As the group discussions continued, the stories were about the non-performance of government. It also emerged quite strongly that the community-based organizations, and the many ordinary persons they represented, had no voice in the decision-making process in the state. Furthermore, after a session of brainstorming around these core issues, the consensus was that there was a serious implication of denial of rights. Therefore, the capacity the CBOs wanted was the ability to mobilize and to advocate. It was also about the skills to do a critical analysis and to be able to package an argument that would help their case.

There was enough information coming from the participants on the poverty of the ordinary people in Birnin Kebbi town and the state in general. So we said, let us see how some of these issues manifest around town. We did a transect walk. We came back and downloaded what we saw onto a map. In the process of interrogating the map the participants were engaged in analysing the issues they had earlier enumerated. They also mapped out relationships, studied locations of different groups and classes in the city and the significance of such spatial difference in relationship to the question of where development was taking place and where was left out. The drawing of the map was itself eventful. Everyone was on their feet arguing, debating in order to reach agreement on the location of features and the sizes of objects to represent them. One of the reasons for the eventfulness of the mapping exercise was the realization by the CBOs that they were all from in or around

Birnin Kebbi and yet did not interact much with each other, and so they did not know what different groups were doing. The map made the CBOs see each other's locations and the spread of activities.

Stage three: interrogating the map and dynamizing the issues

There were two points of interest for me from the exercise. One was the dynamization of the issues (rather than the dynamization of sculpted stories) from inside the map. Participants were asked to locate on the map of Birnin Kebbi the different sites where each of the core issues predominated. Forced marriage was located in the spaces inhabited by the non-literates who were also mostly not enlightened on the issues of rights and choices. Although this phenomenon also took place in the elite locations among the rich and highly educated people, it was euphemistically referred to as matchmaking. When the parallel was drawn between forced marriages and matchmaking, some of the women at the workshop who lived in the district governor quarters where the practice of matchmaking was prevalent vehemently objected to the comparison arguing that matchmaking was different and far more preferable to forced marriage because, in the former, the girl's consent is at least respected. The women also argued that parents know what is good for their children. When reminded that part of the rights which we just discussed had to do with freedom of choice, the women insisted that doing what is right for the child was not a negation of that freedom.

The spaces where the ordinary men and women lived their daily lives and where the very grassroots CBOs engaged in their activities were indicated as notable sites for 'shrunken' personalities. The participants said that this was the case because people in such spaces were constantly downgraded, their knowledges rejected, and their needs ignored. As a consequence they no longer have confidence in what they know and what they are capable of doing. This sense of low worth is further aggravated by the lack of freedom of choice, which authority structures impose on their subjects. Such authority structures were named as the palaces of traditional rulers, government and the elite in the society. One participant observed that, 'They downgrade us so that we do not have the mouth to challenge what they are doing wrong.'

The discussions and analyses coalesced in various drama pieces that focused on the issue of accountability and transparency. They argued that the focus on accountability and transparency was important because they were features of good governance. Secondly, they also said that at the centre of their marginalization and poverty is corruption which is the antithesis of good governance. The participants worked in small groups to tell stories of their experiences as marginalized citizens. They also performed corruption and from within the dramas outlined their ideals of a good government and how that would promote development. A significant point about the dramas was that they performed good governance from two levels. The first level was an internal examination of the operations and administrative strategies of the CBOs themselves. The central question in the drama was, 'To what extent do the CBOs themselves practise a transparent system of governance?' The question demanded that the CBOs tell the truth about themselves. This was difficult as it was too close to home. The members adopted a creative escape of making their dramas about 'other' organizations that did not practise good governance. It was clear that these 'other' organizations were similar to, if not the same ones present at the workshop. But it was safe and comfortable to talk about their organizations from a fictive and third person remove. Then at the second level they brought government down for shredding, based on their knowledge of being either civil servants or unemployed youths with frustrated aspirations.

As part of the examination of participants' organizational and administrative practice, the facilitator asked everyone to turn the searchlight on themselves and to ask whether we are accountable and transparent in our homes, to examine how we relate with our wives and family, etc. Then it dawned on people that the oppressions and problems they complain about may not only be about those in government, but that they could be about each and every one of us. It therefore became clear that we could not separate ourselves, our attitudes and behaviours from the issues we identified. Thus when participants were asked to indicate what was gained from the drama-making exercise and what happened to them in the process of doing the map, they gave the following responses:

- It helped an understanding of the issues.
- It made us think deeply – something you must do with your brain.
- We had to concentrate.
- The thinking together and making the drama in groups encouraged group participation.
- As we talked and worked together it revealed patterns of cultural values and behaviour.
- The map provided good knowledge of the area.
- It made it possible to locate sister organizations and key features in the town.
- The social map enacted the story of Birnin Kebbi in terms of issues of democracy and development.
- Holding the chalk and making the map on the floor made me feel like a good designer; I had a feeling of satisfaction.

This process of communicating and making change as reflected here has two parts to it. One is the process of understanding the issues and the second is building capacity for action.

In this process TFD and PLA were both engaged in enacting communication for change. What was also being heard were the voices of the CBO members drawn from different parts of the state. They were speaking to each other, first as a group with a common predicament. They were also interested in speaking to government about their concerns as citizens of the State. In the dramatizations that critiqued both government and CBO practices, drama was telling the story of development and its failures. The map was an outline of the geography of poverty in Birnin Kebbi. The interrogation of both the map and the dramas was interested in pointing out directions that might be useful for the CBOs in both their desire and attempt to talk to government about participatory governance and development.

It is in this regard of wanting to hold conversations with government that other means of communication are added to TFD and PLA. In our work with CBOs in different urban and rural communities we are always told, 'The government does not talk to poor people like us.' In contrast, they see us as 'people who can talk to government'. We know the truth that not even we are able to talk to government as easily as community members imagine. But we do know the media that government wants to see itself reflected in. These are television and radio. They are also happy to be packaged in videos. So, with 'Encountering Citizens' (an ongoing research by the Theatre for Development Centre – TFDC – into citizenship in Nigeria) we have used these forms of media to disseminate research results to people in power and to other development activists.

With information about what others are doing in an environment where face-to-face sharing is difficult, the voices that are heard are not necessarily that of TFDC. They are the voices of the ordinary people who ordinarily do not enter the spaces where development and policy matters are discussed. In serving as media through which the government is prepared to hear voices of such people, those same people have managed to enter reserved spaces; it is also an act of transgressing the spaces that are usually closed. For example, when on December 4, 2003 the TFDC showed its video, 'Nigeria: In Search of Citizens?', at the Commonwealth People's Forum event as part of the Commonwealth Heads of Government Meeting (CHOGM), the people sitting in the main auditorium of the Yar'Adua Centre in Abuja, Nigeria were a combination of law-makers drawn from the Nigerian National Assembly, and representatives from international development agencies engaged in giving different kinds of development assistance to Nigeria. Also present were civil society activists from all parts of Nigeria and the Commonwealth countries. The video they were watching was a documentation of realities of development problems from Bayelsa, Benue and Kaduna States. The voices they heard in the video were those of the peoples of these different regions talking about ethnicity, religion, gender, their needs and their frustrations.

147

I am not sure that Kande Patrick from Kurmin Jatau in Jaba Local Government Area from Kaduna State would otherwise go beyond the gate of the Yar'Adua Centre without being harassed, insulted and sent away! But the world listened to her that day! When the oil spillage and the flames of burning gas in the Niger Delta filled the screen, the realities of the calamity were beyond denial. The images and the drama that the audience watched that day were of young and old people from Bayelsa in the Niger Delta. The TFDC offered incisive captioning and problematized the three related issues of citizenship, rights and development. In addition, the discussions that followed proved that video can be a useful tool for communicating development. They also showed that such media could bring home issues and generate a lot of discussion. This media dissemination also went beyond the Yar'Adua Centre to the national arena. The Nigerian Television Authority in its annual review of major events showed interviews with key players in the citizenship research from Nigeria, UK, Brazil and India, three different times. Watched by over 40 million people across the nation the issues had engaged national consciousness. In a related manner, when the drama about ginger and the Commonwealth civil society visit to Sab-Zuro in Jaba Local Government Area of Kaduna were shown on the Kaduna State Television station in its prime-time news slot, 'Panorama', on 18 December 2003, the politics of ginger was being heard all over the state and brought the debate to public view.

But beyond mass audiences on television or at major events as happened at the Yar'Adua Centre, such videos may be watched by people in power in the privacy of their offices or homes. They may also be put to use in workshops and conferences to frame discussions and debates on related issues.

Stage four: community action plans – building capacity and planning development

One last step in our making development together with the people is to discuss the catalogue of issues that have emerged, prioritize them and engage in the discussion of actions. There are several rationales around community action plans (CAPs): that development does not have to be something that someone or some authorities out there give to communities. Communities can develop their own societies. We however acknowledge that such development may need the support of others outside their immediate environment. So, when the community action plan starts from identifying priority issues, it explores who the stakeholders are in the project. It is then that we begin to talk about responsibilities and who would take charge of what activity. Then we analyse capacities and capabilities. By the time we have explored budgetary implications and time frames and what outcomes the community is looking for there is a whole picture, as well as the challenges, laid out in front of everyone. In outlining a range of activities, in identifying actors/stakeholders and in allocating roles and responsibilities to members of their organizations, the CBOs are accepting that they are change agents. The journey to this point is a long exercise of challenging attitudes, perceptions and preconceived notions. This journey is a capacity trip.

Conclusion

The communication that takes place in Theatre for Development happens in different arenas, corresponding to the various stakeholders in the agenda defined by any one set of objectives and goals. In general, however, there is always a development issue at the centre of all TFD work in Nigeria. We have also found that sometimes the issues are not necessarily physical infrastructure. They may be located in what Boal has called the 'cop in the head', i.e. internalization of belief or philosophies that may act against critical thinking and change. Development communication in this instance would be about reaching the cranial recess where such internalizations have taken refuge in order to develop a new consciousness that challenges the 'cop'. It is also about developing collective understanding and meanings of the phenomena that underpin our lives. Following these therefore, the group can put out 'messages' to places where they believe there would be positive effect. The media that have made the voices loud have, in our experience, ranged across the indigenous performance arts of storytelling, songs and dance. Others are drama, PLA, radio through to television and video.

[Originally published in *PLA Notes* 50, 2004]

Bibliography

Abah, O. S. (2004) 'Theatre for Development and social change in Nigeria', Unpublished paper presented at a conference on 'Performing Africa', Leeds University Centre for African Studies (LUCAS), University of Leeds, 14–16 May.

Boal, A. (1985) *Theatre of the Oppressed*, New York: Theatre Communications Group.

Freire, P. (1972) *Pedagogy of the Oppressed*, Harmondsworth: Penguin.

Harding, F. (1997) 'Theatre and video for development', in A. Cornwall (ed.), *PLA Notes* 29, London: IIED.

Nigerian Popular Theatre Alliance (NPTA) (2001) 'From capacity potential to capacity building: CBOs and democratic development in Kebbi', Report of the training workshop held at Modiyawa Hotel, Birnin Kebbi, 2–16 June.

Smith, K., S. Wilford and R. O'Connell (1997) 'PRA and Theatre for Development in southern India', in A. Cornwall (ed.), *PLA Notes* 29, London: IIED.

Theatre for Development Centre (TFDC) (2002) 'Encountering citizens: perceptions, realities and practices in Nigeria', Report of research on 'Citizenship, participation and accountability', Ahmadu Bello University, Zaria, Nigeria.

18 | Powerful grassroots women communicators: participatory video in Bangladesh

Renuka Bery and Sara Stuart

Prologue

When Bulu, a village woman, was young, she was deserted by her husband who had tried to sell her 'like a cow'. Now, she is an organizer with years of experience and a steadfast commitment to legal aid for grassroots women. She works at Banchte Shekha, a women's organization in western Bangladesh.

Bulu's involvement in participatory video began in 1992 when she joined a workshop with fourteen other Banchte Shekha group members and field workers. She wanted to make a tape that would tell Nasima's story – a story of domestic violence. Although it would have been easier to interview Nasima at Banchte Shekha's office to avoid crowd control problems, Bulu said, 'No.' She hoped that by taping in the village, word would reach Nasima's husband and that this would make him worry.

Bulu made this tape simply – editing in the camera. She completed the recording in less than three hours and played it back immediately to Nasima and the members of her *somiti* [women's group]. They were excited and inspired by seeing themselves and the story of their sister on a television screen. They gave feedback and permission to show it elsewhere.

Bulu's strategy for using the tape was clear: she planned to show it to Nasima's husband's neighbours to keep Nasima's experience and perspective alive in their minds, as well as to put pressure on them not to give false testimony in the village court where Nasima's case would be heard. In most domestic cases, the court in the husband's village has jurisdiction. As women generally marry outside their own villages, they have very little influence in that court, while their husbands' families may have a great deal. The tape about Nasima gave her a stronger voice in a situation where she would otherwise have had very little power. In addition, the tape is used to raise awareness among Banchte Shekha members and workers about violence against women and women's human rights.

Since 1992, Bulu has used video extensively in Banchte Shekha's legal aid activities. She taped a village court case about a man who had disavowed paternity and refused to give financial compensation. In the village court he reversed his position and promised child support rather than face a suit in the local government court. In another case of desertion, the mere mention that Banchte Shekha planned to make a tape about a particular woman's experience motivated her husband and his family to negotiate a settlement. They didn't want to be embarrassed in front of their neighbours.

In Bulu's hands, a camcorder is a powerful tool to advocate for women's human rights. Her access to and skills with this tool have given her elevated status in the community, just as being associated with an organization that owns these tools has given all Banchte Shekha members increased status in their communities. Her tapes illustrate to grassroots men and women how their sisters, who have been abandoned or abused, have gained justice through village-level mediation or through the formal courts.

Bulu's experience demonstrates the potential and power of grassroots women communicators. She and her sisters in Bangladesh have not only mastered the technical skills, they have integrated participatory communication methods and strategies into their own organizations.

Introduction

Participatory video is a methodology developed over twenty-five years of experience. Communication for Change (C4C, formerly Martha Stuart Communications) began its work keenly aware of the disadvantages inherent in centralized control of media making and media dissemination. In exploring less brokered forms of communication, we produced programmes with real people speaking from their own experience on issues of general concern. This approach challenged the norm, where experts or journalists reported on an issue. We also questioned the concept that communication is a product. We consider it a process – a means not an end. Our work has evolved through experimentation, into what we call participatory communication.

At Communication for Change, we define participatory communication as a process which allows people to speak for themselves. Though the modes of communication vary, in participatory communication the people who control the tools are community members – not outsiders who mediate information and representation. Participatory communication is an exchange among individuals that values each person's perspective and voice. Such communicators can mobilize constituencies and give a stronger collective voice for change at many levels of society.

Communication for Change forms collaborative relationships with people's organizations that are working successfully at the grassroots level on issues of importance to their members or constituents. Together we introduce communication tools and methods to their workers, members and community organizers. This, we believe, establishes a model for communication which strengthens local communities through their organizations and inspires social and economic change.

The objectives and strategies of participatory communication share a great deal with the methods for achieving change that have been developed through the global women's movement. The inclusive stance of the women's movement which values each woman's perspective and experience, and which seeks out and embraces diversity, is consonant with participatory communication. Participatory communication methods enhance the bottom-up strategies used by women's organizations around the world, and aid their efforts to leverage their experience to influence the mainstream.

It is a mistake to ask, 'What is the women's agenda?' We cannot expect a single agenda for half the world's population. There will never be a unified women's front or an equivalent of the World Bank representing women's interests around the world. Diversity must enrich and strengthen the women's movement, or we will have no movement at all.

Given this fluidity and preference for autonomy, women are becoming, by necessity, skilled networkers and coalition builders – active in many alliances. For these strategies to succeed the movement requires a multitude of participatory communicators.

Participatory communication

Participatory communication focuses on who is communicating. Why? Because who creates the message shapes its content, perspective, and impact.

Participatory media are a subset of direct media which are distinct from mass media. We consider mass media as 'big' in terms of budget and numbers of people who can receive the messages (e.g. broadcasts aimed at an audience of millions and mass market video cassettes). Direct media are smaller on all these scales; here the elements of choosing to participate or self-determination are strong, and these forms of communication often enable feedback or exchange. Participatory communication is two-way. It involves dialogue, collaboration and group decision-making. This classification system is not perfect; as the technology changes rapidly, there are more and more hybrids and we must adapt definitions.

To grasp the characteristics and impact of participatory media, it is best to start without preconceived ideas. Assumptions based on the expectations created by mass media are often incorrect. For example, a participatory videotape can be considered successful and even cost-effective by reaching and motivating a handful of viewers. This small audience would be considered a resounding failure in the mass media.

Participatory media have a function in the larger process of organizing, training or advocacy. The goal of such communication might be mobilizing, or awareness raising, or confidence building – not a finished programme. We find that the value and impact of a tape is rarely determined by technical quality. Grassroots organizers with little formal education are often the most effective producers.

With participatory media, people first learn to operate the equipment. They participate in planning and making productions about their own concerns. Seeing their situations framed on a video screen, their perspective on these issues changes. Afterwards they show their programmes to their peers and members of their communities. Such activities are profound experiences for the small media maker. They have the potential for great impact, before one considers the value of the recorded programme to its viewers.

The mass media maker's job is finished once he or she files the story or delivers the final edited tape. But the participatory video maker's work is just beginning. He or she will be involved in facilitating playbacks of the tape, in building on the insight, motivation and understanding the tape creates, and in continuing to work toward the goals that the tape is serving. Participatory media are practically oriented and build on the strengths of local organizers. They can succeed even when time and resources are constrained.

Bangladeshi non-governmental organizations

Bangladesh has a large, vital, and mature community of non-governmental organizations (NGOs) which have played a critical role during the years of authoritarian rule and in the transition to democracy. They address many areas of social concern which includes coordinating relief efforts for the natural disasters which routinely occur and speaking strongly against religious fundamentalist forces that try to infiltrate government structures at all levels. Since 1989, Communication for Change has introduced participatory video to several Bangladeshi NGOs. This chapter documents and analyses the experience of Banchte Shekha and Proshika, two such organizations.

Proshika, the third largest NGO in Bangladesh, has more than half a million members in villages and urban slums throughout the country. The basic organizing unit is a group of up to twenty men or women members. Women comprise a slight majority of Proshika's membership. Human development is the core of Proshika's work. They begin by raising consciousness, analysing the causes of poverty, initiating collective saving and developing income-generating activities. Over a period of years, group members have achieved sustainable improvements in income, health, education, social issues, environment, and other areas. They also participate actively in local and district levels of decision-making and planning.

Proshika's work is broad and therefore difficult to summarize in brief. As the groups form alliances, their collective strength grows. They have opposed powerful interests and exposed inequity and corruption in their communities and on the part of local authorities. They have learned the value of collective strength in the face of conflict. In their work on the environment, the organization has pioneered sustainable agricultural practices and opposed the importation of pesticides that are banned in developed countries. In some cases, by gaining access and rights to public resources, such as water, the poor have increased their income while protecting their environment.

Banchte Shekha is a women's organization with more than 20,000 members in several districts of western Bangladesh. Banchte Shekha began by working with poor, rural women who were struggling to survive on their own. They had experienced violence, desertion, dowry abuse and often their families were unable or unwilling to support them. Banchte Shekha's numerous programme activities reflect their commitment to giving poor women, through awareness raising and skills building, the right to live with dignity.

As with Proshika, Banchte Shekha's central organizing unit is a group of 20–25 members. Their programmes in savings, credit, training and income generation assist the members in attaining economic solvency. Their literacy, health, and legal advocacy programmes assist the women in recognizing and demanding their legal and human rights. Banchte Shekha's legal aid programme has become a formidable force in the area. Their reputation in the communities is that the cases supported by Banchte Shekha never lose in government courts.

Planning

Planning is crucial when developing participatory approaches. Considerable attention and time were given to forming collaborative relationships with Proshika and Banchte Shekha. Participatory video challenged existing assumptions and structures.

Banchte Shekha had almost no previous experience with any communication technology. Like rural women in many parts of the world, Bangladeshi village women have very limited access to information and most have little formal education. The mass media in their country do not represent their experience or issues. Therefore, the opportunity to share relevant experiences of peers inside and outside the organization was compelling.

In 1991 Banchte Shekha sent two young women to a twenty-day participatory video workshop for workers from smaller NGOs. They returned to make their productions with Banchte Shekha members. As a result, many people in the organization gained exposure and first-hand experience with participatory video. Despite this exposure, some found it difficult to separate their thinking about participatory video from promotional video. They saw video as a tool to promote the organization's public image.

In Proshika it was different. Although not everyone understood it, some field workers and members immediately recognized the potential of this tool and methodology for strengthening their work. During an exploratory visit to Bangladesh, C4C spent a day with twelve village women. With Proshika's video team, we introduced the basics of video equipment and discussed some experiences of grassroots producers.

This first exposure generated a great deal of excitement, ideas and energy. The women had no fear of the equipment and eagerly gave it a try. We screened these recordings with several Proshika workers who were at the centre that day. The men were impressed. They had not thought village women could use sophisticated technology.

After the screening, the village women talked about their ideas for using video; their thoughts were insightful. They proposed making tapes to expose exploitation in their communities. One woman wanted to interview leaders making promises. By showing the tape to the communities, she felt they could put enough pressure on the leaders to fulfil the promises they so often break. These women also felt that video could be a very good channel for sharing experiences between communities and for elevating women's status in society.

Their visions convinced all who were present of the value and potential these tools offer. It is one thing to be fascinated and enthused by a new technology; it is quite another – after your first exposure – to have formulated a strategy to apply this technology with potentially far-reaching impact.

Implementation

Both Proshika and Banchte Shekha committed themselves to train grassroots members and field workers. By learning to shoot in-sequence, they avoided the time and expense of editing. The simple methods allowed those directly involved a voice in managing participatory video.

Proshika chose to establish independent rural production units based in seven of their sixty Area Development Centres (ADCs). Each ADC-based team was equipped with a VHS camcorder, a battery monitor, a set of playback equipment, a generator and accessories. Banchte Shekha established a single video team at their office. They have one complete set of equipment and use Hi8mm as their recording format rather than VHS.

In both organizations, grassroots members and full-time field workers received training and access to the equipment. Few of the participants had prior experience with video or any other electronic technology; they all learned by doing. Some participants were sceptical; others were frightened of electronic technology, but all were very curious to try these new tools. A pioneering spirit grew in the groups; we felt we were doing something new in Bangladesh.

The grassroots participants were eager for the workshop to address their issues and social change concerns. Muriam, an organizer who distributes loans, wanted to learn video and train her *somiti* sisters with it. Aklima is the first of nine wives. Deserted by her husband, she struggled to support herself and her three children. She wanted to make tapes about women's legal rights. Tuli, a group leader, had some experience with popular theatre and saw video as another method for increasing the status of women. Their ideas and others ensured that participatory video grew into a relevant and locally valuable process.

During the three-week workshops, the trainees were introduced to participatory video strategies. Each participant learned to operate the equipment: to make simple programmes edited in the camera, to conduct playbacks and to lead discussions about the tapes and the issues in their communities. The trainees returned to their villages to make a video programme on an issue directly related to his or her own work. They also led community screenings of these productions. Through these activities they gained a powerful, new kind of literacy.

The training was intensive. The women participants grew bolder as their self-confidence grew; they deferred less to the men and relied on their own judgement. They were better able to assert their ideas. They often admonished the men for being clannish or insensitive. This change was more evident after six months of practice. The technical quality of their programmes had improved but, more importantly, their ability to conceptualize issues and use video to communicate these issues had developed as well.

Often training is conducted far from the environment where the new skill is to be applied. Thus, when the trainees return home, they face the difficult task of introducing something new, convincing their peers of its merit. The experience of bringing these new skills to their communities during the training was important. There is no substitute for showing your programme to your peers. It is at once humbling, empowering and intensely motivating. Muriam organized all the women in her *somiti* to help with her production on nutrition. The villagers were impressed and suggested other programmes she could make. In Hassina's village the men were extremely critical because they were jealous of the women who were learning new skills that they, themselves, wanted. The participatory video trainees completed their training as confident and experienced teams of producers and communicators whose work was, at least partially, understood by their communities.

Decentralization, participation and empowerment

Proshika's participatory video programme is groundbreaking. We know of no other rural development communication initiative that compares in its scope and its level of decentralized grassroots participation. While occasional follow-up training and technical support is available from Proshika's communication unit in Dhaka, the participatory video teams' work is locally focused and integrated into the overall work of the ADCs.

Video team members in Proshika and Banchte Shekha consult with their peers about important issues in the communities. They discuss how a videotape could assist them in pushing for change and solving problems. In some cases, workers and members from outside the video team initiate ideas for tapes. This type of collaboration increases the scope of the video programme.

For example, a participatory video team documented the destruction of the social forestry income-generating projects of many Proshika members. Tree plantations along the roadside were cut down to widen the road. The members had used many tactics to either stop the road or get compensation, but to no avail. Then they taped the destruction and interviewed people who had lost their livelihood. This video was used successfully to gain just compensation from the local government for the lost trees. The experience won many supporters among the local population and Proshika staff members. They are convinced that grassroots members with access to video have greater power to solve local problems.

Members and workers report that video is a valuable tool because it can make people conscious; when people can visualize, they understand. They say, 'Video cannot be bribed, and it tells honestly *our* stories.'

Video is also a valuable tool for documenting injustice and harassment. As Bulu's experiences illustrate, this application of participatory video is useful in efforts to gain equitable settlements and to protect the rights of women. The potential to be exposed or embarrassed by video in front of one's peers is enough to motivate changes in behaviour, gain financial redress and prevent further acts of violence. Thus, video becomes a powerful deterrent. Peer pressure is an effective force for change and video can help to release this force.

During a cholera outbreak, one video team produced a health tape about the causes of diarrhoea. The video devoted attention to insects as a vector for spreading bacteria, and showed flies on the food available from street vendors and restaurants. Community screenings of this tape educated the population about the causes and remedies for diarrhoea, but they also influenced the owners of restaurants and sweet shops to improve sanitary conditions because their clientele refused to purchase food from unsanitary vendors.

Playbacks in the centres, during training and in villages can unleash the drive and commitment to work for meaningful change. One worker explained, 'We get instant consciousness with video playbacks. It works very rapidly. People come thinking it will be a movie but when they see that the tape is about their lives, they ask to see the tape again and again. They raise lots of questions and get more conscious.'

Village playbacks and the discussions which follow offer rich opportunities for organizing and mobilizing. For example, Shameema and Lailee led a discussion with the villagers after viewing a tape about bamboo handicrafts. The women were amazed to see their sisters in another village working in an occupation traditionally reserved for men. They were excited by this tape and talked about getting a loan from their *somiti* to start a bamboo handicrafts trade. Suddenly they realized they could expand their ideas to include any occupation. Their range of options increased dramatically through this experience.

In addition to introducing new ideas and stimulating consciousness in a group, grassroots videotapes make a strong impression. They are so easy to understand and so relevant that viewers absorb a great deal. One playback in a village attracted more than two hundred people to watch the tapes. Everyone came – from small children to village elders. After watching three tapes the video team led discussions with different groups from the audience. One worker spoke with a twelve-year-old boy who, having seen *The Life Struggle of Aleya*, recited the entire story of Aleya's life. He made connections about how the practice of giving dowry is harmful to all levels of society and said he would not ask for a dowry when he gets married. In another conversation some of the men teased another about his marrying a twelve-year-old girl. People in this village were more conscious of issues portrayed on the tape after the playback session.

Participation takes place at many levels: in planning strategies, in making productions, in showing them, in leading discussions, in managing the video work. While many organizations are reluctant to decentralize responsibility for communication resources, Banchte Shekha and Proshika are doing it.

Banchte Shekha's video team has instituted a policy aimed at increasing the participation and leadership capacity of the grassroots members. There is a rotating 'presidency' for participatory video. The president ensures that the participatory video activities are implemented. She mediates problems within the group, and refers them to the participatory video supervisor if necessary. The president keeps the records and documents the activities with the help of someone more educated. She assigns tasks and responsibilities among the team during her term. This process has stimulated some positive competition. Everyone wants her reports to be the best.

Proshika has also made strides in solving institutional and management issues arising from the ADC participatory video work. New policies have been adopted that give greater status and accountability to these activities. They have defined participatory video in such a way that it relates to the organization's core mission. They agreed on the following ten goals for participatory video:

1　To awaken people's human and ethical values.
2　To ensure the participation of poor villagers and to value their thoughts and beliefs.
3　To disprove the popular belief that poor villagers cannot use sophisticated technology and to create skill among these target people.
4　To project the viewpoints of the villagers about social issues and to ensure their participation.
5　To point out the reasons why the poor are deprived and robbed of power.
6　To ensure that participatory video remains true to life rather than being created as entertainment.
7　To uphold the views of people who are alienated by the mass media.
8　To show that grassroots people are capable of expressing their feelings and their problems.

9 To raise people's consciousness by exchanging video programmes among people of various regions.

10 To show the processes from which people conquer poverty and to show the causes of poverty.

Proshika has redefined participatory video as its own. This ownership extends from the tools, methods and management all the way to the ideology and ethic. Other organizations accomplish a great deal without finding it necessary to digest and institutionalize participatory communication to such an extent. Still, these ten goals indicate the degree to which Proshika has successfully integrated participatory video.

The themes of decentralization, participation and empowerment are interdependent. True participation can lead to empowerment, but without significant decentralization and scope for self-determination, the grassroots people we seek to empower will not be able to participate.

Participatory communication and leadership

While there are people who are natural or gifted communicators, most of us develop our communication skills through education and practice. Generally, when we describe the benefits of participatory video, we focus on empowerment, training, self-representation and advocacy outcomes. Participatory video training provides a forum to learn and use new communication skills. These are all ingredients of leadership.

When people learn to make a meaningful and compelling video programme, to master a new and sophisticated tool, or to facilitate a group discussion after viewing a relevant video programme, they develop communication skills that increase their visibility in the community. Even after putting down the camera, cassettes and VCR, participatory video producers remain experienced communicators. Exercising these communication skills to effect change requires vision and strategy. We see among our partners a growing and strong strategic sensibility – another key element of leadership. As the people we train become more skilful communicators and thus more capable leaders, they will take more responsibility for the goals of their organizations. Strategic thinkers and communicators are important and valuable assets, not only to their organizations, but to their communities and nations as well. They are the ones who will ask challenging questions and inspire others to make changes to improve their lives.

Reaching beyond the local level

Once local-level participation and empowerment have taken root and are succeeding, it is possible to add a second objective for participatory communication: to serve as a channel to communicate beyond the local area. Tapes can flow horizontally from one village to another. This mode of distribution could, if carefully managed, challenge the prevailing top-down flow of media and information in society.

One videotape exchange created healthy competition and increased motivation among Proshika workers for prompt delivery of services. The participatory video team in one ADC documented the ceremony honouring the installation of the forty-fifth sanitary, deep-tube well in the area. When this tape was shown to a number of Proshika field managers, they were impressed. They felt that if their peers had distributed forty-five, then they could certainly do as well or better.

Tapes from Banchte Shekha and Proshika have been screened locally, nationally and internationally. Such recognition and distribution can have both positive and negative outcomes, as Shahnaz Begum's experience illustrates. She is a village woman who was trained in participatory video at Proshika. In 1993 Shahnaz was among eight winners of the British Council's Women in Development video competition. Her production, *The Life Struggle of Aleya*, is a powerful tape. It was one of seventy-eight entries from twenty-three countries. This award illustrated the strengths of participatory video and gave the communities in South Asia, Bangladesh and especially Proshika a concrete reason to acknowledge it as a viable and important communication model.

Shahnaz made the tape about her neighbour, Aleya. Despite being poor, uneducated and abandoned by her husband, Aleya struggled hard and successfully to educate her daughter. Shahnaz felt that her own possibilities in life were greatly limited by her lack of schooling. She wanted the tape to be a positive example to encourage other parents to educate their daughters, even in hard times.

Shahnaz went to Delhi to a screening of all the winning tapes. It was her first time out of Bangladesh and her neighbours warned her to take care not to get kidnapped and sold. 'I was scared at first but then I felt strong. I was afraid I would not be able to walk with the people I met in Delhi because they would be more educated and well dressed. But going to Delhi was one of the greatest experiences in my life!'

Not being able to talk directly with anyone else was the most difficult problem she faced. Shahnaz has lots of new ideas about how video can be used as an organizing and mobilizing tool. In Delhi she saw a tape about people who came together to fight the police. 'In this tape the people were so united the police couldn't do anything. Unity is so important.' While sharing her experiences with the other Proshika video teams she said, 'All the other tapes in this competition used lots of make-up and acting. My tape was about the real life in Bangladesh.'

Although the award brought greater legitimacy to participatory video at Proshika, it has taken attention away from participatory video as a movement by highlighting one tape, one style and one person. It created problems in Shahnaz's community, where Aleya and others accused Shahnaz and Proshika of reaping benefits from Aleya's personal story. Proshika has had to work hard to re-emphasize the value of the methods and process of participatory video, and not just the accomplishments of one tape or story.

While it is important to balance the demands of advocacy and broader distribution in order to retain the benefits of participation and local empowerment, there are times when the former reinforces the latter. The Self-Employed Women's Association (SEWA), for example, has been a leader in advocating for inclusion of the self-employed in national labour policy. Their video unit, Video SEWA, supported them in motivating and educating the women of Gujarat state to stand up and have their work counted in the 1991 census. Video SEWA's fifteen-minute edited programme, *My Work, Myself*, reached an audience of approximately half a million women through community playbacks and a broadcast on Gujarat state television three days before the census was taken.

Proshika will have the capacity and the structure to undertake this sort of advocacy communication campaign. They are establishing an advocacy unit which will receive participatory videotapes on specific issues. They may use excerpts in their campaigns and lobbying initiatives. For instance, the advocacy unit might request grassroots testimony on chemical pesticides for use in lobbying, or to bring the issue to broader public attention. With finite human resources, a balance must prevail to ensure that the work retains its participatory dimension and services both the needs of the larger organization and the grassroots communities.

Conclusions

NGOs are working in many areas for increased education, human rights, gender equity, a sustainable environment, freedom, and economic self-sufficiency. To achieve fundamental change in these areas, organizations created by and for grassroots women and men have a critical leadership role to play. These NGOs are pioneers and advocates. They must create programmes that address the realities of their constituents' needs. In order to succeed, these organizations – and through them their members – need to communicate for themselves. They cannot reach their goals without communication skills and tools.

Participatory communication skills can elevate women's status in their communities by strengthening women's voices. With powerful voices, women can organize, train, take collective action and ultimately build communities and a society based on self-determination. These actions form a chain. Participation leads to empowerment. Proof of empowerment comes from exercising collective strength. Effective deployment of collective strength opens the doors for self-determination. We believe that as individuals and communities become self-determining, they have the capacity to gain social and economic justice in all areas of their lives. They have the strength and experience to demand that their governments and other authorities be responsive and responsible in their policies and decision-making. Our experiences in Bangladesh point to some effective and powerful methods.

[Originally published in Donna Allen, Ramona R. Rush and Susan J. Kaufman (eds), *Women Transforming Communications: Global Intersections*, SAGE Publications, 1996]

Bibliography

Devine, B. (1994) 'Training for social activism', *Community Media Review*, 17(2), March/April.

Fuglesang, A. (1982) *About Understanding: Ideas and Observations on Cross-Cultural Communication*, Uppsala: Dag Hammarskjöld Foundation.

Higgins, J. W. (1993) 'Visions of empowerment, media literacy and demystification', *Community Television Review*, 16(3), May/June.

Protz, M. (1989) *Seeing and Showing Ourselves: A Guide to Using Small Format Videotape as a Participatory Tool for Development*, New Delhi: Centre for Development of Instructional Technology.

Rahaman, R. S. (ed.) (1986) *A Praxis in Participatory Rural Development*, Dhaka: Proshika MUK.

Rao, A. (ed.) (1991) *Women's Studies International: Nairobi and Beyond*, New York: Feminist Press.

Riano, P. (ed.) (1994) *Women in Grassroots Communication Furthering Social Change*, Thousand Oaks, CA: Sage.

Rose, K. (1992) *Where Women are Leaders: The SEWA Movement in India*, New Delhi: Vistaar Publications.

Rush, R. R. and D. Allen (1989) *Communications at the Crossroads: The Gender Gap Connection*, Norwood, NJ: Ablex Publishing Corp.

Shramshakti (1988) *Report of the National Commission on Self-Employed Women and Women in the Informal Sector*, New Delhi: Akashdeep Printers.

'Video for the People' (1989) *Media Development: Journal of the World Association for Christian Communication*, 36(4).

PART THREE

Community and participatory development: principles and practice

19 | Managing local participation: rhetoric and reality

Robert Chambers

[...] Citizens of this land, through various development or planning committees at various levels, participated significantly in preparing the Second National Development Plan. It was a typical example of participatory democracy [...] The Plan is a people's plan. It was designed and formulated by the people for their own development. (Introduction to the Zambian Second National Development Plan 1972–1976)

There is a plan being drawn up now for this area. As soon as it is out, we will let you know what you are expected to do. (A Locational Agricultural Assistant in a public meeting in Migori Division, Kenya, reported by Oyugi 1973: 7)

Definitions and perspective

[...] There is some justification for the vague use by political leaders of phrases like 'self-reliance', 'participatory democracy' and 'local participation' in order to secure support and action; but there is less justification for the imprecise use of these phrases by academics and civil servants, since for them such usage may cover up bad or lazy thinking [...] This chapter seeks to clarify some of the issues involved and to suggest means whereby the gap between rhetoric and reality might be narrowed [...]

Local participation can conveniently be analysed in three ways: who participates; what institutions are involved; and what objectives and functions it has. First, those who participate may be government staff at the local level, the local inhabitants of an area, or a combination of these two. The issue is complicated by the tendency for those government staff who originate in the area in which they work to think and act as local inhabitants (Oyugi 1973: 10). A distinction can be made between (i) 'participation by staff', meaning by those staff who typically do not originate in the area and who are liable to transfers out of it, (ii) 'participation by the people', including both inhabitants and those staff who originate in the area, and (iii) 'joint participation' in which both groups – outside staff and local inhabitants – are involved. To include the range of meanings in common usage, 'local participation' in this chapter is used to include all three categories – participation by staff, participation by the people, and joint participation by both staff and people.

Second, local participation can be analysed in terms of the institutions through which it occurs. In eastern Africa over the past decade these have included local government authorities, development committees, community development committees, self-help groups, public meetings, and local interest groups such as churches, women's groups and political parties.

Third, local participation can be analysed in terms of objectives and functions. The values ascribed to it in its various forms include:

- making known local wishes;
- generating development ideas;
- providing local knowledge;
- testing proposals for feasibility and improving them;
- increasing the capability of communities to handle their affairs and to control and exploit their environment;
- demonstrating support for a regime;
- doing what government requires to be done;
- extracting, developing and investing local resources (labour, finance, managerial skills, etc.);
- promoting desirable relationships between people, especially through cooperative work.

In eastern Africa both the participation sought by governments and the institutions through which attempts have been made to achieve it have changed remarkably over the past fifty years. In the early colonial period the local participation sought by governments was rather limited and negative. This included the handling by surviving or artificial indigenous authorities of many matters that could be described as traditional; and the payment of taxes. However, there was increasing attention to the development of local government institutions, mainly at the district level [...]

Local participation can be analysed in terms of two streams of initiatives, communication and resources; those which are top-down, originating in government headquarters and penetrating towards and into the rural areas; and those which are bottom-up, originating among the people in the rural areas and directed upwards into the government machine. Given our concern here with government organization and local interest groups, the two most notable and important top-down initiatives in eastern Africa have been development committees and block grants; and the most important bottom-up initiatives have been self-help projects. The experience with these will be considered in turn. [*Editor's note*: for the sake of brevity, Chambers' discussion of development committees, block grants and self-help has been cut from this account. Those interested in historical continuities should read Chambers' account against accounts of similar instruments used by the World Bank, such as Social Funds and Community-Driven Development, and decentralized local governance narratives prevalent among development donors in the 2000s.]

Participation and equity

The way in which words are used in the rhetoric of self-reliance and participation encourages the idea that increased participation will mean a more democratic, egalitarian and equitable society. The idea that the participation advocated in plans and policy speeches reaches and benefits all the people is important for the reassurance of political leaders. There is just enough truth in this belief to sustain it; and it is reinforced by the highly selective experience of political leaders, who are usually shown the best of everything, and who usually see that best on its best behaviour. But very often, and far more often than either political leaders or civil servants perceive or wish to perceive, participation means more influence and resources to those who are already influential and better off, while those who are less influential and less well off benefit much less, or do not benefit, or actually lose.

There are many ways in which 'participation' accentuates inequity. Greater local participation in planning tends to widen regional inequalities. It favours those areas which are better able to produce plans and to implement them: the early experience with the Regional Development Fund in Tanzania was that the more prosperous regions (with the more competent staff, better infrastructure, better services) were more effective in spending the fund, while some of the remoter and more backward regions lagged and returned large sums unspent. Participation in planning is also likely to mean plans drawn up either by civil servants or by civil servants together with a few members of the local elite. Participation in development committees can mean that those who are already well off approve projects and programmes which favour and support those who are already well off. Participation in self-help labour can mean that the women, already overworked, turn out while the men find excuses. Participation through 'voluntary' contributions can mean an income-regressive flat-rate tax which hits the poorest hardest; and failure to pay, as with contributions to some of Kenya's institutes of technology, may be penalized through the denial of public services – health treatment, the right to buy a bicycle licence, and so on – until a receipt for a minimum contribution can be shown.

Participation in the local management of economic activities is even more inequitable. In pastoral societies measures for communal management of grazing and water resources have almost invariably benefited the larger stock-owners to the detriment of the smaller men: dam committees set up in Botswana to manage new dams charged a flat rate to all users, regardless of whether they brought hundreds of stock to water, or only one or two, in effect excluding the poorer people from the club; similarly, when council boreholes, which charged on a pro rata basis for numbers of stock watered, were handed over to local syndicate management, rates were changed to a flat rate for each stock-owner regardless of the number of stock he watered. Again, it is notorious that land reform programmes, necessarily (short of a revolutionary situation) working through local committees, are captured by local elites who benefit more than the programme intends. In sum, all too often participation proclaimed on the platform becomes appropriation and privilege when translated into action in the field.

This should scarcely be surprising, except to those who, for ideological reasons or because they are simple-minded, or more commonly from a combination of these causes, reify 'the people' and 'participation' and push them beyond the reach of empirical analysis. The tendency for local elites to capture projects and programmes and use them for their own benefit should indeed be recognized as a fact of life. Moreover, there are benefits as well as costs in this. Leaders are often leaders because they have ability, and projects may be better managed through their participation. Leaders, especially where there is an active political party, may seek support and legitimacy and so have an incentive to spread the benefits of projects to more rather than fewer people. A conflict between the aims of good leadership and management on the one hand, and of distribution and equity on the other, is, however, likely to be a persistent feature which will remain difficult to overcome.

Moreover, there are such variations between conditions in different areas that generalized prescriptions for participation and equity are more shaky and dangerous than in other more uniform contexts such as field staff management. All the same, six measures to mitigate the inequity which flows from participation and to improve its equity effects can be proposed.

First, in allocating support between alternative self-help projects, preferences should be given to those to which all have access, or to which a wider rather than narrower band of the population will have access. A scale of desirability can be drawn up according to this criterion, with at one pole those projects which benefit all members of the community more or less equally – the village well, the health post (if treatment is free), the social hall – moving through those which benefit all but some much more than others – the access road, the nursery school, the primary school, the cooperative store – to those which only benefit a minority of the community or a few individuals who are already better off – the secondary school with high fees, the cash crop processing plant when only a few can grow the cash crop, the institute of technology to which only a few will be able to send their children.

Second, contributions to projects should be related to economic status, the richer paying more and the poorer paying less, and limited to those who are expected to benefit from the services resulting. There are conflicting considerations here. It may be very important for a person's self-respect that he contribute equally with his richer neighbour; and unless carefully handled, the identification of a 'poor' group which contributes nothing or contributes less may be humiliating and resented. If levels of contribution are permissive, then each potential contributor can make his own decision. At one extreme there is little justification for the confiscation of a poor widow's hen to help pay for a secondary school that she will never be able to send her children to. On the other hand, if some degree of persuasive pressure is not exerted, there will be those in the community who could contribute but refuse to do so even though they will use the service later. President Nyerere faced this dilemma and after at first opposing compulsion came to the view that indolent members of a community should be made to work and contribute. 'From each according to his means, to each according to his need' may be an unattainable ideal, but the first half at least is close enough within range in most East African rural communities to justify a determined attempt to achieve it.

Third, policies for participation should be related to the stage of development reached. Typically, different regions within the same country are at different stages. In the first stage, as in Turkana or West Pokot in Kenya, the major tasks are finding and using leaders who will help to get development moving through education, infrastructure, opening up markets and movement into the cash economy; self-help may be impossible and the formation of interest groups premature. In the second stage, as found in much of the Coast Province of Kenya and many of the areas which are marginal for arable agriculture, leaders are still important in decision-making, in setting an example, and in adopting innovations, but increasingly a shift of official extension can be directed towards leaders and groups together. Self-help is active, but follows the tendency for the first projects to benefit all or almost all the community, while later and later projects benefit fewer and fewer. In the third stage, as found in the more highly developed high-potential smallholding areas of Kenya such as Nyeri and Kisii, interest groups form themselves spontaneously and the progressive farmers can rely more and more on specialized commercial services. It is at this stage that a special effort is justified, to leap over the leaders and the elite groups who can look after themselves – the cooperative committee of prosperous farmers, the women's groups (Maendeleo ya Wanawake) of their wives and the wives of civil servants – in order to reach, rouse and help the people who have been left out. In this stage, community development should be less concerned with conventional self-help projects, which will have shown their usual trend towards serving the better-off members of the community (as for example with [livestock] dips and secondary schools), and official liaison, which can be handled by technical officers. Community development workers should, rather, be concentrating on welfare extension programmes which have a reasonable chance of adoption and success among the less well-off members of the community, such as nutrition, vegetable growing, home economics, health and family planning. In this third stage, community development workers often find themselves overtaken by events and initiatives and left standing; but they can, by redirecting their attention to these less privileged groups, again find a useful role.

Fourth, especially in these highly developed third-stage areas, a radical reorientation of staff activities is required. Moris (1972) has shown how central directives can be distorted in the course of application in the field, and their original objectives subverted. To reduce such tendencies, carefully devised procedures and careful supervision can help. But if staff are to behave very differently, shifting their attention and services away from local elites to local non-elites, they must themselves be convinced that this is right merely through the issue of circulars and orders. The Special Rural Development Programme (SRDP) in Kenya showed the potential of a participatory approach to inter-departmental action. Seminars held over periods ranging from three days to three weeks, in which departmental staff heads came together and together thought through problems with some outside assistance, showed that at both divisional and district levels this sort of open participation could yield ideas, consensus and commitment. As so often, the imagination, intelligence and diligence of field staff proved to be far greater than many imbued with the centrist ideology would have supposed. In any reorientation towards equity programmes, a think-tank open-ended seminar approach is a powerful, perhaps essential, means of securing strong commitment on the part of staff.

Fifth, a major if surprising obstacle is the invisibility of poverty to field staff. This can be tackled through preparatory work for the seminars mentioned above. It was through acting as enumerators in a random sample survey of farmers that the SRDP field staff in Vihiga came to perceive the poorer people. To replicate such a survey on any scale might be difficult; but before attending any seminar, staff could be quickly trained to carry out their own small surveys of one or two areas. Various rules of thumb for selecting respondents could be suggested; but in any case it could be a requirement that at the start of the seminar each participant should describe in detail the circumstances of a number of the poorest people in the area where he worked and put forward his suggestions for how they could be helped.

Sixth, as with other aspects of managing rural development, the design, testing and modification of procedures are critical. In its earlier stages, the experimental opportunities of SRDP were not being exploited to explore this vital area; yet such exploration, with experimental testing, is surely a very high priority, especially given the likelihood that equity will be a major preoccupation of the 1970s.

Finally, this concluding section will itself be little better than rhetoric, and far from reality, unless there is a very determined political will to reach the poorer people. Fine phrases in development plans do not feed children; nor does public oratory. In the early 1970s an oversimplified impression is that

Tanzania and Botswana have the political will and are building the machinery to implement it; that Kenya has the machinery in the form of an efficient civil service, but not the will; and that Zambia may still be having difficulty in creating both the will and the machinery. These judgements may be harsh. But they are needed to emphasize that the end which is sought, a more equitable rural society, is very difficult to achieve; that trying to achieve it is kicking against the pricks; and that the non-revolutionary course towards it requires sustained effort, a high level of management in the rural areas, and above all a credible and consistent political will.

[Abridged version of a chapter published in *Managing Rural Development*, Kumarian, 1986]

Bibliography

Almy, S. W. and P. M. Mbithi (1972) 'Local Involvement in the Special Rural Development Programme', in J. Anderson, 'Self help and independency: the political implications of a continuing tradition in African education in Kenya', *African Affairs*, 70(278), January.

Edward, C. G. (1969) 'Understanding the role of Community Development Officer in Embu District, Kenya', 3rd-year dissertation, Department of Political Science, University College, Dar es Salaam.

Hirschman, A. (1967) *Development Projects Observed*, Washington, DC: Brookings Institution.

Holmquist, F. (1970) 'Implementing rural development projects', in G. Hydén, R. Jackson and J. Okumu, *Development Administration: The Kenyan Experience*, Nairobi: Oxford University Press.

Moris, J. R. (1972) 'Administrative authority and the problem of effective agricultural. administration in East Africa', *African Review*, 2: 105–46.

Nyangira, N. (1970) 'Chiefs' Barazas as agents of administrative and political penetration', Staff Paper no. 80, Institute for Development Studies, University of Nairobi.

Oyugi, W. O. (1973) 'Participation in development planning at the local level', Discussion Paper no. 163, Institute for Development Studies, University of Nairobi.

20 | Community participation: history, concepts and controversies

James Midgley

The historical antecedents of community participation

Although it is often assumed that community participation is a new idea in development studies, current community participation concepts are based on a rich legacy of ideas and practical agendas which have helped to facilitate the formulation of present-day proposals for the involvement of local people in social development. It is, of course, impossible to review these antecedents here in any detail, but some of the more important influences on contemporary community participation theory and practice require elaboration. Among these are the Western ideologies and political theories, the Third World community development movement of the 1950s and 1960s and finally Western social work and community radicalism; each requires a brief discussion.

The legacy of Western ideology

Of the various historical influences on the development of current community participation principles, the debt to Western democratic theory would seem to be the most obvious. By arguing that ordinary citizens have a right to share in decision-making, proponents of community participation reveal the inspiration of democratic ideals. However, this inspiration is not based on classical notions of representative democracy (Schumpeter 1942; Dahl 1956; Lucas 1976; Pennock 1979) but rather on a modern variant of liberal democratic theory known as neighbourhood democracy (Dahl and Tufts 1973). Indeed, many proponents of community participation are sceptical of representative democracy and its possibility of providing meaningful opportunities for the involvement of the masses in the political affairs of developing countries. Drawing on the theory of neighbourhood democracy, they advocate the creation of small-scale institutions for the realization of political aspirations in the villages and urban neighbourhoods of the Third World.

The views of the proponents of community participation are also infused with populist notions which, Wiles (1969: 166) pointed out, are characterized by the belief that 'virtue resides in the simple people who are in the overwhelming majority and in their collective traditions'. There are many definitions of populism but as Stewart (1969) observed, common to all of them is the idea that ordinary folk are badly done by. They may be perceived to be the victims of economic disruption or thought to suffer from the arrogance of an inflexible bureaucracy, or it may be believed that they are neglected by an indifferent establishment. In these circumstances, populist movements often arise to champion the cause of the masses to rally their support.

Populism has considerable influence in development studies and also in the developing countries where it has been embraced by political leaders, intellectuals and technocrats. Worsley (1967) pointed out that the development plans of many Third World countries are strongly populist in character, placing emphasis on cooperative and communitarian forms of social and economic organization, stressing values of self-help and self-sufficiency. The mixed economy is accepted and the proclaimed objective of the plans is to promote agriculture and improve the levels of living of the masses. Modernization of the economy through the promotion of heavy industry is regarded as inappropriate to the needs of the people. Kitching (1982) defined populism in a similar way, pointing out that its major exponents in recent time have included President Nyerere, officials at the ILO concerned with the World Employment Programme, Schumacher and the Intermediate Technology Development Group and Lipton (1977).

The influence of populist ideas on the advocates of community participation has been very considerable; indeed, it may be argued that community participation principles are a primary expression of populist ideas in the Third World today. As in populism, current community participation theory suggests that ordinary peole have been exploited by politicians and bureaucrats and that they have been excluded not only from political affairs but from the development process in general. Their simple way of life is threatened by the forces of modernization and rapid social change and they face increasing hardship as a result of economic and political mismanagement. By organizing local people and making them aware of their situation, community participation provides a mechanism for the mobilization of the masses and collective means of redress.

Anarchism has also had an influence on community participation but this influence has been more subtle than that of populism. Anarchist ideas are most noticeable in the work of those writers who have taken an anti-statist attitude, arguing that the formal institutions of the modern state are inimical to the emergence of spontaneous forms of social and political organization. Central to their work is the belief that authority, and particularly the institutionalization of coercive authority in the organs of the state (of whatever ideology or proclaimed intention), is a primary source of oppression. To realize both freedom and welfare, the state must be destroyed.

Of the various forms of anarchism, Kropotkin's version of anarcho-communism, with its romantic and naturalistic tendencies, is probably closest to contemporary community participation ideas. His insistence that cooperation and mutualism are natural human instincts and characteristic of primordial social organization is frequently echoed in the literature. Many contemporary community participation advocates also share his belief that instinctive human capacities for communalism and participation will re-emerge when the corrupting influences of the state are removed. His utopian formulae for the reorganization of society into a voluntary federation of communes run wholly on egalitarian principles is paralleled in the writings of those who urge the creation of small, self-sufficient communities which promote social development and maximize community participation in the Third World.

The influence of community development

The community development movement of the 1950s and 1960s is another source of inspiration for contemporary community participation theory. Indeed, the two approaches have much in common. Like community participation, community development focused on small communities, seeking to establish democratic decision-making institutions at the local level. It attempted also to mobilize people to improve their social and economic circumstances through undertaking a variety of development projects (Brokensha and Hodge 1996). But there are also clear differences. Community participation theory evolved partly in response to the criticisms which have been made of the community development movement. By reacting to its inadequacies, community participation advocates have sought to formulate a more politicized and people-centred approach which conceives of participation in a more dynamic way.

Among the first proponents of community development were missionaries and colonial officials; indeed, as Mayo (1975) pointed out, colonialism itself created the climate in which community development was to take shape. The dual mandate to civilize while exploiting, the use of forced labour under the pretext that it was an indigenous institution and the need to establish durable and responsible political structures, all facilitated the evolution of an early form of community development. In Africa, missionary efforts to promote education led to the creation by the Colonial Office in London of the Advisory Committee on Native Education which produced a number of reports on colonial educational policy. The 1944 report on *Mass Education in the Colonies* was particularly important for it placed emphasis on literacy training and advocated the promotion of agriculture, health and other social services through local self-help. The British government implemented many of the recommendations of the report and established community development programmes in many African countries; it also supported training and research in the field. These latter activities produced a variety of books and manuals on the subject, of which those by Batten (1962, 1965) are perhaps the best known. In India, as Bhattacharyya (1970) observed, community development drew inspiration from both missionary and indigenous sources. Of the indigenous sources, the utopian experiments of Tagore and Gandhi were particularly important; after independence, when the Indian community development programme was launched, the debt to Gandhi's philosophy was obvious.

Drawing extensively on the British literature and the African and Indian experience, the United Nations and the American government contributed further to the refinement of community development ideas. Community development featured prominently in United Nations documents which were published in the 1950s and 1960s and the organization actively encouraged the promotion of these activities. The American aid programme provided liberal financial support to Third World governments establishing schemes of this kind and a number of American academics were recruited as advisers and experts. A particular motive for American finance aid was a desire to contain subversive influences. It is not surprising, as Brokensha and Hodge (1996) pointed out, that American community development expenditures were highest in countries such as Thailand and Vietnam which were considered to be most threatened by communism.

In spite of the rapid expansion of community development, disillusionment with its achievements was widespread by the 1970s. Many governments, particularly in Africa, failed to provide adequate financial support but nevertheless extolled the virtues of self-help. Community development was soon recognized by the people to amount to little more than a slogan which brought few tangible benefits. In many African countries, civil servants came to regard community development as a relatively unimportant field of public service and as ministries of education lost interest, community development activities were promoted on a haphazard basis by poorly funded ministries of social welfare instead. Corruption, maladministration and inefficiency were rampant and it often seemed that the only beneficiaries of community development were the workers and officials who staffed the creaking community development bureaucracies. An indication of the declining fortunes of community development is revealed in the decision of the Indian government in 1978 to restructure its community development programme, renaming it the Integrated Rural Development Programme instead.

Although community development may be regarded as an immediate precursor to the community participation movement, contemporary community participation advocates have been vociferous critics of community development, claiming that it failed because of its bureaucratic administration and superimposed direction. This not only stifled the innate capacities of ordinary people to determine their own destiny but perpetuated the structures of inequality and oppression both at the national and local level. They argue that an alternative grassroots approach, which liberates the powerless and ensures their involvement in community life, is needed to promote genuine participatory development.

The contribution of Western social work and community radicalism

Although social work is primarily concerned with the problems of needy individuals and their families, it has also, since its inception in the late nineteenth century, focused on communities seeking to organize and mobilize people to improve local amenities and social services. Among the first attempts to systematize community work practice and give it a theoretical base were the reports edited by Lane (1939, 1940) for the National Council on Social Work in the United States. Later publications by Ross (1955, 1958), Warren (1955) and Harper and Dunham (1959) refined these ideas and helped to establish community organization (as it became known) as an accepted method of social work. In the 1960s community organization ideas were further developed by writers such as Morris (1964), Ecklein and Lauffer (1972) and Perlman and Gurin (1972) to incorporate notions of social planning into community organization procedures.

The development of community organization in Europe lagged behind and was largely influenced by American ideas (National Council for Social Service 1960; Hendricks 1964; Thomas 1983) even though existing activities such as youth work and community planning in the new towns provided a basis for the development of local practice methods. In spite of this, American-style community organization was never fully adopted and instead a more radical style of community work took root. This approach transformed conventional methods of community work: instead of seeking to help deprived communities to improve their social and environmental circumstances, the new community work activists urged that people take direct political action to demand changes and improvements.

One important source of inspiration for community work radicalism in the West were the ideas and activities of Alinsky (1946, 1971) in Chicago in the 1930s and 1940s. In the Back of the Yards campaign, Alinsky mobilized local people through existing grassroots organizations, teaching them to use a variety of confrontational tactics when dealing with government organizations and commercial interests. Another was the War on Poverty in the United States, which facilitated the institutionalization of radicalism in community work practice. There were similar developments in Britain in the late 1960s, when the Wilson government announced that it would establish community projects in particularly deprived inner-city areas as a part of its Urban Programme. Although the projects were originally based on conventional community organization techniques, they were soon influenced by more radical community action approaches and also by Marxian ideas. The initial assumptions of the projects that poverty could be reduced by local improvements, the provision of better services and the stimulation of community interest soon lost appeal and many workers began to see their task as one of raising the political consciousness of the poor. As Loney (1989: 131) observed, this reflected the influence of an increasingly popular structural approach in community work which 'focused on economic, social and political factors in seeking to account for deprivation rather than on individual, family or cultural factors'. Armed with this ideology, local project activists took control of the community development projects and tensions between them and their governmental sponsors increased.

While the American and British community action experiments resulted in the creation of few really durable projects, they infused community work with a new dynamism which institutionalized radicalism as an essential ingredient of practice. Although this radicalism has seldom been expressed in revolutionary or subversive acts, it has changed the nature of community work in the industrial countries.

It has also had considerable appeal in the Third World. Midgley (1981) noted that community action ideas have had some popularity in social work circles in developing countires and Marsden and Oakley reported that many non-governmental organizations had adopted radical community work methods. Some, such as the Community Action Movement in Maharashtra, India, adopted an explicit Marxian ideology, which rejected 'welfarism' and sought instead to promote a 'political struggle based on class analysis of Indian society and the organization of the oppressed majority' (1982: 158). Although it cannot be claimed that the contemporary community participation movement in the Third World is characterized by a similar ideology, it has been much influenced by community work radicalism in the West.

The emergence of community participation

While the three historical antecedents described already provide a source of inspiration for current community participation theory, its emergence as a coherent approach to social development must be seen as a direct consequence of the United Nations' popular participation programme. Surveying the activities of the Untied Nations in this field, Wolfe (1982) observed that the concept of popular participation was broadly conceived; popular participation not only required the creation of opportunities for political involvement but the adoption of measures that would enable ordinary people to share fully in the development process.

The emphasis on popular participation in United Nations thinking was formalized with the publication of two major documents on the subject in the 1970s. The first, *Popular Participation in Development*, which was published in 1971, reviewed the emergence of the idea with reference to community development in the Third World during the preceding twenty-five years. The second, *Popular Participation in Decision Making for Development*, which was published in 1975, offered a formal definition of the concept with reference to its implementation. The publication of these documents was followed by the creation of a major research programme into popular participation by the United Nations Research Institute for Social Development (UNRISD) in Geneva. As Stiefel and Pearse (1982) reported, participation was to become one of the major themes around which the organization's activities were to develop. Further reinforcement for the idea of popular participation came from resolutions adopted at the World Conference on International Women's Year which was held in Mexico City in 1975 (United Nations 1976), which observed that women had been excluded from participating both in political activities and the development process in the Third World.

Although nebulous and diffuse, the popular participation idea soon inspired more specific conceptions of community-level involvement in social development. Recognizing that the notion of popular participation was very broad, the United Nations convened a meeting of experts in 1978 to consider the specific issue of community-level participation (United Nations 1981).

But a more significant contribution came from agencies such as UNICEF and the World Health Organization, and especially in the adoption of the UNICEF/WHO Declaration on Primary Health Care at the Alma Ata Conference in 1977. The concept of community participation in health featured prominently in this document and, as De Kadt (1982: 573) observed, has become a 'major preoccupation in the health field'. The adoption of this declaration followed growing concern about the inappropriateness of health policies in developing countries; it emphasized the provision of basic services in local communities instead, which would provide basic healthcare, preventive services, nutrition, maternal and child health and the utilization of simple medical technologies. Above all, it called for the mobilization of local communities to take responsibility for their own health. UNICEF and WHO were optimistic that 'health by the people' was feasible; indeed, several collections of country case studies (Djukanovics and Mach 1975; Newell 1975; Hetzel 1978) gave ground for optimism, demonstrating that community-based primary health programmes were already functioning in a number of countries.

During the 1970s, the idea of popular participation also attracted attention from those engaged in housing and urban development research. Although proposals for aided self-help housing had been made earlier by Koenigsberger et al. (1952) and Abrams (1964), it was largely through the work of Turner (1967) that these ideas were popularized. The initiative was taken by the World Bank, which modified its housing sector lending policies to promote self-help housing in the Third World. In 1975 the Bank's *Housing: Sector Policy Paper* stated that squatter upgrading and sites and services schemes 'are primary lending instruments for more equitable urban development' (p. 45). By 1980 the Bank had loaned $US1.3 million to developing countries for schemes of this kind; forty-one projects had been established, and by 1983 another ninety projects would be approved (World Bank 1980).

Through the influence of the international agencies, the governments of many developing countries have acknowledged the need for greater emphasis on community-based development strategies, and some have taken steps to strengthen participatory elements in their social development programmes. Of course, some governments have also established their own programmes based on indigenous populist, nationalist or traditional beliefs. Non-governmental organizations have also been major promoters of community participation ideals. International voluntary agencies ranging from Oxfam to the World Council of Churches have been particularly enthusiastic about community participation ideas, and many academics, especially in the field of development studies, regard community participation as a new and variable approach to social development. Although little is known about the activities of local and national voluntary organizations in the Third World, many of them, including national charities, indigenous populist movements and village-based associations, have popularized the ideals of community participation. But [...] the belief in the undoubted virtue of involving people in development is not as straightforward or uncontroversial as it might at first appear [...]

[Excerpt from *Community Participation, Social Development and the State*, Methuen, 1986]

References

Abrams, C. (1964) *Man's Struggle for Shelter in an Urbanising World*, Cambridge: MIT Press.

Alinsky, S. (1946) *Reveille for Radicals*, Chicago, IL: University of Chicago Press.

— (1971) *Rules for Radicals*, New York: Random House.

Batten, T. R. (1962) *Training for Community Development*, London: Oxford University Press.

— (1965) *The Human Factor in Community Development*, London: Oxford University Press.

Bhattacharyya, S. N. (1970) *Community Development: An Analysis of the Programme in India*, Calcutta: Academic Publishers.

Brokensha, D. and P. Hodge (1996) *Community Development: An Interpretation*, San Francisco, CA: Chandler.

Dahl, R. A. (1956) *A Preface to Democratic Theory*, Chicago, IL: University of Chicago Press.

Dahl, R. A. and E. R. Tufts (1973) *Size and Democracy*, Stanford, CA: Stanford University Press.

De Kadt, E. (1982) 'Community participation for health: the case of Latin America', *World Development*, 10: 573–84.

Djukanovics, V. and E. P. Mach (eds) (1975) *Alternative Approaches to Meeting Basic Health Needs in Developing Countries*, Geneva: World Health Organization.

Ecklein, J. L. and A. Lauffer (1972) *Community Organizers and Social Planners*, New York: Wiley.

Harper, E. and A. Dunham (eds) (1959) *Community Organization in Action*, New York: Association Press.

Hendricks, G. (1964) *Community Organization*, The Hague: Ministry for Social Work.

Hetzel, B. S. (ed.) (1978) *Basic Health Care in Developing Countries*, Oxford: Oxford University Press.

Kitching, G. (1982) *Development and Underdevelopment in Historical Perspective*, London: Methuen.

Koenigsberger, O., S. Groak and B. Bernstein (eds) (1952) *The Work of Charles Abrams: Housing and Social Renewal in the USA and the Third World*, Oxford: Pergamon.

Lane, R. P. (1939) 'Reports of groups studying community organization process', *Proceedings of the 66th National Conference of Social Work*, New York: National Association of Social Workers.

— (1940) 'The field of community organization', *Proceedings of the 67th National Conference of Social Work*, New York: National Association of Social Workers.

Lipton, M. (1977) *Why Poor People Stay Poor*, London: Temple Smith.

Loney, M. (1989) *Community against Government*, London: Heinemann.

Lucas, J. R. (1976) *Democracy and Participation*, Harmondsworth: Penguin.

Marsden, D. and P. Oakley (1982) 'Radical community development in the Third World', in G. Craig, N. Derricourt and M. Loney (eds), *Community Work and the State*, London: Routledge and Kegan Paul.

Mayo, M. (1975) 'Community development: a radical alternative?', in R. Bailey and M. Brake (eds), *Radical Social Work*, London: Edward Arnold.

Midgley, J. (1981) *Professional Imperialism: Social Work in the Third World*, London: Heinemann.

Morris, R. (ed.) (1964) *Centrally Planned Change*, New York: National Association of Social Workers.

National Council for Social Service (1960) *Community Organization: An Introduction*, London.

Newell, K. W. (ed.) (1975) *Health by the People*, Geneva: World Health Organization.

Pennock, J. R. (1979) *Democratic Political Theory*, Princeton, NJ: Princeton University Press.

Perlman, R. and A. Gurin (1972) *Community Organization and Social Planning*, New York: Wiley.

Ross, M. G. (1955) *Community Organization: Theory and Principles*, New York: Harper.

— (1958) *Case Histories in Community Organization*, New York: Harper.

Schumpeter, J. (1942) *Capitalism, Socialism and Democracy*, London: Allen and Unwin.

Stewart, A. (1969) 'The social roots', in G. Ionescu and E. Gellner (eds), *Populism: Its Meanings and National Characteristics*, New York: Macmillan.

Stiefel, M. and A. Pearse (1982) 'UNRISD's Popular Participation Programme', *Assignment Children*, 59/60: 145–59.

Thomas, D. N. (1983) *The Making of Community Work*, London: Allen and Unwin.

Turner, J. F. C. (1967) 'Barriers and channels for housing development in modernizing countries', *Journal of the American Institute of Planners*, 34: 167–81.

United Nations (1971) *Popular Participation in Development: Emerging Trends in Community Development*, New York.

— (1975) *Popular Participation in Decision Making for Development*, New York.

— (1976) *Report of the World Conferences of the International Women's Year*, New York.

— (1981) *Popular Participation as a Strategy for Promoting Community Level Action and National Development*, New York.

Warren, R. L. (1955) *Studying Your Community*, New York: Russell Sage.

Wiles, P. (1969) 'A syndrome, not a doctrine', in I. Ionescu and E. Gellner (eds), *Populism: Its Meanings and National Characteristics*, New York: Macmillan.

Wolfe, M. (1982) 'Participation in economic development: a conceptual framework', *Assignment Children*, 59/60: 79–109.

World Bank (1975) *Housing: Sector Policy Paper*, Washington, DC.

— (1980) *Education: Sector Policy Paper*, Washington, DC.

Worsley, P. (1967) *The Third World*, London: Weidenfeld and Nicolson.

21 | The making and marketing of participatory development

David Mosse

Making a participatory rural development project

In 1990, while working for the British NGO Oxfam in south India, I was invited to join an ODA (Overseas Development Administration, now Department for International Development, or DfID) 'mission' of expatriate consultants to design a new agriculture development project in 'tribal' western India, the Indo-British Rainfed Farming Project (IBRFP). This was a fairly typical consultancy which brought together a group of professionals from different disciplines (economics, soil science, plant genetics and social anthropology) into a 'transitory knowledge building community' (Wood 1998) around ambitious donor 'Terms of Reference': 'to review all available information which may be relevant to the formulation of the approach and technical content [of the project] ... and to produce a detailed proposal for ... a fully participatory and poverty focused rainfed farming project'. Typically ignorant of local and historical detail, our team was attributed high status as international experts, given access to top people, and mobility through the five Indian states and the capital. Working to tight time-frames, the team relied on working assumptions, guesswork, borrowed ideas or past experience to put together a coherent project idea, a viable design and a convincing argument to justify the investment of public money by the donor (see ibid.).

Complex worlds and local histories had to be pressed into the service of current policy debates. And in this case upland *adivasi* ('tribal') communities and regional institutions had to be rendered comprehensible and responsive to planned project inputs in predictable ways – within six weeks. That indeed is what development consultants are well paid to do; to come up with models that reduce disorder and allow rational sense to be made of programme inputs. This sort of 'project design mission' is itself an important subject of ethnographic inquiry. However, here I want to press on to consider the *output* of this consultancy – the project model – rather than the process. What sort of representation was 'the project' and what interests were involved? A few key points:

First, as James Ferguson (1990) argued for World Bank project discourse in Lesotho, the IBRFP project document represented places and people as embodiments of those development problems which are amenable to the donor's currently favoured 'technical' solutions. Two solutions stand out: the first was 'the introduction of improved agricultural *technology*' and the second 'enhancement of farmer capacities through *participation*'. The initial technical design document described the farming system of the project area as an arena of almost unlimited possibilities for increased production through the introduction of agricultural technologies – improved cultivars, crop husbandry, livestock improvement, soil and water conservation techniques (etc.), an inventory extended and detailed by a series of (always hopeful) UK consultants. But, while the project area quickly became known as the environmentally degraded home to a catalogue of deficiencies in existing practice (reduced fallows, cultivation on steep slopes, low inputs, limited knowledge, livestock disease, etc.), development problems could *not* legitimately be traced to farmer ignorance and traditional agriculture.

This was a project in the new 'Farmer First' policy mould. Problems pointed instead to the mistaken priorities and procedures of the Indian agricultural research and extension establishment, which in common with most, or even all, national agricultural research systems, had failed to develop and deliver appropriate technology to the complex, diverse and risk-prone agricultural environment of upland tribal farmers (Witcombe et al. 1998). And one of the root causes of this was the failure to involve farmers in technology development, testing and popularization. This leads, then, to the second 'solution', namely 'participation'. Farmer participation would ensure that more appropriate technologies would be developed and delivered. But this was only one aspect of participation. In a much broader sense our documentation conceived of the project districts as an *area without participation*, meaning, among other things, that they were remote from government administration and services, agricultural technology and inputs, institutional credit and markets. Indeed, in writing the project design I (and my consultant colleagues) found it possible to reframe a variety of political, economic and technical issues in terms of the 'master metaphor', *participation*.

The beauty of this idea was that while it had been made into a powerful interpretive device – not least by my own writing – which legitimized and amplified the meaning of project action, it could at the same time, in *operational* terms, involve a restricted and eminently manageable set of project activities (village-level meetings, PRAs [Participatory Rural Appraisals], workplans, etc.), formalized and 'manualized' as the 'IBRFP Participatory Planning Approach to Farming Systems Development', which I also helped to draft.

Having established a 'people in need of participation' (as much as in need of better technology) our project design then invoked a 'model of change' – that is, a simplified set of problem–solution linkages *causally* connecting activities and objectives, inputs and outputs. These established, for example:

the relationship between farmer-managed trials, widening cultivar choice and crop yield increases; soil and water conservation and yield stability; or farmer organizations and access to credit and reduced debt. Above all, the project was defined by a 'theory of participation'. This asserted that persisting poverty and isolation and inappropriate and unsustainable development programmes were the consequence of 'top-down' planning and the non-involvement of farmers in the process of need identification and programme design. Correspondingly maximizing farmer participation (including the specific involvement of women) would result in better-designed, more effective and sustainable programmes. And, to quote the project document, 'The basic premise is that sustainable development can only be achieved by enhancing local self-reliance through institutional and community development.' Ultimately participation was about the transfer of power.

The project design was synthesized into the currently dominant project formulation model – the Logical Framework (or Logframe), which conveyed to outside decision-makers the idea of manageability based upon the existence of logically and causally related activities and objectives, an ordered sequence of events, the functional integration of different components and institutional actors (donors, implementing agencies, field staff and villagers) within a single knowledge system (see Quarles van Ufford 1993: 139). The logical relations of the model of change were in fact clarified through successive reworking of the Logframe, which was the point of reference to validate approaches, report achievements and negotiate changes in strategy as the project went along. The Logframe was itself part of a carefully negotiated and drafted Project Document which stood for the project and justified it in prescribed form (through separate annexes dealing with economic cost-benefits, technical viability, institutional viability and social policy acceptability – in terms of poverty, equity and gender criteria). Once its elements – approaches, roles, expected outputs, categories of activities – were present in the text, the project existed in our minds and in our conversations, regardless of the actuality of events.

But the project text was only partly and imperfectly written for internal coherence; it was also a container for wider policy argument, both within the donor agency and externally. For example, farmer participation in plant breeding and varietal selection (a core project innovation) was explicitly a challenge to the prevailing regulatory frameworks and bureaucratic practice in the Indian agricultural research establishment (see Witcombe et al. 1998). The emphasis on farmer agency and indigenous knowledge was a critique of monolithic top-down modernist approaches to agricultural development directed at collaborating Indian bureaucrats, while 'sustainability' through self-reliance and farmer control was intended as a critique of subsidy-driven government programmes, and to restrain the dominance of technical agendas over social ones within donor and project agencies. Finally, participation and the poverty focus were aimed at answering public criticism of the British aid programme from NGOs and media in the UK and in India. Indeed, in the early 1990s the project was intended to mark and advertise a major departure from earlier practice. The project design was a policy argument, a discourse of persuasion (Apthorpe 1997).

The project text was both the outcome of social processes of persuasion and enrolment, and a point of reference anticipating future policy arguments. And these were not confined narrowly to project actors. Through regional networks, the nascent project would also serve as a vehicle for other interests – for example, Indian and international NGOs lobbying donors and government. I was myself deputed by Oxfam to connect the emerging official aid agenda with that of Indian NGOs, to exert policy influence and reorientate a public sector implementing agency. Projects are rarely bounded entities. Local planning, open-ended design, a focus on the needs of the poorest and women, and prioritization of the protection of subsistence cropping through low-risk low-cost technologies over investment for commercial agriculture – these were clearly political choices. But they were advanced as technical decisions, concomitants of the paradoxical universal rationality of 'participation', a globally valid development approach endorsed by international donors, the work of NGOs and valorized 'local' knowledge. By reference to this discourse we foreign consultants could effectively de-author potentially threatening change, making it the impersonal demands of the 'system' (i.e. the participatory approach) (see Porter 1995: 79). We stood as guarantors of the universal technical validity of changes that still had to be negotiated within a large bureaucratic public sector project agency.

So, this project design – and its emphasis on 'participation' – was, like most others, a bid for political support, a site for institutional politics (around the competing agendas of technical and 'social' donor advisers, donor and project agency and project management and field staff). Against Ferguson, such institutional politics is as much about coalition building in order to *restrict* bureaucratic and technical power as about its extension. But in order to advance policy arguments at any level, and so acquire and retain political support, project ideas have to meet other criteria. First, a project has to be *consequential*; has to be ambitious and have big effects. IBRFP 'aimed to improve the long-term livelihoods of poor farmers in a drought prone region ... and promote a replicable participatory poverty-focused [and environmentally benign] approach to farming systems development elsewhere'. Programme discourse requires such overambition. Relatedly, a development project has to be *innovative*. It needs the quality of novelty, and has to mark a new beginning. This theme reverberates through IBRFP's initial documentation.

Second, the designed interventions have to be seen to be *technical*. The political nature of the project's participation goals and its critique of existing state policy and programmes are concealed behind the technical expertise of international consultants. As a 'Participation Specialist' my own 'technical' annexes were able to stand alongside those relating to seed technology or soil conservation methods, rendering regional social analysis in terms of the apolitical organizing development idea of 'participation'. More broadly, the language of international development consensus (and ultimately legal and intergovernmental agreement) is always technical and never political. And this is what gives Logical Frameworks such an important position in formal negotiation of development. The project had to be represented *as if* it had no political or institutional context.

Finally, project formulations including objectives have to have a high degree of *ambiguity*, which in project discourse facilitates and helps maintain consensus by allowing the multiplication of criteria of success (see below). As an interpretive device, the project model should function so as to enable a variety of actors and institutions to isolate and claim credit for desirable change. Importantly, the ambiguity of the project idea also allows it to absorb and give expression to shifting agendas. Over its first ten years, the IBRFP project would bear the imprint of successive international development fashions. By 1993/94 watershed development had gained primacy over rain-fed farming technologies and 'farmer first' approaches; by 1995 trends towards micro-finance and 'self-help' groups were strongly mirrored in the project, while from 1998 the project was to exemplify DfID's new Sustainable Rural Livelihoods (SRL) framework. Again one of the key roles of external consultants is to ensure effective reinterpretation of project models in terms of shifting policy trends. Indeed, the project model was characteristically more permeable to such policy trends than to its own constantly reinterpreted field experience.

Donors and their consultants were without doubt the dominant voice in the design and (re-)formulation of this project and its language of legitimacy, even though donor power and imposed designs had to be veiled behind a rhetoric of partnership and rituals of collaboration, including carefully orchestrated 'joint' planning workshops. To gain acceptance, donor-imposed designs have to appear to reflect national policies, or to draw on the emerging aims/approaches of implementing agencies (which are flatteringly cited in project documents). At the same time, the work of international consultants, feasibility reports or studies of various kinds accumulate data that serve to symbolize the rationality of decisions (see Alvesson 1993). Donor project designs, including that of the IBRFP project, however, only have to *appear* to be hegemonic. For this project to work at all, its model had to be porous to the interests of a range of actors and institutions. There *had* to be a *single* project model – given privilege in the text – but there were always several readings of it, several shadow or subordinate models and rationalities validating action from different points of view or operational positions (i.e. of fieldworkers, managers, consultants, etc.).

Indeed, the purpose of the singular, technical-rational, politically acceptable, ambitious and *ambiguous* project model is often precisely to provide a vehicle for very different interests beyond the donor, including (in this case) those of central/state government, a parastatal agency and agro-research centres, among others. Like an international regime (on say trade), the project model with its ambiguous metaphor of participation was able to facilitate coopera-tion between different institutional interests. Moreover, once a vehicle for the different interests of various 'stakeholders', the representations of the official model find many supporters and so acquire greater stability and protection from failure.

In this case, the IBRFP project model, at one level an unstable operating consensus, was secured on diverse institutional interests, which were uniquely underpinned and symbolized by the ambiguous concept of 'participation' itself. What is characteristic of 'successful' projects is a high degree of convergence of disparate interests and priorities on to a single validating and interpretive model; and therefore a shared interest in reaffirming and protecting it. And suc-cessful project ideas are those that provide an interpretive framework (official objectives and measures of progress) broad enough to contain and stabilize the various interests involved. Successful models (and their architects) are those that 'assist in the critical process of creating certainty, of turning arbitrariness into givenness and actuality' (Porter 1995: 74). 'Success' in development is an institutional process, not an objective fact.

Making and marketing participation

The project began work in July 1992. By the end of 1995 a small, highly committed project team was working in a handful of the poorest tribal villages in a remote corner of western India. They had earned local credibility slowly over three years, by helping farmers identify and test improved rice and maize varieties for poor upland soils with few inputs, providing them with credit, in some places establishing low-cost soil and water conservation structures, deepening wells, providing tree seedlings, vegetable seeds and improved breeds of goats and chickens. They had begun by using PRA to identify people's needs and priorities, while exposing local people to new ideas, technologies and options; regularly taking men and women to distant research centres, or bring-ing government experts and administrators to their doorsteps. Staff worked hard to build relationships with groups of poor farmers, meeting again and again, sitting, discussing, explaining ideas, initiating activities and delivering a range of schemes. This was an approach to development understood and increasingly favoured among donors and NGOs, but what did it mean to the KBCL project host?

KBCL was a leading national commercial organization involved in the pro-duction and marketing of fertilizer, with a firm commitment to agricultural development through 'scientific management' and the 'transfer of modern technology' through its own demonstrations and promotional campaigns aimed at expanding its capacity to deliver agricultural inputs and services. Its nationwide marketing operations were concentrated in the same broad region as the project, although its clients were not the poor farming communities that were to be the project's focus. The question is how could KBCL's strong marketing agenda and its understanding that input supply was the principal constraint to agriculture and that low-input demand was a constraint to market development be reconciled with a project model which stressed low/no-cost low-input technology and response to the demands of very poor farming communities (with negligible demand for fertilizer)? How could a fertilizer company, with staffing and procedures evolved to meet the considerable logistical demands of transporting and supplying 1.5 million tonnes of fertilizer (yearly) to a precise schedule, manage to respond to the range and complexity of needs of small tribal farming communities? How could a company with tight systems of control and accountability allow tribal farmers to develop their own development responses? Why would KBCL sign up to the external donor-driven development agenda anyway? What interests did it have in a participatory, poverty-focused project, and how was it to make this project a successful part of its own organizational agenda?

In order to answer these questions, a little more needs to be known about KBCL itself. In its marketing operations, KBCL had only one legitimate channel of distribution, namely local cooperative societies, 2,000 of which from different parts of the country were its members. KBCL marketed its government-allocated quota of fertilizer through apex cooperative societies or directly to lower-level societies at fixed prices. Its marketing strategy could only be geared towards increasing its market share of cooperative sales by gaining and retaining farmer loyalty. But the only difference between KBCL urea and that of its competitors was the 'KBCL' name and logo printed on the bags. There was therefore a fundamental organizational imperative to promote itself and its brand name and to do so through serving the wider interests of farmers as its shareholders and its market. For this reason various farmer services (ranging from warehousing to soil testing) and educational and welfare activities were central to its broader marketing strategy; and these included a network of client-service centres and local input supply nodes, as well as an expanding 'village adoption' welfare programme.

Finally, along with promoting its name in relation to its farmer clients, KBCL had the equally important need to preserve and enhance its profile in relation to the government (at both state and central level) which controlled the allocation of fertilizer quotas and other commercial projects in which KBCL would be interested. In short, senior management could give meaning to the project in terms of KBCL's own enduring concerns with advancing its profile to its client base, extending its capacity to deliver agro-inputs and services, enhancing its link with government and the national goal of increasing agricultural production, as well as straightforward fertilizer marketing. Initially, they were also hopeful of opportunities to exploit additional commercial/ marketing possibilities, for example through large-scale wasteland development and social forestry plantations, or the marketing of agricultural seeds or produce. Indeed, KBCL was far more interested in the value of the project as a high-profile, high-prestige internationally funded venture able to promote its image and relationship with government and other external observers, and to expand its broad patronage role in relation to its farming community clients, than with any potential it had in establishing a (very low-value) local market for fertilizer. What was unexpected was that it was the rhetoric and practice of 'participation' that proved most effective in pursuing these promotional and patronage objectives.

So, why was a *participation* agenda so compatible with the self-promotional goals of a fertilizer company? From one point of view the answer is that the project was able, very effectively, to turn 'participation' into a *commodity*, which, like urea, could be bagged with KBCL's own label on it. This was made possible by the high profile accorded to the project by the donor, and by a rising demand for skills in 'participatory' approaches and a 'package of methods' (mostly PRA) by large-scale state-led development programmes such as the National Watershed Development Programme within India, and the project's ability to deliver these. Through skilful public relations the project management succeeded in establishing 'participation' as a technique/commodity and itself as the primary local source and supplier, and reaped the rewards of high-profile visibility, and reputation. This 'commodification' of participation was inadvertently helped by the efforts of myself and other consultants working with the project team to systematize the processes of village-level planning. And this systematization was itself a means both to validate community-based approaches (within the team) and to deal with considerable pressure to press ahead quickly with the implementation of physical works.

What it meant was that participation (ultimately a matter of shifting relations of power) could be formatted, printed, wrapped (sometimes quite literally in coloured tissue paper) and delivered as a gift.

If the project was able to advance the marketing agenda of its parent organization, it was also clear that it would come under considerable pressure to conform to this organization's systems and procedures, to respect its hierarchy, observe its rules, and to deliver progress in its terms – that is as quantified outputs in compliance with predefined categories – however inconsistent these demands might be with the donor's principles of participatory development. At the level of the IBRFP project unit, considerable management energy was devoted to handling these demands, negotiating flexibility and protecting the project's work and culture from external pressure. Often this meant trying to pursue exploratory approaches at village level, while remaining upwardly accountable and delivering against specified expectations; translating the realities of project experience into categories that would be meaningful to senior marketing and accounts managers. Through its routine monitoring and progress reports, and in its presentations to official visitors, the project constructed a 'plans-targets-output' version of itself in order to satisfy external audit, while preserving autonomy for its own practices. Indeed, the creativity of the new project could only be protected if key people within it were willing to engage with the bureaucratic culture of the parent organization on its own terms; people who could act as buffers and manager-brokers of organizational culture, who were bilingual in the discourse of KBCL bureaucracy and donor policy.

Ultimately it was impossible for the project to resist external control, and its buffers and brokers were also conduits for external institutional demands. Those who interpreted the project and made it meaningful to the marketing agency also brought back expectations; personalized mediation brought personal obligations to control the process and deliver the result. Conflicting demands – the commitment to participation, and its opposite, the imperative to control – appeared to make the project unmanageable; *except* that paradoxically the notion of 'participation' itself brought these incompatible agendas together. The 'participation' framework preserved integrity and made an unmanageable project manageable. How?

As a set of practices, 'participation' proved eminently *manageable*. Practically, 'participation' produced not (as might be expected) a diverse and locally variable development programme, but the strong convergence of activities into a fixed set – crop trials, soil and water conservation, agro-forestry and input supply credit and a range of ad hoc welfare programmes. There is no question that these interventions were important, shaped by project staff's sincere interactions with villagers and pursued with commitment; but choices were also constrained to comply with prevailing organizational systems and procedures. Over time, it was inevitable that priority would be given to familiar, conventional programmes over innovative initiatives where approval might be uncertain or delayed. At the same time the institutional need to maintain relationships with local government, senior management, research institutions or donor advisers, each with distinct development agendas, required the introduction of a stream of other (frequently flawed or inappropriate) schemes for which farmers had little input – the promotion of new winter crops, drip irrigation, grain banks, compost pits, farm machinery, mushroom cultivation, women's handicraft, or first-aid kits.

The point is that the participation framework enabled all of these to be widely perceived as a direct response to 'local needs'. In ways that I have explored elsewhere (Mosse 1996, 2001), participatory techniques allowed the development priorities conveyed by the project (or demanded by its systems) to be mirrored back to them; in fact this was unavoidable. Self-interested villagers would of course collude with project staff in endorsing external assumptions and programme priorities where this guaranteed benefits; the disincentives to innovate or to challenge prevailing preconceptions were shared by staff *and* villagers. And as villagers shaped their needs and priorities to match the project's schemes and administrative realities – validating imposed schemes with local knowledge and requesting only what was most easily delivered – the wider institutional interests of the project (including those of host and donor organizations) became built into community perspectives and project decisions became perfectly 'participatory'. The shift from a relatively open and exploratory system towards a closed one was not intentional but a side effect of institutional factors (including the effects of my own systematizing documentation) that were not perceived by project actors themselves, or even by external observers. Indeed, project actors had become caught up in a system that was increasingly closed and controllable – increasingly impervious to variable local needs, reinforcing preconceptions and narrowing options – but which was, at the time, being widely acclaimed for its participatory processes and the sophistication of its methods.

Once in place, moreover, the 'participation' framework provided a uniquely strong basis for defining programme success. As a normative framework and an ordered set of field techniques (from 'village entry' and PRAs to 'work-plans') participation became embedded in the project's practices, increasingly routinized but providing ready measures of achievement. The publicized record of village meetings, attendance, PRAs, trainings (etc.) provided an unassailable quantitative record of the project's participatory performance. Participation goals were supremely ambiguous – generating multiple criteria by which the project could claim success with authority in ways that did not depend upon field-level verification. Through the discursive practices of the project – notably the reports of its consultants (including myself) – 'participation' had come to represent a range of desired social transformations (people's empowerment, control, voice, awareness, etc.) which could be symbolically invoked by the trivial and routine practice of PRA. My own exhortations on the importance of pursuing 'genuinely' participatory approaches served further to thicken the meaning of 'thin' development practice.

On the basis of its 'participation' methodology KBCL's IBRFP project was given a reputation (by the donor) that generated a steady stream of international visitors. The project found that it could advertise its participatory achievements while (of necessity) retaining control over an increasingly standard set of project activities, reproduced through conservatism and convenience, the risk aversion of both villagers and staff, and administrative pressure from the parent organization. Among donor staff, the project was already a front-runner, a flagship, 'the jewel in the India aid programme crown', and a compelling advertisement for the new face of British aid.

As a model of participation the project served both to enhance the 'symbolic capital' of a donor agency and its new policy agenda, and to provide a new 'commodity' to promote the profile and reputation of a marketing agency. While neither of these organizational concerns was directly encoded in the 'official' project objectives, the ambiguity of these provided a vehicle for both, as well as the basis for strong overt consensus around this successful participatory project. Moreover, the discourse of 'participation' had also made it possible to manage the conflicting pressures on the project implied by these different agendas. Only self-proclaimed participatory development success could marry KBCL bureaucratic pressures and donor policy expectations, rendering an unmanageable project manageable. The satisfaction of key institutional interests of the donor and host agencies had raised the profile of this project; but it had also raised the stakes. The project was trapped in 'success'.

A core contradiction? Participation and the delivery of development

Well-promoted activities in the area of 'participation' – PRAs, village work-plans, meetings, trainings, villager events – were not, however, in themselves sufficient to secure visible and recognized success. What validated the project was the donor-supported *theory* that linked 'participation' on the one hand, and better (more effective/sustainable) physical programmes of soil and water conservation, forestry, minor irrigation and so forth on the other. Success depended crucially upon the timely implementation of measurable quantities of high-quality development schemes that would hold the attention of outside observers, political bosses and paymasters (and continue to secure 'participation' from villagers). But the timely delivery of programme outputs – the construction of kilometres of soil conservation structures, the planting of trees, deepening of wells, purchase of pumps, or the supply of input credit – had become far too important to be left to *participatory* (i.e. farmer-managed) processes.

External pressures were translated into unofficial systems of rewards and punishments which encouraged a strong vertical control of programme activities and implementation, as well as the export of participation 'commodities' (e.g. PRA training, presentations, workshops, manuals). With measures of performance and 'efficiency' linked to the speed and extent of programme completion, staff who tried to be *too participatory* – spending too much time investigating 'real needs', or women's needs, or working at a pace that would ensure local control and the mobilization of local resources – would soon be seen as underperforming by both project and community.

Field staff not only took direct control of programme implementation (in some instances), but also recruited, trained and paid male and female 'village volunteers' or *jankars*. While crucial to the project's delivery system, *jankars* were also key indicators of 'participation'. The operational system of the project demanded quality and quantity: on the one hand, quality control and upward accountability, and on the other, a constant stream of new activities and commitments to 'keep up momentum'. This in turn ensured expanding networks of patronage locally. Field staff found themselves acting as local patrons and benefactors – a role underlined by the high public profile KBCL gave to its welfare activities. Indeed, the identity and credibility of the project locally became consolidated around its role as benefactor, source of technology, inputs or credit. Rather than making subsidies redundant, village workers were the means to acquire subsidies. In a region where tribal farmers were historically predisposed to engage with outsiders as clients – whether labour contractors, traders, moneylenders or development projects – this may be less than surprising.

This then was the operational logic of the project which resulted from the tension between internal participatory development goals and external institutional demands. The need for close control over works schedules, fixed budget calendars, purchasing and expenditure norms, reporting formats, emphasized upward accountability, the proper use of funds, and the planning and delivery of high-quality programmes against quantitative targets. The project system was simply not capable of transferring power to communities or dealing with the uncertainty that would result from allowing Bhil farmers to develop their own ways of doing things, making their own decisions, taking risks and making mistakes. But, when interpreted through the assumptions of the project model, the impressive landscape of well-laid-out soil and water conservation bunds, improved varieties, newly planted wood lots, deepened wells and operating pump sets could nonetheless be read as demonstrating the success of the donor goals of people's participation and farmer-managed development and self-reliance. Both *participation* and its *denial in practice* were necessary to the management of reputation and the marketing of success.

By its second and third year the project management (including consultants) became increasingly oriented towards the management of what could be read as a profound internal contradiction: high-profile 'participation' on the one hand, and the strong control over programme delivery and expanding patronage on the other. Now the key point is that the core validating project model established *ideologically* precisely the link between 'participatory processes' and efficient implementation that was weak or absent in practice. Indeed, this is precisely why the core model was constantly repeated and invoked in meetings, workshops and during donor review visits. Through ritualized expression the model allowed the interpretation of events and landscapes (smartly bunded) that confirmed its presuppositions. We consultants were officiants at these rituals. As with many projects, donor review visits often served as occasions to *explicate* project assumptions, rather than to examine their practices in any detail. And a good deal of management, donor and consultant effort (through monitoring and reviews, project workshops, etc.) went into the rearticulation of the participatory project model.

Not only reports, but also video films and manuals reaffirmed the model [...] indeed, by the third year of the project, *the model* had become so important that it had been restated as *the* key project purpose. Which now read as establishing a 'replicable, participatory ... FSD (Farming Systems Development) *approach – i.e., a model*' (Revised Logframe, 1995) (rather than sustainable increases in production, etc.). The project had developed a dissemination strategy and defined a 'Replication programme' as a key output (including production of manuals, national/regional seminars/workshops, audio-visual productions, training for NGOs and GOs on the now systematized *Participatory Approach*).

As a goal, *replication* further underlined the coherence of the project as model or simulation, emphasizing coherence and generality (see Fairhead 2000: 101) in a way that strengthened the position of the project in the policy circles (donor, government, international) where it sought to command attention. It effectively denied the contingency of project processes and the strong influence of particular institutional interests. Similarly, the emphasis on outward dissemination and upward policy influence underlined the project design as a legitimizing representations rather than an operational model. The effect of the discourse of replication, dissemination and policy influence was further to blur distinction between the normative and the descriptive, event and representation, so that planning manuals could be cited and reproduced in donor texts and elsewhere as project experience.

Now, it is important to stress that there is absolutely no suggestion here of deception or a cover-up on the part of the project. The project's own reporting (its monthly progress reports) itemized the number of 'participation' activities (participants, meetings, PRAs, trainings, etc.) done and the physical programmes implemented (etc.) with strikingly little interpretive justification of the project model (instead it met the requirements of upward accountability within a management hierarchy). In fact the project did not itself need to provide such analysis since its data were produced within a powerful interpretative community constituted by the wider circle of consultants, donor representatives, technical experts or KBCL senior management – all firmly committed to the project's participatory model in one way or another and the meanings it imposed.

Most visitors remained ignorant of the contradictions of the project or unable to criticize the dominant interpretations offered. Every new engagement with the project, including my own critical monitoring of progress in 'participation', served only to add resilience to the model and its core assumptions. Nobody assumed that participation was easy or the project faultless.

Critical writing on the project could be routinely included in information packs, mildly raising eyebrows, but mostly adding extra endorsement to the model by demonstrating openness to criticism. Success was stable, and in the context of donor policy commitments to poverty and participation, rare. Very few senior donor administrators were not taken to this flagship project. In the UK, the project manager was honoured, and in India the project was invited by government to advise on the design of a new large-scale national watershed development programme.

At the same time the project model derived support 'from below'. The Bhil tribal members of the project's selected villages were not passive victims of imposed development that failed to meet their needs. Rather they participated in and concurred with project representations of their needs and their role as 'participants', because only by doing so could they make legitimate claims on project resources, gain access to important benefits (low-interest credit, agro-inputs, pumps, tree nurseries and wage labour, etc.) and win locally influential project patrons. Field staff, by delivering desirable goods and schemes and work, won support from locals – who agreed to 'participate', attend meetings, train as volunteers, host visitors, to save and make contributions, do things for the poor, willingly participate in the hosting of the project visits, donor monitoring missions or evaluation studies, and in other ways to validate both the wider project and staff performance within it. The 'participatory' goals of self-help, local control, low subsidies, local contributions and cost recovery may have been far from self-evident development ideals to villagers accustomed to maximizing gains from high-subsidy state programmes. But then villages in their dealing with local staff had little need to engage with the ideals of the project's participatory 'high culture'– the language of representation rather than operation.

But there was a cost to success, a cost which those 'too participatory' staff who resisted organizational imperatives towards patronage believe that they bore in seeking to resolve the contradictions of participation. While these project workers too endorsed the model, they spoke to me of the frustration and disillusionment experienced within the operational system of the project. Resented by the project as poor implementers, and by villagers as weak patrons, such staff did not then have the luxury of my own type of back-seat critical commentary. Several claim that they resigned from the project out of frustration. Several took the project model with them, set up independent NGOs and began working locally towards participatory development; although often in practice this meant substituting for the constraints of IBRFP those of the government watershed programmes that they were now funded to implement. Anyway, within the project, resignations, internal appointments and a prevailing insecurity of tenure conspired to produced a project team better able to mediate the core contradictions and win the rewards derived from sustained uncritical support from the donor agency and a remote international community, while at the same time institutionalizing a fear of failure.

This is not to imply the culpability of management. Indeed, the project manager perhaps had to work hardest of all to secure the relationships and mediate the contradictory organizational demands necessary to conjure success. He had the near-impossible task of satisfying immediate and urgent demands for short-term quantified outputs (schemes of all kinds) from his bosses whose high-publicity visits had regularly to be hosted, while at the same time delivering on the donor's agenda of sustainable self-reliance, as well as dealing with a multitude of technical recommendations from authorized and unauthorized visiting experts and consultants. He was expected to manage processes of decentralized development while complying with institutional procedures – especially in the area of personnel and finance – which practically speaking made this impossible. He was expected to allow and facilitate devolved power, when he himself was granted very little. He not only had to manage representations, but also constantly to manage his mangers, to be a hidden hand in boardroom battles between the donor/consultants and management, and in other ways to act as a buffer-mediator between a participatory project, a fertilizer company and an international donor. In short, the project manager was a critical broker of organizational cultures; his was a personally demanding task requiring social sensitivity and managerial talent, and made all the more difficult because of his own relatively junior position in the company hierarchy.

A particular institutional nexus made the marketing of success and the fear of failure a necessary management style. Success is perhaps always experienced as fragile (even though it may not be) and praise is reassuring. It is not at all surprising therefore that in its expanding network of links, project management emphasized those with more distant appreciative government officials, donor representatives and international institutions over peer NGOs, especially those working in the region and grappling with the same difficult dilemmas of participatory development, some of whom had the disconcerting confidence to say that 'if we are really honest we have to admit that even after thirty years of work in tribal villages we have failed to achieve our goal of participatory development'.

Impact – a crisis in representation?

The apparently secure foundation of IBRFP project success was, itself, challenged in 1995 when the project faced its *mid-term evaluation*. The report of the independent evaluation study was most striking in its refusal to accept the prevailing criterion of success – namely the concept of 'participation' itself – or to accept the assumptions of the model, namely that more participation equals better programmes and impact. Indeed, the report criticized the project for having *too much* participation and too little impact. The evaluation team was struck by the strong normative stress on participation as the principal project idea and objective, but the isolation of this from concern with people's livelihoods about which the project simply lacked adequate information. The team was perceptive, and the first outsiders to pick up on the self-referring nature of the project's discourse of participation.

Their report coincided with new indications (in the mid-1990s) of donor disenchantment with 'participation', a re-evaluation of the benefits and cost-effectiveness of participation rather that what was coined as the alternative 'investment approach', and criteria of accountability that stressed impact. Participation was regarded by some as human resource intensive, time consuming, limited in scale, non-replicable and expensive. It was clear that the project had become the site for a contest between different development models. But it had to protect itself against the eroding impact of the new critique that assailed its core participation model. The main instrument for this would be information, and particularly a series of impact studies through which it would re-establish and reaffirm the relationship between participatory processes and impact on livelihoods, and, importantly, justify donor decisions in favour of a second phase.

As well as economic surveys of benefits from new crop varieties and soil and water conservation, a remarkably sustained and detailed set of village 'livelihood impact' studies were undertaken. These focused not on indicators of performance, but on what people ('the beneficiaries') had to say about changes they had experienced during the period of the project. Of course, these were influenced by hopes for the future, but they were far from wholly structured by project concerns, and there were plenty of critical comments. Among other things, a view of livelihoods emerged which departed from the dominant model, for example in the centrality it gave to wage labour, debt and seasonal migration (as against low agricultural productivity) in local livelihood strategies. These studies also drew attention to the extremely restricted nature of routine project monitoring, geared as it was to self-reporting success in participation and programme delivery.

Given my own rising sense of the project as a self-referring discourse, I was at the time surprised (and relieved) to find that overwhelmingly the village studies suggested that the project *was* perceived as important and having a significant *positive impact* in the villages in which it was working, even though the distribution of project benefits was uneven. Moreover, programme impacts were not always those expected. For instance, villagers – men and women – emphasized the importance of savings and credit groups set up in hamlets, while the results of impacts from new crop varieties or SWC [soil and water conservation] were more ambiguous. Some impacts were entirely unanticipated; for example, several groups of women valued the savings groups for their effect of reducing men's drinking and consequently domestic violence. A great deal was at stake in the findings of these studies.

Not surprisingly, a fair amount of controversy over methodology and interpretation, and the demand for follow-up re-studies, arose where findings were not in line with project assumptions. For the present, the point that I want to make is that despite a complex and conflicting body of information, the impact assessment studies not only affirmed project impact, but also did so in such a way as to realign the project with a new donor framework which emphasized livelihoods and impact instead of agricultural productivity and participation.

But while these studies confirmed the 'success' of the project, significantly they did not directly validate the participatory model, or investigate the relationship between project practices and the model (i.e. they could not distinguish impacts from patronage and programme delivery from those of 'self-determined change'). Indeed, by this omission, the central contradiction of the project could be evaded and project assumptions could be confirmed. This, indeed, was the case. As the project was reformulated for a second greatly expanded phase, its 'participatory' success appeared almost unassailable. The new project text endorsed project assumptions, smoothed out blemishes, and made contradictions invisible. As Quarles van Ufford and Roth (2003) note, the administrative discourse of the 'project cycle' allows the recovery of optimism. Failure can be relegated to the past, hope reserved for the future.

Conclusion

What can be concluded here? It can be said that participation is a politically desirable development idea to which institutions will sign up for different reasons; that its ambiguities allow contradictory objectives to persist within projects; that some of these contradictions make 'participation' an unimplementable idea; that participation can be made into a commodity and marketed; that it is not difficult to manufacture success; that 'local knowledge' is relational, produced by the interactions between project patrons and villager clients; and more. Above all I have suggested that 'participation' (and the participatory project) is primarily a form of representation oriented towards concerns that are external to the location. Such representations do not speak directly to local practice and provide little clue to implementation.

When first aired, the paper's analysis provoked a stormy response from my managerial and technical colleagues (although it equally won support from others). At one level it was misread as a critique of the project, an accusation of duplicity levelled at its management. But the critique implied here is above all levelled at my own efforts, as the consultant providing advice on how to turn 'participation' from policy text into meaningful practices. I certainly attempted, and to a degree succeeded, in negotiating practices from project theory, and frequently invoked the project's participatory model in arguments over practical matters such as staffing arrangements (the employment of women, village residence, pay scales), work schedules or development strategies (against subsidies, etc.).

But ultimately I was more concerned to impose a normative model and to protect it from the eroding effects of project reality, than to engage with that reality itself. In fact, after two or three years, events on the ground related less and less to the normative rules I was purveying. I would have been less surprised and a good deal less frustrated had it been clearer to me then that the project designs on participation *could* not primarily serve as guides for action. There were too many other pressing institutional needs and agendas to be met. I would have been less surprised that team agreements were rarely reached or implemented, that consensus on future action was deferred as key decision-makers (having to reconcile too many conflicting demands) adopted the tactic of absenting themselves from key meetings, that consultant recommendations were fully acknowledged but largely ignored; acknowledged that is as interpretive *framework*, ignored as guide to *action*. Consultant and donor engagements with the project regularly rearticulated the project rationale but rarely had any effect on practices. Major donor reviews, mid-term evaluations and visits appeared to have even less. My reports, workshops and discussions contributed to project representations and self-representation. They helped to establish valid categories for reporting and the interpretation (or representation) of events. But what they routinely did not do was orientate action. The more critical and ardent I personally became in engaging with the apparent gaps between the 'participatory development' model and practices, the more ineffective my contributions became. Clearly I was misunderstanding something fundamental.

What I was missing, of course, was an understanding of the project's 'participation' goals as a model for representation rather than implementation; indeed, the fundamental *unimplementability* and practical meaninglessness of the community self-reliance ideal. Moreover, my rearticulation of the normative goals of participatory development – my contribution of a rhetorically useful, but practically useless discourse – had made me complicit in this unimplementability. Let me illustrate this. Central to the project was the idea of 'enhancing community self-reliance through institutional development'. This came to mean establishing self-help farmer *groups* capable of independently organizing local development: managing financial resources (savings and credit), supplying agro-inputs (seed and fertilizer supply) or managing natural resources (e.g. irrigation and forest user groups) so that the project would *withdraw* its services from given villages and areas (Mosse et al. 1996). This concept, based on a model adopted from the wider objectives of NGOs in South Asia, became a core principle around which the project's social development strategy revolved. It was also a 'position' in an ongoing argument about the primacy of 'capacity-building' objectives over 'programme and patronage' approaches; a means to contain the technical enthusiasms of colleagues and to challenge the patronage-welfare approach of the project agency. But what it sought to challenge was far too fundamental to budge.

After all, the project's reputation, the validation of the myth of participation, the performance of local field staff, indeed the core rationale of the project from KBCL's point of view, were all based on its network of patronage and welfare, largesse and the delivery of an expanding range of high-quality programmes, increasingly through village 'volunteers' (*jankars*) who operated as the lower orders of the project delivery mechanism. The whole venture required the retention and extension of project power, not its transfer to people. This carefully controlled and intensively managed system was simply not going to be abandoned for the grave risks of allowing independent decisions and financial responsibility, local autonomy and the withdrawal of the project. Why would the KBCL project want to get rid of its best customers; and villagers a serviceable patron? Even assuming it wanted to promote farmer capacities, the project was part of an organization whose hierarchy and system of accountability were not able to take the risks necessary to devolve power to communities.

To be sure the effect of many of the project activities was to expand knowledge, increase confidence, develop new skills, and release a 'spirit of experimentation', but the idea of a systematic devolution of power and responsibility to tribal farmers involved an unreal image of the project as a flexible risk-taking agent, a facilitating presence, rather than a unit of a politically intelligent, strategically operating marketing organization, determined to retain a firm grip on the development process. The project idea of sustainable community development was initially forged (by myself among others) to underpin key negotiating positions in development policy arguments, and as a critique of dominating agrarian modernism. However, this bore little relationship to the institutional possibilities of this project structure, at this time, in this place. Examined critically, the self-reliance model involved a neo-orientalist delegitimizing of all forms of external dependence – subsidies, moneylenders, migration, agro-inputs, or the marketing of commercial crops – as deviation from the primacy of local control, and the protection of low-risk subsistence livelihoods.

Much to the frustration of many (including myself) the group-based *capacity model* (or some version of it) was (during my association with the project, i.e. up to 1998) never procedurally internalized in the project; although it remained a key element in the project's Phase II, newly underscored by a DfID Sustainable Rural Livelihoods model, with the language of 'social capital'. But as is becoming clear, it was quite unreasonable to expect this development goal to have been operationalized (at least within the prevailing institutional arrangement) since it was fundamentally at odds with what was driving the project – namely marketing-oriented networks of patronage.

So the way in which I (and others) constructed project 'failure' was just as ideological as the representation of 'success'; both in fact endorsed the same model and privileged it over practices. This produced ignorance of project impacts. So what if the model (or my version of it) fails? The project can still succeed. Indeed, a more pragmatic appraisal of circumstances – less shaped by ideological debates, or middle-class NGO intellectual distaste for Indian industrialist perspectives in general, let alone those of a fertilizer company – would have seen new avenues of patronage as advantageous in a remote tribal area, providing new input lines for improved technology, marketing possibilities, and a consistency between local needs and the organizational imperatives of KBCL, rather than the failure to meet objectives. These are, indeed, the very things happening – even as the project purveys images of participation and is represented/represents itself (at least to some observers) as either success or failure in terms of this validating paradigm of 'participation'.

Preoccupation with the elevated principles of self-determined change also ignores perhaps the project's most remarkable achievement, namely its identification and development of improved rice and maize varieties through a careful process of consultation and farmer-managed trials. The project benefits of improved seed inputs, assisted seed distribution and storage, mediated links to national and international agricultural research agendas have been highly significant – at least to the individuals or groups who have been lucky enough to receive project patronage.

In order to work, programme designs and policy models have to be transformed in practice, but they also have to be reproduced as stable representations. The impact of the IBRFP project would not have been achieved without an international validating framework, whether participatory development or 'sustainable rural livelihoods'; but at the same time in this form it would/could not have been implemented. The legitimacy, political support and continued funding of the project depended upon maintaining this model.

[Abridged from the original, which was published in Philip Quarles van Ufford and Ananta Kumar Giri (eds), *A Moral Critique of Development: In Search of Global Responsibilities*, Routledge, 2003]

Acknowledgements

This paper is informed by over eight years' work as a consultant (1990–98) supported by the UK Department for International Development (DfID) with the Indo-British Rainfed Farming Project (IBRFP). The views expressed here are my own and do not reflect those of DfID, 'KBCL' or the IBRFP project. Nonetheless I am grateful to all in the project who have given me ideas and critical feedback over the years, and in relation to this paper in particular, Steve Jones, Arun Joshi, P. S. Sodhi and John Witcombe.

References

Alvesson, M. (1993) *Cultural Perspectives on Organisations*, Cambridge: Cambridge University Press.

Apthorpe, R. (1997) 'Writing development policy and policy analysis plain or clear: on language, genre and power', in S. Shore and S. Wright (eds), *Anthropology of Policy: Critical Perspectives on Governance and Power*, London and New York: Routledge, pp. 43–58.

Fairhead, J. (2000) 'Development discourse and its subversion: decivilisation, depoliticisation and dispossession in West Africa', in A. Arce and N. Long (eds), *Anthropology, Development and Modernities: Exploring Disourses, Counter-Tendencies and Violence*, London and New York: Routledge, pp. 100–111.

Ferguson, J. (1990) *The Anti-Politics Machine: Development, De-politicisation and Bureaucratic Power in Lesotho*, Cambridge: Cambridge University Press.

Mosse, D. (1996) 'The social construction of "people's knowledge" in participatory rural development', in S. Bastian and N. Bastian (eds), *Assessing Participation: A Debate from South Asia*, New Delhi: Konark Publishers, pp. 135–80.

— (2001) '"People's knowledge", participation and patronage: operations and representations in rural development', in B. Cook (ed.), *Participation – the New Tyranny?*, London: Zed Books.

Mosse, D. et al. (with the IBRFP project team) (1996) 'Local institutions and farming systems development: thoughts from a project in tribal western India', ODI Agren Network Paper no. 64.

Porter, D. J. (1995) 'Scenes from childhood: the homesickness of development discourse', in J. Crush (ed.), *Power of Development*, London and New York: Routledge, pp. 63–86.

Quarles van Ufford, P. (1993) 'Knowledge and ignorance in the practices of development policy', in M. Hobart (ed.), *An Anthropological Critique of Development: The Growth of Ignorance*, London and New York: Routledge.

Quarles van Ufford, P. and D. Roth (2003) 'The Icarus effect: the rise and fall of development optimisms in a regional development project in Luwu District, South Sulawesi, Indonesia', in P. Quarles van Ufford and A. K. Giri (eds), *A Moral Critique of Development: In Search of Global Responsibilities*, Routledge.

Witcombe, J. R., D. S. Virk and J. Farrington (eds) (1998) *Seeds of Choice: Making the Most of New Varieties for Small Farmers*, London: Intermediate Technology Publications.

Wood, G. D. (1998) 'Consultant behaviour: projects as communities: consultants' knowledge and power', *Project Appraisal*, 16(1): 54–64.

22 | Whose voices? Whose choices? Reflections on gender and participatory development

Andrea Cornwall

Introduction

Holding out the promise of inclusion, of creating spaces for the less vocal and powerful to exercise their voices and begin to gain more choices, participatory approaches would appear to offer a lot to those struggling to bring about more equitable development. Yet claims to 'full participation' and 'the participation of all stakeholders' – familiar from innumerable project documents and descriptions of participatory processes – all too often boil down to situations in which only the voices and versions of the vocal few are raised and heard. Women, many critics argue, are those most likely to lose out, finding themselves and their interests marginalized or overlooked in apparently 'participatory' processes (Guijt and Kaul Shah 1998; Mayoux 1995; Mosse 1995).

Talk about voice and choice, about rights and entitlements, and about obligations and responsibilities, demands, above all, approaches that are sensitive to the complexity of issues of difference. Gender and Development (GAD) ought to be able to teach those involved with participation in development a thing or two. But the relationship between gender and participation is rather more fraught with tensions and contradictions than these commonalities might suggest. The practice of GAD is often rather top-down, superimposing particular (culturally specific, some might suggest) frames of reference and barely allowing for broader participation in agenda-setting or implementation. A simplifying worldview is thus projected on to diverse development situations, whether by superimposing essentialized images of 'woman-as-victim' and 'man-as-problem' or ignoring the lot of marginal men (Chant 2000; Cornwall and White 2000).

Problematizing the way in which 'gender' is used is essential for addressing the transformatory goals of participatory development. The practical equivalence between 'gender' and 'women's issues', and the narrow focus of 'gender relations' on particular kinds of male–female relations, obscures the analytic importance of gender as a constitutive element of all social relationships and as signifying a relationship of power (Scott 1989; Wieringa 1998). Points of tension between participatory and 'gender-aware' approaches to development arise from – and produce – rather different ways of engaging with issues of gendered power. In this paper, I explore dimensions of 'participation' and 'gender' in development, highlighting paradoxes of 'gender-aware' and participatory development interventions.

'Gender-aware' participatory development: tensions and opportunities

Tensions, commonalities and complementarities between approaches to gender and participation complicate any analysis of the gender dimensions of participatory development. Yet it is these very differences and similarities which provoke food for thought and provide entry points for the emergence of new hybrids, new alliances and new tactics for transforming existing practices. One of the most significant lines of tension runs across – rather than between – approaches to gender and participation.

Some participatory approaches, such as Participatory Action Research (PAR; see Fals-Borda and Rahman 1991) emphasize the structural dimensions of power, echoing the focus of some versions of GAD. These approaches seek to question 'naturalized' assumptions, whether discursive or ideological. With the goal of confronting and transforming inequalities, they introduce particular ideas about power and difference, either to create new spaces or transform existing ones. Applying structural models may serve to essentialize gender identities and relations. This can equally produce institutions that 'misbehave' (Harrison 1997), giving voice to elite women who may have little interest in their 'sisters' and deepening the gendered exclusion of others – notably younger, poorer men (Cornwall and White 2000). They can thus serve to reproduce existing relations of inequality between 'women' or 'men' (cf. Moore 1994; Peters 1995) and strengthen compacts between particular kinds of women and their menfolk (Harrison 1997), rather than build the basis for more equitable gender relations.

Other schools of thought, such as PRA, emphasize the importance of tuning into and building on people's own experiences, concepts and categories. Rather than importing concepts from elsewhere, they focus on enabling local people to articulate and analyse their own situations, in their own terms, and focus more on individual agency than on structural analysis. This opens up the potential for a more nuanced and less essentialist approach to issues of power and difference. By seeking to ground analysis and planning in local discourses and institutions, however, PRA-based participatory practices appear to offer the facilitator little scope for challenging aspects of the status quo that feminist practitioners would find objectionable. 'Local people' are presumed to know best, even if they advocate the chastisement of younger women who step out of line or indeed the repression of women considered to be 'loose' (Overs et al. 2002). With their emphasis on consensus, the institutions created as part of participatory development initiatives – whether committees, user groups, community action planning groups and so on – can exacerbate existing forms of exclusion, silencing dissidence and masking dissent (Mosse 1995; Mouffe 1992). The voices of the more marginal may barely be raised, let alone heard, in these spaces.

Women's participation in participatory development projects

The question of who participates and who benefits raises awkward questions for participatory development. The very projects that appear so transformative can turn out to be supportive of a status quo that is highly inequitable for women. Women's involvement is often limited to implementation, where essentialisms about women's caring roles and naive assumptions about 'the community' come into play (Guijt and Kaul Shah 1998; Lind 1997). The means by which women are excluded, equally, may echo and reinforce hegemonic gender norms, as well as replicate patterns of gendered exclusion that have wider resonance. In this section, I look first at a classic mainstream 'participatory' initiative, to explore barriers to participation faced by women and ways they might be overcome. I then turn to a second project that highlights some of the dilemmas that arise in efforts not just to engage women's participation, but to make participatory projects more 'gender sensitive'.

Engaging participation, excluding women

Joint Forest Management (JFM) is in many ways a classic example of participatory development. It involves creating or adapting existing community-based institutions in order to devolve (some) opportunities for local people to participate in sectoral governance, as 'partners', 'stakeholders' and 'owners' (Leach et al. 1997; Poffenberger and McGean 1996). At a time when JFM was being lauded for its prowess with participation, feminist researchers revealed quite a different story (Agarwal 1997; Sarin 1998). Their analyses highlighted the shortcomings of JFM, as 'gender exclusionary and highly inequitable' (Agarwal 1997: 1374). Women were losing out on benefits from JFM and suffering higher workloads as a result of the difficulties in collecting fuelwood. 'To be labelled "offenders" and forest destroyers into the bargain,' Sarin charges, 'is making a parody of participatory forest management' (1998: 128).

Women's opportunities to influence decision-making in forest protection committees rest not simply on getting women on to these committees, but on how and whether women represent women's interests, whether they raise their voices and, when they do, whether anyone listens. Mohanty (2002) suggests that, in Uttaranchal, although there is an emphasis on a certain percentage of women being on the committee, much depends on the goodwill of its head, who is usually a man, and the forest bureaucrat, also usually a man. 'In the lack of any institutional mechanism to ensure this participation, it remains piecemeal, a gesture of benevolence on the part of male members in the committee and the forest bureaucracy' (ibid.: 1). Voice, she reminds us, does not automatically translate into influence. Sarin and Agarwal both document the consequences of lack of voice and of influence. Their studies show that, unable to exert influence over the rules for forest protection, women were effectively denied the usufruct rights that they formerly had.

These rules were formulated by men without either involving the women in framing them or proposing any viable alternatives for how the women could carry out their gendered responsibility of meeting household firewood requirements following forest closure (Sarin 1998: 127). By allocating places on committees to households and assuming equitable intra-household distribution of benefits, JFM institutions largely tended to reproduce existing structures and dynamics of gendered power and exclusion. As such, they served to exemplify 'the problem of treating "communities" as un-gendered units and "community participation" as an unambiguous step toward enhanced equality' (Agarwal 1997: 1374; Sarin and SAARTHI 1996). While those women who did participate in these new spaces gained new opportunities for leadership and for learning (Mohanty 2002), those women who were effectively excluded from decision-making exercised their agency elsewhere, resisting, rebelling and breaking the rules (Sarin 1998).

Two sets of issues arise here. First, the very real barriers to women's participation in decision-making are worth highlighting. Agarwal (1997) draws attention to familiar constraints: time; official male bias; social constraints about women's capabilities and roles; the absence of a 'critical mass' of women; and lack of public speaking experience. She cites a female member of a forest membership group: 'I went to three or four meetings ... No one ever listened to my suggestions. They were uninterested' (Britt 1993, cited in Agarwal 1997: 1375). As Mohanty (2002) points out, women end up taking on the burden of implementation instead, patrolling the forests at night and getting even less rest. What solutions does Agarwal suggest? Practical adjustments to meeting times and membership rules would, she argues, be easily enough addressed with gender-aware planning, although this alone would not enable women to exercise decision-making. Strategies to increase women's confidence and awareness of their rights are needed, in order for them to be more assertive in joining committees. For this, she suggests, the presence of a gender-progressive non-governmental organization (NGO) or women's organization is a major factor: membership makes women more self-confident, assertive and vocal in mixed gatherings. Other spaces outside the officialized public space of the committees thus gain importance as sites for confidence- as well as alliance-building (see Kohn 2000).

On issues that do affect women-in-general, such as access to fuelwood, it is important that women *qua* women are given space to articulate their concerns. Gender-progressive institutions can enable women to challenge their exclusion. Yet here a second issue arises: the extent to which the participation of particular women should be taken as representative of (both in the sense of speaking about and speaking for) women-in-general. Caution may be needed in moving beyond particular concerns that are clearly shared, to identifying female representation with enhancing the position of all women (Phillips 1991). The essentialisms that lurk behind well-intentioned efforts to increase women's participation as women are dangerous as well as wrong-headed: these can deepen exclusion while providing reassurance that gender inequality has been addressed. Moreover, as Mohanty contends, 'the mere presence of women in the decision-making committees without a voice can be counter-productive in the sense that it can be used to legitimise a decision which is taken by the male members' (2002: 1).

Increasing the numbers of women involved may serve instrumental goals, but will not necessarily address more fundamental issues of power. There is no reason to suppose that women, by virtue of their sex, are any more open to sharing power and control than men. Those who represent 'women's concerns' may reinforce the exclusionary effects of other dimensions of difference (Mohanty 1987; Moore 1994; Moraga and Anzaldua 1981). Installing women on committees may be necessary to open up space for women's voice, but is not sufficient: it may simply serve as a legitimating device, and may even shore up and perpetuate inequitable 'gender relations' between women. Female participants may not identify themselves primarily, or even at all, with other women; their concerns may lie more with their sons and their kin. To assume female solidarity masks women's agency in the pursuit of their own projects that may be based on other lines of connectedness and difference.

More controversially, what if, when women raise their voices, they do so to affirm ideals of femaleness that feminists might think of as 'gender oppressive'? What if the 'needs' women profess are connected with fulfilling their duties as wives and mothers? This cuts to the heart of the tension between the feminist agenda of GAD and the emphasis in participation on democratizing decision-making and supporting people's rights to make and shape the decisions affecting their lives, as the next case so vividly illustrates.

The dilemmas of choice As a gender-progressive NGO, Oxfam sought to address women's inclusion as part of their support to the Kebkabiya food security project in North Darfur, Sudan (Strachan and Peters 1997). Oxfam was concerned to avoid increasing workloads, alienating women from the community and causing a backlash from men in the name of empowerment. Men appeared to make all community decisions, and women's involvement was initially limited to helping to build seed banks. In the process of handing the project over to community management, almost all women decided on separate committees. Oxfam responded by supporting these women-only spaces, but also by hiring two female women's coordinators charged with the task of increasing women's participation in the project and representing women's concerns on the management committee. As the women gained confidence in these spaces and began to think about the need to be heard by men for things to change, Oxfam worked to persuade men of the value of women's involvement in the project. Eventually most committees merged.

The tactics used here are typical ones. Working with women's groups separately, then seeking to integrate them with the 'main', male-run committees, is a well-worn route to addressing the issues Agarwal (1997) raises of 'critical mass' and the confidence to speak out. Importantly, however, the Kebkabiya case raises other critical questions. Village women asked for practical help with things like handicrafts and poultry raising. The women's coordinators thought these projects should be supported – this, after all, was what women wanted. Oxfam worried that supporting traditional gender roles would reinforce women's inequality rather than empowering them. Instead, the project coordinator secured a special fund to support those women's projects he regarded as in line with project aims, as a means to securing women's involvement in the main project.

The village women in Kebkabiya were quite explicit about what they wanted. What is significant is that the NGO hesitated. Despite commitment to participatory decision-making, those with the power to allocate resources withheld support and then gave it piecemeal, with other objectives in mind. They believed that it would be in women's interests – even if the women themselves did not see it this way – to participate in the main project. This encapsulates a familiar but unresolved debate in feminist circles over 'objective' and 'subjective' interests (Jonasdottir 1988; Molyneux 1985).

If women prefer interventions that appear to reinforce their subordination, what does the gender-aware participatory development practitioner do? Fierlbeck's (1997) analysis of the concept of 'consent' as used in liberal theory addresses this dilemma. Choices cannot be simply argued away with reference to 'false consciousness'. Nor can arguing about the restricted contexts of choice be sustained, for it breaks down once we examine women's choices in other settings. But her conclusion fails to offer succour: 'we must be willing to probe and to query the choices and decisions of "autonomous" agents', for consent is 'in itself not only a moral construct but, more tangible, a potently political device for ensuring obedience' (ibid.: 43). This rather begs the very questions of agency that she seeks to answer.

Overt compliance may be a strategy enabling subordinates room to manoeuvre: the 'hidden transcripts' (Scott 1990) of those Sudanese women might provide a different perspective. It might well be that the women complied with how the development project sought to construct their interests as 'women' to secure goals that remained consonant with their own projects. Compliance might have given them room for manoeuvre while maintaining important relationships with men (Arce et al. 1994; Villarreal 1990). In any case, '... women's attachment to and stake in certain forms of patriarchal arrangements may derive neither from false consciousness, nor from conscious collusion but from an actual stake in certain positions of power available to them' (Kandiyoti 1998: 143).

Seemingly benign intervention may undermine the strategies of those for whom 'actual stakes' in current arrangements may involve more than initially meets the outsiders' eye. Inviting 'the community' to design their own interventions runs the risk, however, of reinforcing stakes that maintain a status quo that the marginal have tactics to grapple with, but no possibility of realizing strategies for change because they lack the power and agency to do so (see de Certeau 1984). These dilemmas are most apparent in contexts where participatory approaches are used to enable 'the community' to engage more directly in the development process. It is to this, and the implications for what kinds of development projects emerge, that I now turn.

From appraisal to action: gender in participatory planning

Just as the nominal inclusion of women appears to satisfy 'gender' goals, so too the use of participatory methods in planning processes may be tokenistic rather than transformative. Participation in planning ranges from more sustained and deliberative processes of engagement to one-off performances: all the way down Arnstein's (1969) ladder of participation from tokenism to delegated control. PRA is a widely used participatory technology that has become particularly popular as a tool for planning over the last decade, either through use to identify priorities or to construct community action plans. PRA is often conflated with 'doing participation'. The aim of this section is not to suggest that participatory planning can be reduced to the use of PRA. Rather, my focus on PRA here is both to enable me to further explore some of the tensions raised earlier in this paper and to engage with it as an approach that has gained such remarkable popularity in development work.

PRA would seem to promise a lot for work on gender. Its principles emphasize enabling unheard voices to be heard. PRA processes can create spaces where new rules for engagement provide new opportunities for voice and influence (Chambers 1997; Jones and Speech 2001). But a focus on gender is not implicit in the methodology, nor is it often an explicit element of PRA practice (Cornwall 1998; Crawley 1998; Guijt and Kaul Shah 1998). Where gender has been paid attention, it is often through deliberate emphasis on difference (Welbourn 1991) or through other tools alongside PRA (Guijt 1994; Humble 1998; Kindon 1998). The examples given below show that PRA can be used in processes that provide opportunities for poor women to empower themselves. Yet, used by facilitators who lack a concern with process, power and difference, it can exacerbate exclusion and cement existing relations of inequality.

Missing women, masking dissent

Mosse's (1995) insightful account of the early project planning stages of the Kribhco Indo-British Rainfed Farming Project (KRIBP) in India is one of the earliest, and best known, critiques of PRA from a gender perspective. Yet while it is often read as a generalized critique of PRA, it is actually rather more situated. The KRIBP project aimed to identify women's perspectives on farming systems, strengthen their roles in natural resource management and 'open new opportunities for women's involvement in household and community decision-making and resource control' (ibid.: 4). 'PRAs' were used to do so. These activities consisted of three days in villages using visual techniques and interviews with groups, before a plenary village meeting.

As public events, Mosse argues, these 'PRAs' did not permit sufficient articulation of dissent to allow marginal women a voice. Women's participation was minimal. The public location of activities made it difficult for women to attend, let alone participate. The decision to time these one-off events to capture seasonal migrants reflected a concern with maximizing male participation with little regard for women's availability. By effectively creating public performances, the team failed to recognize the extent to which the powerful might take control of the public arena, and the implications for the inclusion of other voices. Concluding that the public 'PRAs' he witnessed 'tend to emphasize formal knowledge and activities, and reinforce the invisibility of women's roles' (ibid.: 21), Mosse contends that 'women's agreement with projections of community or household interests will be tacitly assumed, and the notion of distinctive perspectives overlooked' (ibid.: 21).

Mosse's subsequent critique of what appear to be inherent limitations of PRA illustrates a rather different point. PRA methods in themselves are largely gender neutral. Powerful examples exist of PRA methods being used to facilitate gender awareness, such as Bilgi's (1998) use of daily time routines to enable men to explore and challenge their prejudices. Yet their appealing simplicity allows PRA methods to slot easily into the repertoire of technical methods fieldworkers already use. As Goetz notes of GAD: 'The search for simple formulae and tools to integrate gender-sensitive data and practices to projects and policies implies faith that technique can override forms of prejudice embedded in organizational cognitive systems and work cultures' (1997: 4).

If prejudice about whose knowledge counts and what counts as knowledge structures the use of these methods, then it is not surprising to find these assumptions in the outcomes of these PRAs. Mosse draws attention to the 'aesthetic bias' (1995: 24) of PRA techniques, suggesting that their formality marks out their use 'as the province of men' (ibid.: 19). But the team was not made up of anthropologists who would relish unstructured conversations. They were technicians. It is hardly surprising that they preferred neat charts. Moreover, most were men who may have been predisposed to paying more attention to what men had to say. PRA methods are treated as the source of the problem, but it seems more likely that the composition of the team conditioned their use of these methods and their reactions to what emerged from them. The standardization and rapidity of these PRAs, their public nature, the lack of female staff and the failure to anticipate these challenges effectively excluded women in early planning activities of the KRIBP. Clearly, institutional and personal as well as methodological issues played a part here.

How might women's perspectives have been voiced in this context? One barrier to women's participation is time. Holding sessions at times that women suggest as convenient at least allows the option to participate. Where time is needed most, however, is in building women's capacity to speak and to act. Rushed incursions into communities and hastily cobbled together action plans inevitably fail to address this. Consideration also needs to be given to locating PRA sessions in places where women feel comfortable. Mosse suggests that using PRA in non-public contexts would address exclusion from 'formal', public spaces. But public places are not necessarily less desirable places to hold discussions with women, as Hinton (1995) found in work with Bhutanese refugees in Nepal: women preferred not to have discussions in their own homes, as they were more likely to be interrupted or overheard. Even within the public domain, space can be made for those who are more marginal by structuring the process to include them. One tactic is to work with separate groups, each of whom presents their analysis in turn in open sessions. These strategies can make a difference and provide an important lever for change precisely because they are public. The challenge is to expand beyond the liminal performative domain of the PRA exercise to the everyday fora in which community decision-making takes place (Kesby 1999).

As the KRIBP experience demonstrates, one of the most powerful barriers to women's inclusion is entrenched attitudes and taken-for-granted assumptions among fieldworkers themselves (Chambers 1997; Parpart 1999). Requiring teams to work with women as well as men, younger as well as older people, has helped create awareness among fieldworkers of dimensions of difference (Jonfa et al. 1991; Welbourn 1991). Whether this effectively addresses gender issues remains open to question. Just as handing over control to a highly inequitable 'community' is hardly a recipe for transformation, simply enabling women to speak, as Parpart notes, is not necessarily empowering, and 'can disempower if it removes the ability to control the dissemination of knowledge' (1999: 263). What happens, then, when deliberate efforts are made not simply to 'include women' but to institutionalize measures to address gender equity?

Making space for difference Redd Barna Uganda's (RBU) experience with participatory development projects illustrates how attention to difference can be combined with community-wide participatory planning (Guijt 1997; Guijt et al. 1998; Mukasa 2000). Aware that plans made at the 'community' level often avoid contentious gender issues, Redd Barna created spaces in which gender- and generation-specific issues could be tackled within a broader participatory planning process. High-level institutional commitment enabled RBU to work with an approach that made gender and age differences explicit (ibid.) and emphasized addressing women's subordination directly.

Initial work focused on creating spaces for older and younger men, women and children to analyse their own situations as the basis for a community action plan (Guijt et al. 1994). Priorities were then discussed at a community meeting that shared the groups' findings. This was a significant innovation, but, as RBU found, dividing up communities and then bringing people together to create a single 'community action plan' created the space for younger women and children to speak, but not necessarily for them to be listened to. This suggested the need for a longer process of engagement rooted firmly in local ownership. RBU developed a five-stage planning process: from preparation, initial immersion, analysis of 'intra-communal difference' and planning to implementation with monitoring/evaluation (Guijt et al. 1998). Working with partner organizations, and relating closely to government, RBU supported this process with skills training, making the time to give plans solid foundations, and addressed inclusion through advocacy and conflict-resolution (Mukasa 2000; Sewagudde et al. 1997). Within this process, each group generated its own priorities and engaged in active deliberation on the issues raised by others before deciding which priorities to bring forward, allowing groups to consider the priorities of others without defending their own. Analysis at community level identified shared or group-specific priorities to be taken forward into community or group action plans, creating a layered action planning process whereby major shared concerns could be addressed at a community-wide level, while groups were supported to devise and implement their own plans.

Inevitably, conflicts emerged. Mukasa's (2000) insightful account of how issues of difference emerged in the village of Nataloke reveals the very real threats that such a process opens up. She gives an account of a community meeting that brought together peer groups of women and men of different generations, in which meeting conventions had been addressed to make space for the less powerful to speak. And speak they did. Older women chose a song to convey their views, one that condemned husbands who spent women's hard-earned money on alcohol, gambling and women. Mukasa reports a tense silence, broken by the voice of a respected elder:

> The women have actually raised real issues although it is in a wrong forum ... they have raised issues which we usually settle at 3.00 am [deep in the night]. The women have talked! YES, they have talked! They have brought out the issues that are a taboo in a public forum like this. In front of the visitors! But

since what they have talked is the undeniable truth, for me I appeal to fellow men that we should not become angry, instead we should say we are SORRY and begin afresh. (Muzee Mukama, cited in Mukasa 2000: 13)

Younger women began to speak out against domestic violence and control over their movements. Men fought back:

The response which came entirely from older men was sharply critical of their issues and insisting that they were to blame for their plight. They accused them of being frivolous, lazy and unreliable as wives. The men defended them- selves on polygamy using quotations from the Bible. They again accused them [the younger women] of washing their dirty linen in public by mentioning issues that are strictly private. (Ibid.: 13)

In a review eight months later, women declared their pride at gaining greater access to legal representation for cases of domestic violence, maintenance of children and inheritance. Men, however, spoke of women's violation of cultural taboos by bringing 'private' issues into public fora. There had been a backlash and younger wives had taken the brunt (Guijt 1997; Mukasa 2000). Women had been beaten as a direct result of spending their time in PRA meetings rather than on domestic work. The divorce rate was up as a consequence.

What was needed, RBU realized, was more of a focus on advocacy work with men; sensitivity to the timing and duration of meetings was equally a concern. A realization also emerged of the limitations of treating 'women' as a single group. Older women were giving younger women chores to do to prevent them from going out to meetings, for example, and enjoining them to behave themselves. Mukasa's account highlights the importance of disag- gregating 'gender' and paying attention to the 'differences within': in this case, barriers to participation faced by the younger women as a consequence of intra-household relations with older women. Again, the need for advocacy for the right to participate emerged from this experience; it also highlighted the importance of promoting not only an awareness of difference, but respect for the priorities of others as having equal value – what Cornell (1992) terms 'equivalence' as opposed to 'equality'. The implications for equity are spelled out by Kabeer: '... creating "access" is not enough. Equity requires that poorer women and other excluded groups are not just able to take advantage of such success but do so on terms which respect and promote their ability to exercise choice' (1999: 76).

Reflecting on RBU's experience, Guijt et al. (1998) note that while their focus on age and gender has proved a powerful way to initiate change, it also masked other differences, notably economic differences. Kabeer's point about the terms on which exclusion is addressed is significant. Just as dividing communities along externally defined axes of difference can obscure the intersections between these and other differences, it may take for granted forms of commonality that fail to match people's own concerns, connections and agendas. This raises questions about the salience of a focus on particular axes of difference, such as gender, rather than on dimensions and positions of powerlessness. I will return to this point.

Nevertheless, the Redd Barna case powerfully illustrates how PRA can help address the exclusion of women's voices, raise issues of gendered power, and destabilize 'commonsense' notions about sexual difference. As Kabeer's (1999) analysis of 'empowerment' makes clear, however, it is only when analysis moves beyond the everyday materialities of people's lives to explore issues of gendered power that other choices become imaginable. To do so requires moving beyond the comfort of consensus. It also requires institutional commitment to supporting a longer-term process of social change rather than 'quick fix' development solutions. Participation in policy paradoxically offers both prospects of more lasting change and the domain in which 'quick fix' participation has been most evident in recent years. It is to this that I now turn.

Lending voice? Participation, gender and policy

Over the course of the 1990s, growing awareness of the limited scope of participatory 'islands of success' projects led to the use of participatory methods and processes to influence policy processes. This chimed with shifts in mainstream development discourse that saw a greater recognition of the need to engage with the state, and a convergence of elements of the good governance agenda with a focus on citizen participation (Cornwall 2000a; Gaventa 2002).

Popularized by the World Bank and supported by bilateral agencies and INGOs, Participatory Poverty Assessments (PPAs) gained ascendancy in the 1990s as a means of tapping into poor people's concerns and representing their 'voices' to policy-makers (Booth et al. 1998; Brock 2002; Norton and Stephens 1995; Robb 1999). In some cases, PPAs have simply involved the short-cut use of rapid qualitative techniques. In others there have been more active efforts to bridge the gap between policy-makers and those whom policies affect by engaging a diversity of actors in the research process. 'New generation' PPAs have tended to be more inventive and strategic, opening up spaces for engagement by local government officials and NGOs, 'street-level bureaucrats' who play vital, often unacknowledged, roles in shaping policy (Grindle and Thomas 1991; Lipsky 1980). Perhaps the best-known and most successful of these efforts, the Consultations with the Poor project (Narayan et al. 2001), captured the limelight through its use of sound-bites gleaned through rapid PRA-style encounters with 'the poor' (Brock 2002; Rademacher and Patel 2002). While the extent to which these processes deserve the label 'participatory' remains a moot point, they are especially interesting sites in which to examine some of the assumptions, tensions and challenges of addressing gender.

Two salient issues arise from earlier discussions. First, participatory processes tend to be as 'gender sensitive' as those who facilitate them. Second, gender work tends to make the presumption that when women participate they become the flag-bearers for 'gender issues'; GAD discourse is peppered with gender myths about female solidarity and general community-minded selflessness. Robb claims that 'PPAs are responding to the challenge of inclusion by directly representing the views of the poor to policy-makers' (1999: xii). Yet to claim that the 'views of the poor' are directly represented in these documents would be disingenuous. The 'politics of the encounter' (Jonfa et al. 1991) and the processes of editing and editorializing PPA reports are hardly unmarked by the positionality and perspectives of PPA facilitators. Whether and how gender issues are raised, then, would seem to depend on the agency of those who shape this process and on their understanding of 'gender'. It is with this that the next section is concerned.

Gender in participatory poverty assessment and poverty reduction strategies
Participatory poverty research has highlighted 'intangible' aspects of poverty and given vivid accounts of the differences in poor women's and men's experiences. The UNDP Shinyanga PPA (UNDP/IDS 1998) raised a range of issues, from domestic violence to the impact of male alcohol consumption on household well-being. The Zambia PPA (Milimo and Norton 1993) provided compelling arguments for the disaggregation of the category of 'female-headed household', which the Ugandan Participatory Poverty Process (UPPAP 1999) has taken up. The South Africa PPA focused directly on women's experiences in heterosexual relationships and on a definition of poverty as powerlessness (May 1998). Domestic violence, marital instability, tensions within family relations, lack of legal rights for women (particularly over property), insecurity and concerns about personal safety all emerge, as they do in the 'Consultations with the Poor' project (Narayan et al. 2001).

Whether these findings emerge in the framing of policy, however, depends on how gender is interpreted, something about which there appears to be little consistency (Whitehead and Lockwood 1998). If 'gender' means 'ask the women too', then the product of PPAs will likely be gender-disaggregated data that have been 'gathered' with little attention to gender dynamics, gender relations or the contexts in which the data were produced. If, as is most frequently the case, 'gender' refers to 'women's issues', it would not be surprising to see findings concerning women's access to resources, perhaps some dimensions of institutionalized disprivilege, and suggestions regarding interventions like women's groups or the provision of credit. Razavi and Miller argue that 'the situation of women cannot be improved simply by "asking the women themselves" what their interests are' (1995: 38). The deliberative potential of PPAs is under-realized, exacerbated by the tensions between eliciting local versions and engaging in critical reflection. As Kandiyoti argues: 'Taking "naturalized" categories at face value may enhance adequate communication and promote so-called "bottom-up" approaches to development which are sensitive to local constructions of gender, but it does not necessarily further the goal of putting them into question' (1998: 146).

What is evident from the treatment of gender in many PPAs is that these 'naturalized' categories remain largely unquestioned. The dilemmas of the Kebkabiya project have particular resonance here, as the versions produced in these consultative exercises may go no farther than reaffirming normative constructions. It might be wondered to what extent more marginal women would risk speaking out in brief encounters that generally last no more than a few days: it is easy to seek out 'women's voices' and hear only the more prominent among them. The depth of insight gained in the process is questionable, especially without the contextual knowledge to situate who speaks and what they speak about. And the agency of the facilitator is obscured by the pervasive imagery in PPAs of neutral facilitators simply listening and recording poor people's voices. As in the KRIBP project, Lebrun's (1998) study of the UNDP-funded Shinyanga PPA demonstrates the extent to which fieldworkers' conduct influences what emerges. Her work highlights the limitations of pervasive assumptions of gender-based solidarity between female fieldworkers and local women:

> By being an urban-dweller, working in the formal sector, educated, and from a middle-class background, the female fieldworker had good reason to feel closer to her male colleagues, rather than to village women ... it is also a better move in terms of personal career development to express solidarity with a male colleague, rather than entering into conflict with them on gender issues, especially if the woman holds a lower position than her male colleagues in the hierarchy of the district bureaucracy. (Ibid.: 26)

As this example shows, getting an awareness of gender into the process of generating knowledge for policy is more complex than getting people to use the right tools to gather information. Issues of subjectivity and positionality may have just as much influence on what emerges. Influencing policy, in any case, depends on more than simply feeding information to policy-makers (Keeley and Scoones 1999); getting data on gender issues will not ensure that these issues find their way on to the poverty alleviation agenda. Goetz's (1994) analysis of the ways in which information about women is taken up in development bureaucracies underlines the point that what policy-makers want to know tends to determine how information is used.

Whitehead and Lockwood's (1998) analysis of six World Bank Poverty Assessments (PAs), four with a PPA component, is a powerful example of the limited influence of gender-relevant insights on the shaping of policy recommendations. At every stage, gender issues slipped off the policy agenda. When it came to policy recommendations, gender barely made an appearance. As has become evident in recent reviews of gender in the Poverty Reduction Strategy Papers (PRSPs), this is a tendency that has not gone away despite all the bluster about participation that has accompanied PRSP processes. The attrition of gender issues with the move into policy becomes evident from other recent studies of PRSPs (McGee et al. 2002; World Bank 2001, 2002; Zuckerman 2002). Zuckerman argues that 'the majority of PRSPs produced to date weakly apply an obsolete WID [Women in Development] approach – mentioning a few female problems in isolation such as girls not attending school and women's reproductive health problems' (ibid.: 2). One reason for the lack of attention to gender, she suggests, is the presumption that participatory processes would feed into the PRSPs.

These analyses reinforce the point that what is needed is not simply good tools or good analysis, but advocacy, persistence and influence to accompany the process all the way through to the writing stage. Zuckerman (ibid.) contends that in UPPAP, regarded by many as a very participatory process, the efforts made to address gender were undone at the final synthesis stage. By the time it came to the PRSP, gender had gone missing. In the contrasting example of Rwanda, she argues, advocacy at every stage of the process made the difference. The Rwandan Ministry of Gender and the Promotion of Women played an instrumental role, employing tactics such as co-sponsoring a workshop with the Ministry of Economics and Finance at which a wide range of stakeholders applied gender analysis tools to formulate recommendations on integrating gender into the PRSP, and establishing an inter-agency 'PRSP engendering [sic] committee' which included the PRSP writing team director.

Whitehead and Lockwood (1998) and Zuckerman (2002) draw attention to the role that those who write PPA reports and the PRSPs play in framing the 'voices' they claim to represent. Their analysis makes clear – once again – that without an explicit focus on gender issues, they can simply disappear from view. While Zuckerman's analysis focuses more on tactics for advocacy for gender issues, Whitehead and Lockwood argue that what is needed to make a difference is a gender-focused conceptual lens through which to 'read' empirical findings about the differential effects of poverty on men and women.

Conclusion: making more of a difference

Unless efforts are made to enable marginal voices to be raised and heard, claims to inclusiveness made on behalf of participatory development will appear rather empty. Requiring the representation of women on committees or ensuring women are consulted are necessary but not sufficient. Working with difference requires skills that have been under-emphasized in much recent participatory development work: conflict resolution, assertiveness training (Guijt and Kaul Shah 1998; Mosse 1995; Welbourn 1996). The need for advocacy on gender issues is evident, at every level. Yet there is perhaps a more fundamental obstacle in the quest for equitable development. The ethic of participatory development and of GAD is ultimately about challenging and changing relations of power that objectify and subjugate people. Yet 'gender' is framed in both participatory and 'gender-aware' development initiatives in ways that continue to provide stumbling blocks to transforming power relations.

Kandiyoti notes 'the blinkering and distortion that may result from the importation of Western feminist concerns and units of analysis into gender and development writing' (1998: 146). She argues for the need to 'remain agnostic' over the value of 'gender' if it obscures the diversity of social life and the contexts within which social categories have meaning. Where 'addressing gender' simply involves gathering and presenting sex-disaggregated data, then gender-blindness may be replaced with gender-blinkeredness. This does nobody any good. Yet the category 'gender' remains useful, precisely because it signifies an aspect of all social relationships and a relation of power (Scott 1989). What is at issue here is the slippage between 'gender' and 'women' and the ways in which 'gender relations' come to be understood.

Making a difference calls for an approach that can deal with the diversity of experiences and interactions that are part of everyday life, rather than imposing categories and concepts from conventional 'gender' approaches. To do so calls for strategies that are sensitive to local dynamics of difference and that build on the 'gender issues' that men as well as women can identify with and mobilize around – like gender violence, safe motherhood – rather than essentializing sexual difference (Cornwall 2000b; Greig 2000). In this, I follow Mouffe (1992), in suggesting that identities are always contingent and depend on specific forms of identification. Rather than presupposing some kind of homogeneous identity, then, looking at the ways in which people identify themselves with others or with particular issues can provide a more effective basis for advocacy and for action.

The challenge is to hold together – rather than dispense with, or completely erase – a politics of difference that is premised on the contingent, situational identity claims that make an identification with 'women's issues' possible, with a politics in which identifications provide the basis for action on commonly held concerns. This would not preclude a direct focus on issues that women-in-general might commonly identify with – for example, property rights. But it would go beyond the assumption that all women identify with 'gender issues' and that bringing about change is a zero-sum game in which women-in-general are pitted against men-in-general. It would recognize that some men may also be affronted by the exclusion of women and may prove important allies. Moreover it would tackle some of the consequences of defining interventions in terms that fail to embrace the needs of people who fall outside the boundaries created by assumptions about 'women's needs'.

While the tensions outlined at the start of this paper continue to provide obstacles, they also present opportunities. Seeking to challenge and transform relations of power that turn difference into hierarchy is a common thread that can bring together feminist and participatory practitioners' concerns with voice and choice. Participatory approaches have much to offer, but will make a difference only if they're used with sensitivity to issues of difference. Rather than the 'add women and stir' approach to addressing gender, what is needed are strategies and tactics that take account of the power effects of difference, combining advocacy to lever open spaces for voice with processes that enable people to recognize and use their agency. Whether by reconfiguring the rules of interactions in public spaces, enabling once silenced participants to exercise voice, or reaching out beyond the 'usual suspects' to democratize decision-making, such processes can help transform gender-blindness and gender-blinkeredness into the basis for more productive alliances to confront and address power and powerlessness.

[Abridged version of an article originally published in *World Development*, 31(8), August 2003, pp. 1325–42]

Acknowledgements

Many thanks to Jo Doezema and Naomi Hossain for their research assistance. I would like to thank Karen Brock, Robert Chambers, John Gaventa, Anne-Marie Goetz, Irene Guijt, Naila Kabeer and Shahra Razavi for conversations and comments that helped me clarify some of the ideas that are expressed here. This paper builds substantially on an earlier and longer background paper, commissioned by UNRISD for the Copenhagen Plus Five conference in Geneva, 2000, published as an IDS discussion paper and in Shahra Razavi (ed.), *Shifting Burdens: Gender and Agrarian Change under Neoliberalism*, Kumarian Press, May 2002.

References

Agarwal, B. (1997) 'Re-sounding the alert – gender, resources and community action', *World Development*, 25: 1373–80.

Arce, A., M. Villarreal and P. de Vries (1994) 'The social construction of rural development: discourses, practices and power', in D. Booth (ed.), *Rethinking Social Development Theory: Research and Practice*, London: Longman.

Arnstein, S. (1969) 'A ladder of citizen's participation', *Journal of the American Institute of Planners*, 35(7): 216–24.

Bilgi, M. (1998) 'Entering women's world through men's eyes', in I. Guijt and M. Kaul Shah (eds), *The Myth of Community: Gender Issues in Participatory Development*, London: Intermediate Technology Publications, pp. 93–9.

Booth, D., J. Holland, J. Hentschel, P. Lanjouw and A. Herbert (1998) *Participation and Combined Methods in African Poverty Assessment: Renewing the Agenda*, London: DfID, February.

Brock, K. (2002) 'Introduction', in *Knowing Poverty: Critical Reflections on Participatory Research and Policy*, London: Earthscan, pp. 1–13.

Chambers, R. (1997) *Whose Reality Counts? Putting the First Last*, London: Intermediate Technology Publications.

Chant, S. (2000) 'From "woman-blind" to "man-kind": should men have more space in gender and development?', *IDS Bulletin*, 31: 7–17.

Cornell, D. (1992) 'Gender, sex and equivalent rights', in J. Butler and J. W. Scott (eds), *Feminists Theorize the Political*, London: Routledge, pp. 280–96.

Cornwall, A. (1998) 'Gender, participation and the politics of difference', in I. Guijt and M. Kaul Shah (eds), *The Myth of Community: Gender Issues in Participatory Development*, London: Intermediate Technology Publications, pp. 46–57.

— (2000a) 'Beneficiary, consumer, citizen: changing perspectives on participation and poverty reduction', SIDA Studies 2, Stockholm: SIDA.

— (2000b) 'Missing men? Reflections on men, masculinities and gender and development', *IDS Bulletin*, 31: 18–27.

Cornwall, A. and S. White (eds) (2000) 'Men, masculinities and development: politics, policies and practice', *IDS Bulletin*, 31(2).

Crawley, H. (1998) 'Living up to the empowerment claim? The potential of PRA', in I. Guijt and M. Kaul Shah (eds), *The Myth of Community: Gender Issues in Participatory Development*, London: Intermediate Technology Publications, pp. 24–34.

De Certeau, M. (1984) *The Practice of Everyday Life*, Berkeley: University of California Press.

Fals-Borda, O. and M. A. Rahman (1991) *Action and Knowledge: Breaking the Monopoly with Participatory Action Research*, New York: Apex Press.

Fierlbeck, K. (1997) 'Getting representation right for women in development: accountability, consent and the articulation of women's interests', in A.-M. Goetz (ed.), *Getting Institutions Right for Women in Development*, London: Zed Books, pp. 31–43.

Gaventa, J. (2002) 'Introduction: exploring citizenship, participation and accountability', *IDS Bulletin*, 33: 1–11.

Goetz, A.-M. (1994) 'From feminist knowledge to data for development: the bureaucratic management of information on women and development', *IDS Bulletin*, 25: 27–36.

— (1997) *Getting Institutions Right for Women in Development*, New York: Zed Books.

Greig, A. (2000) 'The spectacle of men fighting', *IDS Bulletin*, 31: 28–32.

Grindle, M. and J. Thomas (1991) *Public Choices and Policy Change*, Baltimore, MD: Johns Hopkins University Press.

Guijt, I. (1994) 'Making a difference: integrating gender analysis into PRA', *RRA Notes*, 19: 49–55.

— (1997) 'Impacts and institutions, partners and principles: third review of the development and use of participatory rural appraisal and planning', Kampala: Redd Barna.

Guijt, I. and M. Kaul Shah (1998) 'Waking up to power, conflict and process', in I. Guijt and M. Kaul Shah (eds), *The Myth of Community: Gender Issues in Participatory Development*, London: Intermediate Technology Publications.

Guijt, I., T. Kisadha and A. Fuglesang (eds) (1994) 'It is the young trees that make a thick forest', London and Kampala: IIED/RBU.

Guijt, I., T. Kisadha and G. Mukasa (1998) 'Agreeing to disagree: dealing with age and gender in Redd Barna Uganda', in I. Guijt and M. Kaul Shah (eds), *The Myth of Community: Gender Issues in Participatory Development*, London: Intermediate Technology Publications, pp. 228–42.

Harrison, E. (1997) 'Fish, feminists and the FAO: translating "gender" through different institutions in the development process', in A. M. Goetz (ed.), *Getting Institutions Right for Women in Development*, New York: Zed Books.

Hinton, R. (1995) 'Trades in different worlds: listening to refugee voices', *PLA Notes*, 24: 21–6.

Humble, M. (1998) 'Assessing PRA for implementing gender and development', in I. Guijt and M. K. Shah (eds), *The Myth of Community*, London: IT Publications.

Jonasdottir, A. K. (1988) 'On the concept of interest, women's interests and the limitations of interest theory', in K. B. Jones and A. K. Jonasdottir (eds), *The Political Interests of Gender*, London: Sage.

Jones, E. and Speech (Society for People's Education and Economic Change) (2001) 'Of other spaces: situating participatory practices: a case study from southern India', IDS Working Paper no. 137, Brighton: Institute of Development Studies.

Jonfa, E., H. M. Tebeje, T. Dessalegn, H. Halala and A. Cornwall (1991) 'Participatory modelling in North Omo, Ethiopia: investigating the perceptions of different groups through models', *RRA Notes*, 14: 24–5.

Kabeer, N. (1999) 'The conditions and consequences of choice: reflections on the measurement of women's empowerment', Mimeo, Institute of Development Studies, Brighton.

Kandiyoti, D. (1998) 'Gender, power and contestation: rethinking bargaining with patriarchy', in C. Jackson and R. Pearson (eds), *Feminist Visions of Development*, London: Routledge, pp. 135–51.

Keeley, J. and I. Scoones (1999) 'Understanding environmental policy processes: a review', IDS Working Paper no. 89, Brighton: Institute of Development Studies.

Kesby, M. (1999) 'Beyond the representational impasse? PRA praxis in the context of gender focused HIV research in rural Zimbabwe', Seminar presentation, Institute of Development Studies, Brighton.

Kindon, S. (1998) 'Of mothers and men: questioning gender and community', in I. Guijt and M. Kaul Shah (eds), *The Myth of Community: Gender Issues in Participatory Development*, London: Intermediate Technology Publications, pp. 131–40.

Kohn, M. (2000) 'Language, power and persuasion: toward a critique of deliberative democracy', *Constellations*, 7(3): 408–29.

Leach, M., R. Mearns and I. Scoones (eds) (1997) 'Community based sustainable development: consensus or conflict', *IDS Bulletin*, 28(4).

Lebrun, N. (1998) 'The politics of needs interpretation at the grassroots: the role of fieldworkers in addressing gender issues in the Tanzanian UNDP PPA, Shinyanga 1997–98', Unpublished MPhil dissertation, Institute of Development Studies, Brighton.

Lind, A. (1997) 'Gender, development and urban social change: women's community action in global cities', *World Development*, 25: 1205–23.

Lipsky, M. (1980) 'Street-level bureaucracy: dilemmas of the individual in public services', New York: Russell Sage Foundation.

May, J. (1998) 'Experience and perceptions of poverty in South Africa', Durban: Praxis.

Mayoux, L. (1995) 'Beyond naivete: women, gender inequality and participatory development', *Development and Change*, 26: 235–58.

McGee, R., J. Levene and A. Hughes (2002) 'Assessing participation in poverty reduction strategy papers: a desk-based synthesis of experience in sub-Saharan Africa', IDS Research Report no. 52, Brighton: Institute of Development Studies.

Milimo, J. and A. Norton (1993) 'Zambia participatory poverty assessment: synthesis report', Mimeo.

Mohanty, C. T. (1987) 'Under western eyes: feminist scholarship and colonial discourses', *Feminist Review*, 30: 61–88.

Mohanty, R. (2002) 'Women's participation in JFM in Uttaranchal villages', Mimeo.

Molyneux, M. (1985) 'Mobilization without emancipation? Women's interests, the state, and revolution in Nicaragua', *Feminist Studies*, 11(2): 227–54.

Moore, H. (1994) *A Passion for Difference*, Cambridge: Polity Press.

Moraga, C. and G. Anzaldua (1981) *This Bridge Called My Back: Writings by Radical Women of Color*, Watertown, MA: Persephone Press.

Mosse, D. (1995) 'Authority, gender and knowledge: theoretical reflections on the practice of Participatory Rural Appraisal', KRIBP Working Paper no. 2, Swansea: Centre for Development Studies.

Mouffe, C. (1992) 'Feminism, citizenship and radical democratic politics', in J. Butler and J. Scott (eds), *Feminists Theorize the Political*, New York: Routledge.

Mukasa, G. (2000) 'Gender and participation: the case of Redd Barna, Uganda', Unpublished MA thesis, Institute of Development Studies, Brighton.

Narayan, D., R. Chambers, M. K. Shah and P. Petesch (2001) *Voices of the Poor: Crying Out for Change*, Washington, DC: World Bank.

Norton, A. and T. Stephens (1995) *Participation in Poverty Assessments*, Washington, DC: Social Policy and Resettlement Division, World Bank.

Overs, C., J. Doezema and M. Shivdas (2002) 'Just lip service? Sex worker participation in sexual and reproductive health interventions', in A. Cornwall and A. Welbourn (eds), *Realizing Rights: Transforming Approaches to Sexual and Reproductive Well-being*, London: Zed Books, pp. 21–34.

Parpart, J. (1999) 'Rethinking participation, empowerment and development from a gender perspective', in J. Freedman (ed.), *Transforming Development*, Toronto: University of Toronto Press.

Peters, P. (1995) 'The use and abuse of the concept of "female-headed households" in research on agrarian transformation and policy', in D. Fahy Bryceson (ed.), *Women Wielding the Hoe: Lessons from Rural Africa for Feminist Theory and Development*, Oxford: Berg, pp. 93–108.

Phillips, A. (1991) *Engendering Democracy*, Cambridge: Polity Press.

Poffenberger, M. and B. McGean (1996) *Village Voices, Forest Choices: Joint Forest Management in India*, Delhi: Oxford University Press.

Rademacher, A. and R. Patel (2002) 'Retelling worlds of poverty: reflections on transforming participatory research for a global narrative', in K. Brock and R. McGee (eds), *Knowing Poverty: Critical Reflections on Participatory Research and Policy*, London: Earthscan, pp. 166–88.

Razavi, S. and C. Miller (1995) 'From WID to GAD: conceptual shifts in the women and development discourse', Occasional Paper no. 1, Geneva: UNRISD.

Robb, C. (1999) 'Can the poor influence policy? Participation in the World Bank's poverty assessments', Washington, DC: World Bank.

Sarin, M. (1998) 'Community forest management: whose participation?', in I. Guijt and M. Kaul Shah (eds), *The Myth of Community: Gender Issues in Participatory Development*, London: Intermediate Technology Publications, pp. 121–30.

Sarin, M. and SAARTHI (1996) 'The view from the ground: community perspectives on joint forest management in Gujarat, India', Forest Participation Series no. 4, London: IIED.

Scott, J. (1989) 'Gender: a useful category of historical analysis', in E. Weed (ed.), *Coming to Terms*, London: Routledge.

— (1990) *Domination and the Arts of Resistance*, London: Yale University Press.

Sewagudde, J., G. Mugisha, R. Ochen and G. Mukasa (1997) 'Mixing and matching methodologies in Redd Barna Uganda', *PLA Notes*, 28: 79–83.

Strachan, P. and C. Peters (1997) *Empowering Communities: A Casebook from Western Sudan*, Oxford: Oxfam.

UNDP/IDS (1998) 'Human development report: Shinyanga Region, Tanzania', New York/Brighton: UNDP/IDS.

UPPAP (1999) *Uganda Participatory Poverty Assessment* (draft), Kampala: Ministry of Finance.

Villarreal, M. (1990) 'A struggle over images: issues on power, gender and intervention in a Mexican village', Unpublished MSc thesis, University of Wageningen.

Welbourn, A. (1991) 'RRA and the analysis of difference', *RRA Notes*, 14: 14–23.

— (1996) *Stepping Stones: A Training Package on HIV/AIDS, Communication and Relationship Skills*, Oxford: Strategies for Hope.

Whitehead, A. and M. Lockwood (1998) 'Gender in the World Bank's Poverty Assessments: six case studies from sub-Saharan Africa', Mimeo, Geneva: UNRISD.

Wieringa, S. (1998) 'Rethinking gender planning: a critical discussion of the use of the concept of gender', Working Paper no. 279, The Hague: ISS.

World Bank (2001) 'Gender in the PRSPs: a stocktaking', Washington: PREM, World Bank.

— (2002) 'External assessment of participation in poverty reduction strategy papers: a synthesis', Washington, DC: Participation and Civic Engagement Group, World Bank.

Zuckerman, E. (2002) 'Poverty reduction strategy papers and gender', Background paper for the conference on Sustainable Poverty Reduction and PRSPs, Berlin, 13–16 May.

23 | Ethnicity and participatory development methods in Botswana: some participants are to be seen and not heard

Tlamelo Mompati and Gerard Prinsen

Introduction

As participatory methods are increasingly preferred in the effort to develop communities, and as development initiatives increasingly take place at the grass roots, practitioners are discovering that ethnicity and ethnic identity are among the most important factors influencing the opportunities for change at village level in most African countries. This article discusses the understanding and practice of participatory development methods in Botswana. In particular, it examines the role that ethnicity plays in determining the involvement of the different ethnic communities in development planning and in community decision-making processes more generally.

After delineating the concept of ethnicity, the article describes the traditional consultation process in Botswana, with the *kgosi* (chief) as the key player in the process. It will be shown how this process systematically excluded ethnic minority groups. The implications of ethnicity for present-day village consultation in rural Botswana will then be analysed. In the concluding section, the authors identify five problem areas for participatory development methods and indicate how such methods could possibly address these problems.

To illustrate ethnic prejudice and exclusion, the article uses experiences from a Participatory Rural Appraisal (PRA) project that was commissioned by Botswana's Ministry of Finance and Development Planning in 1995/96. The general objective of this project was to assess the potential use of PRA in existing development planning practices. Teams of extension workers in four districts were trained in PRA and subsequently applied it in selected villages. Having produced village development plans through these exercises, which took about two weeks per village, the project also assessed their implementation after several months (Prinsen et al. 1996).

Defining ethnicity

Ethnicity can be defined as a social phenomenon concerned with negative interactions between cultural-linguistic groups (ethnic groups). 'It arises when relations between ethnic groups are competitive rather than co-operative'

(Nnoli 1995: 1). Ethnicity develops when ethnic groups compete for rights, privileges and available resources. It is characterized by strong feelings of pride, belonging and the exclusiveness of members of the group. Therefore, ethnicity often manifests itself in phenomena such as cultural stereotyping and socio-economic and political discrimination. Stereotyping does not allow people to be judged and treated as individuals in their own right. Instead, 'the other person is labelled as having certain characteristics, weaknesses, laziness, lack of honesty and so on, and these labels obscure all the other thinking about the person' (Clements and Spinks 1994: 14). These labels result in prejudice, which encompasses negative assumptions and pre-judgements about other groups that are believed to be inferior. As such, prejudice is rooted in power – the power of being a member of a primary group and feeling more important than people in other 'secondary' groups. Ultimately, the feeling of exclusiveness as a group, and the negative images held about other groups, lead to discrimination, which Clements and Spinks (ibid.) see as 'prejudice in action'.

Participatory development

Participatory development methods are born out of the recognition of the uniqueness of an individual as an entity who is capable of making unique contributions to decision-making. Currently, participatory methods are very much in vogue in development thinking. The entire spectrum of development agencies, from grassroots organizations to the World Bank, seems to have embraced the concept of participation in development planning and implementation (Chambers 1994a, b, c; World Bank 1994). The major actor who is expected to participate is the 'community', an entity that is hardly ever described beyond 'all those living in a certain geographic area'. However, although various authors have pointed out that a community is rarely a homogeneous entity (Butcher et al. 1993; Clark 1973; Plant 1974), very little research has been done to determine the precise nature and workings of the heterogeneous rural African village.

PRA is a method that seeks to maximize the equal involvement of all adult members of a community in planning their collective development. It is purported to overcome cultural, political and economic barriers to meaningful participation in development planning. However, the literature on this popular consultation method focuses almost exclusively on the stakes held by different material interest groups (rich versus poor, pastoralists versus settled farmers) or by men versus women (Mosse 1994). It deals far less with the cultural dichotomy of superior versus subordinate ethnic groups. This is probably a result of two factors. First, most writers on participatory methods in Africa are of European or North American origin. Even though they have extensive experience in a particular African country, they are less likely to comprehend the subtle details of ethnic identities in most of these countries. Indeed, the average child in a sub-Saharan African country, having been socialized to ethnic divides from birth, can probably multiply several times over the list of ethnic identities a European or North American is able to identify.

Second, the minority of sub-Saharan Africans who write on participatory methods may be hesitant to address the matter of ethnicity because the concept effectively undermines the foundations of their already rather weak 'nation-states' (Davidson 1992). Indeed, recent history in sub-Saharan Africa shows horrifying experiences of what happens when ethnic identity prevails over national identity.

Notwithstanding the above, the issue of ethnicity cannot be ignored when community participation is becoming a cornerstone for development planning. This is not only because most communities are composed of different ethnic groups, but because if participatory development efforts prioritize the most marginalized areas for intervention, as they often do, then it is likely that it is precisely these areas that are also characterized by strong ethnic divisions.

From the above, it is clear that ethnicity relates antagonistically with the basic concepts underlying participatory methods. Ethnicity has exclusiveness, prejudice and discrimination as core characteristics. Participatory methods, on the other hand, have taken liberal concepts such as 'one person one vote' and 'the freedom of one should not be to the detriment of another' as their cornerstone.

Socio-political realities of ethnicity in Botswana

By custom, the major ethnic groups in Botswana, called *Tswana*, were organized in villages according to distinct subgroups, such as *Bakwena*, *Bangwaketse*, *Bakgatla* and *Batlokwa*. However, villages were not necessarily formed of ethnically homogeneous groups of people. They were further divided into specific sub-ethnic groups (*merafe* and *meratshwana*) that were associated with particular wards according to kinship or common ancestry. In this context, *merafe* refers to people belonging to one of the *Tswana* groups that constitute the regional majority and *meratshwana* refers to all other ethnic groups. A ward was made up of a number of family groups or households, most of whom would be related to the ward head, while others would be family groups from other ethnic groups placed under the head's care (Ngcongco 1989).

The arrangement of wards within a village was such that the highly regarded wards were located close to the *Kgosing* ward (the main ward where the *kgosi* lived) and the ethnically poorly regarded wards were situated in the outskirts of the village. Thus, the subordinate ethnic groups were physically relegated from the social, cultural and political life of the village. The importance attached by villagers to this physical separation extends, at least in some cases, to the deceased. For example, one of the plenary sessions dealing with the village map in Artesia became hotly debated, as one of the villagers reproached the audience that his late aunt, related to the *kgosi*, was buried too close to the graveyard for subordinate ethnic groups. What was contested was whether the two graveyards were or were not too close to each other, not whether there should be two separate graveyards (Botswana Orientation Centre 1996a).

The inhabitants of the subordinate wards were marginalized in many respects. For instance, Datta and Murray (1989: 59) note that *Batawana* and *Bayei* tended to have a master–serf relationship, with *Bayei* seemingly '... accepting their lower status in that they would refer to themselves as *Makuba* (useless people), the *Batawana* term for *Bayei*'. Similarly, *Bakgalagadi* in the *Bangwaketse* and *Bakwena* areas show acceptance of their lower status by referring to the dominant groups as *Bakhgweni*, which connotes 'master'.

This pattern, in which the negative 'image of the other' of the dominant group is incorporated as the 'image of the self' by the subordinate group, completes a cycle of repression to which resistance can develop only with difficulty. If a subordinate group wished to oppose the status quo, it would have to start with the most difficult part of change: reversing its self-perception – that is, thinking of the world upside down (Freire 1972). The situation described above was observed during the PRA project.

The PRA process involved the selection and training of ten villagers in each village to assist in the proceedings and to lead project implementation when the PRA team was gone. As villagers were 'free' to elect their trainees, almost invariably members of the dominant ethnic group were elected. It should be noted that even subordinate ethnic groups generally tended to vote for a candidate of the dominant group. The well-entrenched belief among the ethnic minority groups was 'We cannot speak so eloquently and do not understand things'. In the particular case of Kedia, the authors learnt that once, owing to external pressure, a member of the subordinate ethnic group of *Basarwa* was appointed supervisor of a community construction programme in which most labourers also belonged to the subordinate ethnic group. Soon the labourers requested the *kgosi* to appoint somebody from his own ethnic group, claiming that their supervisor was often absent, could not manage the work, and drank too much. In short, they did not want one of their own group as supervisor (Botswana Orientation Centre 1996b).

As an almost inevitable consequence of these ethnic power imbalances, subordinate ethnic groups were systematically impoverished by being denied the right to own cattle and access to land and water. Consequently, their livelihoods were usually relegated to economically and ecologically marginal areas, and some groups, such as the *Basarwa*, were even forced to become hereditary serfs called *balata*, *balala* or *batlhanka* (Datta and Murray 1989). This relationship relegated *Basarwa* to the level of personal and private property.

Systematic impoverishment is a major source of concern for the ethnic minority communities in Botswana. The introduction of the Tribal Grazing Land Policy (TGLP) in 1975 is a case in point. This policy commercialized huge areas of formally communally owned land around the Kalahari desert, resulting in the annexation of land from the indigenous people of the area, particularly *Bakgalagadi* and *Basarwa*, and its reallocation to the more economically powerful members of the majority ethnic groups from all over Botswana. A majority of the indigenous people of the area were forced to work for the new master-landowners (Mogalakwe 1986).

In Kedia, for example, the PRA exercise stimulated a discussion about opportunities to develop a rather marginal 33,000-hectare area that was 40 kilometres away from the village but nevertheless belonged to it. The introduction of livestock, wildlife management and commercial production of veld products were suggested options. While the dominant ethnic group considered the ideas with enthusiasm, the suggestions were a source of major discomfort to members of the ethnic minorities. They used the land for hunting and for gathering veld products, and were afraid of losing access to it if it was commercialized (Botswana Orientation Centre 1996b).

Stratification of communities according to ethnicity is not only visible in the physical set-up of villages and the social, economic and political relations among ethnic groups, but is also enshrined and protected in Sections 77 and 78 of the Constitution of Botswana (Republic of Botswana 1965). These sections of the supreme law of the country legitimize the superiority of the eight so-called major tribes, all belonging to the *Tswana* (*Bakgatla*, *Bakwena*, *Balete*, *Barolong*, *Bangwato*, *Bangwaketse*, *Batlokwa* and *Batawana*). All other ethnic groups in the country are usually referred to as 'minor', 'subordinate' or 'subject' groups.

Although the Constitution explicitly mentions eight major tribes, the issue of ethnicity is downplayed under the motto 'We are all *Batswana*'. Thus, there is no official government record with data related to ethnicity. For example, population censuses do not contain reference to ethnicity. Therefore, it is difficult to determine how many people belong to a particular ethnic group or know the proportion of the *Tswana* to other ethnic groups in Botswana's 1.5 million population. Consequently, Hitchcock (1992) resorts to extrapolating such figures from 1946 census dating to the colonial Bechuanaland Protectorate Government, which describes 70 per cent of the population as belonging to the eight *Tswana* subgroups and the remaining 30 per cent to minority groups, most of which have their own languages (*Bakgalagadi*, *Balala*, *Basarwa*, *Batswapong*, *Bayei*, *Herero*, *Kalanga*, *Mbukushu*, *Nama*, *Pedi*, *Subiya*, *Teti*).

Consultation in traditional *Tswana* society

The understanding and practice of 'consultation' are not much different in Botswana than they are in the West. Consultation is a process through which decision-makers and planners solicit the views of the people for whom decisions are being made. An important feature of consultation is that the consulting party does not necessarily have to use the views of those consulted. Botswana had, and still has, an extensive consultation system to advise decisions. Traditionally, the key player in this process was the *kgosi* (chief). The *kgosi* headed the governance system, and was the custodian of the custom, culture and welfare of his people. He ruled over his subjects through ward heads who were appointed by him. The ward heads connected their own people to the *kgosi* and vice versa (Ngcongco 1989). However, they were more accountable to the *kgosi* than to their subjects.

Although the strong convention of consultation played an important role in checking the risk of absolutism on the part of the chief, nothing compelled him to consult his advisers. Consequently, while the *kgosi* would from time to time meet with his subjects to 'consult', this consultation meant predominantly the imparting of information or issuing of instructions.

The *kgosi* promulgated new laws at the *kgotla*. The *kgotla* is a traditional meeting place found in all *Tswana* communities, which the *kgosi* used 'to advise or admonish his followers as well as to impart information to them' (ibid.: 44). The persuasive skills and power of the *kgosi* in this regard were critical. So too was the role of the *malope a kgosi* (commoners who do things to be loved by the chief or to receive favours from him), who helped detect and discourage any dissenting views.

The following example from the PRA project illustrates the importance of the continuing role of the *malope a kgosi*. Ethnic conflict was rife in Artesia and the *kgosi* and the ethnic minorities upheld several conflicts. In order to circumvent the effects of power imbalance, the PRA project team organized separate sessions in the ward of the ethnic minority. This proved to enhance their participation greatly on the first day. However, on the second day the villagers observed that one of the village elders (*lelope*) noted down names of villagers who spoke out against the established order. Once villagers became aware of this, most of them withdrew from the meeting. In the evening, the conflict expanded, when all the villagers who were elected to be trainees threatened to quit. They informed the project team that the elder was summoned to the *kgosi* every evening to report on 'who said what'. They did not want to get into trouble with the *kgosi*. The problem was solved after extensive talks with all parties involved (Botswana Orientation Centre 1996a).

In practice, there was very little room for debate once the *kgosi* had issued his orders; 'the *kgotla* after all is not a participatory but a consultative institution' (Molutsi 1989: 115). Participation in this context denotes people actively taking part in the decision-making process, whereas consultation entails being informed about decisions to be or already taken. In short, the word of the *kgosi* was highly respected and was almost always final. Hence the *Setswana* saying '*Lefoko la kgosi le agelwa mosako*', meaning 'The word of the *kgosi* is to be supported and respected by all'. In this regard, the *kgosi* was regarded almost as an omnipotent being. As will be explained shortly, consultation in modern Botswana differs a little from the way it was conceptualized traditionally.

Ethnic exclusionism at the *kgotla*

Theoretically, all adult members of the community have unrestricted right of speech at the *kgotla*. This principle is reflected in the *Tswana* proverb '*Mmua lebe o abo a bua la gagwe*', meaning 'Everybody is free to speak out, and even to make mistakes'. However, practice in traditional communities was very different as subordinate groups were denied participation. The perpetuators took comfort in this practice by blaming the victim. For example, in the case of the discrimination practised by *Bangwaketse* against *Bakgalagadi*, the usual explanation given was that by nature *Bakgalagadi* are timid and bashful, and find it difficult to stand up and speak at gatherings (Ngcongco 1989).

The agenda of the *kgotla* meeting was the responsibility of the *kgosi*, and only on rare occasions could ordinary members of the *merafe* (not the *meratshwana*) add to the *kgosi*'s agenda through their ward heads. Participation, in the sense of 'having a say' in this kind of decision-making process, was restricted. Only a few people could participate, and these included the chief's uncles and brothers (who were also the chief's advisers) and members of the ethnically dominant groups. In an ethnically heterogeneous community, these restrictions were rigidly enforced. For instance, in *Bakwena* and *Bangwaketse* areas, *Bakgalagadi* were not, as a rule, expected to speak at the *kgotla*, even though they were free to attend like any other *Motswana*. 'As children in the home, they were to be seen and not to be heard ... *Bakgalagadi* were children and their overlords were the ones who could and did speak for them' (ibid.: 46).

Even the physical arrangement of the *kgotla* indicated its undemocratic nature. The *kgosi* sat in front surrounded by his advisers – mostly his male relatives and a few hand-picked village elders. Immediately behind the chief's advisers sat the *merafe* and behind them the *meratshwana*. This pattern was observed in all villages where PRA plenary sessions took place at the *kgotla*. The male members of subordinate ethnic groups hardly spoke, and then usually only when directly addressed. Women and youngsters of ethnic minorities almost never spoke. They were seen but not heard. When one of the PRA team members naively suggested once that the *kgosi* also solicit the views of people from the ethnic minority wards, the *kgosi* looked at them and replied: 'Ah, these people never come to the *kgotla*, I cannot see them' (Botswana Orientation Centre 1996a: 3).

In this regard, the *kgotla* provides a forum for the dominant ethnic groups to exercise power and authority. It is natural, therefore, that the groups in power will feel threatened when members of the subordinate groups attempt to speak in this forum, as this is viewed as undermining their power base. This point is illustrated in an interview conducted by Ngcongco (1989: 46) with a *Mongwaketse* elder who related an incident that demonstrated the undemocratic nature of the *kgotla*. 'A member of the *Bakgalagadi* who attempted to speak at a particular *kgotla* meeting was rudely pulled down by *Bangwaketse* who said: *"Nna hatshe o tla re tlholela."* This literally meant: "Sit down, you will bring us bad luck."'

The following example shows how a *kgosi* used a police officer to enforce this practice of ethnic exclusionism during the PRA pilot project. In Kedia the authors observed a participatory planning meeting in which one particular woman from a subordinate ethnic group spoke out loudly against discriminatory practices of the dominant group. Observably, she was helped in breaking gender and ethnic rules by a serious intake of alcohol, but quite a number of other participants were also rather inebriated. The *kgosi* quickly pointed at a policeman, who took the woman by the arm, lifted her off the ground, and brought her to the shade of a tree about fifty metres from the meeting place. Thereafter, the meeting continued as if nothing had happened. Participatory methods aim to change such practices by involving people directly in the decision-making processes that affect their lives and livelihoods.

Consultation in present-day Botswana

In the opening lines of a paper presented to a conference on democracy in Botswana, Mpho (1989: 133) observed that 'Democracy appears to exist in Botswana because the majority of the people belonging to the so-called "minority" tribes have remained peaceful and patient about their oppression.' However, this situation is changing. One reason for this change is the deepening socioeconomic inequality in the country. Botswana receives ever-increasing revenues from diamond mining and the country has risen from being a very low-income country in the 1960s (with a per capita income of US$22 at independence in 1966) to a middle-income country in 1995 (per capita income of US$3,082). Nevertheless, this wealth is very unevenly distributed, with the richest 20 per cent of the population receiving 61 per cent of the total national income, while the poorest 40 per cent, many of whom belong to subordinate ethnic groups, received only 9 per cent (MFDP 1997: 3). At the same time, however, the economic boom led to an extensive and well-developed infrastructure, which increased mobility and educational levels. This development empowered ethnic minorities to challenge the status quo. Increasingly, ethnic groups at the lower end of the ladder now organize themselves and voice protests, even though this is still incomprehensible to members of the dominant ethnic groups.[1]

Against this background of, on the one hand, a rather rigid ethnically stratified social order and, on the other, an increasingly mobile society in which traditional values are being eroded and in which subordinate ethnic groups question the status quo, the government has built a long-standing practice of 'consulting' villagers on development. Since independence in 1966, the government has formulated five-year development plans to inform and guide its path of development. Preceding the making of a new development plan, district-level extension teams visit all villages and hold meetings in which the villagers forward the needs and wishes they would like to see incorporated in the upcoming development plan (Byram et al. 1995). This consultation process takes place along patterns similar to those used by the chiefs. Every village has elected members for a Village Development Committee (VDC), which is a body charged with leading development programmes at village level. In ethnically heterogeneous communities, members of the VDC usually belong almost exclusively to the dominant ethnic group and the *kgosi* is an ex officio member. VDCs are similar, therefore, to the traditional union of the *kgosi* and his advisers. The *kgosi* and ward heads manage the community's internal relations while they gather in the VDC to deal with its relations with government. The exercise where government officers descend on villagers to 'consult' on development plans always takes place at the *kgotla*. The VDC does the groundwork by informing and consulting villagers beforehand, and as such the actual consultation exercise at the *kgotla* bears resemblance to a ritual – pleasing to those who feel comfortable with the customary social order but unappreciated by others.

This consultation process is now facing problems and increasing criticism from various sides. The number of villagers attending the *kgotla* is steadily decreasing. The chiefs complain nationwide that people no longer heed their calls to come to the *kgotla*. This may have two explanations. First, villagers from subordinate groups no longer wish to partake in a ritual in which they have no right to stand up and speak (while the chiefs no longer have the authority to enforce attendance). Second, villagers may feel their input to government's planning is not taken seriously because they hardly get any feedback nor see their input really influencing policies and practices. This problem arose during the PRA project, as described below.

A recurrent complaint of all the chiefs involved in the PRA project was that 'villagers no longer come to *kgotla* when I call them'. Indeed, a low and/or decreasing attendance of villagers at the *kgotla* was a continuous worry for the PRA team (Botswana Orientation Centre 1996a, b, c, d). The matter of low attendance at the *kgotla* has various reasons, one of which is a decreasing authority of the chiefs without the void being filled by others. On the other hand, the pilot project revealed extensive proof that villagers do not feel treated respectfully in the established consultation procedures. Group-interviewed respondents in eight of the nine villages researched almost unanimously concluded that they are 'treated like children' in consultations (Prinsen et al. 1996: 28).

Another criticism of the consultation process comes from government officers. With an increasing frequency and openness the government expresses its disappointment with the disappearing 'self-help spirit', one of the nation's leading principles (MFDP 1994: 7). It is concluded that *Batswana* have become increasingly dependent upon government to provide them with infrastructure and the commodities and amenities of life, without making any contribution themselves. Government sees proof of this in the ever-recurring 'shopping lists' that villages produce after the consultations.

The last criticism comes from planners and analysts. In their view, as government has invested heavily in infrastructure over the past two decades, development now needs to shift focus. First, '... the initiative must be seized by those in the private sector' because too few viable economic enterprises have emerged from the citizenry (MFDP 1991: 28). Second, the time has come to look at the quality of service provision or the 'poor productivity' of civil servants (MFDP 1994: 9). Both these areas need a forum for dialogue between citizens and the state that is qualitatively well beyond the present practice.

Conclusions: problems and opportunities

In view of the problems with the long-practised approach to consultation, the Ministry of Finance and Development Planning piloted Participatory Rural Appraisal (PRA) over thirteen months in 1995/96 in four of the country's ten districts. Besides trying to address the inherent inadequacies of consultation as practised in Botswana, the ministry also felt, in line with international trends, that 'there is significant evidence that participation can in many circumstances improve the quality, effectiveness and sustainability of projects' (World Bank 1994: i).

In the light of the above discussion, it will be clear that the issue of ethnicity was politically far too sensitive to be addressed explicitly in the PRA project. However, the practical experiences acquired during the project clearly revealed the tensions between different ethnic groups and the traditional consultation structures, on the one hand, and the Western liberal values underlying participatory methods, on the other. These tensions create obstacles for meaningful and effective participatory planning exercises. Sometimes during the project, PRA offered opportunities to surmount or circumvent these obstacles. However, there were also instances where it could not offer workable solutions. A preliminary inventory of the obstacles results in five categories of problems related to ethnicity that are listed below with some of the opportunities PRA offers to address them.

Physical segregation Subordinate ethnic groups may be invisible at first glance: their houses, their livelihoods and even their cemeteries may be only subtly separated from those of the dominant groups. Not only can this apparent invisibility lead to overlooking them altogether, but when participatory methods deal with the physical planning of a village, ignorance of minorities' physical segregation may further damage their interests. Even assisting in developing their marginal income resources may require scrutiny, as subordinate ethnic groups may lose their access to these resources to dominant groups once such resources become more attractive. To overcome these pitfalls, some PRA techniques (transects, random household interviews, farm sketches) take the facilitators (i.e. extension workers, planners and other professionals) away from its central meeting places. Provided these outsiders observe well and ask open questions (assuming that their guides feel free to talk in such informal settings), the outcomes of these enquiries may be brought up in plenary PRA reporting to the village at large.

Political exclusion Participatory methods usually require the establishment of a community-based committee to serve as a counterpart or complementary body to outside development agents. These committees play a central role in implementing and following up development activities. Generally, the fact that the community has elected the committees satisfies the participatory requirement by outside development agents of having empowered the community to be the local partner. However, it may well be that subordinate groups are effectively excluded from these committees. Subsequently, the local partner may use its 'empowerment' to further marginalize subordinate groups under the guise of democratic elections.

Temporary and outsider-initiated interventions can rarely change power balances directly. Participatory programmes are no exception. It can only be hoped that subordinate groups gradually develop a claim-making power through small-group work, careful facilitation and confidence-building activities. However, this may well require a continued role for the outsiders in monitoring and carefully following up the activities at grassroots level. This continued involvement in events at village level will be legitimized only as long as the outsiders' contribution to development is appreciated or at least tolerated by the ethnically dominant groups.

Prejudice and feelings of inferiority Even when problems of political and administrative exclusion are overcome through participatory methods, and subordinate ethnic groups take a seat in the community organizations that join hands with development agents, the ethnic minority's contribution may be limited. Their self-esteem and perception of their skills and capacities may be so low that they are prevented from making a significant contribution. Simultaneously, dominant groups will continuously reproduce negative attitudes towards the subordinate groups in these organizations.

Participatory methods are often based on working in small groups. A repressive atmosphere is less likely to be felt and enforced in such groups, especially if their work takes place outside the symbolic courts of power. If properly facilitated, these small groups offer a learning opportunity for subordinate groups to practise negotiating skills and build self-confidence. It should be noted, however, that often the outsiders (especially government officers) also belong to the dominant ethnic groups. Consequently, they may also display prejudices in their interaction with ethnic minorities. It is, therefore, very important for outsiders to be self-critical.

Reprisals Even if outsiders succeed in involving subordinate ethnic groups in local development processes, there may be reprisals against these groups for defying the status quo. It is unlikely that the local powers will take such 'corrective' measures while the outsiders are around. But the danger of reprisals is real as soon as the outsiders have left. It is also unlikely that upon their return to the village the outsiders will be made aware of these reprisals. Subordinate ethnic groups are very conscious of the risk of reprisals and will normally withdraw before they expose themselves to such risks.

One of the central objectives of participatory methods is to give people control over procedures, plans and events. This is especially important when working with subordinate groups. The more these groups feel in control, the less likely they will be to venture into areas where they can expect reprisals. Participatory methods do not offer opportunities to address the problem of reprisals by dominant ethnic groups but, if carefully and properly applied, they can prevent the problem arising.

Risk avoidance Participatory methods are based on the assumption that people are able and willing to voice their interests and that they mean what they say. However, in ethnically divided communities, subordinated ethnic groups may be unwilling to voice their views on their medium- and long-term interests, when this could immediately destabilize or endanger their limited certainties and self-image, however feeble these may seem to outsiders. Development projects usually aim to change, i.e. improve, an existing situation. However, for many ethnic minorities living on the brink of survival, avoiding risk and maintaining the status quo are paramount priorities. This attitude is largely the culmination of all the problems elaborated above and will change only as the weight of these problems decreases.

The above inventory has explicitly been called 'preliminary' because an understanding of the implications of ethnicity for participatory development methods is only beginning to emerge, along with their increased use. This inventory is also preliminary because it is based on experiences in the particular context of Botswana. As explained, the strengthening and expanding state apparatus in Botswana has created tensions between the traditional and ethnically oriented socio-political order, and the modern liberal Western order. In this process, traditional systems seem to lose power to the new order, thus potentially creating room for subordinate ethnic groups to exert themselves politically. However, it is unclear whether this room exists, and whether participatory methods can broaden it in those African countries where the state apparatus is crumbling. Nevertheless, at this stage it is already clear that participatory methods are likely to remain scratches on the surface of the ethnically coloured African rural reality, unless its practitioners are able and willing to address ethnicity and ethnic identity openly.

[Originally published in *Development in Practice*, 10(5), November 2000, pp. 625–37]

Note

1 An assistant minister is quoted in a newspaper as having said to a *Basarwa* delegation: 'You think these outsiders [donor agencies] will always help you. Well, one of these days they will be gone and then there will only be us, and we own you and we will own you till the end of time' (Good 1996: 59).

References

Botswana Orientation Centre (1996a) *Artesia, Village Development Plan*, Gaborone: BOC.

— (1996b) *Kedia, Village Development Plan*, Gaborone: BOC.

— (1996c) *Lentsweletau, Development Planning through PRA*, Gaborone: BOC.

— (1996d) *East Hanahai, Village Development Plan*, Gaborone: BOC.

Butcher, H., A. Glen, P. Henderson and J. Smith (1993) *Community and Public Policy*, London: Pluto Press.

Byram, M., A. Molokomme and R. Kidd (1995) 'Local consultation process', in Ministry of Local Government, Lands and Housing, *District and Urban Planning – the Way Forward: Report of the Proceedings and Evaluation of the 1995 Planners Seminar*, Gaborone: Government Printer.

Chambers, R. (1994a) 'The origins and practice of participatory rural appraisal', *World Development*, 22(7): 953–69.

— (1994b) 'Participatory rural appraisal (PRA): analysis of experience', *World Development*, 22(9): 1253–68.

— (1994c) 'Participatory rural appraisal (PRA): challenges, potentials and paradigm', *World Development*, 22(10): 1437–54.

Clark, B. D. (1973) 'The concept of community: a reexamination', *Sociological Review*, 21(3): 32–8.

Clements, P. and T. Spinks (1994) *The Equal Opportunities Guide: How to Deal with Everyday Issues of Unfairness*, London: Kogan Page.

Datta, K. and A. Murray (1989) 'The rights of minorities and subject people in Botswana: a historical evolution', in J. Holm and P. Molutsi (eds), *Democracy in Botswana*, Gaborone: Macmillan.

Davidson, B. (1992) *Black Man's Burden: Africa and the Curse of the Nation-State*, New York: Times Books.

Freire, P. (1972) *Pedagogy of the Oppressed*, Harmondsworth: Penguin.

Good, K. (1996) 'Towards popular participation in Botswana', *Journal of Modern African Studies*, 34: 53–77.

Hitchcock, R. K. (1992) 'The rural population living outside of recognised villages', in D. Nteta and J. Hermans (eds), *Sustainable Rural Development*, Gaborone: Botswana Society.

MFDP (Ministry of Finance and Development Planning) (1991) *National Development Plan 7*, Gaborone: Government Printer.

— (1994) *Mid-term Review of National Development Plan 7*, Gaborone: Government Printer.

— (1997) *National Population Policy*, Gaborone: Government Printer.

Mogalakwe, M. (1986) *Inside Ghanzi Farms: A Look at the Conditions of Basarwa Farm Workers*, Gaborone: Applied Research Unit.

Molutsi, P. P. (1989) 'The ruling class and democracy in Botswana', in J. Holm and P. Molutsi (eds), *Democracy in Botswana*, Gaborone: Macmillan.

Mosse, D. (1994) 'Authority, gender and knowledge: theoretical reflection on the practice of participatory rural appraisal', *Development and Change*, 25(3): 497–525.

Mpho, M. K. (1989) 'Representation of cultural minorities in policy making', in J. Holm and P. Molutsi (eds), *Democracy in Botswana*, Gaborone: Macmillan.

Ngcongco, L. D. (1989) 'Tswana political tradition: how democratic?', in J. Holm and P. Molutsi (eds), *Democracy in Botswana*, Gaborone: Macmillan.

Nnoli, O. (1995) *Ethnicity and Development in Nigeria*, Aldershot: Avebury.

Plant, R. (1974) *Community and Ideology: An Essay in Applied Social Philosophy*, London: Routledge and Kegan Paul.

Prinsen, G., T. Maruatona, N. Mbaiwa, F. Youngman, N. Bar-on, T. Maundeni, T. Modie and T. Mompati (1996) *PRA: Contract and Commitment for Village Development, Report on the Ministry of Finance and Development Planning's Participatory Rural Appraisal Pilot Project*, Gaborone: Government Printer.

Republic of Botswana (1965) *Constitution of Botswana*, Gaborone: Government Printer.

World Bank (1994) *The World Bank and Participation*, Washington, DC: World Bank.

24 | Towards a repoliticization of participatory development: political capabilities and spaces of empowerment

Glyn Williams

Mainstreaming participation, depoliticizing development

[I]s the new participatory myth acting more like a Trojan horse which may end up by substituting a subtle kind of teleguided and masterly organized participation for the old types of intransitive or culturally defined participation, proper to vernacular societies? (Rahnema 1997: 167)

Writing at the beginning of the 'PRA boom', Majid Rahnema saw participation's rapid growth as an indication that it had already been politically 'tamed', and was serving important economic, institutional and legitimating functions for a mainstream vision of development. Sidestepping his uncritical celebration of 'vernacular societies', Rahnema raises important questions for those finding themselves inside or outside the 'Trojan horse' today. Does the recent explosion of 'participatory' practices and discourse represent a radical paradigm shift, or the active *de*-politicization of international development? Certainly, within its officially recognized forms, participatory development appears to be wholly compatible with a liberalization agenda, able to marshal poor people's voices in support of the World Bank's policy prescriptions.[1] As a result, criticisms of participatory development have been fleshed out carefully over the last ten years, not just in the rhetoric of self-proclaimed anti-developmentalists, but also through careful reflection on field experiences by practitioners and academics alike.

In this chapter, I highlight this depoliticization critique before offering an agenda for the repoliticization of participatory development. The first criticism is that participation stresses personal reform over political struggle, whereby a 'revelatory' moment occurs in which 'communities' uncover their previously hidden knowledge and 'uppers' cast off their professional biases (Chambers 1994). There is little on how such instances of revelation are built into longer-term projects or alliances for change, or indeed the various forms of resistance they might face. A second reservation is that participatory development privileges 'the community' as the site where empowerment is assumed to occur. All too often, 'communities' are treated as fixed and unproblematic and idealized in terms of their content (Mohan 2001). By homogenizing communities, and uncritically boosting 'the local' as the site for action, participatory development both draws a veil over repressive structures (of gender, class, caste and ethnicity) operating at the micro-scale, and deflects attention away from wider power relationships that frame the construction of local development problems (cf. Fine 1999; Mohan and Stokke 2000).

The third criticism, that participation has become the 'new tyranny' of development, deserves slightly longer elaboration. Participation's claims to openness and transparency, combined with its massive institutional reach, have led critics fundamentally to question the 'empowerment' it is intended to achieve. The argument is that participation actively 'depoliticizes' development, incorporating marginalized individuals in development projects that they are unable to question (Kothari 2001); producing 'grassroots' knowledge ignorant of its own partiality (Mosse 2001); and foreclosing discussion of alternative visions of development (Henkel and Stirrat 2001). Alongside this portrayal of grassroots agency, participatory development also denies development experts' role in shaping processes of participation. By obscuring the agency and motivations of development workers, important questions about the nature of management and leadership are bypassed, and key aspects of the development process are thus removed from public scrutiny.

These concerns echo those raised by James Ferguson in his study of the development business in Lesotho (Ferguson 1994). In this reading, participation merely adds to the 'anti-politics machine': it is a Foucauldian exercise of power that rewrites the subjectivity of the Third World's poor, disciplining them through a series of participatory procedures, performances and encounters. At the same time, the discourse of participation legitimizes that power: through their incorporation, swathes of intended 'development beneficiaries' are deemed to have shifted from objects to empowered subjects – or even authors – of their own development. In this way, any blame for project 'failure' is displaced from macro-level concerns, and relocalized on to 'the people', leaving the anti-politics machine free to grind onwards.

There are, however, important limitations to this 'depoliticization' critique. First, in some versions of this argument there is an almost conspiratorial air of intentionality, as implied in Rahnema's phrase: 'teleguided and masterly organized'. Participatory development may have become an international and powerful discourse, but it is not an intentional project capable of being controlled by a narrow set of 'interest groups', be they local Southern elites or policy-makers in Washington. The second point is that some of these critiques suffer almost as much as celebratory accounts of participatory development do from a reductionist view of power. Participatory development projects may well rescript people's subjectivities in terms of others' choosing and incorporate them within a development process far less benign than its promoters might suggest. But while participation may appear to be all-pervasive, this account of its operation is in danger of ignoring the fact that any configuration of power/ knowledge opens up its own particular spaces and moments for resistance.

Seeing these possibilities for resistance, we should not forget the lessons learned from Scott's 'weapons of the weak' (Scott 1985). To take the 'incorpora-tion' of participatory events at face value is to ignore people's ability for feigned compliance and tactical (and self-interested) engagement. Furthermore, there is the ever-present possibility that while participatory development projects can seem all-consuming to practitioners and academics evaluating them, they may play a relatively small part in their intended beneficiaries' lives (Kumar and Corbridge 2002; Williams et al. 2003a). Limited engagement or even exit thus provide means of passive resistance to the 'tyranny of participation'. In a more positive sense, we need to remember that within Foucault's own writing, systems of power/knowledge are practically grounded and evolving, thus pro-viding space within themselves for alternative discourses and knowledges to emerge. By examining the particular ways in which the discourse and practices of participatory development play out in concrete situations, we can look for opportunities for their *re*-politicization. If, as the contributors to *Participa-tion: The New Tyranny?* suggest, participation appears both all-pervasive and fraught with contradictions, it surely also provides the conditions for these contradictions to be exploited by a range of different actors.

Two important questions thus emerge. The first is methodological: how should we evaluate participatory practices as a form of development? The second is more practical: if participation has gained institutional power within development practice, what can this power be made to *do*? Answers to this second question are always inherently political: they are about seeking ways in which the contradictions and opportunities of participation can be exploited to forward particular programmes, values and interests.

In the rest of this chapter I sketch out preliminary answers to both ques-tions. My response to the methodological question is that a more realistic evaluation of participatory development should focus on participation's wider political impact. I then turn to how participation should be used, and take up Mohan and Stokke's (2000) call to 'develop a new political imaginary', highlighting where the potential for a radicalized or repoliticized participatory development might lie.

Re-evaluating participation: institutional analysis and political capabilities

In approaching the first question, two methodological shifts are required in evaluating participatory development. The first is to move beyond individual instances of participation to look at the institutional impact of participa-tory techniques and values. Both proponents and critics alike have perhaps focused too much on the minutiae of participatory methods and events, and too little on their wider context. To some extent, the literature on participation has already begun this analysis through its own internal critique. Blackburn and Holland's collection, *Who Changes?* (1998), reviews initiatives to embed participation more deeply within development practice, and the institutional difficulties that such attempts face. Throughout their collection changes in practice of development professionals themselves are seen as central to better participation. Recommendations to enhance a participatory ethos include institutional change and a set of micro-tactics for reform-minded individuals to push participation within their own institutions (IDS Workshop 1998a, 1998b).

In combination, these individual and institutional changes are intended to spread the 'benign virus' (Blackburn 1998: 167) of participation; we are therefore presented with a series of *managerial* strategies that will deepen participation's impact. However, a discussion of *political* changes needed for participation is largely absent here. It is this absence that suggests a second shift in methodology, towards a more explicitly political analysis of participation. In their work on assessing anti-poverty policies, Whitehead and Gray-Molina outline key issues such an evaluation could draw upon. They examine the degree to which development initiatives improve the *political capabilities* of the poor, defined as 'the institutional and organizational resources as well as collective ideas available for effective political action' (Whitehead and Gray-Molina 1999: 6). In their view: 'an analysis of political capabilities requires a closer examination of the rules of political engagement as actually played, including the transformation or manipulation of rules over time. Critically, political capabilities involve the ability to create new rules, transform social preferences, as well as secure new resources as they become available' (ibid.: 7). In this reading, political capabilities provide the set of navigational skills needed to move through political space, and the tools to reshape these spaces where this is possible. A key distinction here would be a focus on uncovering the knowledge and performances required to (re-)negotiate political space rather than trying to quantify levels of political capital in the abstract. Understanding the processes by which cultural capital (in Bourdieu's sense) is deployed to political ends would therefore be far more important than attempts to produce political 'institutional mappings' equivalent to those of the World Bank's Social Capital Assessment Tool (Krishna and Shrader 1999).

Moore and Putzel (1999) have used Whitehead and Gray-Molina's definition of political capabilities in arguing for the rehabilitation of political analysis within aid and development work more generally. For Moore and Putzel, important criteria for the success of development projects are the degree to which they contribute to the mobilization and sustained political action of the poor. They argue that the structural constraints poor people face (of political exclusion, fractured identities and physical isolation) mean that their political mobilization is largely *re*-active. Despite increased globalization and the privatization of development, developmental activities of the state remain key sites for struggle as it is here that there is a chance that forms of recognized authority can be called to account. For Moore and Putzel, an important part of poor people's political empowerment is thus the degree to which states create and shape opportunities for the poor to engage in government-focused struggles for rights and resources.

These opportunities may not be present everywhere. Whitehead and Gray-Molina (1999: 5) suggest, on the basis of their fieldwork in Bolivia, that their arguments are relevant to a subsection of developing countries where there are 'reasonably stable boundaries, and relatively coherent systems of public policy-making and implementation'. This is because the long-term construction of political capabilities explicitly requires constituencies of the poor (national or sub-national) involved in interaction with a responsive (or 'democratic' in a loose sense) state. Whether political capabilities are relevant within *extreme* cases of authoritarianism or state failure is therefore open to empirical question. However, James Fox's work on Mexico does at least suggest that these capabilities can survive periods of repression (Fox 1996).

Although participation is not central to these authors' work, their wider arguments suggest that political analysis should be given more prominence in the evaluation of participatory development. Some important questions that such an analysis would address include the following:

- *To what extent do participatory development programmes contribute to processes of political learning among the poor?* Equally important here are knowledge of formal political rights and increased awareness of the de facto local rules of the game, which can sharpen understanding of appropriate strategies and allies.
- *To what degree do participatory programmes reshape political networks?* It is often the reshaping of linkages *beyond* the local that will be a key determinant of success/failure for poor participants. The ways in which the existing roles of brokers and patrons are challenged or reinforced is of importance here – and these political intermediaries should not be assumed to be always and everywhere a negative force.
- *How do participatory programmes impact upon existing patterns of political representation, including changes to the language of political claims and competition?* Challenging repressive or exclusionary political norms is crucial to the longer-term success of participatory practice – and here an analysis of local cultures of leadership and governance may be important in understanding both the potentials and limits to this change.

These questions can redirect analysis of participatory projects towards explicit recognition of the political aspects of development, but are also important guides for a self-critical participatory practice. With regard to both, whether or not they are able to produce more 'positive' and effective development in the sense used here, they can at least guide a fuller and more honest evaluation of the outcomes (intended or otherwise) of participation on the ground (see Williams et al. 2003b). At stake here is not merely the effectiveness of participatory processes in accumulating local stocks of social capital, but their contribution to the political empowerment of sections of the poor. As Moore and Putzel argue: 'It is useful to think of empowerment in terms of increasing the political capabilities of the poor ... It is the political capabilities of the poor that will determine whether they can employ social capital ... constructively or create social capital where it is lacking' (Moore and Putzel 1999: 13).

This produces a very different reading of the politics of participation from that in Blackburn and Holland's collection: the central question is not 'how do we strategize to embed participation within development institutions and agendas?', but 'what longer-term political value do participatory processes have for the poor?' In particular, taking poor people's changing ability to engage *with the state* as the analytical end-point focuses attention on the particular sites where decisions are made, influence is held and authority is located. This itself may provide a fruitful contrast with analyses of participation that describe its disciplinary effects as being systemic, and the agency behind them simultaneously both all-powerful and diffuse. As Andrea Cornwall (2002) has indicated, a more careful reading of Foucault would question the particular qualities of different spaces of participation, both within and against/outside the state. Linking this understanding of political space with an assessment of political capabilities can in turn suggest a range of ways in which participation can be used to call state power to account.

In further developing such an approach, the literature on comparative politics is useful. Ethnographic understandings of state power that develop context-specific answers to the three questions posed above are crucial here. Understanding formal political rights and the de facto rules of the game; the constitution of local political society; and discourses of political claims and cultures of leadership are all vital in assessing how participation is being, and could be, used.

Learning from participation: 'success' and 'failure' in South Asia

Reading recent South Asian case studies, one can find numerous instances of the *de*-politicizing effects of participatory development. Mosse's assessments of the Western Indian Rainfed Farming Project show that participatory consultation exercises were both a strategic game whereby villagers tried to second-guess the resources to be won, and simultaneously important events in legitimizing the programme for audiences of powerful outsiders (Mosse 1994,

2001). In their account of the programme's counterpart in eastern India, Kumar and Corbridge note that trying to ensure the participation of the very poorest within the project was always an unrealistic target: 'the Project has been less successful in targeting the poor, than richer families have been in targeting the Project' (Kumar and Corbridge 2002: 14). Furthermore, the project's longer-term effects of 'thinning of the social networks of the poorest and most vulnerable' (ibid.: 18) have undermined the political capabilities of the poor.

If read simply in comparison to their intended outcomes, the failure of these programmes on the ground – through routinization, the capture and co-option of schemes, the reproduction of the power of village elites – is both familiar and unsurprising. In part, the idealism of a naive understanding of participatory development writes 'failure' into such projects from the outset. Insofar as the poor are supposed to become 'empowered' by dint of their engagement in participatory events alone, this view of participation does not merely raise the standard for developmental 'success', it sets it impossibly high. Most participatory development projects simply do not command *enough* power to transform radically the structural inequalities that reproduce poverty. To this extent, judgements of projects that see their problems merely as 'failures' *within the act of participation itself* are tilting at windmills. To blame development professionals for not truly taking on board participatory values, or locally powerful figures for acting in self-interested ways, may protect the purity of a mythic participatory ideal but it fails to elucidate participation's potential and limitations in changing development practice. Instead, and as Mosse, Kumar and Corbridge note, the 'failures' of these projects are to be found elsewhere: they were shaped by donor and Forest Department agendas to provide relatively efficient service delivery rather than any more radical programme of emancipation.

Where more positive examples of the power of participatory development projects exist, some form of transformative political agenda often explicitly underpins their effectiveness. Starting with an example from 'inside' the state, the People's Campaign for Decentralized Planning in Kerala (launched 1996) shows how a more radical version of participatory development can capture the popular imagination. Although the resources made available for local planning are qualitatively different from other experiments in decentralization, the mechanisms (including PRA) and institutions (the *panchayats* or village councils) used to engage the public are widespread in India. In explaining why participatory planning works here rather than elsewhere, Heller (2001) notes the central importance of synergies between political institutions and social mobilization. Specifically, elements of the ruling Communist Party saw decentralization as a means to extend their electoral support beyond its working-class core, and used earlier experience in linking with the mass-based Kerala Popular Science Movement to galvanize mass participation. The wider lesson is that state-sponsored participatory development is effective, because it is associated with a genuine attempt to reshape state power.

In contrast, the Rajasthan-based Mazdoor Kisan Shakti Sangathan (MKSS) shows the potential for participatory mobilization outside and explicitly *against* the state. The MKSS campaigns for the right-to-information on a range of government activities important to the poor, including welfare and development programmes. The movement has used photocopies of official documents to confront corrupt practices. In its *jan sunwais* (public hearings), the MKSS aims at collective, local verification of official accounts to pick up misdeeds that would be invisible through higher-level audit processes. In parallel, the MKSS has organized large-scale protests to put pressure on the state legislature to provide a legal basis for freedom of access to government information. As Jenkins and Goetz (1999) note, the MKSS uses information as a radical resource; rather than using participatory techniques to generate and offer up a 'grassroots viewpoint' to the state, the MKSS's success is explicitly based around participation challenging the official record. Chambers's ideals of 'sharing' are seen as naively consensual by comparison: if knowledge is indeed power, then those (ab)using it are unlikely to give it up lightly.

In both of these 'successful' examples, and in others such as mobilizations around the Maharastra Employment Guarantee Scheme (Joshi and Moore 2000), a number of common points emerge. First, they share a clear political direction and aim to produce fuller and more active citizenship. 'Moving' the state towards a decentralized mode, or opening it up to effective public scrutiny, are examples of *progressive* agendas that could build poor people's political capabilities in the longer run. Second, they reshape political networks by building alliances not limited to the poor themselves and extending beyond the grass roots: cross-class and cross-institutional linkages (with different branches of government, NGOs and/or parties) are part of their success. Third, the poor took these programmes and movements seriously because they at least offered the hope of significant change. Although Moore and Putzel note that poor people's political capital is limited, these examples suggest that they will gamble it on genuine opportunities for constructive engagement when these arise. Finally, in these examples, grassroots participation was not reified, either as the only mode of operation, or as an end in itself. Rather, it was one among several tactics for achieving the empowerment of the poor. In the final section, I expand on this idea of tactical engagement to locate the points at which the growing power of participatory development practice can be harnessed towards progressive political goals.

Towards the repoliticization of participation

An overtly political analysis is not simply useful for evaluating existing projects and programmes; it can also highlight participation's contribution within a more emancipatory practice. Here I expand on participation's potential to develop 'a new political imaginary' of empowerment by thinking through the ways in which it currently works, and can be made to work, within developmental processes and discourses. In doing so, attention must also be given to the spatial and temporal aspects of empowerment that participation is to achieve. It is through this reappraisal that the scope for participation's repoliticization may be explored, and the differences between participatory and other forms of development can be made explicit.

Looking first at the forms of development process demanded by a participatory agenda, the dangers of institutionalized participation are that it can place excessive demands on the time of all concerned. Governmental and NGO resources can be poured into participatory activities that have little influence on key managerial decisions, and build only cynicism among their lay participants. By contrast, when the dynamics of local political society are more supportive, 'official' moments can open up spaces of empowerment at the grass roots; be used to extract public promises from politicians, bureaucrats and managers; and/or make explicit wider political conflicts and agendas. More generally, participatory development's claims to transparency and openness may provide a key pressure-point at which to deploy and build the political capabilities of the poor and their allies.

Intelligent pursuit of these claims could allow both greater public scrutiny of development managers' actions, and opportunities for political learning. With regard to increased public scrutiny, participation's avowed ethic of self-critical reflection turns the spotlight on development institutions' behaviour, values and actions to a greater extent than before. This could provide political leverage to uncover and challenge decisions that would otherwise remain hidden: for example, pressurizing officials to account for their use of discretionary power can be an important way of curbing their excesses. Furthermore, attempts made to contain participation within certain arenas can be opened to question. At the intra-project level, grassroots participants are usually not empowered to criticize or evaluate key decisions concerning project objectives, staffing or finance; at a wider level, participation is generally ghettoized within social development, and absent from other spheres of government activity. A repoliticized practice could explicitly challenge these boundaries, tactically pressing for the extension of participatory 'rules of engagement' into other arenas.

With imaginative use, the practical mechanisms of participation's 'new public management' culture (Desai and Imrie 1998) can also be turned into important resources in building political capabilities. Within Kerala and other examples of mass participation in local government, 'success' is not only found in the individual projects that are completed, or the instances of corruption that are challenged, but also through the wider institutional learning that occurs. 'Moving' the state, or the development agency, to the grass roots can increase the density of contacts between power-holders and the population at large, making the former more visible. Social activism would use this increased visibility to ensure that the everyday and mundane spaces of participation become opportunities to build public understanding of how power works. In terms of the discourse promoted by participatory practice, the picture is again ambivalent. In part because of the focus on participatory processes rather than theoretically informed understandings of power, participation remains a highly malleable discourse in political terms. One possibility is that it could be used to spread debate on the nature of political rights.

If modernist top-down development caused a disjuncture between 'elite' and 'vernacular' ideas of development (Kaviraj 1991), participation could at least hold the possibility of building a common language community between the architects and recipients of development programmes. Here it may well be participation's claims to 'listen' and 'represent' – however problematical – that provide a foothold to place elements of alternative developmental visions on the political agenda. Again, using the claims of participation's idealized self-image as an entry-point to challenge its actual practice may be a useful strategy in forwarding a more radical vision of empowerment. In doing so, explicit and open debate of political values will be required to avoid returning to a romanticized vision of 'local' cultures and to build support for anti-oppressive agendas.

Although a transformative participation can have no predefined or 'tele-guided' goals, some features of a new political imaginary of empowerment can be traced. In spatial terms, this imaginary would require a developmental practice that aimed towards achieving relative levels of empowerment within networks, rather than producing bounded, localized spaces of liberation. As noted above, political analysis guides us towards the range of state and non-state actors engaged in participatory development projects. More radically, thinking in terms of political networks recognizes how the degree to which these actors appear to be at the 'centre' or 'periphery' of any particular struggle over developmental resources is both dynamic and highly context-specific. Majid Rahnema's metaphor of participation as a 'Trojan horse' is thus somewhat inappropriate: instead of the clandestine penetration of 'authentic' local spaces, we have at least a degree of two-way traffic that refashions and reproduces the spaces of political action.

Finally, a change in temporal focus is also needed if an empowering political practice is to be created. Here it is vital that 'empowerment' is not treated as a change in status created at a particular moment in time. Rather, empower-ment should be seen as a relative (and reversible) process built from within longer-term political projects. Development programmes have their own trajec-tories, and political institutions have their own life cycles; participation, and its potential for empowerment, should not be seen outside these. In practice, even where participatory projects are successful, we will witness periods in which their effects are routinizing rather than revolutionary. Similarly, for the poor, everyday participation in democratic forums may appear to do little more than reconfirm the status quo, and provide public acts of legitimation for power brokers.

The challenge for a repoliticized participatory practice is to recognize and develop the political capabilities that may be present within such periods of apparent quiescence. Cornwall provides a typology of spaces of participation, but movement between these categories is always possible. 'Movements and moments' of participation can bed down into 'regularised relations' whereby 'citizens become part of the machinery of governance' (Cornwall 2002: 18), but the latter can also be vital preconditions for the emergence of active mass campaigns. As a result, progressive visions of development have to be tactically agile in their use of participation, carefully combining mass mobilization, the institutionalization of gains, and learning to navigate the reshaped spaces of participation. All are important, and it would be both simplistic and wrong to label any one mechanism as more 'radical' or 'authentic' without careful contextualization.

Conclusions

In this chapter, I have attempted to move beyond both the naive boosting of participatory development and the potentially disabling 'tyranny' critique by thinking through issues of methodology and practice. With regard to the former, I have argued that there is a marked absence of constructive political analysis within current evaluations of participatory development. This silence has in turn perpetuated participation's political malleability, and its ready co-option within processes where underlying neoliberal worldviews are not called into question. The alternative presented here is to highlight questions of politics by examining the effects of participation on political capabilities: how, if at all, do specific instances of participation contribute to processes of political learning, reshape networks of power, and change patterns of political representation? As an alternative basis for evaluation, this focus on political capabilities moves debate on because it takes questions of power seriously. Power over participatory encounters is not simply a result of individual choices and values, but neither is it systemic, totalizing and irresistible in the sense expressed by some of participation's detractors. A careful reading of Foucault draws attention to the particularities of participatory development: both the discourses and practices through which it has spread, but also the space for movement and contestation it creates.

As such, the questions raised in this chapter are not only of use to a detached academic analysis: they can also inform a radicalized development practice. Actually existing participation, for all its shortcomings, provides a range of opportunities through which the power of development can be actively called to account. In exploiting these opportunities a radicalized practice should not only be sure of its underlying values, it must also be imaginative in its forms of engagement, using to the full those elements of participatory processes and discourses that support its political agenda. In doing so, careful attention needs to be given to the contexts of individual instances of engagement. Equally importantly, the spatial and temporal dimensions of empowerment envisaged within repoliticized participatory development need to transcend the search for isolated moments of liberation or professional 'reversals'. Nor should it champion a post-developmental retreat to 'the local' to escape participation's totalizing power. Rather, it should encompass longer-term political projects and reshaped political networks that embed within themselves a discourse of rights and a fuller sense of citizenship.

[Originally published as 'Towards a repoliticization of participatory development: political capabilities and spaces of empowerment', in S. Hickey and G. Mohan (eds), *Participation: From Tyranny to Transformation*, Zed Books, 2004]

Note

1 *Voices of the Poor* gave the Bank's *World Development Report 2000/2001* 'ethnographic interest', but in contrast to the intentions of PRA these voices do little to interrupt the dominant 'expert' voices.

References

Blackburn, J. (1998) 'Conclusion', in J. Blackburn and J. Holland (eds), *Who Changes? Institutionalizing Participation in Development*, London: IT Publications, pp. 167–78.

Blackburn, J. and J. Holland (eds) (1998) *Who Changes? Institutionalizing Participation in Development*, London: IT Publications.

Chambers, R. (1994) 'The origins and practice of Participatory Rural Appraisal', *World Development*, 22(7): 953–69.

Cornwall, A. (2002) 'Making spaces, changing places: situating participation in development', IDS Working Paper no. 170, Brighton: Institute of Development Studies.

Desai, V. and R. Imrie (1998) 'The new managerialism in local government: North–South dimensions', *Third World Quarterly*, 19(4): 635–50.

Ferguson, J. (1994) *The Anti-politics Machine: 'Development', Depoliticization, and Bureaucratic Power in Lesotho*, Cambridge: Cambridge University Press.

Fine, B. (1999) 'The developmental state is dead – long live social capital?', *Development and Change*, 30: 1–19.

Fox, J. (1996) 'How does civil society thicken? The political construction of social capital in rural Mexico', *World Development*, 24(6): 1089–1103.

Heller, P. (2001) 'Moving the state: the politics of democratic decentralisation in Kerala, South Africa, and Porto Alegre', *Politics and Society*, 29(1): 131–63.

Henkel, H. and R. Stirrat (2001) 'Participation as spiritual duty; empowerment as secular subjection', in B. Cooke and U. Kothari (eds), *Participation: The New Tyranny?*, London: Zed Books, pp. 168–84.

IDS Workshop (1998a) 'Reflections and recommendations on scaling-up and organizational change', in J. Blackburn and J. Holland (eds), *Who Changes? Institutionalizing Participation in Development*, London: IT Publications, pp. 135–44.

— (1998b) 'Towards a learning organization – making development agencies more participatory from the inside', in J. Blackburn and J. Holland (eds), *Who Changes? Institutionalizing Participation in Development*, London: IT Publications, pp. 145–52.

Jenkins, R. and A.-M. Goetz (1999) 'Accounts and accountability: theoretical implications of the right-to-information movement in India', *Third World Quarterly*, 20(3): 603–22.

Joshi, A. and M. Moore (2000) 'Enabling environments: do anti-poverty programmes mobilise the poor?', *Journal of Development Studies*, 37(1): 25–56.

Kaviraj, S. (1991) 'On state, society and discourse in India', in J. Manor (ed.), *Rethinking Third World Politics*, New Delhi: Sage, pp. 225–50.

Kothari, U. (2001) 'Power, knowledge and social control in participatory development', in B. Cooke and U. Kothari (eds), *Participation: The New Tyranny?*, London: Zed Books, pp. 139–52.

Krishna, A. and E. Shrader (1999) 'Social capital assessment tool', Paper presented at the Conference on Social Capital and Poverty Reduction, World Bank, Washington, DC, 22–24 June.

Kumar, S. and S. Corbridge (2002) 'Programmed to fail? Development projects and the politics of participation', *Journal of Development Studies*, 39(2): 73–103.

Mohan, G. (2001) 'Beyond participation: strategies for deeper empowerment', in B. Cooke and U. Kothari (eds), *Participation: The New Tyranny?*, London: Zed Books, pp. 153–67.

Mohan, G. and K. Stokke (2000) 'Participatory development and empowerment: the dangers of localism', *Third World Quarterly*, 21(2): 247–68.

Moore, M. and J. Putzel (1999) 'Thinking strategically about politics and poverty', IDS Working Paper no. 101, Brighton: Institute of Development Studies.

Mosse, D. (1994) 'Authority, gender and knowledge: theoretical reflections on the practice of PRA', *Development and Change*, 25: 497–526.

— (2001) '"People's knowledge", participation and patronage: operations and representations in rural development', in B. Cooke and U. Kothari (eds), *Participation: The New Tyranny?*, London: Zed Books, pp. 16–35.

Rahnema, M. (1997) 'Participation', in W. Sachs (ed.), *The Development Dictionary: A Guide to Knowledge as Power*, Hyderabad: Orient Longman (originally published by Zed Books, 1992).

Scott, J. (1985) *Weapons of the Weak. Everyday Forms of Peasant Resistance*, New Haven, CT: Yale University Press.

Whitehead, L. and G. Gray-Molina (1999) 'The long-term politics of pro-poor policies', www.worldbank.org/poverty/wdrpoverty/dfid/whitehea.pdf.

Williams, G., R. Véron, M. Srivastava and S. Corbridge (2003a) 'Participation, poverty and power: poor people's engagement with India's Employment Assurance Scheme', *Development and Change*, 34(1): 163–92.

— (2003b) 'Enhancing pro-poor governance in eastern India: the role of action research in institutional reform', *Progress in Development Studies*, 3(2): 159–78.

World Bank (2000) *World Development Report 2000/2001: Attacking Poverty*, New York: Oxford University Press.

PART FOUR

Participation in governance

25 | Towards participatory local governance: six propositions for discussion

John Gaventa

Introduction

For the last twenty years, the concept of 'participation' has been widely used in the discourse of development. For much of this period, the concept has referred to participation in the social arena, in the 'community' or in development projects. Increasingly, however, the concept of participation is being related to rights of citizenship and to democratic governance. Nowhere is the intersection of concepts of community participation and citizenship seen more clearly than in the multitude of programmes for decentralized governance that are found in both Southern and Northern countries.

Linking citizen participation to the state at this local or grassroots level raises fundamental and normative questions about the nature of democracy and about the skills and strategies for achieving it. The literature is full of debates on the meanings of citizenship and of participation, on the role and relevance of 'the local', especially in the context of globalization, and of course on the problem of governance itself. In this article, I pose six propositions which link to this debate and which raise critical challenges for how it may be pursued further.

Proposition one: relating people and institutions

A key challenge for the twenty-first century is the construction of new relationships between ordinary people and the institutions – especially those of government – which affect their lives.

Recently, a number of studies have pointed to the growing gap that exists within both North and South between ordinary people, especially the poor, and the institutions which affect their lives, especially government. For instance, the recent *Voices of the Poor* report, prepared for the *World Development Report 2000/2001*, finds that many poor people around the globe perceive large institutions – especially those of the state – to be distant, unaccountable and corrupt. Drawing from participatory research exercises in twenty-three countries, the report concludes:

From the perspectives of poor people world wide, there is a crisis in governance.

While the range of institutions that play important roles in poor people's lives is vast, poor people are excluded from participation in governance. State institutions, whether represented by central ministries or local government are often neither responsive nor accountable to the poor; rather the reports detail the arrogance and disdain with which poor people are treated. Poor people see little [relief from] injustice, criminality, abuse and corruption by institutions. Not surprisingly, poor men and women lack confidence in the state institutions even though they still express their willingness to partner with them under fairer rules. (Narayan et al. 2000: 172)

The *Voices of the Poor* study is not alone in its findings. Another study by the Commonwealth Foundation (1999) in over forty countries also found a growing disillusionment of citizens with their governments, based on their concerns with corruption, lack of responsiveness to the needs of the poor, and the absence of participation or connection to ordinary citizens.

The empirical evidence on the crisis in the relationship between citizens and their state is not limited to the South. In a number of established democracies, traditional forms of political participation have diminished, and recent studies show clearly the enormous distrust citizens have of many state institutions. In the UK, for instance, a recent study sponsored by the Joseph Rowntree Foundation points to the

need to build a new relationship between local government and local people. There are two reasons for this. The first has to do with alienation and apathy. There is a major issue about the attitudes of the public, as customers or citizens, towards local government ... This is a symptom of a deeper malaise, the weakness or lack of public commitment to local democracy. (Clarke and Stewart 1998: 3)

Other data in the United States, most notably the work by Robert Putnam, point as well to the decline in civic participation and the growing distance between citizens and state institutions.

Proposition two: working on both sides of the equation

Rebuilding relationships between citizens and their local governments means working both sides of the equation – that is, going beyond 'civil society' or 'state-based' approaches, to focus on their intersection, through new forms of participation, responsiveness and accountability.

As Fung and Wright (2001: 5–6) observe, the right has taken advantage of the decline in legitimacy of public institutions to 'escalate its attack on the affirmative state ... Deregulation, privatisation, reduction of social services and curtailments of state spending have been the watchwords, rather than participation, greater responsiveness, and more effective forms of democratic state intervention.' They and of course many others argue that the response to the crisis should focus not on dismantling the state, but on deepening democracy and seeking new forms for its expression. They argue that the 'institutional forms of liberal democracy plus techno-bureaucratic administration seem increasingly ill suited to the novel problems we face in the twenty-first century'.

However, those who have sought to deepen democratic governance have often been divided on their approach to the problem. On the one hand, attention has been paid to strengthening the processes of citizen *participation* – that is the ways in which poor people exercise voice through new forms of inclusion, consultation and/or mobilization designed to inform and to influence larger institutions and policies. On the other hand, growing attention has been paid to how to strengthen the *accountability* and *responsiveness* of these institutions and policies through changes in institutional design, and a focus on the enabling structures for good governance.

Increasingly, however, we are beginning to see the importance of working on both sides of the equation. As participatory approaches are scaled up from projects to policies, they inevitably enter the arenas of government, and find that participation can only become effective as it engages with issues of institutional change. And, as concerns about good governance and state responsiveness grow, questions about how citizens engage and make demands on the state also come to the fore.

In both South and North, there is growing consensus that the way forward is found in a focus on *both* a more active and engaged civil society which can express demands of the citizenry, *and* a more responsive and effective state which can deliver needed public services. In focus groups around the world, the Commonwealth Foundation study, for instance, found that despite their disillusionment with the state as it is, poor people would like to see strong government which will provide services, facilitate their involvement and promote equal rights and justice. The study argues that at the heart of the new consensus of strong state and strong civil society are the need to develop both '*participatory democracy* and *responsive government*' (1999: 76): the two are mutually reinforcing and supportive – 'strong, aware, responsible, active and engaged citizens along with strong, caring, inclusive, listening, open and responsive democratic governments' (ibid.: 82).

Similarly, Heller (2001: 133) discusses the limits of both the 'technocratic vision', with its emphasis on technical design of institutions, and the 'anarcho-communitarian model', with its emphasis on radical grassroots democracy. Rather, he calls for a more balanced view (the 'optimist conflict model') which recognizes the tensions between the need for representative working institutions, *and* the need for mobilized and demand-making civil society. The solution is not found in the separation of the civil society and good governance agendas, but in their interface. The IDS study by Goetz and Gaventa (2001) extends this argument further by examining over sixty concrete cases of citizen voice and state responsiveness, and discusses further the mechanisms and conditions through which they intersect and interact.

Proposition three: rethinking voice, reconceptualizing participation and citizenship

The call for new forms of engagement between citizens and the state involves a fundamental rethinking about the ways in which citizens' voices are articulated and represented in the political process, and a reconceptualization of the meanings of participation and citizenship in relationship to local governance.

Traditionally in representative democracies, the assumption has been that citizens express their preferences through electoral politics, and in turn, it was the job of the elected representatives to hold the state accountable. In both North and South, new voice mechanisms are now being explored which argue as well for more direct connections between the people and the bureaucracies which affect them. In the UK, for instance, the White Paper on Modern Local Government puts an emphasis on more active forms of citizenship, and on the concept of community governance:

> Local authorities are based on the principles of representative democracy, yet representative democracy has become passive. Rather than expressing a continuing relationship between government and citizen, the citizen is reduced to being a periodic elector. It is as if the idea of representative democracy has served to limit the commitment of the citizen to local government. At the same time, representative democracy and participatory democracy have been argued as mutually exclusive opposites. In fact, an active conception of representative democracy can be reinforced by participatory democracy – all the more easily in local government because of its local scales and its closeness to the local communities. (Quoted in Clarke and Stewart 1998)

Similarly, the Commonwealth Foundation study argues that:

> In the past the relationship between the state and citizens has tended to be mediated and achieved (or thought to be) through the intermediaries, elected representatives and political party structures. But this aspect of participation in governance for a good society requires direct connection between citizens and the state. This interface has been neglected in the past. The connection between the citizen and the state must be based on participation and inclusion. (1999: 82)

Increasingly around the world, a number of mechanisms are being explored which can foster these more inclusive and deliberative forms of engagement between citizen and state. These go under various labels, ranging from 'participatory governance', to deliberative democracy, to 'empowered deliberative democracy' (Fung and Wright 2001: 7), defined as:

- *'democratic* in their reliance on the participation and capacities of ordinary people,
- *deliberative* because they institute reasons-based decision-making, and
- *empowered* since they attempt to tie action to discussion'.

Such an approach, later relabelled 'empowered, participatory governance' by Fung (2002: 3–4), involves linking 'bottom-up' and 'top-down' forms of governance to create 'a new architecture of governance that cuts a middle path between the dichotomy of devolution and democratic centralism'.

Around the world, there are numerous examples of innovations which incorporate this approach, ranging from provisions for participatory planning at the local government level in India and the Philippines, to participatory budgeting in Brazil, to citizen monitoring committees in Bolivia, to forms of public referenda and citizen consultation in Europe. Most of these approaches involve new legal frameworks for local governance which incorporate a mix of direct forms of popular participation with more representative forms of democracy. (For a review of a number of these mechanisms, see Goetz and Gaventa 2001.)

As discussed in previous papers, linking participation to the political sphere means rethinking the ways in which participation has often been conceived and carried out, especially in the development context (Gaventa and Valderrama 1999). In the past within development studies, the drive for *'participatory development'* has focused on the importance of local knowledge and understanding as a basis for local action, and on direct forms of participation throughout the project cycle (needs assessment, planning, implementation, monitoring and evaluation). A wide range of participatory tools and methodologies have grown from this experience which now may have application in the field of *'participatory governance'*.

On the other hand, work on political participation growing out of political science and governance debates has often focused on issues largely underplayed by those working on participation in the community or social spheres. These include critical questions dealing with legitimate representation, systems of public accountability, policy advocacy and lobbying, rights education and awareness-building, and party formation and political mobilization. Yet the political participation literature has paid less attention to issues of local knowledge, participatory process or direct and continuous forms of engagement by marginalized groups.

Each tradition has much to learn from the other. Increasingly, they have been brought together, especially in the development field, under the concept of *'citizenship'*, which links participation in the political, community and social spheres. But the concept of 'citizenship', itself, has long been a disputed and value-laden one in democratic theory (Jones and Gaventa 2002; Gaventa et al. 2002). On the one hand, citizenship has traditionally been cast in liberal terms, as individual legal equality accompanied by a set of rights and responsibilities and bestowed by a state to its citizens. Newer approaches aim to bridge the gap between citizen and the state by recasting citizenship as practised rather than as given. Placing an emphasis on inclusive participation as the very foundation of democratic practice, these approaches suggest a more active notion of citizenship, which recognizes the agency of citizens as 'makers and shapers' rather than as 'users and choosers' of interventions or services designed by others (Cornwall and Gaventa 2000, 2001). As Lister suggests, 'the right of participation in decision-making in social, economic, cultural and political life should be included in the nexus of basic human rights ... Citizenship as participation can be seen as representing an expression of human agency in the political arena, broadly defined; citizenship as rights enables people to act as agents' (Lister 1998: 228).

At the same time, there is a growing recognition that universal conceptions of citizenship rights, met through a uniform set of social policies, fail to recognize diversity and difference, and may in fact serve to strengthen the exclusion of some while seeking inclusion of others (Ellison 1999). With this has come a renewed concern for questions of identity, diversity and inclusion. The DfID paper on *Realising Human Rights for Poor People* calls for participation of the poor in decisions which affects their lives to be included in the list of universal human rights (DfID 2000). The right to participate is also linked to rights of *inclusion*, and to rights to *obligation*, through which poor people may expect to hold governments more accountable and responsive.

Realizing these rights poses enormous challenges for local governance, and the new deliberative mechanisms for citizen engagement increasingly associated with them. Whose voices are really heard in these processes? What about issues of representation and accountability within them? How will various forms of local governance accommodate differing meanings of citizenship that cut across gender, political, cultural and social lines? Without attention to these questions, increased participation in local governance for some may simply reinforce the status quo.

Proposition four: learning about outcomes as we go along

While the search for new democratic processes of local governance is critical, far more needs to be learned about how they work, for whom, and with what social justice outcomes. In general, while there is some evidence of positive 'democracy' building outcomes, there is less evidence about the pro-poor development outcomes of participatory governance.

The promises on behalf of democratic decentralization, especially in its newer, more innovative forms, have been great. As Blair (2000: 23) summarizes one line of argument:

> the hope is that as government comes closer to the people, more people will participate in politics ... that will give them representation, a key element in empowerment, which can be defined here as a significant voice in public policy decisions which affect their futures. Local policy decisions reflecting this empowerment will serve these newer constituencies, providing more appropriate infastructure, better living conditions and enhanced economic growth. These improvements will then reduce poverty and enhance equity among all groups.

On the other hand, the evidence about the degree to which these outcomes have been realised is mixed.

Traditionally, the more pessimistic argument has been that democratic decentralization simply opens up space for the empowerment of local elites, not for consideration of the voices and interests of the more marginalized. Obstacles of power, social exclusion and minimal individual and collective organizational capacity mean that few gains will be made by the poor. As Manor observes, he has 'yet to discover evidence of any case where local elites were more benevolent than those at higher levels' (Manor 1999: 91, quoted in Blair 2000).

On the other hand, more recent studies of participatory forms of local governance have begun to point to some more positive outcomes. Blair's own study of democratic local governance in six countries, for instance, points to some gains in accountability as well as participation and empowerment goals. Moreover, some improvement may be seen in 'universal services', such as education and healthcare – arguably because these served to benefit the local elites as well. Less success was seen in programmes targeted at the poor themselves, as these were more likely to be 'captured' by local elites.

Osmani's review of the literature (2000), however, points to any number of examples of where 'truly participatory decentralisation' has contributed to both greater equity and efficiency of local services, because it allows responsiveness to local services. But he is also quick to point out that attempts to take such cases to scale have faced obstacles both of the unwillingness of those at the top to give up power and the difficulty of gaining the involvement of the poor from the bottom.

Heller's study (2001: 158) of democratic experiences in Kerala, Port Alegre and South Africa is more positive, at least when it comes to what might be termed 'democratic process outcomes'. He finds that the synergy of state and society in local governance:

- creates new associational incentive and spaces;
- allows for a continuous and dynamic process of learning;

- promotes deliberation and compromise;
- promotes innovative solutions to tensions between representation and participation;
- bridges knowledge and authority gap between technocratic expertise and local involvement.

On the whole, the evidence on both the pro-poor and the democratic outcomes of experiments in new forms of participatory governance is as yet inconclusive. Many of the studies that have been done have been on the impact of decentralization in general, not on the more democratic and participatory innovations we have begun to see in recent years. Far more work needs to be done on the impact of these newer sets of innovations.

Proposition five: building conditions for success

The enabling conditions for the better-known 'successful' experiments in participatory governance are limited to a few countries. Effective intervention strategies in most cases therefore must begin with how to create the prerequisite conditions necessary for participatory governance to succeed.

Many of the experiments which are often held up as recent 'success' stories in participatory local governance are limited to a few places in the world, which often reflect contexts and conditions which are not widely found elsewhere. For instance, Heller's study (ibid.) in Brazil, India and South Africa points to three enabling conditions of participatory governance:

- strong central state capacity;
- well-developed civil society; and
- an organized political force, such as a party, with strong social movement characteristics.

In how many countries (or indeed in how many places in these three countries) are such prerequisites found? Of the sixty to seventy countries where experiments of democratic decentralization are taking place, no doubt very few.

This has enormous implications for strategies of replicability, or for intervention in countries where these conditions do not pre-exist. In such cases, more work will need to be done on the preconditions of participatory governance, including awareness-building on rights and citizenship; building civil associations and social movements engaged in governance issues; and strengthening institutions of governance, both at the local and central levels. Merrifield's (2002) work raises important challenges for how to promote 'citizenship learning' in places where strong awareness of rights and responsibilities does not previously exist. Osmani (2000) argues for the ongoing importance of supporting empowerment strategies, through economic livelihoods, social mobilization and advocacy, as a necessary precondition for taking participatory governance to scale.

The work by Fung and Wright (2001) on innovative deliberative mechanisms in the USA, Brazil and India points to three principles that are fundamental to EDD (empowered deliberative democracy) and three 'design principles' for institution-building. They are perhaps helpful starting points for democracy-building strategies:

Principles of EDD
- focus on specific, tangible problems
- involvement of ordinary people affected by these problems and officials close to them
- deliberative development of solutions to these problems

Design principles for EDD
- devolution of public decision making authority
- formal linkages of responsibility, resource distribution and communication
- use and generation of new state institutions to support and guide these efforts.

However, they also point to one background enabling condition, which is by no means universally found in work on participation and local governance. That is, 'there is a rough equality of power, for the purposes of deliberative decisions, between participants' (ibid.: 25). To gain such conditions means that the work on local democracy-building must also be linked to work on empowerment, especially of oppressed and marginalized groups, as discussed briefly above.

Proposition six: contesting the 'local' in an era of globalization

While the 'local', and related themes of 'participation' and 'empowerment', are increasingly part of the development discourse, the 'local' has many conflicting political meanings, and is itself a problematic concept, especially in an era of increased globalization.

Historically, the 'local' has been considered a key site for democracy-building and citizen participation. It has been there that 'people usually come into contact with politicians or public officials, receive services and benefits from the state, and organize together in communities' (Lowndes 1995: 161). Citizenship was thought to derive largely from community identification and membership; civic action and political participation were thought to be concentrated at the local level; and local governance provided a learning ground for broader understandings and forms of citizenship (ibid.).

However, in the current climate, the focus on the 'local' is increasingly problematic, for at least two reasons. First, as Mohan and Stokke (2000) remind us, we need to carefully examine the concept of locality, and how it is being used by a variety of non-local actors. Increasingly, ideas of participation and local governance are being promoted by a wide variety of actors, ranging from grassroots social movements and political parties, to mainstream development organizations, such as the World Bank, UNDP, USAID and many others. As concepts of local participation are being mainstreamed throughout development discourse, they are also being used to support and justify a variety of agendas, ranging from consolidation of central powers, to support for a neoliberal agenda and structural adjustment, to promotion of more progressive notions of development and democracy-building. Again quoting Mohan and Stokke (ibid.: 263–4):

> the paradoxical consensus over the role of 'local participation' in a globalizing world is fraught with dangers. Local participation can be used for different purposes by very different ideological stakeholders. It can underplay the role of the state and transnational power holders and can overtly or inadvertently cement Eurocentic solutions to Third World development. There is a need for critical analysis of the political use of 'the local', but also a need to develop a political imaginary that does not repeat these weaknesses.

Given the widespread adoption of the discourse of participation, we need both to critically examine how and for what purposes the agenda is being used, and also to develop a clearer analysis of under what conditions the mainstream development discourse creates spaces for positive engagement. That is, how do we assess when engagement with large institutions which are promoting participation discourse will widen the opportunities for genuine democracy-building at the local level, and under what conditions will it risk co-optation and legitimization of the status quo?

A second problem surrounding a narrow focus on the local is the way in which the discourse may screen out the importance of extra-local factors that equally shape the possibilities for democratic participation locally.

At one level, of course, this is seen in the importance of national legal frameworks, and strong central governments, for making local democratic innovations more effective. At the same time, a focus on the local without attention to the national may in fact diffuse national reform strategies. Some see the decentralization agenda as a way of undercutting work on human rights, especially for women, much of which has been carried out at the national and international levels. In such situations, work on national-level reforms, such as participatory constitutionalism, may be a prerequisite for local work. But there are important strategic questions: How can national-level advocacy groups and reform processes build and support a local constituency? Conversely, how can local groups scale up their demands for reform in the national legal and political process? What are the enabling legal frameworks created 'from above' that strengthen the possibility of effective democracy building 'from below'?

The problem becomes more complex when questions of global governance and global citizenship are also taken into account. Increasingly assertions of universal global rights (of the woman, of the child, for participation, etc.) may shape or conflict with understandings of local rights and citizenship. Local actors may use global forums as arenas for action (e.g. Narmada Dam; Chiapas) just as effectively – or more effectively – as they can appeal to institutions of local governance (Edwards and Gaventa 2001). Conversely, expressions of global civil society or citizenship may simply be vacuous without meaningful links to the local. The challenge is not only how to build participatory governance at differing levels, but how to promote the democratic and accountable *vertical links* across actors at each level. As Pieterse puts it, 'this involves a double movement, from local reform upward and from global reform downward – each level of governance, from the local to the global, plays a contributing part' (quoted in Mohan and Stokke 2000: 263).

Conclusion

The widespread engagement with issues of participation and local governance creates enormous opportunities for redefining and deepening meanings of democracy, for linking civil society and government reforms in new ways, for extending the rights of inclusive citizenship. At the same time, there are critical challenges – to ensure that the work promotes pro-poor and social justice outcomes, to develop new models and approaches where enabling conditions are not favourable, to avoid an overly narrow focus on the local, and to guard against co-optation of the agenda for less progressive goals. These are important challenges for the broader agenda of promoting *both* participatory democracy *and* development, for theorists and practitioners alike.

[Originally published as a background paper prepared for the Ford Foundation Local Governance network retreat at Buxted Park, Sussex, June 13–15, 2001]

References

Blair, H. (2000) 'Participation and accountability at the periphery: democratic local governance at the periphery', *World Development*, 28(1): 21–39.

Clarke, M. and J. Stewart (1998) *Community Governance, Community Leadership, and the New Local Government*, London: Joseph Rowntree Foundation.

Commonwealth Foundation (1999) *Citizens and Governance: Civil Society in the New Millennium*, London: Commonwealth Foundation.

Cornwall, A. and J. Gaventa (2000) 'From users and choosers to makers and shapers: repositioning participation in social policy', *IDS Bulletin*, 31(4): 50–62.

— (2001) 'Bridging the gap: citizenship, participation and accountability', *PLA Notes*, 40: 32–5.

DfID (2000) *Realising Human Rights for Poor People*, London: DfID.

Edwards, M. and J. Gaventa (2001) *Global Citizen Action*, Boulder, CO: Lynne Rienner Publishers.

Ellison, N. (1999) 'Beyond universalism and particularism: rethinking contemporary welfare theory', *Critical Social Policy*, 19(1): 57–83.

Fung, A. (2002) 'Creating deliberative publics: governance after devolution and democratic centralism', *The Good Society*, 11(1): 66–71.

Fung, A. and E. O. Wright (2001) 'Deepening democracy: innovations in empowered participatory governance', *Politics and Society*, 29(1): 5–41.

Gaventa, J. and C. Valderrama (1999) 'Participation, citizenship and local governance – background paper', Conference on Strengthening Participation in Local Governance, Institute of Development Studies, Brighton, www.ids.ac.uk/ids/particip/research/localgov.html.

Gaventa, J., A. Shankland and J. Howard (2002) 'Making rights real: exploring citizenship, participation and accountability', *IDS Bulletin*, 33(2), April.

Goetz, A. M. and J. Gaventa (2001) 'From consultation to influence: bringing citizen voice and client focus into service delivery', IDS Working Paper no. 138, Institute of Development Studies, Brighton.

Heller, P. (2001) 'Moving the state: the politics of democratic decentralisation in Kerala, South Africa, and Porto Alegre', *Politics and Society*, 29(1): 131–63.

Jones, E. and J. Gaventa (2002) 'Concepts of citizenship – a review', *IDS Development Bibliography*, 19.

Lister, R. (1998) 'Citizen in action: citizenship and community development in Northern Ireland context', *Community Development Journal*, 33(3): 226–35.

Lowndes, V. (1995) 'Citizenship and urban politics', in D. Judge, G. Stoker and H. Wolman, *Theories of Urban Politics*, London: Sage, pp. 160–80.

Merrifield, J. (2002) 'Learning citizenship', IDS Working Paper no. 158, Institute of Development Studies, Brighton.

Mohan, G. and K. Stokke (2000) 'Participatory development and empowerment: the dangers of localism', *Third World Quarterly*, 21(2): 247–68.

Narayan, D., R. Chambers, M. K. Shah and P. Petesch (2000) *Voices of the Poor: Crying Out for Change*, Washington, DC: World Bank.

Osmani, S. R. (2000) 'Participatory governance, people's empowerment and poverty reduction', Conference Paper Series, United Nations Development Programme.

— (2001) 'Participatory governance and poverty reduction', in A. Grinspun (ed.), *Choices for the Poor: Lessons from National Poverty Strategies*, New York: UNDP.

26 | The politics of domesticating participation in rural India

Ranjita Mohanty

In the last two decades, a variety of institutional spaces have been created by the Indian state at the village level to invite, encourage and enhance the participation of poor, low-caste (*dalit*) and tribal groups and women. Claiming to be based on democratic principles and procedures, such spaces promise to include the excluded people in deliberations and decision-making. The spaces are attractive to people for the sheer logic that they are created by the state, yet there are caveats, problematics and challenges that characterize their participation in these democratic institutions and the processes that take place within them. Often the existence of other spaces created by movements, NGOs or people themselves, where they practise participation, enable them to transfer their learning and skills to state-created spaces and energize them (Mohanty 2004). However, in the absence of other spaces, the state is possibly the only actor that is expected to create conditions for the actualization and animation of the institutional spaces it constructs. If the state fails to do that, the spaces remain largely empty ones, where otherwise excluded groups, such as women, may never gain entry to actualize participation, despite their eagerness.

This chapter examines the presence and absence of women in three institutionalized spaces created by the state to promote development and democracy: sectoral institutions of health and watershed development, and the constitutionally mandated institutions of local government called *panchayats*. It traces the practices and dynamics of representation, inclusion and voice within these spaces in three villages in Karuali district in the state of Rajasthan: Khubnagar, Akolpura and Bhikampura. The first is the home of the local *panchayat* headquarters, the second is a revenue village which has basic service institutions, and the third is a hamlet. All three are mostly populated by scheduled castes (SCs) and scheduled tribes (STs) in a context marked by extremes of poverty and exclusion.

My analysis raises questions about how women are represented in these institutions, whether their inclusion leads to substantive participation and voice, and whether these spaces are capable of enhancing the political agency of women, fashioning their political imagination and resulting in their political empowerment. In analysing women's experiences of participation in this setting, I explore the challenges of building genuinely inclusive and substantive representation and voice for marginalized actors.

Visions of the state

Women in Karuali have known the state in many forms: as provider of essential services such as the post office, school, health centre and roads. They have images of the state as it manifests itself in ostentatious election campaigns – cascades of motor cars on the dusty and uneven roads, shining flags, larger-than-life photographs of future leaders, and public meetings where people gather in their millions. They have also known the state as the police, and as the revenue officer, essential in ensuring legal order. The might of the state, despite its non-performance, is a seductive force. The idea of the state as the powerful big brother is also in the post-colonial imagination. A combination of welfarism, developmental and social justice agendas is also associated with the state. Out of both fear and respect, people would like to associate with the state. Hence, despite being a merely formal presence, and notwithstanding all the humiliations that they are subjected to, women may still want to be part of the institutional spaces created by the state.

The contemporary democratic revival, with its emphasis on building and strengthening local institutions, has brought the role of the state into sharp focus. Studies have shown that, in many contexts, poor and resourceless people continue to look to the state to intervene and solve their problems when it comes to the fulfilling of basic needs, physical security and conditions of dignified living. For historical reasons, the state still looms large in the perception of millions of people. Notwithstanding the retreat of the state under a globalized and liberalized economy, in countries like India the state is an everyday presence in the lives of poor and vulnerable sectors such as low castes, women and tribal people. As codified power, ultimate decision-maker and resource mobilizer, the state impinges on the lives of people more than any other force, thereby determining how affairs in society are to be managed.

As Chandhoke puts it, political preferences for the state over other actors are 'the outcome of historical processes ... that preference formation takes place in a historical context, that of specific institutions or systems of rules. These shape interest, fix responsibility and guide the formation of expectations' (2005: 1037). To understand participation in state-created developmental spaces, it is important to understand the nature of the post-colonial state and the depth of people's relationships of dependence and patronage with it. It is important to capture how the state features in the imagination of people, since it is their relationship with the state, ranging from disillusionment and despair to seeing it as a patron and a benefit, which is reflected in their relationship with state-created institutions. Despite the failure of the state to erase unequal material and social relationships, it has instilled a sense of political consciousness among the deprived section, though that consciousness is often played out on the basis of groups, which try to compete with each other for social and political dominance. In this competition and negotiation for power, women in general and low-caste and tribal women in particular are left at the margins. It is only with the creation of local institutions and reinforcement of affirmative action through reservations in political, educational and development institutions that their political participation has gained some impetus.

The local institutional spaces that I explore in this chapter have come into existence through different traditions of thought and policy decisions. Sectoral development projects, such as for watershed management and health, are guided by the state's mandate of uplifting the socio-economic conditions of the rural poor. The health institutions are part of the Integrated Child Development Scheme (ICDS) in which women are selected by government functionaries to run *anganwadi*, which are children's schools and health centres for expectant mothers and small children. The watershed project is a time-bound sectoral project. It has a village-level committee in each village to implement the project, to which representation of women and men is sought through nomination; each village committee has a total of ten or eleven members, out of which three or four members are women.

The *panchayats*, unlike the development committees, were created as units of local governance though the 73rd Constitutional Amendment in 1992. Understood variously as the grassroots units of governance, village republic and local governance (Sinha and Nandy 2000; Hiremath 1997; Mathew and Nayak 1996; Jain 1996; Rai et al. 2001), the *panchayats* are part of a three-tier system of governance that begins at the village and ends at the district. Each *panchayat* consists of several revenue villages and hamlets, and is divided into several wards from which candidates are elected to the *panchayat*. These members are referred to as ward members/*panch*, and the head of the *panchayat* is called *sarpanch*. *Gram sabha*, or the village council, which is the general body of all the adult residents in the villages of which the *panchayat* is constituted, is the body to which the *panchayat* members are accountable. A third of the seats in each *panchayat* are reserved for women. Women are expected to stand for the seats that are reserved for them, as well as for the general/open seats. Provisions are also made to reserve seats for SCs and STs in accordance with their numerical presence in a particular *panchayat*.

The different routes through which these spaces have evolved historically explain some dimensions of the way women's membership is constructed within them. Watershed development projects, which are fixed-duration target-oriented projects, constitute the committee to engage women actively in the project so that they can influence poverty outcomes through effective resource management, decision-making and ensuring an equitable distribution of benefits. The new policy guidelines are based on a process of change approach and call for the state to change from a controlling authority to becoming a provider of technical advice and support services in the development of the watershed. To strengthen the local institutions, the policy speaks of developing the institutional, managerial and technical capacity of people so that they can manage natural resources. It calls upon the state to develop a new role based on a spirit of partnership with the users of the natural resources in the village.

The ICDS of the Department of Women and Child Development has a thirty-year history, and aims to improve the nutritional and health status of vulnerable groups through a package of services, including supplementary nutrition, preschool education, immunization, health check-ups, referral services, and nutrition and health education. It provides an integrated approach for converging basic services through community-based *anganwadi* workers and helpers, through supportive community structures/women's groups and the *anganwadi* centre, which is a meeting ground for mothers and front-line workers. At the village level, the *anganwadi* centre has become a pivot of basic healthcare activities, contraceptive counselling and supply, nutrition education and supplementation and preschool activities. As part of its thrust on building the community organization of women, the ICDS forms self-help groups of women to engage in saving and credit activities.

Panchayats, in contrast to these two developmental spaces, have a constitutional mandate to encourage political participation of women and engage them in governance so that they can participate as well as ensure democracy at the local level. Evolved as a result of decentralization of decision-making, *panchayats* are supposed to engage people in assessing local needs, planning and executing solutions. While development projects have a welfarist approach in providing for women's membership in the committees, membership in *panchayats* is guided by the principles and legalities of affirmative action emanating from the state's agenda of social justice. Developmental thinking, directed towards changing the socio-economic landscape, engages women as committee members, users and beneficiaries; governance institutions, directed towards involving rural communities in local democracy, engage women as elected representatives in the framework of democracy. In their normative orientation, both institutions have a transformative agenda and women, at least theoretically, come to occupy different categories and are expected to enact roles that make them agents in influencing the developmental and democratic outcomes of the institutions.

Invited spaces as empty spaces 'Invited spaces' are conceptualized by Cornwall (2002) as spaces created by external agencies such as the state into which people are invited to participate. She contrasts invited spaces with the social and associational spaces of everyday life by suggesting that externally created spaces can be sites in which participation is domesticated, and in which the dynamics of power between actors within them offer very different possibilities for exercising voice and agency from those spaces people create for themselves. In the villages where this study is located, women's visibility in public spaces and their participation in state-created local institutions are negligible. Situations of chronic poverty together with rigid caste hierarchies, entrenched patriarchy and an apathetic bureaucracy have given rise to a situation where women have failed to participate in a meaningful way. Hence when we look at these institutional spaces through the lens of gender we find them largely empty and non-functional for women. One way of analysing this is through the conceptual category of *empty spaces*, a subcategory of invited spaces, denoting contexts where a marginalized group fails to populate an official invited space. The procedures and structures are there; also in some cases formal membership of women can be found. Yet all these do not translate into meaningful political participation.

In reality, an empty space is seldom completely empty. Even in the dismal scenario where women are purposely kept outside the boundaries of officially created spaces, in their own ways they try to enter that space. In my earlier research in Uttaranchal, where I could see traces of women's engagement, I argued that institutional spaces such as these can be considered as necessary though not sufficient conditions for participation and democracy (Mohanty 2004). In the context of empty spaces, can we hold the same argument that institutional spaces, despite all their shortcomings, have a normative grounding which *can be* activated to create conditions for women's engagement in development and democracy? What would explain the 'emptiness' of the *panchayat* and watershed committees as participatory spaces for women? And how can we best understand women's engagement with these spaces – either in seeking entry, or in maintaining their 'emptiness'? What do *they* see as the benefits of engagement, and how do they view the barriers they experience to inclusion and voice?

In what follows I describe my own standpoint in investigating this question, and point to three key elements that explain the failures of these invited spaces to secure the meaningful political participation of women: the control by men of the recruitment of women and of women's representative voices; women's relegation to being beneficiaries and wage earners within invited spaces; and stereotypes of women's public roles that go unchallenged by a putatively neutral state.

Investigating women's roles in participatory spaces Conducting research, I would like to think, is a different experience for a researcher who is also an activist. At one level it is a deeply satisfying act, to visit the villages, talk to the women, develop a relationship. At another level, it is frustrating to see the poor conditions: to contrast it with the urban centre where I live. I am acutely aware of my personal and professional locations that drive me to Karuali: my academic training in the university in social sciences and my long years of working with NGOs. I try to be a disciplined, systematic scientific researcher; I also try to be empathetic and sensitive. The cognitive and emotive threads run inside me, making research at once a cathartic and a disturbing experience.

I visit the Society for Sustainable Development, an NGO based in the district town of Karuali. I spend long hours talking to them, before I visit the villages. I tell them that I want to visit villages where they are not working, in fact where no NGO has ever gone and worked. I had a mental picture of what the villages would look like. But regrettably the reality is somewhat different. The roads are dusty, dust from stone mines casting a thick veil over our heads. When we step into the first village, I decide almost intuitively that I will just make a round of the village talking to people informally. I do not want to be, at the moment, pressured with the thought that I have a research agenda. The *varanda* where I am sitting is a post office, and I develop a friendship with the person who distributes the mail. I know from my days spent with my grandparents in their village that this is a person whom everybody likes, who knows who lives where and who does what. I am fortunate to have met him. We fall into conversation. I request that he accompany me to the village. He agrees and we start walking. We meet many people on the way and greet them. People are friendly and courteous, inviting us to their homes for tea. I am not constrained by time or research methodology. I sit drinking tea, chatting. Preethi, my colleague, who is still researching her MPhil, is excited, but thinks I am crazy: 'We have not yet met a single woman – Ranjita, let's try to meet them.'

By now it is obvious that we have to meet the women in their homes; I have gathered some sense of the social positioning of women, which – it is not difficult to make the link – influences their political position in local institutions. But women reveal, during that first meeting, a far deeper fracture in their relationship with the spaces that exist at the local level for their participation:

> *roji roti mein sari jindagi nikal gayi ham garibon ki, kya pata kameti mein kya hota hai- furshat ho to pata Karen* ('Poor people like us spend all their time in pursuing their livelihood; if we had the luxury of time, we would find out what happens in the committees')

> *Jab apne ghar aour samaj ham par pabandi lagata hai to ham use kaise todien* ('When our family and our community restrict us, how can we break that?')

> *Ham kuchh kaehn koi sunta bhi hai* ('Does anyone listen to what we say?')

> *Jab ham aksham hai, jab hamra sajma aisa hai to sarkark ko hi to kosis karna*

chhiye na? Aour kaun karega ('When we are poor and not capable of engaging our society, government must act')

Hame bas itna malum hai ki ham kameti ke sadshya hai, uske bad pata nahin ('I only know this much, that I am a member, nothing beyond that')

Ghar ke longon ne kha kin mahil ke liye arkshan hai – tum choonab mein khadi ho jayo, baki uske bad ham smbhal lenge ('Family members said that there is a seat reserved for women; you contest the election, we will manage it after that')

A vivid picture of Uttaranchal comes to my mind, different people, different narratives: women visible in public spaces, eager to do things, have belief in their own agency. I return to my hotel room and start arranging my thoughts. A few things become clear: looked at through women's eyes, the institutional spaces created by the state are largely empty, women trying but not gaining inclusion; the state, except for creating these spaces, has done nothing to actualize the spaces; women's identities are being manipulated in a manner that restricts their participation in these spaces. These impressions shaped the contextual background and analytical constructs I developed for the study.

I have my own understanding of what participation is. I try not to impose, but to find threads of similarities, albeit in different contexts. Does exclusion create similar feelings, does inclusion mean similar struggle? Intuitively we achieve a rapport – the urban educated middle-class researcher and the women in the villages. Despite our belonging to different places, wearing different kinds of clothes, speaking different languages, we begin to talk. I am aware, like many of these women, that there are many differences and barriers between us that cannot be dismantled; yet there is an element of trust that I will understand their stories. They, as much as I, know that there is nothing to offer except an empathetic ear. A comradeship grows – after a few meetings, women open up, pour out their stories. I am aware that when I go back to Delhi, my university colleagues will tease me for turning social science research methods upside down, but I am convinced that there could not have been a better methodology to study participation.

Recruiting members: denial of choice, imposition of choice

The genesis of representation in the Indian context has its base in the principles of affirmative action. Special efforts in the form of affirmative action to ensure political participation are meant to rescue excluded groups such as SCs, STs and women from social discrimination. Thus political participation and social participation are meant to reinforce each other – that is, political participation, by bringing excluded identities into the political spaces of decision-making, would bring them political equality that would negate some of the social inequalities they are subjected to, and social equality would equip them to seek inclusion in political spaces of decision-making and achieve political equality. Both are essential for citizenship and participation and both require that women, low castes and tribals as ascribed social categories be recognized by the state.

In practice, however, these norms of representation are dissonant with the realities of the inclusion – and indeed exclusion – of women from local institutional spaces. In the watershed developmental committee, women members are often selected in the village meeting. Selection is an informal process even though it takes place in the formal meeting. At times, the project bureaucracy selects women to be representatives because they are educated, or part of the *panchayat* system, or family members of 'influential' people in the village who have economic, political and/or social dominance at village level. At times, project bureaucrats ask these influential people to select women members. Women's willingness to be part of the committee is often taken for granted, and they are never asked about their choice as representatives. Representation in the ICDS is of a different nature to that of the watershed committee. Women from the community are recruited to implement the project – that is, they run the health-centre-cum-school and provide healthcare assistance to women. Hence there is a professional aspect to ICDS and it is treated as a salaried job. The community worker at village level is called the *anganwadi* worker; as education is a requirement, it is often the most educated woman from the community who is recruited. The project also has provisions to recruit widows and women who are 'deserted' by their husbands, and in such cases education no longer remains the sole criterion.

It is all too obvious that women are recruited to the watershed committee to meet procedural requirements. It seems ironic to talk about 'choice', since most women members are not even aware that they have membership of the committee. Both the project bureaucracy and male members know that women will merely be decorative members, leaving men the prerogative to rule the committee. Thus from the very beginning, the stage is set for keeping women outside and excluded from the committee. Women, too, get this sense; hence during the course of the project when meetings take place in their absence and they are sent papers to sign, endorsing decisions taken by male members, they do not resist.

Even in *panchayats* where women get elected, who will stand for election is a matter rarely decided by women. The 'politics' of representation in these invited spaces is a combination of local dominance, cultural codes of patriarchy and the working of the local administrative bureaucracy. The study villages are mostly populated by SCs and STs who live together with upper-caste Hindus. Often there is a village hierarchy in which groups who have numerical strength, together with economic and political resources, come to dominate. For example, most women from Bhikampura, which is densely populated by Jatavs, an SC community, are of the opinion that they are not treated very well in the *panchayat*, where an open seat for the *sarpanch* is occupied by Rajputs, the higher-caste Hindus from Harngar, which is a *panchayat* village. Men obviously want their family members to stand for the reserved seats so that the 'power' of *panchayat* membership remains within the family. Though being elected gives women representatives a political and constitutional legitimacy, in the micro-contexts of the village, these are inconsequential as men determine not only who will be given representation but also 'who will be represented by whom'. We therefore find husbands, brothers and sons conducting all the affairs in the village meeting on behalf of actual members.

When participation is imposed because there is a seat reserved for women, women are subjected to multiple humiliations. Women remain formal members, but men from their families exercise all the power associated with that membership. At the same time other women in the village find the situation difficult to accept. It is of course not a good feeling, even in a patriarchal system, to know that they are being used and domesticated by the very system that is intended to bring them empowerment and emancipation. I heard about Rajana Jatav, a low-caste woman, who contested and won election to the *panchayat* in the village of Akolpura, but whose husband attends the meetings to represent his wife. He also takes all the decisions which, as a *panchayat* member, she should be taking.

I wanted to meet Rajana, but she never came to any meeting I organized with women in the village. 'She is shy,' they said; 'you must meet her at her home.' I asked if someone could take me to her home. There was a surge of excitement among them as they walked with me towards her house. We reached Rajana's house. She came out into the courtyard to greet us – a young woman, certainly shy, with a long veil. I asked her if she is required to keep that on while talking to us. She nods silently, but does not remove the veil. We begin talking; she hardly answers the questions. All she has to say is that she never attends the meetings, adding that her husband is quite active. Why did she contest the election, then, I ask. Her voice chokes: 'Family members insisted, but you see, it's so humiliating. All these women make fun of me all the time and tell me that I am no more than a peon in the *panchayat*.' I refrain from hurting her sensibilities further, promising that I will see her when I come to her village next time, and leave quietly.

I am tempted to compare Rajana with Ankuri Jatav, the only woman member who claims to have subverted the male local bureaucracy's agenda of using women only as 'proxy' representatives. A Jatav low-caste woman, Ankuri says that she has the support of her community and therefore could win the election. There probably is some truth in that since the SCs in Bhikampura actively compete with upper-caste Rajputs of Harngar, particularly because the post of the *sarpanch* in Harngar *panchayat* is an open post occupied by a Rajput. The

Jatavas, working as labourers on the farms of Rajput, have found Ankuri an ally in their determination to challenge their Rajput masters politically. However, her own persona has to a certain extent shaped her political aspirations. She says that she is not intimidated by men or local bureaucrats, she goes to meetings and makes her point; she has struggled, but has created a space in which she has won acceptance. 'Why, then, have other women not followed you?' I ask. She responds thoughtfully: 'It is not often easy for women to ignore or even infuriate their family and society.' That simple truth indicates how the choices that women might exercise in fulfilling their political ambition are hijacked by the state and the larger society to keep women confined to what the culture demands of them.

Creating identities and assumptions: reinforcing stereotypes

Cultural roles of subservience within the family support a dynamic whereby women tend to be relegated to the roles of beneficiaries, wage earners and proxy representatives within the invited spaces under study (Cornwall 2004). Mere formal membership, stripped of the choices and freedoms that might come with representative authority, creates a scenario in which women come across as formal members in development committees, and as beneficiaries and users of the project, which often takes the shape of their being employed by the project as wage workers, and as proxy representatives in the *panchayat*, who legitimize the use of their position and power by male members of the family.

In the spaces provided by the *panchayat*, women's inclusion in *gram sabha* meetings merely serves the purpose of including their physical presence. They are neither encouraged nor discouraged to attend meetings. Men do not show overt aggression to women attending meetings or speaking in public, but there is an indifference which women find very humiliating. In watershed committees their role is even further diminished as even women's physical presence is not considered desirable by male members. The head of the institution, together with his allies in the committee and in local administration, sets the agenda for the meeting, and this often determines who will be included or excluded. Women in watershed projects are often found attending meetings when work is to be distributed during implementation, thereby reducing themselves to no more than labourers, ironically in the very context that is designed to give them ownership and participation in the project (Mohanty 2004). While membership of the *panchayat*, and therefore inclusion, is largely driven by the male members of the family, in the watershed committee membership is required to fulfil formal provisions. Inclusion is therefore never thought of as important, or as something that women may find desirable and on which basis they might make their claim. More than their presence and inclusion, it is their signature on official documents that is valued. 'What stops them refusing to sign such documents?' I ask. 'The fear and risk involved in annoying powerful people in the village and one's own family members,' Nirmala, an *anganwadi* worker, argued:

> Few women here have awareness about their rights. Some of us who are educated and are aware about our rights, we are seen as a 'nuisance' and a constant threat within the village. Hence, while women who are silent and docile will be called to meetings, we will be deliberately kept outside.

In Akolpura, one of the women members – wife of the chairperson of the watershed committee – looked embarrassed to talk about her role in the committee. 'I do not need to be there all the time – my husband plays an important role in the committee. We do not have disagreements on issues,' she says. In the social relations of power within patriarchy, women often echo what men think appropriate. Earlier on that day, talking to a group of women in the village, I gathered that in their view 'power' is transferred from a man to a woman – if a man is powerful in the public domain, so is his wife. Why, then, must women claim their 'own share of power'?

While women are not encouraged to take part in deliberations in the watershed committee meeting and influence decisions in the project, they are encouraged to step out of their homes to earn extra income for their families. Since most people have very small landholdings and work as wage labourers, women often go out of their houses to work. Hence watershed projects, which create this opportunity for local employment in dam construction, building rain-harvesting structures, maintaining plantations, raising nurseries, and so on, are able to include women only as labourers. Further reduction of their agency takes place in the *panchayats*, where, except for the rare occasions where they come across as elected members, women behave as good supportive wives and mothers, transferring their position and power in the *panchayat* to their husbands and sons.

In the case of the ICDS, women are actively included – indeed, it is not difficult to find women in a programme exclusively designed for them. Women have no hesitation in frequenting the *anganwadi* centre. Since the programme reinforces the traditional images and assumptions that families and society have of women as wives and mothers, it is considered safe for women to visit the *anganwadis*. Everyone seems to be happy as long as women are part of a programme that prepares them to be better wives and mothers; it is even better if they can build some savings and credit that the family can fall back upon during times of crisis. No one seems to mind women frequenting a non-threatening space where they interact only with other women. Yet the ICSD has had effects on the agency of women recruited as *anganwadi* workers. We find Nirmala, for instance, very vocal, often raising issues during my meeting with her: 'We have started from scratch – there was nothing available to women in this village to prove that they could excel in education and prove their capabilities. Projects like this have given us this space.' One can appreciate their sense of self-worth being acknowledged by the project. But the 'professional identity' that ICDS constructs for women like her and the sense of professional satisfaction that the work gives them do not translate into any radical possibilities for the large number of women receiving healthcare in ICDS, who participate only as 'mothers' eulogizing the domesticated conflict-free identity which is so valued by the larger society and their own families.

These identities of beneficiaries, wage earners and proxy representatives are intricately linked with the assumptions that go with them, and these assumptions then begin to govern the local institutions:

> *Auraten ghar mein khus rahti hain* ('Women are happy serving their family')

> *Jo faishla uske pati aur putra kartein hain, bahi uska bhi faishal hota hai* ('She would naturally want to support her husband's and son's decisions')

> *Parivar ki khushali ke liye woh ghar ke bhar bhi kam kar leti hai, lekin rajniti uske bas ki bat nahin, yah woh bhi smmajhti hai* ('She has an obligation to work to fulfil livelihood demands, but she also understands that politics is not her cup of tea')

> *Unhe samaj aur sanskriti ki parvah karni chahiye – unko ijjat usi mein milta hai* ('They are taught to respect society and its culture – that is where they have to gain her respect')

Constructions of gendered participation

Stereotyped understandings of women's public roles restrict their participation in invited spaces, so long as the state – in its role as space-maker – acts as a putatively neutral facilitator of this participation. The state sides with the dominant social forces, groups and individuals to avoid conflicts. The process take place in such a manner that women are excluded from its sphere. A dominant construction of gendered participation manipulates the state institutions and shapes participation, and is premised upon four critical aspects of participation: wisdom, space, power and voice.

I am talking to a group of women, some of them quiet, some eager to talk. It is impossible to keep men out of such meetings. They are curious to know what is going on. The men are trying to assess my identity and are anxious to be party to the conversation that is going on. Some of them watch from a distance, some gradually draw closer. They interrupt the women, give their version of the issue. The presence of men makes women self-conscious. I ask the men not to interrupt a woman while she is talking. One of them is sharp. He says: 'Then you have to talk to us separately after you finish here.' Then they withdraw; a few more men gather meanwhile and wait at a distance. I finish talking to the women; it is getting dark, but I will have to talk to these men who have waited patiently for so long. So I join them. More tea is served. First they want to know whether or not I am a government officer. It takes a while to convince them that I am just doing a study. 'What are you going to do with the study?' one of them asks. 'Let's see,' I try to be evasive, 'maybe some good recommendation for your village will come up.' We begin talking. Gradually the suspicion gives way to a kind of temporary camaraderie.

Seen through the lens of these forces, we get a particular picture of the *wisdom* that women exercise in the pursuit of participation, the *spaces* where women seek inclusion, the *power* that participation offers to those who pursue it, and the *voices* that can be raised to animate participatory spaces:

Wisdom Unki samajh mein nahi ayega ('they will not understand') is the common refrain from men regarding women's interest in what goes on in the village meetings. The institutional space is seen by men as technical in its content, masculine in its manner of deliberation, and external in its goal, as opposed to the generic discussions women have within the household, which more often than not refer to the feminine pursuits of nurturing and caring for family members.

Space: Women's space is never seen as external – it is always space within the four walls of the house where they are expected to participate. If women seek inclusion, it has to be within the family; if they seek deliberation and negotiation, it has to be with family members. The family space is almost sacrosanct, and women seeking inclusion in the external spaces offered by the institutions are looked upon as transgressing the boundaries of their defined spaces.

Power: The majority of men feel that the power a woman has is directly proportional to that which her husband wields. If the male is powerful, so is his wife. Making men the reference point for power also gets its impetus from the fear that empowering women can have political consequences. Hence we find men happy with their women so long as they are part of the saving and credit group, which is perceived as non-threatening and non-political, and do not aspire to be watershed committee members or *panchayat* members, where deliberation and negotiation of a different kind take place.

Voice: Male reactions to female voices raised outside of the home are either indifferent, or amused, or simply dismissive. The reactions understandably are directed towards keeping women silent. As the *sarpanch* of Harngar says, *hamri gaon ki aurtaen to bas baat karna janti hai, sauk hai unki* ('Oh, they love to talk and talk. That, after all, is their habit!'), implying that women's speech is without much substance. A common reason men cite for keeping women silent is their lack of political language – 'they do not know what to say in a meeting'. Hence the fear is that women may annoy government officials and influential people in the village by uttering something 'useless'.

If participation is all about political negotiation, democratization and empowerment, certainly these conventional patriarchal notions of participation do not offer much possibility to women. But things are worse when these notions get transferred to state institutions created to promote participation. The state, rather than critically looking at the forces that subvert its developmental and democratic agenda, poses as innocent, pretending that everything is all right with the way its institutions function. For instance, it is fairly well understood that women are often silent in public spaces because cultural codes do not allow them to speak in front of older men – fathers, fathers-in-law, brothers and uncles. It is considered disrespectful and brings dishonour to families if women are found talking in public meetings. Hence one of the ways to keep women silent is by not bringing any women-related issues to the meeting for discussion.

In institutions where women find representation following specific directives issued by the state, discussion of women's issues, where women might represent a collective interest, has been superseded by discussion of more generic issues. Two women *sarpanch* who won *panchayat* elections because seats were 'reserved' for women have spent their five years' tenure planning the construction of school buildings and roads, because in popular perceptions that is what village development is all about and the *sarpanch* is expected to develop infrastructure facilities in the village. In ICSD, since it is a health project targeted at children and women, women's issues are understandably represented in meetings. In the watershed committee, which is a forum to implement a highly specialized project, however, discussion invariably centres on issues pertaining to that project. It is seldom that women, as a collective or as individuals, or their issues, are represented in committee spaces. By treating certain issues as 'non-decisionable' and thereby keeping them outside the institutional decision-making process and concentrating on popular 'safe' issues, which will not result in conflict because women will not participate in such deliberations, the institutions help society exercise its power over women (Kabeer 1994). This eventually turns women into absentee members or silent spectators.

It is not only that women speak or do not speak, but the extent to which when they do speak they are comprehensible to men and the local bureaucracy. Women are not encouraged to speak because they do not know the political language of the public space or the language of the state. In the context of distance between the state and people, activists have often worked as interpreters. In our particular context, where a highly negligent state distances itself from poor, *dalit* and tribal women and the activist interpreter is not present, women's voices are virtually absent from official institutional spaces.

Conclusion

State-created spaces are attractive because they are grounded in the normative principles of equality, justice and empowerment. However, in contexts where these institutions reproduce stereotyped identities, assumptions and expectations for women, women – instead of fashioning their political imagination and democratic aspirations – come to experience multiple doses of humiliation, discrimination and exclusion. As a result, and despite the provision for representation, looked at from rural women's vantage points, these spaces appear largely empty. In such situations, even the normative grounding of these spaces is not enough to create the necessary conditions for participation to take off. Women, incapacitated by poverty and social exclusion, display a sense of resignation, and it seems unlikely that they will organize on their own to negotiate and claim their equitable stake in these local participatory institutions. The state, which is expected to facilitate women's participation, has failed them in many ways.

Let me, at the risk of sounding prescriptive, end this chapter with a small note on what would help in such contexts to mobilize women's substantive representation, inclusion and voice. My earlier research in Uttaranchal shows that women's participation, facilitated by NGOs, movements and at times even by the state, in 'other supportive spaces', enables them to participate in the invited spaces of development and governance institutions. Their participation receives further impetus when local bureaucrats, particularly those placed at the higher level, encourage, mobilize and create conditions for women's participation by directly intervening at the village and district levels. The coexistence of these two conditions is essential, because the absence of one will result in too much dependency on the other. Too much dependency on the state, as the three villages in Rajasthan indicate, creates a situation where women will unquestioningly accept what the state offers to them. Likewise, too much dependency on women's organizations or NGOs will result in bypassing the state. When these organizations facilitate women's participation, they help in creating a larger supportive environment for women to gain entry to and participate in the official invited spaces. When the state, through its local bureaucracy, accommodates women's genuine interests in the local institutional spaces, it helps in building the participatory character of these spaces to *institutionalize* such interests as women's rightful stake in processes of development and democracy.

[Originally published as 'Gendered subjects, the state and participatory spaces: the politics of domesticating participation in rural India', in Andrea Cornwall and Vera Schattan Coelho (eds), *Spaces for Change*, Zed Books, 2007]

References

Chandhoke, N. (2005) 'Seeing the state in India', *Economic and Political Weekly*, 12 March.

Cornwall, A. (2002) 'Making spaces, changing spaces: situating participation in development', IDS Working Paper no. 170, Institute of Development Studies, Brighton.

— (2004) 'New democratic spaces? The politics and dynamics of institutionalised participation', *IDS Bulletin*, 35(2): 1–10.

Hiremath, U. (1997) 'Women in grassroots politics', *Social Welfare*, 44(2).

Jain, D. (1996) *Panchayati Raj: Women Changing Governance*, New Delhi: UNDP.

Kabeer, N. (1994) *Reversed Realities: Gender Hierarchies in Development Thought*, New Delhi: Kali for Women.

Mathew, G. and R. Nayak (1996) 'Panchayat at work: what it means for the oppressed', *Economic and Political Weekly*, 6 July.

Mohanty, R. (2004) 'Institutional dynamics and participatory spaces: the making and unmaking of participation in local forest management in India', *IDS Bulletin*, 32(2).

Rai, M., M. Nambiar, S. Paul, S. Singh and S. Sahni (2001) *The State of Panchayats: A Participatory Perspective*, New Delhi: Samskriti.

Sinha, D. and B. Nandy (2000) 'From spectators to participation: panchayat as public domain for dispute settlement', *Journal of the Anthropological Survey of India*, Kolkata.

27 | Aiding policy? Civil society engagement in Tanzania's PRSP

Elaina Mack

Over the last decade, a shift has gradually taken shape – leading to what is now being referred to as the 'new aid paradigm'. Along with a new emphasis on strengthening the capacity of the state has been an attempt to expand the role of Southern civil society actors – not just to provide services to *aid the poor*, but also to contribute to *aid policy* to help reduce poverty. While some attention has been paid to the policy process, more focus is needed to address the other side of civil society engagement. That is, the influence those civil society organizations are actually having on policy. In particular, very little is known about how and why civil society organizations engage in policy, how they use different strategies to exert policy influence, and what outcome such efforts have had. This chapter explores the contexts, capacities and experiences of civil society policy engagement in Tanzania, drawing on interview material and secondary literature gathered in 2006. It seeks not only to reflect on how to strengthen the capacity of civil society organizations to get involved in policy, but also how to create an enabling environment in which they can get involved.

Civil society, Tanzania and the 'new aid paradigm'

The twenty-first century has ushered in a new series of policy approaches, practices and politics for international aid. Together, they have amounted to a dramatic shift that is now being touted as a 'new paradigm of aid'. This paradigm involves strengthening the role of the state in the name of bolstering national ownership, governance, partnership, accountability and pro-poor rights. It involves policy taking a much more prominent position, whereas projects, previously central to the delivery of aid, now become just one aspect of a broader development agenda (Groves and Hinton 2004). Further, the new paradigm calls for poverty reduction to become the overarching goal of all development actors – challenging various stakeholders to think more pragmatically and holistically about how to help improve the lives of poor people in more substantive, systemic and sustainable ways.

At the same time, these shifts and others have expanded the role of civil society actors in trying to aid the poor and reduce poverty. For instance, the donor focus on democratization and governance has encouraged (and perhaps even pressured) civil society to assume such roles as: providing checks and balances vis-à-vis the state, fostering political participation among citizens, nurturing democratic institutions and playing a leadership role in resisting authoritarianism. Furthermore, recent development trends have encouraged civil society to assume an advocacy role to promote the interests of the poor, and build social capital to advance pro-poor development, much like its efforts to promote civic action. These new responsibilities have been added to civil society's already large portfolio of tasks involving the delivery of social services to specific recipients.

With all these changes, the development community has been in a steep learning curve to help nurture civil society engagement in policy. Initially, donors and academics in particular focused on trying to establish and create a more conducive *process* for which civil society could engage in development policy. This work was especially evident after the first round of many developing countries' Poverty Reduction Strategy Papers (PRSPs). While it is important that this work continues, more attention is needed to address the other side of civil society engagement – namely, the influence that non-governmental organizations are actually having on policy. In particular, very little is known on how and why civil society organizations engage in policy, how they use different strategies to exert influence on policy, and what outcome such efforts have had. There are, however, signs that interest in these issues is growing. For instance, a recent study conducted by the Overseas Development Institute (ODI 2006) indicates that civil society organizations (CSOs) in developing countries are only achieving a 'limited impact' and are often failing to influence policy processes and practices, even in countries with more liberal political systems.

Why are CSOs in developing countries having such limited impact, even with the new spaces afforded to them? Do CSOs have enough capacity to fulfil these new wide-ranging roles? And even if they do have the capacity, are they equipped with enough power to influence policy, especially when donors aren't involved?

Understanding 'civil society' involvement

The term 'civil society' has become quite a contested concept. There seems to be very little agreement on its definition. In particular, the only consensus that appears to have emerged is that civil society means different things to different people and that it functions differently at different times. While this is not the place for a lengthy discussion of this debate, several aspects are worth highlighting. More generally, civil society is a space where people can come together to pursue common interests because they care enough about something to take collective action. In theoretical terms, Edwards suggests that definitions of civil society break down into three different camps: analytical models focusing on *associational life*, including the separation from the market and state; *normative models*, such as thinking about the kind of society that is to be strived for; and the arena of *public sphere* where public deliberation and 'active citizenship' play a role (2004: vii–viii).

There is an enormous amount of diversity in civil society organizations. In practical terms, civil society is composed of a range of organizations, including non-governmental organizations, community-based organizations, trade unions, chambers of commerce, professional associations, churches and many more. This diversity is also evident in the range of interests, resources, organizational structures, objectives, values and scope of organizations. In the context of development cooperation, there has been a growing shift over the last thirty years in terms of refocusing the strategic roles that Southern CSOs play. There is increasing overlap between CSOs in the South and North owing to the greater interconnectedness, convergence and expansion of CSO efforts. As a result of these changes, Tomlinson (2006a: 2) believes that the most significant CSO strategic roles involve:

- collaborating in solidarity with poor and marginalized citizens;
- articulating and coalescing of citizen interests for democratic governance in the South;
- advancing gender equality, particularly the rights of poor and marginalized women;
- expanding space for citizens' voices, particularly in the South, in policy dialogue;
- stimulating innovations grounded in the realities of where poor people live and work;
- building capacity in various areas relevant to social change;
- networking and learning, leveraging CSO knowledge and CSO policy perspectives;
- mobilizing and leveraging Northern financial and human resources; and
- promoting expressions of global citizenship and exchange for global social justice.

This is by no means an exhaustive list, but it does give us a sense of the context, number of roles and competing goals for which CSOs in the South must prioritize.

Policy: process, engagement, influence

Policy, like civil society, is contested terrain. For the purposes of this chapter, public policy is defined as a 'course of action or inaction chosen by public authorities to address a given problem or interrelated set of problems' (Pal 2001: 2). The policy process, on the other hand, is generally understood as the steps followed to shape policy from problem identification to implementation and evaluation. While this chapter does not *systematically* review Tanzania's civil society engagement in all stages of the policy process, it is important to be aware of them all and to remember that each phase plays a unique role, that the policy process can start from many different places and that it can involve a wide range of different elements.

Given the growing expectations of civil society, this chapter suggests that a new understanding of *policy engagement* is needed for the field of international development. The term proposed by this chapter borrows from several other concepts, such as participation, advocacy, citizen engagement, governance, etc. It involves the interplay between the following roles:

- participating in the formulation, implementation and evaluation of aid policies to strengthen their relevance and quality (engagement in invited space);
- undertaking advocacy work to identify, raise awareness or lobby decision-makers on issues of importance either to the organization or to its constituents (trying to create new space for public debate);
- providing checks and balances on aid and other policies in the spirit of good governance (the watchdog function); and
- fostering civic education or political engagement to help citizens exert their rights or to hold the government to account (promoting the 'demand' side of development).

The global and regional policy context

Over the years, several international papers, agreements and commitments have created a broad policy and resource framework for the delivery of aid. Particularly significant for the purposes of this analysis is the 2005 Paris Declaration on Aid Effectiveness, and the resultant focus on the delivery of results in the form of the Millennium Development Goals, Poverty Reduction Strategy Papers and programme-based approaches (PBAs), such as Sector-wide Approaches (SWAPs) and Budget Support.

The broad goal of the 2005 Paris Declaration on Aid Effectiveness is to customize large-scale development assistance to the particular requirements of recipient countries. The Declaration builds on the 2002 Monterrey UN Summit on Financing for Development and the 2003 Rome High-level Forum on Harmonization. A series of commitments, indicators and targets focus on five key areas:

1 ownership: recipient or partner countries exercise effective leadership over their development policies and strategies and coordinate development action;
2 alignment: donors base their overall support on partner countries' national development strategies, institutions and procedures;

3 harmonization: donors' actions are more harmonized and transparent;
4 management for results: managing resources and improving decision-making for results; and,
5 mutual accountability: donors and partners are accountable for development results.

It is important to note that this aid effectiveness agenda was largely developed under the premise of what donors (and developing country governments) believed would lead to a more efficient and effective aid system. And while CSOs have welcomed key aspects, particularly ways to strengthen donor practices and the state in poor countries, concerns have emerged both in terms of how the Declaration will affect CSOs and how it will meet the goals of poverty reduction. As a vehicle for reducing poverty vis-à-vis effective aid, Tomlinson argues that because the bulk of the Declaration focuses on the capacities of the state, it is an 'unfinished and narrow agenda for reform' and further it 'ignores the role of citizens and CSOs as development actors in their own right who have a long history in organizing economic, social and political initiatives with and on behalf of the poor' (2006b: 3). The crux of the argument then becomes 'aid effectiveness for whom', 'on what basis' and 'defined by whom'.

Some of the most concerning elements of the Declaration for civil society organizations include the aid alignment and harmonization agendas. The discourse surrounding these agendas suggests that there will be genuine benefits for recipient and donor governments. Yet these agendas raise important concerns about the role of civil society organizations, as donor countries increasingly assign more of their funding for direct support to recipient governments. These concerns are based on several problematic assumptions (Pratt 2006: 2; Tomlinson 2006b: 6–8):

- state development strategies may not be a product of applying democratic principles or practices, including seeking the input of diverse citizens;
- given the instability of governments in many countries, new types of aid may become 'unstuck' through corruption and/or other undemocratic structures – even despite donor countries' best efforts to prevent this from happening;
- a disproportionate amount of focus on alignment with state policy and reliance on administrative harmonization may have grave consequences for achieving the Millennium Development Goals;
- harmonized aid may make the poor more vulnerable to political change;
- these agendas may 'de-prioritize civil society' as the focus on the state continues;
- it is not always clear how civil society will be funded under the new 'aid paradigm';

- civil society may increasingly be seen as an extension to the state, helping governments to meet *their* targets;
- alignment and harmonization may mean that gender issues are ignored. In particular, the funding for women's organizations to analyse budgets and other public issues may be jeopardized and marginalized; and
- organizations may reorient their priorities to meet those of the government to secure funding, potentially blurring the boundaries between the state and civil society.

Two observations stand out for civil society organizations in Tanzania. First, donors are placing more emphasis on government partnerships; yet they are also struggling to find better ways to relate to and make a difference to the lives of the poor. Groves and Hinton (2004) suggest that there are contradictions here as the new policy approach has actually *reduced* the opportunities for donor–citizen and donor–civil society interaction as agencies continue with the shift away from projects. Second, this new focus on donor–government partnerships has created some degree of uncertainty for many civil society organizations, both in terms of how they might be financially supported and in how they might be able to play an active role under the 'new aid paradigm'.

Many new ways of delivering aid have resulted from priorities identified in the Paris Declaration and its predecessors. Three such mechanisms merit discussion as they significantly affect *all* civil society organizations working on international development issues. The first is the Millennium Development Goals (MDGs), which influence nearly all practical aspects of today's aid system. MDGs tend to frame government and donor investment preferences and policies. Consequently, CSO activities often need to coincide with these goals to secure funding. As Bissio (2003) points out, CSO involvement in the MDGs tends to concentrate on the *implementation* of national poverty eradication programmes, a role that they are already playing. While CSO participation may not be institutionalized, the MDGs have provided civil society with new forums for dialogue and advocacy with governments and donors. Indeed, global civil society has been quite active and has tried to capitalize on these forums. In 2004 alone, over 1,800 NGO representatives from across the globe took part in a UN conference focusing on the MDGs (UN Non-Governmental Liaison Services 2006). Other NGOs have drawn attention to the MDGs through such initiatives as the worldwide Make Poverty History campaign.

The second is the Poverty Reduction Strategy Papers (PRSPs), which are national strategies that outline the macroeconomic and social policies and programmes to be undertaken by poor countries as a way of fostering growth and reducing poverty over a specified number of years. PRSPs are to be drawn up by governments through a participatory process involving domestic stakeholders (private sector, civil society, etc.) and external development partners, especially the IMF and the World Bank (IMF 2005). The idea was adopted as a qualifying condition for countries to participate in the Heavily Indebted Poor Countries (HIPC) initiative, starting in 1999. Consistent with the priorities laid out in the Paris Declaration, international financial institutions envisage that PRSPs will be:

- country-driven, promoting national ownership of strategies through broad-based participation of civil society;
- result-oriented and focused on outcomes that will benefit the poor;
- comprehensive in recognizing the multidimensional nature of poverty;
- partnership-oriented, involving coordinated participation of development partners (government, domestic stakeholders and external donors); and
- based on a long-term perspective for poverty reduction (ibid.).

Several critical issues have been raised with respect to the participation of civil society in developing, implementing and monitoring PRSPs. First, the strategies have provided new policy spaces for civil society to engage with and question the state in almost every country. Yet in practice spaces for participation have been seen by many civil society organizations as limited and not guaranteed. A concern is that organizations may in fact be *legitimizing* donor-led policy processes rather than trying to create new space for civil society involvement. Criticism has been made that donors have kept a tight rein on too much of the policy content. Thus, CSOs were invited to participate only in discussions related to a predetermined agenda. Finally, new opportunities for CSO dialogue on policy remain very fragile and tied to donor interests.

The third mechanism is programme-based approaches (PBAs), such as SWAPs and Budget Support. These are sometimes seen as a central tool in contributing to implementing PRSPs and making progress towards the MDGs. As the name implies, sector-wide approaches provide a funding window for a sector (e.g. health) or sub-sector (e.g. HIV/AIDS). Often they are implemented through the coordination of partner governments, donors and some NGOs, to use donor resources to support an agreed policy and expenditure programme. Budget support focuses on key exchanges between partner governments and donors to emphasize *broader budget priorities and policy objectives*, such as through a national budget (OECD 2005).

While there is surprisingly little academic and donor attention paid to civil society involvement in PBAs (until quite recently), some significant implications have emerged. The development of the plan is supposed to involve key stakeholder groups, including civil society and the private sector, through a well-developed participatory process. Yet the practice of 'piggybacking' off the agenda, design and implementation of the PRSP may not only undermine PBA principles but also reduce opportunities for civil society involvement in major development issues. This has understandably raised concerns that PBAs (particularly Budget Support) are obliging governments to become more accountable to donors rather than to citizens.

Participation in the PRSP process

With some consultation experience in processes such as Vision 2025, Tanzania Assistance Strategies and the National Poverty Eradication Strategy, NGOs reviewed and provided input to the draft government PRSP in 2000. The government of Tanzania led rushed consultations with the help of three NGOs, which organized the discussions. Consultations included representatives of five NGOs at each of seven zonal workshops (Curran 2005). The hastily organized consultations, as might be expected, were roundly criticized by NGOs in Tanzania and analysts elsewhere. In particular, critics argued that NGOs were not given sufficient time, information or opportunity to engage in a meaningful policy debate. It was perceived that their participation was largely an instrumental one-off event. It is important to note that the government of Tanzania was eager to finish the strategy in order to access the HIPC funds. The philosophy and concepts underpinning the PRSP process were also new and confusing for everyone, including the government itself.

Even so, a handful of NGOs did engage in the policy process. A coalition was formed under the Tanzanian Coalition for Debt and Development (TCDD), which enabled these groups to participate in analysing the state of Tanzania's poverty and to recommend specific areas for sector improvements. However, it is important to be mindful of *which* NGOs participated as part of the TCDD and the first PRSP process. There is a general consensus within the literature that only a small number of 'elite' civil society organizations were involved. In particular, international NGOs were provided with substantial opportunities to contribute to the process, while smaller local ones were virtually excluded. Equally concerning was the fact that the local professional NGOs that represented the poor needed to attract and secure support from international NGOs and donors in order to support their activities at these meetings (Mercer 2003). On the whole, NGO diversity and discourse in the first PRSP process were rather limited.

Beyond the policy formulation stage, civil society organizations were also involved in the implementation and evaluation of the PRSP, but arguably in even more limited ways. For instance, CSOs were allowed to read the government's Annual Progress Reports prepared on the implementation of the strategy. Other larger, more professional CSOs conducted their own independent primary research, which was then used in town-hall-style forums such as Poverty Policy Weeks and Public Expenditure Reviews (Curran 2005). Despite these experiences, a 2001 civil society workshop identified several challenges. Perhaps most significant was that many CSOs found it difficult to get involved in monitoring efforts when their constituents or they themselves did not understand the PRSP process, content and jargon (Hakikazi Catalyst 2004).

The majority opinion suggests that CSOs did not have much influence on the content of the first PRSP and that the strategy does not include civil society views or contributions in a meaningful way (Curran 2005). A 2003 study by Gould and Ojanen found that not only were the PRSP consultations 'shallow and tendentious', but the document itself was written by a 'small, homogeneous "iron triangle" of transnational professionals' made up of elite government, donor and non-state (NGOs) representatives in Dar es Salaam (Gould and Ojanen 2003: 7). Consequently, CSOs were essentially sidelined when they identified issues that were not already on the donor-state agenda.

Despite these views, there were three important contributions that stemmed from CSO involvement in Tanzania's PRSP process. First, the PRSP process enabled key CSOs to push for the elimination of school fees to be put on the policy table and to raise its profile, though the government's position did not immediately change as a result of their efforts. Further evidence gathered by CSOs helped to put pressure on the government to abolish school fees in 2001. Thus, while CSOs had limited influence during the PRSP process, they managed to position the school fees issue and keep it fixed on government and donor radars.

Second, CSOs were vital in raising the level of awareness and understanding of the PRSP document through developing and distributing plain language documents, television and radio information across the country. This information, written in English and Swahili, helped to demystify the technical language and in some cases these versions were used by local governments as *the strategy* to be followed (Curran 2005). Furthermore, the popular versions seemed to do a good job of capturing complex development problems like HIV/AIDS, trade, health equity and other issues by using cartoons and interesting anecdotes. See Figure 27.1 below for two examples from the plain version of the PRSP.

Finally, while it has been established as part of regulation guiding the sector, the PRSP process provided a focus for the new NGO Policy Forum. Bringing together some seventy NGO voices, the Forum used the PRSP process as a vehicle for discussing such issues as policy influence and advocacy (IMG 2005). The establishment of this coordinating body would prove useful for the second round of the strategy, locally known as the MKUKUTA.

Organizing and coordinating: the MKUKUTA policy process

The role of civil society in this final policy episode, the MKUKUTA (PRSP II), was quite different to its predecessor. Such changes included:

- Renaming the PRSP MKUKUTA in Swahili or the 'Economic Growth and Poverty Reduction Strategy'. This is fairly significant because it seemed

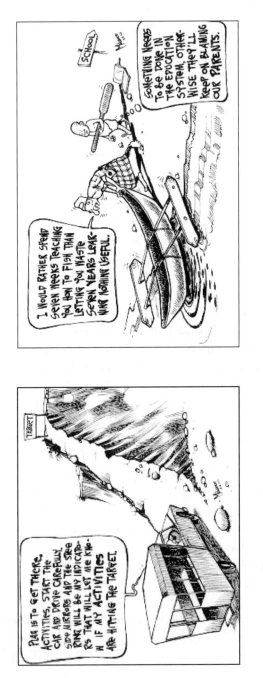

FIGURE 27.1 The plain language version of Tanzania's PRSP: (a) Illustrating the rationale for evaluation; (b) Illustrating the need for education reform (*source*: Hakikazi Catalyst 2002: 10, 20)
Note: Zanzibar had its own PRSP process but was included in the main PRSP for Tanzania

to create more local ownership and effectively moved the leadership (and language) of the policy from donors to the government of Tanzania, at least at a surface level.

- Slower and more strategic consultations (approximately one year) allowed more time for CSOs to get involved in the revision process and created more opportunities for groups to participate in meetings, working groups and committees. Central to this consultation process was a 'roadmap' that the government prepared to maximize civil society participation as much as possible (Curran 2005). For instance, consultations were organized around themes, so it was much easier for NGOs to develop policy statements and to generally understand where they could 'fit in to the process'. Those involved in the participation process contributed to each of the three pillars, such as:
  a. Growth and Income Poverty → inclusion of employment and livelihoods, and commitment to revise land rights polices;
  b. Social Wellbeing → more attention to children, HIV/AIDS and gender; and,
  c. Good Governance and Accountability → consideration of policies to address domestic violence issues (ibid.: 12)
- The inclusion of the third pillar, in particular, has been attributed to NGO advocacy efforts. However, it is important to acknowledge that the government was not necessarily opposed to the idea and it was not always clear how much sway donor agencies had behind the scenes. Moreover, as one donor put it, CSO involvement in the MKUKUTA can be assessed at the 'outcome level'. This means that CSOs speak of feeling that they are 'having their say and are being heard', but it is not yet clear, as one put it, how their 'contributions will translate into sustainable impacts'.
- There was an increase in the number of non-state actors involved, including fifteen identified stakeholder groups. These groups ranged across NGOs, business groups, church-based groups and trade unions (ibid.). Umbrella and network groups such as the National Policy Forum (NPF), Tanzanian Gender Networking Programme (TGNP) and the Tanzania Association of NGOs (TANGO) worked to coordinate and collect member views at the national and district levels.
- Public education became a priority. Following the lead of CSOs in the first PRSP, the government developed a communications strategy to reach target groups with tactics such as holding regular media briefings and putting up information on village noticeboards (URT 2006).
- Cross-Sectoral Technical Working Groups were created to support the implementation phase. Civil society organizations are now responsible for heading the monitoring and evaluation group on the mainland and for the advocacy group on Zanzibar. A recent report, however, indicates that

while NGOs on the mainland have been invited to participate and lead these groups, their involvement has been welcomed only on 'light technical issues'. Therefore, they are being prevented from lobbying the government, much to the dismay of the NGOs. Yet the same study goes on to note that the mere fact that the government is talking about the nuances of policy engagement is a sign that NGOs are 'no longer having to demand access to processes from the start' (ActionAid and Care International 2006: 21).

The attitudes, role and contributions of civil society in making the MKUKUTA were seen as more positive than in the first PRSP. Civil society organizations are beginning to recognize government efforts to widen policy spaces and are even saying they are fairly satisfied with how the government undertook the MKUKUTA participatory process. Likewise, the government is starting to appreciate CSO contributions. In fact, ministries are no longer automatically taking a 'hostile stance' towards CSOs in such processes, though there is a 'long way to go for both government and development partners' (IMG 2005: 35). There was also some evidence suggesting an improvement in government–CSO relations during the consultation process of MKUKUTA (ActionAid and Care International 2006).

Three brief caveats and challenges must be pointed out. First, this positive (and surprising) feedback may not necessarily be related to improvements to the participatory process. Rather, it might be *because* the majority of the same players were involved in improving the second round of the PRSP. A related caveat, second, is the often unspoken concern that professional NGOs might not be representing many of Tanzania's diverse population groups. This might be tied to the reality that the majority of key NGOs are based in Dar es Salaam, but the capacity of these organizations to gather local input is still weak (IMG 2005). Exacerbating the problem are international and professional CSOs, which may be increasingly 'crowding out' smaller, local groups from direct participation in the aid policy process (although working with professional CSOs may be the only effective way at present, given the capacity of local CSOs and the nature of aid policy processes). Finally, while the intention of the MKUKUTA was to focus on priority *outcomes* versus priority *sectors*, participation was sometimes limited to CSOs specializing in a specific area (e.g. education). This approach made it difficult to explore the many cross-cutting issues of poverty such as HIV/AIDS and gender equity (ibid.).

Conclusions

There seem to be two schools of thought on the prospects for civil society participation in PRSPs. The first camp sees Tanzania's civil society participation in the development process as an important opportunity for CSOs to get involved in national policy processes. Through these new opportunities, civil society organizations can potentially strengthen their associational autonomy vis-à-vis state power (Tripp 2000). At the same time, the process provides a mechanism for civil society to hold the state to account (Piron and Evans 2004). Thus, this view contends that civil society participation in development policy helps to *create new space* for influencing the domestic arena. The second school of thought asserts that the new spaces should really be seen as a *response* to governance trends that emphasize civil society organizations as important players in policy-making (Mercer 2003). According to this view, there are several consequences related to this 'pseudo-form' of democracy. For instance, it is widely argued that when CSOs participate in such processes they are in fact lending *legitimacy* to donor-driven policy-making. Similarly, organizations are arguably letting the government 'off the hook' from their essential responsibilities to identify, analyse and execute national policies. For the sector, this has meant that CSOs are increasingly standing in as 'stakeholders' and 'representatives' of the people – marginalizing their role as 'watchdogs' at the same time (Shivji 2004). Moreover, according to this perspective, participation in development policy has actually *impaired* the sector's capacity to influence domestic policies.

What lessons, then, emerge from the Tanzanian case?

The adoption of top-down approaches In this case study, CSOs adopted strategies that targeted government or donors rather than grassroots groups. For instance, in the PRSP process professional CSOs were often 'going to the people' instead of the 'people going to them'. Though high-profile CSOs certainly demonstrated good intentions, adopting top-down approaches rather than mobilizing from the bottom may have inadvertently weakened the process and affected the outcome of the policy. Adopting more grassroots approaches, however, would require strong community leaders and would likely take longer. The NGOs may also have undertaken both 'top-down' and 'bottom-up' strategies.

Building coalitions and allies Establishing coalitions, such as in the MKUKUTA process, helped CSOs to amplify their voices on specific issues. Building strong allies with the more progressive and like-minded civil servants and with representatives of donor agencies also proved useful. For example, in the first PRSP process it was noted that 'sympathetic officials' helped to feed CSO input close to more powerful political ears (Curran 2005: 9). Similarly, having strong ties to donor agency employees and priorities allowed CSOs to essentially 'box in' a sometimes resistant government by capitalizing on pressure from multiple stakeholders, as in the land case. It is important, though, to ensure that coalitions are cohesive. In the first, fifth and sixth episodes reviewed here, for instance, it became somewhat problematic when coalitions formed along sectoral lines. This seemed to harm CSO activities, not only because the coalitions were competing against each other for space and attention, but also because this approach narrowed the position of each group when it was essential to view critical issues holistically (e.g. land rights, HIV/AIDS). Then again, this approach may have been tactical for a number of reasons, among them shaping the issue, time constraints, relationship conflicts, differences in organizational cultures, financial limitations and other reasons.

Leveraging from evidence and policy commitments Finding and using evidence, and/or reminding the government of its commitments, provided civil society organizations with some useful policy leverage. For instance, the government seemed to take CSOs more seriously when they lobbied with hard evidence for abolishing school fees after the first PRSP process. While there were many factors at play and there are still concerns, these efforts may have contributed to the government's final decision – resulting in dramatic increases in pupil enrolment rates from around 50 per cent in 2001 to roughly 95 per cent in 2005 (DfID 2005). Though its dispute with the state is still unresolved and contentious, HakiElimu is increasingly calling on the government to hold to the promises made in the Primary Education Development Strategy (PEDS) and MKUKUTA. Thus, following the first school of thought described above, development participation may provide some CSOs with more weight or 'policy teeth' to argue their case against the state.

Making use of diverse communication channels Civil society organizations used the media as a central vehicle to promote popular discussion and analysis of issues such as through booklets, posters, newspapers, radio, TV and other tools. This was seen in the Hakikazi Catalyst's plain language PRSP. The media were also used to mobilize support and to draw attention to priority issues – both locally and internationally.

Invited, uninvited and declined policy spaces A final lesson relates to how CSOs approach policy spaces. First, civil society organizations were, for the most part, 'invited' to participate in the policy processes. This meant that the government and/or donors had nearly all of the control to decide which, when and how CSOs were to be involved. This has become particularly challenging given that the government has often been inconsistent in inviting NGOs, and such groups still feel that they need to be 'invited', as opposed to participating in an open forum, for example. Increasingly, CSOs are dealing with this challenge by becoming proactive and 'knocking on the Government's door' when they sense that something is 'being processed behind the curtain' (IMG 2005: 35).

CSOs have been unwelcome when policy spaces are 'uninvited'. This is a major problem because CSOs have needed to resort to either bypassing the government altogether or confronting a defensive state head-on and assuming the associated risks. This aligns with Shivji's (2004) view that CSOs should work toward *expanding* space for democratic participation versus focusing all their efforts on one-off donor/government-led policy dialogues and stakeholder workshops. A continuous process of 'reforming and reconstituting' government, she argues, is the only way to 'ensure genuine people's participation and to deter the abuse of state power' (ibid.: 691).

[This chapter was written for this reader]

References

ActionAid Care International (2006) 'Where to now? Implications of changing relations between DfID, recipient governments and NGOs in Malawi, Tanzania and Uganda'.

Bissio, R. (2003) 'Civil society and the MDGs', *Development Policy Journal*, pp. 151–61.

Curran, Z. (2005) 'Civil society participation in the PRSP: the role of evidence and the impact on policy choices?', *PPA Synthesis Study*, London: Overseas Development Institute (ODI).

DfID (Department for International Development) (2005) 'Tanzanian success in education and health brings further UK support', News release, 6 October.

Edwards, M. (2004) *Civil Society*, Oxford: Blackwell.

Gould, J. and J. Ojanen (2003) 'Merging in the circle: the politics of Tanzania's poverty reduction strategy', Policy Papers 2, Institute of Development Studies, University of Helsinki, www.valt.helsinki.fi/kmi/english/pub_merging.htm.

Groves, L. and R. Hinton (2004) *Inclusive Aid: Changing Power and Relationships in International Development*, London: Earthscan.

Hakikazi Catalyst (2002) 'Zanzibar without poverty: a plain language guide to the Revolutionary Government of Zanzibar's Zanzibar Poverty Reduction Plan (ZPRP)', January, www.hakikazi.org/plain_language.htm.

— (2004) 'Poverty Reduction Strategy Review: consultation of civil society organisations from the Southern Highlands regions of Iringa, Mbeya, Rukwa and Ruvuma', Conference held at Rift Valley Hotel, Mbeya, 29/30 March.

IMF (International Monetary Fund) (2005) 'A Factsheet: Poverty Reduction Strategy Papers (PRSP)', Washington: IMF, September. Available at: http://www.imf.org/external/np/exr/facts/prsp.htm.

IMG (International Monitoring Group) (2005) 'Enhancing aid relationships in Tanzania: IMG Report 2005'.

Mercer, C. (2003) 'Performing partnership: civil society and the illusions of good governance in Tanzania', *Political Geography*, 22: 741–63.

OECD (2005) 'DAC Guidelines and Reference Series: harmonizing donor practices for effective aid delivery, volume 2: Budget Support, Sector Wide Approaches and capacity development in public financial management', Paris: OECD.

Overseas Development Institute (ODI) (2006) Julius Court, Enrique Mendizabal, David Osborne and John Young, 'Policy Engagement: How Civil Society Can be More Effective'. Available at: www.developmentgateway.com.au/jahia/Jahia/pid/3496<http://www.developmentgateway.com.au/jahia/Jahia/pid/3496>.

Pal, L. (2001) *Beyond Policy Analysis: Public Issue Management in Turbulent Times*, Scarborough: Nelson Thomson Learning.

Piron, H. and A. Evans (2004) 'Politics and the PRSP approach: Synthesis Paper', London: Overseas Development Institute.

Pratt, B. (2006) 'Aid harmonization: challenges for civil society', *Ontrac: The Newsletter of the International NGO Training and Research Centre*, 33.

Shivji, I. (2004) 'Reflections on NGOs in Tanzania: what we are, what we are not, and what we ought to be', *Development in Practice*, 14(5): 689–94.

Tomlinson, B. (2006a) 'Determinants of civil society and aid effectiveness: a CCIC Discussion Paper', www.ccic.ca.

— (2006b) 'The Paris Declaration on Aid Effectiveness: donor commitments and civil society critiques – a CCIC Backgrounder', www.ccic.ca.

Tripp, A. M. (2000) 'Political reform in Tanzania: the struggle for associational autonomy', *Comparative Politics*, 32(2): 191–214.

United Nations Non-Governmental Liaison Services (2006) Website, www.un-ngls.org/, accessed August 2006.

URT (United Republic of Tanzania) (2006) Official website, www.tanzania.go.tz/, accessed August 2006.

28 | Participation without representation: chiefs, councils and forestry law in the West African Sahel

Jesse C. Ribot

Participatory development aims to redress the failures and inequities of top-down centralized development strategies. But what is community participation without representation? Does it redress central control? Does it include community in decision-making, resource control or benefits? Can there even be community participation without some form of locally accountable representation? Community or popular participation is about communities having decision-making powers or control over resources that affect the community as a whole, such as forests and grazing commons or community development. But for such decisions to internalize social and ecological costs or to assure equitable decision-making and use, they must be devolved to a body representing and accountable to the community.

Across Africa responsibilities for natural resource management are being devolved to rural communities in the name of decentralization and popular participation. This movement is based on efficiency, equity and development arguments in which community management is seen to improve performance in each of these spheres. But a closer look at participation in West African forestry reveals that it is less inclusive than the name implies. In the wooded savannahs and forests of the West African Sahel participatory forestry projects and policies devolve a limited set of responsibilities and benefits to commercially interested, non-representative groups and individuals, as well as to largely unaccountable state and non-state local authorities. These local authorities are often given only a tangential role in decision-making. Community participation, however, requires the devolution of real powers of decision to representative bodies.

This article explores representation and decision-making in so-called participatory forestry projects and policies in four Sahelian countries: Burkina Faso, Mali, Niger and Senegal. It examines existing structures of representation in all four countries and then presents two sketches of how representation is integrated into participatory forestry. The article concludes that participatory forestry does not integrate community representatives even in the few cases where such representatives exist. Without accountable representation, these participatory policies and projects become forms of covert privatization of forest use rights or a modern reproduction of indirect rule – replete with labour obligations. Real participation must begin with generalized rural democratization – it is about enfranchisement and cannot only be done project by project or through forestry policy alone.

Existing structures of local representation

Village chiefs and the rural councils of local state governance structures are frequently taken to represent rural populations in participatory development and natural resource management projects. In the countries of the West African Sahel, villages are the most common unit of social aggregation around which local use and management of woodlands is organized both by local populations and by outside agents. Each village, averaging 100 to 500 people, typically has a chief, and some have specialized chiefs overseeing forest use. There are also other poles of authority within villages, such as imams, marabouts, griots, pastoral chiefs and caste heads who may be involved in resource management. Colonial rulers relied on and thereby shifted powers to village chiefs rather than these others. Most state and outside organizations still privilege chiefs as their primary village interface.

In all four countries most chiefs gain their position through inheritance via a male lineage tracing back to warriors, the founding family of the village, or families chosen by colonial powers to replace antagonistic local leaders. In Senegal and Burkina Faso there are state-sanctioned processes for choosing village chiefs. In Senegal village chiefs (usually the head of the hereditary male line) are elected by heads of households, who are virtually all male. In Burkina Faso each village is divided into committees of youth (men or eighteen- to fifty-year-olds), elders (men over fifty), and women (over eighteen). At national elections, each committee elects its representatives and these representatives constitute a village council. The village council then elects from its members a village council president. All of these processes systematically under-represent or exclude women, but to a much lesser degree in Burkina Faso, where women have one third of the village vote.

In Mali, Niger and Senegal chiefs hold their position for life. Neither do they represent nor are they systematically accountable to the village as a whole. In Burkina Faso the process for choosing village council presidents appears more accountable than for other village chiefs within these Sahelian countries, owing to regular periodic elections. Although there are various local mechanisms of accountability, the accountability of chiefs is by no means assured. Some are despots; others are responsive leaders, depending on the personality of the chief, the specific history of the village in question, and its location in a larger political economy.

Local government is another form of rural governance in the Sahel. Since independence from France in early 1960s, Burkina Faso, Mali, Niger and Senegal have established local units of representative government. The smallest unit of government in study countries regroups five to fifty villages (similar in scale to US counties). These local governments have both elected governance bodies, or 'rural councils', and an appointed central government administrator, or a 'prefect'.

In Burkina Faso the rural council is constituted from elected representatives of village committees. These representatives form a council and elect a president from among themselves. In the other three countries the candidates for rural councils are presented for election by nationally registered political parties. Each party presents a slate of candidates to fill each council. The slate with the majority of votes takes the council and elects a president from among its members. While there is universal suffrage, independent candidates cannot run for election to these councils (nor can any individual or group present lists without a party's endorsement). Since villagers have little influence over national political parties, nor the resources to form parties, they are unable to choose their own candidates. Indeed, villagers I work with in eastern Senegal feel that rural councils do not represent them, they represent political parties. Further, few parties have the resources to organize local government slates, so there is little competition in local elections.

The official role of rural councils in all four countries is to advise and assist the prefect on political and administrative matters. Decisions of the rural councils of local governments must be approved by the prefect. So, even in Burkina Faso, where rural councils are relatively representative of local populations, they are simply not autonomous decision-making bodies.

Participatory forestry policies and projects

Given the limitations on existing forms of representation, how do 'participatory' policies and projects construct local control? Who makes decisions and who benefits? In Burkina Faso and Niger, projects are creating village-level participatory structures. Mali and Senegal are using local government as the basis for participatory forestry. Burkina Faso is presented as an example of the village-based approach and Mali as a local government-based example.

Burkina Faso: participation by committee in Nazinon Burkina's new participatory forestry laws are being modelled on a joint United Nations Development Programme and Food and Agricultural Organization project in the forest of Nazinon, thirty miles south of the capital, Ouagadougou. This scheme is based on the creation of cooperatives in villages surrounding the forest of Nazinon and a union coordinating the cooperatives.

In Nazinon village-level cooperatives are responsible for forest management. In each village the project constitutes a cooperative filled with villagers interested in wood-fuel production. Each cooperative elects a president, secretary, treasurer and manager. The project also set up a union of Nazinon cooperatives with a general assembly constituted of all managers, secretaries and treasurers of the village cooperatives. The union's Administrative Council is constituted of the cooperative managers and a president elected from the general assembly. The administrative council is empowered to make the daily administrative and business decisions of the union and is responsible for surveying the implementation of all laws concerning the union and forest management.

A technical office of the union is set up by the national Forest Service to develop forest management plans in collaboration with the administrative council. These plans must be approved by the Forest Service. The manager from each cooperative is charged with assuring the plan's implementation, under the guidance of the technical office. In addition, a control committee, including representatives from the national government's Control Service, the minister responsible for cooperatives, the Minister of Territorial Administration, and a village council representative, surveys the union's and cooperatives' accounts.

In general, the new policies place some responsibilities for and powers over wood-fuel management into the hands of a group of economically interested individuals. Decisions over the disposition of forests and over revenues from forest exploitation are in the hands of these individuals and of the Forest Service. The Forest Service maintains complete control of all production and management decisions through required approval and through control of the rules by which production and management can take place. A local representative (from the village council) is only brought into the national Control Committee, where she or he is just one member among many. In a study on decentralization, Burkina Faso's prime minister's office pointed out that these committees should be representative of the village community, but are not. Further, this committee makes no decisions over forest use. In short, little control is devolved to local authorities. It stays with the Forest Service and private groups.

Mali: participation through local government Mali's 1994 forestry laws assign responsibilities for forest management to local government (called Decentralized Territorial Collectives). The new laws give local governments a forested domain within their territorial jurisdiction and the right to protect or conserve part or all of their forested domain. According to the new laws, any individual or group of individuals wishing to commercially cut for wood fuels within the forest domain of a local government must organize a Rural Wood Management Structure (WMS – Structure Rurale de Gestion de Bois). A WMS can be a cooperative, corporation, association or any other form of organization recognized by the state. In private (as in Burkina Faso's and Niger's committees) these are groups of private individuals interested in practising or investing in commercial woodcutting.

Before a WMS can begin using the forest, the Forest Service must propose a management plan for approval by the local government. This plan includes an annual wood-fuel production quota which, according to forestry officials, is to be determined by the sustainable potential production of the forested domain of the local government in question. The annual quota will be set by an ad hoc commission composed of two representatives of the WMSs, one from local government, and one member of the Forest Service. Recognizing the contentious political nature of quota allocation, the new laws also create a regional commission to resolve conflicts over the fixing and distribution of quotas. This commission is to be organized by the minister responsible for forests. Finally, once a management plan and quota have been established and approved, a cutting permit can be delivered by the Forest Service upon the payment of a forest exploitation tax.

Mali's new participatory forestry laws, replacing a system in which the Forest Service delivered permits to whom, where and when it chose, give local governments considerable power over the disposition of forests. Indeed, Mali has developed the most progressive forestry laws in the Sahelian region. Local government representatives can decide to protect the forests by decree or they can control exploitation through approval or rejection of forest management plans. They can also use these powers to control which WMSs can exploit local forests. The Forest Service, however, has maintained control over how much wood can be cut, where, when and how (via quotas and management plans).

As in Burkina Faso, Mali's local government representative on the quota committee is only one among four members and is not guaranteed a controlling role. The 'mode of allocating the quota' in this committee is left to the order of the Regional Governor (a central government appointee). The Forest Service has also reserved the role of quota dispute resolution for itself, a role better for a more neutral body such as the courts.

In sum, in Mali some significant decisions have been devolved to local government bodies. But two factors cancel the most progressive aspects of these new policies. First, since independent candidates cannot present themselves for local elections, local government is not representative or locally accountable – so these 'local' decisions are not necessarily community decisions. Second, jurisdiction over forests may not be devolved to local government, but rather to intermediate-level governance structures such as circles and regions (many forests will also remain under central government control). These governance structures, which are also not representative, cannot even be considered local.

Participation: by whom in what? Who participates in what benefits? The benefits in these cases include labour opportunities in woodcutting, income from these labour opportunities and from wood-fuel sale, and some role in forest decision-making. Labour opportunities are important since this work often has gone to migrant or urban workers from outside the woodcutting area. Integrating local labour increases village income. There is also profit from the sale of wood. In Burkina Faso, firewood prices fixed by the Minister of Commerce keep prices in participatory projects above those received by independent woodcutters. These opportunities and profits go largely to the private individuals who make up management committees and woodcutting organizations. Membership is self-elected or influenced by foresters and village elites – these are effectively private organizations. In addition to private income and profit, in two cases some benefits are directed at the community as a whole. In Burkina Faso, each cooperative has a fund fed by a firewood tax, part of which is earmarked for public works serving the larger village community. In Niger, 10 per cent of non-tax revenues from wood fuel sales go to the village chief – this, too, is ostensibly to benefit the community as a whole.

While some villagers benefit from labour opportunities, local wood-fuel sale and fees collected for community funds, most profit in West African wood-fuel markets accrues through access to transport and urban trade. Unfortunately, the Forest Services in all of these countries have maintained tight control over the delivery of transport permits and have refused to assist local woodcutters in gaining access to transport or merchant licences. Villagers in all four countries have expressed their desire to operate in transport and urban markets. This most lucrative segment of the wood-fuel sector is currently dominated by urban merchants and truckers. In short, villagers are permitted to 'participate' in forest labour but only in a limited portion of forest-based profits.

Who participates in decisions? Management plans and quotas reserve decisions over where, when and how much wood will be cut for the Forest Services. In Mali and Senegal, local government representatives participate in the daily decisions of plan implementation and have some control over the plans. In Burkina Faso and Niger it is the village-level committees of cooperatives and unions which can make daily implementation decisions. But the rules of cutting and management that they must follow and the quantities they can cut are defined by the Forest Services, based largely on questionable ecological grounds.

The most critical decision, whether forests surrounding a given community will or will not be cut, has been reserved by Forest Services in all cases but Mali. In Mali's new forestry laws rural councils have the definitive right to protect all or any of their forested domain (although the proportion of forests in the local domain will be determined by what a national committee decides is in the national interest). In Burkina Faso, Niger and Senegal, however, the Forest Service can give woodcutting rights in any forest to anyone they chose, regardless of local wishes.

In these latter countries local communities have no legal mechanism for protecting local forests. Foresters can allocate exploitation rights via parastatals, concessions, state sale of parcels and the delivery of exploitation permits. Communities in project areas who choose not to accept the conditions of 'participation', and those simply not chosen for projects, have no legal control over the disposition of forest resources. Forest Services can sell the forests out from under them. These local governments and village communities simply do not have the right to say 'no' to Forest Service-sanctioned cutting in surrounding forests. This is hardly participatory forestry.

In short, participation amounts to the Forest Services managing forests with the assistance of private groups within local communities, with increased labour opportunities and profit for these private groups and some income earmarked for whole communities. Critical decisions over forest disposition are devolved into 'local' hands only in Mali. But even in Mali it is only over the limited area of forests assigned to local governments by a national committee.

Ecology of central control

Forest Services' control of woodcutting may seem to make ecological sense. Indeed, the maintenance of Forest Service control over management plans and quotas is often argued on 'technical' ecological grounds to protect the national good. But the ecological evidence does not support the need for such centrally controlled management. Sahelian vegetation is resilient. The little evidence that has been collected indicates robust natural regeneration after woodcutting. Villagers and woodcutters in each country say they return to cut in the same area after five to twelve years. They are not cutting gallery forests. The main anthropogenic cause of permanent deforestation in this zone is agricultural policy. Instead, they focus their attention on woodcutting even if it is not the problem. There is also no scarcity of wood fuels in this region, so micro-management is not essential even to accelerate regeneration.

The ecological evidence brings into question the need for detailed management plans or production quotas. The 'participatory' (rather, centralized) distribution of decision-making powers and forest control among foresters, private groups and representatives cannot be justified on ecological knowledge or grounds that their decisions threaten the forests. Further, national governments, Forest Services and state agents in all four countries have long histories of profiting legally and illicitly from forest control. There is a danger that withholding management plans and quotas or allocating them to powerful figures could become new extractive tools in the hands of foresters. Technical ecological arguments, it seems, are helping Forest Services maintain a long-standing stake in this lucrative sector. They help justify central control and also happen to attract donor financing.

In the West African Sahel, much more forest control could be devolved to local communities without threatening the forests.

Representation with or without participation

Without locally accountable representation the ostensible objectives of participatory approaches are unlikely to be met. There are no guarantees that the social or ecological externalities of commercial forestry will be internalized, and there is a great risk that the benefits will not return to the community as a whole. Devolving control or decision-making powers to non-accountable or non-representative bodies or individuals (such as hereditary or male-elite-picked chiefs, party-picked local councils, cooperatives, village associations or NGOs) is just a new, slightly obscured form of 'privatization' via privatized use rights. It is not devolution to the community as a whole. Rather, it gives powers over community resources to groups within the community with an economic interest in the forest or to individuals in positions of authority.

Participation without representation is tantamount to forced labour when it involves responsibilities without choice. By assigning responsibilities in the name of participation, for example, Senegal's new forestry laws give the Forest Service the means to mobilize rural labour. They do so with no checks or balances, creating a potential for what might be dubbed 'participatory corvée'. Further, when villagers' alternative to participating is the potential loss of forests to outsiders, labour in 'participatory' forestry can hardly be considered voluntary. Further, participation is a modern reproduction of indirect rule when it uses local non-state authorities to legitimize and carry out external projects of the state and international organizations (such as environmental management). Like colonial rule, it can also strengthen and legitimize the non-representative, unaccountable governance forms it relies on.

Until local authorities become more systematically accountable to local populations, governments, NGOs and donor agencies involved in participatory approaches must ask themselves if they are unwittingly supporting and strengthening non-representative or unaccountable governance – which is unlikely to accomplish the ostensible goals of participation. Indeed, by problematizing local representation these groups could support the emergence of more spatially and temporally generalized, participatory rural governance processes. Conditions for locally accountable representation, for example admitting independent candidates in local elections, are prerequisite to generalized rural participation. This is not to say that accountably structuring representation can guarantee community inclusion. Rural elites always try to manipulate candidacies, electoral processes and those in elected positions. Inclusive processes cannot create accountable representation. They simply make it a possible outcome of struggle among village classes, castes, interest groups and elites. Unfortunately, given the electoral codes in most of the Sahel, this is not yet even a possibility. Indeed, current laws block such possibilities. Enfranchisement through rural democratization is a first step towards participation.

With locally accountable representation participation becomes meaningful when these representatives have powers of decision over valuable resources. In Mali local government has some real powers, but is not representative. In Burkina Faso there is accountable (although gender-biased) representation, but no local decision-making powers. Representation without powers is as much of a farce as powers without representation. Popular participation requires both.

[Originally published in *Cultural Survival Quarterly*, 20(3), 1996, pp. 40–44]

Bibliography

Baland, J.-M. and J.-P. Platteau (1996) *Halting Degradation of Natural Resources: Is There a Role for Rural Communities?*, Oxford: Clarendon Press.

Burkina Faso (1993) 'Loi No. 007/93/ADP Portant régime electoral des conseillers de village, de secteur communal, de département et de province', Government of Burkina Faso.

Ouali, F., P. Kiemdé and D. Yaméogo (1994) 'Etude de base sur l'état de la decentralisation au Burkina', Summary report, Commission Nationale de la Decentralisation, Premier Ministère, Burkina Faso, June.

Ouédraogo, H. M. G. (1994) 'Les coutumes relatives a la gestion des resources naturelles au Burkina Faso', Programme de Cooperation Technique, FAO-LEG: TCP/BKF/2352, Rome, March.

Republic of Senegal (1972) 'Décret no. 72-636 du 29 mai 1972 relatif aux attributions des chefs de cironscriptions administratives et chefs de village', *Journal Officiel de la République du Sénégal*, 17 June.

Ribot, J. C. (1995a) 'From exclusion to participation: turning Senegal's forestry policy around?', *World Development*, 23(9).

— (1995b) 'Local forest control in Burkina Faso, Mali, Niger, Senegal and the Gambia: a review and critique of new participatory policies' (see also Senegal and Mali country studies), Africa Region Working Paper, Washington, DC: World Bank.

Thomson, J. and C. Coulibaly (1994) 'Decentralization in the Sahel: regional synthesis', SAH/D (94) 427, Regional conference on Land Tenure and Decentralization in the Sahel, Praia, Cape Verde, CILSS, OECD, Club du Sahel, January.

29 | Talking politics in participatory governance

Gianpaolo Baocchi

Some studies on citizenship have noted that the idea of participation in community affairs evokes romantic images of virtuous citizens engaged in selfless discussions that may not reflect the conflict inherent in such exchanges (Mansbridge 1980). Despite this unrealistic image, 'participation in government' has become in recent years a ubiquitous catch-phrase for policy-makers and social scientists from various orientations. As policy, participation is advocated because of its potential to enhance governance or to promote efficiency and redistribution (Fung and Wright 2000). The growing scholarship on the topic focuses on the efficiency, fairness and sustainability of governmental participation and has rarely addressed a central question: Is participation in government limited to addressing governmental decisions, or can it become a setting for the broad, public-minded and open-ended discussion prized by democratic theorists and evoked by the concept of the 'public sphere' (Habermas 1987, 1989)?

I examine instances of open-ended community deliberations in government-sponsored assemblies in two poor districts of the city of Porto Alegre, Brazil, which I will call for the purposes of this article 'Pôr-do-Sol' and 'Nazaré'. These deliberations provide a useful test for considering the relationship between participatory governance and the public sphere. Porto Alegre is home to a participatory experiment that has achieved academic notoriety for its novel institutional forms and for the tens of thousands of participants from under-privileged neighbourhoods. The participatory budget process in Porto Alegre was introduced by the Partido dos Trabalhadores, or Workers' Party, in the early 1990s as a set of reforms that would allow significant citizen input into the decision-making processes of municipal governance. This action was, in part, a move to legitimize the administration's redistributive municipal policies. It subsequently evolved into a structure of assemblies in each of the city's sixteen districts that combined elements of 'direct and represented democracy'.

Understanding these community gatherings expands our understanding of democracy and civic participation in a number of ways. First, it broadens our conception of who are 'proper candidates' for civic action. The participants here are generally not formally educated, are poor, and have lived through two decades of authoritarian rule. These characteristics make them entirely different from the participants of the *salons* (Habermas 1989) and dispel misconceptions about the urban poor in Latin America, who have often been portrayed as being entangled in social pathology and client–patron relationships (Pearlman 1976). Second, this study points to the importance of government-sponsored settings in enabling community practices. Government sponsorship provides materials and logistical support for continued discussions and makes available a language of common problems as a marker for the public interest. This begins to address a crucial unanswered question about whether state reforms can 'conduce to democracy in the absence of a self-organized citizenry or an autonomous associational realm' (Emirbayer and Sheller 1999: 147), and also corrects the notion that the only place for open-ended community discussion is within the networks of civil society or in its 'free-spaces' (Evans and Boyte 1992; Polletta 1999). Third, while theorists have correctly emphasized the importance of formal rules and institutional features of participatory settings (Cohen 1996; Cohen and Rogers 1992; Elster 1998), I point to the importance of interactions of the local associational context with these participatory institutions in creating a stage for civic discussions.

The city of Porto Alegre and the participation experiment

Since the 1970s, the city of Porto Alegre has had a history of significant social movements and neighbourhood association activity (Baierle 1992). And since the mid-1980s, these movements had proposed participatory reforms to municipal governance (ibid.). The participatory institutions were introduced in 1991, after the Workers' Party assumed the administration of the municipality, and succeeded, after a few years, in drawing very large numbers of participants from the city's less privileged neighbourhoods. Early difficulties included organizational matters within the participating institutions, the city's poor financial situation, the lack of organizational experience in some of the city's districts, and conflicts with established civil society networks that opposed the participation of new entrants to civil society (Fedozzi 2001). Participating institutions focused on budgeting matters, and they evolved over the years to accommodate more participants. By 2000, upwards of 20,000 participants were counted in the first yearly assembly of the participatory budget.

Regular assemblies take place each year beginning in March and involve broad segments of the population in each of the city's districts. With the mayor in attendance, the previous year's projects are reviewed and neighbourhoods or organized groups in attendance select delegates for the subsequent proceedings. These delegates then regularly attend the assemblies to learn about the criteria and costs involved in various city projects and to discuss their district's needs and overall priorities. All areas of the municipal budget are eventually decided this way, and common projects range from the construction of new roads to the delivery of social services and healthcare (Prefeitura Municipal de Porto Alegre 1998). Meetings are run by a non-voting City Hall-appointed facilitator, and forty to sixty delegates regularly attend weekly assemblies in most districts. At the end of the yearly budget cycle in July, votes among delegates finalize decisions on the district's projects, set priorities, and select representatives from the district to serve on a municipal Budget Council that is responsible for the ultimate decisions over budget items, such as the overall allocation of municipal funds for each district. While the Budget Council makes decisions over the next months, delegates from the districts continue to meet often to monitor the outcome of chosen projects.

Few studies have addressed whether and how participants carry out open-ended community discussions in such community settings. While some studies have considered the orientation of individuals who participate in these discussions and have observed change over time in associational patterns, none has addressed the actual process of participation. If these experiments in Porto Alegre contribute to the formation of a genuine Brazilian 'public space' (Avritzer 2002) or to a novel form of democracy (Santos 1998), then understanding how open-ended public-minded discussions take place in the Brazilian setting becomes a crucial question.

Nazaré and Pôr-do-Sol: the two districts

Almost a third of the population of Porto Alegre resides in 'irregular settlements' and *favelas* (slums) in socially vulnerable situations (Oliveira and Barcellos 1990; Oliveira 1996; Panizzi 1990; Prefeitura Municipal de Porto Alegre 1998), and these areas cover much of the two districts studied here. The Nazaré district is poor and remote: among its 30,000 residents are some of the city's most violent and destitute people, and there are few businesses in the district. In contrast, Pôr-do-Sol, a district of 100,000, has many slum areas but also has lower-middle-class neighbourhoods, a business area and several churches. While about 65 per cent of households in Nazaré are below the poverty line, in Pôr-do-Sol the percentage is closer to 40 per cent. Political party competition is similar in both districts – the Workers' Party is the dominant party among the urban poor in both districts.

The socio-economic background of regular assembly participants in the two districts is also similar: the median participant in both districts had between six and seven years of formal education and a household income between 1 and 1.5 times the income for the poverty line. Men and women were equally represented at these assemblies (CIDADE 1999), and the racial composition of the assemblies reflected that of the districts, with approximately 15 per cent of participants identifying as 'non-white'. There is no evidence of discrimination on racial grounds throughout these participatory institutions, or that racial divisiveness is a factor in discussions. The primary difference between the two districts has to do with civic networks; Nazaré has fewer civic networks and they are more recent, while Pôr-do-Sol has a strong tradition of activism and, at the time of this study, had one functioning district-level setting where activists from different neighbourhoods would meet, bridging the district's various civic networks.

I spent a year and a half on this ethnographic investigation. I attended district assemblies and as many other meetings in civil society as possible, including meetings held at neighbourhood associations, churches and community centres. Asking questions about the types of discussions and community activities at these meetings required direct observation, echoing recent work on civic networks and political practices that has begun to rely on participant observation and ethnographic methods for specific insights. Despite its limitations, ethnography does answer a number of questions not accessible by other research methods: questions of meaning, intent, purpose and implicit rules, among others, that cannot be answered by interviews alone. Knowing the unspoken rules of these social contexts also becomes important to apprehending the possible drawbacks of participatory democracy. I collected documents and life-history accounts, carried out interviews, and conducted a number of surveys to supplement my ethnographic evidence.

Emergent public spheres; the meeting takeover

Assemblies took place weekly or semi-monthly in a central public setting in both Nazaré and Pôr-do-Sol, drawing an average of fifty participants for each meeting much of the year. These assemblies lasted up to two hours, and for several months the agenda included the technicalities and relative merits of certain projects for the district. In Pôr-do-Sol, meetings were held on a weeknight in a church hall, and in Nazaré, they were held in a school on a weekend afternoon. In both districts, participants tended to come from a range of neighbourhoods within the district. The agenda for the meetings was usually drawn up in advance by the facilitator, and time was allotted at the start of each meeting for announcements. A typical meeting might also include presentations by technical experts from each of the various municipal departments, followed by discussions when participants could ask questions or comment on the topic. The facilitator was responsible for keeping to the agenda and calling on participants who would sign up for a turn to speak.

Despite the fact that non-governmental community items of common interest were not part of the scheduled agenda, 'meeting takeovers' frequently occurred in both districts. Often while announcements were made during the meetings, participants would request to discuss a 'news' item. In Pôr-do-Sol, participants made a habit of bringing newspaper clippings, which often led to discussions that had to be closed off to keep to the agenda. One participant [Walter] who always brought newspaper clippings told me that 'you are always learning something' because otherwise 'people are in the dark about injustice'. For him, whose civic engagement dates to pro-democracy social movements in the 1970s, the assemblies were a forum to discuss news in order to foster the 'critical consciousness' prized by liberation theology activists.

While participants seldom seemed to mind these 'interruptions', facilitators sometimes described them as disruptive: 'Some of these interruptions are childish, people just want to create problems.' But the facilitators did not prevent interruptions 'to avoid creating a bigger problem'. The discussion of a specific 'news' issue sometimes became a discussion of politics and economics, government policy or macroeconomic problems, not to mention specific community problems, and a meeting sometimes would be taken over by problems that could potentially embarrass the administration or the Workers' Party.

Such was the case in the Nazaré district, where a school shooting had taken place a few days prior to the assembly. The agenda of this particular meeting was to discuss education projects for the next year, but participants kept returning to the subject of the shooting. Early on in the meeting, Carla used the announcements period to begin a long discussion about having received an inadequate response from the police about future safety in schools. Then, throughout the meeting, participants repeatedly raised the issue with a representative from the education department, who dismissed their advances, remarking that it was a police issue. Carla spent most of the meeting in the back of the room discussing school safety with several other women, and towards the end of the meeting, she asked to make an announcement. First, she apologized for interrupting the meeting:

> I have an announcement. Tomorrow we will have a demonstration to protest the lack of respect for human rights in this city and this district. I know lots of you are with the Workers' Party, but it needs to respect workers and tomorrow we are calling all mothers to march all the way to the police station to demand a police officer at the school.

Her announcement was applauded. The next day, fifty mothers marched to the police station, where they were greeted by the press as well as by council persons from the Workers' Party and other parties. Carla made a statement to the press that appeared in the newspaper, and a police officer was then put on duty at the school. Although Carla's topic was more instrumental than Walter's newspaper clipping reading, it was clearly a public-spirited presentation on a collective problem. Implicit in Carla's actions is the understanding that these assemblies had become one of the central settings for engaging with others in civil society. Her presentation also illustrates that there was no censure of participants for discussing issues that, in principle, could hurt the administration, while showing that community activists like Carla knew the strategic importance of these settings.

Needs as public problems

The examples above show how participants took over meetings with the awareness of the importance of the district assemblies as a civic network structure. I now explore the communicative aspect of this process, as participants stitched together a language of public interests and public goods at these assemblies, turning 'needs' into 'public problems'. The creation of 'public concerns' out of specific needs helped create a language of citizenship that made public-spirited discussion possible. This language of citizenship, however, was not based on the abstract rights and duties of citizenship, but was based on sharing common problems and working toward common solutions at the assemblies. It was also not a language explicitly based on religious notions of social justice, as might be expected given the historical importance of liberation theology in social movements in Brazil. Nor was it based on a socialist discourse of class empowerment, such as might accompany a Workers' Party experiment. Rather, this language of citizenship emphasized 'the good of the community' and valued collective and pragmatic problem-solving. It defined the community as constituted of persons with similar problems and living situations. For example, at one meeting, a long-time participant tried to motivate a group of new participants to stay at the meeting.

> For 10 years many people have come here to solve problems ... We fought for it, mobilized for it, and achieved it. We focused on the closed sewer because we got together with our neighbours and fought for it. And after that, we learned that we have to fight for larger things. We have many problems we need to still solve.

This language was often deployed in discussions, when participants wished to convince other participants to become more involved in the process, or to persuade others of the value of a certain position. But discussions about the 'hows' and 'whys' of social problems emerged in conversation that made use of this language, as discussion of specific needs and issues led to discussions of broader issues. It was not uncommon for a discussion about funding a cooperative to lead to a discussion on unemployment, or a discussion about a park to lead to a discussion on the environment, while a discussion about building up a slum might lead to a discussion on land tenure and migration.

Often, the discussion of a social problem implicit in an investment project became a discussion about the limits of municipal government. In the Nazaré district, for example, an agenda on social service projects for the district was limited to a small number of projects for senior citizens, thus prompting a participant to attempt to create an ad hoc committee to coordinate the provision of social services generally. Laura signed up to ask a question of the technical expert from City Hall, but when her turn came to speak, she decided instead to make a plea for the creation of a social services committee for problems with children. She addressed the whole group present, arguing:

We have at least 500 children in the district needing daycare. Without daycare and without schools we are bringing up violence in the district, but by then it's too late. We need to bring the community to debate these issues and participate.

The discussion momentarily turned to violence and crime in the district, with several people sharing stories about a wave of violent robberies. In this discussion, people's private needs for daycare and stories of being robbed were linked to public problems of crime and a lack of social services. Josué collected the names and addresses of volunteers for a committee. Participants often mentioned a sense of belonging to a larger community of citizens who are facing problems together, as a result of having worked together over the year to decide on projects. A relatively new participant, Ana, described how the sense of sharing common problems was important: 'You participate and you realize that your problems are the same as everyone else's problems, and you work because your problems are the same.'

For Ana, whose participation in these assemblies is her only involvement in civic affairs, the sense of 'public' comes from having worked collectively to make decisions throughout the year and from developing a sense of belonging to a community of others with similar needs or problems. Her vocabulary, as mentioned, was not an explicit vocabulary of social justice based on religious or political ideologies, however. This fact bothered older community activists linked to church social activism, one of whom found people 'these days too only talking about projects and not enough with the big questions'. Indeed, another participant I interviewed discussed how participating in these assemblies had shown him how he 'had rights', by which he meant 'rights to ask for projects and rights to ask the mayor and the engineer why [projects] don't come'. The language deployed by participants was based on needs and common problems and was used to create a sense of public and public-minded speech.

Buffering conflict: the role of civic networks

Thus far I have discussed emergent community discussions as being similar in both the poorer Nazaré district and the Pôr-do-Sol district. In Pôr-do-Sol, however, the existence of denser social networks and the presence of experienced activists meant that conflict was buffered and informal rules of conduct were enforced so that interruptions of meetings occurred within certain topical and behavioural boundaries. Experienced participants worked in the background to resolve conflicts and create compromises, and they enforced certain unspoken rules to prevent interruptions that might otherwise have derailed meetings. As one of these experienced participants described to me, if it were not for people 'like he' in the background, 'meetings would be much more full of conflict. We try to discuss issues ahead of time and find compromises.' In addition to 'working in the background', these experienced participants also actively curtailed certain kinds of interventions.

Pôr-do-Sol had a number of functioning neighbourhood associations and other civic organizations, and evidence suggested that there were significant connections among them. Three-quarters of the participants of the assemblies at Pôr-do-Sol, for example, participated in one of these other associations, and over half of them participated in an organization beyond their neighbourhood. It was not uncommon for participants to meet each other at other meetings throughout the week. Participants had significant experience with the assemblies and civic life in general; on average, participants in Pôr-do-Sol had six years of experience with the assemblies and had been participating in civic associations for ten years. Out of the forty-odd regular participants, almost one quarter had been participating in associations of one kind or another since the 1970s, according to my survey. These more experienced participants helped facilitate meetings in Pôr-do-Sol, going as far as preparing the meeting agenda and spending time outside of meetings discussing the various projects. As a City Hall facilitator in the district put it, 'Working in the Pôr-do-Sol was very easy, I would show up there and they would have all the meetings' agendas all set up.' Another facilitator noted that 'the level of experience in the Pôr-do-Sol makes a difference, a lot of these guys have many years of experience, ... which avoids problems'. A number of incidents during my fieldwork confirmed that it was experienced participants, not the official facilitator, who commanded the respect to keep meetings in line.

In Pôr-do-Sol, a conflict erupted at a meeting over the placement of a traffic light, and some residents from a small nearby slum, the Ave Maria settlement, threatened to stop traffic at a busy thoroughfare at rush hour unless the traffic light was moved to the front of their slum. The thoroughfare was a very busy one, where cars passed by at very high speeds. More than one child from this slum had been injured trying to cross the street, and for safety the residents wanted a traffic light in front of their settlement. According to technical criteria, however, a light would not be possible. Residents from Ave Marie nonetheless continually raised this issue at several meetings, interrupting other discussions.

In the middle of an assembly in which a member of the municipal planning department was present, Jaírson, a resident of the settlement, interrupted the meeting with a threat, addressing the municipal bureaucrat:

> I am glad you are here today because I hope you are ready to admit your mistake in turning down our demand. Three children have been hurt at this road, and we are going to take action until you solve this problem.

The City Hall planner was taken aback, but proposed that a meeting be scheduled in Ave Maria to discuss the technical criteria that made the traffic light unfeasible. Jaírson pressed on and promised that residents of the slum would step out into traffic at rush hour the next day and every day after that until a traffic light was installed. The meeting quickly deteriorated into a shouting match, until some of the older activists in the district managed to quiet it down. The next day, Jaírson and Ave Maria residents blocked traffic during rush hour, though they were dissuaded from continuing the action by activists from other neighbourhoods shortly after they had begun.

At another assembly a few days later, whose agenda was dedicated to sewage projects, Jaírson brought up the topic again during the period for announcements:

> I want to announce that last week we stopped traffic because we never received adequate explanation for why we didn't have the traffic light put in place for us last year. I want to let everyone know that we will do it again next week if we have to, and the week after that.

Other community activists intervened, saying that they intended to 'investigate the matter'. Another activist intervened, mentioning that he hoped 'Jaírson would call some other people before anyone decides to stop traffic again' because 'a lot of workers need to get home to their families on the bus that goes past'. The matter was not resolved right away and dragged on for several weeks. Although the administration's planners scheduled a number of further meetings and proposed options like speed-bumps, Ave Maria residents continued to threaten to stop traffic. Community activists from the other neighbourhoods in the district continued to try to prevent another stoppage, while pressuring the administration at assemblies to address the matter. By the end of my fieldwork in 1999, there had been no other traffic blockages, but the traffic light question had not been resolved.

Several other times during my fieldwork, experienced community activists enforced informal rules of participation, which included avoiding personal attacks and allowing only certain kinds of interruptions. At an assembly, during a discussion about the agenda for the next meeting, Marcos claimed that the next agenda ought to include an item to prevent Arno from making comments because 'he talks too much' and 'is always trying to show off'. Marcos and Arno had had disagreements in the past and often clashed over issues. To other participants, their disagreements now seemed to be personal. Both men were community activists with a long history in their respective communities; they were known throughout the district. Since an incident involving a clinic a few months before, they now appeared to contradict each other at almost every turn. This time, however, others vocally interfered, coming to the defence of Arno and telling Marcos that 'you can disagree, but this is not how you do it'. At other times, similar potential conflicts were diffused, as certain types of behaviour were criticized for being inappropriate for 'people who work for the community'.

Activists enforced other informal rules preventing certain kinds of open-ended discussions deemed to be occurring 'at the wrong place'. Discussions that were deemed 'overly personal', such as those having to do with particular complaints or personal intrigue, were usually interrupted. During the assembly's announcements, if a participant tried to start a conversation about a broken pipe in front of her house or on the rudeness of a bus driver, it would likely be curtailed by one of the more experienced participants with a suggestion of where to deal with this problem, telling the person that 'this is not the place for this. We can try to figure out where to go with this problem, but right now the agenda is something else.' Similarly, complaints about other participants or accusations of improprieties in a neighbourhood association were also often stopped.

While these activists curtailed certain discussions and activities, there was little evidence that they tried to dominate other participants. While these activists commanded significant respect from others, nothing indicated that they used this respect to advance a particular agenda or to gain particular benefits. And although these activists limited certain discussions, they did not do so on the basis of political allegiances, as might be expected. Rather, the standard seemed to be that if a certain issue was framed as a 'public issue' – that the impropriety at the neighbourhood association or the broken pipe represented a problem for the community – discussions on that issue were much more likely to be allowed to run their course.

'The only place in the community': a drawback of participatory institutions

There was little evidence in the assemblies of the drawbacks of participation most often noted by scholars such as the *domination* of the less eloquent by the culturally better equipped or the emergence of an oligarchy of movement experts who retained social power by controlling meetings (Lipset 1997). In fact, meetings were often unruly and sometimes difficult to call to order. Nevertheless, the evidence points to a specific disadvantage to participation in the Nazaré district assemblies: the fact that the budgeting assembly was 'the only place in the community' meant that it was a setting so important to community activists that it was there they felt they must air certain grievances and where individuals' reputations in the community were determined. A number of conflicts between municipal bureaucrats and participants took place during fieldwork, and a Nazaré participant described his district as one that 'was not intimidated by administrators with college degrees and was not afraid of fighting with them'. While theorists of the public sphere might find conflict and disagreement to be fundamental, not all disagreements and conflicts here were public-spirited ones. Without a core of experienced and respected activists to manage these conflicts, the interruptions in Nazaré took over meetings, created personal conflicts between activists, and at times caused other participants to leave feeling that these meetings 'were pointless' or 'too disorderly'. These kinds of interruptions were at odds with the public-spiritedness of other interruptions and sometimes completely derailed the agenda of the meetings.

My survey evidence shows that in Nazaré the district assemblies were meeting places for networks that would otherwise have little contact. For over half of the participants at Nazaré assemblies, the assemblies were the only meeting they participated in during an average week. For most of the other half, the other main forum in which they participated was in their home neighbourhood. Fewer than 10 per cent of participants at the assemblies participated in any kind of regular meeting outside of their neighbourhood other than the budgeting assembly. Although there were probably informal settings where participants from different neighbourhoods might meet, it is not an exaggeration to describe these budgeting assemblies as the only district-wide meeting event, which lent these settings a certain importance. Community life in Latin American urban peripheries is one in which calculations of honour, reputation and respect before others become particularly important, especially as persons become involved in politics and the processes that bring benefits to one's community. In these assemblies, interruptions were staged both by participants and others who were vigilant of their reputation before the community. One participant, Maurício, who interrupted a meeting to 'clear his name' about a rumour, explained he did this because this 'is where the community meets. There is no other place in our district. What happens here is important for the whole district.'

Not all the participants I interviewed were happy with the overwhelming importance of the participatory budget meetings in community life. Some expressed a wish for a greater separation between participatory budget activities and civil society. One person told me that because Nazaré, as a district, does not have any other meeting place, 'there is a lot of confusion about what we're supposed to do. Instead of public investments, all kinds of topics are discussed' that often caused the meeting 'to serve no real purpose'. In fact, meetings did serve a purpose for some participants, though not a public-oriented one. Because budgeting assemblies were the 'only place for the whole community', it was there that participants developed and maintained reputations, resolved disputes and jockeyed for prestige in the community. Without a significant number of experienced participants to curtail these interruptions, they continued to occur.

Other settings

Government-sponsored assemblies of the participatory budget were not only settings where community activists and other citizens met, they were the *principal* setting for each district and were more successful than independent settings at drawing a broad range of participants and eliciting regular conversations on community matters. Just as the past history of both districts shows how difficult it is to establish regular discussions with the character of a public sphere, even after state-sponsored meetings, interviews showed that it was difficult to establish such public-minded discussions on a regular basis in settings outside of the state-sponsored institutions.

In Pôr-do-Sol, where there was already significant neighbourhood activity, the advent of the budgeting assemblies facilitated the creation of an *additional* parallel and independent forum that was closely linked to the budgeting assemblies. In Nazaré, however, community activists were unable to establish such a forum despite numerous tries, and the budgeting assemblies remained the only such forum for the district. It is the connection of budgeting assemblies to decision-making power, or the perception that meetings accomplished something, that accounts for their relative success in both districts.

In Pôr-do-Sol, the advent of budgeting assemblies in 1991 made possible the regular functioning of a *Conselho Popular*, or popular council, although it had been attempted since 1998. The *conselho* was an autonomous umbrella organization dedicated to fostering discussion on common problems in the district, and it drew participants from various neighbourhoods. Community activists involved in the *conselho* described its early difficulties, stating that 'before the budget assemblies it was almost impossible to count on people showing up to a meeting'. Several of the principal community activists in the new *conselho* had been active in the community for a number of years before the budgeting assemblies, principally with local, neighbourhood-level activities, and the establishment of the budgeting assemblies provided the impetus for a district-level forum. The budgeting assemblies regularly drew together a range of community activities, creating a setting where they discussed common problems. In time, these ongoing conversations led to the activation of the *conselho*.

Although the *conselho* was, during my fieldwork, a district-level setting where open-ended conversations about community affairs took place, it was a setting that was closely related to the budgeting assemblies and was dependent on them. Its yearly schedule was always tied to that of the budgeting assemblies, and at the times of the year that budgeting assemblies did not meet, the *conselho* did not meet. The principal community activists in the *conselho* were the same as those in the budgeting assemblies, and activities between the two settings were coordinated. In addition, a significant portion of activities at the *conselho* was dedicated to the budgeting assemblies, and the City Hall facilitator of the budgeting assemblies was often in attendance. A few times during my fieldwork, entire meetings were dedicated to solving a community dispute, such as the one between Arno and Marcos that erupted in the budgeting assembly. In other words, the *conselho* provided a complement to the budgeting assemblies.

As in Pôr-do-Sol, in Nazaré, before the advent of the participatory budget assembly, it was difficult to establish a meeting place for community discussions. All evidence shows that there simply was no such prior setting. Since the advent of the budgeting assemblies, activists had tried several times to create a similar *conselho*, but unlike in Pôr-do-Sol, they never succeeded. According to several interviews, it was clear that the idea of an independent *conselho* did not appeal to a number of assembly participants. One told me, 'Why do we need a *conselho*? We already have the budgeting [assemblies] and that's where the government comes, not somewhere else.' This feeling was echoed by other community activists.

In Pôr-do-Sol, the previous existence of neighbourhood-based activism meant that the establishment of the budgeting assemblies facilitated the creation of another, non-governmental, setting, the *conselho*. In Nazaré, the establishment of budgeting assemblies created a setting where citizens could meet and carry out discussions, although the paradox is that the presence of other autonomous networks, as in Pôr-do-Sol, was important in the quality of discussions in the participatory budget.

Conclusion

The government-sponsored participatory assemblies in poor neighbourhoods in Brazil appear a potential redress to the paradox that 'neighbourhoods with the most serious need for community organization are the ones with the least capacity to create and sustain them' (Logan and Molotch 1987: 136). Although some scholars have argued that in the context of Latin America, 'total independence and the construction of an autonomous social project from the grassroots have proved to be unworkable' (Schönwälder 1997: 765), it is clear from Porto Alegre that state-sponsored institutions have proved important in fostering open-ended discussions in unlikely settings. I have addressed the question of whether and how such arrangements afford the conditions for participants to engage in the open-ended public-minded discussions heralded by democratic theorists.

I have provided an ethnographic investigation into the conditions necessary for the appearance of the public sphere. In concert with the predictions of theories on the 'social bases of democracy', the past history of two Porto Alegre districts showed difficulties in establishing the regular communication characteristic of the public sphere. Drawing on ethnographic evidence, I examined how participants in district assemblies of the participatory budget created the fragile talk of open-ended public-minded discussion in two of the city's poor districts. Participants regularly used these spaces for civic discourse and deliberation, deploying a language of the commonality of needs to signify the community and the public interest. While both Nazaré and Pôr-do-Sol districts were home to open-ended discussions, some of Pôr-do-Sol's activists had substantial histories of activism prior to the budgeting meetings, while Nazaré's residents, on the whole, had their first involvement in civic life through budgeting meetings. This was a significant difference. Organized networks of civil society played an important role in Pôr-do-Sol, most clearly in terms of managing and curtailing conflict, while in Nazaré the assemblies became the only place in the community, and thus became a staging ground for some participants to manage their reputations.

A comparison with a prior period in both districts, shows that before the budgeting assemblies, it was more difficult to sustain any kind of regular meeting place beyond individual neighbourhoods to carry out these discussions. According to community activists like Arno, this was because 'people have difficulty, they don't have experience and then after working the whole week they don't want to go to another meeting'. As serious impediments in the past, activists also pointed to the transient lives of those living in squatter settlements and to their lack of experience with civic affairs. During the time of my research, however, on a regular basis both districts were home to open-ended and public-spirited discussion on common affairs at the participatory assemblies, a context that would be considered unlikely according to mainstream sociological accounts, given their citizens' material difficulties, their lack of education and the lack of a liberal political culture.

This essay also highlights the role of state-sponsored institutions as enabling the public sphere in otherwise difficult settings. Although participatory institutions may be more relevant in those societies where the state historically has played a larger role in nation-building than in North Atlantic societies, instances of participation in government are increasingly common in many countries. Fraser (1992) has criticized the conception of the public sphere for precisely neglecting the possible connections with empowered state settings, and I have also raised this issue, but in a slightly different way. Here I argue that empowered state settings, such as this one in Brazil, are important objects of investigation because they have the potential to foster the participation of unlikely candidates in the public sphere. By providing material support and fostering a 'sense of public', these empowered settings have the potential to bring in those participants otherwise relegated to subaltern spheres.

Finally, I call attention to the importance of interactions between participatory arrangements and the civil society surrounding them. The tendency of some scholarship on participatory governance and deliberative democracy is to focus on the rules and institutional design of participatory arrangements at the expense of the surrounding social context (Elster 1998). Attention to these interactions may significantly qualify both the criticisms and praise for instances of participation in government as they shed additional light on the desirability of such arrangements in a variety of contexts. One of the insights from my research is that whether participatory sites are prone to certain downsides or patterns of communication may have as much to do with the surrounding civil society as the institutional participatory rules. In this case, while the assemblies were not prone to previously noted drawbacks of participatory democracy, such as the domination of the assemblies by the articulate few, they were prone to another drawback of participation in government specific to settings without already established civic networks. The social networks in Pôr-do-Sol were important, not so much in turning an 'I into We' (Putnam 1995), but in preventing the 'We' of the discussions on collective projects from turning into an 'I' of personal disputes, as happened in Nazaré.

[Abridged version of an article originally published as 'Emergent public spheres: talking politics in participatory governance', *American Sociological Review*, 68, February 2003, pp. 52–74]

References

Avritzer, L. (2002) *Democracy and the Public Space in Latin America*, Princeton, NJ: Princeton University Press.

Baierle, S. (1992) 'A explosão da experiencia: a emergencia de um novo principio etico-politico em Porto Alegre' [The explosion of experience: the emergence of a new political-ethical principle in Porto Alegre], Master's thesis, Department of Political Science, Universidade de Campinas (UNICAMP), Campinas, Brazil.

CIDADE (Centro de Assessoria e Estudos Urbanos) (1999) 'Orçamento participativo – quem é a populacão que participa e que pensa do processo' [The participatory budget: who participates and what they think of the process], Porto Alegre: CIDADE.

Cohen, J. (1996) 'Procedure and substance in deliberate democracy', in S. Benhabib (ed.), *Democracy and Difference: Contesting the Boundaries of the Political*, Princeton, NJ: Princeton University Press, pp. 95–109.

Cohen, J. and J. Rogers (1992) *Associations and Democracy*, London: Verso.

Elster, J. (ed.) (1998) *Deliberative Democracy*, Cambridge: Cambridge University Press.

Emirbayer, M. and M. Sheller (1999) 'Publics in history', *Theory and Society*, pp. 145–97.

Evans, S. and H. Boyte (1992) *Free Spaces: The Sources of Democratic Change in America*, New York: Harper and Row.

Fedozzi, L. (2001) *O Poder da Aldeia* [The power of the village], Porto Alegre: Tomo Editorial.

Fraser, N. (1992) 'Rethinking the public sphere: a contribution to the critique of actually existing democracy', in C. Calhoun (ed.), *Habermas and the Public Sphere*, Cambridge, MA: MIT Press, pp. 109–42.

Fung, A. and E. O. Wright (2000) 'Deepening democracy: innovations in empowered participatory governance', *Politics and Society*, 29: 5–42.

Habermas, J. (1987) *The Theory of Communicative Action*, vol. 2: *Lifeworld and System: A Critique of Functionalist Reason*, trans. T. McCarthy, Cambridge: Polity.

— (1989) *The Structural Transformation of the Public Sphere*, Cambridge, MA: MIT Press.

Lipset, S. M. (1997) 'The iron law of oligarchy', in S. Buechler and F. K. Cylke Jr (eds), *Social Movements: Perspectives and Issues*, New York: Mayfield, pp. 385–92.

Logan, J. R. and H. L. Molotch (1987) *Urban Fortunes: The Political Economy of Place*, Berkeley: University of California Press.

Mansbridge, J. (1980) *Beyond Adversary Democracy*, Chicago, IL: University of Chicago Press.

Oliveira, N. dos Santos (1996) 'Favelas and ghettos: race and class in Rio de Janeiro and New York City', *Latin American Perspectives*, 23: 71–89.

Oliveira, N. and T. Barcellos (eds) (1990) *O Rio Grande do Sul Urbano* [Urban Rio Grande do Sul], Porto Alegre: FEE.

Panizzi, W. M. (1990) 'Da legalidade para a ilegalidade: a formacão de micro territorios urbanos' [From legality to illegality: the creation of urban micro-territories], in N. Oliveira and T. Barcellos (eds), *O Rio Grande do Sul Urbano*, Porto Alegre: FEE, pp. 190–214.

Pearlman, J. (1976) *The Myth of Marginality*, Berkeley: University of California Press.

Polletta, F. (1999) 'Free spaces in collective action', *Theory and Society*, 28: 1–38.

Prefeitura Municipal de Porto Alegre (1998) 'Regimento interno do orçamento participativo' [Internal regulation of the participatory budget], Porto Alegre: PMPA.

Putnam, R. D. (1995) 'Bowling alone: America's declining social capital', *Journal of Democracy*, 6: 65–78.

Santos, B. de Souza (1998) 'Participatory budgeting in Porto Alegre: toward a redistributive democracy', *Politics and Society*, 4: 461–510.

Schönwälder, G. (1997) 'New democratic spaces at the grassroots? Popular participation in Latin American local governments', *Development and Change*, 28: 753–70.

30 | Co-governance for accountability: beyond 'exit' and 'voice'

John Ackerman

Introduction

In the contemporary world of second-wave reforms and democratic transitions, the construction of an honest, efficient and effective government apparatus has moved to the top of the international policy agenda. Unfortunately, most contemporary pro-accountability reforms exclude the 'voice' of societal actors. On the one hand, 'old' public management strategies such as civil-service reform and strict procedural monitoring are explicitly designed to insulate the state from society. On the other hand, New Public Management (NPM) policies such as managed competition and performance contracts also keep society far away from the core activities of the state. Although NPM does have a participative or 'social control' current within it (Bresser and Cunill 1999; Peters 2001), this is usually marginalized in favour of marketization strategies. Marketization itself allows citizens to let their opinions be known through 'exit' options, but it prohibits their active participation in government. Indeed, recent studies have shown that such policies may even undermine community organization and social capital in the developing world (Cunill 2000; Wallis and Dollery 2001).

Governments and international development agencies have recently moved 'participatory development' up their discursive agendas (cf. UNDP 2002; World Bank 2003), but actual practice has lagged far behind. Participation is usually seen to be important only insofar as it reduces government costs and responsibilities. It suddenly appears to be 'practical' and attractive when governments can offload service delivery to non-governmental organizations (NGOs) and community groups or convince local residents to donate volunteer labour or materials. The direct involvement of citizens and societal groups in the core functions of government continues to be extremely rare.

This article argues that the opening up of the core activities of the state to societal participation is one of the most effective ways to improve accountability and governance. Through an exploration of case studies from a wide variety of contexts and policy areas, the article shows that state reformers should move beyond strategies based on 'exit' and even 'voice' (Hirschman 1970; Paul 1992) to establish spaces of full 'co-governance' with society. Instead of sending sections of the state off to society, it is often more fruitful to invite society into the inner chambers of the state. The article concludes with a summary of the principal lessons for institutional reformers and development professionals interested in strengthening government accountability through the involvement society.

Accountability and society

Good government does not emerge spontaneously or naturally out of the good hearts of individual bureaucrats and politicians. It is the result of a tough, and often conflict-ridden, process of institutional design. The principal element that assures good government is the accountability of public officials. This involves both answerability, or 'the obligation of public officials to inform about and to explain what they are doing', and enforcement, or 'the capacity of accounting agencies to impose sanctions on powerholders who have violated their public duties' (Schedler 1999a: 14). Although some individual officials may never need institutional structures to assure their commitment to the public good, most do need it at least some of the time. The only way to guarantee good government is by institutionalizing powerful accountability mechanisms that hold every public official responsible for his/her actions as a public servant.

The celebration of free and fair elections is one of the most powerful pro-accountability mechanisms in existence. Through periodic elections, political leaders who work for the common good are supposed to be re-elected, and leaders who use public office for particularistic ends are supposed to be removed from office. Nevertheless, there are both structural and contextual problems with elections in the contemporary world. First, elections only hold elected officials accountable. The vast majority of public officials are appointed bureaucrats who are not directly accountable to the public through the electoral process. Second, because elections only occur once every few years and force an incredible diversity of opinions and evaluations together into a single ballot, it is virtually impossible for elections to give clear accountability signals to individual office holders (Przeworski et al. 1999). Third, even if the accountability signal were somehow clearly discernible, the fact that most politicians are elected by only a small portion of the population often forces politicians to favour patronage, 'pork' or corruption over initiatives that would bring long-term benefit to the public as a whole (Varshney 1999). The effectiveness of elections as mechanisms of sanction and control is weakened by the distance between political and civil society, the clientelistic nature of many political parties, the excess private funding for candidates, and the lack of public information about the general workings of government and even less information about the specific behaviour of individual office holders.

As a result, 'vertical accountability' mechanisms, such as elections, that require government officials to appeal 'downwards' to the people at large have been complemented by 'horizontal accountability' mechanisms that require public officials and agencies to report 'sideways' to other officials and agencies within the state itself. Guillermo O'Donnell has defined horizontal account-ability in the following manner.

> The existence of state agencies that are legally enabled and empowered, and factually willing and able, to take actions that span from routine oversight to criminal sanctions or impeachment in relation to actions or omissions by other agents or agencies of the state that may be qualified as unlawful. (O'Donnell 1999: 38)

Examples of horizontal accountability mechanisms include human rights ombudsmen, corruption control agencies, legislative investigative commis-sions and administrative courts.

There has been a phenomenal growth of such institutions throughout the world in recent years. Unfortunately, as with elections, these many new agencies of horizontal accountability are plagued by both structural and contextual problems. Structural difficulties include the impossibility of monitoring the almost infinite number of government actions (and inactions) as well as the political isolation that results from these agencies' statutory or constitutional independence (Maor 2004). Contextual difficulties include the lack of adequate funding, limited enforcement capacity, the absence of second-order account-ability (i.e. holding accounting agencies accountable) and the overall weakness of the rule of law needed to enforce agency sanctions.

Fortunately, there is a third way to hold government accountable. In addi-tion to elections and horizontal accountability agencies, societal actors can directly oblige government actors to answer for their actions and sanction them for wrongdoing. Samuel Paul's (1992) article in *World Development* on 'Accountability in public services: exit, voice and control' was one of the first to put forth such an agenda. The traditional public accountability mechanisms such as expenditure audits and legislative reviews seem unequal to the task of ensuring accountability for public services at the micro level ... Public service accountability will be sustained only when the 'hierarchical control' (HC) over service providers is reinforced by the public's willingness and ability to exit [i.e. marketization] or to use voice [i.e. direct participation] (ibid.: 1047–8). Paul here simultaneously articulates the accountability function of marketization strategies and, even more importantly, makes the crucial argument that direct societal participation is often even more effective than strategies based on 'exit'.

The 1996 symposium on 'Development strategies across the public–private divide', also published in *World Development*, then expanded and filled out this initial discussion of society's pro-accountability role. This series of articles argued that 'state–society synergy' (Evans 1996a, 1996b) is one of the best ways to strengthen government accountability. 'In sum, the image of the good bureaucrat – carefully insulated from constituents – has its usefulness, but openness to the role of the "co-producer" ... may be the best way to increase effectiveness and ultimately the best way to preserve the integrity of increasingly besieged public institutions' (Evans 1996b: 1131). This literature performed a great service insofar as it pushed academics and development professionals to take societal participation seriously. No longer was society viewed as a 'bother', a 'contaminant' or as the source of bureaucratic 'capture'. States and societies could be strengthened simultaneously. Nevertheless, this first wave of writings was also limited in scope insofar as it tended to emphasize depoliticized forms of participation, circumscribed societal action to specific local services and to the implementation phase of government projects, and left out the important discussion of the legal institutionalization of participative mechanisms.

In recent years, two different currents of research have arisen that expand on this earlier literature. First, authors such as Catalina Smulovitz, Enrique Peruzzotti, Nuria Cunill and Sylvio Waisbord have argued that more political forms of societal participation such as mass mobilization, media exposés and the use of the courts are also effective ways for society to improve government accountability. Smulovitz and Peruzzotti distinguish this form of accountability from the electoral and the horizontal forms by calling it 'societal account-ability'. They define this as a non-electoral yet vertical mechanism of control that rests on the actions of a multiple array of citizens' associations and movements and on the media, actions that aim at exposing governmental wrongdoing, bringing new issues into the public agenda, or activating the operation of horizontal agencies (Peruzzotti and Smulovitz 2000b: 150; 2002: 32).

For example, in their analysis of the social response to two extrajudicial killings in Argentina, the authors have documented how the combination of mobilization, legal action and media exposure can effectively guarantee that the judicial system operates impartially, even when the perpetrators are well connected or even part of the government apparatus itself (Peruzzotti and Smulovitz 2000a, 2000b, 2002). Waisbord has complemented this analysis by focusing on the role of investigative journalists and media scandals in obliging public servants and politicians to be more accountable (Waisbord 2000). Cunill (1997, 2000) follows this same line of research but focuses more on the action of citizens in general than on that of organized civil society. For her, the most important society-driven pro-accountability mechanisms are legal reforms such as popular referendum laws, administrative procedure acts that require public consultations, 'amparo' laws, and freedom of information acts (Cunill 2000: 25–39). Since such laws open up the state to the action of the common citizen they create space for the active enforcement of accountability by the public.

This literature is a welcome addition to the accountability debate since it obliges us to look beyond 'well-behaved' local participation in specific govern-ment projects to a more openly political and even confrontational engagement with the government apparatus as a whole. Nevertheless, these writings still envision and defend an arms-length relationship between state and society. As Cunill has written, 'co-management is irreconcilable with control. The efficacy of [social control] is directly dependent on the independence and the autonomy that societal actors maintain with respect to state actors' (Cunill 2000: 9, my translation).

The second alternative current of research is more 'transgressive' insofar as it explicitly violates the separation between state and society. For instance, Ernesto Isunza has recently written about 'transversal accountability' in which societal actors participate directly in the leadership and operation of state pro-accountability agencies (Isunza 2003). This parallels Anne Marie Goetz and Robert Jenkins' description of the 'The New Accountability Agenda' which emphasizes 'hybrid' or 'diagonal' forms of accountability (Goetz and Jenkins 2001, 2002a) in which 'vertical' actors carry out intrastate 'horizontal' accountability functions. In a similar spirit, Leonardo Avritzer has put forth the idea of 'participatory publics', which occur when societal participatory practices are taken up by and embedded within the state (Avritzer 2002). Archon Fung and Eric Olan Wright have also followed this line of research in arguing for 'empowered participatory governance' which expands the sphere of democratic participation beyond formal electoral politics to involve society at large in deliberation over the design and operation of fundamental government services such as schooling, policing, environmental protection and urban infrastructure (Fung and Wright 2001). In addition, Jonathan Fox has argued for an 'interactive approach' to state–society relations which envisions the improvement of accountability through the participation of society in the core functions of government (Fox 2000).

This group of authors goes beyond the circumscribed participation implicit in the 'co-production' literature as well as the arms-length action of the 'societal accountability' literature to posit a full 'co-governance for accountability' which confuses the boundary between state and society. In addition to co-producing specific services and pressuring government from the outside, societal actors can also participate directly in the core functions of government itself. This form of civil society participation is special because, as Goetz and Jenkins have written, it 'represents a shift towards augmenting the limited effectiveness of civil society's watchdog function by breaking the state's monopoly over the responsibility for official executive oversight' (Goetz and Jenkins 2001: 365). The present article looks both to bring together these various texts into a coherent literature and to demonstrate the salience of this budding 'transgressive' school of thought by offering some examples of how it works in practice.

Case studies

(a) *Participatory budgeting in Porto Alegre, Brazil* The Porto Alegre city government represents one of the most effective schemes of state–society collaboration for accountability in the developing world. Since 1989, when the Workers' Party (PT) first won the city government, Porto Alegre has placed spending decisions for over 10 per cent of its annual budget in the hands of the people. Every year, more than 14,000 citizens in this city of 1.3 million participate in neighbourhood meetings as well as sixteen regional and five thematic assemblies to set priorities for government investment in infrastructure and basic social services. Each assembly then elects two councillors to serve on a city-wide Council of Participatory Budgeting (COP), the organ responsible for putting together the final citywide budget plan. At each level of the process (neighbourhood, district, citywide) decisions are made through intense negotiation and the use of sophisticated weighted voting systems designed to ensure a fair distribution of resources. At the end of the process, the proposed budget is then submitted to the local legislature for final approval and promulgation. During the following year, the regional and thematic assemblies, councillors and neighbourhood groups evaluate the previous year's negotiation process and monitor the implementation process of the previous year's budget.

The participatory budgeting (PB) process is an excellent example of 'co-governance for accountability'. Normal citizens are involved directly in the planning and supervision of public spending, activities normally under the exclusive purview of public officials. This arrangement is clearly a step beyond both the 'co-production' and the 'societal accountability' models of civil society participation. Instead of trying to influence policy from the outside or only at the local community level, the citizens of Porto Alegre are invited inside the governmental apparatus itself.

This arrangement has had an important impact on accountability. First, it has drastically reduced the possibilities and incentives for corrupt behaviour on the part of bureaucrats. Each neighbourhood and region is informed as to the exact amount of funds that will be invested in which products and services in its area and, even more importantly, since the citizens themselves participate in designing the budget, they feel they have a personal stake in making sure the government complies with its commitments (Navarro 1998: 70–71). Second, the budgeting process reduces the political use of public funds by opening up alternative channels for the participation of civil society. The crucial element is the entirely open and public nature of the budget assemblies. Any adult can attend, speak and vote in the assemblies (Avritzer 2000: 18). Moreover, it is easy to form a new group and thereby gain access to special organizational representation. This leads to easy 'exit' options for members of clientelistic groups where 'voice' is not an effective form of protest.

Third, PB limits the capture of state institutions by wealthy interests. Popular participation itself does this by replacing the power of money with the power of voice. In addition, the special design of Porto Alegre's system reinforces this tendency even further. The algorithm used for determining budget priorities intentionally tilts investments towards poorer neighbourhoods. Owing to this built-in pro-poor bias, the same need presented by two neighbourhoods is much more likely to be implemented in the poorer one than the wealthier one (Baiocchi 2001: 48). Marquetti (2003) has recently empirically demonstrated the significant redistributive impact of the PB.

The origins of this successful pro-accountability arrangement can be found in society. First, the idea of instituting a participatory budget had its origins within civil society. It was the Union of Residents' Associations of Porto Alegre (UAMPA) that first advocated the introduction of such a mechanism in the city in 1986 (Avritzer 2002: 145). Second, Avritzer documents how the expression 'participatory budget' did not exist in the PT's electoral platform for city government in 1988. The design of today's PB arrangement arose only after a period of intense negotiation and participation between the new government and civil society groups (Avritzer 2000: 9). Third, the particular institutional form developed by the Porto Alegre government was largely modelled on already existing practices of deliberation and negotiation in civil society (Navarro 2002).

The Porto Alegre experience offers many lessons for pro-accountability state reformers. First, poor, uneducated people can and do effectively participate in the core activities of governance. Abers (1998) documents that while in 1991 29 per cent of Porto Alegre's residents earned three times the minimum wage or less, 45 per cent of the budget participants fit this profile. The underprivileged not only actively participate, they even participate more, relative to their size in the population, than better-off groups. Second, governments can only get back as much as they put in to efforts to activate civil society participation for accountability. In Porto Alegre, citizens are taken out of their usual role as only 'advisers' or information providers to government projects and thrust directly into the decision-making process itself. In addition, the government actively encourages the participation of unorganized citizens through the use of government-employed community organizers (ibid.: 514).

As has been shown to be the case in other cities that have tried participatory budgets, without such full involvement by the government, 'participation' schemes can easily end up only strengthening previously existing clientelistic networks and unbalanced intra-community power relations (Goldfrank 2002; Nylen 2002). Third, governments need to take civil society into account in the design of the participative mechanisms themselves. The PB did not spontaneously arise out of the minds of enlightened bureaucrats. It originated in civil society, was pushed forward by social actors and was ultimately modelled on previously existing practices in civil society by a new government that itself consisted mostly of individuals who had made their careers as community and social activists. Participatory mechanisms usually hold the mark of their birth.

Fourth, according to Fung and Wright (2001), the Porto Alegre experience is an excellent example of how a healthy balance can be struck between 'devolution' and 'centralized supervision and coordination'. Although devolution and decentralization are important because they bring government closer to the people, if carried out blindly, they tend to reinforce inequalities both within the newly 'autonomous' local units as well as between them. Decentralization is productive only if the centre remains responsible for the supervision and coordination of the activities in the local units.

(b) *Mexico's Federal Electoral Institute* Mexico's Federal Electoral Institute (IFE) stands out as an example of successful 'co-governance for accountability'. The principal activities of the IFE include organizing federal elections, distributing public funds to the political parties, monitoring the use of both public and private funds by the parties, checking for media bias in the coverage of political campaigns, putting together and cleaning up the official electoral roll, and running public education campaigns (IFE 2000a).

The IFE actively involves societal actors at five different levels. First, the IFE is run by an independent, nine-member 'citizen-run' General Council that serves as both a special horizontal accountability agency for electoral affairs and as the IFE's principal directive body (Schedler 1999b). Second, the meetings of the General Council are public. The minutes and decisions are widely publicized, reported on by the media, and are available via the Internet. Third, one representative from each registered political party sits on the General Council. These party representatives can fully participate in the discussions of the General Council and have access to most of the same information as the councillors but do not have the power to vote on initiatives or decisions. Fourth, the IFE councils that are responsible for organizing and supervising the federal elections at the state level are also 'citizen-run' insofar as they are appointed by the General Council without any formal interference from local or state governments (Isunza 2003). Fifth, during its most important moment of 'service delivery', the organization of the federal elections, the IFE recruits a huge army of citizen volunteers. During the months leading up to the 2000 elections, more than one million citizens were mobilized to ensure the realization of free and fair elections.

Overall, the IFE has been remarkably successful. The lack of significant post-electoral protests and mobilizations in the year 2000 was unprecedented for a presidential election in Mexico. In addition, the fact that there has not been a new electoral reform since 1996 is a testament both to the great breakthrough of this reform and to the legitimacy that the institution continues to enjoy up through the present. Other than the 1933–42 and 1963–70 periods, the seven years during 1996–2003 mark the longest period the Mexican political system has gone without an electoral reform since the promulgation of the Mexican constitution of 1917 (Molinar 1996). Finally, the IFE's recent historic US$100 million fine imposed on the Party of the Institutional Revolution (PRI) and its aggressive investigation of the irregular financing of the campaign of sitting president Vicente Fox demonstrates its ability to stand up to even the most powerful interests.

This case study offers a number of important lessons for state reformers. First, it confirms the willingness and capacity of poor people to participate in the core activities of governance. Second, the rule of equal and opposite reaction applies here once again. Normal citizens will participate at such massive levels only if the policies being implemented are seen to respond to demands that have originated in civil society, are designed with the participation of a broad range of actors, and actively incorporate citizens into the process of implementation itself. Third, none of the achievements of the IFE would have been possible without a significant amount of resources dedicated to the reform and operation of the IFE itself. Societal participation is best stimulated when it is perceived as a complement to rather than as a replacement for government action. Without a core group of 2,500 civil servants, significant salaries for the General Council and a large operating budget of US$480 million in the year 2000 (IFE 2000b), the IFE would not have been able to successfully carry out its tasks nor stimulate the popular legitimacy it needed in order to involve the active participation of civil society.

Fourth, the case of the IFE forces us to question the commonly accepted idea that neutrality arises exclusively out of the absence of partisanship. Although some of the effectiveness of the IFE does indeed arise out of the professionalization and non-partisanship of its staff, a great deal of its legitimacy also arises out of the saturation of partisanship or the radical plurality of those who participate in the decision-making processes of the IFE. The General Council is made up of nine citizen councillors, but also surrounded by a whirlwind of party representatives and media 'intrusions'. Each voting booth is staffed by trained members of civil society, but also intensively watched by representatives from each political party. One of the principal reasons why the electoral reform of 1996 was more effective than the reforms of 1990 and 1994 is because a greater diversity of political positions were taken into account at the negotiating table in 1996 than during the other two reforms.

(c) *Police and school reform in Chicago* Like many cities in the developing world, Chicago has a 'tradition of machine politics, insular administrative bureaucracies installed in reaction to political manipulations, a vibrant tradition of neighborhood activism [and] extreme socioeconomic inequality' (Fung 2001: 73). Research by Archon Fung shows how the Chicago city government has improved the performance of its schools and police forces by actively incorporating the participation of civil society, going far beyond methods of consultation, co-production and protest to open itself up to full 'co-governance' with the citizenry at large.

In 1988 the city assembly passed the Chicago School Reform Act, which created a 'local school council' (LSC), five for each of the Chicago Public School's (CPS) 530 elementary and high schools. The LSC's principal tasks are hiring and firing school principals, approving school budgets, developing long-term strategic planning documents called School Improvement Plans (SIPs) and dispersing funds (ibid.: 77). These reforms have made the Chicago school system one of the most open to participation in the entire United States. Chicago's police reform also involved a significant increase in citizen participation. The 1995 reform of the Chicago Police Department (CPD) organized police officers into 279 'beat teams' that are required to hold open 'community meetings' each month in which police officers and citizens work together to identify problems and plan solutions (Fung 1999; Skogan and Hartnett 1997). Here the mode of participation is more akin to 'societal accountability'. Citizens are not given any direct legal power over the operations of the police. They simply provide information and pressure the officers to attend to specific problems. Nevertheless, the close citizen oversight of police activities does serve as a powerful accountability mechanism since citizens' complaints can trigger existing internal mechanisms of supervision and control (Walker 2001).

There is evidence that both school and police services have greatly improved as a result of the reforms. During 1994–98 the murder rate declined 24 per cent, robbery fell 31 per cent and sexual assault fell 21 per cent in Chicago, results that are comparable to radically different 'zero-tolerance' strategies like those imposed by Rudolph Giuliani in New York (Fung 1999; Skogan and Hartnett 1997). In addition, school performance as measured by a specially developed 'metric of school productivity' shows that during 1987–97 'while students entering the system have become increasingly disadvantaged and less well prepared, the majority of schools have become more effective in educating them' (Fung 2001: 99).

The origins of the two reforms are quite distinct. School reform arose out of conflict between state and society and was driven by social protest. In the Chicago schools, reform resulted from a pitched battle that pitted a diverse social movement composed of parent organizations, 'good government' civic groups, educational reform activists, and a coalition of business groups against traditional school insiders such as the Chicago Teachers' Union and the Board of Education (ibid.: 77). In contrast, police reform arose out of consensus between government and civil society and was principally directed by reformers within the state.

Nevertheless, neither of these reforms was the independent creation of 'far-sighted' bureaucrats. Both state and society actors were crucial in the development of each participation mechanism, and the more actively civil society was involved in the development of the reform proposals the more complete was the opening up of the state to society.

These institutions are excellent examples of what Fung calls 'accountable autonomy'. For both cases, the role of central power shifts fundamentally from that of directing local units (in the previous hierarchical system) to that of supporting local units in their own problem-solving endeavours and holding them accountable to the norms of deliberation and achievement of demanding but feasible public outcomes (ibid.: 87). For example, while local school councils in Chicago are responsible for drawing up budgets and sanctioning principals they are also simultaneously monitored and evaluated by central agencies. This adds an interesting new twist to our theoretical discussion of accountability because here local participative bodies are accountable to centralized bureaucratic agencies. Instead of civil society holding government accountable it is now government that is holding civil society accountable.

The Chicago cases reinforce the above lessons. First, the most active participants in Chicago are once again the poor and uneducated. Minority dominant areas tend to have higher participation rates than white dominant areas (Fung 1999). Second, the success of these Chicago cases also depended on the government opening the process beyond already organized civil society organizations and employing community organizers to stimulate participation and facilitate community decision-making. Third, civil society participation in the design phase of participatory structures proved to be crucial here as well. Neither of the Chicago reforms arose purely out of the minds of social planners and their relative success depended on the ability of the government to involve social actors from the very beginning. Fourth, the supply side of the equation is crucial. Without a capable and well-financed state apparatus that can actually respond to popular demands and participation, such accountability mechanisms would create more disenchantment than hope.

Finally, these cases push us farther towards the conclusion that the supposed either/or choice between centralization and decentralization is a false dichotomy that needs to be reanalysed. Although devolving power is important, there is an equal need to strengthen the centre, at least in its coordinating and monitoring capacities. Nevertheless, the local school councils are elected bodies that do not bring a clear popular mandate arising out of popular assemblies and the police 'community meetings' do not have any direct legal authority over police behaviour as does the IFE's General Council. An average of only twenty to twenty-five people participate in each beat meeting per month and there are only an average of 1.5 candidates in the elections for each open spot in the school councils (ibid.).

(d) *Decentralization and rural development in Mexico* Decentralization on its own is just as likely to strengthen corrupt local networks as it is to promote participation and accountability. Pro-accountability arrangements cannot be expected to arise spontaneously from devolution, but need to be intentionally structured. This is the central lesson of Jonathan Fox's research on the use of World Bank funds for municipal development projects in rural Mexico.

The Mexican Municipal Funds Programme has been almost entirely financed by two large loans received from the World Bank, one for US$350 million for 1991–94 and a second for US$500 million for 1995–99. This money was targeted for use in basic infrastructural improvements for the poorest communities in the rural areas of the poorest states and was implemented through municipal governments. Autonomous 'solidarity committees' were to be organized in each community in order to supervise government spending, decide which projects would be funded and contribute the necessary labour power. Unfortunately, since the solidarity committees did not have any legal standing or formal authority over the Municipal Funds Programme itself, the actual level of participation and the effective autonomy of the committees from the municipal, state and federal government depended entirely on the whims of local bureaucrats. Many committees were therefore entirely ignored or allowed to participate only in the implementation phase of the projects.

Nevertheless, this participatory mechanism was actually relatively successful in the state of Oaxaca. In this state the community assemblies made the project selection decisions in 63 per cent of the cases (Fox and Aranda 1996: 37). Fox and Aranda argue that one of the principal reasons for this high level of participation is that Oaxaca is an area that is endowed with a very high level of 'horizontal social capital' owing to a long and rich indigenous tradition of community collaboration and self-governance. Equally important, the government of the State of Oaxaca was flexible and open to working with these traditions. Instead of imposing a new organizational structure on society, a healthy mixing between state and social forms was permitted (Fox 1994). Indeed, in Oaxaca this tolerance of autonomous social forms goes back much farther than the Municipal Funds Programme. The state's municipal structure itself, with 570 municipalities based in local organizational forms, demonstrates the government's long-standing commitment to accommodating legal forms to traditional practices.

The communities that had higher levels of participation had more effective development projects. When the community was directly involved, it tended to monitor the use of funds more closely and to pick projects that were more useful for the population as a whole. In contrast, when the selection process was manipulated from the outside, investment tended to be shifted towards highly visible although not always useful projects (Fox and Aranda 1996: 37). A few years into the programme the government intervened in order to increase community participation and make the distribution of resources fairer. The formulas used for poverty measurement and funds distribution were improved and, even more importantly, made public. Moreover, the amount of funds that could be spent in the municipal capital was limited to 25 per cent, thus requiring municipalities to channel funds to the most needy, isolated areas.

Finally, the required amount of community contributions was made variable depending on the impact on poverty the selected project would have. High-impact projects required less community contribution than low-impact projects, thus encouraging investment in true 'public goods' (ibid.: 12; Fox 2002: 104–5).

These changes stimulated community participation and strengthened social capital. This occurred because the reforms made communities aware of their right to a precise amount of funds, actively involved the poorest areas, and empowered those actors who looked beyond their particular interests and towards the development of the community as a whole. Here institutional reform had a direct impact on trust, fairness and participation (Fox 2002). Nevertheless, the origins of this particular scheme of state–society synergy for accountability were entirely 'top-down'. Instead of arising out of intense negotiations between social actors and government reformers, the participation scheme was thought up and designed by the federal government in consultation with World Bank staff. This may go a long way in explaining why community participation has not been more dynamic in the Municipal Funds Programme, and why the case of Oaxaca is more of an exception than the rule.

There are various lessons to be learned from this case study. First, as we have already seen above, the direct involvement of social actors and practices from the design stage greatly contributes to the success of accountability mechanisms that depend on active participation from civil society. Second, this case also confirms the importance of the formal, legal empowerment of participatory bodies. Without a clear institutionalized location in the decision-making process, these bodies are left open to the winds of manipulation and are quickly bypassed by unwilling or authoritarian public officials. Third, government transparency and institutional design have an important impact on community participation. Co-governance for accountability stands a much better chance at success when government actors respect social actors enough to fully inform them about the details of development programmes and design participatory institutions so as to ensure the active involvement of the most marginal actors. Finally, this case also demonstrates the value of what Norman Long has called 'interface analysis'. This type of analysis pushes us to focus upon intervention practices as shaped by the interactions among the various participants, rather than simply on intervention models, by which is meant the ideal-typical constructions that planners, implementers or their clients put upon the process (Long 1999: 4).

(e) *Grassroots anti-corruption initiatives in India* One area of government that seems to be particularly resistant to societal participation is the auditing of government expenditure. This task is usually thought to be far too technically sophisticated and politically delicate for the average citizen. Freedom-of-information acts have recently started to sprout up around the world, and citizens are encouraged to use public information to pressure corporations or governments from the outside to comply with their duties or to decide their votes (e.g. Fung and O'Rourke 2000). But it is difficult to find examples in which normal citizens are as directly involved in the activity of auditing government expenditure as they are, for example, in the activity of budget design in Porto Alegre.

Nevertheless, as Anne Marie Goetz and Rob Jenkins argue, the cases of the Mazdoor Kisan Shakti Sangathan (MKSS) movement in Rajasthan, India, and the Rationing Kruti Samiti (RKS), or Action Committee for Rationing, movement in Mumbai, India, show that when reformist bureaucrats are faced with an active pro-accountability movement in civil society it is possible to make important inroads into the area of social auditing. The central accountability problem that both of these organizations face is widespread corruption in the provision of government services to the poor. Wages for public works projects are frequently skimmed off by public managers and the materials used in these projects are often artificially overpriced and of bad quality so as to allow the maximum room for kickbacks. In addition, the country's Public Distribution System (PDS), which is in charge of channelling basic food items and other fundamental household goods like kerosene to the poorest households, is rife with corruption.

Most communities in India already have local 'participatory' institutions that are supposedly responsible for monitoring the performance of government programmes. Nevertheless, these 'Vigilance Committees' and 'Village Assemblies' are often captured by actors who are implicated in the process of corruption itself. For instance, they are frequently chaired by the representative of the municipal ward and their members are appointed in a top-down fashion. In addition, many government ration shops are owned or controlled by the very same politicians who are on the committees that are supposed to supervise them (Goetz and Jenkins 2001: 371).

As a result of the failure of these state-run participatory mechanisms, movements such as MKSS and RKS have found it necessary to create their own autonomous society-driven mechanisms for auditing public projects. The MKSS has developed a methodology through which it independently investigates government spending practices and then exposes and compares this information to reality through public hearings (*jan sun wai*) (Goetz and Jenkins 2002a: 41–2). In the hearings obvious discrepancies and missing accounts are presented and the public is given the opportunity to check their own personal experience as public employees or suppliers with the accounts. Public officials often attend and many cases exist in which this process has worked to directly shame them into returning large amounts of 'misdirected' funds.

Goetz and Jenkins present the case of the RKS in Mumbai as another example of what they call 'diagonal accountability', or the participation of 'vertical' actors in 'horizontal' enforcement activities. Since the official 'Vigilance Committees' are ineffective, the RKS has developed its own parallel system of informal vigilance committees. For each ration shop, five local women who are clients of the shop monitor and evaluate the quality and prices of the goods being sold. This activity has been facilitated by the RKS citywide campaign to oblige shop-owners to display prices publicly as well as samples of the goods on sale. The reports of the informal committees are then put together and presented both to the user community and to the central coordinating bureaucracy of the PDS in the city (Goetz and Jenkins 2002b).

This process was particularly successful during the period immediately following the 1992 riots in Mumbai, after which the city government was very interested in being perceived as being responsive to the poor. In addition, during this period an important reform-minded bureaucrat held the job of Regional Controller of Rationing. Nevertheless, once this reformist left his post the process became much less effective. The authors therefore claim that the RKS's experience with 'diagonal accountability' has been only a 'limited success story' (Goetz and Jenkins 2001). As we saw with the case of the MKSS, society-driven pro-accountability initiatives that confront the state and demand inclusion in the basic activities of government can be highly effective. Nevertheless, the RKS experience also shows us that ultimately the success of these movements often also depends on constructing alliances with progressive government officials as well.

As Goetz and Jenkins argue, such initiatives are grounded in a fundamentally naive view of politics and bureaucratic inefficiency because they assume that bureaucrats are simply ignorant of the problems with government (Jenkins and Goetz 1999). Bureaucrats need to be made directly accountable to the citizenry and the best way to do this is to allow citizens to get involved in the activity of auditing from the inside and to confront bureaucrats face to face with their complicity in bad performance or corruption. Second, co-governance for accountability does not need to begin with reformist or progressive governments. Success can also arise out of the action of independent organizations and social movements that press their demands on the state and push their way into the auditing of government programmes. Third, it seems that at some point in the process these movements do need allies within the government. Without state support or at least tolerance, such movements will most likely be repressed or rendered ineffective by state action. Finally, both of these cases confirm that sensitive and complex activities such as public auditing are not beyond the capacity of poor, illiterate citizens.

Lessons for institutional reformers

This article has argued that the active involvement of civil society and the strengthening of the state apparatus are not mutually exclusive or even contradictory initiatives. This is the central idea of 'co-governance' as a concept. If institutions are properly designed, a virtuous cycle that reinforces both state and society is possible. This is particularly important to emphasize today given the thrust of much of the NPM literature that proposes the devolution of state responsibilities to social actors via the market.

In addition, this article questions those strands of the 'old' public management literature that emphasize the insulation of bureaucracy from societal actors. As Kaufman has recently argued:

> The implication of accountability reform is different, however, when it refers to the establishment of popular assemblies and other forms of direct grassroots participation in administrative decisions. Although some forms of inclusion, such as partnerships with non-governmental organizations (NGOs), may enhance capacity, others, such as popular assemblies, may be a step backward in terms of the efficiency, effectiveness, and even the accountability of state organizations. (Kaufman 2003: 284)

The above case studies challenge this sort of circumscription of societal participation to 'well-behaved' or 'enlightened' actors such as NGOs and argues for the full inclusion of the citizenry as a whole in the core activities of government.

This article has shown that the first step for government reformers looking to construct co-governance for accountability should be to trust and actively involve societal actors from the very beginning of the process. Reformers should not wait for civil society to start trusting government nor should they wait to involve society until after the government has already designed a new participatory mechanism 'from above'. As the case studies show, the earlier societal actors are involved in the design process the more effective participatory measures tend to be. The best 'entry points' are therefore those issues and locations where there are previously existing social demands and practices surrounding a specific accountability issue.

In addition, when designing participatory mechanisms government reformers should be aware that transparency is not enough. Governments cannot expect information provision to generate single-handedly the positive feedback loops between state and society outlined in the above case studies. Governments should directly stimulate the participation of society. Otherwise, the only actors who will put to use the new information are journalists, academics, nonprofit organizations and already existing community organizations. Although these groups are indeed crucial in maintaining accountability, the cases above show that there is a qualitative forward leap when the population at large and the poor in particular are directly involved in enforcing accountability.

Once initiated, the best way to ensure the sustainability of a participatory framework is through its full institutionalization. As we saw in the case of the

Municipal Funds Programme, the formalization of even limited 'top-down' participatory schemes allowed for the development of much fuller participation. The case of the RKS in Mumbai, India, provides us with important negative examples of this same point. Here the absence of a clear legal framework left participation up to the whims of individual bureaucrats, leading to the eventual overturning of participatory schemes once there was a change of heart on the part of government. The difference between the two Chicago cases also reveals the importance of formalizing participatory procedures. One of the major reasons why the school reform has been more effective than the police reform is because the former institutionalized the involvement of civil society in the formal legal structure much more clearly and explicitly than the latter.

There are three different levels at which participatory mechanisms can be institutionalized. First, participatory mechanisms can be built into the strategic plans of existing government agencies. Second, new agencies can be created whose goal is to ensure societal participation in government activities. Third, participatory mechanisms can be inscribed in law. Although the first level of institutionalization is more or less widespread in the developing world and the second level is relatively common, the third level is extremely rare. Why this is the case is more or less evident. Law-making under democratic conditions involves the messy process of legislative bargaining and a full role for political parties. State reformers and multilateral agencies tend to shy away from such arenas, especially when they are dominated by opposing parties or factions. Therefore, reformers usually settle for executive procedures, special agencies or innovative individual bureaucrats to carry out their participative strategies.

This is a mistake. If dealt with in a creative fashion, partisanship can be just as effective as isolation in the search for effective accountability mechanisms. It is necessary to involve political parties and the legislature in order to institutionalize fully participative mechanisms through the law. Professionalism and independence are necessary but by no means sufficient to ensure the long-term survival of accountability. Effective pro-accountability structures need to be legitimized by society both at their founding moment and during their everyday operations. This requires the multiplication, not the reduction, of 'external eyes' (Smulovitz 2003) and the diversification, not unification, of political and ideological perspectives.

Finally, decentralization alone does not automatically lead to an increase in societal participation or an improvement in government accountability. Although devolution and decentralization are important because they bring government closer to the people, if carried out blindly they tend to reinforce inequalities both within the newly 'autonomous' local units and between them. Decentralization is only productive if the centre remains responsible for the supervision and coordination of activities in the local units.

If carefully applied, co-governance can be much more rewarding than alternatives such as marketization, bureaucratic insulation, 'co-production' or 'societal accountability'. Co-governance for accountability is usually more difficult to implement, but it is well worth the effort. By transgressing the boundaries between state and society, institutional reformers can unleash invaluable pro-accountability processes which are almost impossible to tap into through less ambitious strategies.

[Abridged version of an article that first appeared in *World Development*, 32(3), 2004, pp. 447–63]

References

Abers, R. (1998) 'From clientelism to cooperation: local government, participatory policy, and civic organizing in Porto Alegre, Brazil', *Politics and Society*, 26(4): 511–38.

Avritzer, L. (2000) 'Civil society, public space and local power: a study of the participatory budget in Belo Horizonte and Porto Alegre', IDS-Ford website, www.ids.ac.uk/ids/civsoc/index.html.

— (2002) *Democracy and the Public Space in Latin America*, Princeton, NJ: Princeton University Press.

Baiocchi, G. (2001) 'Participation, activism, and politics: the Porto Alegre experiment and deliberative democratic theory', *Politics and Society*, 29(1): 43–72.

Bresser, L. C. and N. Cunill (1999) 'Entre el estado y el mercado: lo público no estatal', in L. C. Bresser and N. Cunill (eds), *Lo Público no estatal en la reforma del estado*, Buenos Aires: Paidos, pp. 25–58.

Cunill, N. (1997) *Repensando lo público através de la sociedad: nuevas formas de gestión pública y representación social*, Caracas: Nueva Sociedad.

— (2000) 'Responsabilización por el control social', United Nations Online Network in Public Administration and Finance (UNPAN), un- pan1.un.org/intradoc/groups/public/documents/clad/unpan000183.pdf.

Evans, P. (1996a) 'Introduction: development strategies across the public–private divide', *World Development*, 24(6): 1033–7.

— (1996b) 'Government action, social capital and development: reviewing the evidence on synergy', *World Development*, 24(6): 1119–32.

Fox, J. (1994) 'The difficult transition from clientelism to citizenship: lessons from Mexico', *World Politics*, 46(2): 151–84.

— (2000) 'Civil society and political accountability: propositions for discussion', Presented at the conference 'Institutions, Accountability and Democratic Governance in Latin America', Helen Kellogg Institute for International Studies, Notre Dame University, 8 May.

— (2002) 'La relación recíproca entre la participación ciudadana y la rendición de cuentas', *Política y Gobierno*, 9(1): 95–133.

Fox, J. and J. Aranda (1996) *Decentralization and Rural Development in Mexico: Community Participation in Oaxaca's Municipal Funds*, La Jolla: Center for US-Mexican Studies.

Fung, A. (1999) 'Street level democracy: pragmatic popular sovereignty in Chicago schools and policing', Paper presented at the American Political Science Association Annual Meeting, Atlanta, 2–5 September.

— (2001) 'Accountable autonomy: toward empowered deliberation in Chicago schools and policing', *Politics and Society*, 29(1): 73–103.

Fung, A. and D. O'Rourke (2000) 'Reinventing environmental regulation from the grassroots up: explaining and expanding the success of the toxics release inventory', *Environmental Management*, 25(2): 115–27.

Fung, A. and E. Wright (2001) 'Deepening democracy: innovations in empowered participatory governance', *Politics and Society*, 29(1): 5–41.

Goetz, A. M. and R. Jenkins (2001) 'Hybrid forms of accountability: citizen engagement in institutions of public-sector oversight in India', *Public Management Review*, 3(3): 363–83.

— (2002a) 'Voice, accountability and human development: the emergence of a new agenda', Background paper for *Human Development Report 2002*, New York: United Nations Development Programme.

— (2002b) 'Civil society engagement and India's public distribution system: lessons from the Rationing Kruti Samiti in Mumbai', Paper presented at 'Making Services Work for Poor People', World Development Report Workshop (WDR) 2003/04, Oxford, 4/5 November.

Goldfrank, B. (2002) 'The fragile flower of local democracy: a case study of decentralization/participation in Montevideo', *Politics and Society*, 30(1): 51–83.

Hirschman, A. (1970) *Exit, Voice, and Loyalty: Responses to Decline in Firms, Organizations, and States*, Cambridge, MA: Harvard University Press.

IFE (2000a) 'The Mexican electoral regime and the federal elections of the year 2000', Mexico City: IFE.

— (2000b) 'Proceso electoral federal 2000: datos y numeralia más importantes', Mexico City: IFE.

Isunza, E. (2003) 'Construcción de la democracia y rendición de cuentas: una mirada regional de nuevas interfaces socio-estatales en el contexto de la transición política mexicana', Presented at the 2003 meeting of the Latin American Studies Association, Dallas, 27–29 March.

Jenkins, R. and A. M. Goetz (1999) 'Accounts and accountability: theoretical implications of the right-to-information movement in India', *Third World Quarterly*, 20(3): 603–22.

Kaufman, R. (2003) 'The comparative politics of administrative reform: some implications for theory and policy', in B. Schneider and B. Heredia (eds), *Reinventing Leviathan: The Politics of Administrative Reform in Developing Countries*, Miami, FL: North-South Center Press.

Long, N. (1999) 'The multiple optic of interface analysis', Background paper on interface analysis, Paris: UNESCO.

Maor, M. (2004) 'Feeling the heat. Anti-corruption mechanisms in comparative perspective', *Governance: An International Journal of Policy, Administration, and Institutions*, 17(1): 1–28.

Marquetti, A. (2003) 'Participação e redistribuição: o orçamento participativo em Porto Alegre', in L. Avritzer and Z. Navarro (eds), *A Inovação democratica no Brasil: orçamento participativo*, São Paulo: Cortez Editora, pp. 25–58.

Molinar, J. (1996) 'Renegotiating the rules of the game: the state and political parties', in M. Serrano and V. Bulmer-Thomas (eds), *Rebuilding the State: Mexico after Salinas*, London: Institute of Latin American Studies, University of London, pp. 24–40.

Navarro, Z. (1998) 'Participation, democratizing practices and the formation of a modern polity – the case of "participatory budgeting" in Porto Alegre, Brazil (1989–1998)', *Development*, 41(3): 68–71.

— (2002) 'Decentralization, participation and social control of public resources: "participatory budgeting" in Porto Alegre (Brazil)', Presented at a workshop on Citizen

Participation in the Context of Fiscal Decentralization: Best Practices in Municipal Administration, Inter-American Development Bank and Asian Development Bank, Tokyo and Kobe, 2–6 September.

Nylen, W. (2002) 'Testing the empowerment thesis: the participatory budget in Belo Horizonte and Betim, Brazil', *Comparative Politics*, 34(2): 127–45.

O'Donnell, G. (1999) 'Horizontal accountability in new democracies', in A. Schedler, L. Diamond and M. F. Plattner (eds), *The Self-restraining State: Power and Accountability in New Democracias*, Boulder, CO: Lynne Rienner, pp. 29–52.

Paul, S. (1992) 'Accountability in public services: exit, voice and control', *World Development*, 20(7): 1047–60.

Peruzzotti, E. and C. Smulovitz (2000a) 'Societal and horizontal controls: two cases about a fruitful relationship', Presented at the conference 'Institutions, Accountability and Democratic Governance in Latin America', Helen Kellogg Institute for International Studies, Notre Dame University, 8 May.

— (2000b) 'Societal accountability in Latin America', *Journal of Democracy*, 11(4): 147–58.

— (2002) 'Contabilidad social: la otra cara del control', in E. Peruzzotti and C. Smulovitz (eds), *Controlando la política: ciudadanos y medios en las nuevas democracias latinoamericanas*, Buenos Aires: Editorial Temas.

Peters, G. (2001) *The Future of Governing*, 2nd edn, revised, Lawrence: University Press of Kansas.

Przeworski, A., S. Stokes and B. Manin (eds) (1999) *Democracy, Accountability and Representation*, New York: Cambridge University Press.

Schedler, A. (1999a) 'Conceptualizing accountability', in A. Schedler, L. Diamond and M. F. Plattner (eds), *The Self-restraining State: Power and Accountability in New Democracies*, Boulder, CO: Lynne Rienner, pp. 13–28.

— (1999b) 'Las comisiones y la pirámide: notas sobre la conflictiva recentralización del poder en el IFE', *Política y Gobierno*, 6(1): 187–222.

Skogan, W. and S. Hartnett (1997) *Community Policing: Chicago Style*, New York: Oxford University Press.

Smulovitz, C. (2003) 'How can the rule of law rule? Cost imposition through decentralized mechanisms', in J. M. Maravall and A. Przeworski (eds), *Democracy and the Rule of Law*, New York: Cambridge University Press.

UNDP (2002) *Human Development Report 2002: Deepening Democracy in a Fragmented World*, New York: Oxford University Press.

Varshney, A. (1999) 'Democracy and poverty', Presented at the conference on the 2000 *World Development Report*, UK Department for International Development and Sussex Institute of Development Studies, Castle Donington, 15–16 August.

Waisbord, S. (2000) *Watchdog Journalism in South America: News, Accountability, and Democracy*, New York: Columbia University Press.

Walker, S. (2001) *Police Accountability: The Role of Citizen Oversight*, Belmont: Wadsworth/Thompson Learning.

Wallis, J. and B. Dollery (2001) 'Government failure, social capital and the appropriateness of the New Zealand model for public sector reform in developing countries', *World Development*, 29(2): 245–63.

World Bank (2003) *World Development Report 2004: Making Services Work for Poor People*, New York: Oxford University Press.

PART FIVE

Participation as collective action: mobilization, insurgency and struggle

31 | Users as citizens: collective action and the local governance of welfare

Marion Barnes

Introduction

This paper considers the significance of self-organization among users of mental health services and among disabled people in the context of renewed interest in notions of community and citizenship in public policy-making.[1]

As the twentieth century draws to a close the welfare states of most Western countries are facing fundamental challenges. In the UK questions are being raised about the services individuals can expect to receive as social rights of citizenship (Plant 1992). Welfare reform is one of the major items on the agenda of the Labour government elected in the UK in 1997 and has provided an early indication of the conflicts engendered by attempts to change the balance between public and private responsibilities for welfare. While the experiment in welfare markets, particularly within the National Health Service, is being gradually abandoned, this is unlikely to lead to a reversal of the view that responsibilities for service provision do not lie solely in the public sector (Ham 1996). 'Partnership' – between different parts of the public sector and between public, private and community sectors – is being urged as the way forward (EL 97 (65) 1997; NHSE 1997).

Concern about a democratic deficit in the governance of public services, and about the low level of people's participation within democratic processes, is also contributing to a reanalysis of the relationship between individuals and the state (Burton and Duncan 1996). Within all parts of the public sector there is a search for renewed legitimacy through the opening up of decision-making processes to more direct public involvement (e.g. Barnes 1997a; Coote and Lenaghan 1997; Harrison et al. 1997; Stewart 1997). The 1980s saw the 'empowered consumer' come to pre-eminence as a means of increasing the responsiveness of public services. The later part of the 1990s is seeing a rediscovery of 'the community' as both a resource and a focus for empowerment within contexts such as action to reduce health inequalities (e.g. Douglas 1996; Smithies and Adams 1993), initiatives to develop safer communities (Bright 1997) and urban and rural regeneration (Department of the Environment 1995).

Within this context it is particularly pertinent to consider the experiences of those who not only have limited power to exert influence as consumers in welfare markets, but who have also often been excluded from 'community'. Such exclusions have resulted both from social policies which have been deliberately designed to separate those regarded as deviant or different, and by public attitudes which have reinforced such policies (e.g. Barham 1992; Oliver 1996; Prior 1993).

Consumerism and user involvement in community care

The 1990 NHS and Community Care Act sought to achieve a shift in favour of consumer rather than producer interests in social care services. This was to be achieved through encouraging user and carer involvement in the process of assessment by which services are accessed; requiring social services authorities to consult with users, carers and voluntary organizations during the production of community care plans; the introduction of a complaints procedure containing an element of independent review; and the establishment of inspection units, organizationally at 'arm's length' from service providers, with input from lay members – who could be, but are not necessarily, users of services.

By the early 1990s user involvement had developed from something encouraged by the more innovative social services authorities (e.g. Barnes and Wistow 1994a) to a statutory requirement. But if there was now top-down encouragement to listen to what service users were saying, there was also a growing movement among those who were dissatisfied not only with the nature of the services they were receiving, but also with their lack of control over them. Not all those involved in user movements were convinced that user involvement as practised by statutory agencies was consistent with their objectives.

User groups and social movements

The British Council of Organizations of Disabled People (BCODP) was formed in 1981, in response to dissatisfactions with statutory services, and with able-bodied control of voluntary organizations. In the same year Disabled People's International held its first congress in Singapore (Campbell and Oliver 1996). 'People First', an organization promoting self-advocacy on the part of people with learning difficulties, was established in this country in 1984, encouraged by self-advocacy developments in the USA (Williams and Shoultz 1982). The mid-1980s also saw the first UK mental health patients' councils following contact with Dutch users who provided the inspiration for action to support independent organization (Gell 1987). The consumerist changes being introduced 'top-down' provided some legitimation for autonomous action on the part of these developing user groups. But locally, nationally and internationally user groups have been articulating their own objectives which are not always consistent with those of officials promoting user involvement (Barnes 1997b). Together such groups constitute part of a growing 'user movement' with links throughout Europe (van der Male 1995) and in the USA.

User groups are variously described by their members and by those they seek to influence. They may be called self-help groups, pressure groups, advocacy groups or consumer groups. Some analysts have suggested such self-organization can be understood by reference to theories of new social movements (e.g. Oliver 1990; Rogers and Pilgrim 1991; Shakespeare 1993). In our research into disabled people's organizations and groups of mental health service users (Barnes et al. 1996) we found this a helpful framework to distinguish user self-organization from interest groups (Phillips 1993). We also found it useful to draw on new theories of citizenship, particularly those which emphasize the practice of citizenship (Prior et al. 1995) and the need for theories of citizenship to incorporate private as well as public roles (Siim 1994). Users of welfare services may be excluded from citizenship – both formally in terms of actual constraints on their citizenship rights (Law Commission 1995), or through social organization which makes it impossible for people to realize the substantive rights of citizenship (Plant 1992; van Steenbergen 1994).

New social movements seeking change within public policy face a number of tensions in their choice of strategies. Jenson and Froestad (1988) explored this in their study of client organizations in Norway. One danger is that of co-option, which may be especially great in the case of organizations among those who are least powerful: 'In addition to the general problems tied to poverty of resources the clients suffer from lack of self-confidence which is often a result of a long-lasting career as a client. An organization of the powerless will also be more susceptible to influence. This creates dangers for the growing of oligarchy and different kinds of co-optation from professions, political organizations, bureaucracies and companies' (ibid.: 87).

Movement from oppositional action to action to develop new forms of institutions also demands different types of organization and thus change in the nature of the movements themselves. Lovenduski and Randall (1993) consider this in the context of the development of feminist political action. They discuss how those involved in the women's refuge movement faced dilemmas of both principle and organization when statutory authorities started to incorporate approaches originally developed in opposition to existing practices adopted by local authorities, the police and other agencies concerned with domestic violence. Similarly, those involved in the establishment of Women's Therapy Centres have been faced with compromise in order to gain acceptance for their ideas by statutory agencies (Barnes and Maple 1992: 151, 154), and to adopt different organizational strategies when seeking to provide services directly (Sturdy 1987). Similar dilemmas are faced by autonomously organized groups of users once they seek to impact on mainstream welfare services, or seek funding from the statutory sector.

Drawing on theories of new social movements and new theories of citizenship, two issues emerge as central to an understanding of the nature and significance of self-organization among groups based in experiences of exclusion, oppression or disadvantage which seek to impact on service systems:

1   the significance of identity as a factor defining both motivation to act collectively – to develop groups in which identities can be formed and expressed, and the objectives pursued by such groups; and
2   changes within local governance which have provided space in which user groups can act, but which have prioritized the identity of service users as consumers rather than citizens.

This paper examines the objectives and strategies of disabled people's groups and mental health service user groups in relation to both issues. Both operate in a context in which community care policy provides a focus for much of their effort to influence both services and policies. There is uncertainty among the mental health users' or survivors' movement about identifying themselves with the disabled people's movement in the UK, and it is possible to highlight differences in the priorities and tactics adopted by different groups. For example, disabled people have sought to celebrate the value of diversity and have rejected attempts to make them 'approximate to normality' (Davis 1995; Oliver 1996). In contrast, people who have experienced mental illness have sought to emphasize that mental distress is a part of normal human experience (Barnes and Shardlow 1996a; Chamberlin 1988). 'Becoming ordinary' is a useful tactic to adopt by people who have been labelled mentally ill as a result of apparently deviant behaviour (Lorencz 1991). 'Coming out' as a user of mental health services has been important for service users who have gained a presence in forums from which they have hitherto been excluded. Some have identified themselves as 'survivors' of oppressive services. However, it is both a shared experience of using services and of the broader impact of mental distress or disability on their lives which motivates many to participate in both movements, and it is the commonality of experiences with which I am concerned here.

Negotiating identities

Renewed interest in the concept of community within academic discourse reflects not only the communitarian thinking popularized by Etzioni (1995), but also the emergence of analyses which reflect on the different identities from which community membership can derive. As well as referring to a locality within which people interact in their daily lives, community can refer to shared identities as members of a particular religious or ethnic group, a shared sexuality, or a shared identity as disabled people. Such communities of identity may consist of people who do not live within the same locality and who may not interact frequently on a face-to-face basis.

Literature produced by disabled people reflects both the cultural and political significance of identity for disabled people's organizations. Campbell and Oliver (1996) reflect on diversity within the disability movement, but also the centrality of the social model of disability and of the necessity of disabled people defining themselves rather than submitting to a definition imposed by welfare professionals. At a political level that may involve direct action, such as the action taken early in 1998 by activists who threw red paint at the entrance to Downing Street in opposition to suggestions that benefits to disabled people might be withdrawn. Others express it through disabled arts (Morris and Finkelstein 1993) or through the development of a sociology of disablement which provides a theoretical basis for an analysis of disabled people's experiences (Oliver 1990). Deaf people in particular have emphasized a deaf culture as a distinct cultural identity (Davis 1995; Rose and Kiger 1995).

Campbell and Oliver (1996) accept the definition of the disabled people's movement as a new social movement and point to the link between the development of a disability consciousness and action within the movement:

> We ... consider how this process has required the redefinition of self and a rec-
> ognition that the personal is the political. Finally we consider the challenges to
> negative disability imagery that this personal liberation has produced, and the
> attempts to develop a positive imagery through the newly emerging disability
> culture. Central to this will be the role of the social model and the recognition
> of disability as oppression. It is also worth making the point here that, for us,
> transforming both personal and political consciousness is one of the key fac-
> tors that separates new social movements from the old, more traditional social
> movements. (Ibid.: 105)

Melucci (1985) has suggested that a shared identity 'constructed and negoti-ated through a repeated process of "activation" of social relationships connect-ing the actors' distinguishes 'new' from 'old' social movements. The emphasis is on agency, rather than class location, and as Melucci suggests, identities are created and re-created not simply by 'being', but through action within such movements. Scott (1990) has suggested a very diffuse view of the identities which might form the bases for social movements: 'the possible number of social movements is limited only by the potential range of collective identities people are willing to adopt (for example, as women, rate payers, animal-lovers, inner city dwellers etc.)'. This confuses the difference between identity and interest. While having a physical impairment is not the same as accepting an identity as a disabled person or choosing to act within the disabled people's movement, the element of choice in adopting or accepting an identity is surely different in the case of disabled people from that of animal-lovers.

In contrast to Scott's view, Phillips (1993) emphasizes the distinction between identity-based social movements and interest groups. In her essay 'Pluralism, solidarity and change', she writes:

The new pluralism homes in on identity rather than interest groups: not those gathered together around some temporary unifying concern – to defend their neighbourhood against a major road development, to lobby their representatives against some proposed new law – but those linked by a common culture, a common experience, a common language. These links are often intensely felt, and, more important still, are often felt as opposition and exclusion. Identity groups frequently secure their identity precisely around their opposition to some 'other' focusing on a past experience of being excluded, and sometimes formulating a present determination to exclude. (Ibid.: 146–7)

Underpinning this distinction is the fact that action around a particular 'interest' can be engaged in by anyone, regardless of their personal or social identity. However, white people cannot join some black people's organizations, nor, in many cases, can men participate in action undertaken within the women's movements. The extent to which membership of groups is exclusive to those sharing the characteristics which define the relevant identity varies within movements. It is one example of the diversity which exists within new social movements. Nevertheless, for groups for whom oppression, difference and exclusion provide a focus for action, the issue of identity based on a common experience is a key motivating factor. Some may accept others as allies, as associates or as supporters, but not allow them to participate in decision-making. Control rather than membership is what makes the difference. Hasler (1993) wrote of the early years of the disability movement: 'What characterized all these groups was that their leadership was made up of disabled people, and they believed that disabled people should and could develop solutions to the problems they encountered.' While some of the groups we studied (Barnes et al. 1996) welcome non-disabled people or people who have not used services as members or allies, they are not given the same status, for example when it comes to voting on issues of policy.

Legitimate pressure?

The confusion between identity and interest groups was evident in responses of officials to the groups studied in our research (ibid.). Organized groups of users were seen as self-interested and atypical and this was used to question the legitimacy of the position they take. This is illustrated in the following response from an official to one of the mental health groups in the study:

I think that in collecting the views of users you have to throw your net more widely than just the pressure groups. That you need, that into your audit systems the user view and not the *representative's* view, that the actual person there who is using the service at the time. (Our emphasis, quoted in Barnes et al. 1999)

The term 'pressure group' used here to describe an organized group of mental health service users is applied to distinguish the so-called legitimate voices of unorganized users from the allegedly 'unrepresentative' voice of those who collectively draw on their experiences to seek improvement in the mental health system. The irony of this is that hitherto unorganized service users or citizens who become participants in health service decision-making can also be berated for expressing personal views and reflecting personal experiences rather than taking the wider view and reflecting, for example, on the needs of populations. Barnes and McIver (1998) have identified such a response in the context of public participation in primary care. Organizing within user movements can create the conditions in which it is possible for people to act as genuine 'representatives' of communities of identity, but it can also be used to undermine the legitimacy of such representations by constructing them as expressions of self-interest in the context of pressure group activity.

An activist in a disabled people's organization reflected on how he inter-preted the notion of 'pressure' in the context of action taken by the disabled people's coalition in which he was engaged:

> Pressure to me as it applies to organizations like ours is really resistance ... It's pressure to remove barriers so it's pressure applied to public opinion, barriers to public awareness, perpetuated by the media and so on; it's pressure to over-come the barriers of the administrative systems and information ... pressure to overcome the physical exclusions that have built up around disabled people ... it's pressure to overcome resistance and obstacle. (Disabled activist)

This analysis distinguishes interest-group politics, in which powerful lobbies seek to influence policy in order to reinforce their own already powerful posi-tion, from action among groups excluded from power which aims to enable them to reach the same starting point as everyone else. Such action requires collective organization and (as discussed below) the development of confidence and skills within groups and in individual members.

Objectives of self-organization

Building community capacity to enable community participation is an ex-pressed objective of policy in increasingly diverse contexts. The participation of communities is seen both as a means and an end to promoting health, reducing crime and rebuilding the social and economic infrastructure of inner cities. In this context, a perception of user groups as simply one among a number of self-interested stakeholders lobbying in a pluralistic policy system may run counter to emerging policy trends.

A key aspect of the theorization of new social movements concerns the objectives or purposes of such movements. Most analyses emphasize the ideo-logical nature of such goals, placing practical changes within the context of a much wider purpose which presents a fundamental challenge to dominant goal structures. For Melucci (1985) such goals are symbolic and cultural, concerned with the meaning and orientation of social action and providing a vision for future models of social interaction. Cohen (1985) suggests: 'they target the social domain of "civil society" rather than the economy or state, raising issues concerned with the democratization of structures of everyday life and focusing on forms of communication and collective identity' (ibid.: 667).

User groups seek cultural and ideological objectives relating to the way in which mental distress and disability are understood – both within service systems and in society as a whole. They also seek to democratize the structures through which services are designed and delivered. Their targets include both the state as commissioner and provider of welfare services, and civil society from which, uncivilly, they have often been excluded. Much of the action in which user groups are involved is directed towards 'the public' rather than to welfare systems. For example, one mental health group in our study had conducted a public awareness campaign using the concept of 'stress' to emphasize the 'normality' of mental health problems. Other action was directed at organizations or institutions outside the state, for example the media.

But it is not really possible to separate out cultural objectives (such as the media representation of disabled people) from objectives of securing change within systems of welfare. One particular dimension of the cultural objectives of user movements is that of epistemology – the value of experiential knowledge as a way of understanding and explaining mental health problems and disability, and for determining appropriate service models.

Self-organization provides space for reflection on shared and different personal experiences. This may develop into theorization which produces new explanatory models to provide a reference point both for self-development and for campaigning (Morris 1989; Oliver 1996). Activists recognize that the development of 'disability consciousness' cannot be forced, but that it is important to create a context in which people could make connections:

> We want the Coalition to embody this collective experience of exclusion and
> we want to be able to represent it at every level from the very simple local level
> where, for example, someone realizes that very small changes in their local
> environment like the ability to get in a corner shop can make a very significant
> difference to their lives in that they might not be dependent on people to do
> their shopping for them, they wouldn't have to wait for their home helps to get
> basic everyday things that other people get when they want them. And all the
> way from that experience, that awareness of daily obstacles, to the developed
> political awareness of activists and all stages in between. (Disabled activist)

Whether or not people develop a sophisticated political analysis of their situation, the opportunity to share experiential knowledge provides access to an expert resource which is different from that available from health and social care professionals (and may be considered more useful than professional input). The value of information and experience sharing is commonly identified by those engaged in user groups of all types (see, e.g., Barnes and Bennet 1998, in relation to older people's experiences of this). Beyond the exchanges that take place between disabled people and others involved in user groups, the establishment of dialogue between users and producers of services provides forums in which experiential and professional knowledge can be shared. Through dialogue comes at least the possibility of transformation and change, described by Iris Marion Young as follows:

> By giving voice to formerly silenced or devalued needs and experiences, group representation forces participants in discussion to take a reflective distance on their assumptions and think beyond their own interests. When confronted with interests, needs and opinions that derived from very different social positions and experience, persons sometimes come to understand the limitations of their own experience and perspective for coming to a conclusion about the best policy for everyone. (Quoted in Phillips 1993: 156)

This notion of deliberative or communicative democracy is gaining increasing attention within both academic political science and public policy circles, and in practical projects to increase citizen participation in public decision-making (see, e.g., Gutmann and Thompson 1996; Phillips 1995; Stewart 1997). But there are particular challenges associated with developing dialogue and deliberation between those who may be defined as 'incompetent' and who have been excluded from decision-making about key issues affecting how they are able to live their own lives, and those who may be gatekeepers to the services they need.

Dialogue between users and officials can often be uncomfortable for professionals unused to being questioned by their clients or patients:

> They are not used to being accountable to the member of an organization, they are not used to being asked awkward questions and so it is a very difficult environment. (Disabled activist)

Professional defensiveness has been evident in many initiatives which have sought to empower service users, in particular those involving users of mental health services (Barnes and Wistow 1994b). Power imbalances also mean that users who speak out put themselves at risk, and need the support of peers if they are not to suffer as a result. Thus user self-organization is critical as a foundation on which deliberation to increase understanding can be built. Activists spoke of supporting people to take on limited roles within specific services before building the confidence to engage in more strategic decision-making processes. Once people recognize that their own knowledge and understanding of their situation might lead to alternative solutions to those suggested by professionals, the groups provide both the opportunities and support necessary to enable dialogue to develop. This is capacity-building among communities of people whose identities have been devalued and who, individually, have been largely powerless to achieve change.

Governance and citizenship

Collective action based in common experiences of oppression, disadvantage or social exclusion should be distinguished from an assertive consumerism which seeks to maximize individual self-interest. But once user groups engage in dialogue with producers of public services they enter the territory of public service decision-making. It is at that point that the issues of identity and governance come together in the tension around the disputed identities of 'consumer' or 'citizen'.

Collective action among service users provides a means through which citizenship can be expressed in three ways:

1 seeking to achieve social rights associated with the status of citizenship (Marshall 1950; Plant 1992);
2 providing a forum from which excluded individuals can contribute to the practice of citizenship (Lister 1998; Prior et al. 1995);
3 enhancing the accountability of public services to their citizen users (Ranson and Stewart 1994).

Elsewhere I and others have discussed ways in which individual user groups seek to enhance the citizenship rights of those they represent (Barnes and Shardlow 1996b; Barnes et al. 1999). The disability movement has explicitly adopted a civil rights position in relation to campaigns for disabled people's rights and has used the discourse of citizenship to argue for anti-discrimination legislation (Barnes 1991). But here I want to focus on the practice of citizenship and how user groups can play a role within systems of governance. Ranson et al. (1995) describe the defining quality of citizenship as agency: 'citizens are makers and creators as well as members of the worlds in which they live'. Lister also considers the relationship between agency and citizenship in her work on feminist perspectives on citizenship:

> To act as a citizen requires first a sense of agency, the belief that one can act; acting as a citizen, especially collectively, in turn fosters that sense of agency. Thus, agency is not simply about the capacity to choose and act but it is also about a conscious capacity which is important to an individual's sense of self-identity. The development of a conscious sense of agency, at both the personal and political level, is crucial to women's breaking of the chains of victimhood and their emergence as full and active citizens. (Lister 1998: 38)

A similar analysis can be applied to the role played by user groups. Citizenship is not just about having certain rights (and concomitant responsibilities), but about being able to participate in the community. The concept of citizenship is not only a political but also a sociological one (van Steenbergen 1994). People with mental health problems and disabled people experience discrimination which affects their capacity to engage as active citizens within the lives of their communities. Groups organized around these identities seek to achieve social justice and to enable people to participate as citizens within their communities – by taking part in determining the nature of welfare services, by supporting users to take on other roles, and by action intended to overcome stigmatizing and exclusionary practices among members of the communities in which they live. The following quote from a disabled woman interviewed during our research clearly expresses citizenship aspirations which go beyond influencing services related to personal impairment:

> More [disabled] women are having relationships ... getting married ... having children. So it is obvious to anybody that we need access to healthcare, we need access to schools, disabled parents need to be able to go on to boards of governors and things like that to have a say in their child's education ... But we still can't get the message over to everybody ... (Disabled activist)

Interviews with user group activists in our study also provided personal testimony of 'breaking the chains of victimhood':

> ... it's given me a life and without it I wouldn't have dreamed of doing half the things I do now. It's given me confidence, assurance ... I get up now and speak at a conference quite happily. A few years ago I would have no more done that than fly! (Mental health activist)

> I've seen disabled people who have been in a position of receiver and they've come into the position to do something for the community, the change is just tremendous. Their self-esteem comes back ... [they] really enjoy life. And it does them good. (Disabled activist)

Participation in the groups demonstrates that being disabled or experiencing mental health problems does not also imply incompetence:

> One of the major roles that we can play is actually to say, we are users, we can participate at this level, we can articulate, we can challenge, we can negotiate, we can write papers, we can do this, instead of [being] some bumbling idiot that doesn't know what they are doing. (Mental health activist)

Participation quite literally gives people a 'voice'. As confidence develops they are able to play a role in organizing the group, in planning forums involving service purchasers and providers, and in representing the group at conferences and seminars. Some user groups have become involved in training professionals, some in providing advice and advocacy services, some provide user-led services and others jointly manage services with statutory agencies. Group members may become active participants in strategic decision-making about health and social care services at local and national level (e.g. the Mental Health Task Force established by the Department of Health to support the implementation of community care policies within mental health services included a national user group), as well as in supporting individuals to play a more active part in decision-making about the services they receive directly.

Thus, as well as addressing discrimination directly (through public awareness campaigns as well as by individual advocacy), the active involvement of service users in public service decision-making systems demonstrates their capability to be active agents 'making and creating' the services they receive, rather than simply 'consuming' them.

Enhancing accountability

At this point the objectives of user groups can be seen to come close to those of public service officials who seek, through engagement with user organizations, to enhance the legitimacy of their decision-making processes and to improve the responsiveness of the services produced. This can be considered in terms of the role of user groups in contributing to a process of accountability based in dialogue. A relationship of accountability implies an important shift in the balance of power between users and providers. While none of the interviewees in the user group study claimed that the influence of these groups had resulted in a fundamental shift in the balance of power within the health and social care system, they did believe that the groups had provided a challenge and forced those in positions of power to reconsider their practices (Barnes et al. 1999). Through their presence within the different forums in which they meet with purchasers and providers, users can require public officials to give account of their actions and to be questioned on this. A member of one of the mental health user groups which had a well-established relationship with the local health authority and mental health trust described one way in which this can happen:

> I think it is very easy for professionals to write a really glowing document
> saying this is what we are providing, but if the end result is that it is not what
> is really happening, then they have to be made accountable for that particular
> statement and so one of the roles I think we play is to actually challenge the
> quality assurance issues, for instance, laid down in the contract between the
> mental health unit and the purchasing group of the health authority. And if
> they don't meet that then we will actually raise it ... with the purchaser and say,
> you know, what are you going to do about this? (Mental health activist)

Here the direct experience of mental health service users is being used to question the extent to which service providers are meeting their contractual obligations. They are seeking answers as users or potential users of those services who may be directly affected by any failure to deliver what was intended. But in so doing they are also acting in the public interest, providing a means through which public service providers are required to give account.

Dilemmas and tensions

Changes in systems of governance associated with new public management provided opportunities for users to play a more active role in influencing the nature of health and social care services. However, those changes emphasized the creation of more effective consumers as a spur to increasing service responsiveness, rather than community development as a basis for collective empowerment. Most user groups seek to engage with the state in order to achieve change in the nature of services, and 'user involvement' has achieved widespread acceptance as a task to be undertaken by public service officials. However, while officials involved in health and social services might increasingly look to user involvement as a source of legitimation for their decisions, they also tend to place qualifications on the legitimacy of user groups as representatives of service users (Harrison et al. 1997). Apart from questioning the organizational capacity and coherence of individual user groups, becoming organized per se is seen to distinguish activists from the majority of 'ordinary' service users (see above). The wider purposes encompassed by user movements are rarely acknowledged by officials concerned primarily or solely with the more effective functioning of one particular service.

User self-organization is significant in its own right as a means of enhancing the citizenship of excluded groups, not simply as a means through which producers can access users to provide consumer feedback. This creates a number of dilemmas for user groups seeking to engage with the state in order to achieve change in service systems, as well as other objectives. The particular dilemmas which have been identified by user activists can be summed up as follows:

1   The potential for their energies to be dissipated by engaging with an increasingly diverse set of bodies resulting from the fragmentation of systems of governance. The purchaser/provider split created an increase in the number of forums in which decisions might be made, and the possibility (referred to as a reality by some of the officials interviewed in our study) that purchasers and providers might seek to 'play the user card' in competition with each other (Mort et al. 1996). As 'user involvement' becomes more widespread and more public agencies start to realize the necessity of consulting with or more directly involving those who use their services, this danger increases.

User groups not only speak of 'consultation overload', but ask how they can encourage public agencies to collaborate in working with user groups.

2 The danger of becoming reactive to official agendas, rather than determining their own priorities for action. While officials might question the representativeness of user groups, groups are nevertheless a convenient source of views for officials who are expected to demonstrate that they have consulted users. Constantly responding to the agendas of officials could take up all the limited resources of groups.

3 Groups are often dependent (at least in part) on statutory agencies for financial support (either grant aid or finance linked to contracts to provide specific services such as advocacy). Activists are aware of the potential inhibition on campaigning activities as a result of funding from statutory agencies they could be criticizing. As groups mature and are being drawn into better-established and sometimes formal relationships with statutory authorities, they are starting to face dilemmas which have been experienced by more traditional voluntary organizations in seeking to maintain independence while also needing to secure funding (Lewis 1993).

4 While a consumerist philosophy provides legitimacy for user involvement, it also encourages a model of competing interest groups, or the pursuit of individual rights, rather than encouraging collective action to achieve social change. This was evident in the distinction drawn by some officials between 'user involvement' and 'user group involvement'. It can also provide a point of difference and sometimes conflict within user groups themselves.

Conclusion

Changes within systems of governance have provided opportunities for user groups to engage with processes from which their members have previously been excluded. User participation within systems of decision-making is enabled and supported by separate organization – users are often more effective participants if they have the support of others and can link into shared and common experiences, rather than speak solely from personal experience. While participation carries the dangers of incorporation, there is also evidence of transformation taking place both in the processes of governance and the service models emerging from dialogue between users and producers (see Barnes 1997b).

Lovenduski and Randall wrote of the experience of those involved in the women's refuge movement in the 1980s:

> Because the government wanted to reduce the powers of the state by devolving responsibilities to the community in the form of the voluntary agencies, the refuge movement was able to gain financial support from the state. This enabled refuge collectives to assert feminist values. In other words, as the form of

the state changed, space was created for feminist interventions. But the welfare bureaucracy was bound to contest the erosion of its authority. The resulting political struggle is at the heart of disagreements between feminist Women's Aid workers and welfare professionals. (1993: 316–17)

Similar conclusions can be drawn about the relationship between user movements and the local governance of welfare in the 1990s. Space has opened up within the state which has enabled user movements to come in to develop new forms of welfare, but that space is not being occupied without a struggle. Nevertheless, becoming part of processes of governance is important in itself. An underlying purpose of such groups is to campaign for the inclusion of people previously excluded from mainstream society. Inclusion within processes of governance is significant because of the recognition of competence, and the legitimacy of the presence of people previously regarded as incompetent to participate within decision-making processes. The election of a Labour government in May 1997 saw some evidence of a shift from market competition as a lever for service improvement towards a reassertion of (new) public service values. Two aspects of this suggest that the relationships between user groups and health and social care services may undergo some change as a result. First, community development is enjoying something of a renaissance – particularly in the context of regeneration initiatives and as a means towards health improvement. Broader acceptance of the collective ethos of community development may lead to increased recognition of the value of collective organization among what I have called here 'communities of identity' among users of welfare services. Second, public agencies are being enjoined not only to develop partnerships with each other in order to deliver public policy objectives which are not capable of achievement within the boundaries of any one agency, but also to develop partnerships with community organizations for a similar purpose. Communities are no longer only a target for policy, but are also seen as a means of delivering it.

But important questions remain. How feasible is it to talk of a real 'partnership' with agencies which not only have substantially more power in terms of both resources and influence, but also power to control access to the services needed by group members? While the discourse is no longer that of competitive markets within health and social care, competitive bidding is becoming even more established as a route to new resources or preferential treatment by government. The competitive bidding process introduced in relation to the Single Regeneration Budget has been considered a valuable model to adapt and adopt in contexts such as Health Action Zones, 'Best Value' sites within local government and the identification of 'Beacons of Excellence' within the health service. There is increasing scope here for statutory authorities to seek to play the user card in support of their applications for the benefits associated with special status. And, since communities can exclude as well as include, will the different voices of disabled people and people with mental health problems be heard as locality-based community groups enter into partnerships with public and private sector agencies?

[Originally published in *Social Policy and Administration*, 33(1), 1999, pp. 73–90]

Acknowledgements

The research referred to in this paper, 'Consumerism and citizenship amongst users of health and social care services', was funded by the ESRC as part of its Local Governance Programme, award no. L 311253025.

Note

1 The article draws on research looking at self-organization among disabled people and people with mental health problems, and the response of local 'officials' to such groups. Where quotes are not referenced, they come from interview transcripts from that project. References to publications arising from the research are included in the references.

References

Barham, P. (1992) *Closing the Asylum: The Mental Patient in Modern Society*, Harmondsworth: Penguin.

Barnes, C. (1991) *Disabled People in Britain and Discrimination: A Case for Anti-Discrimination Legislation*, London: Hurst/Calgary.

Barnes, M. (1997a) *The People's Health Service?*, Birmingham: NHS Confederation.

— (1997b) *Care, Communities and Citizens*, Harlow: Addison Wesley Longman.

Barnes, M. and G. Bennet (1998) 'Frail bodies, courageous voices: older people influencing community care', *Health and Social Care in the Community*, 6(2): 102–11.

Barnes, M. and S. McIver (1998) *Public Participation in Primary Care*, Birmingham: Health Services Management Centre, University of Birmingham.

Barnes, M. and N. Maple (1992) *Women and Mental Health: Challenging the Stereotypes*, Birmingham: Venture Press.

Barnes, M. and P. Shardlow (1996a) 'Identity crisis? Mental health user groups and the "problem" of identity', in C. Barnes and G. Mercer (eds), *Accounting for Illness and Disability: Exploring the Divide*, Leeds: Disability Press.

— (1996b), 'Effective consumers and active citizens' strategies for users' influence on services and beyond', *Research, Policy and Planning*, 14(1): 33–8.

Barnes, M. and G. Wistow (1994a) 'Achieving a strategy for user involvement in community care', *Health and Social Care in the Community*, 2: 347–56.

— (1994b) 'Learning to hear voices: listening to users of mental health services', *Journal of Mental Health*, 3: 525–40.

Barnes, M., S. Harrison, M. Mort, P. Shardlow and G. Wistow (1996) *Consumerism and Citizenship amongst Users of Health and Social Care Services*, Final Report to the ESRC of award no. L311253025.

Barnes, M., S. Harrison, M. Mort and P. Shardlow (1999) *Unequal Partners: User Groups and Community Care*, Bristol: Policy Press.

Bright, J. (1997) *Turning the Tide: Crime, Community and Prevention*, London: Demos.

Burton, P. and S. Duncan (1996) 'Democracy and accountability in public bodies: new agendas in British governance', *Policy and Politics*, 24(1): 5–16.

Campbell, J. and M. Oliver (1996) *Disability Politics. Understanding our Past, Changing Our Future*, London: Routledge.

Chamberlin, J. (1988) *On Our Own*, London: MIND.

Cohen, J. (1985) 'Strategy or identity: new theoretical paradigms and contemporary social movements', *Social Research*, 52(4): 663–716.

Coote, A. and J. Lenaghan (1997) *Citizens' Juries: Theory into Practice*, London: IPPR.

Davis, L. J. (1995) *Enforcing Normalcy: Disability, Deafness and the Body*, London: Verso.

Department of the Environment (1995) *Involving Communities in Urban and Rural Regeneration: A Guide for Practitioners*, London: DoE/Partners in Regeneration.

Douglas, J. (1996) 'Developing with Black and minority ethnic communities, health promotion strategies which address health inequalities', in P. Bywaters and E. McLeod (eds), *Working for Equality in Health*, London: Routledge.

EL 97 (65) (1997) *Health Action Zones*, Leeds: National Health Service Executive.

Etzioni, A. (1995) *The Spirit of Community: Rights, Responsibilities and the Communitarian Agenda*, London: Fontana.

Gell, C. (1987) 'Learning to lobby: the growth of patients' councils in Nottingham', in I. Barker and E. Peck (eds), *Power in Strange Places*, London: Good Practices in Mental Health.

Gutmann, A. and D. Thompson (1996) *Democracy and Disagreement*, Cambridge, MA: Harvard University Press.

Ham, C. (1996) *Public, Private or Community: What Next for the NHS?*, London: Demos.

Harrison, S., M. Barnes and M. Mort (1997) 'Praise and damnation: mental health user groups and the construction of organizational legitimacy', *Public Policy and Administration*, 12(2): 4–16.

Hasler, F. (1993) 'Developments in the disabled people's movement', in J. Swain, V. Finkelstein, S. French and M. Oliver (eds), *Disabling Barriers – Enabling Environments*, London: Sage.

Jenson, T. O. and J. Froestad (1988) 'Interest organizations – a complex answer to political poverty', *Tidskrift for Rattssociologi*, 5(2): 85–117.

Law Commission (1995) *Mental Incapacity*, London: HMSO.

Lewis, J. (1993) 'Developing the mixed economy of care: emerging issues for voluntary organizations', *Journal of Social Policy*, 22(2): 173–92.

Lister, R. (1998) *Citizenship: Feminist Perspectives*, Basingstoke: Macmillan.

Lorencz, B. (1991) 'Becoming ordinary: leaving the psychiatric hospital', in J. M. Morse and J. L. Johnson (eds), *The Illness Experience*, Newbury Park: Sage.

Lovenduski, J. and V. Randall (1993) *Contemporary Feminist Politics: Women and Power in Britain*, Oxford: Oxford University Press.

Marshall, T. H. (1950) *Citizenship and Social Class and other Essays*, Cambridge: Cambridge University Press.

Melucci, A. (1985) 'The symbolic challenge of contemporary movements', *Social Research*, 52(4): 789–816.

Morris, J. (ed.) (1989) *Able Lives: Women's Experience of Paralysis*, London: The Women's Press.

Morrison, E. and V. Finkelstein (1993) 'Broken arts and cultural repair: the role of culture in the empowerment of disabled people', in J. Swain, V. Finkelstein, S. French and M. Oliver (eds), *Disabling Barriers – Enabling Environments*, London: Sage/Open University.

Mort, M., S. Harrison and G. Wistow (1996) 'The user card: picking through the organizational undergrowth in health and social care', *Contemporary Political Studies*, 2: 1133–40.

NHSE (National Health Service Executive) (1997) *The New NHS*, Cm 807, London: Department of Health.

Oliver, M. (1990) *The Politics of Disablement*, Basingstoke: Macmillan.

— (1996) *Understanding Disability: From Theory to Practice*, Basingstoke: Macmillan.

Phillips, A. (1993) *Democracy and Difference*, Cambridge: Polity Press.

— (1995) *The Politics of Presence*, Oxford: Clarendon Press.

Plant, R. (1992) 'Citizenship, rights and welfare', in A. Coote (ed.), *The Welfare of Citizens*, London: Institute for Public Policy Research.

Prior, D., J. Stewart and K. Walsh (1995) *Citizenship: Rights, Community and Participation*, London: Pitman.

Prior, L. (1993) *The Social Organization of Mental Illness*, London: Sage.

Ranson, S. and J. Stewart (1994) *Management for the Public Domain: Enabling the Learning Society*, Basingstoke: Macmillan.

Ranson, S., J. Martin, P. McKeown, J. Nixon and R. Mitchell (1995) *Citizenship for the Civil Society*, Paper presented to the ESRC Local Governance Workshop, Participation, Citizenship and New Management, University of Birmingham, 4/5 October.

Rogers, A. and D. Pilgrim (1991) '"Pulling down churches": accounting for the British Mental Health Users' Movement', *Sociology of Health and Illness*, 13(2): 129–48.

Rose, P. and G. Kiger (1995) 'Intergroup relations: political action and identity in the deaf community', *Disability and Society*, 10(4): 521–8.

Scott, A. (1990) 'Ideology and the New Social Movements', London: Unwin Hyman.

Shakespeare, T. (1993) 'Disabled people's self-organization: a new social movement?', *Disability Handicap and Society*, 8(3): 249–64.

Siim, B. (1994) 'Engendering democracy: social citizenship and political participation for women in Scandinavia', *Social Politics*, 1(3): 286–305.

Smithies, J. and L. Adams (1993) 'Walking the tightrope: issues in evaluation and community participation for Health for All', in J. K. Davies and M. P. Kelly (eds), *Healthy Cities: Research and Practice*, London: Routledge.

Stewart, J. (1997) *More Innovations in Democratic Practice*, Occasional Paper 9, Birmingham: School of Public Policy, University of Birmingham.

Sturdy, C. (1987) 'Questioning the Sphinx: an experience of working in a women's organization', in S. Ernst and M. Maguire (eds), *Living with the Sphinx: Papers from the Women's Therapy Centre*, London: Virago.

Van der Male, R. (1995) 'Client movement in Europe: its past, present and future', *Psychiatria et Neurologia Japonica*, 97(7): 517–21.

Van Steenbergen, B. (ed.) (1994) *The Condition of Citizenship*, London: Sage.

Williams, P. and B. Schoultz (1982) *We Can Speak for Ourselves*, Bloomington: Indiana University Press.

32 | Insurgency and spaces of active citizenship: the story of the Western Cape anti-eviction campaign in South Africa

Faranak Miraftab and Shana Wills

It was in the year 2000. And that same day, we saw that they had a book with them with the addresses of the next families that they were going to evict. And we got a hold of that book. When we got a hold of that book, we saw the addresses there – the next address was on Jones Street, and so we sent some of our civic members to Jones Street. We told them to ... do a sit-in in that house, and don't let anyone touch the people's furniture to carry it out. ... We were so busy because ... we had to carry the old lady in. ... She was with her neighbours and sick in bed. The old lady didn't want us to leave because she thinks that if we were going to leave now then they were going to evict her again. So we had to stay by her and ... we knew they were going to Jones Street. So, we said: 'You go into that house and you stay there and don't let them touch anything. We will be there soon. When they leave here, we will come there.'

And then myself and another member of the campaign went to the state office and ... we phoned the city of Tygerburg and the people in charge of housing just to explain to them that this was an old lady of over eighty years. We wanted to know if we could go to the office to make an arrangement for the old lady to see how she was going to pay. Because definitely we were not going to have her be evicted and staying outside. Fortunately, they understood. The person in charge, I think it was Mr ... of the City of Tygerburg that I spoke to. Then he ordered the law enforcement and the sheriff to leave there. I told him that they have got more addresses and more people that they were going to evict, and we are saying that they are not going to evict those people. Understand? Then they left the area. ... They were forced to leave the area because then people started throwing stones at them. ... And that was how we stopped them. (Gertrude Square, interview, 2002)[1]

This is one of many stories illustrating the struggles by poor people around the world to maintain adequate shelter and to access minimum services. This particular story belongs to Gertrude Square, a forty-something-year-old woman living in one of the many disadvantaged townships of Cape Town, South Africa, an area categorized as 'coloured' under the apartheid urban planning system. During the era of apartheid, Gertrude was evicted on three separate occasions when her ZAR150 income as a single mother of three small children was not sufficient to pay the monthly ZAR80 for the council house she rented from the state. Still vivid in her memory is that experience of coming home from work and finding her children, too young to comprehend the calamity, crawling on their furniture, which had been removed from her house and piled up on the street. She and many others in her community are members of a community-based group colloquially referred to as a civic (shorthand for community-based civic association). They also participate in the Western Cape Anti-Eviction Campaign (hereafter referred to as AEC or the campaign), which resists the evictions of poor residents who are unable to meet their housing or service payments. Until due legal procedures and court hearings can take place, the AEC moves evicted families back into their homes and reconnects their water services (Western Cape Anti-Eviction Campaign 2002). This campaign approach aims to defend the constitutional right of all South African citizens to access adequate housing and sufficient food and water (see Articles 26 and 27 of the 1996 Constitution of the Republic of South Africa).

The present article is an attempt to better understand spaces of popular assertion of citizenship through which individuals strive to practise their constitutional right beyond those formal spaces that often exclude their needs and priorities. Drawing on a series of semi-structured, in-depth interviews with members and leaders of the anti-eviction and anti-privatization movements in Cape Town, South Africa, this article attempts to render a clear portrait of people like Gertrude and their struggles for shelter and services. Concentration is given to the particular grassroots actions engaged against evictions in the Western Cape to illuminate the processes and reasons by which such campaigns are created. Who participates in and creates them? What are the internal compositions of these movements, particularly with respect to race and gender? What are their practices of citizenship and collective action? How do they perceive their rights, and how are they perceived by others, namely by the state and the media? And what are the implications of these spaces of insurgency for planning thought?

[...] In this article, we hope to bring to light insurgent practices of the poor in their struggle for shelter and reintroduce the conceptual notion of this act of creating spaces of inclusive and active citizenship. As the urban poor defy policies imposed on them from above, they shape their environment through resistance and insurgency. The effects of these practices on urban space and urban processes cannot go unexamined. We use insurgent urbanism and insurgent citizenship, a concept first introduced by James Holston (1995) and further articulated by Leonie Sandercock (1998a) and John Friedmann (2002), as our conceptual guide in this endeavour [...]

Citizenship and insurgent movements

Cities under different conditions create varied citizenship dramas, write Holston and Appadurai (1999). The protagonists of the drama of citizenship created under the conditions of neoliberal urban policies are the urban poor, mobilized through their social movements to shape a distinct form of citizenship. As opposed to a statist citizenship that assumes the state as 'the only legitimate source of citizenship rights, meanings and practices' (Holston 1998: 39), this alternative drama of citizenship is active, engaged and 'grounded in civil society' (Friedmann 2002: 76). It moves beyond formal citizenship to a substantive one that concerns an array of civil, political, social and economic rights, including the rights to shelter, clean water, sewage discharge, education and basic health – in short, the right to the city (Lefevbre 1996). This new drama of citizenship is performed not only in the high courts of justice and ministerial corridors of government institutions but also in the streets of the city, the squatter camps of hope and despair, and the everyday life spaces of those excluded from the state's citizenship project. Cities are breeding grounds for these emerging citizenship practices (Isin 1999), which aim to expand the public sphere (Rose 2000) to generate 'new sources of laws, and new participation in decisions that bind' (Holston and Appadurai 1999: 20). The protagonists of this citizenship drama use non-formalized channels, create new spaces of citizenship, and improvise and invent innovative practices, all of which attract a captive constituency that embraces their just demands.

This alternative model of citizenship emerges from the existing disjunctions between the form and substance of citizenship. It challenges the assumption made by liberal citizenship models of a nearly linear progression of citizenship rights (Marshall 1964) and depicts the internal contradictions of liberal and formal citizenship. For example, it highlights the experiences of those eastern European citizens who lost much of their social and substantive rights despite their newly attained civil and political rights (Friedmann 2002) or the experiences of the poor, black majority in post-apartheid South Africa who cannot access much of their constitutionally inscribed, basic social rights, while their newly attained political and civil rights are buried under the devastating social and economic impacts of neoliberalism (ibid.: 70).

Feminists have been some of the most vocal critics of liberal citizenship, providing significant contributions to the construction of an alternative inclusive model (Young 1990; Fraser and Gordon 1994; Yuval-Davis 1997; Lister 1997; Sandercock 1998b; Tripp 1998; Wekerle 2000; Werbner and Yuval-Davis 1999). Their critiques expose the fallacy of the liberal model, which assumes citizens are a single, all-right-bearing entity with equal rights and obligations. This becomes particularly cogent within the framework of the current eroding state of citizens' social rights and their fragile social safety net, whereby the state shifts its responsibilities on to households, thus relying on women's increased citizenry obligations (Miraftab 2001).

Scholars of citizenship in the global South have further pursued this critique by highlighting the irrelevance of the Western liberal definitions of citizenship rights and obligations to the realities of Third World countries (Mamdani 1995, 1996; Kabeer 2002; Gaventa 2002; Cornwall 2002). Through his examination of the relationship between state and civil society in the former colonies, leading scholar in this field Mahmood Mamdani (1996) shows that unlike in Western modern societies, the distinction between state and civil society is blurred in colonies functioning under their colonizers' indirect rule. The state has a bifurcated character and a dual relationship with civil society: as citizens, constituted by colonial settlers and the minority native elites, and as subjects, constituted by the majority natives.

Reconceptualizing the notion of citizenship, shifting its centre from the state to the people, and stressing a pluralist model (Young 1990) have led to a plethora of new definitions of citizenship, including participatory citizenship, inclusive citizenship (Gaventa 2002; Kabeer 2002), active citizenship (Kearns 1995; Lister 1997), and citizenship from below or 'insurgent citizenship' (Holston 1998). These definitions signify an alternative conceptualization of citizenship, in which new meanings, agencies and practices of citizenship are articulated. In this alternative model, practices of citizenship extend beyond 'taking up invitations to participate' in what Cornwall calls 'invited' spaces of citizenship; they extend to forms of action that citizens innovate to 'create their own opportunities and terms of engagement' (Cornwall 2002: 50). Miraftab (2004), referring to these alternative spaces of participation as 'invented' spaces of citizenship, has underlined the significance of expanding the arenas of practising citizenship to include both invited and invented spaces of citizenship. By highlighting in this article the practices of the AEC, we hope to contribute to this recognition of insurgency as a fair and legitimate practice of citizenship by active citizens participating in the construction of inclusive citizenship from below.

As neoliberal practices privatize the city, its infrastructure and its life spaces, and increasingly exclude urban citizens who are not deemed 'good-paying customers', insurgent citizenship challenges the hypocrisy of neoliberalism: an ideology that claims to equalize through the promotion of formal political and civil rights yet, through its privatization of life spaces, criminalizes citizens based on their consumption abilities. Insurgent citizenship is a strategy employed by the poor to hold city officials accountable to their civil and political rights to decent housing conditions, as well as to the city itself, and to reclaim their dignity despite the hypocrisy. The accounts of the AEC members, their visions and dreams, their situated practices and their agency and identity, are presented here with hopes to influence and assist planning theory and education to cultivate a grounded understanding of the range of citizenship spaces and the insurgent urbanism that emerges as an alternative response to neoliberal urbanism.

Historical context: struggle for shelter and basic services

In the South African context, the exclusionary concept of citizenship has been woven together with the accessibility of housing and basic urban services to urban dwellers (Mabin 1993; Parnell 1993; Maharaj 1992). Hence, in any formulation or discussion of citizenship in post-apartheid South Africa, the question of housing and basic services occupies the centre stage. This recognition is reflected in both the 1994 electoral platform proposed by the African National Congress (ANC) for the Government of National Unity and the 1996 South African Constitution, which recognizes the rights of all citizens to access adequate housing and basic services (Articles 26 and 27).

Insurgency and spaces of active citizenship

To overcome the ugly history of apartheid and tackle the state's nation-building agenda, the new government of South Africa initially promised to prioritize equitable access to land, housing and services through its proposed Reconstruction and Development Programme (RDP), which placed the responsibilities of redistribution precisely on the state to achieve a universal and inclusive citizenship. Since access to socio-economic resources has been at the core of apartheid stratifications of citizenship, RDP guaranteed universal citizenship through the granting to all citizens substantive rights to socio-economic resources. Later, however, as explained by numerous scholars and researchers, the redistributive agenda of RDP was abandoned for a growth agenda made public in the state's more market-driven fiscal plan, known as Growth, Employment and Redistribution (GEAR; see Bond 2000a, 2000b; Cheru 1997; Moore 2001). The subsequent shift to this market-led development framework left the notion of universal citizenship in South Africa limited to its formal channels of participation, which are particularly inadequate in a society with some of the world's largest socio-economic gaps and ranks of disparity.

Clear indications of the government's abandonment of a redistributive agenda include the stagnated state of low-cost housing production and the dwindling budget allocation to housing, which has gradually decreased from the promised 5 per cent to 3.4 per cent in 1995/96, 2.4 per cent in 1997/98 and 1.6 per cent in 1999/2000 (Khanya College 2001: 4041). Together with this idle assisted-housing delivery system and shrinking budget have come escalating housing demands owing to the influx of urban populations and a growing number of evictions. Consequently, the housing deficit has not improved, still standing at around 3 million units for the whole of South Africa compared to the 3.4-million-unit shortage estimated in 1994, and basic shelter is still beyond the reach of the impoverished majority.

Furthermore, despite the constitution's declared right for all citizens to access decent shelter and basic services, the neoliberal state's prescription of 'cost reflective pricing' for municipal services has led to extensive service cut-offs for disadvantaged households. Most important, only 1 per cent of South African land, the key issue cementing apartheid's exclusionary citizenship, has been redistributed as of today despite the RDP's land redistribution goal of 30 per cent.

It is true that service provision in South Africa has increased substantially. According to a report reviewed by the Government Communication and Information System in 2000, access to clean running water has been expanded to more than 5 million South African households, and 2.8 million households have gained access to electricity since the government came into power in 1994. However, the ability of vast numbers of poor residents to actually afford services has decreased tremendously. In fact, a recent *New York Times* article reports water taps are often shut to South Africa's poor (29 May 2003, front page). Installation in impoverished townships of state-of-the-art public taps requiring prepaid cards for their operation has created an unprecedented case in the developing world, whereby a growing number of the poor in informal settlements have been cut off and thus denied access to water because of their inability to afford prepayments and their lack of alternatives once money has run out on their cards. Large numbers of township residents also require similar prepaid meter cards to access electricity. Stretches of time without lights or clean water are not uncommon for populations living 'hand to mouth', yet these periods between earnings often brew disastrous public health consequences, such as the devastating cholera outbreak [of] 2000 [...]

An extensive body of literature has adopted the task of analysing the ways in which neoliberal policies lead to such devastating results for the poor [...] With respect to housing, several studies specifically interrogate the South African housing policy and the manner in which its neoliberal, developer-driven goals have undermined the constitutional inspiration for housing as a human right (Miraftab 2003; Jenkins 1999; Mackay 1999; Lalloo 1999; Ruiters and Bond 1996; Tomlinson 1999). A synthesis of these studies will be offered below to provide a foundation from which we can discuss the two eviction conflicts focal to this article concerning the local government (council houses in Mitchell's Plain) and the private banks (bond houses in Mandela Park).

First, the post-apartheid housing policy mobilizes housing subsidies through private developers, instead of community-based groups and non-governmental organizations (NGOs), with the assumption that the private sector can accomplish fast and massive delivery. Yet developers have failed in terms of both speed of delivery and quantity, and the housing backlog persists; see Miraftab (2003) for a detailed discussion regarding this aspect of South African housing policy.

Second, the state offers a range of risk-reducing mechanisms to private financial institutions in efforts to entice their participation in housing loan provisions to the poor. However, banks have not only failed to deliver on their low-cost bonds, but the government's support schemes have been used against low-income residents through mass evictions from poorly constructed bank units, as will be seen in the case of SERVCON in Mandela Park.

Finally, local governments adopt the cost recovery principles of the market by aggressively evicting poor households from the existing stock of rental units for reasons of non-payment. This takes place despite the fact that most of those evicted are unemployed and without job prospects, as will be seen in the case of council houses in Mitchell's Plain. In short, market-led principles that place cost recovery at the centre of local governments' policies and that prioritize the interests of the banks and private developers over the shelter needs of the poor have resulted in the failure of the housing policy to rectify the injustices of the past or to secure the new constitutional right to basic shelter [...] The anti-eviction movement has emerged within the poor townships of Cape Town in direct response to such threats against the more vulnerable populations of South Africa, creating spaces of resistance for average citizens to protect their livelihoods and claim their constitutional rights to access decent living conditions.

The birth of the AEC

The AEC is a grassroots agglomeration of organizations whose members have been victims or face the threat of evictions or service cuts. Since arrears from non-payment of utility services frequently constitute an eviction, the AEC resists service disconnections in addition to fighting evictions. The poor families threatened by these two concerns usually work collaboratively; thus, the people mobilized to resist evictions are often the same as those mobilized to oppose service disconnections.

These grassroots initiatives against evictions and service cuts work closely with a movement coalesced under an Anti-Privatization Forum (APF), which started in Johannesburg in late 1999, and launched an independent forum in the Western Cape in 2000. The Cape Town APF is an umbrella organization that incorporates an array of members including unions, NGOs, political groups and activists opposed to the privatization of shelter and basic services. It is a voluntary organization that binds its members in only a few basic principles, the most prominent of which demands the provision of essential services on the basis of people's needs and not their ability to pay. While the grassroots campaign (AEC) maintains a grounded focus, concerning itself mainly with the immediate day-to-day problems of its member communities with respect to the singular issue of shelter (housing and services), the APF covers a wide range of struggles against neoliberal capitalism, which includes but also goes beyond housing, water and electricity (e.g. access to education).

It also organizes mass protests locally and nationally and collaborates with other global movements opposed to neoliberal policies.

Most campaign activists were involved in the township struggles against apartheid and have maintained active membership in their communities' civic organizations since then. For example, Max Ntanyana and Fonky Goboza currently lead the Mandela Park AEC and participate in the Western Cape APF but have been active in their civic organization in the black township of Khayelitsha since their teenage years. Their involvement with the AEC is a natural continuation of their community development activism, which previously had been mobilized by NGOs and community-based organizations. They see their role in the prevention of evictions and service disconnections as no different from their responsibility for ensuring the provision of shelter and services.

> What we want is community development. ... We've got rich experiences and the community knows us. ... People in large numbers come here reporting their cases to us ... where they are robbing our people or criminals are shooting people. They will come to us before going to the police. They come to us when their water is cut off. They will ask us how to open the water [taps]. (Fonky Goboza and Max Ntanyana, interview, 2002)

Similarly, Valhalla Park AEC activist and local civic leader Gertrude Square builds on her past involvement in the rent boycotts and protests of the apartheid struggle. She underlines her all-encompassing activities as a member of the campaign and the civic body in her community:

> I'm doing anything and everything. I'm just not only busy with evictions and all that stuff. In the civic body, I'm busy with people that are struggling to receive pensions, disability grants, [or] rent-payment grants, abandoned children, with everything. (Interview, 2002)

The vision that drives the campaign can best be described as one of achieving a just city, a city in which both the political and economic rights of its people are ensured and respected and where all residents feel confident that their voices will be heard and their basic needs will be met. Fonky Goboza of the Mandela Park AEC describes the campaign's vision:

> We don't have supporters. We don't have followers. We have active participants. That is participatory democracy ... The statement that we are putting across is that we as a people want open transparency where everyone participates and everybody knows what is taking place ... Our struggle is genuine. We want to make justice in housing programmes. (Interview, 2002)

However, despite this grand aspiration for social justice, the campaign's composition and its internal dynamics with respect to gender are not much different from other community-based movements in that it is composed of mostly female members but led primarily by men. At the AEC's first annual general meeting, during which a management committee of ten members was voted into office, only one woman was selected for the committee. Although a third of the forty attendees were women, the first eight members nominated and voted into office were men, consequently filling the more demanding positions of chair, vice-chair, secretary and treasurer. When at one point a vocal female member spoke up about the gender disparity within the newly established management committee, another female activist disagreed, and the issue was not followed up. One highly regarded female member, however, turned down the offer to serve on the committee, explaining that the position commanded too much responsibility and that she would be more effective maintaining her current role as a grassroots mobilizer for her community. An active female campaign activist illustrates this gender controversy:

> It is mostly women and not a lot of men [who participate] ... but men have got all of the front-line things to do. There are no women going to the council or going to parliament or going to the Unicity or what have you. ... I get very cross [because] I feel that I should also be there. Why not? ... Most women are probably feeling like that ... [but] I am the only one that says it. ... I've been in the campaign since it started. I want to be all over the place and I'm not. ... They [male leaders] do that because they know how to. I would if I could. ... I also want to be there ... in the front line!

Racially, however, the campaign has been able to bridge the colour lines among the poor townships despite the deep and entrenched social divides between groups stratified under apartheid as 'blacks' and 'coloureds'. Since the eviction crisis affects most disadvantaged ethnic groups in Cape Town today, the movement against evictions derives strength from the camaraderie among its racially diverse campaign members. Although at first it was exclusively composed of residents from 'coloured' townships, as evictions focused on defaulting tenants in council houses, the AEC later incorporated mass membership among black households when bond houses in black townships such as Mandela Park were seized, and black owners were evicted. Considering that the majority of its constituency is unemployed and consequently struggles with transport fees to travel anywhere, the campaign's ability to recruit members of African townships to support evicted 'coloured' families in Mitchell's Plain (and vice versa) is particularly remarkable. The participation of campaign members in mass rallies and their demonstrated support to communities outside of their own townships involve notable sacrifice and illustrate a commitment and solidarity that likely ameliorate racial divides.

Deeply entrenched patterns of social exclusion and hierarchy cannot naively be expected to swiftly change through processes of active participation or popular education. However, there is hope that creating and participating in spaces of insurgent citizenship and prolonged struggle might afford certain steps, though tiny and slow, towards a broader social transformation, which may influence changes in individual identity and consciousness.

The AEC and APF as spaces of active citizenship

[...] South Africa is situated well in this particular discussion as its recent history of constitutional change has created a heightened awareness about rights among those who were historically denied a citizenship. They are fully aware of their constitutional rights to shelter and basic services: the needs for which they have fought throughout their struggle against apartheid. 'Water is a necessity. We must have water. And a roof over our heads, we must have it. These are not privileges,' says pensioner and member of the Tafelsig AEC Siyaam Cassiem, who has lived through the difficult, 'bossy days' of apartheid. Ironically, though the contemporary history of South Africa has established a foundation for people's increased awareness of their right to have rights, this has not been sufficient in creating spaces and avenues for claiming and practising those rights.

The AEC members are disenchanted with the main formal channel allotted to them for voicing their concerns and making demands: the local government and its councillors. Much of the hope that local activists had invested in these recently established, decentralized, formal structures to facilitate their greater participation in decision-making and inclusive governance has weathered in the past few years. 'They [councillors] have forgotten where they came from. ... They don't care a damn about the people on the ground ... They just want to be in a position to fill their pockets and to empower themselves,' states a Valhalla Park resident (interview, 2001).

This sort of commentary regarding local councillors has been common among township residents with whom we interacted in Cape Town. Threatened by evictions and service cut-offs, they find their local councillors more committed to party politics than to the fellow community members who put them in power. Referring to local councillors' incompetence at addressing the urgent problems of the poor, an AEC activist and civic leader explains, '[When people need things], it's to us that they turn ... to the people who are on the ground, volunteers, who don't get paid, who are nothing and nobody. We are just people like them. When they are in a struggle and things get hot, then they run to us' (woman in Elsie's River, interview, 2002).

Undoubtedly central to the ability of excluded residents to make citizenship claims is the creation of a progressive pro-poor constitution that expands 'human rights' to include substantive 'rights to livelihood' in South Africa (Beall et al. 2002). But the existing spaces created from above for making these rights real are insufficient (Cousins 1997). The following extract from an interview with a member of the Cape Town APF Steering Committee is illustrative of the shortfall of legal procedures as formal, claim-making channels for the poor and the ineffectiveness of the existing 'invited spaces' for practising citizenship. [...] The legal procedures and formal channels provided by the new constitution are not entirely ignored by the poor. Instead, they are used when advantageous and defied when they are found unjust. Excluded South Africans take advantage of these formal channels whenever possible, but in many cases they find these invited spaces of practising citizenship, created from above by the state, ineffective at addressing the immediacy of their needs and concerns and enforcing just laws. When formal channels fail, the poor use extremely innovative strategies, which create alternative channels and spaces to assert their rights to the city, negotiate their wants, and actively practise their citizenship.

Invented spaces of citizenship

The AEC activists describe their activities as a spontaneous response to the immediate problems and basic needs of the poor. Their strategies constitute a collection of ideas and actions, stretching from informal negotiations, capacity-building and training to mass mobilizations in the form of peaceful protests, sit-ins and land invasions; to defiant collective action such as illegal reconnection of services and repossession of housing (Oldfield 2003). In certain respects, they perpetuate the strategies of anti-apartheid resistance and its tradition of mass mobilizations and non-violent direct action, which included the boycott of rent payments for housing and services in protest against the poor quality of services and the illegitimacy of an oppressive state (Adlers and Steinberg 2000; Seekings 2000; Mayekiso 1996).

The campaign activists claim their rights to the city and to basic shelter and services by resisting the unjust exclusionary actions of the state. One of the main strategies employed is defiant collective action. For example, when they are unable to stop service disconnections, male and female members of the campaign, referred to as 'struggle plumbers' and 'electricians' in the Durban context, simply reconnect those services (Desai 2002). The campaign also helps evicted households reoccupy their homes by breaking the new locks and returning removed furniture and belongings to the units.

Interestingly, the campaign does not follow a uniform blueprint. Their tactics are flexible and innovative and vary in each specific situation (see also Oldfield and Stokke 2004; Oldfield 2003). For instance, Valhalla Park civic member and AEC activist Gertrude takes pride in her community's ability to display force and demonstrate power through spontaneous, cooperative action or informal, persuasive negotiating:

> If someone saw a white man or somebody just hanging around a letterbox or by the water meter, then they [would] just call the people. A lot of people are out of work here and that is what makes us so strong. If something happens

during the day, then we get all of the people together and we hop in our cars and we chase them right out. And we warned them, if ever you come in here again, there is going to be trouble … [But in one case] we talked [to them], and they said: 'No, we don't want to come here to cut people's water off, but we are the contractors. The contract is a piece of bread.' [We said to them:] 'It's a shame … you leave me without water, you leave me thirsty with children, yet it's your piece of bread.' [Then] they made an agreement with us. [They said:] 'So, that my children can eat, we will come in here and we will issue the water cut-off papers.' So they asked us nicely, can they come in here and issue the papers to the people, but if it comes to the point when the people don't pay, then they won't cut the water off. So we said fine. (Gertrude Square, interview, 2002)

Recent negotiations between a bank representative and Mandela Park residents over a long-term dispute regarding the structurally faulty, low-cost bond houses provide another keen example of how campaign strategies are inventing new spaces for practising citizenship. On 12 June 2002, nearly three hundred residents of Mandela Park gathered at their community civic centre to meet visitors from the Johannesburg office of Khayeletu Home Loans – senior Outsourcing Manager Henry Warden and a second bank representative – to discuss the scrapping of certain arrears. During that meeting, Warden verbally agreed to the cancellation of accumulated arrears and interests and the halting of evictions for all elderly and disabled residents. However, the campaign activists, aware of the limited credibility of verbal promises, insisted, 'We do not take anything verbally. We want it in black and white … Please write it down now. Very simply, write it out, A, B, and C.' Because of the community's persistent demands, the two representatives left the centre only after a dictated statement on official bank letterhead was faxed to the meeting and signed by Warden.

Instances like this are helpful in understanding 'citizenship not as a given but as a practice' (Gaventa 2002: 4) – the sort of practice that Holston and Appadurai (1999: 20) describe as aspiring to 'new kinds of citizenship, new sources of laws, and new participation in decisions that bind'. Although the 1996 constitution entitles all South Africans to basic political citizenship rights, including accountability from leaders, campaign activists are trying to create spaces of citizenship from which their rights can be ensured and actually practised. Unlike lengthy legal procedures, informal innovative spaces for practising citizenship created from below are far more responsive to the immediate needs and demands of the poor. These spaces emphasize the agency of poor people and are relevant to and inclusive of their personal realities.

But peaceful negotiations and clever, persuasive tactics are not always effective at expanding the spaces of citizenship practice. For example, in 2001 the campaign's resistance strategies incited more violent events in Tafelsig, the township in which the AEC was first established, when community members barricaded entrances to the township with burning tyres in efforts to prevent the disconnection of water supplies to more than 1,800 homes. Tyres and mattresses were set alight on nearly every street, and enraged residents chanted protest slogans as firefighters and police units appeared at the scene. Police security forces further agitated Tafelsig residents by firing teargas and rubber bullets at protesters, resulting in a brutal confrontation that injured one young boy (*Cape Argus*, 27 September 2001).

Expanding the public sphere

[...] Capacity-building and training sessions organized by the AEC and participated in by campaign activists are important strategies, which not only respond to the immediate needs of their members but also serve towards the long-term campaign goal of a just society. Persistently striving to assert their rights, trained AEC activists have created their own local database of vulnerable households by conducting door-to-door surveys of residents and recording those households that have experienced or been threatened with evictions and service cuts. This information functions as an important tool, enabling the campaign to substantiate their acts of resistance, mobilize AEC members in solidarity, and challenge the officials in charge. Through participation in skill-enhancing initiatives, members take advantage of invited spaces of citizenship created from above by local and international donors and governmental interventions and participate in invented spaces of citizenship, spaces that are chosen, demanded and seized through collective action from below.

Participation in capacity-building and leadership training workshops also helps members to overcome some of the obvious hierarchical barriers within the organization, an example of which exists in the context of gender. A campaign activist who had expressed dismay regarding the apparent male domination of the AEC admits certain levels of change have been achieved through participation in the campaign's advocacy and education workshops. Reflecting on her personal experience, she states,

> I always thought that I better come up with the right words and stuff. But [now] I feel that if people talk out of the dictionary with expensive words ... I must stop them and tell them, 'Listen, I don't understand you and we speak plain language here.' Because those people use words to get around. This is what I learned at the [leadership] workshop. ... I [also] learned to speak in front of people. ... I'm very proud of myself.

Identity and agency

While conceptualizing the AEC as a space of active citizenship invented from below by the poor as an alternative to those invited spaces of citizenship organized and formulated from above by the governments or donors, we also need to recognize how others are characterizing the circumstances. The ways in which the media, the state and city officials portray these movements and respond to them are likely to influence the ability of campaign members to exercise the agency needed to challenge exclusion [...]

The media play an important role in the construction of the movements' identities. The mainstream media's portrayals of the AEC and APF as '"ultra-left" and "freeriders" embedded in a culture of nonpayment' discredit them as relevant voices of civil society and delegitimize their actions. Presented as 'outcasts of civil society', movement members are stripped of the celebratory status that other organizations within civil society are granted. While NGOs and community-based organizations that take part in the invited spaces of citizenship are presented as 'rightful' or 'authentic' voices of the poor, the grassroots movements that create the innovative and invented spaces of citizenship are presented as 'inauthentic', and their agency is often criminalized.

State [...] responses to AEC and APF actions vary depending on its existing internal power dynamics and political context, and they range from direct oppression of the movements, to appropriation of their discourse, to accommodation of their demands.

The mass mobilizations organized by the AEC and APF have in some cases faced the state's repressive machinery. Those who courageously voice their dissent have been routinely beaten, shot at, arrested and charged, and banned from associating with the two movements [...] But such criminalization of the poor's declaration of its inability to afford service and shelter costs ultimately criminalizes poverty and amalgamates with the dehumanization of the poor. From the perspective of APF activists, the state's policies of privatization and cost recovery should be understood as policies that in and of themselves dehumanize the poor.

> Privatization ... is the commercialization of human rights. You are not entitled to things as a human being. It depends on your ability to pay. If you can't pay, you virtually become a criminal. The poor are being criminalized for being poor. That is the case in Mandela Park now. And that [is what] we believe must be resisted. (Robert Wilcox, interview, 2002)

The state's response, however, is not always through direct oppression. It also retaliates through the appropriation of the opposition's discourse in efforts to diffuse the effects of their defiance.

The significance of the AEC exists precisely in its ability to disseminate knowledge about these rights among the poor and to hold the state accountable for its constitutional promises and policy provisions. For that, its strategies promote governing through citizenship, contributing to a notion of inclusive governance. But the immediate actions of the present are not risk free. As Nikolas Rose (2000: 100) poses, they 'may connect up and destabilize larger circuits of power. [But they may also] be refused, or reversed and redirected as a demand from citizens for modification of the games that govern them, and through which they are supposed to govern themselves.'

[... D]espite the uncertainties that the future holds, the processes of their resistance create spaces of active citizenship that need to be valued as legitimate voices within the civil society. This recognition, consequently, raises critical questions for planners about the ways in which they define their roles and their arenas for action. These questions require careful consideration and are addressed below.

Conceptual implications for planning education and research

The global neoliberal policies of privatization and state withdrawal in the provision of basic services discussed in this article have launched simultaneous and contradictory processes of exclusion and inclusion for the poor. On one hand, they have brought about the erosion of their livelihood, in which they are excluded from access to the most essential of the services, and on the other, they have opened up certain public realms of decision-making that they were previously excluded from. This simultaneous opening of certain spaces and closing of others has important implications and deceptions for the planning practice that need careful attention.

Traditionally, urban planners, assuming a 'problem-solving' role, worked for the state, and their practices centred primarily on the state's definition of needs and priorities. In the 1960s, this planning paradigm started to be challenged, and alternative formulations of planning were offered on the grounds that planning needs to foster the disadvantaged groups (Davidoff 1965; Krumholz and Clavel 1994; Webber 1983). These critical strays within the planning theory and practice advocating for public participation, however, gained strength in the 1980s with the withdrawal of the neoliberal state from its role as provider of public services, which shifted many of the state's previous responsibilities to non-state actors such as private corporations and civil society organizations. Community participation consequently inherited increased rationale within mainstream planning processes.

Within this heightened attention to and interest in participatory planning, some have challenged the possibility of achieving meaningful change, warning against co-option of processes that need to stay within the community and independent of the state and its power brokers, referring to the planning professionals (Piven 1970; Krumholz 1994). Others, problematizing the notion of 'public' and the contradictory interests within it, warned against conflating the community and deceptively using the notion of participation. They have underlined the role of planners in the present era as facilitators who enable the inclusion of diverse and often conflicting interests in the planning practice (Sandercock 1998b; Marris 1998; Friedmann 1998; Forester 1988).

The more recent reinterpretation of the notion of citizenship has started to offer planning theory new understandings to conceptualize planning beyond participatory planning to one of insurgent planning. Holston (1995, 1998), Sandercock (1998a, 1998b) and Friedmann (2002), articulating this influence for planning theory, stress an expansion of the realm of planners' inquiry and commitment. 'If modernist planning relies on and builds up the state, then its necessary counter-agent is a mode of planning that addresses the formations of insurgent citizenship' (Holston 1998: 47). This alternative insurgent mode of planning, writes Sandercock (1998b: 189), recognizes 'the contradictions between formal and substantive citizenship and works on behalf of the expansion of citizenship rights'. Planning practice centred primarily on the state's identification of needs and priorities among modernist planners for whom the state had a monopoly in the construction of citizenship. But for an emerging wave of planners who take into account an expanded realm of citizenship construction, the sources of information and guidance for planning practices are the everyday spaces of citizenship (Douglass and Friedmann 1998; Marris 1998; Friedmann 1998; Sandercock 1998a; Beard 2002). This wave within planning thought tries to uncover/recover the insurgent practices that shape the cities and their environments, and thus understand the processes of insurgent urbanism. A planning practice that relies not merely on the high commands of the state but on situated practices of citizens entails an epistemological shift (how we know what we know) with important implications for planning education, moving away from the notion of an expert and scientific knowledge to an ethnographic one (Holston 1999: 158).

Echoing them, this article stresses the need to rethink how the planning profession possibly engages certain community-based groups that are celebrated as civil society representatives and concurrently licensed for inclusion in participatory processes and, perhaps, disengages others who are criminalized as 'ultra left' and excluded from decision-making processes. It uncovers that the revision of planning's role from a problem-solving exercise to an actual facilitating approach needs to be refined further to include a range of spaces for public participation. Planning theory and education in articulation of citizen participation need to be explicit about working with both the resources of the state and the resources of citizens, but the latter should not be limited to those spaces of public participation sanctioned by the state as invited spaces of citizenship but needs to include the invented spaces of citizenship. Inclusion of those who are in direct conflict with policy-makers and planners and who resist their displacing policies may indeed be the most effective strategy to guarantee accountability, democratization, participatory decision-making and inclusive governance.

The insurgent grassroots actions by the poor to protect the roofs above their heads and their access to basic services, as described in this article, are as important as officially sanctioned grassroots actions to produce shelter. Should the planning profession hope to improve its relevance to those grassroots processes that shape and reshape the urban reality, it will need to include in its recognition of the poor's self-help strategies those insurgent practices they employ to achieve their right to the neoliberal cities. The elimination of the latter from planners' scopes of investigation and education will only defeat their effectiveness in situations of this kind, which they are bound to face. Tension undoubtedly exists between these arenas but can certainly be productive, and as Holston (1998: 54) advises, 'planning needs to encourage a complementary antagonism between these two engagements'.

The story of the AEC aims to contribute to this recent opening in the planning inquiry by overcoming the selective definition of what constitutes people's organizations and civil society and underlining the significance of both invited and invented spaces of citizen participation in the formation of inclusive cities and citizenship.

[Abridged version of an article published in the *Journal of Planning Education and Research*, 25(2), 2005, pp. 200–17]

Note

1 Where the consent of the respondent has been acquired, real names have been used; otherwise, for reasons of confidentiality, this has been avoided.

References

Adlers, G. and J. Steinberg (2000) 'Introduction: from comrades to citizens', in G. Adlers and J. Steinberg (eds), *From Comrades to Citizens: The South African crisis Movement and Transition to Democracy*, New York: St Martin's Press.

Beall, J., O. Crankshaw and S. Parnell (2002) *Uniting a Divided City: Governance and Social Exclusion in Johannesburg*, London: Earthscan.

Beard, V. (2002) 'Covert planning for social transformation in Indonesia', *Journal of Planning Education and Research*, 22(1): 15–25.

Bond, P. (2000a) *Cities of Gold, Townships of Coal: Essays on South Africa's New Urban Crisis*, Trenton, NJ: Africa World.

— (2000b) *Elite Transition: From Apartheid to Neoliberalism in South Africa*, London: Pluto.

Cheru, F. (1997) 'Civil society and political economy in South and Southern Africa', in S. Gill (ed.), *Globalization, Democratization and Multilateralism*, New York: St Martin's Press, pp. 219–44.

Cornwall, A. (2002) 'Locating citizen participation', *IDS Bulletin*, 33(2): 49–58.

Cousins, B. (1997) 'How do rights become real? Formal and informal institutions in South Africa's land reform', *IDS Bulletin*, 28(4): 59–68.

Davidoff, P. (1965) 'Advocacy and pluralism in planning', *Journal of the American Institute of Planning*, 31: 331–8.

Desai, A. (2002) *We are the Poors: Community Struggles in Post-Apartheid South Africa*, New York: Monthly Review Press.

Douglass, M. and J. Friedmann (eds) (1998) *Cities and Citizens*, New York: John Wiley.

Forester, J. (1988) *Planning in the Face of Power*, Berkeley: University of California Press.

Fraser, N. and L. Gordon (1994) 'Civil citizenship against social citizenship', in B. Van Steenbergen (ed.), *The Condition of Citizenship*, London: Sage, pp. 90–107.

Friedmann, J. (1998) 'The new political economy of planning: the rise of civil society', in M. Douglass and J. Friedmann (eds), *Cities and Citizens*, New York: John Wiley.

— (2002) *The Prospect of Cities*, Minneapolis: University of Minnesota Press.

Gaventa, J. (2002) 'Exploring citizenship, participation and accountability', *IDS Bulletin*, 33(2): 1–11.

Government Communication and Information System (2000/01) *South Africa Yearbook*, www.gcis.gov.za.

Holston, J. (1995) 'Spaces of insurgent citizenship', *Planning Theory*, 13: 35–52.

— (1998) 'Spaces of insurgent citizenship', in L. Sandercock (ed.), *Making the Invisible Visible: A Multicultural Planning History*, Berkeley: University of California Press.

— (1999) 'Spaces of insurgent citizenship', in J. Holston (ed.), *Cities and Citizenship*, Durham, NC: Duke University Press.

Holston, J. and A. Appadurai (1999) 'Cities and citizenship', in J. Holston (ed.), *Cities and Citizenship*, Durham, NC: Duke University Press.

Isin, E. F. (1999) 'Cities and citizenship', *Citizenship Studies*, 3(2): 165–72.

Jenkins, P. (1999) 'Difficulties encountered in community involvement in delivery under the new South African housing policy', *Habitat International*, 23(4): 431–46.

Kabeer, N. (2002) 'Citizenship, affiliation and exclusion: perspectives from the south', *IDS Bulletin*, 33(2): 12–23.

Kearns, A. (1995) 'Active citizenship and local governance: political and geographical dimensions', *Political Geography*, 14(2): 155–75.

Khanya College (2001) 'GEAR and housing in South Africa', Khanya College Economic Literacy Series no. 3, Johannesburg: Khanya College.

Krumholz, N. (1994) 'Advocacy planning: can it move the center?', *Journal of the American Planning Association*, 60(2): 150–51.

Krumholz, N. and P. Clavel (1994) *Reinventing Cities*, Philadelphia, PA: Temple University Press.

Lalloo, K. (1999) 'Arenas of contested citizenship: housing policy in South Africa', *Habitat International*, 23(1): 35–47.

Lefevbre, H. (1996) *Writings on Cities*, trans. E. Kofman and E. Lebas, Oxford: Blackwell.

Lister, R. (1997) *Citizenship: Feminist Perspectives*, New York: New York University Press.

Mabin, A. (1993) 'Conflict, continuity and change: locating the "properly planned native townships" in the frontiers', in Planning Study Group, *Proceedings of the Symposium on South Africa Planning History*, pp. 305–37.

Mackay, C. J. (1999) 'Housing policy in South Africa: the challenge of delivery', *Housing Studies*, 14(3): 387–99.

Maharaj, B. (1992) 'The "spatial impress" of the central state: the Group Areas Act in Durban', in D. M. Smith (ed.), *The Apartheid City and Beyond? Urbanisation and Social Change in South Africa*, London: Routledge, pp. 74–86.

Mamdani, M. (1995) 'Introduction', in M. Mamdani and E. Wamba-dia-Wamba (eds), *African Studies in Social Movements and Democracy*, Dakar: CODESRIA.

— (1996) *Citizens and Subjects: Contemporary Africa and the Legacy of Late Colonialism*, Princeton, NJ: Princeton University Press.

Marris, P. (1998) 'Planning and civil society in the twenty first century: an introduction', in M. Douglass and J. Friedmann (eds), *Cities and Citizens*, New York: John Wiley, pp. 9–18.

Marshall, T. H. (1964) *Class, Citizenship and Social Development*, Chicago, IL: Chicago University Press.

Mayekiso, M. (1996) *Township Politics: Civic Struggles for a New South Africa*, New York: Monthly Review Press.

Miraftab, F. (2001) 'Risks and opportunities in gender gaps to access shelter: a platform for intervention', *International Journal of Politics, Culture, and Society*, 15(1): 143–60.

— (2003) 'The perils of participatory discourse: housing policy in post-apartheid South Africa', *Journal of Planning Education and Research*, 22(3): 226–39.

— (2004) 'Invented and invited spaces of participation: neoliberal citizenship and feminists' expanded notion of politics', *Wagadu: Journal of Transnational Women's and Gender Studies*, web.cortland.edu/wagadu/.

Moore, D. (2001) 'Neoliberal globalisation and the triple crisis of "modernisation" in Africa: Zimbabwe, the democratic republic of the Congo and South Africa', *Third World Quarterly*, 22(6): 909–29.

Oldfield, S. (2003) 'Polemical politics and the practice of community organising in Cape Town, South Africa', Paper presented at Contested Urban Futures: Grassroots Activism and Neoliberalization in Europe, North America and the Global South, Center for German and European Studies and the Institute for Global Studies, University of Minnesota.

Oldfield, S. and K. Stokke (2004) 'Building unity in diversity: social movement activism in the Western Cape Anti-Eviction Campaign', Case study for the UKZN project 'Globalization, Marginalization and New Social Movements in Post-apartheid South Africa', www.nu.ac.za/ccs/default.asp 6,20,10,1458/.

Parnell, S. (1993) 'Creating racial privilege: public health and town planning legislation, 1910–1920', in Planning Study Group, *Proceedings of the Symposium on South Africa Planning History*, pp. 97–120.

Piven, F. F. (1970) 'Whom does the advocacy planner serve?', *Social Policy*, 1(1): 32–7.

Rose, N. (2000) 'Governing cities, governing citizens', in E. F. Isin (ed.), *Democracy, Citizenship and the Global City*, London: Routledge.

Ruiters, G. and P. Bond (1996) 'Failure in the townships? The development bottleneck', *Southern Africa Report*, April.

Sandercock, L. (1998a) 'Framing insurgent historiographies for planning', in *Making the Invisible Visible: A Multicultural Planning History*, Berkeley: University of California Press.

— (1998b) *Towards Cosmopolis*, New York: John Wiley.

Seekings, J. (2000) 'After apartheid: civic organizations in the "new" South Africa', in G. Adlers and J. Steinberg (eds), *From Comrades to Citizens: The South African Crisis Movement and Transition to Democracy*, New York: St Martin's Press.

Tomlinson, M. R. (1999) 'From rejection to resignation: beneficiaries' views on the South African government's new housing subsidy system', *Urban Studies*, 36(8): 13–49.

Tripp, A. M. (1998) 'Expanding "civil society": women and political space in contemporary Uganda', in N. Kasfir (ed.), *Civil Society and Democracy in Africa: Critical Perspectives*, London: Frank Cass.

Webber, M. (1983) 'The myth of rationality: development planning reconsidered', *Environment and Planning B: Planning and Design*, 10: 89–99.

Wekerle, G. (2000) 'Women's rights to the city: gendered spaces of pluralistic citizenship', in E. F. Isin (ed.), *Democracy, Citizenship and the Global City*, London: Routledge.

Werbner, P. and N. Yuval-Davis (1999) 'Women and the new discourse of citizenship', in N. Yuval-Davis and P. Werbner (eds), *Women, Citizenship, and Difference*, London: Zed Books.

Western Cape Anti-Eviction Campaign (2002) 'Campaign statement: what is the AEC? Western Cape Anti-Eviction Campaign', www.antieviction.org.za/, accessed 22 September 2002.

Young, I. (1990) *Justice and the Politics of Difference*, Princeton, NJ: Princeton University Press.

Yuval-Davis, N. (1997) 'Women, citizenship and difference', *Feminist Review*, 57: 4–27.

33 | Pedagogical guerrillas, armed democrats and revolutionary counter-publics: examining paradox in the Zapatista uprising in Chiapas, Mexico

Josee Johnston

> You must struggle. Struggle without rest. Struggle and defeat the government. Struggle and defeat the government. Struggle and defeat us. If the peaceful transition to democracy, dignity, and justice wins, never will there have been a defeat so sweet. (Subcomandante Marcos, in the opening speech to the National Democratic Convention, August 1994 [Zapatista Army of National Liberation 1995: 250])

The Zapatista Army of National Liberation (EZLN) has consistently defied popular expectations of guerrilla struggle. On 1 January 1994, EZLN soldiers used armed means to capture temporarily Chiapas' major urban centres. Since that initial uprising, the EZLN has not launched any military offensives, and has instead struggled to mobilize civil society. Defying expectations of rigidity and violence, the Zapatistas embraced pluralism, eschewed Marxist rhetoric, maintained a relatively horizontal organizational structure, and even introduced a revolutionary law on women. They demanded democracy, yet steadfastly refused to turn in their arms. At the same time, the EZLN members have not acquired any new weapons since the ceasefire, but have instead used their resources to alleviate poverty in the indigenous communities.

The paradoxical nature of the Zapatista uprising befuddled academic observers, and prompted a somewhat predictable reaction of high-minded nomenclature. On numerous occasions, the Zapatista rebels were referred to as 'postmodern'. The politically ambiguous postmodern terminology belied the politically directive nature of their struggle, and provided little under-standing of the empirical obstacles to democratization, or the precise nature of the Zapatistas' democratic aspirations. At the same time, it is not clear that the Zapatistas can be accurately described as 'modern', even though they demand the services of a modern welfare state, and employ modern political discourses like nationalism, socialism and feminism. Not only is the modern label ambiguous, but it disguises the extent to which the EZLN is rebelling against a particular model of modernization that has been responsible for the marginalization of small-scale rural producers in Mexico. A better analytical starting place is not abstract Western theoretical debates about modernity and postmodernity, but the actual substantive demands put forward by the Zapatista rebels. Democracy is one such demand, and is the focus of this article.

To explore what is both old and new in this particular case of peasant resistance to economic marginalization and political exclusion, I address three issues: pedagogy, violence and democracy.

Armed pedagogy

> Fighting at birth, fighting while growing up, loving and dying fighting, and, yes, even writing is combat. (Subcomandante Marcos)[1]

To understand the paradox of armed democrats, it is first necessary to explicate the pedagogical motivations behind the Zapatistas' uprising. Although the Zapatistas engaged in very real military manoeuvres, complete with real guns, ammunition and human blood, they were more motivated by the desire to communicate the truth of their suffering than by a programme to obliterate their enemy. When questioned by a reporter from the *New Yorker* about their 'delusional' aspirations to capture Mexico City, Marcos responded, 'Weren't we there already by January 2nd? We were everywhere, on the lips of everyone – in the subway, on the radio. And our flag was in the Zócalo.' Marcos describes their pedagogical military strategy even more explicitly in these words:

> [Intellectuals] are right when they say that things exist only when they are named. Until someone names it, Chiapaneco death doesn't exist. But now it exists ... [the Zapatistas] named it by dying [in a military struggle], because no matter what, we were dying. It wasn't until you turned around to see, the press that is, that you named it ... We didn't go to war on January 1 to kill or to be killed. We went to war to make ourselves heard.[2]

If the Zapatistas were pursuing the traditional goal of guerrilla movements – conquering the state – we would surely have to be pessimistic about the impact of these pedagogical strategies. Even the most eloquent poetry is not capable of defeating a federal army equipped with the latest military technology. Viewing the pedagogical intent as primary, however, gives a much different perspective on the uprising's accomplishments. In Marcos's words:

> we weren't expecting the Mexican people to say: 'Oh, look, the Zapatistas have taken up arms, let's join in,' and that then they would grab kitchen knives and go after the first policeman they found. We believed that the people would respond as they did, that they would say, 'Something is wrong in this country, something has to change.'[3]

The question then arises: how do we best conceptualize such a guerrilla movement, without dismissing its military component, or minimizing its pedagogical intent? In his prison writings, Gramsci contemplated the nature of revolutionary change, and saw a historical shift in strategy occurring from the 'war of movement' to the 'war of position'. In a war of movement, a ruling group seizes control of the state, as in the Bolshevik or Cuban revolution. Gramsci suggested that a war of movement was less feasible in the democracies of western Europe, and saw possibilities opening up through a war of position that targets ideas, attitudes, the state and civil society. In a war of position, counter-hegemonic organizations merge together to form a new historic bloc and build up the social foundations of a new state. The goal is to build a broad counter-hegemony, while resisting co-optation by more powerful hegemonic forces. This is an admittedly slow and onerous task, requiring effective political organization capable of organizing new groups of working classes, and building bridges between peasants and urban marginals.

It is obvious that the Zapatistas cannot by themselves form a historic bloc that provides comprehensive counter-hegemonic organization on the level of ideas, institutions and resources. It also seems clear that in a strict sense, the Zapatistas cannot serve as exemplars for peaceful protest. Even so, the Zapatistas' armed struggle was fought on the level of a Gramscian war of position. The rebels did not aim to take over the centres of government, but instead sought to capture the hearts and minds of Mexican civil society in order to rearrange power relations at a more profound level. The Zapatistas hoped to use military means to catalyse the formation of a new historic bloc, comprising new democratic ideas, institutions and equitable material strategies. Their struggle was based on the premise that a real 'revolution' could not occur through a change in the reins of power, but must involve long-term change at the level of individual consciousness, state institutions, material structures and civil society.

The success of this strategy is an open question. What I hope to explore here are the motivations underlying this strategy. Why did an armed group wage a war of position? Or to put the question a slightly different way, why did a pro-democratic organization feel that a military strategy was the only means to enter into dialogue with the national public sphere? The history of failed social revolution in Mexico partially explains the Zapatistas' decision to wage their war on the level of civil society. The Zapatistas' choice of armed pedagogy may also have been based on an understanding of the weak social basis underlying the Mexican state's implementation of a globalization project – a topic to which I now turn.

Blurred boundaries: violence and democracy under a globalization project

We want to say, in case anyone doubts it, that we do not regret rising up in arms against the federal government, and we say again that they left us no other way, and that we neither deny our armed path nor our covered faces; that we do not lament our dead, that we are proud of them and that we are ready to shed more blood and suffer more deaths if that is the price we must pay for democratic change in Mexico. (Subcomandante Marcos, August 1994 [Zapatista Army of National Liberation 2005: 47])

The Zapatistas are often portrayed as a social movement, distinct from a truly revolutionary guerrilla struggle. This depiction is usually a laudatory one. Following the end of the Cold War, many left intellectuals declared that the age of armed uprising was over and gone (Castañeda 1995). Out went the Guevera model of the guerrilla *foco*, and in walked new social movements, usually posited as the new, non-violent weapons of social change. The military tradition was deemed a Cold War vestige, an artifact that the left should disown given the seemingly obvious incompatibility between armed struggle and democracy. Jorge Castañeda, among others, has insisted that the Zapatistas should not be characterized as an armed struggle, but should instead be conceptualized as a political movement. Much of the analysis on the Zapatistas focuses on their peaceful use of armed tactics, especially the Internet aspect of their struggle. In a *Time* magazine report on 'Cyberwar', the Zapatista uprising was given a typical spin – as a struggle that is primarily occurring over the Internet, characterized by a new 'mode of battle that involves the Internet and other forms of telecommunication'. An interview with American Zapatista activist 'Dominguez' (one of the organizers of the virtual 'sit-ins' on Mexican government websites) presented cyberwar as a more civilized alternative to blood-and-guts fighting. In Dominguez's words, 'I'd much rather see extremists take down an Internet server than go around killing people.'[4]

Clearly the Zapatistas should be differentiated from those using more violent methods of guerrilla warfare. Although the EZLN believed armed uprising was necessary, they used violence cautiously in the initial miltary attacks, and since the ceasefire have vigorously supported non-violent, educational tools of struggle to achieve their pedagogical objectives without bloodshed. The EZLN have been extremely careful to abide by the ceasefire agreement signed by the federal government, deliberately refusing to respond when provoked by the Mexican military and paramilitary organizations. The Zapatistas have eschewed the traditional goals of obtaining state power. All of these symptoms lead Castañeda to hypothesize that 'any leftist movement in Latin America today is necessarily reformist – even if it is armed, indigenous, and encircled in that heart of darkness that is the Lacandon jungle' (1995: 85–6).

Even so, insisting that the Zapatistas are socio-political actors, completely distinct from armed revolutionaries, obscures the context of violence and exclusion that forced them to consider armed struggle, and that stops them from turning in their weapons. Although the Zapatistas' democratic aspirations are central to their struggle, we must not forget that they orchestrated an armed uprising, complete with guns, bullets, military strategies and loss of human life. What is significant about the Zapatista case is not their 'non-violent' nature, but how the lines between armed struggle and democracy cannot be neatly separated, no matter how much intellectual observers want social movements to be moving into a post-violence era. Speaking at a round table entitled 'From the underground culture to the culture of resistance' on 26 October 1999, Marcos was insistent that he was not speaking as an expert on culture, but rather as part of a guerrilla movement. In his words:

> We are *guerreros* [guerrillas]. Some very otherly *guerreros*, but, at the end of the day, some *guerreros*. And we *guerreros* know a few things. And among the few things that we know, we know about weapons. So, better that I talk to you about weapons. Specifically, I'm going to talk to you about the weapon of resistance.[5]

Academic analyses often fail to appreciate both sides of the Zapatista struggle – their democratic aspirations, as well as their deliberate, self-conscious use of military tactics. Although it is important to recognize the significance of the Zapatistas' choice to use armed strategies, romantic portrayals of armed struggles for democracy – even relatively self-conscious struggles like the Zapatistas' – should be avoided. Even though the EZLN supported greater democracy in Mexico from the beginning of their armed struggle, choosing the paradox of a pro-democratic military strategy was risky. Recognizing these risks is important since they caution against glamorizing a military approach to democracy, and remind us that using war to bring peace is a paradox in the true sense of the word: an absurdity that contains truth – a self-contradiction. To understand the paradox of armed, pro-democratic movements, we should see the Zapatistas' use of violence as part of a broader context of globalization, and the related phenomenon of low-intensity democracy, and low-intensity warfare. The decision of the Salinas government in 1992 to pave the way for NAFTA by amending Article 27 of the Mexican constitution – officially ending land reform, and opening the door to the privatization of campesino land – was the straw that broke the camel's back, and pushed the Zapatista communities towards the 1994 declaration of war.

Globalization was not an abstract concept for campesinos, but a concrete socio-economic phenomenon that made campesino survival more precarious, frustrated efforts at political participation, undermined any semblance of democratic legitimacy, and ultimately shaped a context where poor farmers took up arms. With the trade liberalization and constitutional amendments of the Salinas years, poorly paid farmers were forced to compete with cheap imports of American corn, while landless farmers saw their hopes of owning land officially dissipate. While the state retreated from its traditional corporatist responsibilities to the peasant sector, campesinos' political efforts to hold peaceful protests and influence state decision-making were consistently stymied. Although claiming to open up the political process to greater democracy, elites refused to redistribute land, wealth or political power. Zapatista major Ana Maria describes their frustrated efforts to obtain some measure of popular participation in government decisions:

> we could not find any other way out of this situation. We had spent years struggling peacefully, we held marches, we had meetings, we went to the municipal palaces and the Government Palace, and we went to Mexico [City] to the National Palace of Mexico to shout, to ask, to agitate in front of the government. They never paid attention to us. They always gave us papers full of promises. Then, what good is a piece of paper, filled with promises, to us?[6]

Liberation theology, a project of peaceful change, also had its limits in bringing justice for the campesinos in a context of state indifference and even outright hostility. Marcos reports:

> What happened is that the Church-led projects failed, and the *compañeros* realized that even this strategy didn't offer them many options. If they organized into cooperatives, they get harassed, and the cooperatives are broken. If they organize themselves to ask for land, they are rejected. If they organize to take over the land, they are killed. They don't have good health; they're dying. That's the source of the 'boom,' the source of thousands of Zapatistas.[7]

By emphasizing the theme of death in their communiqués, the Zapatistas tried to communicate that their decision to wage an armed struggle grew out of the misery that ends life for many campesinos in Chiapas. In addition to the violence of poverty and malnutrition, campesinos faced the deliberate violence of the cattle ranchers and armed guards who forcibly took control of cleared land. The evidence suggests that the EZLN did not originate in an idealistic plan to take over the federal state, but instead had more practical origins as a self-defence force protecting villages against hired thugs.[8] Their willingness to face death in warfare grew out of these early skirmishes with hunger, armed paramilitary organizations and an unresponsive state. The Zapatistas were prepared for a long period of warfare, and were surprised by the rapid response of civil society demanding an end to incursions by the Mexican army.

The transnationalized Mexican state, combined with the heightened marginalization of the peasant sector, proved to be a highly volatile combination in Chiapas, ultimately leading to guerrilla violence and a state policy of low-intensity warfare. This strategy comprised four primary elements: 1) strengthening the army, 2) attempting to legitimize the government, 3) 'taking the water away from the fish' (e.g. working to coerce and co-opt Zapatista supporters through means of assassinations, intelligence gathering, development projects for PRI supporters, psychological warfare and bribery, and other means of violence carried out by paramilitary organizations), and 4) minimizing international solidarity with the Zapatistas. The state has moved at least 70,000 troops into Chiapas (an estimated one third of the entire army) and received substantial amounts of US military aid and advice to wage the war of counter-insurgency.[9]

Since 1994, paramilitary groups have executed at least 1,500 indigenous opponents of the government in Chiapas.[10] This violence has created at least 20,000 internal refugees, mainly indigenous people forced from their municipalities in order to escape paramilitary attacks. Unemployed indigenous youths are offered lucrative bribes to participate in these paramilitary groups, and are trained on the myriad army bases in the area. These groups are used to terrorize Zapatista families and supporters, forcing them to flee from their communities and live in fear – as seen in the terror tactics of the December 1997 massacre in Acteal, Chenalhó, when forty-five indigenous persons, mainly women and children, were assassinated by paramilitary groups as they prayed for peace.[11]

In late August of 1999, the army moved to tighten the noose around the neck of the Zapatista communities, attempting to build major roads into the Zapatista-occupied territory under the guise of 'social-development' projects. Protests followed, with participants including striking UNAM students and television personalities like television actress Ofelia Medina. State governor of Chiapas Roberto Albores Guillen responded by stating that he would no longer allow the presence of national or international observers in the region.

The unresponsiveness of governance at all levels to their concerns created the strong belief among a significant portion of the indigenous campesino population that there was no other option but to rise in arms to fight for democracy. For all the myopia of resource mobilization theorists, they have been right to emphasize the importance of local opportunity structures for understanding the formation of protest movements. A great deal of the paradox of armed struggle for democracy can be understood by an examination of the limited opportunity structure in the context of low-intensity democracy and low-intensity warfare in Chiapas.

Today, the Zapatistas and their supporters continue to face limited options for peaceful protest, or implementing progressive reforms within the semi-authoritarian, low-intensity warfare in Chiapas. Looking at the violence perpetrated by socialist regimes throughout history, Parekh (1992) concludes that for the revolution to maintain legitimacy by promising to introduce a humane social order, it cannot rely on violence alone, and must have alternative strategies to armed struggle. He writes, 'a revolution requires violence: at the same time it is constantly tempted to misuse it, and runs the risk of losing its legitimacy and sense of direction. Every theory of revolution therefore needs a well-considered theory of violence' (ibid.: 107).

The EZLN fulfil Parekh's criterion of a 'well-considered theory of violence' to an impressive degree. Although the ELZN felt that armed struggle was an appropriate path for them, they did not see violence as the singular key to unlock emancipation, and they do not hold the seizure of state power as the primary objective. In an interview Marcos explained:

> We don't understand armed struggle in the classic sense of the previous guerrillas. That is, we do not see armed struggle as a single path, as one single almighty truth around which everything else spins. Instead, from the start, we have seen armed struggle as one in a series of processes or forms of struggle that are themselves subject to change; sometimes one is more important and at times another is more important.[12]

By limiting violence, and targeting change at the level of civil society, the Zapatistas' armed pedagogy was a particularly effective strategy. By keeping their military actions minimal, and developing a close relationship with Mexican civil society, the Zapatistas were able to maintain the moral high ground in their conflict with the state, and legitimize their overarching demand for greater democracy in Mexico. Understanding the empirical context of violence and unaccountable governance has helped us make sense of the strategic considerations of armed democrats in Chiapas. To understand the normative component of the Zapatista struggle, we require a more thorough exploration of their struggle to deepen the meaning of democracy in Mexico beyond low-input governance.

Rethinking democracy: the democratizing effect of Zapatista counter-publics

> they said nobody in their right mind would answer this call from a rebel group, outlaws ... whose obsessive language is now trying to recover old, used-up words: democracy, freedom, justice ... (Subcomandante Marcos, August 1994 [Zapatista Army of National Liberation 1995: 243])

The Zapatistas' unconventional combination of pedagogy and armed violence has led some to argue that they are not really guerrillas per se, but 'armed reformists' (Castañeda 1995: 86). While the traditional guerrilla taxonomy may not apply, the Zapatistas have certainly not applied a 'reformist' label to their own struggles. Instead, they have insisted that they are not just fighting for a bigger piece of the economic pie, or a shot at governance, or simply a clean-up in the electoral process. The vision of democracy advocated by the Zapatistas is not the minimalist Western conception of periodic voting, or what Marcos calls 'democracy white-washed with imported detergent and the water from anti-riot tanks' (Zapatista Army of National Liberation 1995: 246). They insist that they are fighting for something more difficult to achieve: a new world, comprising more democratic institutions, ideals, systems of governance and socio-economic outcomes. When asked to comment on the current political panorama in Mexico, Marcos clearly articulated that what they were contesting was not the holder of power, but the inequitable nature of power itself in Mexico: 'What we want is an alternative country and not an alternative in power. We are not struggling against the PRI. We are struggling against the system of the Party-State.'[13] Struggling for an alternative country? This vision of grandeur makes it tempting to dismiss the Zapatistas' democratic vision as a naive remnant of more radical times. Their failure to engage in party politics has also led to criticism that they are disconnected from the struggle over actually existing democracy in Mexico (Esteva 1999).

In light of their armed tactics, and unwillingness to become directly involved in electoral battles, how are we to understand their paradoxical claim to be democratic champions? In the following section, I argue that the Zapatistas are, in fact, democratic rebels, even though they don't run for office, or endorse political parties. To understand their democratic aspirations, we need a notion of democracy that is more substantive than the hegemonic version of low-intensity democracy, and that can account for the important role of the public sphere in the democratization process.

The positivist tools of mainstream democratic thought – 'minimalism' – don't provide us with a satisfactory analysis of the Zapatista's democratic aspirations. Minimalist conceptions of democracy (also known as the school of competitive elitism, or polyarchy) are based on the works of Joseph Schumpeter and Robert Dahl. These two theorists focused on democracy as a political procedure, and saw the ballot box as the exclusive channel for citizen participation in modern societies. Although few democratic theorists today would call themselves 'Schumpeterians', the minimalist vision of democracy is the hegemonic paradigm in political science, and in international policy-making circles. Minimalist conceptions of democracy are divorced from issues of economic democracy or social equality, and elections are used as the primary litmus test to evaluate a country's democratic status. Minimalism tends to neglect the role of social movements in the struggle for deeper, more participatory democratic systems, and views democracy more as a system of elite governance than an ethic of popular participation or equality (Apter 1992).

My contention is not that electoral obstacles to Mexican democracy do not exist, or that the procedures of liberal democracy are unimportant. My objection is that the standard minimalist approach to Mexico's politics portrays democracy in a flat, two-dimensional fashion, focusing exclusively on state control of electoral politics, and using a narrow criterion of democracy based on Western experience. A photo of Mexico's semi-authoritarian state is taken, the variables are precisely measured against procedural criteria, the relative ranking is calculated, and the positivist theorist looks no farther.

There are much richer traditions of democratic thought that we can draw from to understand the Zapatista struggle. Minimalist interpretations tend to obscure the dialectical nature of the struggle for democracy, and the role of pro-democratic forces in civil society. To understand armed democratic rebels, democracy needs to be understood outside the minimalist framework of electoral politics, in a more substantive sense that refers to the idea of returning power and self-determination back to people. In this expanded view, traceable back to the classic Greek definition as well as numerous Rousseauian-Marxist traditions, democracy is about more than just occasional voting. Democracy refers to a way of life where individuals and communities have relative autonomy, and are able to set the conditions for their own social, moral, ecological and economic development.

To begin to capture the notion of popular democracy, the idea of democracy as a fixed, finite system of regular elections, universally applicable across time and space, should be soundly rejected as an imperialist fiction. A post-orientalist viewpoint conceptualizes democracy as a three-dimensional matrix of pro- and anti-democratic forces that struggle to deepen the meaning of democratic participation beyond proceduralism, and towards a more substantive vision of equal participation and autonomous self-determination. In this view, democracy is a moving target, a contested space where material and discursive struggles are fought, and where different groups compete for cultural, political and economic leadership in the public sphere. Like the Gramscian struggle for hegemony, the struggle for democracy is never complete, and cannot be decided by force or fiat. For the Zapatistas, this is 'a struggle that does not aim to conquer "democratic power" but to widen, strengthen and deepen the space where people can exert their own power' (Esteva 1999: 154). The conditions for a democratic life are never completely resolved, but instead are continually negotiated and renegotiated by competing interests in the public sphere – a concept that is critical to understanding the possibilities for late-capitalist democracy. As Lummis poetically writes:

> Radical democracy envisions the people gathered in the great public space, with neither the great paternal Leviathan nor the great maternal society standing over them, but only the empty sky – the people making the power of Leviathan their own again, free to speak, to choose, to act. (1996: 27)

A notion of public space, or the 'public sphere', can help us reconceptualize the role the Zapatistas play in the struggle for a more substantive, participatory democracy in Mexico. This concept can help us better understand the Zapatistas' role as pedagogical rebels. They promote democracy not through party politics, but by interacting with the official public. This interaction broadens the conceptualization of democracy in the public sphere beyond a narrow minimalist vision, and consolidates a stronger indigenous and campesino identity demanding the rights and conditions for self-determination. The Habermasian conception of the public sphere is a useful starting point, which Fraser defines clearly as: 'a theatre in modern societies in which political participation is enacted through the medium of talk. It is the space in which citizens deliberate about their common affairs, and hence an institutionalized arena of discursive interaction' (1992: 110).

As feminist theorists and post-colonial theorists have noted, a strict Habermasian conception of a singular 'bourgeois' public sphere, where inequalities and status distinctions are bracketed and neutralized, is problematic (Felski 1989; Benhabib 1992). The ideal of an inclusive bourgeois public sphere is tarnished by the historic exclusion of people lacking proper credentials for participation (women, blacks, property-less males). Even when formal barriers to participation were erased, participation in public debates was (and is) barred by inadequate resources, and unspoken cultural assumptions about proper participation styles (rational, 'objective', should address 'public' rather than 'private' matters, etc.). In addition, the ideal of a singular public sphere is cast into doubt by revisionist historiography that documents the long-standing existence of alternative publics where subordinated groups gathered, formed opinions and challenged the dominant interpretations of the bourgeois public (Fraser 1997). Under critical scrutiny, the dominant public sphere comes to seem less like a space for open, democratic interaction, and more like an arena where hegemony is enforced, where dominant powers make their own interests appear like common sense, and where the architecture of domination comes to rely less on coercion, and more on public means of consensus production. Fraser writes:

> We can no longer assume that the liberal model of the bourgeois public sphere was simply an unrealized utopian ideal; it was also an ideological notion that functioned to legitimate an emergent form of class (and race) rule ... the official public sphere then was – indeed, is – the prime institutional site for the construction of the consent that defines the new, hegemonic mode of domination. (Ibid.: 76)

But should we then dismiss the notion of the public sphere as an idealistic fantasy that has always been coercive in practice? Real-life situations such as the one in Mexico do not meet the Habermasian ideal of a singular, institutionalized arena of public negotiation. Even so, the Zapatistas' actions and declarations, and their revitalizing of civil society, suggest that a process of public negotiation over the meaning of democracy is occurring in Mexico on multiple levels (Esteva 1999). Further, the increasing prevalence of state coercion (as opposed to consensual co-optation) suggests that the Zapatistas' democratic interventions have not been successfully incorporated into state hegemony. How do we describe such a fragmented process of public contestation?

In contrast to the Habermasian assumption that a multiplicity of publics is a deviation from the democratic ideal, Fraser (1997) articulates a different ideal of the public sphere: inequality is not bracketed but explicitly 'unbracketed'; private issues are not de facto excluded, but any issue has the potential to become a public issue; the normative ideal is not a singular public, but multiple 'subaltern counter-publics'. Fraser argues that a singular public sphere tends to heighten the tendency of dominant groups to control the public debate. In the history of modern industrial societies, women, gays, lesbians and people of colour have found it necessary to forge subaltern counter-publics to generate identities and a sense of collective interests. Subaltern counter-publics exist in a parallel universe involving a complex relationship of contestation with the official public, and have historically scored many victories by transforming 'private' suffering (e.g. rape, racial discrimination) into public issues.

Subaltern counter-publics not only expand the total area of discursive contestation, bringing new issues to the fore of democratic discussion and state regulation, but they provide a space where marginalized groups develop a sense of their identities and interests. Subaltern counter-publics thus serve a dual function. First, they help consolidate identity and resistance among subaltern counter-publics. Second, they serve to widen and revitalize democracy by training and encouraging members of subaltern counter-publics to broaden the official public sphere, and confront the tension between universal principles and particular oppressions. They are respites from the dominant culture, and a training ground for interaction with the dominant public, and '[i]t is precisely in the dialectic between these two functions that their emancipatory potential resides' (ibid.: 82).

I offer these details on Fraser's theory of subaltern counter-publics because of its important contribution to our understanding of armed democratic rebels. Although the electoral realm is an important terrain of struggle that should not be abandoned, we need to turn our attention towards the Zapatistas' role-building subaltern counter-publics. This is true in terms of the first function of building a subaltern counter-identity based on indigenous and campesino identities, and in terms of the second function of interacting with the official public to broaden the meaning of democracy in the dominant public sphere.

Part I: The construction of subaltern counter-publics

The Zapatista rebellion has played an important role in consolidating subaltern counter-publics in Mexico, especially campesino and indigenous counter-publics focused on the right to democratic self-determination. Although not ratified, the San Andres accords on indigenous self-determination negotiated between the federal government and the EZLN in the autumn of 1995 have become a critical manifesto of indigenous rights to autonomous cultural and material development. The Zapatistas have refused to continue negotiations with the federal government until these accords are carried out in the form originally agreed to by the EZLN and the federal representative. The Zapatista uprising and the EZLN's presence in the Mexican public sphere has helped consolidate a more important sense of indigenous identity. In the words of the Zapatistas:

> The indigenous peoples are national actors today, and their destinies and their platforms form part of the national discussion. The word of the first inhabitants of these lands now holds a special place in public opinion. The 'indigenous' is no longer tourism or artisanry, but rather the struggle against poverty and for dignity.[14]

The democratic demands of the San Andres accords were not created out of thin air, but reflected the Zapatistas' desire to preserve indigenous traditions of consensus-building and community-level democracy. The accords themselves were not unilaterally declared by the Zapatistas, but came out of a process of dialogue between various indigenous groups. Zapatista supporters see democracy as both a way of organizing social life on a local communal level, and as a weapon capable of building identities to resist the historic authoritarianism of the Mexican state. Marcos writes: 'Collective work, democratic thought, and majority rule are more than just a tradition among indigenous people; they have been the only way to survive, to resist, to be proud, and to rebel' (Zapatista Army of National Liberation 1995: 46).

The Zapatistas continually attempt to establish a group identity based on democratic principles. This is manifest in the organizational structure of the EZLN. Although the evidence is somewhat contradictory, the EZLN appear to be a relatively democratic organization that resists vanguardism, and is rooted in indigenous traditions of direct, participatory democracy through community assemblies. One reason that the guerrillas wear ski-masks is the Mexican tradition of *caudillismo*, where one personality functions as the paramount leader. Although clearly the personality of Marcos has stood out and intrigued the international press, he functions as a spokesperson and military strategist, and is not the head of the EZLN. On numerous occasions Marcos has emphasized his subsidiary role in the uprising:

> I have the honor to have as my superiors the best men and women of the various ethnic groups: Tzeltal, Tzotzil, Chol, Tojalabal, Mama and Zoque. I have lived with them for over ten years and I am proud to obey and serve them with my arms and soul ... They are my commanders and I will follow them down

any path they choose. They are the collective and democratic leadership of the EZLN, and their acceptance of a dialogue is as true as their fighting hearts and their concern about being tricked once again. (Ibid.: 84)

The top council of the EZLN, the CCRI-CG (Clandestine Revolutionary Indigenous Committee, General Command), is democratically elected by base communities, and these members can be recalled if they do not comply with the popular will. The CCRI is a council of indigenous leaders who are informed by an unknown number of clandestine committees representing the major ethnic groups, and who are in turn responsive to the indigenous communities. Although the military is organized in a typical hierarchical command structure, strategic political and organizational decisions are made at the community level, rather than by military leaders. The decision to hold the uprising itself was made democratically by the involved indigenous communities.

Efforts to consolidate collective democratic identities are also seen in EZLN's strategies to mobilize civil society. In June of 1995, the EZLN became frustrated with the government refusal to negotiate any national demands, so they responded by organizing a massive plebiscite (*Consulta*), letting Mexicans and foreigners vote on the EZLN demands and the future strategies of the rebel group. The *Consulta Nacional e Internacional* was carried out in August 1995, with participation by 1.2 million Mexicans and more than 100,000 people outside Mexico. The *Consulta* voted that the EZLN should convert itself into an independent political force, and in response the Zapatista Front of National Liberation (FZLN), an independent civilian political force, was formed at the end of December. The EZLN also consulted its entire membership when it was time to decide whether or not to sign the federal government's proposal for peace. In March of 1999 the FZLN organized another *Consulta* that allowed 3 million Mexicans at home and abroad to vote on the San Andres accords on indigenous rights and culture.[15]

Not only have the Zapatistas helped strengthen identities based on democracy and resistance within their own organization, but they have inspired and helped develop this identity within campesino and indigenous counterpublics more generally. Several important movements towards indigenous and campesino self-determination have been inspired by the Zapatista uprising, the most notable being the move towards autonomous municipalities. The National Indigenous Convention, established in response to the Zapatistas' National Democratic Convention (CND), holds as its primary goal a national plan to establish autonomous multiethnic regions.[16] Besides these overt constructions of alternative, democratic institutions, the Zapatista uprising encouraged a wave of land seizures, as landless campesinos were inspired to commit courageous acts to promote their right to self-determination in the form of a piece of land. Sebastian Lopez, a Tzotzil Indian peasant who led the seizure of a 300-hectare ranch, said, 'They [the Zapatistas] have opened the doors for all of us. The government has to take us into account.'[17]

Although the Zapatistas have not orchestrated all of these movements, there is clearly an element of EZLN inspiration, and a commonality of spirit with the general principles of indigenous and campesino self-determination and autonomous development espoused by the EZLN. Although the Zapatistas are a military movement, they have inspired tremendous debate, discussion and construction of democratic counter-publics in the state of Chiapas. These counter-publics work to resist the authoritarian powers of local and national elites and the dominant visions of a globalized economy where campesinos serve as wage labour on corporate plantations.

Part II: Interacting with the official public. The Zapatistas' democratic vision

A subaltern counter-public is not only a place of identity formation. It is not an 'enclave', but a 'public', interacting with the official public in the hopes of expanding its discourse into broader political, economic and cultural settings. Although the Zapatistas do not want to become the state, they do want to become a stronger public that provides input into decision-making at varying levels of government, and contributes to legally binding decisions on important matters, such as the rights to indigenous self-determination embodied in the San Andres accords.

To understand why the Zapatistas have not converted themselves into a political party, we need to consider two factors: 1) the difficulty of equal participation in the electoral process, and 2) the fact that the EZLN's democratic objectives exceed electoral strategies. Participation in the electoral process would be risky, given the extreme level of inequity, and the strong chance that the final outcome would be tainted by corruption and vote-buying. Their reluctance to directly participate in electoral politics also requires a broader understanding of democratic struggle as not just about free and fair elections, but including efforts to deepen debate in the official public, and strengthen the participation of subaltern counter-publics. Although the Zapatistas demand fair elections, they realize that elections are not enough to achieve meaningful democracy:

> The struggle for democracy in Mexico is not only a struggle for fair, free, and just elections; multi-party participation; or a change in power. It is, above all, the struggle for politics to be 'citizenized' if you will. The struggle to find new ways, to create spaces, to nurture initiatives which give voice and a place to those who make a nation: the workers of the field and the city, the indigenous, the squatters, the housewives, the teachers, students, retired and pensioned, small businessmen, professionals, employees, handicapped, HIV positives,

intellectuals, artists, researchers, unemployed, homosexuals, lesbians, youth, women, children and elderly, the everyone who, under different names and face, dress and name themselves, the people.[18]

Yet even with the inequality of opportunity between publics, Zapatista-inspired subaltern counter-publics have not remained isolated in a jungle fortress. Instead, they have challenged the conception of democracy provided by the official public, and put forth a more radical conception that unites demands for political democracy with economic justice, and emphasize the importance of a participatory democratic process. The Zapatistas recognize that democratization requires a process of numerous subaltern counter-publics operating within the public sphere to challenge the hegemony of the PRI and its globalization project. The Zapatistas have put forward an alternative conception of social struggle that is not based on a revolutionary vanguard, but on a loose network of autonomous social movements working together towards common goals, at the same time respecting their differences. Support for the Zapatistas does not require subordination to an ultimate military cause, or even to one political party. In the first month of the Zapatista uprising, the EZLN issued a statement calling for the solidarity and support of the 'North American people and government', as well as 'all workers, poor peasants, teachers, students, progressive and honest intellectuals, housewives, professionals, and all independent political organizations' in Mexico' (Zapatista Army of National Liberation 1995: 59, 61). They weren't asking that these diverse elements of national and transnational civil society come to the Lacandon rainforest and join their armed struggle. Instead, the Zapatistas asked these groups to join their struggle 'in your own way using your own methods, so that we can win the justice and freedom that all Mexicans desire' (ibid.: 61). Although the Zapatistas consistently make appeals for struggle on multiple levels, they also insist on the need for unity around certain normative ideals like democracy and justice.

As Michael Walzer has observed, 'the one and the many are often described in philosophical literature as if they were opposed to each other, but in politics and society what we must hope for is their cooperation' (1999).[19] The Zapatistas deliver this hope to us, and suggest that economic equality, political participation and cultural recognition are not separate agendas, but part of a larger democratic project. This comprehensive and complex vision of democracy provides inspiration in our 'post-socialist' intellectual age – a time characterized by a general suspicion towards overarching emancipatory projects, a divide between the politics of redistribution and recognition, and decentring of materialist struggles (Fraser 1997).

The Zapatistas' democratic vision provides particularly valuable insights about the important connections between political and economic rights that are obscured in minimalist democratic thought. A democratic system of inclusion and participation is fundamentally at odds with a socio-economic situation of impoverishment, a situation that is inherently characterized by exclusion, inequality, violence and the absence of personal autonomy. As is often noted, the Zapatistas have not used conventional Marxist rhetoric. Even so, they continually emphasize the importance of a democratically controlled economic system to possessing substantive political rights. Political rights cannot exist without economic rights.

Achieving the goal of economic and political citizenship will be difficult, if not impossible, under the reins of a transnationalized state operating a very thin type of procedural democracy. For this reason, 'neoliberalism' is a particularly important Zapatista target, representing the powerful imperative to obey the dictates of global financial powers, instead of listening to the demands of national citizens. Self-determination and the preservation of specific indigenous identities are inextricably linked to struggles against global capital.

The Zapatistas have called for a shift of power away from supranational institutions like the World Trade Organization (WTO) and the IMF, and back towards democratically accountable state structures. The Zapatistas do not make these calls for democratic economic control in isolation, but have had tremendous success mobilizing other subaltern counter-publics in Mexico and around the world. The spark of an international Zapatista counter-public was lit in 1996 when the Zapatistas hosted 4,000 activists from five continents at the first 'Inter-continental Gathering for Humanity and Against Neoliberalism'.

In short, the Zapatistas have made strong connections between globalized economies and the lack of meaningful democratic participation. These connections contest the official public's vision of low-intensity democracy, and have inspired the struggles of subaltern counter-publics in Mexico and abroad to put forward a more substantive, radical notion of popular democratic control over political and economic development.

Conclusion

Given the intensity of actions by the Mexican military and paramilitary organizations in Zapatista territory, it seems patently clear that the Zapatistas' struggle for democracy is far from over. There is nothing to be gained from idealizing their struggle, or minimizing the severity of recent military efforts to crush the Zapatistas and terrorize their social support base. The Zapatistas' attention to multiplicity and cautious use of violence might earn them the respect of Western political theorists (present author included), but the results are paradoxical. The Zapatistas' unwillingness to 'lead' the revolution makes them more democratic, but this is a slow and onerous struggle, which leaves them open to criticism, persecution and co-optation. It would not be the first time a revolutionary group has been absorbed into state hegemony

– one need only look to the numerous precedents in Mexican history, from the development of corporatism after the Mexican revolution, to the state incorporation of student protesters after 1968.

Aware of the danger of co-optation, the Zapatistas have refused to accept the government's offer to buy peace, insisting that their goals are much larger than just material improvement for their communities. In Marcos's words:

> If we had done so, if we had surrendered, if we had sold ourselves, we would now have good houses, good schools, hospitals, machinery for working the land, better prices for our products, good food. But we chose not to sell ourselves, we chose not to surrender. Because it so happens that we are indigenous and we are also *guerreros*. And *guerreros* are *guerreros* because they are fighting for something ... If we had surrendered, if we had sold ourselves, we would no longer have been poor, but others would have continued to be so.[20]

Even with all the obstacles, it is important to see their struggle as a critical piece of a pro-democratic movement that challenges the shape of actually existing Mexican democracy. This can only occur when theorists move beyond a narrow conceptualization of democracy as electoral politics, and consider the importance of subaltern counter-publics and the public sphere in the democratization process. Although the EZLN continues to endure the violence of so-called low-intensity warfare, their battle to broaden the conception of democracy within the public sphere to include the demands for indigenous and campesino self-determination has been at least partially successful. The Zapatistas have demanded a redistribution of resources, the right to self-determination, and the participation of civil society in the governance of Mexico. The Zapatistas have also helped put issues of land, economic redistribution and indigenous self-determination squarely back in the public sphere, and challenged the authority of the PRI to govern using centralist, authoritarian measures. The Zapatistas have helped loosen the PRI's hold on Mexico and helped indigenous people gain visibility. Most EZLN demands remain unfulfilled, but they are now more firmly on the public agenda. In an interview, Marcos recognized the partial success of the EZLN strategy of armed pedagogical struggle:

> This approach has worked. Proof of its effectiveness can be found in the changes that have taken place since the first of January [1994]. The federal government's sudden attention to Indian questions comes only after the first of January. The cult of social-liberalism and everything it implies has been suddenly set aside ... all of a sudden, the success of the Mexican economy is being questioned ... We have a clear sense of the uprising's impact, and we think that non-militarized organizations at the national level also understand that these changes are a product of the armed uprising of desperation.[21]

[Abridged version of an article published in *Theory and Society*, 29(4), 2000, pp. 463–505]

Acknowledgements

This research was partially supported by a doctoral fellowship from the Social Science and Humanities Research Council (SSHRC) of Canada.

Notes

1 Subcomandante Marcos, 'Duality and remembrance', Newsgroup: chiapas-n@ burn.ucsd.edu. Posted 24 September 1999. Accessed 2 November 1999.

2 Zapatista Army of National Liberation, *Zapatistas! Documents of the New Mexican Revolution*, online publication, Autonomedia, 1995, ch. 5, accessed May 1997; available from gopher://lanic. utexas. edu/ll/la/Mexico/Zapatistas.

3 Ibid., ch. 5.

4 Tim McGirk, 'Wired for warfare. Rebels and dissenters are using power of the Net to harass and attack their more powerful foes', *Time* Special Report, 'The communications revolution. Languages of technology, 154(15), 11 October 1999, www.pathfinder. com/time/magazine/articles/0,3266,32558,00. html.

5 Subcomandante Marcos, 'Marcos on underground culture and resistance' (1999), Listserve: chiapas-n@burn.uscsd.edu. Posted 28 October 1999. Accessed 29 October 1999.

6 Zapatista Army of National Liberation, *Zapatistas!*, ch. 5.

7 Ibid.

8 Subcomandante Marcos, 'Interview: Subcomandante Marcos' (Katzenberger 1996: 65).

9 Brian Wilson, 'The slippery slope: US military moves into Mexico', Chiapas96-lite@mundo.eco.utexas.edu. Posted 17 June 1997. Accessed 18 June 1997.

10 Diego Cevallos, 'IPS/army tightens noose around EZLN', Newsgroup: chiapas-l@ burn.ucsd.edu. Posted 21 August 1999. Accessed 23 August 1999.

11 The majority of the victims of the Acteal massacre had entry wounds in the back. Jaime Aviles, 'Zedillo: la guerra perdida', *La Jornada*, 10 January 1999, online.

12 Zapatista Army of National Liberation, *Zapatistas!*, ch. 5.

13 'Subcomandante Marcos interview with UNAM Radio, La Jornada, 11-7-95', Newsgroup: Chiapas95@mundo.eco.utexas.edu. Posted 8 November 1995. Accessed 1 November 1999.

14 EZLN, 'V Declaration of the Lacandon Jungle', 1998, www/ezln. org/archive/ quinta-lacandona-eng. html.

15 Laurence Iliff, 'DMN/Mexican referendum a success, rebels say', Newsgroup: chiapas-1@burn.ucsd.edu. Posted 24 March 1999. Accessed 25 March 1999.

16 Ibid.

17 Kieran Murray, 'The last resort', *New Statesman and Society*, 18 March 1994, p. 20.

18 EZLN, 'Some reflections about FOBAPROA', Newsgroup: Zapatistas Online. Posted 30 October 1998. Accessed 1 November 1998.

19 www.dissentmagazine.org/article/?article=1525.

20 EZLN, 'V Declaration of the Lacandon Jungle'.

21 Zapatista Army of National Liberation, *Zapatistas!*, p. 141.

References

Apter, D. (1992) 'Democracy and emancipatory movements: notes for a theory of inversionary discourse', *Development and Change*, 23(3): 141.

Benhabib, S. (1992) *Situating the Self: Gender, Community and Postmodernism in Contemporary Ethics*, Minneapolis: University of Minnesota Press.

Castañeda, J. G. (1995) *The Mexican Shock*, New York: New Press.

Esteva, G. (1999) 'The Zapatistas and people's power', *Capital and Class*, 68: 153–83.

Felski, R. (1989) *Beyond Feminist Aesthetics: Feminist Literature and Social Change*, Cambridge, MA: Harvard University Press.

Fraser, N. (1992) 'Rethinking the public sphere: a contribution to the critique of actually existing democracy', in C. Calhoun (ed.), *Habermas and the Public Sphere*, Cambridge, MA: MIT Press.

— (1997) *Justice Interruptus*, New York: Routledge.

Katzenberger, E. (ed.) (1996) *First World, HA HA HA! The Zapatista Challenge*, San Francisco, CA: City Lights Books.

Lummis, C. D. (1996) *Radical Democracy*, Ithaca, NY: Cornell University Press.

Parekh, B. (1992) 'Marxism and the problem of violence', *Development and Change*, 23(3): 103–20.

Walzer, M. (1999) 'Rescuing civil society', *Dissent*, pp. 62–7, www.dissentmagazine.org/article/?article=1525.

Zapatista Army of National Liberation (1995) *Shadows of Tender Fury. The Letters and Communiqués of Subcomandante Marcos and the Zapatista Army of National Liberation*, trans. F. Bardacke, L. Lopez and the Watsonville, California, Human Rights Committee, introduction by J. Ross, afterword by F. Bardacke, New York: Monthly Review Press.

34 | Bodies as sites of struggle: Naripokkho and the movement for women's rights in Bangladesh

Shireen Huq

Introduction

Women in Bangladesh suffer both an unequal legal status with regard to many important rights and an inferior position with regard to cultural beliefs and practices. This situation is aggravated further by what appears to be a lack of social and political will to deliver justice on violations that women routinely suffer, and, on the part of women themselves, by a lack of knowledge, confidence and skills to challenge such situations. The most frequent violations that women suffer in Bangladesh have to do, first, with their personal status and cultural identity as females – they are frequently treated as minors with few rights but disproportionate responsibilities – and, second, with their legal status as unequal citizens, because of which they are routinely and systematically the recipients of lesser resources, opportunities and rights.

Attempts to challenge women's subordination in Bangladesh reflect a number of different forces. Bangladesh's independence in 1971, a few years prior to the United Nations International Year of Women, meant that, from the outset, policy interest in 'women's issues' tended to be subsumed within the rubric of 'women and development', in particular women's contribution to production and a preoccupation with family planning. The interest in women's issues among even progressive political parties tended to be rhetorical and limited in scope, these limitations arising out of their own adherence to middle-class norms of gender propriety.

This chapter deals with the experiences of Naripokkho,[1] a women's organization that seeks to carve out an autonomous space for feminist politics in Bangladesh that is neither driven by the women and development agenda nor subsumed within a male-dominated party politics. This has allowed the organization to bring on to the public agenda various new, often controversial, issues that emerge out of the organization's commitment to link the personal experiences of women to a political analysis of their subordination. One of the issues, one that constitutes a continuous and central thread in its activism, is related to women's bodies as a site of oppression. This chapter will deal with the reasons why this politics emerged and the form it has taken.

The founding of Naripokkho

A number of us, all women who were engaged in one way or another with the situation of rural women in Bangladesh, had come together in 1980 to try to forge a collective identity from wherein we could intervene on the woman question. We wished to pursue, both professionally and politically, our vision of social change and women's emancipation. The choices we had made in our personal lives reflected our desire and our determination to be free and different from what was destined for women in Bangladesh.

Naripokkho was founded as a result of that collective desire. The catalyst was a three-day workshop on women and development, organized in 1983 by the Asian Cultural Forum on Development (ACFOD), that brought together thirty-three women development workers from non-governmental organizations (NGOs) all over the country. They came to the workshop expecting to make, and listen to, the usual presentations about their organizations: how many women 'beneficiaries' they were reaching, what kind of income generation programmes they were supporting, and so on. However, a number of us felt that there were ample opportunities to talk about what development NGOs were doing about 'poor and disadvantaged women', but few or none to talk about the women employed to reach them.

Despite initial resistance to the idea of talking about 'ourselves', I was able to use my influence as one of the facilitators to help transform the workshop into a first-person discussion of the life and experiences of the women who were attending: the women *in* development work. Who were these women? How did they end up in jobs that represented a dramatic and often unacceptable break with tradition?[2] What life circumstances had led to the choice of a job or a career that required women to be visible and mobile in unprecedented ways? Front-line female development workers, going from village to village, many on bicycles, were considered by some as pariahs and a bad omen. They represented a significant departure from the cultural norm of remaining within the confines of one's home and at best venturing out into 'accepted' female occupations, such as teaching in schools. What did these women face that their male colleagues did not? What problems and challenges did they face in the villages they worked in? What problems and challenges did they face within the organizations that employed them? These questions had never been addressed.

The workshop allowed us to reflect on a number of questions that touched on our personal experiences: our first memories of being discriminated against as females; the circumstances that had led us to opt for a role different from those destined for the majority of women in Bangladesh; and the problems we faced in our personal and professional lives that male colleagues did not. We had no idea of the intensity of the sense of injustice that lay beneath the surface, ready to explode. Many women had *literally* never spoken about themselves before. A few still could not say the words, and simply cried. Others could not stop speaking, describing events and situations that testified to how deep, how widespread and how constant the experience of discrimination was, and how poignant and long-lasting the pain it inflicted.

Charting new territory: the first 'small steps'

By the end of the workshop, we were clear that we did not want this process of discovery to end and that we wanted to stay connected. The genesis of Naripokkho was thus in the realization of the links between personal experience and societal discrimination, and this formed an important dimension of its organizational strategy from the outset. The seeds of the organization were laid at a workshop, and workshops have remained an important way in which the organization has sought to achieve its goals.[3]

The discussions at our workshops have evolved over the years to encompass a number of different issues. One set of discussions, which stems from the questions we set ourselves at that first workshop, focuses on women's observations and experiences of gender discrimination at home and at work, and what these might have in common with those of the women who were targeted as beneficiaries by the development NGOs that employed them. This helps both to establish the grounds for a personal engagement with the issues of discrimination, violence and injustice, and to form the basis for identification with 'others'. This has become a significant feature of Naripokkho's strategy for change – *a first-person engagement in the movement for change and the emergence of a collective 'we'.*

A second set of discussions focuses on the position and treatment of women in law. The first workshop had revealed how little women knew about their legal rights and how little they understood about discrimination in the content of the law itself. Personal law in Bangladesh, as in India, is governed by religion. This means that religious rather than civil law governs such areas as marriage, the dissolution of marriage, custody and guardianship of children, and inheritance. Given that all religions discriminate against women, women from different religious communities not only enjoy different rights from each other but also have fewer rights than men in their communities. Legal discrimination thus formalizes and justifies customary inequality.

These discussions have a subversive potential. They open women's eyes to the injustices encoded in law and suggest that litigation and courts cannot always be relied on for justice. This was a revelation for many, who until then had thought the only problem women faced in relation to the law was lack of access to the judicial system. These discussions have brought out the important distinction between 'law' and 'justice' (*ain o nyaybichar*); a distinction that enabled us subsequently to evaluate everything from the point of view of *nyaybichar* and *nyajjota* (justice and fairness).

And finally, the workshop discussions focus on women's bodies, providing a safe space in which women are able to share some of the more private and intimate aspects of their 'embodied' experiences of deprivation and discrimination, and re-examine their personal lives. Understanding and appreciating their bodies, unravelling their attitudes to their own bodies and sexuality, and analysing how others have treated them, have been an important part of this re-examination. These discussions have clarified how much of the discrimination, ill treatment and violence women suffer is connected to the ways in which their bodies, their sexuality, their reproductive roles and their health are perceived, valued and constructed by their families, their colleagues and by society at large.

These discussions have also revealed how little so many women in Bangladesh know about or understand their bodies, and how little they acknowledge their sexuality and sexual needs. The discovery by some women of where their uterus was located was a revelation! For others, it was the idea of sexual pleasure which proved to be revolutionary! The opportunity to talk about these aspects of their lives opened the floodgates to other more private areas of suffering. In some cases, women described unwanted sexual advances by men taking advantage of their vulnerability in particular situations. In other cases, they spoke of rejection, often in hurtful and abusive terms, by their husbands when they expressed their desire for sexual pleasure. One woman said that she had been married for seven years and did not know that women could have orgasms. Another described how her husband had thrown her off the bed, shouting *'Aami ki bajaarer meyelok ghorey anchi naki?'* ('Have I brought home a woman from the brothel?')[4] The common refrain during these discussions has been 'the pleasure is not for us to have, it is always for them to take'. The issue of sexuality has become central to our discourse on rights and freedoms, and women from the brothels have become our sisters in struggle.

What has transpired in these workshops has helped to determine who we have become as an organization. First of all, from the start, we opted for a strategy that stressed process over blueprint, and a process that entailed continuous learning and clarification based on the participation of women and the sharing of first-hand experiences. We wanted engagement on the basis of personal identification with the issues. As a result, every issue that we have taken up has a basis in the reality of our lives and of women's lives more generally. We say that 'we speak *about* ourselves and we speak *for* ourselves'.

Second, our concern with various aspects of women's self-determination – their right to freedom of speech and movement, to freedom from violence, to control over their bodies and their sexuality, and so on – meant that we were, in effect, redefining ideas about *personhood* as they related, in the first instance, to women, and by extension to men. The first understanding of rights for most of the women we work with comes from the recognition of discrimination, and with it the understanding of discrimination as injustice. The right not to be discriminated against – that is, the right to non-discrimination – was then our starting point; the basis on which we demanded equality and justice. Our experience of discrimination as *women* led us to demand fair treatment and respect for our dignity as *human beings*, and only thereafter to claim our rights and entitlements as *citizens*. It was only through the process of seeking redress for unfair treatment and discrimination, demanding changes in the law and cultural behaviour, and requiring accountability from the state, that we became aware of ourselves as citizens and bearers of rights.

And finally, given our approach, it was inevitable that a concern with 'body politics' would be an important theme in Naripokkho's work. The centrality of women's bodies in the countless trivial, as well as significant, instances of oppression that have been recounted in our workshops was striking. Over time, the connection between these instances and the processes by which male power over women is maintained and reproduced in Bangladesh has become increasingly clear, and we have come to realize how profoundly our bodies affect every aspect of our being, experience and consciousness as women.

Bangladesh has long been characterized by the dramatic absence of women in public spaces. Women were not visible in the streets, on public transport or in markets. In rural areas, women rarely ventured beyond the boundaries of their *bari*,[5] and in towns and cities women stayed away from streets and parks. Although this scenario has changed considerably in the past two decades, the norm continues to relegate women to the 'shelter' of the family and the home; their enforced dependence on men for both protection and provision reinforces their cultural devaluation.

We are socialized into 'becoming women' on the basis of a combination of Islamic strictures and Bengali cultural norms of gender propriety whereby we are not to be seen or heard. We are expected to speak quietly, to keep our eyes downcast, to cover ourselves in the presence of strange men and to eat when everyone else has eaten. Despite constitutional provisions and policy declarations regarding the advancement of women, and the entry in recent years of large numbers of women into the formal workforce, societal norms continue to value women primarily as bearers of children – or, rather, sons – even though many have died from too early, too frequent and too many pregnancies.

Although economic pressures have forced women to defy social, and often family, expectations, and take up work in public space, it is assumed that only women without male provision or protection do this. A woman outside the boundaries of her family and home is therefore either destitute – an object of pity – or immoral – an object of shame. And yet, despite this stress on the protection of women and their confinement to the 'safety' of the domestic sphere, we have found that violence against women appears to be a part of everyday life, within the domestic sphere and outside it: wife beating, dowry deaths, assaults, rapes and, more recently, fatwa-related violence and acid attacks are common. Consequently, although Naripokkho has been active on a variety of issues and on a number of different fronts, body politics has remained a continuous thread in its work.

The 'politics of the body' in Naripokkho's agenda

Making violence against women visible Not surprisingly, the first issue around which Naripokkho mobilized, and one that continues to dominate our agenda, is that of violence against women. Not only was this woven into the everyday experiences of the women who came together in the workshops, but also more generally: fear about their personal safety acts as a crippling constraint on what women can be and do in Bangladesh.

Our standpoint on violence has evolved partly as a critique of the way the issue has been handled by the mainstream women's movement, and partly as a response to the specific instances that have come on to our agenda. The mass rape of women by the Pakistan army during Bangladesh's independence war in 1971 continues to be referred to by our politicians, intellectuals and public leaders as 'the loss of honour' of Bangladeshi women rather than as a war crime. We challenged this interpretation. If 'loss of honour' was at all an issue, then surely it was that of the rapist. The *raison d'être* for protest on the issue of rape should surely be the necessity to shame the rapists. However, the idea that women are the repositories of family, community and national honour is a deep-rooted one. It continues to dominate the political discourse about the national struggle for independence. And it leads to communities to congratulate themselves upon successfully forcing the rapist to marry his victim! This practice is common, especially in rural communities, and is seen as the only way of recouping lost honour.

Naripokkho's first involvement in a campaign on the issue of violence against women was in 1985, when the then military government had imposed a temporary ban on all political activities. Denied their usual source of news, journalists filled the front pages with reports of crimes, including violence against women, that previously had been relegated to obscure sections of their papers. Opposition groups saw this as an opportunity to mobilize public opinion against the ruling regime. By choosing to focus on violence in terms of women's safety in public space, it was able to define the issue as a law and order problem and cast it in terms of the failure of the government to maintain law and order. The fact that most of the violence reported in the media occurred within the home and had been perpetrated by family members offered little possibility for political capital. Thus the issue of domestic violence was ignored.[6]

At about the same time that year, newspaper reports of the sale into prostitution and subsequent death of a ten-year-old girl named Shabmeher sparked off unprecedented public anger. In the same week, newspapers reported the rape of a five-year-old girl. The fact that both these incidents represented the violation of 'innocent minors' evoked unprecedented sympathy, even among those who appeared to have become immune to the daily reports of violence against women all over the country. A high-profile campaign against violence against women was mounted by various women's organizations and other social groups, convened by Bangladesh Mahila Parishad, the largest women's organization in the country. Naripokkho was invited to join the eighteen-member National Steering Committee.

Naripokkho's concern with women's safety and security, our belief that violence against women was a product of systemic discrimination rather than a purely individual act, and our conviction that women had to be both visible and audible in the fight against violence if they were to transcend their status as passive victims, led us initially to become involved in this campaign, and also explain our subsequent decision to leave it. From the outset we found ourselves at odds with the politics and strategy that animated the campaign organizers, in particular their reluctance to take on board the issue of domestic violence and their desire to promote 'important men' as patrons of the campaign in a bid to give it social acceptability and defuse any 'feminist' connotations.

We were not happy with this framing of what is a critical issue for the women's movement. The focus on law and order as the fundamental problem was, in our view, born out of a partisan politics that sought to use the campaign to mobilize against the government in power. It reflected neither an analysis of the patriarchal power relations that permitted, condoned and even encouraged various forms of violence against women, both within the home and in the public domain, nor any intention of building a serious campaign against such violence. We welcomed the support of men, but not their leadership or patronage. We wanted the public face of the campaign to be female, and we wanted the campaign to project the image of women fighting back. We suggested that the campaign highlight positive programmes that contributed to reducing women's economic dependence. We also proposed the promotion of martial arts training for girls so they could defend themselves rather than wait passively for male protection. The slogan we mobilized our members around was *'nari nirjaton rukhbo shobey, haath achey hatiar hobey'* ('we will fight violence against women, our hands will be our weapons').

We also wanted to give space in the campaign to survivors of violence. Our proposal to have one such survivor speak at one of the main public meetings organized by the committee was turned down in favour of their chosen 'important' men. We did manage, however, through 'guerrilla action', to bring someone who had experienced such violence onstage and have her speak.[7] We felt that it was important to give those who were perceived as 'victims' the opportunity to take back control over their lives through such engagement in public action. However, our attempt to include the issue of domestic violence in the campaign agenda met with strong opposition, and we were effectively silenced.

The abrupt collapse of the campaign with the lifting of the government's ban on political activities confirmed to us that it had merely been a stick to beat the government with at a time when other sticks had been banned. This made us keenly aware of the use, and misuse, of women's issues to further partisan interests, and wary from an early stage about coalition politics. We have, since then, stayed clear of coalitions, and instead opted to work with others in alliances formed on the basis of shared stands on particular issues.

Action on acid violence

For reasons not fully understood, among the many different forms of violence against women in Bangladesh is the deliberate use of acid as a weapon. While this is not the most common form of violence, it is significant both because there is a much higher incidence of such attacks in Bangladesh than anywhere else in the world, and because of the horrific physical and psychological damage they can inflict. Given the importance of appearance to women's chances in life, and to their chances of marriage – long considered the only acceptable destiny for women in Bangladesh – the psychological damage can be particularly devastating.

In 1995, a journalist following up on the case of Nurun Nahar, a young girl who had been attacked by a rejected suitor, first drew Naripokkho's attention to the devastating effects of acid violence. Naripokkho mobilized government action to ensure that Nurun Nahar received appropriate medical treatment, and that those responsible for the attack were prosecuted. Above all, Naripokkho provided her with the emotional support she so badly needed not to give up on life.

In 1997, Naripokkho organized the first workshop of acid survivors. A total of nine young girls from different parts of the country and their mothers were invited to participate in the workshop. We were determined to avoid any media sensationalization of this event, so we decided not to inform the press about it. Instead, we focused our energies on arranging meetings with the ministers of health and family welfare, home affairs, women's affairs and law, justice and parliamentary affairs. We needed government action to ensure that these girls and others like them received appropriate medical treatment and that police investigation of the crime and prosecution of perpetrators was taken seriously. We also arranged a meeting with UNICEF to urge it to take on board what was largely (at that time) a form of violence targeting young girls.[8] These meetings succeeded in bringing home to ministers and government officials the severe consequences of this crime, and motivated them to make declarations about the serious nature of it and their intention to take stern action. UNICEF followed this up by supporting an initiative to set up the Bangladesh Acid Survivors Foundation in 1998, to provide support for acid survivors in the form of medical treatment, prosecution and rehabilitation.

Our encounter with acid survivors on this first occasion taught us a number of important lessons. First of all, our attention had been on the girls themselves, and on their mothers, because we thought they were the ones who suffered most from the attack itself and from dealing with its aftermath. However, at a meeting held at the start of the workshop to introduce the survivors and their families to members of Naripokkho, we found that many fathers and brothers had also come. We had not thought of inviting them at all.

As we went around the room introducing ourselves, some of the girls broke down, saying they wished they had died instead of having to live with the consequences of the attack. One girl in particular said she wanted to die because she could not stand the pain this had inflicted on her mother and her family. At this point, we were startled by a heart-rending cry from one of the young men, a brother. He broke into what can only be described as inconsolable weeping. Then the older man sitting next to him, a father, started crying. Soon we were all crying. Why hadn't we thought of the pain that fathers and brothers suffered? We understood then that our most important allies in the fight against violence against women were the fathers and brothers of women who had suffered.

The second thing that took us by surprise was when some of the family members asked that we organize a meeting of the acid survivors with the press. While we had been bending over backwards to avoid giving the media any opportunity for sensationalism, one of the fathers told us firmly, 'People need to see and know what kind of damage acid attacks can cause.' On the last day of the workshop, we organized a meeting with selected journalists who were known to us and who we felt would be sensitive. We also invited the Secretary of the Ministry of Women's Affairs.

At this meeting, the girls presented on a flip chart what they had identified during the workshop as the causes and consequences of such attacks, what their needs were, what they wanted to achieve and what they dreamed for themselves. It was front-page news the next day, and apart from one newspaper that actually printed a photograph of one of the girls at the flip chart, all the other papers carried close-ups of their badly disfigured faces. We had not been able to prevent the sensationalism we had feared. From then on it was a snowball effect: special features, television, CNN, ABC and so on. We tried wherever possible to inject our real and serious concerns about all forms of violence against women, but violence against women was too common an occurrence. The acid story, by contrast, had shock value.

Our focus in the workshop was to make these girls want to live again,

34 | Huq

411

and to know that there is a lot to live for. On their last evening with us, the Theatre Centre for Social Development – a theatre group that has been a friend and partner for Naripokkho through the years – organized an evening of entertainment. A drag show was followed by music, and a makeshift dance floor helped to transform these girls, who had become used to hiding behind veils and holding back from living, into young teenyboppers having fun. Selina's mother beamed as she watched her daughter, who had not spoken since the attack six months prior to the workshop, laugh and begin to speak a few words. Empowerment for these women has meant the journey from victim to survivor, and then from survivor to activist. We wanted not only to let the survivors find their voices but also to bring them into the movement against violence against women. The torchlight procession organized by Naripokkho on the eve of International Women's Day in 1998 was led by Bina, Nurun Nahar and Jhorna, victims who had made the journey to activists and no longer covered their faces.

Advocacy around services for women

The work with acid survivors saw an expansion of Naripokkho's activism from protest to advocacy. We lobbied the government for better services for women who had suffered violence, and for changes in both the policies and institutional arrangements through which services were delivered and justice administered. We began a new project called 'Monitoring state interventions to combat violence against women' in 1999; this has regularly monitored all twenty-two police stations in the Dhaka metropolitan area, the two major public hospitals (emergency, gynaecology, burns and forensic medicine departments) and the special court which tries all cases involving violence against women.

At quarterly meetings with service providers, findings from the monitoring are presented in a spirit of dialogue. Representatives from these institutions, together with Naripokkho, prepare recommendations for improvements, and the dialogue is sustained on the basis of trust. Naripokkho's commitment to constructive engagement with the problems has meant an unwritten agreement on our part not to publicize these findings in the media. It has also helped that we present this work as action research rather than as 'monitoring'. Most service providers put forward lack of resources as the major problem. While the resources issue is often a real one, and we do offer to lobby to address it, we also try to get providers to focus on their own behaviour and attitudes (identified by violence survivors as a primary problem).

Naripokkho has also been active around women's health and reproductive rights. The urgency attached to population control in the country had led to the imposition on family planning providers of numerical targets, a practice fraught with potential for abuse. In 1987, one of our members reported the death of a woman from tetanus infection following a sterilization operation in a Model Family Planning Clinic. Closer investigation revealed that the woman had actually approached the clinic for an abortion. The clinic staff decided she was a good candidate for sterilization and did not want to miss the opportunity of increasing their performance figures. Instead of giving her the anti-tetanus serum with her abortion, which would take a number of days to take effect and require her to come back for the sterilization, they decided to operate there and then.

This incident raised serious questions regarding the government's preoccupation with numerical targets over women's right to choose and the safe delivery of services. In 1989, we documented abuse in the Norplant[9] programme: doctors were reported to be refusing to remove the implant when women complained of side effects. Our concerns around safe contraception, reproductive rights and sexual freedom have come to be clustered around the theme 'shorir amaar shiddhanto amaar' ('my body, my decision').

In 1996, Naripokkho took up the issue of the accountability of health service providers to women on an experimental basis, in connection with monitoring the government's commitment to the Programme of Action of the International Conference on Population and Development (ICPD). Health constitutes a key arena of women's suffering, and represents the end results of discrimination, violence and inequality. Naripokkho sought to activate the Upazila Health Advisory Committee, set up by the government to monitor and improve health services at local level. This committee, composed of a cross-section of society, public representatives and government functionaries, proved to be effective in bringing about improvements, once activated.

Solidarity with sex workers

The rights of sex workers is another aspect of our politics of the body. Sex workers occupy an uneasy marginal status in Bangladeshi society. In a culture that is built on the repression of women's sexuality, confinement to the home, and marriage as women's ultimate destiny, sex workers appear to defy every precept of 'normal' Bengali womanhood. Although treated in the popular press as victims, they often appear to enjoy a peculiar autonomy denied to other women: they mix freely with men, they speak their minds assertively on television, they live on their own earnings, have children outside marriage and bring them up without male guardians, and even, occasionally, declare an active sexuality. Sex workers have appeared periodically in the media over the past decade because of attempts by the government or self-motivated groups of citizens to demolish brothels and evict their occupants.

The first threat of eviction that Naripokkho associated itself with was that of Tanbazaar in 1991. Although this threat was successfully resisted, six years later the Kandupatti brothel in old Dhaka was attacked and its residents were evicted by the hired musclemen of local vested interests. The most recent attempt took place in 1999, when the government evicted sex workers and their children from a complex of brothels, over a century old, located in the Tanbazaar and Nimtoli areas of Narayanganj. This action was met by an unprecedented mobilization of development NGOs and human rights organizations to defend the rights of sex workers. For the first time in the country's history, a major public debate took place in the newspapers over the meaning of sex work and the status of sex workers. All the major dailies carried news and features on the topic for nearly a month after the eviction.

The mobilization was led by Naripokkho and led to the formation of Shonghoti, a broad-based human rights alliance protesting against the government actions and demanding that sex workers be respected as citizens. Eighty-six organizations of various types joined Shonghoti. They provided active support in mobilizing protests against the unlawful eviction, as well as assistance for those rendered homeless. The formation of Shonghoti marks a new chapter in the struggle for women's rights as human rights in Bangladesh. However, the successful alliance-building effort of 1999 had a ten-year history behind it, involving various attempts at brothel evictions and Naripokkho's encounter and *porichiti*[10] with sex workers.

The public response to sex work has conventionally taken two forms: moral condemnation of 'loose' women, or moral benevolence towards 'hapless' victims. In 1991, women from Tanbazaar had themselves attempted to claim their rights as citizens, as workers and as women, and condemned attempts to evict them as violations of these rights. Their voice at that time, however, was drowned by the dominant discourses of moral outrage and benevolence. In the ensuing ten years, however, their assertion of their citizenship has been heard several times; finally in 1999 it found a place both within the struggle for universal human rights and women's emancipation, and in the public discourse on prostitution.

Recognition of the human rights of all, including women engaged in prostitution, brought the issue of work and what constitutes work to the centre of the public debate. This has been a thorny issue for many, including Shonghoti members. Even as we declared unequivocal support for upholding the rights of women in prostitution, we were arguing over some basic questions among ourselves. Can sex be considered work? If sex in prostitution is work, then is sex in marriage work as well? If sex in prostitution is not work, then what is it? Naripokkho's strategy in trying to hold together this unprecedented mobilization of a diverse range of organizations was to deliberately avoid public discussion of these issues. It was felt that public debate on this complex issue carried the danger of prompting simplistic public stands and unnecessary polarization. Instead, we focused our campaigning on the human rights of sex workers, their status as citizens, the rights of citizenship and the obligations of the state.

Talking to sex workers, however, has left us in no doubt that for them sex *is* work, sometimes pleasurable, more often not. Moreover, it is work that offers higher returns for their labour than many other work opportunities available to poor women with no assets of their own.

And finally ... working on ourselves

Public claiming of rights, and accountability, are important aspects of the assertion of women's citizenship in a culture where women are defined as dependants, politically, culturally and economically, and where they are expected to accept their position without protest. However, while a great deal of our energy as an organization has been devoted to body politics in the public domain, we have also accepted from the outset that our own bodies were implicated in this politics in particular ways.

Our beginnings in the shared life experiences of women working in development NGOs focused our subsequent work in particular ways, and helped to bring a different dimension into the politics of gender in development, based on the concrete experiences of discrimination, inequality and resistance of women development workers themselves. This raises uncomfortable issues around the 'culture' and body politics of development organizations, including issues of sexual harassment, recognition of women's reproductive and caring responsibilities, and issues of physical security. Naripokkho has brought discussion of these issues, previously relegated to the realm of the personal – and hence the private – into the realm of the professional – hence public – domain, raising them as matters that NGOs had to address within their own organizational structures: a process not always welcomed by the organizations in question.

We have also used our workshops to think through the politics of our own bodies. We try to provide participants with a variety of skills that will strengthen their self-confidence in the public domain, such as chairing sessions (a function normally monopolized by men), taking responsibility for devising cultural events and producing a daily 'wallpaper' bulletin. Above all, we use workshops to give them a place to be themselves – the selves they have not been allowed to be. They write and draw whatever they wish on the wallpaper provided. The cultural sessions provide them with a space to sing, dance, recite poetry and generally express the imaginative side of themselves. The idea of 'play' does not feature much in women's lives in Bangladesh, and in many parts of the country they are not permitted to sing and dance. Allowing themselves to throw off their inhibitions, to let their bodies move as they wish and not worry about how their saris fall is an exhilarating experience for many of the women, who have been brought up since childhood to take up as little space in the world as possible.

These workshops have produced over time a body of testimonies that provide us with the knowledge, anger and conviction to fight 'for women', as well as with the hope, energy and inspiration to do so in a way that remains true to our collective voice. Looking back on over two decades of activism, we find that our interactions with each other, our willingness to stand out against mainstream ideas about women's politics, our determination to counter cultural ascriptions of passivity to women – the *bhadramahila*[11] paradigm that mainstream women's organizations continue to operate within – have given us an energy that makes us appear bold and uninhibited to the wider public. This public perception was brought to our attention by journalists covering our movement against the 8th Amendment to the Constitution, which sought to make Islam the state religion. They commented on the speed with which we took our first procession down from Shahid Minar to the Press Club. What they did not know, however, was that this was not entirely intentional. Because of our inexperience with banners, we had not cut holes in them for the wind to pass through, so they caught the wind and the procession sailed through the streets of Dhaka at an amazing speed. The predominant image of Naripokkho members since then has been one of women 'with saris worn high and no make-up', moving with an agility out of keeping with the customary decorous walk expected of women.

Although we are perceived as a threat to the established paradigm of how women should behave, we have also invoked a reluctant admiration. Our energy, our apparent audacity, our *'damn care bhaab'* ('couldn't give a damn attitude') have been described by many of our friends and colleagues outside the movement as possessing a certain appeal – *'bhalo lagey kintu bhoyo lagey'* ('attractive but dangerous'). The causes we take up and the politics we bring to them have reinforced this public image. In particular, our decision to take up the cause of the 'bazaar women', a despised social group living on the margins of society but apparently exercising some degree of autonomy in their lives, appears as yet another example, to those who disapprove of us, of our willingness to flout convention and align ourselves with women who deserve pity or condemnation perhaps, but certainly not the solidarity one extends to one's own kind.

[Originally published in Naila Kabeer (ed.), *Inclusive Citizenship: Meanings and Expressions*, Zed Books, 2005]

Acknowledgements

I wish to express my gratitude to Professor Naila Kabeer and Professor John Gaventa at the Institute of Development Studies, Sussex, for insisting that activists can write and not giving up on me, and especially to Naila for insisting that the Naripokkho story needed to be heard and helping to pull out a coherent piece from the longer 'stream of consciousness' narrative I had embarked on.

Notes

1 Naripokkho means 'pro women'.

2 There has been a considerable expansion in the scale – and visibility – of female employment since that workshop. The erosion of male incomes, the rising cost of living, the pressure on women to contribute to household income and the emergence of new opportunities for them to do so – particularly in the export-oriented garment industry, but also within the NGO sector itself – have all led to a far more visible involvement by women in paid work.

3 We often observe that Naripokkho began as it meant to go on: by challenging externally determined agendas to create a space for women to find their own voice.

4 There are two revealing equations at work here. There is the explicit equation between the behaviour of a wife wanting sexual pleasure and that of a prostitute. The second equation is implicit in the colloquial use of the term 'bajaarer meyelok', which literally means 'woman from the marketplace', to describe women in prostitution. In other words, women who go out to work (enter the marketplace) can only be selling sexual services.

5 The bari is the shared compound in which members of an extended family reside, usually in independent houses.

6 In fact, Naripokkho's study on violence against women, conducted during 1995–97, found that 60 per cent of the women interviewed across all classes had experienced conjugal violence, and that 63 per cent of violence-related injuries requiring hospitalization occurred within the home.

7 We had the support of a leading woman lawyer in Bangladesh who was a speaker at this meeting, and who at the end of her speech invited the survivor to come onstage and address the auditorium. It was not possible at this point for the organizers to intercept her.

8 Acid is now used as a weapon for vengeance in all kinds of enmity arising out of marital discord and dowry demands, family feuds and land disputes and the number of male victims is on the increase.

9 Norplant is a contraceptive implant, which has to be surgically placed and removed.

10 The Bangla word porichiti can mean both 'acquaintance' and 'identity'. Interestingly for Naripokkho, it was both an acquaintance and identification with sex workers.

11 The bhadramahila is the equivalent of the Victorian gentlewoman. Historically the term refers to the women of the bhadrolok class (gentry), a Western-educated urban middle class whose emergence in mid-nineteenth-century Kolkata was characterized by a break with the feudal class.

35 | Citizenship: a perverse confluence

Evelina Dagnino

Citizenship has become an increasingly recurrent term in the political vocabularies of social movements, and more recently NGOs, governments, and international development agencies. In Latin America, its emergence is linked with the experiences of social movements during the late 1970s and 1980s, reinforced by democratization efforts, especially in those countries still under authoritarian or military regimes. It swiftly became a common reference point among a range of social movements such as those of women, black people and ethnic minorities, gays, older people, consumers, environmentalists, urban and rural workers, and those organized around urban issues such as decent housing, health, education, unemployment and violence (Foweraker 1995; Alvarez et al. 1998).

For Latin American social movements, the reference to citizenship was not only a useful tool in their own specific struggles but also a powerful link among them. The general claim for equal rights already embedded in the conventional concept of citizenship was both expanded and given particular meanings in relation to specific claims. The process of redefinition placed a strong emphasis on the cultural dimension of citizenship, incorporating contemporary concerns with subjectivities, identities and the right to difference. This new citizenship was seen as reaching far beyond the acquisition of legal rights: it depended on citizens being active social subjects, defining their rights, and struggling for these rights to be recognized. At the same time, the emphasis on culture asserted the need for a radical transformation of cultural practices that reproduce social inequality and exclusion.

As a result of its growing influence, citizenship soon became a contested concept in Latin America (Dagnino 2004). From the 1990s onwards, it has been appropriated by the elites and by the state to encompass a variety of meanings. In the neoliberal perspective, citizenship is understood primarily as the integration of individuals into the market, while at the same time previously acquired rights, in particular labour rights, are being progressively eroded. Meanwhile, in response to increasing poverty and social exclusion, there has been a resurgence of philanthropic endeavours from the so-called Third Sector, which convey their own version of citizenship.

The contested definitions of citizenship are the principal axis of political struggles in Latin America today, a reflection of the confrontation between a democratizing, participatory project to extend the meaning of citizenship and the neoliberal offensive to curtail any such possibility. In this article, I draw on the experience of Brazil in relation to these issues in order to highlight the challenges and contradictions to be addressed in using the term citizenship in international development discourse.

A perverse confluence

Today's democratization processes are locked in a perverse confluence of two distinct political projects. On the one hand, many countries have seen the increasing involvement of civil society in discussion and decision-making about public policy. In Brazil, in particular, efforts to enlarge democracy through participation have been recognized and incorporated in the 1988 constitution. As a result, the confrontational relations between the state and civil society have been largely replaced by an investment by social movements in the possibility of joint initiatives and in institutional participation in the newly created participatory spaces (see, for example, Abers 1998; Dagnino et al. 1998; Fedozzi 1997; Santos 1998). At the same time, neoliberal governments throughout Latin America are bent on achieving a reduced, minimal state[1] that progressively abandons its role in guaranteeing universal rights by rolling back its social responsibilities and transferring them to civil society, now envisaged as a mere implementer of social policies.

The perverse nature of the confluence between the participatory and the neoliberal projects lies in the fact that both not only require a vibrant and proactive civil society, but also share several core notions, such as citizenship, participation and civil society, albeit used with very different meanings. The common vocabulary and shared institutional mechanisms obscure fundamental distinctions and divergences. The apparent homogeneity conceals conflict and contradictions by displacing dissonant meanings.

The neoliberal project has also redefined meanings in the cultural sphere. The notion of citizenship offers perhaps the most dramatic case of how such meanings are displaced. First, because it was precisely through the notion of citizenship that the participatory project managed to achieve its most important political and cultural gains, to the extent of generating an innovative definition that has penetrated deep into Brazil's political and cultural fabric (Dagnino 1994a; Dagnino et al. 1998). And second because such a displacement determines how the most critical challenge facing Latin America – inequality and poverty – is addressed.

Participatory citizenship

Citizenship came to prominence as a crucial weapon in the struggle against social and economic exclusion and inequality, and in broadening the prevailing conception of politics. Thus, the struggles for a deepening of democracy that were undertaken by social movements in Latin America sought to redefine citizenship by challenging the existing definition of what constituted the political arena – its participants, its institutions, its processes, its agenda and its scope (Alvarez et al. 1998).

Adopting as its point of departure the notion of a right to have rights, this new definition of citizenship enabled new social subjects to identify what they considered to be their rights and to struggle for their recognition. In contrast to a view of citizenship as a strategy by the elites and by the state for the gradual and limited political incorporation of excluded sectors of society, or as a legal and political condition necessary for the establishment of capitalism, this is a definition of non-citizens, of the excluded: a citizenship 'from below'.

Much of the attraction of citizenship and its core category of rights lies in the dual role that it has played in the debates on democracy that characterize contemporary politics in Latin America. The struggle for the recognition and extension of rights helped to make the argument for the expansion and deepening of democracy much more concrete. And the reference to citizenship provided common ground and shared principles for a huge diversity of social movements that adopted the language of rights as a way to express their demands. This in turn helped these movements to avoid fragmentation and isolation. Thus the building of citizenship was always conceived as a struggle for the expansion of democracy that could incorporate both a broad range of demands and particular concrete struggles for rights, such as the rights to housing, education and healthcare, whose achievement would further deepen democracy.

The focus of social movements on the need to assert the right to have rights is clearly related to extreme levels of poverty and exclusion, but also to the pervasive authoritarianism and hierarchical organization of Brazilian society. Class, race and gender differences have historically underpinned the social classification that pervades our cultures by establishing each person's 'place' in the social hierarchy. Thus, for marginalized sectors, the political relevance of cultural meanings that are embedded in social practices is part of their daily life. As in most Latin American societies, to be poor means not only to experience economic or material deprivation, but also to submit to cultural rules that convey a complete lack of recognition of poor people as subjects, bearers of rights. In what Telles (1994) called the incivility embedded in that tradition, poverty is a sign of inferiority, a form of existence that makes it impossible for individuals to exercise their rights. The cultural deprivation imposed by the absolute absence of rights – which is essentially the denial of human dignity – finds its expression in material deprivation and political exclusion.

The perception of cultural social authoritarianism as a dimension of exclusion, in addition to economic inequality and political subordination, constituted a significant element in the struggle to redefine citizenship. First, it made clear that the struggle for rights, for the right to have rights, had to be a political struggle, thus enabling the urban popular movements to establish the link between culture and politics which became embedded in their collective action. The experience of the Assembléia do Povo (People's Assembly) from 1979 to the early 1980s, a movement of *favelados* (shanty-town dwellers) in Campinas in the state of São Paulo, illustrates this. Right from the start of their struggle for the 'right to the use of the land', *favelados* knew that they would have to struggle first for their very right to have rights. Thus, their first public initiative was to ask the media to publicize the results of their own survey of the *favelas*, in order to show the city that they were not idlers, misfits or prostitutes, as they were assumed to be, but decent working citizens who therefore should be seen as bearers of rights (Dagnino 1994b).

Making this connection made it possible to establish alliances with other social movements – such as ethnic, feminist, gay, ecological and human-rights movements – in seeking more egalitarian social relations and helping to articulate a distinctive, enlarged view of democracy. Rights and citizenship (Santos 1979) became the core of a common ethical–political field in which many of these movements and other sectors could share and reinforce each other's struggles. For instance, the emergence of the Sindicato Cidadão (Citizen Trade Unions) in the early 1990s shows that this vision penetrated even the Brazilian labour movement (Rodrigues 1997), traditionally associated with a more strictly class-based stance.

Second, the broader scope of citizenship went far beyond the formal legal acquisition of a set of rights within the political–judicial system. Rather, it represented a project for a new sociability: a more egalitarian way of organizing all social relations, new rules for living together in society (new ways to deal with conflicts, and a new sense of a public order, of public responsibility, a renewed social contract), and not only the incorporation into the political system in the strict sense. More egalitarian social relations imply recognizing the other as having valid interests and rights, and the constitution of a public domain in which rights determine the parameters for discussion, debate and the negotiation of conflicts, thus bringing in an ethical dimension to social relations. Such a vision is profoundly unsettling for both the social authoritarianism that characterizes Brazilian society and for more recent neoliberal discourses that elevate the importance of private interests at the expense of an ethical dimension to social life (Telles 1994).

Third, once rights are no longer limited to legal provisions, access to existing rights or the implementation of formal rights, it is possible to include new rights that emerge from specific struggles or campaigns. In this sense, the definition of rights and the assertion of something as a right become themselves the objects of political struggle. The rights to autonomy over one's own body, to environmental protection or to housing, for instance, illustrate something of the diversity of these new rights. The inclusion not only of the right to equality, but also the right to difference, specifies, deepens and broadens the right to equality (Dagnino 1994a).

Fourth, an additional element in this redefinition transcends a central reference in the liberal concept of citizenship: the claim to access, inclusion, membership and belonging to an already given political system. What is really at stake in struggles for citizenship in Brazil is more than the right to be included as a full member of society; it is the right to participate in the very definition of that society and its political system, to define what we want to be members of. The direct participation of civil society and social movements in state decisions constitutes one of the most crucial aspects in the redefinition of citizenship, because it conveys a potential for radical transformations in the structure of power relations that characterize Latin American societies.

A further consequence of such a broadening in scope is that citizenship is no longer confined to the relationship between the individual and the state, but becomes a parameter for all social relations. This may be more evident for social movements of women, blacks or gays, for example, since such a significant part of their struggles is concerned with fighting the discrimination and prejudice that they face in every aspect of daily life. The process of building citizenship as the affirmation and recognition of rights was seen as a way to transform deeply embedded social practices. Such a political strategy implies moral and intellectual reform: a process of social learning, of building new kinds of social relations in which citizens become active social subjects. It also means that all members of society have to learn to live on different terms with citizens who refuse to accept the social and cultural places previously ascribed to them.

Social movements, whether organized around basic claims such as housing, water, sewerage, education and healthcare, or broader interests such as those of women, blacks or ecological movements, emphasized that citizenship meant the constitution of active social subjects who can thus become political actors. Some even defined citizenship as consisting of this very process. Thus consciousness, agency and the capacity to struggle are evidence of one's citizenship, even if other rights are absent. Among fifty-one activists interviewed in Campinas, São Paulo, in 1993, most members of popular movements and of workers' unions expressed this view. By contrast, answering the same question – 'Why do you consider yourself a citizen?' – members of business organizations stressed the fact that they 'fulfil their duties' and 'have rights', whereas the middle-class activists highlighted their 'position in society', derived from their professional activities, as indicators of citizenship. Interestingly, while a large majority of these two sectors considered that they were treated as citizens, a similar majority of those belonging to social movements and workers' unions expressed the opposite view (Dagnino 1998: 40–41).

The role of the social movements of the 1970s and 1980s in shaping this redefinition of citizenship is obviously rooted in their own struggles and practices. Although they drew on a history of rights that had given rise to regulated citizenship (Santos 1979), they reacted against the conception of the state and of power embedded in that history. They also reacted against the control and tutelage of the political organization of popular sectors by the state, political parties and politicians. Their conception of rights and citizenship embodied a reaction against previous notions of rights as favours and/or objects of bargain with the powerful (as in the case of citizenship by concession, *cidadania concedida*) (Sales 1994). In this sense, the struggle for rights, also influenced by the 1970s human-rights movements against the military regime, encapsulated not only claims for equality but the negation of a dominant political culture deeply rooted in Brazilian society.

This notion of citizenship and the participation of civil society as a mechanism for its extension were formally recognized in the 1988 constitution. The Collor government, brought to power in 1989, began the move to neoliberalism, which reached its peak under Cardoso from 1994 to 2002, and created what we have referred to as the perverse confluence between the two political projects. Citizenship was once again redefined in neoliberal terms, in order to neutralize the meanings that the term had acquired in its use by social movements while trying to retain its symbolic power.

Neoliberal versions of citizenship

Some neoliberal definitions of citizenship retrieve the traditional liberal conception, while others address new elements in the contemporary political and social configurations in Latin America. First, the collective meaning given by the social movements is reduced to a strictly individualistic understanding. Second, neoliberal discourses establish an alluring connection between citizenship and the market. To be a citizen is equated with individual integration in the market, as a consumer and as a producer. This seems to be the basic principle underlying the vast number of projects to enable people to 'acquire citizenship': that is to say, to learn how to start up micro-enterprises, or how to become qualified for the few jobs still available. As the state retreats from its role as guarantor of rights, the market is offered as a surrogate for citizenship. Hence, social rights enshrined in the Brazilian constitution since the 1940s and reaffirmed in 1988 are now being eliminated, on the grounds that they impede the freedom of the market and therefore restrict economic development and modernization. This rationale effectively casts bearers of rights/ citizens as unpatriotic, privileged enemies of political reforms intended to shrink state responsibilities. Previously guaranteed rights to social services are increasingly viewed as commodities to be purchased by those who can afford them. This effectively turns the market into a surrogate for citizenship, the incarnation of modernizing virtues and the sole route for the Latin American dream: inclusion in the First World.

A further aspect of neoliberal versions of citizenship is in the formulation of social policies on poverty and inequality. Many of the struggles organized around the demand for equal rights and the extension of citizenship focused on how such policies should be defined. The participation of social movements and other sectors of civil society was a fundamental claim in the struggles for citizenship, in the belief that this would contribute to social policies that would ensure that all citizens enjoyed universal rights. With the rolling back of the state, these social policies are increasingly formulated as emergency responses for those whose very survival is at risk. The targets of these policies are not seen as citizens who are entitled to rights but as 'needy' (*carentes*) human beings requiring public or private charity. In the face of the gravity and urgency of the situation, reinforced by cuts in social spending, many sectors of civil society called upon to participate in the name of 'building citizenship' choose to subordinate their belief in the universality of rights and surrender to the immediate practical possibility of helping a handful of the destitute.

The notion of a 'Third Sector' (the others being the State and the Market) as a surrogate for civil society is particularly expressive of this attempt to implement a 'minimalist' politics and to collapse the public spaces for political deliberation that had been opened up by the democratizing struggles of previous decades (Avritzer 2002). The relationship between the state and NGOs exemplifies this perverse confluence. Endowed with technical competence and social insertion as 'reliable' interlocutors in civil society, NGOs are frequently seen as the ideal partners to assume the responsibilities handed over by the state to civil society or to the private sector (see also Alvarez 1999 for the impact of this process in depoliticizing feminist organizations in Brazil). Parallel to this is the government's tendency to 'criminalize' social movements that remain combative and well organized, such as the Landless Movement (MST) and some trade unions. Reinforced by the mass media and international aid agencies, there is a growing sense that 'civil society' is synonymous with NGOs, if not equated with the 'Third Sector'. In this scheme of things, 'civil society' is thus reduced to those sectors whose behaviour is 'acceptable' to the government, or to what one analyst referred to as 'the five-star civil society' (Silva 2001).

Conclusion

This analysis has important consequences for the contested conceptions of citizenship, such as the displacement of issues such as poverty and inequality: in being addressed solely as technical or philanthropic issues, poverty and inequality are effectively withdrawn from the public (political) arena and so from the proper domain of justice, equality and citizenship, and reduced to a problem of ensuring minimum conditions for survival.

Moreover, the solution to the problem of poverty and inequality is presented as an individual moral duty. The idea of a collective solidarity that underlies the classical reference to rights and citizenship is being replaced by an understanding of solidarity as a strictly private moral responsibility. This is why civil society is being urged to engage in voluntary and philanthropic work. It is no coincidence that voluntary work is becoming the favourite hobby of the Brazilian middle class. This understanding of citizenship also accords with that held by corporate foundations. Seeking to maximize profits while also nurturing a public image of 'social responsibility', these foundations also view solidarity as a question of individual ethics, with no reference to universal rights or to the political debate on the causes of poverty and inequality.

This 're-signification' of the notions of citizenship and solidarity blocks off their political dimension and erodes the sense of public responsibility and public interest that had been so hard won in the democratizing struggles of Brazil's recent past. As the targeted distribution of social services and benefits comes to occupy the place formerly held by rights and citizenship, so the institutional channels through which to claim rights are closed down; instead, distribution depends only on the goodwill and competence of those involved. It becomes increasingly difficult, therefore, even to formulate the notion of rights within the public sphere (Telles 2001). The symbolic importance of rights as the cornerstone of an egalitarian society is thus being dismissed in favour of social relations based on individualism.

A second set of consequences relates to the participation of civil society, another central plank of the democratizing project that has been re-signified. While the neoliberal project requires the participation of civil society, this increasingly means that organizations of civil society take over the role of the state in providing services. The effective sharing of decision-making power, i.e. the full exercise of citizenship as conceived by democratizing forces, takes place in most cases within the limits of a neoliberal framework, with decision-making power remaining the preserve of the 'strategic nucleus' of the state (Bresser-Pereira 1999). The political meaning of participation has thus been reduced to management, and related concerns with efficiency and 'client satisfaction' have come to replace the political debate on inequality and social justice.

The perverse confluence described here constitutes a minefield in which sectors of civil society, including NGOs, that do not support the project of the minimal state, feel deceived when, motivated by the shared vocabulary of citizenship, they get involved in initiatives with government sectors that are committed to rolling back the state. Many of the social movements that participate in public spaces to formulate public policies share the same reaction. Some of them define this situation as a dilemma, and several contemplate rejecting altogether any further joint initiatives, or being extremely cautious with respect to the correlation of forces within these initiatives and the concrete possibilities opened by them (Dagnino 2002).

Under an apparent homogeneity of discourse, what is at stake in these spaces is the advancement or retreat of very different political projects and conceptions of citizenship. Although the election in 2002 of Luís Inácio Lula da Silva of the Workers' Party (PT) renewed hopes that the democratic participatory project would advance, his broad coalition government has not been immune to the effects of the perverse confluence described in this article. Ironically, since the PT itself emerged in the 1980s as a result of civil society's struggles around the building of citizenship, the government's social policies – an increase in their number and scope notwithstanding – are still largely following the same neoliberal directions. Resolving the perverse confluence and reaffirming a radical conception of citizenship is the difficult and urgent task now facing social movements and democratic sectors of civil society.

[Originally published in *Development in Practice*, 17(4), 2007, pp. 549–56]

Note

1 Clearly, this state is only selectively minimal: it is minimal regarding social policies towards the poor, but not with respect to the protection of capitalist interests, as in the case of government efforts to save banks from financial failure.

References

Abers, R. (1998) 'From clientelism to cooperation: local government, participatory policy, and civic organizing in Porto Alegre, Brazil', *Politics and Society*, 26(4): 511–37.

Alvarez, S. E. (1999) 'Advocating feminism: the Latin American feminist NGO "boom"', *International Feminist Journal of Politics*, 1(2): 181–209.

Alvarez, S. E., E. Dagnino and A. Escobar (eds) (1998) *Cultures of Politics/Politics of Cultures: Revisioning Latin American Social Movements*, Boulder, CO: Westview Press.

Avritzer, L. (2002) *Democracy and Public Spaces in Latin America*, Princeton, NJ: Princeton University Press.

Bresser-Pereira, L. C. (1999) 'From bureaucratic to managerial: public administration in Brazil', in L. C. Bresser-Pereira and P. Spink (eds), *Reforming the State: Managerial Public Administration in Latin America*, Boulder, CO: Lynne Rienner, pp. 115–46.

Dagnino, E. (1994a) 'Os movimentos sociais e a emergência de uma nova noção de cidadania', in E. Dagnino (ed.), *Os Anos 90: Política e Sociedade no Brasil*, São Paulo: Brasiliense.

— (1994b) 'On becoming a citizen: the story of D. Marlene', in R. Benmayor and A. Skotnes (eds), *International Yearbook of Oral History and Life Stories*, Oxford: Oxford University Press.

— (1998) 'Culture, citizenship, and democracy: changing discourses and practices of the Latin American left', in S. Alvarez, E. Dagnino and A. Escobar (eds), *Cultures of Politics/Politics of Cultures: Revisioning Latin American Social Movements*, Boulder, CO: Westview Press.

— (2002) *Sociedade Civil e Espaços Públicos no Brasil*, São Paulo: Paz e Terra.

— (2004) 'Sociedade civil, participação e cidadania: de que estamos falando?', in D. Mato and I. García (eds), *Políticas de Ciudadania y Sociedad Civil en Tiempos de Globalización*, Caracas: Universidad Central de Venezuela.

Dagnino, E., A. C. Chaves Teixeira, D. Romanelli da Silva and U. Ferlim (1998) 'Cultura democrática e cidadania', *Opinião Pública*, V(1), November, pp. 11–43.

Fedozzi, L. (1997) *Orçamento Participativo – Reflexões sobre a experiência de Porto Alegre*, Porto Alegre: Tomo Editorial/FASE.

Foweraker, J. (1995) *Theorizing Social Movements*, London: Pluto Press.

Rodrigues, I. J. (1997) *Sindicalismo e Política: A Trajetória da CUT*, São Paulo: Scritta/ FAPESP.

Sales, T. (1994) 'Raízes da desigualdade social na cultura Brasileira', *Revista Brasileira de Ciências Sociais (ANPOCS)*, 9(25): 26–37.

Santos, B. de Souza (1998) 'Participatory budgeting in Porto Alegre: toward a redistributive democracy', *Politics and Society*, 26(4): 461–510.

Santos, W. G. dos (1979) *Cidadania e Justiça*, Rio de Janeiro: Campus.

Silva, C. A. (2001) Comment during a debate transcribed in *Os Movimentos Sociais, a Sociedade Civil e o 'Terceiro Setor' na América Latina: Reflexões Teóricas e Novas Perspectivas* (co-ed. with S. E. Alvarez), 1st edn October 1998, Campinas: IFCH/ UNICAMP, pp. 1–77.

Telles, V. da Silva (1994) 'A sociedade civil e a construção de um espaço público', in E. Dagnino (ed.), *Os Anos 90: Política e Sociedade no Brasil*, São Paulo: Brasiliense.

— (2001) *Pobreza e Cidadania*, São Paulo: Editora 34.

Sources

1 S. R. Arnstein, 'A ladder of citizen participation', *The Journal of the American Institute of Planners*, 35(4), July 1969, pp. 216–24. By permission of Taylor & Francis.

2 M. Stiefel and M. Wolfe, *A Voice for the Excluded: Popular Participation in Development*, Zed Books, 1994, ch. 2.

3 N. C. Saxena, 'What is meant by people's participation?', *Journal of Rural Development*, 17(1), 1998, pp. 111–13.

4 J. Cohen and N. Uphoff, 'Participation's place in rural development: seeking clarity through specificity', *World Development*, 8, 1980, pp. 213–35. By permission of Elsevier.

5 S. C. White, 'Depoliticizing development: the uses and abuses of participation', *Development in Practice*, 6(1), 1996, pp. 6–15. By permission of Taylor & Francis.

6 P. A. Leal, 'Participation: the ascendancy of a buzzword in the neo-liberal era', *Development in Practice*, 17(4), 2007, pp. 539–48. By permission of Taylor & Francis.

7 O. Fals Borda, 'Learning to recognize oneself', in *Knowledge and People's Power: Lessons with Peasants in Nicaragua, Mexico and Colombia*, Indian Social Institute, New Delhi, 1985, ch. 4.

8 R. Tandon, 'The historical roots and contemporary tendencies in participatory research: the implications for health care', in Korrie de Koning and Marion Martin (eds), *Participatory Research in Health*, Zed Books, 1996, ch. 2.

9 'New Paradigm Research Manifesto', available at http://www.peterreason.eu/Papers/New_Paradigm_Manifesto.pdf. By permission of Peter Reason.

10 P. Maguire, 'Proposing a more feminist participatory research: knowing and being embraced openly', in Korrie de Koning and Marion Martin (eds), *Participatory Research in Health*, Zed Books, 1996, ch. 3.

11 P. Reason, 'Cooperative inquiry', in Jonathan A. Smith (ed.), *Qualitative Psychology: A Practical Guide to Methods*, SAGE Publications, 2008, ch. 10. By permission of SAGE.

12 R. Chambers and I. Guijt, 'PRA five years later', *Forests, Trees and People Newsletter*, 26/27, April 2005, pp. 4–15.

13 I. Scoones, 'PRA and anthropology: challenges and dilemmas', *PLA Notes*, 24, 1995, pp. 17–20.

14 J. Symes and S. Jasser, 'Growing from the grassroots: building participatory planning, monitoring and evaluation methods in PARC', *PLA Notes*, 31, 1998, pp. 57–61.

15 S. Patel, 'Tools and methods for empowerment developed by slum and pavement dwellers' federations in India', *PLA Notes*, 50, pp. 117–30.

16 T. Wakeford, 'Citizens juries: a radical alternative for social research', *Social Research Update*, Issue 37, summer 2002 (biography revised November 2005). *Social Research Update* is published by Department of Sociology, University of Surrey, Guildford GU7 7XH, United Kingdom. Tel.: +44 (0) 1 483 300800; Fax: +44 (0) 1 483 689551. Edited by Nigel Gilbert. © University of Surrey.

17 O. S. Abah, 'Voices aloud: making communication and change together', *PLA Notes*, 50, 2004, pp. 45–52.

18 S. Stuart and R. Bery, 'Powerful grassroots women communicators: participatory video in Bangladesh', in Donna Allen, Ramona R. Rush

and Susan J. Kaufman (eds), *Women Transforming Communications: Global Intersections*, SAGE Publications, 1996. By permission of SAGE.

19 R. Chambers, 'Managing local participation: rhetoric and reality', in *Managing Rural Development*, Kumarian, 1986, ch. 4. By permission of the Nordic Africa Institute.

20 J. Midgley, 'Community participation: history, concepts and controversies', in *Community Participation, Social Development and the State*, Methuen, 1986, ch. 1 By permission of the author.

21 D. Mosse, 'The making and marketing of participatory development', in Philip Quarles van Ufford and Ananta Giri (eds), *A Moral Critique of Development: In Search of Global Responsibilities*, Routledge, 2003, pp. 43–75. By permission of Taylor & Francis.

22 A. Cornwall, 'Whose voices? Whose choices? Reflections on gender and participatory development', *World Development*, 31(8), August 2003, pp. 1325–42. By permission of Elsevier.

23 T. Mompati and G. Prinsen, 'Ethnicity and participatory development methods in Botswana: some participants are to be seen and not heard', *Development in Practice*, 10(5), November 2000, pp. 625–37. By permission of Taylor & Francis.

24 G. Williams, 'Towards a repoliticization of participatory development: political capabilities and spaces of empowerment', in Samuel Hickey and Giles Mohan (eds), *Participation: From Tyranny to Transformation*, Zed Books, 2004, ch. 6.

25 J. Gaventa, 'Towards participatory local governance: six propositions for discussion', Background paper prepared for the Ford Foundation Local Governance network retreat at Buxted Park, Sussex, June 13-15, 2001 (see www.logolink.org). By permission of the author.

26 R. Mohanty, 'Gendered subjects, the state and participatory spaces: the politics of domesticating participation in rural India', in Andrea Cornwall and Vera Schattan Coelho (eds), *Spaces for Change*, Zed Books, 2007, ch. 4.

27 This chapter was written for this reader.

28 J. Ribot, 'Participation without representation: chiefs, councils and forestry law in the West African Sahel', *Cultural Survival Quarterly*, 20(3), 1996, pp. 40–44. By permission of the Cultural Survival Quarterly.

29 G. Baocchi, 'Emergent public spheres: talking politics in participatory governance', *American Sociological Review*, 68, February 2003, pp. 52–74. By permission of the American Sociological Association.

30 J. Ackerman, 'Co-governance for accountability: beyond "exit" and "voice"', *World Development*, 32(3), 2004, pp. 447–63. By permission of Elsevier.

31 M. Barnes, 'Users as citizens: collective action and the local governance of welfare', *Social Policy and Administration*, 33(1), 1999, pp. 73–90. By permission of John Wiley and Sons.

32 F. Miraftab and S. Wills, 'Insurgency and spaces of active citizenship: the story of Western Cape anti-eviction campaign in South Africa', *Journal of Planning Education and Research*, 25(2), 2005, pp. 200–17. By permission of SAGE Publications.

33 J. Johnston, 'Pedagogical guerrillas, armed democrats, and revolutionary counterpublics: examining paradox in the Zapatista uprising in Chiapas Mexico', *Theory and Society*, 29(4), 2000, pp. 463–505. By permission of Springer.

34 S. Huq, 'Bodies as sites of struggle: Naripokkho and the movement for women's rights in Bangladesh', in Naila Kabeer (ed.), *Inclusive Citizenship: Meanings and Expressions*, Zed Books, 2005, ch. 10.

35 E. Dagnino, 'Citizenship: a perverse confluence', *Development in Practice*, 17(4), 2007, pp. 549–56. By permission of Taylor & Francis.

Index

Kropotkin, Peter, 173

land reform, 168
land rights, 294
land seizures, 396
Landless Movement (MST) (Brazil), 424
Laura from Porto Alegre, 311
leadership, 104, 159; informal, 49
learning: through participation, 32; through risk-taking, 92
learning loop, 128–9
legal aid, 154; for women, 150
legal procedures, as claim-making channels, 373
Lele, Uma, 40–1
Lesotho, development in, 239
Lewin, Kurt, 89
liberation theology, 310, 311, 388
Life Struggle of Aleya, The, video, 158, 160
linkage diagrams, 117
Lipton, M., 173
Lister, R., 354
literacy, 21, 49, 154, 156 *see also* illiteracy
livelihood impact studies, 197
local, contestation of, 261–3
local leaders, 48–9
local level, going beyond, 159–61
local residents, as category, 48
Locke, John, 40
logical framework analysis (LFA), 129, 184, 186
Lopez, Sebastian, 396–7
Lovenduski, J., 358
low-intensity warfare, against Zapatistas, 388–9, 400
Lummis, C. D., 392

Magna Carta, 134
Maharastra Employment Guarantee Scheme (India), 245
Mahila Milan savings cooperative (India), 131
mainstreaming of participation, 57–8, 238–40
Make Poverty History campaign, 286
male bias in participatory research literature, 96
Mali: forestry laws in, 300–1; participatory forestry in, 297–305; Rural Wood Management Structure, 300–1
malope a kgosi, 229

Mamdani, Mahmood, 366
management of participation practices, 165–71, 190
Mandela Park (South Africa), 369, 371, 374, 376
manipulation, participation as, 4, 6–7
mapping and modelling, 116, 118, 144, 146–7
maps, interrogating of, 145–8
Marcos, Subcomandante, 383, 384, 386, 387, 388, 390–1, 395, 400; subsidiary role of, 395–6
marginalization, of minority ethnic groups, 227
market, surrogate for citizenship, 424
marketization, 322, 324
marriage, forced, 144, 145
Martha Stuart Communications, 151
martial arts training for girls, 409
Marx, Karl, 40, 61
Marxism, 25, 29, 176, 177, 383, 399
Mass Education in the Colonies report, 174
mass mobilization, 325
matchmaking, 145
Mazdoor Kisan Shakti Sangathan (MKSS) movement (Rajasthan), 245, 335
media exposure, 325
Medina, Ofelia, 389
meeting takeover, 309–10
meetingitis, 12
men, as potential allies of women, 411
mental health patients' councils (UK), 346
mental health services, users of, 345–62
Mental Heath Task Force, 356
meter cards for service access, 368
methodological conversations, 142–3
methodology for study of participation, 271
Mexico, 21, 383–402; decentralization in, 332–4; electoral supervision in, 329–30; political capabilities in, 242
micro-finance, 186
Millennium Development Goals (MDGs), 74–5, 284, 285, 286
minimalist view of democracy, 399
minorities, rights of, 20, 28
Mitchell's Plain (South Africa), 369
MKUKUTA policy process (Tanzania), 289–92
Model Cities program, 8, 10–13, 14, 15, 18
modernization, 22, 38, 70, 76, 173; models of, 383

rural poor: differentiation of, 48; participation of, 48
Rwanda, Ministry of Gender and the Promotion of Women, 217

Sahel, forestry law in, 297–305
San Andres accords (Mexico), 395; voting on, 396
Sandercock, Leonie, 364
savings groups, 133; importance of, 197
school shooting (Brazil), 310
Schumpeter, Joseph, 391
scope of participation, 50
seasonal calendars, 116
secondary sources, analysis of, 116
Sector-wide Approaches (SWAPs), 284, 287
segregation: of ethnic groups, 233–4; of women, 269
Self-Employed Women's Association (SEWA) (India), 161; Video SEWA, *My Work, Myself*, 161
self-help, 167, 173, 175, 186, 233; groups, 168, 347; localized, 23; strategies of the poor, 379
Self-Help Support Programme (Intercooperation), 114
self-initiated actions, 32
self-liberation, 25–6
self-organization, 345; objectives of, 351–4
self-reliance, 24, 184, 196, 200; unimplementability of, 199–200
self-sufficiency, 174
Senegal: famine in, 118; participatory forestry in, 297–305
services, struggle for, 367
sex work, meaning of, 414
sex workers: rights of, 414; solidarity with, 413–15
sexuality, construction of, 406
Shabmeher, death of, 409
Shack/Slum Dwellers International, 133
Shahnaz Begum, 160–1
Shonghoti organization (Bangladesh), 414
silence, culture of, 78
Silva, Luis Inácio da, 'Lula', 426
Sindicato Cidadão (Brazil), 421
Single Regeneration Budget (UK), 359
skill-enhancing initiatives, 375
slum and pavement dwellers, in India, 131–3; changing tactics of, 132
slums, assembly participation in, 308

Smulovitz, Catalina, 325
social capital, 200
social forestry, 189
Social Funds, 166
social movements, 26–7, 398, 420, 422, 423, 424; alliances between, 421; criminalization of, 376, 378, 424
social work, Western, model of, 176–7
Society for Sustainable Development, 270
solidarity: collective, replacement of, 425; of women, 413–15
solidarity committees (Mexico), 333
Somaliland, 118
songs and dance: not permitted to women, 415; use of, 212
South Africa, 259–60; anti-eviction campaigns in, 363–82; PPA in, 215
South Asia, participation in, 243–5
South–South workshops, 114
Southwest Alabama Farmers' Cooperative Association, 17
space occupied by women, minimal, 415
spaces: invited, 294, 366, 378 (and empty, 268–9); of active citizenship, 367–9, 372–3; of citizenship, invented, 373–5, 376; of women, domestic, 277; participatory, expansion of, 295; provision of, 348; public, in Brazil, 308
SpaceTimes, of the people, 79
SPARC organization (India), 131
Square, Gertrude, 363–4, 370, 373–4
squatter settlements, 319; upgrading of, 178
Sri Lanka, 114
staff activities, reorientation of, 170
Stakeholder Analysis, 70, 76
state: capacity of, 23; destruction of, 173; devolving responsibilities to community, 358; distinction from civil society, 366; engaging with, 243; in the popular imaginary, 266–7; many forms of, 266; minimal, 419, 425; party-state, 391; relation to civil society, 419; retreat of, 387, 424 (as guarantor of rights, 423); role of, 253–4, 265, 285, 318 (as space-maker, 276); synergy with society, 324, 326, 331, 334; transnational, 399; under modernity, 378
stereotypes, reinforcing of, 274–6
sterilization, forced, 413
story-telling, 86–7, 143
strategic sensibility, development of, 159

About Zed Books

Zed Books is a critical and dynamic publisher, committed to increasing awareness of important international issues and to promoting diversity, alternative voices and progressive social change. We publish on politics, development, gender, the environment and economics for a global audience of students, academics, activists and general readers. Run as a co-operative, Zed Books aims to operate in an ethical and environmentally sustainable way.

Find out more at:

www.zedbooks.co.uk

For up-to-date news, articles, reviews and events information visit:

http://zed-books.blogspot.com

To subscribe to the monthly Zed Books e-newsletter, send an email headed 'subscribe' to:

marketing@zedbooks.net

We can also be found on **Facebook**, **ZNet**, **Twitter** and **Library Thing**.